MW01199498

INTRODUCTION TO
THE HISTORY OF INDIAN BUDDHISM

BUDDHISM AND MODERNITY
A series edited by Donald S. Lopez Jr.

Recent books in the series:

Critical Terms for the Study of Buddhism, edited by Donald S. Lopez Jr. (2005)
The Madman's Middle Way: Reflections on Reality of the Tibetan Monk Gendun Chopel, by Donald S. Lopez Jr. (2006)
The Holy Land Reborn: Pilgrimage and the Tibetan Reinvention of Buddhist India, by Toni Huber (2008)
Buddhism and Science: A Guide for the Perplexed, by Donald S. Lopez Jr. (2008)
Shots in the Dark: Japan, Zen, and the West, by Shoji Yamada, translated by Earl Hartman (2009)
In the Forest of Faded Wisdom: 104 Poems by Gendun Chopel, a Bilingual Edition, edited and translated by Donald S. Lopez Jr. (2009)

INTRODUCTION TO THE HISTORY OF INDIAN BUDDHISM

EUGÈNE BURNOUF

Translated by Katia Buffetrille
and Donald S. Lopez Jr.

The University of Chicago Press | Chicago & London

The University of Chicago Press, Chicago 60637
The University of Chicago Press, Ltd., London
© 2010 by The University of Chicago
All rights reserved. Published 2010.
Paperback edition 2015
Printed in the United States of America

24 23 22 21 20 19 18 17 16 15 2 3 4 5 6

ISBN-13: 978-0-226-08123-6 (cloth)
ISBN-13: 978-0-226-26968-9 (paper)
ISBN-13: 978-0-226-08125-0 (e-book)
10.7208/chicago/9780226081250.001.0001

The University of Chicago Press gratefully acknowledges the generous support of the Institute for the Study of Buddhist Traditions at the University of Michigan toward the publication of this book.

Library of Congress Cataloging-in-Publication Data

Burnouf, Eugène, 1801–1852.
[Introduction à l'histoire du Buddhisme indien. English]
Introduction to the history of Indian Buddhism / by Eugène Burnouf ; translated by Katia Buffetrille and Donald S. Lopez Jr.
p. cm. — (Buddhism and modernity)
Includes bibliographical references and index.
ISBN-13: 978-0-226-08123-6 (hardcover : alk. paper)
ISBN-10: 0-226-08123-0 (hardcover : alk. paper)
1. Buddhism—India—History. I. Title. II. Series: Buddhism and modernity.
BQ334.B9713 2010
294.30954—dc22
2009008382

♾ This paper meets the requirements of ANSI/NISO Z39.48-1992 (Permanence of Paper).

Contents

Acknowledgments *vii*

Introduction to the Translation, by Donald S. Lopez Jr. *1*

A Note on the Translation *29*

INTRODUCTION TO THE HISTORY OF INDIAN BUDDHISM

Table of Contents *39*

Analytical Table of the First Two Memoranda *41*

Foreword *51*

First Memorandum: Preliminary Observations *55*

Second Memorandum: Description of the Collection of the Books of Nepal *81*

Appendixes *535*

Index *595*

Acknowledgments

Over the course of this project, we received the assistance and support of many colleagues. These include Stéphane Arguillère, Timothy Barrett, Anne Chayet, Eugen Ciurtin, Christopher Cüppers, Madhav Deshpande, Catherine Despeux, Isrun Engelhardt, Marie-Dominique Even, Jean-Philippe Geley, Roberte Hamayon, Paul Harrison, Guo Liying, William Paulson, Jean-Noël Robert, Alexander von Rospatt, James Robson, the Société Asiatique (especially Jeanne-Marie Allier and Pierre-Sylvain Filliozat), John Strong, and Hartmut Walravens. Helpful comments on the translation were provided by the anonymous reviewers for the University of Chicago Press. Finally, we gratefully acknowledge the assistance of the Lumbini International Research Institute, which provided a generous grant in support of the translation.

Introduction to the Translation

Introduction à l'histoire du Buddhisme indien by the great French scholar Eugène Burnouf (1801–1852) was the most influential work on Buddhism to be written during the nineteenth century. In important ways, it set the course for the academic study of Buddhism, and especially Indian Buddhism, for the next century. Burnouf's *Introduction* would influence two audiences: it offered scholars both a method of analysis and a massive amount of information about Buddhism; it offered the educated public a wealth of Buddhist literature, and a portrait of the Buddha, that would captivate the European imagination for decades. For both scholars and the public, it also played a key role in the creation of Buddhism as a "world religion," one that set forth an ancient philosophy that seemed simultaneously to be most modern. This masterpiece, first published in 1844, is largely neglected today. One might argue that the book has all but disappeared and remains unread and unexamined, not because it is outdated or has been superseded (although it is and has been on a number of individual points), but because it became so fully integrated into the mainstream representation of Buddhism, which it helped to create, that it is no longer visible.

Burnouf's massive work (647 pages in the original edition) is of high historical value, providing a clear window onto how Buddhism was understood in the early decades of the nineteenth century, just when the Buddhist traditions of Asia were beginning to be studied by the philologists of Europe. At the same time, it is not simply a monument of antiquarian scholarship; the work offers a vast fount of still accurate information and insight into Buddhist religion and philosophy, as well as hundreds of pages of translations from important Bud-

I would like to thank Harmut Walravens and especially Katia Buffetrille for their assistance in the preparation of this introduction.

dhist texts. And Burnouf's theories on the Buddha's teachings and the development of his doctrine remain both fascinating and instructive. Indeed, Burnouf's *Introduction* was a seminal text in Europe's formation of Buddhism as a textual object—a tradition properly understood first from its ancient texts, rather than from the words and practices of its contemporary adherents. Since the time of Burnouf, the primary task of the scholar of Buddhism has been the acquisition, editing, translation, and interpretation of texts.

As its modest title suggests, *Introduction à l'histoire du Buddhisme indien* was the first work to introduce Indian Buddhism to Europe. The significance of Burnouf's achievement was immediately recognized. In 1845 one of the first substantial reviews of the work, by Eduard Roer (1805–1866) in the *Journal of the Asiatic Society of Bengal*, began:

> It is with great satisfaction, that we hail the appearance of a work, which will, we suspect, form an epoch in our knowledge of Buddhism. . . . As a fortunate combination of circumstances had concentrated at Paris all the first and secondary sources for the history of Buddhism, a man was required who united to a profound knowledge of the ancient languages of India, an acquaintance with modern languages and literature of the Buddhists, the critical tact of the philologist and historian, and the comprehensive grasp of the philosopher, qualities, which in E. Burnouf are most happily blended together.[1]

Indeed, what Burnouf published in 1844 would both establish the foundation and set the agenda for the study of Indian Buddhism for the next century and beyond. He provides lengthy discussions of the discourses of the Buddha, the *sūtras*; the code of monastic conduct, the *vinaya*; and the metaphysical treatises, the *abhidharma*. Burnouf offers extended passages translated from a great variety of texts, including many tales of the Buddha's disciples, the *avadānas*. There are essays on topics that continue to draw the attention of scholars, such as the meaning of terms like *nirvāṇa* and *pratītyasamutpāda* (dependent origination). There are also discussions of obscure terms for weights and measures and of varieties of sandalwood. Yet Burnouf does not simply summarize the contents of the manuscripts. He presents acute analyses, most of which remain compelling, seeking always to understand Buddhism within its historical, cultural, and geographical context as, above all, an Indian religion, rather than a free-floating philosophy untouched by the circumstances of its time and place, as it would come to be regarded by so many.

1. Eduard Roer, review of *Introduction à l'histoire du Buddhisme indien*, *Journal of the Asiatic Society of Bengal* 14, no. 2 (1845): 783–84.

Burnouf's book was studied assiduously not only by his illustrious students, but by the next generations of European scholars of Buddhism, such as Sylvain Lévi, Otto Franke, Hermann Oldenberg, Émile Senart, Theodor Stcherbatsky, F. W. Thomas, E. J. Thomas, Louis de la Vallée Poussin, and Alfred Foucher. A work of similar scope would not be produced for more than a century, when in 1958 the Belgian scholar Monseigneur Étienne Lamotte, a direct heir of Burnouf's legacy, published *Histoire du Bouddhisme indien* (no longer in need of an introduction), a work that remained untranslated into English for only thirty years.[2]

The influence of the *Introduction* extended well beyond France, and beyond the infant discipline of Buddhist studies. It was read in America by Ralph Waldo Emerson and Henry David Thoreau.[3] On May 28, 1844, the year of the *Introduction*'s publication, the Sanskrit instructor at Yale, Edward Eldridge Salisbury (1814–1901), a Congregationalist deacon and student of Burnouf, delivered a lecture entitled "Memoir on the History of Buddhism" at the first meeting of the American Oriental Society. This fifty-page report, based largely on Burnouf's work (and would be published in the *Journal of the American Oriental Society* that same year), was the first scholarly article on Buddhism to be written by an American.

Burnouf's *Introduction* was read in Germany by Schopenhauer, Nietzsche, and Schelling, who praised it for refining his understanding of nirvāṇa and noted how remarkable it was that France, with its political instability, could produce a man like Burnouf. Wagner wrote, "Burnouf's *Introduction to the History of Indian Buddhism* interested me most among my books, and I found material in it for a dramatic poem, which has stayed in my mind ever since, though only vaguely sketched."[4] The material for this poem came specifically from Burnouf's description of the *Śārdūlakarṇāvadāna* (pp. 222–23). Wagner's Buddhist-themed opera, *Die Sieger*, although listed in the timetable he had presented to King Ludwig II, was unfortunately never completed.

Before the publication of the *Introduction*, the few academic studies of Buddhism had taken the form of scholarly articles in journals such as *Asiatick Re-*

2. See Étienne Lamotte, *History of Indian Buddhism from the Origins to the Śaka Era*, trans. Sara Webb-Boin (Louvain: Institut Orientaliste, 1988).

3. In 1844 Thoreau published "The Preaching of the Buddha" in Emerson's Transcendentalist journal *The Dial*. It included a translation from the French by Elizabeth Palmer Peabody of the fifth chapter ("Herb") of the *Lotus Sūtra*, drawn from two articles published by Burnouf in the *Revue indépendante* in April and May 1843. The translation itself is often mistakenly attributed to Thoreau. See Roger C. Mueller, "A Significant Buddhist Translation by Thoreau," *The Thoreau Society Bulletin* (Winter 1977): 1–2.

4. Richard Wagner, quoted in Raymond Schwab, *The Oriental Renaissance: Europe's Rediscovery of India and the East, 1680–1880* (New York: Columbia University Press, 1984), p. 439. On the history of Buddhist studies, see J. W. de Jong, *A Brief History of Buddhist Studies in Europe and America* (Delhi: Sri Satguru Publications, 1987).

searches, *Transactions of the Royal Asiatic Society*, *Transactions of the Literary Society of Bombay*, and *Journal des Savans*. Dr. Francis Buchanan of the East India Company drew heavily on information from the Italian missionary to Burma, Father Vincenzo Sangermano, in his "On the Religion and Literature of the Burmas," published in *Asiatick Researches* in 1801. Julius von Klaproth's life of the Buddha, based largely on Mongolian sources, appeared in two installments in the 1824 *Journal Asiatique*. Consequently, in surveying European knowledge of Buddhism in his 1845 review, Eduard Roer noted that the initial understanding of Buddhism in Europe had come from "secondary sources," that is, works in Chinese, Burmese, and Mongolian, leading him to observe, "Our first acquaintance with Buddhism was in fact not a kind to invite research; the mixture of extravagant fables, apparent historical facts, philosophical and religious doctrines was so monstrous, that it seemed to defy every attempt to unravel it."[5]

Burnouf was the first to attempt to "unravel" Buddhism from Sanskrit sources. He would do so, not in a scholarly article, but in the first European monograph, and a huge monograph, devoted entirely to the subject of Buddhism.[6]

It was a work that would be deployed in a variety of ways in the decades after Burnouf's death. In the second half of the nineteenth century, many sought to find links between Buddhism and Christianity. Such links were sometimes sought in an ecumenical spirit; the great historian Jules Michelet, a close friend of Burnouf's, wrote that in his words he "plainly saw the unique miracle of the two Gospels, the one arising from the Orient, the other from the Occident."[7] At other times, Burnouf's work was used by missionaries seeking to understand the spirit of Buddhism in order to convert its followers. Still others read Burnouf with different motives, as certain European and American scholars attempted to locate an Aryan, rather than Semitic, origin for Christianity.[8]

Yet despite its influence, Burnouf's *Introduction* was not reprinted until 1876, and has not appeared since. Apart from an inadequate translation of a small portion of the text, it has never been translated into English.[9]

5. Roer, review of *Introduction à l'histoire du Buddhisme indien*, p. 783.

6. One would likely exclude from consideration here Edward Upham's eccentric work, *The History and Doctrine of Budhism, Popularly Illustrated: With Notices of the Kappooism or Demon Worship and of the Bali or Planetary Incantations of Ceylon, embellished with 43 lithographic prints from the original Singalese designs* (London: R. Ackermann, 1829).

7. Jules Michelet, quoted in Schwab, *The Oriental Renaissance*, p. 291.

8. This was the project of Burnouf's cousin, with whom he is often confused, the classicist and Sanskrit scholar Émile Burnouf (1821–1907), known on this topic for his *Science des religions*. The Comte de Gobineau cited Burnouf in his four-volume *Essai sur l'inégalité des races humaines* (1853).

9. The only "translation" of any portion of Burnouf's text sought to bring some of its Buddhist stories to an Anglophone audience. In 1903, L. Cranmer-Byng and S. A. Kapadia published *Legends of Indian Buddhism*, a rough and sometimes inaccurate paraphrase of the legends of the Indian emperor Aśoka, drawn from pp. 358–434 of Burnouf's text.

THE LIFE OF BURNOUF

Eugène Burnouf was born in Paris on April 8, 1801, the son of the distinguished classicist (and translator of Tacitus) Jean-Louis Burnouf (1775–1844). He received instruction in Greek and Latin from his father and studied at the Lycée Louis-le-Grand. In 1822 he entered the École des Chartes, receiving degrees in both letters (*licence-es-lettres*) and law (*licence en droit*) in 1824. He then turned to the study of Sanskrit, both with his father and with Antoine Léonard de Chézy (1773–1832). In 1814 chairs in Indology (Langues et littératures sanscrites) and Sinology (Langues et littératures chinoises et tartares-mandchoues) had been established at the Collège de France, with Chézy appointed to the first and Jean-Pierre Abel-Rémusat (1788–1832) appointed to the second. Burnouf published his first translation from the Sanskrit in the *Journal Asiatique* in 1823, the legend of the snake and the frogs from the *Hitopadeśa*, a famous anthology of animal tales. In 1824 he published "Sur un usage remarquable de l'infinitif sanscrit" in the same journal.

In 1826 Burnouf published, in collaboration with the young Norwegian-German scholar Christian Lassen (1800–1876), *Essai sur le pâli*[10] (on Pāli, the canonical language of Theravāda, or, as it was called at the time, Southern Buddhism). By his subsequent standards, it was a brief 222 pages in length, and included some examples of Pāli alphabets. The work is devoted mainly to grammar and orthography, as well as discussions of the origins and extent of Pāli, and comparisons of Pāli with other Prakrits. Although Buddhism is not the chief focus of the study, it is often mentioned, especially its role in the dissemination of Pāli in Southeast Asia. There is also a discussion of various Buddhist traditions concerning the date of the death of "Shakya Mouni Bouddha," a topic to which Burnouf would return. The appendixes include descriptions of several Buddhist manuscripts in Pāli.

Also in 1826, Burnouf was appointed adjunct secretary of the Société Asiatique, which had been founded in 1822; he would become secretary in 1832. And in that same year, he married Reine Victoire Angélique Poiret, with whom he would have four daughters. In 1829 Burnouf was named professor in general and comparative grammar at the École Normale. While there, he received an award from the Count de Volney for his work in "the transcription of Asiatic scriptures in Latin letters."

10. The full title of the work is *Essai sur le pâli, ou langue sacrée de la presqu'île au-delà du Gange: Avec six planches lithographiées, et la notice des manuscrits palis de la bibliothèque du Roi* [Essay on Pāli, or the Sacred Language of the Peninsula beyond the Ganges, with six lithographed plates and a note on the Pāli manuscripts in the Bibliothèque du Roi].

In addition to his work in Sanskrit and Pāli, Burnouf was an accomplished scholar of Avestan, the sacred language of Zoroastrianism, practiced by the Parsis in India. Between 1829 and 1833 (with a final volume in 1843) he published, at his own expense and with fonts of his own design, a lithograph (in 562 pages) of the *Vendidad Sadé* (or *Videvdat*) from a manuscript in the Bibliothèque Royale, brought to Paris by Abraham Hyacinthe Anquetil-Duperron (1731–1805). This collection contains works on myth, doctrine, and law, in the form of dialogues between Ahura Mazda and Zoroaster. Between 1833 and 1835, Burnouf published *Commentaire sur le Yaçna, l'un des livres liturgiques des Parses*, a translation of a commentary on the *Yasna* ("worship" or "oblations"), the main liturgical section of the Avestan canon. Composed of seventy-two chapters, it contains the *gathas,* or verses, the oldest section of the *Avesta*, traditionally regarded as having been composed by Zoroaster himself.

A deadly cholera epidemic struck Paris in 1832, during which both Chézy and Abel-Rémusat died. Burnouf was appointed to succeed his teacher as chair of Sanskrit at the Collège de France; Burnouf's friend Stanislas Julien (1797–1873) was selected to succeed Abel-Rémusat. In his inaugural lecture on February 1, 1833, Burnouf made no mention of Buddhism, but he expressed the enthusiasm of the age, describing ancient India as possessing "perhaps the richest literary history that a people can offer to the curiosity and admiration of Europe."[11] He concluded:

> It is India, with its philosophy and myths, its literature and laws, that we will study in its language. It is more than India, gentlemen, it is a page from the origins of the world, of the primitive history of the human spirit, that we shall try to decipher together. . . . There is no philology without philosophy and history. The analysis of the operations of language is also a science of observation; and if it is not the very science of the human spirit, it is at least one of the most astonishing faculties with whose aid the human spirit manifests itself.[12]

Although now occupying the chair of Sanskrit, Burnouf continued to publish studies of Avestan language and literature. His major project, however, was *Le Bhâgavata Purâṇa ou histoire poétique de Krĭchṇa*, which contained the Sanskrit text, translation, and learned comments on the *Bhāgavata Purāṇa*, the famous Hindu compendium of the legends of Kṛṣṇa. He published three large volumes (of 768, 725, and 681 pages, respectively) between 1840 and 1847 and planned as many as three more volumes in order to present all twelve cantos of the text.

Burnouf was also renowned for his erudition and dedication as a teacher. In

11. Eugène Burnouf, "De la langue et de la littérature sanscrite. Discours d'ouverture, prononcé au Collège de France," *Revue des deux mondes* 2nd ser., 1 (Février, 1833): 273.

12. Ibid., p. 275.

a letter to Lassen in 1835, he wrote, "My students in Sanskrit are still not sufficiently advanced to take part in my work in a useful manner. They do me the honor of believing what I tell them; but I need them to discuss it and, through their doubts, force me to find something new."[13] His students included some of the greatest scholars of the day from both France and elsewhere in Europe, and at least one from America, figures such as Philippe Edouard Foucaux (1811–1894), who translated the *Lalitavistara* from the Tibetan in 1848; Hippolyte Fauché, translator of the *Rāmāyaṇa* and the *Mahābhārata*; Théodore Pavie, author of *Les Babouches du Brahmane*; the brilliant and controversial biblical scholar Ernst Renan; the Belgian Félix Nève, student of the *Ṛg Veda* who went on to become professor at the Catholic University of Louvain; Adolphe Pictet, Swiss scholar of comparative linguistics; Gaspare Gorresio, who would hold the first chair of Sanskrit in Italy; Alexandre Langlois, who provided the first translation of the *Ṛg Veda* into French; and Édouard Lancereau, translator of the *Pañcatantra*. In his diary entry of March 20, 1845, Friedrich Max Müller described his first meeting with his future teacher: "Went to see Burnouf. Spiritual, amiable, thoroughly French. He received me in the most friendly way, talked a great deal, and all he said was valuable, not on ordinary topics but on special. I managed better in French than I expected. 'I am a Brahman, a Buddhist, a Zoroastrian. I hate the Jesuits'—that is the sort of man. I am looking forward to his lectures."[14]

It was shortly after his appointment to the chair of Sanskrit at the Collège de France that the Société Asiatique, of which Burnouf was then secretary, received a communication from Brian Houghton Hodgson, British resident at the Court of Nepal, offering to send Sanskrit manuscripts of Buddhist texts to Paris. The receipt of these texts would change the direction of Burnouf's scholarship for the last fifteen years of his life (described in the next section). It is the case, however, that either his studies of Avestan texts—he is also credited with deciphering the Old Persian cuneiform inscriptions of Darius and Xerxes found at Persepolis—or his studies of Sanskrit literature would have assured his place in the history of Oriental studies in the nineteenth century, even if he had not turned to the Buddhist studies that would be his most enduring legacy.

Until a full study can be made of the "Fonds Burnouf" in the Bibliothèque Nationale—twenty volumes of correspondence (including some of his father's papers)—an account of Burnouf's life is largely an account of his scholarship. Apparently suffering from poor health for most of his short life, he left France on only two occasions, and both times for research. He traveled to Germany briefly

13. Eugène Burnouf to Christian Lassen, 1835; quoted in Léon Feer, *Papiers d'Eugène Burnouf conservés à la Bibliothèque Nationale* (Paris: H. Champion, 1899), p. xix.

14. *The Life and Letters of the Right Honourable Friedrich Max Müller, Edited by His Wife*, 2 vols. (London: Longmans, Green, and Co., 1902), 1:34.

in the late summer of 1834 and to England in the spring of 1835, where he visited the British Museum, the library of Haileybury (the college of the East India Company), and the Bodleian. Although Burnouf was a devoted husband and father, his life was dedicated to study: he was at his desk each day by 3:00 AM, a practice that his contemporaries blamed for his early death. Even by the high standards of Paris in the first half of the nineteenth century, both the breadth and the depth of his learning are impressive. The 358-page catalogue of his library, prepared for an auction held in 1854, lists 2,730 books and 218 manuscripts divided into the following subjects: theology; jurisprudence; philosophy; natural sciences; fine arts; linguistics, languages, and literatures; geography and voyages; history of religions; history; archaeology; biography; bibliography; texts printed in India; and manuscripts (in the following categories: Zend, Sanskrit, Nepalese Buddhist, Pāli, Indian dialects, Burman, Siamese, Sinhalese, Tibetan, French).[15] Among the manuscripts were fifty-nine Buddhist writings from Nepal, to which we shall shortly turn.

Despite his health problems, Burnouf persisted in his work on the Nepalese manuscripts, publishing the present volume in 1844. He continued to add appendixes to his *Lotus Sūtra* translation. And he continued to translate Pāli texts for his planned volume on the Buddhist canon of Sri Lanka. He died, apparently of kidney failure, on May 28, 1852. The *Lotus de la bonne loi* appeared that same year. It was dedicated, as Burnouf had instructed, to Brian Houghton Hodgson, *fondateur de la véritable étude du Buddhisme par les textes et les monuments*, "founder of the true study of Buddhism through texts and monuments"—an appellation that over the passing decades has come to more accurately describe its author.

THE STORY OF THE *HISTOIRE*

In his "Third Anniversary Discourse" delivered on February 2, 1786, to the Asiatick Society of Bengal in Calcutta, Sir William Jones had famously declared:

> The *Sanscrit* language, whatever be its antiquity, is of a wonderful structure; more perfect than the *Greek*, more copious than the *Latin*, and more exquisitely refined than either, yet bearing to both of them a stronger affinity, both in the roots of verbs and in the forms of grammar, than could possibly have been produced by accident; so strong indeed that no philologer could examine them all three, without believing them to have sprung from some common source, which, perhaps, no longer exists.[16]

15. *Catalogue des livres imprimés et manuscrits composant la bibliothèque de feu M. Eugène Burnouf* (Paris: Benjamin Duprat, 1854). The Buddhist manuscripts from Nepal are listed on pp. 330–36.

16. William Jones, "The Third Anniversary Discourse, Delivered 2 February, 1786, By the President," in *Asiatick Researches, or Transactions of the Society, Instituted in Bengal, for Inquiring into the History and Antiquities, the Arts, Sciences, and Literature of Asia* 1 (1801): 422–23. This is the London reprint of the original Calcutta edition.

Jones went on to claim that is was impossible "to read the Vedanta, or the many fine compositions in illustration of it, without believing that Pythagoras and Plato derived their sublime theories from the same fountain with the sages of India."[17] In his influential 1808 essay, *Über die Sprache und Weisheit der Indier*, Friedrich Schlegel wrote, "The Renaissance of antiquity promptly rejuvenated all the sciences; we might add that it rejuvenated and transformed the world. We could even say that the effects of Indic studies, if these enterprises were taken up and introduced into learned circles with the same energy today, would be no less great and far-reaching."[18] But Buddhism remained largely excluded from the first wave of European enthusiasm for Indian wisdom, occasioned by such works as Charles Wilkins's 1785 translation into English of the *Bhagavad Gītā* (as *Bhăgvăt-Gēētā; or, Dialogues of Kreeshna and Arjoon*), followed by the French translation two years later; Anquetil Duperron's 1786 translation of four *Oupnek'hat* (*Upaniṣad*) from the Persian into Latin; and Jones's own 1794 translation, *Institutes of Hindu Law; or, The Ordinances of Menu.*

By the fourteenth century, and before the arrival of Portuguese explorers, Buddhism had all but disappeared from India. By the time that European scholars (notably those of the British East India Company), trained in Persian and Sanskrit, began a sustained study of the culture and history of that country, Buddhism was an artifact. There were no Buddhists in India. Instead, there were what Burnouf would call "monuments": reliquaries (stūpas) of the Buddha, cave temples, the ruins of monasteries, and statues. The British found stone inscriptions to be deciphered, but they did not find Sanskrit manuscripts. European travelers and missionaries encountered Buddhism elsewhere in Asia, and in languages other than Sanskrit: Chinese, Japanese, Tibetan, Mongolian, Pāli, Thai, and Burmese.

Burnouf's interest in Buddhism was in evidence as early as 1826 and his *Essai sur le pâli.* But Pāli was no longer a language of India; it was the sacred language of neighboring Sri Lanka. And Pāli was not Sanskrit (literally, the "perfected" language); it was a Prakrit (literally a "natural" language), one of the several Indian vernaculars derived from Sanskrit. By Burnouf's day, European scholars understood that Buddhism had originated in India; whether the Buddha himself was of Indian or African origin remained an object of debate. Brian Houghton Hodgson's "discovery" would thus have major consequences.

Hodgson (1800–1894) was nominated for Bengal service in the East India Company and studied at Haileybury before being sent to Calcutta in 1818, where he continued his training at the College of Fort William. Health problems required his posting to cooler climes, and in 1820 he was appointed as-

17. Ibid., p. 425.

18. Friedrich Schlegel, *Über die Sprache und Weisheit der Indier*; quoted in Schwab, *The Oriental Renaissance*, p. 13.

sistant resident at the Court of Nepal. The appointment of the British Resident was a concession made by the Nepalese under the 1816 Treaty of Sugauli, following the British victory in the Gurkha War. However, they resented the British presence, and consequently limited their travel, leaving Hodgson with time for other pursuits. In a letter of August 11, 1827, he wrote:

> Soon after my arrival in Nipál (now six years ago), I began to devise means of procuring some accurate information relative to Buddhism: for, though the regular investigation of such a subject was foreign to my pursuits, my respect for science in general led me cheerfully to avail myself of the opportunity afforded, by my residence in a *Bauddha* country, for collecting and transmitting to Calcutta the materials for such investigation. There were, however, serious obstacles in my way, arising out of the jealousy of the people in regard to any profanation of their sacred things by an European, and yet more, resulting from Chinese notions of policy adopted by this government. I nevertheless persevered; and time, patience, and dexterous applications to the superior intelligence of the chief minister, at length rewarded my toils.[19]

Although Nepal was a predominantly Hindu kingdom, the Kathmandu Valley was home to the Newar community, which had continued to practice Buddhism, based on Sanskrit texts, after the demise of Buddhism in India. With the aid of the distinguished Newar pundit Amṛtānanda, in 1824 Hodgson began to collect Sanskrit manuscripts of Buddhist sūtras (as well as Tibetan block prints), which he would eventually send around the world, beginning with the gift of 66 manuscripts to the library of the College of Fort William in 1827 and continuing until 1845: 94 manuscripts to the Library of the Asiatic Society of Bengal, 79 to the Royal Asiatic Society, 36 to the India Office Library, 7 to the Bodleian, 88 to the Société Asiatique, 59 to Burnouf. A total of 423 works were furnished.

When word reached Paris of Hodgson's offer of a set of manuscripts to the Société Asiatique, Burnouf wrote to him directly on July 7, 1834, initiating what would become a long correspondence. This first letter begins, "Monsieur"; eventually, Burnouf would address Hodgson as "Mon cher et savant ami." In the letter, Burnouf both thanks Hodgson for his generosity and requests that Hodgson also send "not less than twelve or fifteen" manuscripts directly to him; after offering to cover all the costs, he adds, "I would be most obliged to you to have written on the first page 'Volume belonging to M. Eug. Burnouf.' This measure is necessary so that the book is not sent by mistake to other people or to some learned body." He expresses his "great satisfaction in learning that the books of Buddha (Sâkya) existed in Sanskrit," and confesses:

19. Brian H. Hodgson, "Sketch of Buddhism, derived from Bauddha Scriptures of Nipál," *Transactions of the Royal Asiatic Society of Great Britain and Ireland* 2 (1830): 222.

> Since then, I had the hope to be able, using the knowledge of this language that I had begun to gain through several years of study, to directly approach the Buddhist works; but I would have probably left this world without having been able to carry out this hope, because of the impossibility of my ever going to India, if the so liberal proposal that you wish to kindly address to the Société Asiatique did not embolden me to resort to your benevolent kindness.[20]

On or around April 20, 1837, twenty-four Sanskrit manuscripts of Buddhist texts arrived in Paris, sent by Hodgson seven months before. On July 14 another sixty-four texts would arrive, which Hodgson had had copied in Kathmandu and then sent to the Société Asiatique. He would eventually provide Burnouf with another fifty-nine manuscripts. Suddenly, Burnouf had before him more Buddhist Sanskrit manuscripts than had been available to any previous European scholar, with the obvious exception of Brian Hodgson in Kathmandu. But unlike Hodgson, Burnouf was able to read them. These texts included sūtras and tantras of Sanskrit Buddhism, composed for the most part during the first six centuries of the common era, largely lost in India but preserved in Nepal—works that in India, and in translations into Chinese and Tibetan, were among the most important in the history of Buddhism. To list just ten of the works that arrived in Paris, the manuscripts included the *Aṣṭasāhasrikāprajñāpāramitā* (the *Perfection of Wisdom in Eight Thousand Lines*), one of the earliest and most influential of the perfection of wisdom (*prajñāpāramitā*) texts; the *Gaṇḍavyūha*, regarded as the Buddha's most profound teaching by the Huayan schools of East Asia; the *Sukhāvatīvyūha*, the fundamental sūtra for the Pure Land traditions of East Asia; the *Laṅkāvatāra*, a central text for the Yogācāra school in India and the Chan and Zen traditions of East Asia; the *Lalitavistara*, a baroque account of the Buddha's early life; the *Guhyasamāja*, among the most influential of Buddhist tantras; the *Abhidharmakośa*, Vasubandhu's important compendium of doctrine; the *Bodhicaryāvatāra*, an eighth-century poem by Śāntideva on the practice of the bodhisattva; the *Buddhacarita*, Aśvaghoṣa's second-century life of the Buddha; and the *Saddharmapuṇḍarīka*, the famous *Lotus Sūtra*.

On June 5, 1837, Burnouf wrote to Hodgson. He explained that the Société Asiatique had instructed him and Eugène Jacquet (1811–1838) to examine the twenty-four volumes that had arrived in April. They determined which ones were most important, divided them between themselves, and began reading. Burnouf was initially put off by the *Perfection of Wisdom in Eight Thousand Lines*, "be-

20. Eugène Burnouf to Brian Hodgson, July 7, 1834; in Feer, *Papiers d'Eugène Burnouf*, p. 148. For the French text of this and the preceding passages from Burnouf's letter, see also Akira Yuyama, *Eugène Burnouf: The Background of His Research into the Lotus Sutra* (Tokyo: International Research Institute for Advanced Buddhology, Soka University, 2000), pp. 59–60.

cause I saw only perpetual repetitions of the advantages and merits promised to those who obtain *prajñāpāramitā*. But what is this *prajñā* itself? This is what I did not see anywhere, and what I wished to learn."[21] He next considered the *Lalitavistara*, the important life of the Buddha, but knew that "a Russian friend" (presumably Robert Lenz, 1808–1836) was working on a translation. He continued reading.

> I turned to a new book, one of the nine *dharmas* [the sacred texts of Nepal], the *Saddharmapuṇḍarīka*, and I can promise you that I have not repented my choice. Since about April 25, I have without reserve devoted every moment that I could steal from my occupations as professor of Sanskrit and academician to this work, of which I have already read rather considerable portions. You will not be astonished that I did not understand everything; the material is very new to me, the style as well as the content. But I intend to reread, with pen in hand, your excellent memoirs of the *Asiatic Researches* of London and Calcutta, as well as the *Journal* of Prinsep. Though many things are still obscure to my eyes, I nevertheless comprehend the progression of the book, the mode of exposition of the author, and I have even already translated two chapters in their entirety, omitting nothing. These are two parables, not lacking in interest, but which are especially curious specimens of the manner in which the teaching of the Buddhists is imparted and of the discursive and very Socratic method of exposition. . . . I confess to you that I am passionate about this reading, and that I would like to have more time and health to attend to it day and night. I will not, however, set aside the *Saddharma* without extracting and translating substantial fragments, convinced that there is nothing I could better do to recognize your liberality than to communicate to the scholars of Europe part of the riches that you have so liberally placed at our disposal. I will exert myself in that until this winter, and I will try to dig up some printer in Germany to bring out an *Analysis* or *Observations on the Saddharmapundarīka.*[22]

This "Analysis" or "Observations" would evolve over the next seven years. In a letter of October 28, 1841, he wrote to Hodgson that he had finished printing his translation of the *Lotus Sūtra*, "but I would like to give an introduction to this bizarre work."[23] Three years later, he would publish *Introduction à l'histoire du Buddhisme indien.*

By October 27, 1837, Burnouf had finished all but the final fifteen folios of his translation of the *Lotus Sūtra*. On November 3, he began translating the

21. Feer, *Papiers d'Eugène Burnouf*, pp. 157–58.
22. Ibid., pp. 158–59.
23. Ibid., p. 174.

Kāraṇḍavyūha, an important *sūtra* about Avalokiteśvara, completing the project just ten days later. After taking a day off, on November 14, 1837, apparently able to overcome his initial aversion, he began to translate the *Perfection of Wisdom in Eight Thousand Verses*, eventually completing 90 percent of the text. An incomplete listing of Burnouf's translations of Buddhist texts found among his papers at the time of his death would include the *Mahāvaṃsa* (Great Chronicle) of Sri Lanka from Pāli into Latin; the monastic code (*pātimokka*) translated from Pāli and Burmese; large portions of the *Divyāvadāna* and the *Avadānaśataka*, two important Sanskrit collections of Buddhist legends; and hundreds of pages of translations from the Pāli and Burmese of *jātaka* (or "birth") stories.[24] Only one of these would be published, and then only after Burnouf's death: the *Lotus Sūtra*.

Having completed the translation of the sūtra in November 1839, he had it printed (without notes) in 1841; the translation of the sūtra itself required 283 pages; there would be 149 pages of notes. Burnouf did not publish them, however, for two reasons. The first was that he wanted to wait until he could provide a number of appendixes; he completed twenty-one of these before his death. They range from short discourses on topics such as the six perfections, the bodhisattva Mañjuśrī, and the term *dhātu*, to a ninety-four-page discussion of the thirty-two major marks of the Buddha and a 129-page examination of the Aśokan inscriptions. The appendixes are yet another monument to Burnouf's erudition, meriting their own translation and study. They were edited by his student Julius von Mohl and published in 1852, the year of his death, as *Le Lotus de la bonne loi traduit du Sanscrit accompagné d'un commentaire et de vingt et un mémoires relatifs au Buddhisme*. A massive work, it is 897 pages in length.

Burnouf also delayed the publication of his translation of the *Lotus Sūtra* because he felt that it would not be comprehensible to European readers without an introduction. That introduction grew to become the 647-page work translated here. Or to be more precise, the present text, whose title page reads "Tome Premier," represents what Burnouf envisioned as the first volume of that introduction. As he explains on pages 78–79 at the end of the First Memorandum, he intended at least one more volume, and perhaps as many as three (depending on how one interprets the term *memorandum*; the present volume is composed of only two memoranda). Just as the present volume is devoted to the Buddhist literature of Nepal, preserved in Sanskrit, the second volume, which he says would have five sections, would be devoted to the Buddhist literature of Sri Lanka, preserved in Pāli. The thousands of pages of translations from Pāli texts found among Burnouf's papers provide some sense of the materials he planned to draw

24. For a detailed description of Burnouf's papers, see Feer.

on for the second volume. This study would be followed by another memorandum comparing the Sanskrit collection of Nepal with the Pāli collection of Sri Lanka. Finally, he would compose yet another memorandum, in six sections, that would analyze various traditions concerning the date of the Buddha's death and then go on to examine the fate of Buddhism in India after his death as well as the various periods of Buddhism's emigration from India to other regions of Asia. He often refers to this final memorandum as his *Esquisse historique* (Historical Sketch). Burnouf alludes repeatedly to these various subsequent memoranda in the present volume, suggesting that he fully intended to complete them all.[25]

This book, volume 1 of *Introduction to the History of Indian Buddhism*, was published in Paris in 1844. Burnouf completed it shortly after the death of his father, and he dedicates the volume to his memory in a moving tribute in the final paragraph of the foreword. In the subsequent 165 years, the *Introduction* has been reprinted only once, in 1876, in an edition that added an essay about Burnouf by his student Jules Barthélemy-Saint Hilaire, and introduced a number of typographical errors into Burnouf's text. Burnouf himself provided a very detailed Table Analytique to the volume, such that it is not necessary to provide an extensive description of its contents here. However, a brief survey may prove useful to the reader.

Perhaps the most important sentence in the entire volume occurs on the first page of the foreword, where Burnouf declares that the belief called Buddhism is completely Indian, literally "a completely Indian fact" (*un fait complètement indien*). As noted above, prior to Burnouf, Buddhism was understood to have originated in India, but no original Indian texts (that is, Sanskrit texts) had been discovered. For Burnouf, Hodgson's discovery restored "to India and to its language the study of a religion and a philosophy whose cradle was India." Hodgson discovered the texts, and Burnouf read them and then set out to demonstrate in the *Introduction* that the life of the Buddha and the tradition that he founded can only be fully understood as a product of Indian culture, and expressed in an Indian language. Burnouf's choice of the term *fact* (*fait*) is telling, suggesting his conviction that the Buddha and Buddhism are historical rather than mythological, and that the true Buddhism, as he declares repeatedly, is a human Buddhism that arose not in heaven but on the often contested soil of ancient India. Furthermore, he argues that much about the historical circumstances and social milieu of Buddhism's origins, as well as the chronology of its subsequent development, can be gleaned from reading its scriptures. In doing so, he takes a strong stand

25. A clearer understanding of the process by which Burnouf produced the *Introduction* as well as a more precise view of what he intended for the subsequent volumes would be possible with a detailed study of the extensive notes preserved among his papers, described briefly in Feer.

against a view popular in his day, that India had no history. Clearly the title he gave to his book, *Introduction to the History of Indian Buddhism*, was not randomly chosen.

Burnouf divides his book into two memoranda. He begins the first by explaining why Hodgson sent the manuscripts to Paris:

> Mr. Hodgson certainly had not dispatched two collections of such size to Paris in order for them to sleep peacefully on the shelves of a library. He wanted to see the research that he had himself begun with such success in Asia be pursued in Europe; and it would have been a poor acknowledgment of the efforts he had made to procure these manuscripts, and the generosity with which he favored France with them, not to attempt to bring light to some of the works contained therein. I felt, for my part, as a member of the Société Asiatique of Paris, all the honor and urgency in Mr. Hodgson's appeal, and I resolved from that time on to respond with everything I had to offer.

Burnouf goes on to demonstrate that the most important Buddhist texts preserved in Tibetan, Mongolian, and Chinese are in fact translations of works originally composed in Sanskrit. The remainder of the memorandum is devoted to a detailed argument for the importance of reading Buddhist texts in the language in which they were originally composed. He does not dismiss the use of translations into other languages, but demonstrates what can be lost in the process. As he states: "The genius of India has marked all its products with a character so special that whatever the superiority of mind and whatever freedom in the use of their methods one grants to the Oriental translators, one cannot prevent oneself from recognizing that they must necessarily have brought to their versions certain features of the original that often will remain unintelligible to the reader who does not have the means to resort to the Indian text itself." Burnouf's argument proved compelling for future generations of scholars of Buddhism, who would regard Sanskrit as the *lingua franca* of the tradition.

The Second Memorandum, which comprises the remainder of the book, treats various categories of the manuscripts in the Nepalese collection. Here, Burnouf intersperses his descriptions and analyses with extended translations from various Buddhist texts; almost 40 percent of the entire volume is composed of these translations and Burnouf's copious notes. He had clearly translated a substantial number of texts before he began writing the *Introduction* and deftly incorporated passages from them into his discussion. In addition to its sustained analysis of Buddhist Sanskrit literature, the *Introduction* was the first work of European scholarship to provide translations of Sanskrit Buddhist texts.

The first section of the Second Memorandum is devoted to the various traditional categories for classifying Buddhist texts. For his own purposes, Burnouf chose the most famous of these, the division into the *tripiṭaka*, or "three baskets." These are the *sūtras*, or discourses of the Buddha; the *vinaya*, or works on monastic discipline; and the *abhidharma*, works on philosophy or, as Burnouf renders the term, "metaphysics."

Perhaps Burnouf's most important point in his discussion of the sūtras is the distinction he draws between what he calls the simple sūtras and the developed sūtras. The former (which he draws in fact from the *avadānas*) he considers the older and the more authentic, in the sense that they derive from the Buddha himself or his direct disciples. These are the sūtras that provide both the clearest sense of the Buddha's true teachings and the most valuable information on the early history of Buddhism. The developed sūtras, in contrast, clearly derive from a later period and are filled with mythological elements. The simple sūtras depict the Buddha above all as a teacher of ethics and morality, speaking directly to a human society in which his teachings are not always welcomed. The complicated metaphysics of the developed sūtras derive not from the Buddha but from the musings of monks safely cloistered from the society in which the Buddha fought his battles against the vested interests of the brahmans. "The ordinary sūtras show us Śākyamuni Buddha preaching his doctrine in the midst of a society that, judging from the legends in which he plays a role, was profoundly corrupt. His teaching is above all moral; and although metaphysics is not forgotten, it certainly occupies a less grand position than the theory of virtues imposed by the law of the Buddha, virtues among which charity, patience, and chastity are without objection at the first rank." Burnouf makes a pointed distinction between the two classes of sūtras, and does not hesitate to express his preference for the simple sūtras.

> The scene of the first is India, the actors are humans and some inferior divinities; and save for the power to make miracles that Śākya and his foremost disciples possess, what occurs there seems natural and plausible. On the contrary, everything that the imagination can conceive as immense in space and time is still too confining for the scene of the developed sūtras. The actors there are these imaginary bodhisattvas, with infinite virtues, with endless names one cannot pronounce, with bizarre and almost ridiculous titles, where the oceans, the rivers, the waves, the rays, the suns are coupled with qualities of unmerited perfection in a manner most puerile and least instructive, because it is without effort there. No one is left to convert; everyone believes, and each is quite sure to become a buddha one day, in a world of diamonds or lapis lazuli. The consequence of all this is that the more developed the sūtras are, the poorer they are in historical details; and the farther they penetrate into metaphysical doctrine, the more they distance themselves from society and become estranged from what occurs there.

The first section also contains Burnouf's long and fascinating discussion of the role of caste in Buddhism. In introducing the topic of social class in Indian Buddhism, he observes that European authors had long portrayed the Buddha as a firm opponent of the caste system. Yet, he notes, they had done so without access to any Indian Buddhist sources. He then begins an erudite discussion of the Buddha's attitude toward caste, demonstrating that the simple representation of the Buddha as a social reformer (which persists to the present day) requires substantial qualification. After making it clear that the Buddha's attitude toward caste was a good deal more nuanced than it had been portrayed by previous writers (and would be portrayed by subsequent writers), Burnouf concludes, "We now see, if I am not mistaken, how this celebrated axiom of Oriental history, that Buddhism has erased all distinction of caste, must be understood."

Throughout the long section on the sūtras, and indeed throughout the book, Burnouf is ever concerned with the history that can be gleaned from the texts, considering, for example, how the analysis of linguistic forms can help determine the date of a text and how the presence of predictions of historical figures proves that the texts in which the predictions occur postdate the figures they prophesy.

The section on the Vinaya is largely devoted to stories about monks, with lengthy passages from the stories of the monks Pūrṇa and Saṃgharakṣita, and of the emperor Aśoka. The Sanskrit manuscripts received by Burnouf did not contain any texts specifically concerned with monastic discipline. This led Burnouf to conclude that in the Nepalese collection, it was the *avadānas* or legends that functioned as the Vinaya, with the rules of monastic life implied rather than codified. He devotes considerable attention in this section to a variety of monastic titles as well as the stages of advancement along the Buddhist path. He is aware of the existence of monastic codes in other Buddhist languages and attempts to reconstruct what the key terms would be in Sanskrit. In perhaps the most interesting discussion in this section, Burnouf speculates about the origins of what he considers the only authentic forms of Buddhist worship: the veneration of the Buddha image and the veneration of the stūpa. Here, as elsewhere, it is clear that Burnouf does not confine his evidence to Sanskrit manuscripts. He demonstrates both great familiarity with, and a great interest in, the excavation of stūpas and the analysis of their contents by scholars such as Charles Masson, Alexander Cunningham, and James Prinsep.[26]

The section devoted to the Abhidharma is concerned not so much with the topics specifically associated with these scriptures, such as epistemology and

26. For a popular history of these figures, see Charles Allen, *The Search for the Buddha: The Men Who Discovered India's Lost Religion* (New York: Carroll & Graf Publishers, 2003).

the function of cognition, but more broadly with Buddhist philosophy. As was the case with the Vinaya, Burnouf sought to describe the contents of the texts he received from Hodgson, what he calls the Nepalese collection. The only text in that collection concerned with the Abhidharma in a strict sense was Yaśomitra's commentary (dated by some as late as the eighth century) on Vasubandhu's *Abhidharmakośa.* If this was the only Abhidharma text that Burnouf could have, it was a fortuitous acquisition, and he makes good use of it here and in a subsequent section. He also considers the doctrine of emptiness set forth in the *prajñāpāramitā* corpus as a constituent of the Abhidharma, and he provides a long extract from the beginning of the *Perfection of Wisdom in Eight Thousand Lines.* Ever faithful to Hodgson, Burnouf again discusses the four schools of Buddhist philosophy that Hodgson had set forth in his essays, politely noting that he has been unable to find any mention of them in the Sanskrit manuscripts. The final part of this section is devoted to a detailed exposition of the twelve links of dependent origination (*pratītyasamutpāda*). Ever the generous scholar, Burnouf felt obliged here to include long notes containing the fanciful interpretations of the young German Sanskritist Theodor Goldstücker (1821–1872).

The next section, on Buddhist tantra, is particularly important. Here, Burnouf expresses a disdain that scholars would echo for the next century. He writes, "It is not my intention to long dwell on this part of the Nepalese collection, which I am inclined to regard as the most modern of all, and whose importance for the history of human superstitions does not compensate for its mediocrity and vapidity. It is certainly not without interest to see Buddhism, which in its first organization had so little of what makes a religion, end in the most puerile practices and the most exaggerated superstitions." Indeed, he is incredulous that Alexander Csoma de Kőrös finds some of the tantras beautiful. Burnouf is especially disappointed to see Buddhism, which had for so many centuries distinguished itself from Brahmanism, here make an alliance with "Śivaism." He goes to some lengths to try to understand the origins of this unfortunate alliance. Also included in this section is Burnouf's summary of the *Sūtra of Golden Light* (*Suvarṇaprabhāsa*). Although it is an important and influential Mahāyāna sūtra, especially in East Asia, Burnouf found it listed as a tantra in Csoma de Kőrös's description of the Tibetan canon and regards it as such, finding fault with it on a number of scores. For example,

> This book is so filled with praises of itself made by the Buddha or his listeners, and with the account of the advantages promised to one who studies and reads it, that one searches for it in vain beneath this mass of praise, and one arrives at the last page, almost without knowing what the *Suvarṇaprabhāsa* is. This feature is, to my mind, quite decisive. Nothing, indeed, better shows to what mediocre proportions Buddhism was reduced by the tantras than this tiresome repetition of the advantages

> and merits assured to the owner of a book which, in itself and apart from these developments, would be almost reduced to a few pages.

This fault is clearly not confined to the tantras, and is endemic to many Mahāyāna sūtras; it is noteworthy that Burnouf does not seem to discern the same problem in his beloved *Lotus Sūtra*, although it is rampant there as well.

The penultimate section is devoted to those works that, unlike the sūtras, bear the names of their authors. Here Burnouf returns to the commentary on the *Abhidharmakośa*. He also discusses Nāgārjuna; it appears that among his manuscripts was the *Prasannapadā*, Candrakīrti's commentary on Nāgārjuna's *Madhyamakaśāstra* (*Treatise on the Middle Way*), but carrying the wrong title: *Vinayasūtra*. He ends this section with a passage from Yaśomitra refuting the existence of God. Burnouf seems pleased to observe that Yaśomitra shows no familiarity with the concept of the *ādibuddha*, the primordial buddha that Hodgson described.

The seventh and final section of the Second Memorandum, "History of the Nepal Collection," provides a fascinating insight into Burnouf's historiography. When he had delivered his inaugural lecture in 1833, Burnouf had noted the lack of a single historical text among all the Sanskrit classics. He lamented, "Among so many riches, one feels regret at not finding the history of the nation that they forever glorify."[27] In 1844 he would argue that the history of India only begins to become clear at the time of the Buddha, a development that he credits to "the realistic spirit of this doctrine, its materialism and even its ordinariness." As he explains: "Never descending from heaven and remaining constantly in the vague regions of mythology where the reader grasps only vain forms that are no longer possible for him to fix in time or space, the sacred books of the Buddhists ordinarily present us with a series of entirely human events, a kṣatriya who makes himself an ascetic, who does battle with brahmans, who teaches and converts kings whose names these books have preserved for us."

Also in this section, Burnouf considers the three Buddhist councils at some length, speculating on their respective roles in the formation of the texts that have been preserved to the present and on how a fuller understanding of the councils would allow us to better date the texts. He wonders whether a correspondence could be drawn between the three councils and three genres of Buddhist literature that he discerns: the simple sūtras, the developed sūtras, and the tantras, or whether the tantras arose long after the councils. Speaking of the time when Buddhism was banished from India, he writes with a certain nostalgia: "It is clear, indeed, that as Buddhism moved away from its cradle, it lost a portion of

27. Eugène Burnouf, "De la langue et de la littérature sanscrite. Discours d'Ouverture, prononcé au Collège de France," *Revue des deux mondes*, 2nd ser., 1 (Février, 1833): 271.

the life that it drew from its long abode in the country where it had flourished for so many centuries, and, obliged to use, in order to propagate among new peoples, diverse idioms sometimes little amenable to the expression of its own conceptions, little by little it hid its original forms under borrowed cloths."

The final section closes not with grand conclusions or even a summation of the six hundred pages that have come before, but with a series of questions, especially about the date of the death of the Buddha, questions that Burnouf clearly intended to take up in a subsequent volume of the *Introduction.*

The work ends with a series of appendixes on a variety of Sanskrit terms, ranging from nirvāna to *kārṣāpaṇa*, a form of currency in ancient India that Burnouf calculates at 175 English troy grains and thus worth approximately five centimes in France in 1844. Much of the appendix on nirvāṇa is devoted to Burnouf's ultimately unsuccessful attempt to make sense of the terms *sopadhiśeṣa nirvāṇa* and *anupadhiśeṣa nirvāṇa.* The first of these terms, rendered perhaps as "nirvāṇa with remainder," refers to the state of destruction of all future rebirth while one is still living. The latter, rendered perhaps as "nirvāṇa without remainder," refers to the state of final nirvāna after death, in which the "remainder" of mind and body no longer exists. The longest of the appendixes is devoted to an attempt to bring consistency to several conflicting descriptions of the hierarchy of Buddhist heavens, including that provided by the Augustinian friar Antonio Georgi of Rimini (1711–1797) in his *Alphabetum Tibetanum.* Here, Burnouf's anticlerical sentiments occasionally overwhelm his usually charitable attitude toward the work of other scholars.

Because Burnouf read everything that had been published about Buddhism in a European language, the *Introduction* presents a fascinating survey of the state of European knowledge in the early decades of the nineteenth century. During these decades, Buddhist scholarship occupied a small domain (Burnouf would sign a short article in the January 1824 issue of *Journal Asiatique* simply "Burnouf fils"). But it was a domain populated by the pioneers of the field. Five scholars were of particular importance to Burnouf and appear most often in the *Introduction*'s footnotes. It is against the background of their work that the extent of Burnouf's achievement comes into focus.

The first was the great French Sinologist Jean-Pierre Abel-Rémusat (1788–1832), appointed in 1814 to the new chair in Chinese at the Collège de France. The single most cited work in Burnouf's *Introduction* is the *Foe koue ki*, whose full title is *Foĕ Kouĕ Ki ou Relation des royaumes bouddhiques: Voyage dans la Tartarie, dans l'Afghanistan et dans l'Inde, exécuté à la fin du IV*[e] *siècle, par Chỹ Fă Hian*, published in Paris in 1836. This was Abel-Rémusat's translation of the *Foguo ji* (Record of Buddhist Kingdoms), the travel journal of the Chinese monk Faxian (ca. 337–ca. 422), which provides an invaluable description of Buddhism in India and Sri Lanka at the beginning of the fifth century. The Chinese text is relatively short, but Abel-Rémusat provided detailed notes, in which he sought to identify and explain the many Buddhist persons, places, and doctrines that occur in Faxian's work. When Abel-Rémusat died in the cholera epidemic of 1832, the book was only half finished. Heinrich Julius von Klaproth (1783–1835) took over the project until his own death. It was completed by Ernest-Augustin Xavier Clerc de Landresse (1800–1862) and published in 1836. Until the publication of Burnouf's *Introduction* in 1844, this was the most detailed study of Buddhism to be produced in Europe, and is Burnouf's main source on Chinese Buddhism.

The second scholar was Isaak Jakob Schmidt (1779–1847), a German-Russian born in Amsterdam who served as a Moravian missionary in the Kalmyk region of Russia, whose Mongol population practiced Tibetan Buddhism. He learned both Tibetan and Mongolian, and went on to establish both Tibetan studies and Mongolian studies in Russia. In 1837 he published a translation of the *Diamond Sūtra* from the Tibetan into German, and wrote extensively on Mahāyāna Buddhism. Burnouf held him in high esteem and cites both his essays and his translations of the *Erdeniin Tobchi* (The Chronicles of Sagang Sechen) from Mongolian and the *Sūtra of the Wise Man and the Fool* from Tibetan.

Burnouf's chief source on Tibetan Buddhism was the itinerant Transylvanian scholar Alexander Csoma de Kőrös (1784–1842). His search for the home of the Magyar people led Csoma eventually to Ladakh, where he studied Tibetan texts from 1827 to 1831 before proceeding to Calcutta. His essays on Tibetan Buddhism, published in the *Journal of the Asiatic Society of Bengal* and in *Asiatic Researches*, as well as his Tibetan-English dictionary, are repeatedly cited by Burnouf. It was Csoma's essays on the Tibetan canon that led Burnouf to conclude that the sūtras were translations of works originally composed in Sanskrit.

Although Burnouf read Pāli, the sacred language of Theravāda Buddhism (as noted above, he and Christian Lassen had published *Essai sur le pâli* in 1826), he placed great faith in the work of the leading Pāli scholar of the day, George Turnour (1799–1843). Turnour was born in Sri Lanka, the son of a British civil servant, and after being educated in England spent most of his brief career there, studying Sinhala and Pāli literature. In the *Ceylon Almanack* of 1833 and 1834, he published "Epitome of the History of Ceylon, and the Historical Inscriptions." This contained a translation of "the first twenty chapters of the Mahawanso and a prefatory essay on Pali Buddhistical literature." These writings were his first publications on the *Mahāvaṃsa*, the Great Chronicle of Sri Lanka, which recounts the life and teachings of the Buddha and the history of the transmission of Buddhism from India to Sri Lanka. Although he did not complete his study of the text before his untimely death, he was able to contribute important essays to the *Journal of the Asiatic Society of Bengal*, which Burnouf cites as authoritative.

Finally, there was Brian Hodgson (1801–1894), from whom Burnouf received the Sanskrit manuscripts that would serve as the foundation of his *Introduction*, and to whom Burnouf would dedicate his translation of the *Lotus Sūtra*. Hodgson is remembered today for having sent the Sanskrit and Tibetan texts that he acquired in Kathmandu to Calcutta, London, Oxford, and Paris, but between 1827 and 1841, he published a number of essays on Buddhism. Two of these were particularly important: "Notices of the Languages, Literature and Religion of the Bauddhas of Nepal and Bhot" (*Asiatic Researches*, 1828) and "Sketch of Buddhism, Derived from the Bauddha Scriptures of Nipál" (*Transactions of the Royal Asiatic Society*, 1830) while serving as Assistant Resident and Acting Resident to the Court of Nepal. In these essays, Hodgson describes four schools of Indian philosophy, which later research has shown to have been fabrications (whether willful or not) by either Hodgson or his Newar colleague, Amṛtānanda. Burnouf dutifully discusses these schools in the *Introduction* while acknowledging his inability to find reference to them in the Sanskrit manuscripts that Hodgson had provided.[28]

THE BUDDHISM OF BURNOUF

If the most consequential sentence in the *Introduction* appears on the first page of the foreword, perhaps the second most consequential is buried in a footnote about halfway through the volume. There Burnouf writes, "The present volume is dedicated in its entirety to put in relief the purely human character of Buddhism."

The European encounter with the Buddha had passed through several phases. The travelers and missionaries to the various Buddhist cultures of Asia knew him only as an idol, represented in different forms and known by different names. For Marco Polo, making port in Sri Lanka on his return voyage to Venice after years at the court of the Great Khan, he is Sagamoni Borcan. For St. Francis Xavier, preaching the Gospel to the Japanese, he is Xaca. For Matteo Ricci, donning the robes of a Buddhist monk in an effort to convert them, he was Sciequia. For Simon de la Loubère, envoy of Louis XIV to the court of Siam, he was Sommona-Codom. These were different idols, with different names, representing different gods.

It was only around the turn of the eighteenth century that the conclusion came to be drawn that these were different names, and different images, of the same god. We read in volume 15 of Diderot and d'Alembert's *Encyclopédie, ou Dictionnaire raisonné des sciences, des métiers et des arts*, published in 1765:

28. Also appearing in the notes are Stanislas Julien, Christian Lassen, and Horace Hayman Wilson (1786–1860), the British Sanskritist who, after serving in the East India Company, was appointed to the newly established Boden Chair of Sanskrit at Oxford.

"SIAKA, religion of, (Hist. mod. Superstition) this religion, which is established in Japan, has as its founder *Siaka* or *Xaca*, who is also called *Budso*, & his religion *Budsodoism*. It is believed that the *buds* or the *siaka* of the Japanese is the same as the *foë* of the Chinese, & the *visnou*, the *buda* or *putza* of the Indians, the *sommonacodum* of the Siamese; for it seems certain that this religion came originally from the Indies to Japan, where previously only the religion of the *sintos* was professed."

Much of the speculation about the Buddha in the eighteenth century considered whether this god had once been a man and, if so, where he had come from. When the British arrived in India, they learned that the Buddha was the ninth incarnation of the god Viṣṇu, remembered for his opposition to both animal sacrifice and the caste system. The Buddha was thus revered by the brahmans (with a certain ambivalence), but Buddhists were scorned. This led Sir William Jones to speculate that there were two Buddhas, one of whom—based on the thick lips and curly locks of the statues—likely came from Ethiopia; the other was from India. He would also argue that the Buddha was of Nordic origin. Jones's African hypothesis continued to hold sway, forcing Abel-Rémusat to publish an essay in 1825 (just two decades before the *Introduction*) entitled "On Some Descriptive Epithets of Buddha Showing that Buddha Did Not Belong to the Black Race."[29]

By the time Burnouf published the *Introduction*, the leading European scholars understood that the Buddha was a historical figure and that he was of Indian origin. The basic story of his life had been repeated many times in the accounts of travelers and missionaries, but this story was derived largely from oral reports provided by Buddhists outside India in various local vernaculars. Burnouf was the first to read a large corpus of Indian Buddhist texts in Sanskrit, and it is from these sources that he paints his portrait of the Buddha.[30]

Burnouf played a crucial role in demythologizing and humanizing the Buddha, portraying a compassionate man who preached to all who would listen, without dogma and ritual. Burnouf writes on page 328, "I speak here in particular of the Buddhism which appears to me to be the most ancient, the human Buddhism, if I dare call it that, which consists almost entirely in very simple rules of morality, and where it is enough to believe that the Buddha was a man who

29. "Sur quelques épithètes descriptives de Bouddha qui font voir que Bouddha n'appartenait pas a la race nègre," in Jean-Pierre Abel-Rémusat, *Mélanges Asiatiques* (Paris: Librarie Orientale de Dondey-Dupré Père et Fils, 1825), 1:100–128.

30. It is important to note that although he believed that Buddhist texts should be read in the language in which they had been composed, Burnouf did not disdain the use of translations into Chinese, Japanese, Mongolian, or Tibetan, as he makes clear in the First Memorandum. Nor does he reject in principle the aid of Buddhist scholars, noting that the scholars of Europe are forced by circumstance to work without "the assistance of natives, among whom are some learned men who have preserved the repository of traditional interpretation faithfully."

reached a degree of intelligence and of virtue that each must take as the exemplar for his life."

Yet the Buddha's humanity, for Burnouf, does not make him ordinary. Indeed, what is perhaps most human about the Buddha is that he attained his extraordinary state through his own virtues and efforts, rather than having been divine from birth.

> The authority on which the monk of the Śākya race supported his teaching was entirely personal; it was formed of two elements, one real and the other ideal. The first was the consistency and the saintliness of his conduct, of which chastity, patience, and charity formed the principal features. The second was the claim he made to be buddha, that is to say, enlightened, and as such to possess superhuman science and power. With his power, he performed miracles; with his science, he perceived, in a form clear and complete, the past and the future.

Buddhism for Burnouf was completely Indian, and much of the volume is dedicated to the demonstration of this fact. However, he also seeks to demonstrate the many ways in which Buddhism differed from the dominant Indian religion, Brahmanism (what we refer to today as Hinduism). Brahmanism is negatively portrayed by Burnouf as a tradition controlled by complacent clerics obsessed with protecting the privilege of their caste system at all costs, restricting access to an arid sacred knowledge to those who receive it through the accident of birth. Indeed, for Burnouf, Brahmanism is the persecutor of Buddhism, eventually driving it from Indian soil. This is something that Burnouf clearly regrets, and he distinguishes Buddhism from Brahmanism at almost every turn.

> Written generally in a form and a language that is very simple, the sūtras retain the visible trace of their origin. They are dialogues related to morality and philosophy, in which Śākya fills the role of master. Far from presenting his thought in this concise form so familiar to the Brahmanical teaching, there is no doubt that he expounds it with tiresome repetitions and diffuseness, but which give his teaching the character of a real preaching. There is an abyss between his method and that of the brahmans. Instead of this mysterious teaching confided almost secretly to a small number of listeners, instead of these formulas whose studied obscurity seems made to discourage the acumen of the disciple as much as to exercise it, the sūtras show us a large audience around Śākya, composed of all those who desire to listen to him and in his language, with this need to make himself understood, having words for all intelligences and, through its perpetual repetitions, leaving no excuse to less attentive minds or more rebellious memories. This profound difference is at the very essence of Buddhism, a doctrine whose characteristic feature is proselytism, but proselytism is itself only an effect of this sentiment of benevolence and universal charity which

animates the Buddha, and which is at once the cause and the aim of the mission he gave himself on earth.

For Burnouf, this humanity of the Buddha distinguishes him from the Hindu gods: "Śākya does not come, like the Brahmanical incarnations of Viṣṇu, to show the people an eternal and infinite God, descending to earth and preserving, in the mortal condition, the irresistible power of the divinity. He is the son of a king who becomes a monk and who has only the superiority of his virtue and his science to recommend him to the people." It is true that the Buddha occasionally performs miracles, but he does so only to favorably dispose his audience to what he has to say; what distinguishes the Buddha from his Brahmanical opponents (who also perform miracles) is his teaching, a simple teaching of charity and morality, which he offers freely to members of all castes.

Thus, although Buddhism is thoroughly Indian, there is something about the Buddha that distinguishes him from other teachers who have appeared in India. Throughout the simple sūtras, that is, the sūtras that most accurately represent the teachings of the historical Buddha, the Buddha is above all human, and the power of his humanity was such that it could overthrow the great weight of the culture in which he appeared. Burnouf writes, "He lived, he taught, and he died as a philosopher; and his humanity remained a fact so incontestably recognized by all that the compilers of legends to whom miracles cost so little did not even have the thought of making him a god after his death." Indeed, the power of the Buddha's humanity was so great that it protected history from being overwhelmed by myth: "This respect for human truth in Buddhism, which prevented the disciples of Śākya from transforming the man into God, is quite remarkable for a people like the Indians, among whom mythology has so easily taken the place of history."

Buddhism is for Burnouf an Indian religion, yet one that departs from the tradition from which it emerged. It does so through the powerful humanity of the Buddha, a humanity that seems to transcend both the time and the place of his birth.

CONCLUSION

A full evaluation and analysis of the *Introduction* is not possible here. In the more than a century and a half since its publication, it has been superseded on many topics that, it must be noted, Burnouf often was the first to introduce to European scholarship. When viewed in the light of the current state of knowledge, it is clear that Burnouf made mistakes of interpretation and of fact (for example, he refers to Ārya Asaṅga, the famous Yogācāra master, as Ārya Saṃgha, and he conflates Nāgārjuna and Nāgasena). The manuscripts he received from Hodgson were for the most part modern copies, filled with scribal errors (about which he repeatedly complains); the discovery of earlier manuscripts in Central Asia in subsequent decades has provided clearer insights into the histories of these texts. But given the state of knowledge about Buddhism in 1844 and the sources Burnouf had before him, the *Introduction* is a remarkable achievement; for almost every topic he considers, he provides a more informed and sustained discussion than had appeared previously. It must also be said that the *Introduction* is the work of a superb Sanskritist. Burnouf notes in passing, "I can assert that there is nothing in all the Sanskrit literature as easy to understand as the texts of Nepal, apart from some terms the Buddhists used in a very special way; I will not give any proof of this other than the considerable number of texts that it was possible for me to read in a rather limited time." The "considerable number of texts" included many lengthy and—at least in the estimation of lesser mortals—difficult sūtras and tantras.[31] Also in evidence is the quality of Burnouf's mind. Despite the eloquence of his prose and the complexity of his sentences, there is a generosity about his style, as if Burnouf were conversing with a colleague, reading texts and speculating about what can, and cannot, be concluded from them about the Buddha and his teachings. He often presents his thinking rather than stating a conclusion; his writing recounts his reflections. His scrupulous scholarship, even in its elaborate style, is the mark of a deep intellectual integrity.

In some ways, the *Introduction* is the work of the scholar's scholar, and in this sense its specific contributions to the field of Buddhist studies are many. Yet Burnouf was not just writing for his fellow Orientalists; he wrote also for the educated European public. And for the public in Europe, and beyond, he described the Buddha and Buddhism for the first time in ways that would become so ingrained and natural that their origins in an 1844 French tome would eventually be forgotten. These would include that Buddhism is an Indian religion, that the Buddha is a historical figure, and, perhaps of particular consequence, that the Buddha was the human teacher of a religion (or perhaps a philosophy) that preached ethics and morality, without recourse to dogma, ritual, or metaphysics. The consequences of his portrayal of the Buddha and his Buddhism would be profound.

The task that Burnouf set for himself was unlike anything he, or anyone, had previously attempted. He was not editing, translating, and annotating a single text, no matter how substantial, as he had with the *Yasna* or the *Bhagavata Purāṇa*. He was attempting something entirely new, with very few resources available to him. Furthermore, he did not have a tradition of reliable scholar-

31. As Roer noted in his 1845 review, "It is certainly not an easy task to go through eighty large manuscript works, written in a barbarous language, made often unintelligible by the ignorance of the copyist, to analyse the contents of all, to bring them in their true chronological order, to compare them with the documents of other nations, written in a different language, and lastly use them as sources for the history, religion, and philosophy of the Buddhists" (Roer, review of *Introduction à l'histoire du Buddhisme indien*, pp. 784–85).

ship to serve as his foundation. At the time that he wrote the *Introduction*, there were some who were still debating whether Brahmanism or Buddhism came first, whether the Buddha was of Ethiopian or Nordic origin. We might then conclude this introduction to the *Introduction* with Burnouf's own description of his undertaking:

> The task I impose on myself, although different, is equally arduous. It is necessary to browse through almost one hundred volumes, all manuscripts, written in four languages still little known, for whose study we have only lexicons, I could say of imperfect vocabularies, one of which has given birth to popular dialects even whose names are almost unknown. To these difficulties of form, add those of content: an entirely new subject, innumerable schools, an immense metaphysical apparatus, a mythology without boundaries; everywhere disorder and a dispiriting vagueness on questions of time and place; then, outside and among the small number of scholars whom a laudable curiosity attracts toward the results promised to this research, ready-made solutions, opinions that are immovable and ready to resist the authority of the texts, because they pride themselves in resting on an authority superior to all others, that of common sense. Do I need to recall that, for some people, all the questions related to Buddhism were already decided, when no one had read a single line of the books I shall analyze shortly, when the existence of these books was not even suspected by anyone? For some, Buddhism was a venerable cult born in Central Asia, and whose origin was lost in the mists of time; for others it was a miserable counterfeit of Nestorianism; the Buddha has been made a Negro, because he had frizzy hair; a Mongol, because he had slanted eyes; a Scythe, because he was called Śākya. He has even been made a planet; and I do not know whether some scholars do not still delight today in recognizing this peaceful sage in the traits of the bellicose Odin. Certainly, it is permissible to hesitate, when to such vast solutions one promises only to substitute doubts, or only explanations that are simple and almost vulgar. The hesitation can even lead to discouragement, when one retraces one's steps and compares the results obtained to the time they have cost. I would like, nevertheless, to rely on the indulgence of serious persons to whom these studies are addressed; and while they leave me with the feeling of my insufficiency, with which I am affected more than ever, the hope for their benevolent consideration has given me the courage to produce these rough drafts, destined to open the way to research, which, while still not having a numerous public, is nonetheless in itself of incontestable value for the history of the human spirit.

A Note on the Translation

Eugène Burnouf's *Introduction à l'histoire du Buddhisme indien* is written in the prose of the French academy of his day, as practiced by philologists like Burnouf, well trained in Latin rhetoric. Its often difficult and antiquated style can seem both erudite and archaic to the modern reader, with lengthy and complicated sentences in which the referent is often ambiguous. Burnouf employs many grammatical forms and syntactic structures that are no longer used in modern French; the difficulty of the language is one of the factors that has contributed to the work's oblivion. Burnouf's prose style therefore requires a special attention from even the educated native speaker. It also requires painstaking precision on the part of a translator to arrive at a clear and exact rendering into English.

As translators of the present text, we have attempted to preserve the form, and the formality, of this classic work of scholarship. For that reason, we have not sought to shorten the sentences or "modernize" the language. In order to convey the deliberate and discursive (and at points laborious) quality of Burnouf's prose, we have preserved each sentence as a single unit while changing the syntax to provide a smoother rendering. We have made every effort to determine the meanings of words as they were used among the savants of Paris in the early nineteenth century, relying heavily on the four-volume *Dictionnaire de la langue française* (1877) by Émile Littré, a close friend of Burnouf's.

To make the translation more accessible to the modern reader, Burnouf's archaic renderings of Sanskrit, Chinese, and Tibetan terms have been changed to reflect modern academic conventions. Thus, for example, Tchandra kîrti has been changed to Candrakīrti, and Mañdjuçrî to Mañjuśrī; Hiuan thsang has been changed to Xuanzang, and Keou li thai tseu to Juli taizi; *Hdjig-rten-skyong-ba bji* has been changed to *'jig rten skyong ba bzhi*. When Burnouf identifies misspellings, as in the case of Georgi's *Alphabetum Tibetanum*, the transliteration has been changed to the modern form, but the error has been retained. His phonetics, like Kah-gyur, have also been retained. Sanskrit terms have also been lowercased and combined, changing, for example, Burnouf's Pratyeka Buddha to *pratyekabuddha*. In addition, place-names have been converted to the modern spelling whenever possible. Burnouf's spelling has been corrected in two instances. His *Śāriputtra* and *Vātsīputtrīya* have been changed to *Śāriputra* and *Vātsīputrīya*, and his *phāṭimokkha* (which he read in Burmese manuscripts, where the aspirated and unaspirated *p* are difficult to distinguish) has been changed to *pātimokkha*.

Burnouf often quotes, in French, from English-language sources, especially Hodgson, Wilson, and Turnour. We initially planned to restore the original English rather than translating Burnouf's translations. In comparing Burnouf's French to the original English, however, it became clear that he was not translating passages from British scholars, but paraphrasing them—in some cases augmenting them, and in rare cases misreading them. Consequently we have translated Burnouf's translation, rather than restoring the original English.

Burnouf's numerous translations from the Sanskrit have not been checked against the original texts, as important as that task is; the purpose of this translation is to bring his influential understanding of Buddhism to an Anglophone audience, even when that understanding may not be that of the modern scholar.

Introduction à l'histoire du Buddhisme indien was originally published in 1844 and reprinted in 1876, with an introduction by Jules Barthélemy-Saint Hilaire. The 1876 edition contains typographical errors absent in the 1844 text. We have translated the original edition, making one addition from the 1876 text. Burnouf provided a number of pages of "Additions" at the end of the book (pages 579–93). Their presence is not noted in the 1844 edition, whereas the 1876 edition adds footnotes that say, "See the additions at the end of this volume." Those footnotes have been included here. In "Additions and Corrections," which is the final appendix, augmentations to bibliographical citations and corrections of spelling errors have been incorporated into the body of the text, leaving those additions that add substantive points to Burnouf's discussion.

Burnouf's often inconsistent and occasionally cryptic abbreviations of his sources in the footnotes have been provided in full. The *Introduction* did not contain an index, but instead a detailed "Table Analytique" at the end of the volume (which has moved to the beginning here). However, Burnouf's *Le Lotus de la Bonne Loi* contains a combined index for both that text and the *Introduction*, so the index to this volume has been extracted from that and provided here.

Translating a work of the size, age, and complexity of Burnouf's *Introduction à l'histoire du Buddhisme indien* required us to make thousands of difficult decisions about the rendering of terms from French into English. Two might be mentioned here. Burnouf uses the word *vase* (vase or vessel) to describe vessels as different in shape and purpose as the begging bowl used by a Buddhist monk, the urn used to hold the relics of the Buddha, and a pitcher used for pouring water. This term has been translated as "bowl," "urn," and "pitcher," depending on the context. Second, Burnouf makes frequent use of the noun *religieux*, in both the singular and the plural. It is clear from context that in most cases he is referring to a Buddhist monk, and in such cases it is translated accordingly. However, he uses the term elsewhere to describe Hindu ascetics and Newar priests, neither of whom are technically monks. In those cases, the term is translated as the somewhat archaic English noun "religious."

INTRODUCTION TO THE HISTORY OF INDIAN BUDDHISM

INTRODUCTION
TO THE HISTORY
OF INDIAN BUDDHISM

BY E. BURNOUF

Of the Institut de France
And of the Academies of Munich and of Lisbon,
Correspondent of Those of Berlin, St. Petersburg, Turin, etc.

FIRST VOLUME
PARIS
IMPRIMERIE ROYALE
1844

In memory of

MR. JEAN-LOUIS BURNOUF

My Father

A Token of Gratitude and Regret

Table of Contents Contained in the First Volume

Analytical Table of the First Two Memoranda *41*
Foreword *51*

FIRST MEMORANDUM
Preliminary Observations *55*

SECOND MEMORANDUM
Description of the Collection of the Books of Nepal *81*

SECTION 1 General Description *83*
SECTION 2 *Sūtras*, or Discourses of Śākya *115*
SECTION 3 *Vinaya*, or Discipline *245*
SECTION 4 *Abhidharma*, or Metaphysics *411*
SECTION 5 Tantras *479*
SECTION 6 Works Bearing the Names of Authors *505*
SECTION 7 History of the Collection of Nepal *523*

APPENDIXES

No. 1. On the Word *Nirvāṇa* *535*
No. 2. On the Expression *Sahalokadhātu* *541*
No. 3. On the Words *Purāṇa* and *Kārṣāpaṇa* *545*
No. 4. On the Names of Gods among the Buddhists *547*
No. 5. On the Sandalwood Called *Gośīrṣa* *569*
No. 6. On the Name Śākala *573*
No. 7. On the Expression *Pratītyasamutpāda* *577*
No. 8. Additions and Corrections *579*

Analytical Table of the First Two Memoranda

FIRST MEMORANDUM
Preliminary observations, p. 55.

Occasion of this research, p. 55.—Discoveries of Mr. B. H. Hodgson, p. 55.—His memoranda in the *Asiatic Researches* of Calcutta, p. 56; in the *Asiatic Transactions* of London, p. 56.—His catalogue of Buddhist books, p. 57.—He sends a collection of them to London, p. 57.—Another to the Société Asiatique of Paris, p. 58.—He has another more considerable collection of them copied for this society, p. 58.—These works are the original texts of the books translated among most of the Buddhist peoples of Asia, p. 59.—Proofs of this fact related to the Tibetans, p. 60; the Mongols, p. 60; the Chinese, p. 61—Importance of the Tibetan, Mongol, and Chinese translations, p. 62.—Superiority of the Sanskrit texts, p. 64.—The translations do not take into account the varieties of dialects, p. 65.—Details drawn from the *Lotus of the Good Law*, p. 65.—Examples borrowed from the Tibetan versions, p. 67—On the word *nirvāṇa*, p. 68.—On Indian proper nouns, p. 72—On the systematically faulty translations, p. 73.—Incontestable utility of these various translations for chronology, p. 75.—That the Sanskrit originals have been, for the most part, written in India, p. 76.—Necessity to study them in order to reach certainty on this point, p. 77.—General plan of the present work, p. 78.

SECOND MEMORANDUM
Description of the collection of the books of Nepal, p. 81.

Section 1. General description, p. 83.

Catalogue of the Nepalese collection by Mr. Hodgson, p. 83.—Extent of this collection, p. 84.—The religious books divided into three collections, p. 85;

The *sūtras*, or first collection, p. 85, regarded as the word of Śākyamuni Buddha, p. 86.—The *vinaya*, or discipline, second collection, p. 87. Lack of so named books in the collection of Mr. Hodgson, p. 88. They are replaced there by the *avadānas*, p. 88.—The *abhidharma*, or metaphysics, is the third collection, p. 89.—The origin of the Abhidharma, p. 90.—It is included in the sūtras, p. 91.—These three collections attributed to the last human buddha, p. 91.—They were collected by his disciples, and not written by the Buddha, p. 91.—On another division called *mātṛkā*, p. 94.—On the four *āgamas*, p. 95.—Summary of the general character of these various divisions, p. 97.—More detailed classification, common to the Sinhalese Buddhists and to the Chinese, p. 98.—*sūtra* and definition of these books, p. 98.—*geya*, p. 98.—*vyākaraṇa*, p. 100.—*gāthā*, p. 101.—*udāna*, p. 102. *nidāna*, p. 104.—*ityuka*, p. 105.—*jātaka*, p. 106.—*vaipulya*, p. 106.—*adbhuta*, p. 107.—*avadāna*, p. 108.—*upadeśa*, p. 109.—Summary of this last classification, p. 109.—Other more general divisions in sūtra and tantra, p. 110.—On the nine dharmas of Nepal, p. 111.

Section 2. *Sūtras*, or discourses of Śākya, p. 115.

Description of a sūtra, p. 116.—On the sūtras properly speaking, the *mahāvaipulya sūtras*, and the *mahāyāna sūtras*, p. 117.—Specimens of these books; translation of the *Sūtra of Māndhātṛ*, with a contemporary preamble of Śākya, p. 118.—Translation of the mythological *Sūtra of Kanakavarṇa*, p. 130.—Form and object of these sūtras, p. 137.—Specimen of the Mahāyāna sūtras, p. 137.—Analysis of the *Sukhavatīvyūha*, p. 138.—Analogy of these sūtras with the mahāvaipulyas, p. 140.—Comparison of the Mahāyāna sūtras (great vehicles) and mahāvaipulyas (of great development) with the simple sūtras, p. 140.—Exterior form of the great sūtras, p. 140.—They are formed from a double redaction, one in prose, the other in verse, p. 140.—They are much more developed than the sūtras properly speaking, p. 141.—They are different in the nature of the language peculiar to the parts in verse, p. 142.—This language is not pure Sanskrit, or Pāli, but an altered Sanskrit, p. 142.—Character of the Sanskrit in which the sūtras and other books in general are written, p. 142.—Analogy of this language with Pāli, p. 144.—On some personages who figure in the preamble of the developed sūtras, p. 145.—On bodhisattvas, p. 145.—On Maitreya, p. 146.—On other bodhisattvas who the developed sūtras made listeners of Śākya, p. 147.—On Mañjuśrī, p. 148.—On Avalokiteśvara, p. 150.—System of the superhuman and the contemplation bodhisattvas, p. 150.—On the supreme Ādibuddha, p. 151.—All these personages and this system are totally foreign to the simple sūtras, p. 154.—Other traits of difference between the simple sūtras and the developed sūtras, p. 155.—On mantras and dhāraṇīs, p. 155.—That the simple sūtras belong to another epoch than the developed and Mahāyāna sūtras, p. 156.—The simple sūtras are the most ancient, p. 157.—Reasons in favor of this sentiment, p. 157: the title *developed* itself, p. 158; the redaction of the books that bear this title, p. 158; the exclusively mythological details with which they are filled, p. 159.—The simple sūtras, on the contrary, represent in the greatest detail, the state of the society where Śākya appeared, p. 159.—This society is the one that the monuments of Brahmanical literature make known to us, p. 161.—Its organization is prior to the coming of Śākya, from which one concludes that Brahmanism is more ancient than Buddhism, p. 162.—Proofs of these assertions, p. 162.—On the Brahmanical gods, p. 163.—Adopted by Śākya but submitted to his power, p. 163.—Their cult inferior to the practice of morality, p. 164.—Extract of a sūtra on this subject, p. 165.—Independence of the Buddha with regard to the gods, p. 165.—Utility of the Buddhist books for the history of Indian mythology, p. 166.—Absence of the name Kṛṣṇa in these books, p. 167.—The sūtras contemporaneous with a form of Brahmanism prior to that described by the Purāṇas, p. 167.—On Indian society according to the sūtras, p. 168.—On the castes and, first, on the brahmans, p. 168.—On the word *brahmacarya* peculiar to the brahmans and adopted by the Buddhists, p. 171.—On the kṣatriyas, p. 172.—On the kings and their absolute power, p. 174.—Details borrowed from the story and the punishment of Vāsavadattā, p. 175.—On the prejudices of the royal caste, proofs extracted from the legend of Aśoka, p. 178.—On the inferior castes, p. 179. Mission that Śākya gives himself in Indian society, p. 180.—Śākya is a simple ascetic, p. 181.—He shares the majority of Brahmanical opinions, p. 182.—He is different from his adversaries only by the definition he gives of salvation, p. 182.—Proofs of these assertions, p. 183.—First beginnings of Śākya, p. 183. Equality of the listeners of Śākya with Brahmanical ascetics, p. 184.—They also give themselves to a life of penance and retreat, p. 185.—Voluntary sacrifices, p. 186.—Similarities and differences between Buddhism and Brahmanism on this particular point, p. 186.—Grievances of the brahmans against the Buddhists, p. 187.—Proofs drawn from the sūtras, p. 187.—Battle of the brahmans against Śākya; miracles and examples borrowed from the sūtras, p. 188. Jealousy of the brahmans against Śākya; proofs borrowed from the legends, p. 188. On the means employed by Śākya to convert the people, p. 213.—On the preaching and newness of this means, p. 213. On miracles and faith, p. 213.—Other means of conversion, p. 214.—Śākya receives the ignorant, p. 215, the poor, and the unfortunate of all conditions: proofs extracted from the sūtras and the legends, p. 215. He attracts people with the grandeur of the reward he promises, p. 217.—Proofs borrowed from a legend, p. 217.—Influence of the preaching of Śākya on the system of castes, p. 221.—Śākya is accused of looking to the lowest classes for his disciples, p. 221.—Detailed proofs extracted from a legend, p. 222. How Śākya freed himself from the distinction of castes, p. 226.—He accepts it but explains it by the theory of pains and rewards, p. 226.—Śākya does more than the other Brahmanical philosophers Kapila and Patanjali, p. 227.—In admitting into the religious life men of all castes, he annihilates *de facto* the influence of the first among all, that of the brahmans, p. 227.—How to understand this axiom that Buddhism effaced all distinction of caste, p. 227.—Coexistence of the castes with Buddhism in Ceylon; explanation of this fact, p. 229.—Refutations of some opinions on this subject, p. 229. Śākya did not appeal to a principle of equality, almost unknown in Asia, p. 229.—Opinion of the Buddhists on the castes, borrowed from a modern treatise of Aśvaghoṣa, p. 230.—Summary of the discussion related to the simple sūtras, p. 232.

Examination of the question of knowing whether the simple sūtras can be regarded as all belonging to the same epoch, p. 233.—Those sūtras in which Śākya predicts future events are later than those in which it is only a matter of him and his disciples, p. 233.—From that, three categories of sūtras: 1. those in which the events are contemporary with Śākya; 2. those that are later than him; 3. the sūtras of great development and of the Mahāyāna, where it is almost no longer a matter of human events, p. 233.—One must add a fourth category of sūtras in which opinions foreign to the primitive institution of Buddhism dominate, p. 234.—Proofs drawn from the analysis of the *Guṇakaraṇḍavyūha*, p. 234.—Presentation of these proofs, p. 239.—Outward analogy of this book with an Indian purāṇa, p. 240.—The Sinhalese tradition is mentioned in it but altered, p. 241.—On two redactions of this work, one in prose and the other in verse, p. 241.—The redaction in prose is prior to the other, p. 242.—Summary of the second section, p. 243.

Section 3. *Vinaya*, or Discipline, p. 245.

The *avadānas*, or legends, of the collection of Nepal take the place of the section called *vinaya*, or discipline, p. 245.—Analogy of the avadānas and the sūtras; possibility to establish the same divisions in the first category of books as in the second, p. 245.—The discipline is not dogmatically set forth there, p. 245.—General conditions to fulfill in order to be admitted among the listeners of Śākya according to the avadānas, p. 246.—Proofs borrowed from the legend of Pūrṇa, and translation of this legend, p. 247.—On the title *bhikṣu*, or mendicant, given to the monks, p. 279.—On the title *śramaṇa*, or ascetic, p. 279.—On *śrāmaṇera*, or novice, p. 279.—On the conditions for admission into the body of monks, p. 280.—On cases of exclusion, p. 280.—Constitution of the assembly of the listeners of Śākya and of the *bhikṣunīs*, or nuns, p. 281.—On *upāsakas* and *upāsikās*, or devotees of the two sexes, p. 282.—The meaning of these terms, p. 282.—Difference of these terms and that of *upasthāyaka*, p. 284.—Opinion of Mr. Hodgson on the upāsakas, p. 284.—On the *saṃgha*, or the assembly of the listeners of Śākya, p. 285.—Opinion of Mr. von Humboldt, p. 285 and note 91.—On the meaning of this term in the formula *Buddha*, *dharma*, and *saṃgha*, p. 286 and note 93.—The monks seek solitude, p. 286.—Circumstances that have favored their meeting in a regularly organized assembly, p. 287.—On *varṣa*, or the retreat of the rainy season, p. 288.—On *vihāras*, or the monasteries, p. 288.—An almost nomadic state of Buddhism, p. 288.—The attacks and persecutions of their adversaries favor the gathering of monks in a hierarchically organized body, p. 289.—On the hierarchy and *sthaviras*, or elders, p. 289.—Explanation of this title, p. 289.—On the influence of merit on the hierarchy, p. 290.—On different degrees of monks regarded according to the order of their merit, p. 290.—On *āryas*, or venerables, p. 291.—On *śrotāpannas*, p. 291.—Explanation of this term, p. 292.—Translation of Mr. Schmidt, p. 292.—On *sakṛdāgāmins* and *anāgamins*, p. 293.—On arhats, p. 294.—Explanation of this term and refutation of the opinion of the Buddhists, p. 295.—On *bodhi*, or the intelligence of a buddha, p. 295.—On *mahāśrāvakas*, or great listeners, p. 296.—On *pratyekabuddhas*, or individual buddhas, p. 296.—Summary of the composition of the assembly of the listeners of Śākya, p. 297.—On some religious institutions, and in particular on confession, p. 298.—On the distinction and the classification of faults according to the *Prātimokṣa Sūtra*, p. 299.—Titles of the eight sections of this work, p. 299.—Comparison of these titles with those that the Sinhalese and the Chinese make known to us, p. 300.—On *śikṣāpadas*, or precepts of the teaching, p. 302.—Examination of the titles of the book of the twelve observances, p. 302.—Analysis of these titles according to the Vocabulaire Pentaglotte, p. 303.—Summary of the principal observances imposed on monks, and in particular on retreat, robes, and chastity, p. 308.—On the life of monks in monasteries according to the legend of Saṃgharakṣita, and translation of this legend, p. 310.—On the moral character of these prescriptions and of Buddhism in general, p. 327.—Comparison of Buddhism and Brahmanism in this particular regard, p. 327.—On the character of the discipline in religions where there is little dogma, p. 327.—On worship and the objects to which it is addressed among the Buddhists, p. 329.—Śākya probably did not occupy himself with the cult, p. 330—On religious ceremonies and the absence of blood sacrifices, p. 330.—On the two sole objects of adoration, statues of Śākya and edifices that contain his relics, p. 330.—Origin of this cult set forth according to a fragment translated from the legend of Rudrāyaṇa, p. 331.—The image of Śākya is accompanied with a summary of the Buddhist faith, p. 334.—This image has the aim of awakening the memory of the teaching of the master, p. 334.—Proofs of this alliance of the doctrine with the teaching of the master borrowed from figurative monuments, p. 334.—On the physical beauty of the Buddha, p. 335.—Successive changes brought to this part of the cult, and adoration of other personages, like Avalokiteśvara, p. 336.—On the relics and the edifices that contain them, caityas and stūpas, p. 337.—On the antiquity of the cult of relics in Buddhism, p. 339.—It cannot go back to Śākya, p. 340.—On the influence that certain Brahmanical usages could have had on the erection of stūpas, p. 340.—The cult of relics cannot have come from the brahmans, p. 341.—The adoration of the relics of Śākya is the invention of his first disciples, p. 341.—Why they have assimilated their master Śākya with a sovereign monarch, p. 341.—Reasons for the great number of stūpas still found in India and Afghanistan; personages in whose honor such mausoleums were erected, p. 343.—Observations on the legends that attribute to Śākya himself the institution of the cult of his relics and other remains, p. 343.—On the changes that time introduced in this part of the cult, p. 343.

Examination of the question of knowing if, in the books said to be *inspired*, there are no legends where events are later than the epoch of Śākya, p. 344.—Existence of these legends proved by that of the king Aśoka and translation of this legend, p. 345.—Translation of another fragment related to this same king Aśoka, p. 404.—Succinct comparison of the historical elements contained in these two fragments, p. 407.—In one, it is placed one hundred years, in the other two hundred years after the Buddha, p. 408.—One concludes from this that among the canonical books there are treatises of very different dates, p. 408.—Summary of the third section, p. 408.

Section 4. *Abhidharma*, or Metaphysics, p. 411.

Abundance of books related to the Abhidharma, p. 411.—On the *Prajñāpāramitā*, which represents the Abhidharma in the Nepalese collection, p. 411.—On other books related to metaphysics, p. 411.—Analogy of the books of *Prajñā* with the developed sūtras, p. 412.—On the length and form of the books of *Prajñā*, p. 412.—On the work of Mr. Hodgson and Mr. Schmidt on Buddhist philosophy, p. 413.—On the present philosophical schools of Nepal, according to Mr. Hodgson, p. 413.—On the *Svābhāvikas*, the *Aiśvarikas*, the *Kārmikas*, and the *Yātnikas*, p. 413.—These various schools rely on the same texts, which they interpret differently, p. 417.—On four other philosophical sects, according to Csoma de Kőrös, p. 417; and according to the *Abhidharmakośa*, p. 419.—These four sects are those the brahmans mention in refuting the Buddhists, p. 421.—Summary and comparison of these two categories of schools, p. 422.—On the *Mahāvastu*, a book belonging to one of these schools, p. 423.—Origin of the Abhidharma; that it was extracted afterward from the preaching of Śākyamuni, p. 424.—The books of the *Prajñāpāramitā* are in part the development of the doctrine of the sūtras, p. 425.—Necessity to return to the sūtras for the study of metaphysics, p. 426.—Proof of this assertion borrowed from a fragment of a translated legend, p. 426.—On the different redactions of the *Prajñāpāramitā*, p. 431.—Explanation of this title, p. 431.—Fragment extracted and translated from the *Prajñāpāramitā*, p. 434.—Succinct summary of the doctrine set forth in this fragment, p. 447.—On the theory of causes and effects, called *nidāna* and *pratītyasamutpāda*, p. 449.—Fragment of the *Lalitavistara* related to this theory, p. 450.—Analysis of each of these terms, *jarāmaraṇa*, p. 454; *jāti*, p. 454; *bhava*, p. 455; *upādāna*, p. 456; *tṛṣṇa*, p. 459; *vedanā*, p. 460; *sparśa*, p. 461; *ṣaḍāyatana*, p. 461; *nāmarūpa*, p. 462; *vijñāna*, p. 463; *saṃskāras*, p. 464; *avidyā*, p. 466.—On the existence of the thinking subject proved by various texts, p. 467.—Analogies of the metaphysics of Buddhism with Sāṃkhya doctrine, p. 470.—On the five *skandhas*, or intellectual attributes, p. 470.—Explanation of this term, p. 470.

On other books that can be used for the study of the metaphysics of Buddhism, and in particular of the *Saddharmalaṅkāvatāra*, p. 472.—Succinct analysis of this work, p. 472.—Extract of this work touching on nirvāṇa, p. 473.—Another fragment on the same subject, p. 476.—The method that predominates in this work, p. 477.—Relation of the metaphysical doctrine of Śākyamuni with some dominant opinions of Brahmanism, p. 477.

Section 5. Tantras, p. 479.

The tantras form a separate section in the classification of the Tibetans, p. 479.—Character of this part of the Nepalese collection, p. 479.—Mr. Hodgson has learned of it only at the end; probable reasons for this fact, p. 479.—One can judge the nature of these works from translations provided by Messrs. Wilson and Hodgson, p. 480.—The tantras belong to the most complicated form of Northern Buddhism, p. 481.—One sees in them the cult of Śākyamuni, of the dhyāni buddhas, and the Ādibuddha, allied with the cult of Śiva and the female divinities of the Śivaists, p. 481.—The tantras cannot be books emanating from the teaching of Śākya, p. 482.—Proofs of this fact drawn from the content of these books and from the character of their language, p. 482.—General judgment about this part of the Nepalese collection, p. 483; justified by the analysis of some books and in particular of the *Suvarṇaprabhāsa*, p. 484—Existence of two redactions of this book, p. 484.—Analysis of the Sanskrit redaction that we have in Paris, p. 485.—Summary of this work, p. 490.—On the *Saṃvarodaya Tantra*, p. 491.—On the *Mahākāla Tantra*, p. 492.—On the utility of the study of tantras for the literary history of Buddhism, p. 493.—On the *Kālacakra*, p. 493.—On the *Ārya Mañjuśrīmūlatantra*, p. 493.—On the mantras and dhāraṇīs, or magical formulas, p. 493.—On the existence of dhāraṇīs in the Mahāyāna sūtras, p. 494.—On a compilation of dhāraṇīs, p. 494.—On the various treatises found in them, p. 495.—On the *Vajramaṇḍā dhāraṇī*, p. 495.—Fragment translated from this work, p. 496.—

Summary of the doctrine of the tantras, p. 498.—These books are the result of a rather modern syncretism, p. 498.—Alliance of Buddhism with Śivaism, p. 498.—Opinions of Messrs. Schmidt and W. von Humboldt, p. 498.—What is meant by the alliance of Buddhism with Brahmanism, p. 499.—The relations of Buddhism with Śivaism are presented in a double aspect in the books of Nepal, p. 502.—To this double aspect correspond different books, the Mahāyāna and the tantras, p. 502.—One concludes that these books cannot have been written at the same epoch, p. 502.—On the utility of the study of monuments for the examination of the relations of Buddhism with Śivaism, p. 503.—Insufficiency of the present descriptions, p. 504.—The tantras do not provide commentary on scenes represented on monuments, p. 504.—The alliance of Buddhism with Śivaism is explained by the predominance of this latter cult in the provinces and in the epoch when these monuments have been erected, p. 504.

Section 6. Works bearing the names of authors, p. 505.

Utility of the study of these works for the history of Buddhism, p. 505.—These books are rather rare in the Nepalese collection, p. 505.—They take up and develop subjects treated in the canonical books, p. 505.—One finds in them a certain number of avadānas, among others the *Avadānakalpalatā*, p. 506.—On the *Saptakumārikāvadāna* and the *Buddhacarita*, p. 506.—On the *Sragdharāstotra*, p. 507.—On the *Pañcakrama* and its commentary, p. 507.—Immoral doctrine of this work, p. 508.—On the *Vinayapatra* or *Vinayasūtra*, attributed to Nāgārjuna, p. 509.—On some monks who are cited in it, p. 510.—On the gloss of Candrakīrti, p. 510.—Philosophical fragment extracted from this gloss, p. 510.—Appreciation of this fragment, p. 511.—Another quotation borrowed from the same work, p. 511.—True title of the *Vinayasūtra*, p. 512.—On the collection entitled *Abhidharmakośavyākhyā*, p. 512.—General character of this collection, p. 512.—On the ancient authors of metaphysical treatises according to this work, p. 513.—On the collection called *Kṣudraka* and the sūtras called *Arthavargīya*, p. 514—Extract of the commentary of the *Abhidharmakośa*, p. 515.—Names of several monks who are cited in it, p. 515.—On the monk Vasumitra, p. 516.—Works and sects cited in this commentary, p. 516.—The Kashmiri monks, those of Tāmraparṇa and the Vātsīputrīyas, cited, p. 517.—Details on these latter, p. 518.—Nāgārjuna mentioned, p. 518.—Summary of the matters dealt with in this gloss, p. 519.—Philosophical fragment on the absence of a creator God, p. 520.—The author of this gloss does not mention the school of the Aiśvarikas, p. 520.—This work seems to have been composed between the sixth and the tenth centuries of our era, p. 521.

Section 7. History of the collection of Nepal, p. 523.

The history of the collection of Nepal is not recorded in any book of this collection, p. 523.—Is it true that history is even more foreign to Buddhist books than to those of the Brahmans? p. 523.—How the contrary can be asserted, p. 524.—Factual character of the information that the most authentic of these books contains, p. 525.—Starting from the propagation of Buddhism the history of India begins to become clear, p. 525.—On the tradition of Northern Buddhism, and that the Tibetans are its repository, like the Nepalese, p. 526.—On the dates of the Tibetan translations, p. 526.—On the three councils by which the canonical books were redacted, according to the Tibetans, p. 526.—What we have is probably the work of the last council, p. 527.—The last council could have introduced into the canon some new books, but it must have respected the greatest number of ancient books, p. 527.—This supposition is confirmed by the previous study of the sūtras, p. 528.—Opinion of the Mongols on the succession of the books and their triple destination, p. 530.—The tantras were redacted by neither the first nor the second council, p. 531.—On the ancient times of Northern Buddhism since the death of Śākya to four hundred years after this event, p. 532.—On the Middle Ages of Buddhism, p. 532.—The expulsion of Buddhism from India marks the beginning of modern times for this belief, p. 532.—Character of the preceding dates, which are purely relative, and the necessity to fix the initial point from which they start, p. 533.—This initial point is the death of Śākya, on which date the Buddhists do not agree, p. 533.—Necessity to study the Buddhism of Ceylon, which was preserved, like that of the North, in books of Indian origin, p. 533.—Interest of this study from the historical point of view, p. 533.—General survey of the results that the comparison of the two Buddhist collections, that of the North that uses Sanskrit, and that of the South that uses Pāli, must bring, p. 534.—

Foreword

The subject and plan of the research to which this volume is dedicated are set forth in sufficient detail in the first of the memoranda contained herein, such that any further clarification is superfluous here. Nonetheless, I owe the reader some explanation regarding the collective title under which I have assembled these memoranda.

The belief to which the name Buddhism was given, after that of its founder, is entirely Indian. It is in India that it was born; it is in this country that it developed and flourished over more than twelve centuries. Nevertheless, by the third century B.C., Buddhism had begun to spread beyond India, and in the fourteenth of our era it was almost entirely banished from it. Transported, in different epochs, among the Sinhalese and Burmese in the south, among the Chinese and Japanese in the east, among the Tibetans and Mongols in the north, it put down deep roots among these nations, most very different from the people in whose midst it was born. Although it affected their social state in a very palpable manner, it could itself sometimes be influenced by it.

For a history of Buddhism to be complete, it should, therefore, after having explained the origin of this religion and set forth the vicissitudes of its existence in India, follow it beyond its native soil and study it among the peoples who successively received it. I do not know if, at the present time, it is possible for a single man to embrace this immense subject, but it is hardly necessary for me to declare that I have not claimed to do so. I have especially focused on Indian Buddhism; and once having limited my subject in that way, I have restricted my desires in order to compose an introduction that opened the way to broader and deeper research.

This observation will, in the eyes of the reader, justify my being so reserved in the use of materials that scholars of the first rank have drawn from books foreign to India, with the intention of explaining the religious and philosophical dogma of Buddhism in general. It is farthest from my mind to disregard the grandeur and merit of these endeavors; and one will see in the course of these memoranda the eagerness with which I declare my indebtedness to the most illuminating clarifications in the ingenious and profound research of an Abel-Rémusat and a Schmidt. But one will recognize as well that I have appealed to their testimony only when it seemed to me that it accorded with that of the Indian books which provide the basis of my memoranda, or when, because of its very divergence, it could cast some light on an obscure or controversial point. What I wish to say here is that being able, thanks to the liberality of Mr. Hodgson, to consult a considerable collection of Buddhist books written in Sanskrit, I believed that my first duty was to analyze these books, and to extract from them what could be used for the knowledge of the Buddhism of India. In a word, since I had Indian materials to study this Indian religion, it seemed to me that I must resort to foreign sources only in cases of absolute necessity. This choice, to my eyes, has had another advantage: it has spared me from having to pretend to the public that I am able to speak of things of which I could not make a special study.

This first volume leads the reader to the point at which Buddhism is about to enter history. I have thus not needed to set forth here the chronological system that applies to the facts that marked the birth and developments of this religion; the exposition of this system, according to the plan of my work, has its place marked after the analysis of the sacred collection of the Sinhalese. Nonetheless, since all my research has led me to the conclusion that, between the two prevailing opinions touching on the date of Śākyamuni, that of the Chinese, or Buddhists of the North, who place it in the eleventh century before our era, and that of the Sinhalese, or Buddhists of the South, who place it in the seventh, the only one that is true is the opinion of the Sinhalese; I frankly confess that it is from this point of view that the facts that I have had to discuss in the present volume have been envisaged. I plan to demonstrate elsewhere the inconsistencies of this system foreign to India, which gives the founder of Buddhism four more centuries of antiquity than the Sinhalese recognize for him; their Indian annals, preserved with remarkable care and consistency since about the fourth century before our era, offer us the only original and authentic information that we possessed until now on the origin and the history of Buddhism. I believe that I owe this declaration to readers who would be surprised not to find more precise dates in a work of literary and philosophical criticism. I also could not avoid doing so without sanctioning by my silence the opinion already too widespread, and that people endeavor to spread even more widely each day: that it is impossible to find in India anything that is truly historical. If an illustrious scholar could explain and, to a certain point, could excuse the indifference of the French public with regard to Indian studies based on this opinion, then perhaps

I will be forgiven in turn for having some reservations about assertions that, doubtless without the knowledge of their authors, tend to propagate and justify this indifference.

Moreover, one understands the motivations I have had in attaching the greatest value to the memoranda of Mr. Hodgson and Mr. Turnour, which are written with the aid of Indian materials; this is why I have drawn fully on them. However, I have not used Mr. Turnour's dissertations as frequently as those of Mr. Hodgson, because I am only occupied in this first volume with Northern Buddhism. When I arrive at the analysis of the Pāli books from Ceylon, one will see how many discoveries and works one owes to the zeal of Mr. Turnour; it will also be necessary to recognize that if he has given Europe few original manuscripts, he has provided many accurate translations for it to read. Then, it will be possible for me to do equal justice to the efforts of these two eminent men who have clarified the origin and the dogmas of Indian Buddhism with more illumination than all those who had undertaken its study up to that point, without marking with sufficient precision the boundaries and field of their research.

Finally, I dare rely on the indulgence of the reader for such a new endeavor on so difficult a subject. I would have liked to bring as much knowledge to it as I have put good faith, but too often I have encountered obstacles that were impossible for me to overcome. I have taken great care with the correction of the texts and the Oriental terms I have cited; yet I fear the severity of criticism on this point above all. The printing of this volume has been accomplished in the midst of the most painful preoccupations. Struck by the unexpected blow that, by taking away from our family a respected chief, has so bitterly disturbed the happiness it owed to him, it was only with prolonged effort that I could tear myself away from the discouragement that touched me. It was necessary that the ever-present memory of my father remind me of the work that he encouraged. Those who knew him will not ask me to tell them the reasons I have to weep for him, because they know everything he was able to do for the ones he loved; and they will easily understand that I have regarded as the most pressing duty the obligation to place this work under the protection of this dear and venerated name.

Paris, November 10, 1844

FIRST MEMORANDUM

Preliminary Observations

The research to which these memoranda are dedicated has been undertaken with the aid of a voluminous collection of Sanskrit books that the Société Asiatique of Paris received, near the end of the year 1837, from Mr. Brian Houghton Hodgson, English Resident at the Court of Nepal. Situated by the duties of his post in the center of a country where Buddhism still flourishes, it occurred to Mr. Hodgson, as early as the year 1821, to profit from his sojourn in Kathmandu by studying this religious and philosophical doctrine that was then so little known; and although his leisure time was taken up almost entirely with the works on natural history that have made his name famous, he was still able to find enough time to gather more original documents concerning Buddhism than had been collected up to that time, either in Asia or in Europe. Mr. Hodgson made contact with an educated Buddhist from Patan and obtained from him the most curious accounts of the fundamental dogmas of the religion of Nepal as well as precise information concerning the existence of Buddhist books written in Sanskrit, from which were drawn the details received from the religious of Patan.[1] He spared nothing to see these books: he acquired a certain number of them, with great difficulty; had others copied; and after several years of effort and research, he found himself in possession of a considerable collection of Buddhist Sanskrit treatises, whose existence was not even suspected before him, with

1. Hodgson, "Quotations from Original Sanskrit Authorities," in *Journal of the Asiatic Society of Bengal*, vol. 5, p. 29.

the sole possible exception of the *Lalitavistara*, a type of life of Śākyamuni Buddha, which W. Jones and Colebrooke had either seen or possessed a copy of.

Mr. Hodgson did not delay in communicating the results of his discoveries to the scholars of Europe. The *Asiatic Researches* of Calcutta, the *Transactions of the Asiatic Society* of London, the journal published by this society, and the one under the direction of James Prinsep, the Secretary of the Bengal Society, received in succession communications of the highest interest from Mr. Hodgson. As early as 1828, the *Asiatic Researches* of Calcutta published a dissertation by this scholar replete with completely new notions about the languages, literature, and religion of the Buddhists of Nepal and Bhot, or Tibet; and this first essay already included a presentation of the different philosophical schools of Buddhism of this country that has not been surpassed or even equaled since.[2] At the same time, Mr. Hodgson placed at the disposal of the society of Calcutta three Buddhist treatises written in Sanskrit, which Mr. Wilson published in this same volume of *Researches* and translated with a commentary.[3] This first memorandum revealed, among other important discoveries, this principal and until then unknown fact: that there existed in the monasteries of Nepal great collections of books composed in Sanskrit, that is to say, in the language of the country where Buddhism was born several centuries before our era and from which the brahmans had long since expelled it. Mr. Hodgson published an initial list of these books with the classifications given them by the Nepalese, and he added to it an analysis of and an extract from those of these works dealing with the philosophical views of Buddhists and that make known the different schools that divide them.

In 1829, Mr. Hodgson presented an essay on Buddhism derived from the works he had found in Nepal to the committee of the Asiatic Society of London.[4] By conveying this memorandum to the society, with Dr. Nathaniel Wallich serving as intermediary, the author made known in detail for the first time both the plan he had followed upon his arrival in Nepal to procure precise information about the religion said to be that of the Buddha, and the success that had crowned his efforts. The letter addressed to Mr. N. Wallich that precedes the essay of which I speak must be read in order to appreciate the disinterested zeal that animated Mr. Hodgson and the perseverance with which he pursued the object of his research. I recall this here, less for the honor it brings to its author, than because it marks the point of departure for his work and demonstrates the care he took to put himself in the position to verify in the sacred texts the information he obtained from the Buddhist of Patan. Indeed, while precisely sum-

2. Hodgson, "Notices of the Languages, Literature and Religion of the Bauddhas of Nepal and Bhot," in *Asiatic Researches*, vol. 16, p. 409ff.

3. Wilson, "Notice of Three Tracts Received from Nepal," in *Asiatic Researches*, vol. 16, p. 450.

4. "Sketch of Buddhism Derived from the Bauddha Scriptures of Nipal," in *Transactions of the Royal Asiatic Society*, vol. 2, p. 222ff.

marizing the answers that the Buddhist gave to his questions, he had a list drawn up of the Buddhist books, written in Sanskrit, which were known in Nepal, and procured copies of those of these books to which it was possible for him to gain access, for the purpose of sending them to Calcutta and London. He wished thereby to offer to the learned bodies devoted to Asian history the means to control, extend, and bring to completion, through the study of original texts, the results he had gathered in his conversations with the Buddhist of Patan.

A fortunate circumstance assisted him in the composition of the list of the Buddhist scriptures of Nepal he sought to establish. He learned that the copyists or the owners of religious books had the practice in former times of adding at the end of their copies a type of list of the sacred works known to them. The discovery of these lists put him in a position to compile the catalogue of a veritable Buddhist library that includes no fewer than two hundred eighteen items, several of which are of considerable length, as was subsequently verified. This catalogue, much more important and complete than the one he had sent to the society of Bengal, was printed in the *Transactions* of the society of London in devanāgari characters.[5] I do not speak of other communications that enriched the *Transactions of the Asiatic Society of Great Britain*, as well as the other scientific collections cited above; I hasten to come to the result which, for Mr. Hodgson, had always been one of the most important objects of his research: I mean the gift he wished to make to the Asiatic Society of London, as he had made some time ago to that of Calcutta, of the collection of Buddhist manuscripts discovered through his care.[6]

At the beginning of the year 1830 he had delivered to London seven volumes of Bhotea (Tibetan) manuscripts, as they are designated without any other description in the list of gifts to the Asiatic Society inserted at the end of the third volume of his memoranda.[7] A short time later, in 1835, publishing in the journal of this society a series of texts extracted from the Sanskrit books of Nepal in order to vindicate, with authentic proof, his essay on Buddhism, Mr. Hodgson announced that the collection of Sanskrit books that he had gathered in Nepal comprised about sixty large volumes, and he added to this point these generous words: "I shall be happy to provide copies of the works that form this collection to learned bodies who desire to possess them."[8] Toward the end of this same year, Mr. Hodgson had delivered to London twenty-six volumes containing the great compendium entitled *Prajñāpāramitā*, in one hundred thousand articles, which

5. *Transactions of the Royal Asiatic Society*, vol. 2, p. 224ff.

6. From 1824 to 1839, Mr. Hodgson had sent to the Asiatic Society of Calcutta about fifty volumes in Sanskrit and four times as many in Tibetan. ("European Speculations on Buddhism," in *Journal of the Asiatic Society of Bengal*, vol. 3, p. 885, note.)

7. *Transactions of the Royal Asiatic Society*, vol. 3, *Appendix*, p. xlij.

8. *Journal of the Royal Asiatic Society*, vol. 2, p. 288, note 2.

was part of the previously announced collection,[9] and he promised to send in succession to the Asiatic Society of Great Britain, not only the nine works that are considered canonical in Nepal, but also all of the Sanskrit books he had been able to gather relating to Buddhism.[10] Indeed, a year had hardly passed since this promise when the society received a second set of sixty-six Sanskrit volumes, all related to the religion and to the philosophy of the Buddhists of Nepal.[11]

But it was not enough for Mr. Hodgson to have given this abundant proof of his liberality to an English society of which he was a member; he wished also to invite the Société Asiatique of Paris to partake of the fruits of his discoveries, and in 1837 he gave twenty-four Sanskrit works, among which were several of considerable length.[12] This present was followed by an even more precious shipment: it was composed of sixty-four manuscripts, including almost everything that the Asiatic Society of London had recently acquired.[13] Mr. Hodgson had these manuscripts copied for the Société Asiatique of Paris, which, as early as 1836, had hastened to accept this scholar's offer to convey copies of the manuscripts he had discovered to learned societies who would desire to possess them. Thus, thanks to this double act of liberality and zeal, the Société Asiatique of Paris, to which that of Bengal had just dispatched, one year before, the great collection of Buddhist works translated into Tibetan, known by the name of *Kah-gyur* (*bka' 'gyur*), possessed the greatest part of the Sanskrit texts which, according to the Buddhists of Bhot as well as to those of Nepal, are considered to be the originals from which the Tibetan translations were made.

The Société Asiatique neglected nothing in showing its gratitude to Mr. Hodgson; but it was evident that one of the surest means to express it was to respond in a scientific manner to the appeal he had felt himself authorized to make. Mr. Hodgson certainly had not dispatched two collections of such size to Paris in order for them to sleep peacefully on the shelves of a library. He wanted to see the research that he had himself begun with such success in Asia be pursued in Europe; and it would have been a poor acknowledgment of the efforts he had made to procure these manuscripts, and the generosity with which he favored France with them, not to attempt to bring light to some of the works contained therein. I felt, for my part, as a member of the Société Asiatique of Paris, all the honor and urgency in Mr. Hodgson's appeal, and I resolved from that time on to respond with everything I had to offer. These are the circumstances that have led to the research that is the object of the memoranda contained in

9. *Ibid.*, vol. 2, p. iij.
10. *Ibid.*, vol. 3, pp. vij and viij.
11. *Ibid.*, p. lxxiij.
12. *Journal de la Société Asiatique de Paris*, 3rd ser., vol. 3, p. 316.
13. *Journal Asiatique*, 3rd ser., vol. 3, p. 557, and vol. 4, p. 91.

this volume. One will see, or so I hope, that this research has its place marked in the frame of the studies related to ancient India that I traced some time ago, at the end of my introduction to the *Bhāgavata Purāṇa*.

When Mr. Hodgson made his discoveries known for the first time, he presented to the scholarly world the works that were their fruit, just as they were the original texts from which the books were translated that have authority among most of the nations of Asia that have converted to Buddhism.[14] Not one voice rose against this assertion that so much evidence would soon confirm. Indeed, a short time after Mr. Hodgson published his list of Sanskrit books from Nepal, Csoma de Kőrös, whose studies, pursued with heroic devotion, had made him a master of the Tibetan language, published in the *Journal of the Asiatic Society of Bengal*, and particularly in the *Researches* of this learned company, exact and detailed analyses of the great Tibetan library of the Kah-gyur which, as its title *Translation of Precepts* indicates, is composed of versions made from Sanskrit works, almost all of which are found in the collection of Mr. Hodgson.[15] It is in this way that the part of the Kah-gyur entitled *Sher-chin* (*sher phyin*), which, in twenty-one volumes, deals with the metaphysics of Buddhism, is included entirely, except perhaps for the final volumes, in the different editions of the *Prajñāpāramitā* in Sanskrit discovered by Mr. Hodgson.[16] The same must be said for a good number of volumes belonging to the section of the Kah-gyur called *mdo sde*, corresponding to the large division of the Buddhist scriptures of Nepal called *sūtrānta* or simply *sūtra*. For example, the second volume of the Tibetan section is the translation of the *Lalitavistara*, that is to say, a religious exposition of the life of Śākyamuni.[17] A portion of the fifth volume contains the version of the Sanskrit philosophical treatise entitled *Laṅkāvatāra*,[18] a work that, one might mention in passing, exists also in China.[19] The seventh volume provides the translation of the *Saddharmapuṇḍarīka*, or the "White Lotus of the Good Law," the French translation of which I shall soon publish.[20] This same volume contains, among other treatises, a translation of the *Karaṇḍavyūha*, the Sanskrit text of which also

14. Hodgson, "Quotations in Proof of His Sketch of Buddhism," in *Journal of the Royal Asiatic Society*, vol. 2, p. 288; and in *Journal of the Asiatic Society of Bengal*, vol. 5, p. 29.

15. "Abstract of the Contents of the Dul-va," etc., in *Journal of the Asiatic Society of Bengal*, vol. 1, p. 1ff. "Analysis of the Kah-gyur," *ibid.*, p. 375. "Analysis of the Dul-va," in *Asiatic Researches*, vol. 20, p. 41ff. "Analysis of the Sher-chin," etc., *ibid.*, vol. 20, p. 392.

16. Csoma de Kőrös, "Analysis of the Sher-chin," in *Asiatic Researches*, vol. 20, p. 393ff., compared with Hodgson, "Sketch of Buddhism," in *Transactions of the Royal Asiatic Society*, vol. 2, p. 224ff.

17. Csoma, *ibid.*, p. 416ff., compared with Hodgson, "Sketch of Buddhism," p. 224.

18. Csoma, *ibid.*, p. 432ff., compared with Hodgson, "Sketch of Buddhism," p. 224. We will see below that the true title of this book is *Saddharmalaṅkāvatāra*.

19. A. Rémusat, "Recherches sur les langues tartares," 1:206. *Mélanges Asiatiques*, 1:181. "Observations sur trois Mémoires de M. de Guignes," in *Nouveau Journal Asiatique*, vol. 7, p. 295.

20. Csoma, "Analysis of the Kah-gyur," *ibid.*, p. 436ff., compared with Hodgson, "Sketch of Buddhism," p. 224.

exists in the collection of Mr. Hodgson.[21] The twenty-ninth volume provides a most literal Tibetan version, which I have checked myself, of a collection of legends entitled *Avadānaśataka*, which I shall deal with elsewhere in more detail, and of which I have already translated two books.[22] I do not mention a considerable number of pieces found dispersed, either in the section called *mdo*, of which the *Divyāvadāna* of Mr. Hodgson gives the original Sanskrit, or in the *Dul-va* (*'dul ba gzhi*) section. The parallels I have just indicated are sufficient to prove how worthy of confidence is the testimony of the Nepalese when they assert that their Sanskrit texts are the originals of the Tibetan versions. These citations at the same time provide great likelihood to this opinion of Mr. Hodgson, that in the collection of Tibet there is hardly a single treatise that one does not hope to find one day in the original Sanskrit.[23] If Mr. Hodgson expressed himself in this way before Csoma de Kőrös had published his excellent analysis of the Kahgyur, this assertion cannot be an object of doubt after this analysis has provided us, along with the title of the Tibetan treatises contained in this huge collection, that of the Sanskrit originals of which these treatises are only the translation.

What I have just said about the Tibetan books applies also to the Mongol books, at least as far as I can determine for those religious treatises whose titles I can verify. The beautiful collection of Tibetan and Mongol printed material and manuscripts that Mr. Schilling von Canstadt presented in 1837 to the Institut de France contains the Mongol translation of some Sanskrit treatises of Nepal. I shall cite among others, the *Prajñāpāramitā in Twenty-five Thousand Stanzas*, the Mongol version of which forms two large volumes;[24] the *Suvarṇaprabhāsa*, the Mongol version of which is mentioned by Mr. Schmidt under the title *Altan gerel*;[25] the *Vajracchedikā*, whose translation from the Tibetan we owe to Mr. Schmidt,[26] and two collections of small treatises or formulae of lesser importance.[27] If I do not mention other books, this is because I do not have a greater number at my disposal; but I in no way pretend to limit this necessarily incomplete information to the list of books that the Mongols must have translated from the Sanskrit, or at least from the Tibetan. It is to Mr. Schmidt, who has extracted from the Mongol books such precious information on the Buddhism of

21. Csoma, *ibid.*, p. 437ff., compared with Hodgson, "Sketch of Buddhism," p. 225.

22. Csoma, *ibid.*, p. 481ff., compared with Hodgson, "Sketch of Buddhism," p. 224.

23. "Letter to the Secretary Asiatic Society," in *Journal of the Royal Asiatic Society of London*, vol. 3, p. viij. "Quotations from Original Sanscrit Authorities in Proof," etc., in *Journal of the Asiatic Society of Bengal*, vol. 5, p. 29, note †.

24. Manuscript catalogue of the Schilling Collection, nos. 80 and 81.

25. I. J. Schmidt, *Grammatik der Mongolischen Sprache*, p. 142. *Geschichte der Ost-Mongolen*, p. 307. Manuscript catalogue of the Schilling Collection, no. 83.

26. Manuscript catalogue of the Schilling Collection, no. 86. Schmidt, *Mémoires de l'Académie des sciences de Saint-Pétersbourg*, 4:126ff.

27. Manuscript catalogue of the Schilling Collection, nos. 84 and 85.

Central Asia, that it falls to determine the extent of the borrowing the Mongols have made from the Buddhist literature of Northern India. This task would be even less difficult for this capable Orientalist since, as early as the year 1830, he asserted that among the two hundred and eighteen Buddhist works whose list Mr. Hodgson provided, most of them had been translated into Mongol, and that almost all were in his hands or well known to him under their Sanskrit titles.[28]

I possess even less information on the relation of the Buddhist literature of China to that of Nepal, because thus far the books of the Chinese Buddhists have not been analyzed in detail as have those of the Tibetans, and the titles of those we know cannot be easily rendered into their original form without the double knowledge of Chinese and Sanskrit. But what we can discover from them, without having direct access to the sources, shows that in China, as in Tartary, many of the books renowned to be sacred by the Buddhists are just translations from Sanskrit treatises of Nepal. Thus, it has already been a long time since Mr. Abel-Rémusat noted the existence of a Chinese translation of the *Laṅkāvatāra*, one of the works on the list of Mr. Hodgson that belongs to the Bibliothèque royale.[29] My learned colleague, Mr. Stanislas Julien, was kind enough to bring to my attention a Chinese translation of the *Saddharmapuṇḍarīka* that belongs to the same library.[30] Mr. Landresse mentions, in his notes on the *Foe koue ki*, another religious treatise known under the title the *Splendor of the Golden Light*, which is doubtless none other than the *Suvarṇaprabhāsa* of Nepal or of the Mongols.[31] We must still recall here a book that the Chinese designate with the title *Great*

28. "Über einige Grundlehren des Buddhismus," in *Mémoires de l'Académie des sciences de Saint-Pétersbourg*, 1:92, 93.

29. "Recherches sur les langues tartares," 1:206, and the above quotations, p. 6, note 4, compared with Hodgson in *Transactions of the Royal Asiatic Society*, vol. 2, p. 224, and Csoma, in *Asiatic Researches*, vol. 20, p. 432.

30. Mr. Stanislas Julien was obliging enough to pass on to me a note on this subject that will doubtless be as pleasant to read as it is for me to quote: "The information that this note contains is borrowed from the foreword of *Miaofa lianhua jing* (The Sacred Book of the Excellent Law), a foreword written under the Tang Dynasty (between 618 and 904) by the Samanéen *Daoxuan*. The *Sacred Book of the Lotus of the Excellent Law* was composed in the country of *Da xia* (Bactria) one thousand years ago. It was brought to the East around three hundred years ago, to *Zhendan* (China). Under the reign of Huidi, in the first year of the Taikang period of the Western Jin (280 A.D.), a sage bearing the title *Dunhuang pusa zhuhufazhe* (that is to say, the bodhisattva of Dunhuang, the defender of the law of India) who resided (in China) at Chang'an, translated this work for the first time under the title *Zheng fahua* (The Flower of the Right Law). Under the Eastern Jin, in the Long'an period of the reign of the Emperor An di (between 397 and 402), Jiumo luo shi (Kumāra . . .), a Samanéen from the kingdom of Qiuci, translated this work for the second time and gave it the title: *Miaofa lianhua* (Lotus of the Excellent Law). Under the Sui Dynasty, in the Jin Zhou period of the Emperor Wendi (between 601 and 605), *Dunajueduo*, a Samanéen of Northern India, attached to the monastery of *Daxing shansi* (Monastery where Virtue Flourishes), translated this work for the third time and called it *Miaofa* (The Excellent Law). This is the second Chinese translation made, between 397 and 402, in accordance with an imperial order, which is at the Bibliothèque royale of Paris; it comprises seven oblong notebooks." I shall return to this interesting note in the foreword to *Le lotus de la bonne loi.*

31. Landresse, *Foe koue ki*, p. 322.

Āgama and which is certainly none other than the *Dīrghāgama* of which I shall speak below, just as the book they call "Āgama Adding from One" is the Sanskrit book, or rather the collection, called *Ekottarāgama.*[32] I have no hesitation in believing that, if it had been possible for me to compare the names of the Buddhist Chinese books often mentioned by various authors with the titles in the lists of Mr. Hodgson, I would have again found a good number of Sanskrit titles concealed under the translations or under the more or less altered transcriptions of the Chinese.

The ongoing study of Buddhist works accepted as authoritative by the Mongols and the Chinese will certainly later add a very great number of facts to those I mention here only in passing, and it is very probable that if not the totality, then at least most of what the Tibetans possess will be found in the monasteries of Tartary and China. But however limited the previous indications may be, as for the present, they are sufficient to place the collection of the Sanskrit books of Nepal in the perspective from which Mr. Hodgson wished it to be envisaged by the scholars of Europe. Yes; it is a fact, demonstrated through the evidence itself, that most of the books held sacred by the Buddhists of Tibet, Tartary, and China are but translations of the Sanskrit texts newly discovered in Nepal, and this fact alone definitively marks the place of these texts among the group of documents that the nations of Asia just mentioned furnish to the general history of Buddhism. He presents them to us as the originals, of which these documents are only copies, and he restores to India and to its language the study of a religion and a philosophy whose cradle was India.

If I insist on this fact because it gives to Buddhist studies their true and more solid basis, in no way do I wish to contest the importance that the Tibetan, Mongol, and Chinese books have for this study. Moreover, knowledge of these last three categories of books is absolutely essential for the general history of a system that, received in ancient epochs by peoples of diverse origin and civilization, must have undergone modifications that are important for the historian-philosopher to recognize and note. I have acquired the personal conviction that, for one who wishes to confine himself to the study of Indian Buddhism, the translations of the Sanskrit books of Nepal made in Tibet, like those of the Pāli books of Ceylon made in Burma, have an incontestable utility. I shall not recall, in order to enhance the value of these translations, that they were carried out when Buddhism was still flourishing and by those who had studied Sanskrit and Pāli with the care that the mission with which they charged themselves required. I shall not indicate the various circumstances that assure the superiority of the versions of Sanskrit texts of the North made in ancient times in Asia over those

32. A. Rémusat, "Essai sur la cosmographie et la cosmogonie des bouddhistes," in *Journal des Savans*, 1831, pp. 604, 605, and 726 and several times in the notes of the *Foe koue ki*.

that can be produced today in Europe, although it must cost the philologists, accustomed by their studies of the Sanskrit language, nothing to recognize this superiority, distant as they all are from the assistance of natives, among whom are some learned men who have preserved the repository of traditional interpretation faithfully. I shall not speak further of the difficulties that the explanation of some philosophical terms presents, together with the inconceivable incorrectness of the manuscripts, for which almost all of the Sanskrit texts of Nepal are unique. But I will say that, in themselves, and by virtue of the fact that they are only translations, the Tibetan, Mongol, Chinese, and Burmese versions must, in a good number of cases, successfully serve the intelligibility of the Sanskrit and Pāli originals that they reproduce.

The difference of idioms alone in which these versions are written furnishes the European reader with unexpected means of interpretation that would ordinarily be most difficult to discover through the isolated study of the original text. And to cite only one example, the more or less metaphorical character of the language in which the translator expressed himself, whether he be Chinese, Tibetan, or Mongol, must have forced him to make a decisive choice about some purely Indian expressions, as far as the content and form are concerned, for which his mother tongue offered him only incomplete equivalents or did not offer him any at all. Therefore, since it was necessary to translate, one must believe that the interpreters sacrificed the form for the meaning, and that they put all their efforts into rendering one, even at the expense of the other. Now, if one of these purely Indian expressions appears in a Sanskrit text of Nepal, if there is no dictionary, if there is no philological analogy to aid in suspecting the meaning, will one not expect to find the means to interpret it in the Chinese, Tibetan, or Mongol version of this text? These cases of profound obscurity, moreover, are rather rare, and I can assert that there is nothing in all Sanskrit literature as easy to understand as the texts of Nepal, apart from some terms the Buddhists used in a very special way; I shall not give any proof other than the considerable number of texts it has been possible for me to read in a rather limited time. Nevertheless, we have also to acknowledge, assuming these books to be as little difficult as they are, that it is possible that the foreign interpreters were rather well served by their love for exactitude in discovering and employing an expression in their own language as obscure as the one employed in the Sanskrit text. The version will thus be even less useful to us to the extent that it is more faithful, just as its importance will increase in the eyes of a European reader in general because of the freedom with which the translator dealt with the original. But there is no need to exaggerate the difficulty of the texts in order to heighten the value of the versions the Tibetans, Chinese, and Mongols made; these versions will always in themselves have an incontestable value as a means to interpret the texts, even the less difficult.

After these observations, which it is sufficient for me to indicate summarily, I shall be more free to assert that, in my opinion, the true sources from which one must draw knowledge of Indian Buddhism, the original sources and the most pure, are the Sanskrit texts from Nepal and, as I shall say later, the Pāli books from Ceylon. If I have had to acknowledge that the Chinese, Tibetan, and Mongol versions could, in a more or less great number of cases, shed some light on the study of the originals, one will equally agree with me that in a much more considerable number of cases these versions must remain as obscure to the European philologists who deal with Chinese, Tibetan, and Mongol as the texts written in Sanskrit are for those who have made a special study of this language. I even dare to say that if some differences exist between these two categories of scholars, all conditions of knowledge and talent being recognized as equal, this difference must be to the advantage of those who have the ability to read in the original itself what others can perceive only through the medium of languages whose processes and character often have so few relations to those of the idiom in which the texts were originally written.

The genius of India has marked all its products with a character so special that whatever the superiority of mind and whatever freedom in the use of their methods one grants to the Oriental translators, one cannot prevent oneself from recognizing that they must necessarily have brought to their versions certain features of the original that often will remain unintelligible to the reader who does not have the means to resort to the Indian text itself. Furthermore, the very aim of these translators must have been to reproduce, as faithfully as they could, the Indian color so strongly imprinted in the works they wanted to popularize. Hence, these are versions in which the proper names, and also often the special terms of the religious and philosophical language of Buddhism, have been retained with an attention that is dispiriting to one unable to seek signification in the idiom to which they belong. Hence, these translations are materially exact imitations of the original, but while retracing the outward features, they express no more of the soul than a tracing of a painting that would stop at the outline of the figures without reproducing the colored and living part would represent this painting. In this respect, the original texts have an incontestable advantage over the translations that repeat them; and, all things being equal, moreover, the translator of a Buddhist book written in Sanskrit finds himself in conditions less unfavorable to understanding it well than the translator of the same text reproduced in the language of one of the peoples of the Orient among whom Buddhism established itself.

But it is not solely due to the features it retains from the Sanskrit original that a Chinese, Tibetan, or Mongol translation will sometimes be more obscure than the text, and consequently must be inferior to it in the eyes of the critic; again, and in particular, it is from all that it effaces that the inferiority of the version, compared to the original, results. When, for example, the Chinese designate a Buddhist work as translated from the *fan* language, that is to say, as was recognized by Mr. A. Rémusat, from the language of Brahmā,[33] we learn without doubt that the original text was written in some Indian language; but they do not tell us which language it is. And since they could have translated a good number of books from Pāli originals, and because Pāli is just as much an Indian language as Sanskrit, it happens that the designation *fan* language, while expressing a true fact, suppresses the distinction that would allow one to grasp with this fact another secondary fact, which is no less important than the first but which remains in profound obscurity, namely, whether the text was in Sanskrit or in Pāli. This inconvenience, which has already been indicated,[34] and whose effect is easily sensed because it is historically necessary to know from which source a given book was drawn, must have quite serious consequences when it is a question of certain texts composed in a mélange of different styles and even often of several dialects; because by putting a uniform color on a work whose several parts carry the trace of diverse origins, the translation causes the sole index with which the critic can recognize the authenticity or even the age and the homeland of the work to disappear. It is enough to make this observation, of which I do not have the means to determine the full impact as far as the Chinese and Mongol translations are concerned. There is, nevertheless, at least one book in the Nepalese collection that justifies these remarks and allows one to conjecture that the Tibetan translators did not always accurately render certain features of the original that constitute one of the most interesting and the most innovative characteristics of the primitive text.

This work is entitled *Saddharmapuṇḍarīka*, or the "White Lotus of the Good Law"; it forms part of the nine *dharmas*, or books regarded as canonical by the Buddhists of Nepal. It is composed of two distinct parts or, in fact, two redactions, one in prose and the other in verse. The second does nothing in general but reproduce the content of the first, with the difference that poetic exposition necessarily entails. These two redactions are interspersed with each other in such a way that when a story or a discourse has been set forth in prose, it is reprised anew in verse, sometimes in an abridged manner, sometimes with developments that add a few things to the first redaction. This genre of composition, which is so reminiscent of the combination of prose and verse in the Sanskrit works called *campū*,[35] is not the only interesting characteristic of this book; what makes it even more remarkable is that the poetic parts are widely interspersed with popular forms, sometimes analogous to those of Prakrit dialects derived

33. *Mélanges Asiatiques*, vol. 2, p. 242. *Nouveau Journal Asiatique*, vol. 7, pp. 298 and 299. *Foe koue ki*, p. 15.
34. Abel Rémusat, *Foe koue ki*, p. 14, note 9.
35. Colebrooke, *Miscellaneous Essays*, 2:135 and 136.

from Sanskrit, rather like the half-Sanskrit, half-Prakrit stanza that Colebrooke has mentioned in his treatise on Indian poetry.[36] These forms do not appear only where the needs of meter call for them, the rules of which, moreover, are not very strict; on the contrary they are very frequent and sufficiently numerous to characterize the style of the poetic parts of this work in a distinct manner.

What I have just said about the *Saddharmapuṇḍarīka* applies equally to a great number of works in the Nepalese collection. The books called *mahāyāna sūtras*, of which I shall speak shortly, and in general all the treatises whose core is doubled by the addition of poetic writing, offer this mixed style of Prakrit and Pāli popular forms; one observes it again, and even to a higher degree, in a work composed in prose—the *Mahāvastu*, or the "Great History," a voluminous collection of legends related to the founder of Buddhism and to several of his contemporaries, which will be taken up below. This work is generally written in prose, and the presence of altered forms is certainly not justified by the necessities of metrics.

I do not need to insist strongly to make one understand the interest the critic has in verifying the existence or the absence of a characteristic of this type. It is still an obscure question to know in which language the books attributed to the founder of Buddhism were written for the first time. In the North, the Tibetans, as I will say later, affirm that several Indian dialects were employed at once by the first disciples of Śākya,[37] but without debating in detail this opinion here, the examination of which will find its place in the Historical Sketch of Buddhism, I can already say with Lassen[38] that the classification of the dialects whose use the Tibetans attribute to the first redactors of the sacred scriptures is something that is too systematic and too artificial to be accepted as the complete expression of the truth. Its only merit, to my eyes, is to note the simultaneous use of scholastic language and popular dialects. Thus, this fact, of which Mr. Hodgson has already demonstrated the possibility[39] with good arguments, is in itself too plausible not to be recognized, at least in a general manner; the continuation of our research will only have to set it forth with more details and mark the limits and the significance. It will thus be necessary to take into account the existence of ancient Buddhist inscriptions written in Pāli, and to see in them the proof that in an epoch near the establishment of Buddhism, Sanskrit was no longer the popular language of central and northern India and that the new religion, to be understood by all, was compelled to use a vulgar dialect. It will be equally necessary to weigh facts like that which Lassen's sagacity has already indicated, when he

36. *Ibid.*, 2:102 and 103.

37. Csoma, "Notices on the Different Systems of Buddhism," in *Journal of the Asiatic Society of Bengal*, vol. 7, p. 143ff.

38. *Zeitschrift für die Kunde des Morgenlandes*, vol. 3, pp. 159 and 160.

39. "Note on the Primary Language of Buddhism," in *Journal of the Asiatic Society of Bengal*, vol. 6, p. 682ff.

suspected that a formula that is part of the profession of faith of Buddhists must have been conceived originally in Pāli and from it transported to Sanskrit.[40] If, as I shall show in a special dissertation, very numerous and very important passages of Sanskrit texts from the North allow inductions of the same type, it will be necessary to recognize that the vulgar dialect of central India exerted on the redaction of texts composed in Sanskrit an influence that could only have been produced in ancient times, before Buddhists separated into two great schools, that of the North in which the books are written in Sanskrit and that of the South in which they are in Pāli.

The matter is thus not as simple as it seems to be at first glance. It is complicated further by that of the councils whose history is so closely connected to that of the redaction of the books. What would happen if, widening the horizon of our research, we would compare the Northern tradition with what we learn from the Sinhalese tradition? There, that is to say, among the peoples where Pāli prevails exclusively as the sacred language, we would recognize that a notable part of the Buddhist books, before being written in Pāli, was preserved for a long time in Sinhalese versions. In short, we would find at the end of our research, on the one side, the easily recognizable action of the vulgar dialect on the scholarly language employed at the time of the redaction of the books of the North; on the other side, the proof that the collection of the books of the South was not written entirely at its origin in the dialect called *pāli.* One sees, in this difficult matter, the monuments, the texts, and the memories of the tradition mingle, contradict themselves sometimes, and rarely explain themselves; but each of them always presents itself in the costume that is its own: some speak in Sanskrit, others in Pāli, others in a dialect between Sanskrit and Pāli, and it is on these characteristics that one must focus if one wishes to seek to determine their age and origin.

Now, I ask, in a Chinese, Tibetan, or Mongol translation, what can remain of these characteristics and the questions that they raise? The translator, without doubt, was aware of them, since he was able to translate; but it is difficult to recover some trace of them in his version, which, effacing this difference of style, suppressed all the means that the original delivered to the critic for the solution to the various questions I just recalled. Perhaps, moving to the interpretation of the poetic parts of the *Saddharmapuṇḍarīka,* for example, the interpreter signaled that these pieces are written in a different style and in another dialect. This fact, which I am unable to affirm, is doubtless possible; but it must be acknowledged that such an indication would again not suffice, and that unless the translator gave a specimen of the style with the name of the dialect, one would not be able to decide from this single indication that the style changes. Without engaging myself, moreover, in useless conjectures on the care the Chinese and Mongol

40. *Zeitschrift für die Kunde des Morgenlandes*, vol. 1, pp. 228 and 229, note.

interpreters could take to indicate this important circumstance, I am in a position to affirm that the *lotsavas,* or Tibetan interpreters to whom we are indebted for the version of the *Saddharmapuṇḍarīka* contained in the Kah-gyur, did not resort to any of the precautions indicated above to arouse the attention of the reader concerning the varieties of dialects. They translated in Tibetan prose the Sanskrit prose, in Tibetan verses the Sanskrit verses without signaling that, moving from the first part of the original to the second, one entered somehow into a style and a work that is entirely new.[41]

Since I spoke about the Tibetan interpreters, may I be permitted to justify the general judgment just brought upon the Asiatic translations of the Sanskrit works of Nepal, to show with a small number of precise examples in which manner they are unfaithful to the original, either in translating too much, if I can express myself in such a way, or in not translating enough? It is clear that it is not a question here of criticizing the system followed by these translators; this system is irreproachable: it is one of a perfect literality; and when it is applied with rigor, a Tibetan version represents every feature of the Sanskrit text. I even concede for the moment a point that still appears to me highly debatable, namely, that enough is known in Europe about all the resources of the Tibetan language to translate a book written in this language with as much surety as is possible with the original Sanskrit text and without needing to resort to this text itself. It will suffice for me, for the present, to borrow from these versions, in general so faithful, a small number of passages where the Sanskrit original has, at least to my eyes, an obvious superiority to the Tibetan interpretation. I have so little intention to delineate the difficulties of this comparison that I have chosen the term that occurs most often in the texts, the most important term of all, one that the lotsavas must have understood best, the one we will have the greatest difficulty to explain, the term *nirvāṇa.*

Nirvāṇa, that is to say, in a general way, liberation or salvation, is the supreme aim that the founder of Buddhism proposed for the efforts of man. But what is this liberation and what is the nature of this salvation? If we consult the etymology, it will respond to us that it is annihilation, extinction. Now, how can we understand this annihilation and with what is it concerned? Is it with the conditions related to existence or with existence itself, with life? For a man, is nirvāṇa this state of repose in which he finds himself when through meditation he has broken the bonds that tie him to the external world and enters into possession of his own power, in and of itself, independent of everything surrounding him?

41. This is what the Mongol translators also appear to have done. They have brought, nevertheless, enough accuracy to their work to reproduce versified portions of the Sanskrit books without deviating from the character of the original as far as the position of words is concerned, sacrificing the spirit of their own language. This interesting fact did not escape the attention of Mr. Schmidt, who has not failed to indicate it. (*Grammatik der Mongolischen Sprache*, pp. 161 and 162.)

Or is it the higher state where, isolated from the external world as well as from the internal, he detaches himself from the phenomena of his own life, as he has detached himself from the phenomena of his relative life, and no longer feels in himself anything more than the universal existence within which all the parts of the universe coexist? In other words, is the man in nirvāṇa in the state of individual life, maintaining, along with the sense of his personality, that of his activity? Or is he in the state of universal being, in such a way that having lost the sense of his personality together with that of his activity, he can no longer be distinguished from absolute existence, this existence being either God or nature? In the end, in the hypothesis in which annihilation is concerned with existence itself, is nirvāṇa extinction, the disappearance not only of individual life but also of universal life: in short, is nirvāṇa nothingness?

One sees that the etymology of the word *nirvāṇa* does not respond to any of these questions, which are nothing other than the expression of very different theological systems. It is from the use that Buddhists have made of this term, it is from the definitions they have given to it, that we must demand the explanation of these great problems. Hence, since the Buddhists, for many centuries, have been divided into sects or schools, the explanation of the term *nirvāṇa* varies according to the different points of view of the sectarians. And without entering here into a delicate discussion that will occur elsewhere, I can already say that nirvāṇa is for the theists the absorption of individual life into God and for the atheists the absorption of this individual life into nothingness. But for both, nirvāṇa is liberation, it is supreme freedom.

This is so true that the idea of freedom is the only one that the Tibetan interpreters saw in the word *nirvāṇa*, because it is the only one they translated. In the versions they give of the Sanskrit texts of Nepal, the term *nirvāṇa* is rendered by the words *mya ngan las 'da' ba*, which literally means "the state of one who is freed from suffering" or "the state one is in when thus free." Let us open all the Tibetan dictionaries we possess, that of Schröter, that of Csoma de Kőrös, and that of Schmidt; you will find them all to be unanimous on this point. The first translates this expression as "to die, to put an end to troubles and to the afflictions,"[42] and he renders one of the compound locutions where it appears as "to attain eternal salvation." Csoma renders it as "the state of being delivered from pain," and in another place, "a being delivered from pain, death, emancipation."[43] Mr. Schmidt, finally, interprets it as "to be free from grief" and in another place as "the state of being free from the law of transmigration."[44] The Tibetan inter-

42. *A Dictionary of the Bhotanta or Boutan Language*, p. 200, col. 1.

43. *Dictionary, Tibetan and English*, p. 134, col. 2, and p. 194, col. 2.

44. *Tibetisch-deutsches Wörterbuch*, p. 270, col. 1. Mr. Schmidt saw correctly that the Tibetan expression corresponded to the word *nirvāṇa*.

preters thus understand *nirvāṇa* as freedom and in particular, as Mr. Schmidt says, freedom from the law of transmigration; but they do not indicate what type of freedom this is, and their interpretation does not respond any more than the term *nirvāṇa* does to the numerous questions that arise from this difficult term.

Let me say still more: this version teaches us less than the original Sanskrit word because strictly speaking it is not a translation; it is a commentary. If the word *nirvāṇa* does not show us what is destroyed in the state of nirvāṇa, it allows us to see at least that there is destruction. The Tibetan, when it says that nirvāṇa is freedom from suffering, informs us about the effect of which nirvāṇa is the cause and leaves this cause as well as its mode of action in the shadows. Thus here, we can boldly advance, the Tibetan interpreters translated too much and too little: too much because they saw in nirvāṇa more than the term says, namely the effect of nirvāṇa; too little because they have passed over in silence nirvāṇa's mode of action and the true state that this term expresses, annihilation. All of this at bottom comes almost to the same thing; but when it is a matter of the appreciation of the religious systems of antiquity, this great and beautiful page in the history of the human spirit, it is not possible to bring too much rigor to the interpretation of fundamental terms, and it is of utmost importance to know the primitive meaning of these terms and to see them with their color and in their true costumes. It is all the more necessary when the systems are more antique and more original, for there is an epoch where it is possible to say of theology: *nomina numina.*

A translation of this kind is thus all the more satisfactory, since it is easier to recover the original and to go from the translating term to the translated term. Therefore, as one sees, this advantage is entirely lacking in the Tibetan translation of the word with which we are occupied. Indeed, if we did not have in our possession a single text, a single word of the Sanskrit books of the Nepalese Buddhists, if the word *nirvāṇa* was entirely unknown to us, it would be impossible for a reader versed in the Tibetan language to reconstruct the lost term *nirvāṇa* from the actual elements of the Tibetan *mya ngan las 'da' ba.* The only Sanskrit expression that rendered them exactly would be *śokamukti* or *śokamuktatva* (deliverance from grief), and the word *śoka* (grief) would be such a good equivalent to *mya ngan* that this very term *śoka*, which appears in the royal proper name Aśoka (the king without grief), is represented by the Tibetans with the *mya ngan* in question here. And vice versa, if it was the name Aśoka which was lost and that of *nirvāṇa* which was preserved, when one would encounter the royal name in which the monosyllables *mya ngan* figure, a translation of the most significant part of the word *nirvāṇa*, we would be induced to naturally believe that the term *nirvāṇa* forms the basis of this name. Hence, here are two terms, one for *nirvāṇa* and the name of king Aśoka, the most important half of which, according to the Tibetans, is figured in one and same expression, a circumstance that, I do not hesitate to say, creates for one who would study Buddhism only in Tibetan formulas independent of Sanskrit, a confusion from which it would be quite difficult if not completely impossible to escape.

The term I have just examined belongs as much to the language of the brahmans as to that of the Buddhists; but the latter somehow appropriated it through the use they made of it. They could thus modify its meaning according to the ensemble of their ideas, and it is easy to understand that they provided a translation of it that is so removed from the true etymology. I even imagine that the vague character I just indicated was left in this translation by design; the interpreters, afraid of being forced to take sides among the different sects, would confine themselves to a generality accepted by all, which contributes with other historical elements to establish that the Tibetan versions are subsequent to the full development of the great Buddhist sects. I will now cite a word that properly belongs to the Brahmanical language, and that the interpreters of Tibet treated with a liberty that embarrasses the European reader. In a most remarkable text in which the founder of Buddhism wishes to establish the superiority of morality in the fulfillment of religious duties, he teaches his disciples that homes where children honor their father and mother are as holy as if Brahmā, a spiritual preceptor, the god of the family, and the domestic fire were in their midst. Hence, in this enumeration, which one will read below in the very form the text gives it, appears the word *āhavanīya*, which is a special term among the brahmans, and whose meaning is beyond any doubt: it is, one knows, according to Manu, the consecrated fire lighted in the household and prepared for oblations; it is, in a word, the sacrificial fire.[45] The etymology and the use of the term are entirely in accord here, and there is no possible doubt about the one or the other. But how did the Tibetan interpreters translate this term? By an expression composed of three words: *kun tu sbyin pa'i 'os su gyur ba*, which according to the existing dictionaries does not mean anything other than "has become worthy of complete alms."[46] Perhaps a Tibetan, thanks to the sentiment he has for his language and to the frequent use he makes of this term, knows how to recover here the figurative signification of "sacrificial fire"; because by substituting the word *offering* for *alms*, one arrives, although in a roundabout way, at this very idea, and the Tibetan locution comes down to this: "that which has become worthy of complete offering," that is to say, "the fire prepared for the offering." I ask, nevertheless, all impartial readers: is this term not in itself less perfect and more obscure than the original Sanskrit word *āhavanīya*, whose meaning, apart from being determined with precision by good lexicons, is justified through the value that is perfectly recognizable in the elements of which it is composed? Here again I doubt that it

45. *Manavadharmaśāstra*, 1.2, st. 231.
46. *Bka' 'gyur*, sec. *Mdo*, vol. *ba*, or 29, fol. 413a.

is very easy for a European reader to go from the Tibetan expression back to the Sanskrit term, and nevertheless it is to this term itself that one must return if one wishes to understand the true meaning of the passage in which it is found.

What I have just said applies equally to proper names that are ordinarily difficult to recognize in the Tibetan versions, because their authors translate all the elements of which the names are composed. I content myself with citing one example here, the one that among all reappears most often and in which the original Sanskrit is most easily recovered. There was in the time of Śākyamuni, in the city of Śrāvastī,[47] not far from modern Fizabad, a merchant or, as the Sanskrit books of Nepal call him, a householder celebrated for his wealth and his liberality. He was called Anāthapiṇḍada or Anāthapiṇḍika, "he who distributes food to the indigent," and he owned a garden near the city that he had given to Śākyamuni; and so the latter retired to it very frequently with his disciples to teach them the Law. This is why, in ten legends, there are some eight that commence with this formula: "One day, the Blessed One was in Śrāvastī, at Jetavana,[48] in the garden of Anāthapiṇḍika." Certainly here this last word, although significant in each of its elements, although doubtless being given to this powerful householder afterward in consideration of his liberality, must be taken as a proper name, and

47. We have here the name of one of the cities most frequently cited in the preachings and in the Sanskrit legends of the North. Faxian, at the beginning of the fifth century of our era, speaks of it as a city that has very much fallen from its ancient splendor (*Foe koue ki*, p. 171); thus it would probably be very difficult to recover some of its remains today. It was the capital of Kośala and the abode of Prasenajit, king of this country, or to speak more precisely, king of Northern Kośala (Lassen, *Indische Alterthumskunde*, 1:128 and 129), a province that is distinguished from Kaśikośala or from the Kośala that contains Benares in the Buddhist legends as well as in the books of the brahmans (*Viṣṇu Purāṇa*, p. 186). Wilson establishes with good reasons that it is necessary to look for the site of Śrāvasti not far from Fizabad (*Journal of the Royal Asiatic Society*, vol. 5, p. 123). I must not fail to say that this city is mentioned in the *Viṣṇu Purāṇa* (p. 36, note 16), and in the *Kathāsaritsāgara* (Sanskrit text p. 200, st. 63, Brockhaus ed.). It is often a topic in the *Daśakumāra*, the story of Pramati (*Quarterly Oriental Magazine* 9 [June 1827]: 281). In this account, in which the name of this celebrated city figures several times, it speaks of a great cockfight, a most Brahmanical pleasure, which Śākyamuni prohibited to his disciples, as the Pāli books of Ceylon teach us, notably in a treatise entitled *Brahmajāla sutta*. The name of this city is written Sāvatthi in the Pāli texts of Ceylon (Clough, *Pāli Grammar and Vocabulary*, p. 24, chapter 2).

48. This name designates the most celebrated monastery and temple of Kośala province; it was located near Śrāvasti. It is constantly mentioned in the legends of the *Divyāvadāna* and the *Avadānaśataka*, and the Chinese travelers Faxian and Xuanzang speak of it with admiration (A. Rémusat, *Foe koue ki*, p. 179). One always finds this name written as *Jetavana*; and the Chinese, according to Mr. A. Rémusat, translated it as "the garden (or the temple) of victory, or of the victorious." I cannot restrain myself from seeing, in the orthography of this name, a trace of the influence of the vulgar dialects. If, indeed, *Jetavana* means "the wood of the Conqueror," it should be written in Sanskrit *Jetṛvana*; and it is only in a popular dialect like Pāli that the sound *ṛ* can disappear and yield a short *a*. The *Mahāvaṃsa* of Turnour reproduces it, indeed, always in this form. The redactors of the legends written in Sanskrit received the name as the people gave it to them, and they did not restore it to the form it would have in the classical language. I conclude from it that this designation is not anterior to the establishment of Buddhism, a conclusion that, moreover, accords with the tradition. This is not how, indeed, the Buddhists writing in Sanskrit dealt with the names of places in current use in India before the coming of Śākyamuni: they scrupulously respected their Brahmanical orthography, however contrary it was to the habits of the popular dialect. This is clearly recognizable in words like *Śrāvastī*, *Srughnā*, *Tāmralipti*, *Sūrpāraka*, *Kanyākubja*, and others.

it is my deep conviction that the Tibetans never misunderstood that. Indeed, in the legends in which this personage plays a role, the lotsavas, who always translate his name in the same manner, cannot be unaware that this name is that of a householder contemporary to Śākyamuni. But if they did not commit an error in this regard, they did nothing to prevent European readers from becoming lost, or at least from hesitating when they wish to translate the Tibetan version. Thus one of the scholars whose studies make him most familiar with Buddhist ideas, Mr. Schmidt, has rendered in his Tibetan grammar the expression that corresponds to the Sanskrit terms *anāthapiṇḍikasya ārāme* in this manner: "In the enclosure of eternal joy where food is offered to the indigent."[49] There is certainly nothing to be said against this translation; it reproduces the Tibetan version to the smallest detail; but although it is literally exact, or rather because it is materially faithful, it deceives the reader in the sense that it brings into relief the meaning of "universal joy" concealed beneath the term *ārāma* (Tibetan: *kun dga' ra ba*) and which must disappear following the particular acceptation that this word takes on, that of *pleasure garden* or *hermitage.* I say as much about the proper name of the merchant, and, moreover, I indicate here an imperfection in the Tibetan language, which, not distinguishing clearly enough the substantive in the genitive from the adjective preceding a substantive, does not allow one to decide if the garden in question is that of a personage who distributes alms or rather that where the alms are distributed. I hesitate all the less to make this observation, since Mr. Schmidt himself, in a work most recently published, provides me the opportunity to verify the accuracy.[50] There, indeed, while rendering with his usual exactitude the Tibetan monosyllables that represent the name of the generous merchant, he has very judiciously recognized that these words formed a proper name that should not be translated. This is why I do not need to repeat that these remarks are not addressed to Mr. Schmidt, since he himself later recognized an error that is not his; they concern the Tibetan interpreters, who by the very fact that they rendered all the elements of which these two words are

49. *Grammatik der Tibetischen Sprache*, p. 224.

50. *Der Weise und der Thor*, Tibetan text, p. 18, German translation, p. 21, and at the beginning of the greatest number of the legends that form this interesting volume. There are, moreover, few personages more celebrated among the Buddhists of all schools than this householder, who is also called Anāthapiṇḍika. His name is, properly speaking, only a title which expresses his liberality; because, according to the Sinhalese, he was called Sudatta, the name by which the Chinese also know him (*Foe koue ki*, p. 178). These two names, Sudatta and Anāthapiṇḍika, are passed into the Pāli dictionary, where they designate, according to Clough, the husband of a woman who owes her fame to her dedication to the Buddha (*Pāli Grammar and Vocabulary*, p. 57). One sees that this designation is not sufficient; because it is certain that Anāthapiṇḍika is much more well known than his wife, who was called Viśākhā and who is named in a list of nuns (Turnour, *Journal of the Asiatic Society of Bengal*, vol. 7, p. 933). He was not, as Mr. Rémusat believed, one of the ministers of Prasenajit, king of Kośala, but a simple householder, possessor of immense wealth. His garden, the use of which he gave to the Buddha Śākyamuni, is the theater of most of the preaching of the sage. In the seventh century Xuanzang saw the ruins of the monastery he had built in it and which bore the name Jetavana (*Foe koue ki*, pp. 178 and 179).

composed, translated too much, if I can express myself in that way, for the reader who does not have the Indian original at his disposal.

I have good reason to believe that the Chinese interpreters must also sometimes overshoot the mark in the same manner, because I found in the drama entitled *Pipa ji* a passage that reproduces without doubt the standard preamble to the greatest number of Buddhist books regarded as canonical in Nepal. Here is the passage: "Is it not said, at the beginning of the book of Fo, that in the garden of a certain prince who gives alms to old men and orphans, resides the great religious mendicant Biqiu, with one thousand two hundred fifty people."[51] The words "the garden of a certain prince" represent the word *Jetavana* (the Wood of the Conqueror) and the following phrase, "who gives alms, etc.," is only the development of the name Anāthapiṇḍika itself represented in its etymological elements. Finally, "the great religious mendicant" is the *mahābhikṣu*, or rather the *mahāśramaṇa*,[52] that is to say, Śākyamuni himself. Here again the European translator is shielded from all reproach, and on the contrary one must approve of the exactitude that he has brought to his version, since one can go back without great difficulty from this version to the Sanskrit original. But it is necessary to know this original in advance, and I doubt that it was possible, without having it before one's eyes, to reconstruct from the French translation, which is a faithful image of the Chinese translation, the proper names of places and persons indispensable to retain for fear of not recognizing the true meaning of the original text.

It is by design that I have not spoken here about radically flawed translations of some important Sanskrit words, which one observes in the Tibetan versions, because these translations are found equally among all Buddhist peoples. They start thus from a unique system of interpretation that belongs to the different schools into which Buddhism is divided, and consequently they are not relevant to the interpretative critic but to the philosophical and historical critic. There are such faulty etymologies that could be adopted in response to a system of ideas that it favored, without the translator who gave it current use being culpable of infidelity to the text. These mistakes, which to a certain point are voluntary, are rare and they did not invalidate the authority or the veracity of the Tibetan lotsavas, the only ones, together with the Burmese interpreters, whose accuracy I could verify myself. I repeat, their translations are of an extreme literalness; they render, as much as possible with an instrument as dryly analytical as Tibetan and Burmese, all the features of this fortunate synthesis contained in the expressive unity of a Sanskrit term. But the previous remarks allow me to conclude nonetheless that in spite of the merit of these versions, it is always indispensable to

51. Bazin, *Le Pi pa ki*, p. 118.
52. These terms will be explained later.

resort to the originals from which these versions were made, and that it is solely from the study of the text itself that must result the appreciation of its true character and the solutions to very numerous and very delicate questions that these texts cannot fail to bring out. This conclusion, which has never been contested for any genre of writing or for any literature, needs to be recalled at the moment when there is the question of indicating the place that the books written in Sanskrit, which we owe to the zeal and the liberality of Mr. Hodgson, must occupy in the ensemble of material destined for the study of Buddhism.

The facts that I have just established give rise to two observations of great importance for the continuation of the research of which the Nepalese collection must be the object. The first is that the translation of Sanskrit books carried out in Tibet, Tartary, and China, by fixing the different epochs during which these books began to spread beyond India, furnish a precise limit below which it is not possible for the redaction of the original Sanskrit text to descend. The relish that the Chinese and the Tibetans, for example, have always had for historical precision promises precious aid to the European critic in this respect. It is permissible to hope that at least in the greatest number of cases, the date of the translations of the Sanskrit books, which in their capacity as works reputed to be inspired, are all equally attributed to Śākya, was marked with exactitude by the interpreters. I do not need to observe that no indication of this type is to be neglected, since the work of interpretation was not accomplished at the same time among the diverse nations that adopted Buddhism. What I content myself to indicate here can already verify itself through the examination of the Tibetan Buddhist library, to which the so exact and so substantial analysis of Csoma de Kőrös has given us access. One knows now with certainty that it is between the seventh and thirteenth centuries of our era that the Buddhist books were translated into the language of Bot.[53] This fact, which I recall relying on the knowledge of Csoma, will doubtless need to be studied in all its detail. It will be necessary to investigate if the work of interpretation has not continued into more modern times, and if it has had as its object either ancient Sanskrit texts or works composed subsequent to the epochs just indicated, or even books foreign to India. But this research itself will bear the fruit I anticipate: it will fix the limits and indications useful for the still obscure history of Buddhist literature. I add that if I do not speak here about the light that the examination of the previously mentioned versions must shed on another history no less interesting, that of the migration and propagation of Buddhism beyond India, it is just because the only issue at the moment is to determine in a general way which kind of authority is attached to the Sanskrit books preserved by the Nepalese. I shall indicate later the advantages that the history of Indian Buddhism will derive from the study of monuments

53. "Analysis of the Dul-va," in *Asiatic Researches*, vol. 20, p. 42.

that seem, at first glance, to belong exclusively to the exterior history of this belief.

The estimation of the degree of authority that the Nepalese collection possesses is again the object of the second of the observations I announced above. This observation is that if the Buddhist books are written in Sanskrit, the result is that they were written in India. This is what Mr. Hodgson asserts in more than one place; he does not hesitate to conclude from the language of the books the country where they must have been written; and we have to acknowledge that, presented in such general terms, this conclusion has in itself a great likelihood; but when one examines things more closely, one finds that the issue is less simple than it appears at first sight. The difficulty it presents comes from the fact that it relates to another issue far more vast, the history of Indian Buddhism. If Buddhism had traversed all the phases of its existence in a narrow theater and in a brief span of time, the presumption that it must have been fixed by scripture in the place where the language that serves as its organ was spoken would be, to my mind, almost unassailable. But since Buddhism lived long in India; since it long flourished also in neighboring countries and notably to the west of the Indus and in Kashmir, the redaction of the books that we are at first tempted to regard as a fact accomplished at once and in only one country could have been performed at several times and in several countries. This is only a conjecture, and perhaps this supposition presents fewer probabilities in its favor than the opposite supposition. The facts will teach us at which point this must be verified. For my part, if I am allowed now to advance a personal opinion, I believe that the truth will be found in the conciliation of the two hypotheses. No, the corpus of the Buddhist scriptures of Nepal cannot have been written entirely outside India. It is not permissible to suppose that Śākyamuni's disciples thought about writing down the teachings of their master only when they saw themselves expelled forever from their homeland. There would be something too bizarre in believing that exiles would have written such a considerable mass of books in Sanskrit, in order to translate them almost immediately into the languages of the people who offered them asylum. All these considerations, combined with the circumstances of the language, militate in favor of the first hypothesis. But, on the other side, it is not credible that Buddhism remained stationary from the moment it was transported beyond its native land. One cannot accept that the monks who were its apostles had immediately forgotten the language in which the repository of the teachings of their master was preserved. It is necessary to believe that the usage of this language continued to be familiar to them, since they took part, as the catalogue of the Tibetan library attests, in the versions that were carried out around them.[54] Everything must not be inspired in the Sanskrit collection

54. Csoma, "Analysis of the Dul-va," in *Asiatic Researches*, vol. 20, pp. 78, 85, 92, etc.

of Nepal; the attentive study of this collection may perhaps discover there works that ordinary authors could claim; nothing, finally, prevents Buddhist monks from having written outside India, in neighboring countries when proselytism, reawakened by persecution, animated them with a new ardor. From these two series of hypotheses, neither excludes the other absolutely, because they are most reconcilable with each other. One hypothesis assumes possible for a portion of the books that which the other declares impossible for the totality of the collection; but adopting both of them within just limits moves us equally away from absolute affirmations, as they return us to the examination of facts that alone must verify the hypotheses and mark in each its legitimate part in the solution of the complicated problem that each, taken in isolation, is insufficient to resolve.

But, where will the facts be found, whose testimony we invoke, if it is not in the books themselves, whose origin is the question to resolve? And how does one go from these general affirmations that allow the systematic mind to have the freedom of contradiction, if one does not enter into these verifications of detail that limit each other, and whose results are no less useful in their opposition than in their agreement, in order to narrow the fields of hypothesis and of error? We cannot hope to arrive at some definitive conclusions concerning the country where the Nepalese collection must have been redacted before having examined in detail the different works of which it is composed. We must search in each of them for indices to enlighten us concerning their character and consequently their origin; to note if all present themselves equally as inspired; to distinguish those that bear the names of authors from those supposed to be canonical; then, among the latter, to establish, if possible, a chronological succession based on the succession of the schools to which they are connected and on the age of the events and personages whose memory they have preserved. Such is the most general expression of the conditions of the problem; it is only when one has thoroughly satisfied these conditions that it will be resolved in a definitive manner; until then, and as long as one has not determined the homeland of a given work, either by the direct testimony of this work itself, or by accepted methods of the critic, the assumption will be in favor of the opinion that regards as having been written in India the works written in the learned language of this country.

Now that I have indicated the place the collection of Mr. Hodgson occupies in the ensemble of materials that the Orient furnishes us for the study of Buddhism, nothing remains but for me to sketch rapidly the order in which I believe I must present the results of my research. To familiarize myself with the ideas and with the style that distinguish Buddhist books from other products of Sanskrit literature, I have chosen a work that was accepted as an authority in Nepal, and I have translated it for the purpose of later presenting it to the public as a specimen of this still unknown literature. But before settling on it, I had to browse through almost all of the collection, and it is only after three years of preliminary reading that I decided on the book that I shall publish shortly under the title the *Lotus of the Good Law.* Independent of the interest it can have as a canonical book, this work has put me in a position to understand a good many details that had escaped me during the brief examination I made of Mr. Hodgson's collection. It has become for me a point of comparison to which I have related the notions that my first readings had provided me; and these notions in turn, compared among themselves, then with those one can draw from the books of another Buddhist people, the Sinhalese, have enabled me, if not to resolve definitively the most important questions to which the Nepalese collection gives rise, at least to pose these questions with a greater precision than would have been possible through the knowledge of one work alone.

This is, then, in a few words, the order I propose to follow. I shall describe, in a general manner, according to the Nepalese tradition, the Buddhist collection discovered by Mr. Hodgson. I shall go into necessary detail touching on the three great divisions of the sacred scriptures accepted by the Buddhists of the North, and I shall treat separately the books in which the practices of Śivaist ascetics are mixed with Buddhism. Then, I shall review some of the treatises that bear the names of authors. By examining those works of Nepal that claim the title of inspired books, I shall focus on investigating whether all can be taken as having been written in the same epoch. For this examination, I shall make use of the information furnished by the books themselves, and then I shall assemble what it is currently possible to know about the history of the Nepalese collection. This will be the subject of a memorandum divided into seven parts: the first dedicated to the general description of the books of Nepal; the second, third, and fourth to the three divisions of the inspired books; the fifth to the books in which the worship of Śiva intermingles with that of the Buddha; the sixth to the works bearing the names of authors; and the seventh to the history of the Nepalese collection. This memorandum, which will be composed of texts borrowed from the most important works sent by Mr. Hodgson, will cast some daylight on the early times of Buddhism; and in offering the most characteristic features of the picture of India's social and religious state at the moment of the preaching of Śākyamuni Buddha, it will solve in a definitive way, or so I hope, the long debated question, though no longer one for any Indologist, of the relative antiquity of Brahmanism and Buddhism.

In another memorandum that will follow the one I have just summarized, I shall make for the Pāli collection of Ceylon an examination similar to the one to which I will have subjected the Sanskrit collection of Nepal. I shall set forth what the tradition teaches us concerning the existence of this collection and notably on that of the ancient councils during which the doctrine of Śākya was fixed in a standard manner. This memorandum will be composed of five sections. Then I shall dedicate another memorandum to the comparison of the collections of

Nepal and Ceylon and to the traditions preserved in the North and in the South related to these collections. This comparison will give us the means to recognize that we possess in the Sanskrit library of Nepal and in the Pāli library of Ceylon two redactions of Buddhist scriptures whose difference consists, in general, less in the content than in the form and the classification of the books. From this examination it will result that the fundamental and truly antique elements of Buddhism must be sought in what the two Indian redactions of the religious books, that of the North, which uses Sanskrit, and that of the South, which uses Pāli, have kept in common.

The determination of the different epochs in which the councils were held, during which the Buddhist books were collected, will conduct me naturally to the investigation of the epoch on which they depend, that of Śākyamuni Buddha. This will be the subject of a memorandum divided into six sections, in which I shall compare the opinions of the principal peoples of Asia on this important point of Oriental history. Taking advantage of the synchronisms that the history of Sinhalese Buddhism and some Tibetan texts of the Kah-gyur indicate, I shall use those that are already recognized by the most capable critics in order to make a choice among the different dates assigned to the death of the last buddha. Once this point is established, I shall summarize what is known of the most definitive of the fates of Indian Buddhism; and in order not to omit anything that can shed some light on them, I shall trace the different epochs of emigrations that successively transported it beyond India, where it was never to enter again.

SECOND MEMORANDUM

Description of the Collection of the Books of Nepal

FIRST SECTION

General Description

The Buddhist collection of Nepal is composed of a great number of works whose titles announce treatises of very different genres. These titles have been known for some time through the memoranda of Mr. Hodgson, and this scholar has published two extensive lists of them in the *Asiatic Researches* of Calcutta[1] and in the *Transactions of the Asiatic Society* of London.[2] This double catalogue must be augmented further by one that could be drawn up following the analysis that Csoma de Kőrös has provided of the great Tibetan collection in the *Journal of the Asiatic Society of Bengal*,[3] and especially in the *Asiatic Researches* of Calcutta.[4] Indeed, since, with the exception of some treatises whose Sanskrit titles are not reported by the Tibetan editors, the books that compose this collection are translations of Indian works, and since, following the opinion of Mr. Hodgson, these works must have existed or may even be preserved in some monasteries of Nepal or Tibet, it is understandable that the catalogue of the Sanskrit collection of Nepal could find material for a considerable supplement through the analysis of the Tibetan Kah-gyur.

In Paris, we do not possess the totality of the works whose existence would be made known by a catalogue formed by these three lists combined, and even if

1. "Notices of the Languages, Literature and Religion of the Bauddhas of Nepal and Bhot," in *Asiatic Researches*, vol. 16, p. 426ff.

2. "Sketch of Buddhism," in *Transactions of the Royal Asiatic Society*, vol. 2, p. 229.

3. "Abstract of the Contents of the Dul-va," in *Journal of the Asiatic Society of Bengal*, vol. 1, pp. 1 and 375.

4. "Analysis of the Dul-va," etc., vol. 20, p. 41ff., and "Analysis of the Sher chin," etc., *ibid.*, p. 393ff.

Mr. Hodgson has not been able to procure all the books that his double list indicates, then it is probable that one would have some difficulty to discover in Nepal today all the originals of the Tibetan versions of the Kah-gyur. Be that as it may, the double dispatch, which we owe to Mr. Hodgson, has placed in our possession about eighty-eight Buddhist works composed in Sanskrit, either in verse or in prose, which contain, in all likelihood, what is most important in the religious collection of Nepal. Indeed, these works are for the most part included in the great divisions of the Buddhist scriptures, whose Nepalese tradition, in accord with the testimony of the books themselves, has preserved for our memory.

We would still not be in a position to judge the extent of Buddhist literature based on what we possess, if we are to believe a tradition widespread generally among the Buddhists of the North and those of the South, a tradition that increases the collection of the books of the law to eighty-four thousand treatises.[5] I find in a philosophical compilation, the *Abhidharmakośavyākhyā*, of which I shall speak later, a passage related to this tradition, which proves that it is not solely oral: "'I have received from the mouth of the Blessed One,' says a sacred text, 'eighty thousand texts of the law and more.' In another volume, the commentary adds, one reads eighty-four thousand. The corpus of the law is composed of books accepted as authoritative; now, these books reach, according to some, the number six thousand, and they are designated with the title *dharmaskandha*, or the corpus of the law. As for the eighty thousand texts of the law, they are lost; the only one that survives is this single corpus [of six thousand volumes]. Others understand by *dharmaskandha* each of the articles of the law and they count eighty thousand."[6] It is rather in this latter sense that one must take the term *skandha*. If we had to admit that such a voluminous collection ever existed, a matter that Mr. Hodgson judiciously questions,[7] we would be forced to imagine it as including works of very diverse proportions, from a treatise properly speaking to a simple stanza. Thus we know a work on Buddhist metaphysics, the *Prajñāpāramitā*, of which we have two redactions, one in one hundred thousand articles and the other in a single vowel, *multum in parvo*.[8] The tradition to which I have just referred is, moreover, ancient among the Buddhists. It even gave a kind of consecration to the number eighty-four thousand, for one knows that they have applied this number to objects other than their religious books.

Whatever these eighty-four thousand texts of law may be, their reality can be believed, if by *texts* one understands *articles*; the books that survive to the

5. Hodgson, "Notices of the Languages," etc., in *Asiatic Researches*, vol. 16, p. 421.

6. *Abhidharmakośavyākhyā*, p. 38b of my manuscript. Compare with Turnour, *Journal of the Asiatic Society of Bengal*, vol. 6, p. 526.

7. *Asiatic Researches*, vol. 16, p. 425.

8. Csoma, *Asiatic Researches*, vol. 20, p. 393 compared to p. 396; it is A, which contains everything!—"Analysis of the Kah-gyur," in *Journal of the Asiatic Society of Bengal*, vol. 1, p. 376.

present day are divided into three categories called collectively *tripiṭaka*, that is to say, "the three baskets or collections." These three categories are the *sūtra piṭaka*, or the Discourses of Buddha, the *vinaya piṭaka*, or the Discipline, and the *abhidharma piṭaka*, or the Manifested Laws, that is to say, metaphysics.[9] This division, which is justified by the texts, is one of the bases of the classification of the Kah-gyur, and among the seven corpuses that form the hundred volumes of this great library, the Vinaya is the first, the Abhidharma, under the special title Prajñāpāramitā, is the second, and the collection of Sūtras is the fifth.[10] It is no less familiar to the Chinese Buddhists, whose testimony agrees in general so exactly with that of the Tibetans; they explain it with three words signifying "sacred books, precepts, and discourses,"[11] and we find it elucidated in a learned note of Mr. A. Rémusat, which reproduces exactly the details that the Buddhist books of Nepal furnish us on this subject.[12] But it is necessary that we pause for a moment over these three titles to bring together what the Sanskrit texts and the Nepalese tradition teach us about their value and their application.

The word *sūtra* is a quite well-known term in the literature of ancient India; it designates these short and obscure sentences that contain the fundamental rules of Brahmanical science, from grammar to philosophy.[13] This signification is not unknown to the Buddhists, because Mr. Rémusat defines the term in this way: "Principles or aphorisms that form the basis of the doctrine, the authentic and unchanging texts."[14] I find, moreover, in the collection of Mr. Hodgson a work entitled *Vinayasūtra* or *Vinayapatra*, which is composed of very brief sentences and conceived according to the system of Brahmanical axioms. I shall return to this work below; but I must first hasten to remark that it is not only in this way that the Buddhists understand the word *sūtra,* and that the treatises to which this title is applied are of a very different character from those that it designates in the orthodox literature of ancient India. The sūtras, according to the Nepalese authorities cited by Mr. Hodgson, contain everything that the buddhas have said; this is why they are often called *buddhavacana*, "the word of the buddhas," or *mūlagrantha*, "the book of the text."[15] The Chinese explain this term in the same manner. The sūtras are, according to an interesting note of Mr. Landresse, "the attached or sewn doctrines; it is the general name for all the holy teachings; they are the texts of the sacred books, which deal with the law simply in continuous

9. *Abhidharmakośavyākhyā*, fol. 10a of the MS of the Société Asiatique.

10. Csoma, "Abstract of the Contents of the Dul-va," in *Journal of the Asiatic Society of Bengal*, vol. I, pp. 1ff., 37ff, and *Asiatic Researches*, vol. 20, p. 42.

11. *Foe koue ki*, pp. 3, 78, and 108.

12. *Ibid.*, p. 108.

13. Wilson, *Sanscrit Dictionary*, 2nd ed., s.v. "Sūtra," p. 940.

14. *Foe koue ki*, p. 108.

15. "Notices of the Languages," in *Asiatic Researches*, vol. 16, p. 422.

discourses, long or short."[16] One recognizes in this explanation the trace of the etymological signification of the word *sūtra,* and at the same time the Buddhists' application of it to what they specifically call their sūtras. These books are attributed to the last of the buddhas recognized by all Buddhists, that is to say, to Śākyamuni or Śākya, the recluse of the Śākya race, who is represented conversing with one or several of his disciples in the presence of an assembly composed of other disciples and listeners of all types, from gods to humans.[17] I shall soon show that Buddhist texts determine the proper form of all sūtras, and I shall establish that among several of these books there are differences likely to cast light on their origin and their development. At the moment, it suffices for me to note the most general characteristics and to indicate briefly the place that the sūtras occupy in the ensemble of the Buddhist scriptures of Nepal.

This place is, as one sees, most elevated, since the sūtras are considered the very word of the last buddha, and according to the report of Mr. Hodgson, there is no title that enjoys more authority than this.[18] Written generally in a form and a language that is quite simple, the sūtras retain the visible trace of their origin. They are dialogues related to morality and philosophy, in which Śākya fulfills the role of master. Far from presenting his thought in this concise form so familiar to the Brahmanical teaching, there is no doubt that he expounds it with tiresome repetitions and diffuseness, but which give his teaching the character of a real preaching. There is an abyss between his method and that of the brahmans. Instead of this mysterious teaching confided almost secretly to a small number of listeners, instead of these formulas whose studied obscurity seems made to discourage the acumen of the disciple as much as to exercise it, the sūtras show us a large audience around Śākya, composed of all those who desire to listen to him and in his language, with this need to make himself understood, having words for all intelligences and, through its perpetual repetitions, leaving no excuse to less attentive minds or more rebellious memories. This profound difference is at the very essence of Buddhism, a doctrine whose characteristic feature is proselytism, but proselytism is itself only an effect of this sentiment of benevolence and universal charity which animates the Buddha, and which is at once the cause and the aim of the mission he gave himself on earth.

One should not believe, however, that these brief maxims, so appreciated by antiquity, are entirely lacking in the teaching of Śākya; on the contrary, in the sūtras one still finds several traces of this sententious exposition that summarizes a long development in a few words or in a concise stanza. But these maxims,

16. *Foe koue ki,* p. 321, note 6.

17. Hodgson, "Notices of the Languages, Literature," etc., in *Asiatic Researches,* vol. 16, p. 422.

18. Hodgson, "Quotations from Original Sanscrit Authorities," in *Journal of the Asiatic Society of Bengal,* vol. 6, p. 87, note †.

which one could call real sūtras according to the Brahmanical acceptation of this term, are fairly rare in the sūtras of Nepal, and one must search for them over a long time amid the flood of words beneath which thought sometimes disappears. It is permissible to believe that Śākya must not have abstained from using these sentences, and that the memory of the use he made of them in his teaching favored the entirely special application his disciples made of the term *sūtra* through extending it to his moral and philosophical preaching.

The title of the second category, that of *vinaya*, signifies "discipline," and one constantly encounters in the texts the various forms of the root from which this word is derived employed in the sense of "to discipline, to convert." The Chinese Buddhists understand this term in the same manner, and Mr. Rémusat defines it in this way: "the precepts, the rules, the laws or the ordinances, literally good government."[19] The signification of this word thus cannot create any difficulty; but due to a peculiarity that seems difficult to understand, apart from some short treatises related to religious practices of little importance, Mr. Hodgson's collection does not offer works that take their place in the category of the Vinaya, in the way it possesses those belonging to that of the Sūtras. In the two lists I have cited above, the name *vinaya* does not appear more than once and even then is not employed with this character of generality that it has in the expression *vinaya-piṭaka*, "collection of the discipline." It figures solely in the title of a philosophical treatise, the *Vinayasūtra*, whose existence I have just indicated and of which it suffices for me to say at the moment that it is not attributed to Śākyamuni.[20] Thus how is it that the category of the Vinaya is not, like that of the Sūtras, represented in Mr. Hodgson's collection? Might it have been that works related to the discipline are missing from this collection, either because Mr. Hodgson could not find any, or because these works might have indeed been far less numerous than the sūtras? The careful examination of some of the volumes of the Nepalese collection, compared with the list of the works contained in the Tibetan Kahgyur gives, if I am not mistaken, the solution to this difficulty.

While studying the analysis made by Csoma of the Tibetan library, I have recognized there a certain number of treatises bearing titles that one can find in the Sanskrit collection discovered in Nepal by Mr. Hodgson. These treatises, some of which have been mentioned at the beginning of the present work, belong in general to the same category in both collections; and such a book, which is called *sūtra* according to the double authority of the Nepalese tradition and the very manuscript that contains it, belongs, according to the Tibetans, to the category of *mdo*, that is to say, of Sūtras. But one encounters frequent exceptions to this usual regularity, and there are examples of works that, according to their

19. *Foe koue ki*, p. 108.
20. *Asiatic Researches*, vol. 16, p. 431. *Transactions of the Royal Asiatic Society*, vol. 2, p. 225.

Sanskrit titles, should be attributed to a category other than the one the Tibetan translators have assigned to them. Some examples will suffice to make myself understood. Mr. Hodgson's collection contains a great number of treatises of a small length that bear the title *avadāna*, a title that I will examine later, and about which I content myself in remarking that its application is almost as frequent as that of *sūtra.* I even believe that by combining the two great anthologies of the *Divyāvadāna* and the *Avadānaśataka* with all the treatises with this name dispersed through the Nepalese collection we have in Paris, we would find many more avadānas than sūtras. But several of these treatises have the exact form of sūtras, and following a rigorous classification, it would be necessary to separate them from works that have the title *avadāna* and which do not offer the constitutive characteristics of a true sūtra. Nevertheless, the confusion I indicate here recurs in the Tibetan collection, and one finds among the *mdo*, or the sūtras, a very great number of treatises that bear the title *avadāna.* The distinction between these two categories of books is thus not so definite that they could not stand near each other in a very large classification of Buddhist scriptures.

Assuming this to be the case, it would seem that all of the Sanskrit avadānas that we have should also be found in the thirty volumes of the Tibetan *mdo.* It is not the case, however, and several Sanskrit texts that qualify as avadānas have found a place in the Dul-va of the Tibetans, which is nothing other than the Sanskrit *vinayavastu.* I will mention among others the *Pūrṇāvadāna*, the *Saṃgharakṣitāvadāna*, the *Sūkarikāvadāna*, treatises to which it would doubtless be easy to add others if we possessed exactly in Sanskrit everything contained in Tibetan in the library of the Kah-gyur.

Now, in order for some avadānas to be comprised in Tibet within the framework of the Vinaya, it must have been the case that these avadānas were related more or less directly to the discipline. I conclude from this observation that if the category of the Vinaya seems to be quite absent in the collection of Mr. Hodgson, it is because the general title of this category is masked by the particular titles of some books that must be included in it. The list of Buddhist books given by Mr. Hodgson, and which will be discussed frequently below, provides us with two examples of avadānas that necessarily belong to the class of the Vinaya; these are the *Kaṭhināvadāna*, which deals with the bowl, the staff, and the robes of monks, and the *Piṇḍapātrāvadāna*, which is related to the bowl for collecting alms.[21] The Nepalese cannot be unaware of the great division of the Buddhist scriptures into three categories, since their books themselves, canonical texts and commentaries, speak of it as something of common knowledge. But we do not possess a catalogue of the Sanskrit books of Nepal in which these books are arranged under one or the other of the categories to which they belong. This fact,

21. *Asiatic Researches*, vol. 16, p. 430.

however, must not prevail over what is right, and in the absence of all definitive information on this point, we can with full assurance appeal to the Tibetan tradition, which, fixed in writing between the seventh and the thirteenth century of our era, offers us information prior by almost eleven centuries to the tradition recorded some twenty years ago in Nepal. I am even less hesitant to fill in the lacunae of the Nepalese tradition with elements provided by the library of the Kah-gyur, because this library contains almost nothing other than translations of Sanskrit books, and because the books of Nepal derive their authority from the language in which they were written much more than from the country where Mr. Hodgson has discovered them.

I pass now to the third division, that of the *abhidharma piṭaka*. The commentary to the *Abhidharmakośa* I have mentioned above explains the word *abhidharma* by *abhimukho dharmaḥ*, "the present or manifest law,"[22] and it is in this way also that the Tibetan interpreters of the Kah-gyur understand it.[23] The Chinese Buddhists do not offer such a clear explanation when they say that *abhidharma* means "discourse, conversation" and add that "these are treatises where, by means of answers and responses, one settles on an alternative among different processes indicated by the law."[24] I shall demonstrate later, in setting forth the elements preserved by the Sinhalese tradition concerning the Buddhist scriptures, that the signification of "discourse" is not unknown to the Buddhists of the South; but in translating *abhidharma* as "discourse spoken for the gods," the Sinhalese have tried to heighten the importance of these books that contain in reality the highest part of the Buddhist doctrine. The Abhidharma, indeed, contains metaphysics, and in general the opinions of the Buddhists on everything that exists. This title does not appear in either of the two lists of Mr. Hodgson; abhidharma, however, is not absent from his collection, and it is represented by the *prajñāpāramitā*, "the perfection of wisdom" or "the transcendental wisdom," according to the explanation the Tibetans give of this term,[25] and according to Mr. Schmidt, the Mongols.[26] I shall return below to this title when I examine the books that bear it; first it is necessary to conclude describing the three largest divisions of the Buddhist scriptures in a general manner.

Presented as it is in the previously cited passage of the commentary on the *Abhidharmakośa*, and in the analysis of the Kah-gyur by Csoma de Kőrös, this classification of the books of Śākya seems to encompass works of a legal authority, and nothing indicates that any difference exists among the three collections that it contains. A more careful examination, nevertheless, allows one to sus-

22. *Abhidharmakośavyākyā*, fol. 8b of the MS of the Société Asiatique.
23. Csoma, *Asiatic Researches*, vol. 20, p. 43.
24. A. Rémusat, *Foe koue ki*, p. 108.
25. Csoma, "Analysis of the Dul-va," in *Asiatic Researches*, vol. 20, p. 43.
26. *Geschichte der Ost-Mongolen*, p. 355.

pect the existence of some useful distinctions for understanding the books gathered under these three principal headings. Thus I find several passages in the *Abhidharmakośa* from which it is right to conclude that the collections that contain abhidharma do not emanate directly, or in the same manner as the sūtras, from the preaching of Śākya. The author of the treatise I discuss, for example, expresses it in those same terms: *abuddhoktam abhidharmaśāstram* ("the book that contains metaphysics was not set forth by the Buddha").[27] The elements of this part of the Buddhist doctrine are, according to him, dispersed through various books in which Śākya, while dealing with other subjects, incidentally enunciates several principles of metaphysics, such as this one: "every composite is perishable," a fundamental axiom in all Buddhist schools that the commentator chose to prove this point: that without having expressly set forth the abhidharma, or metaphysics, Śākya nonetheless founded that part of the science through his teaching. We even know sūtras, like the *Arthaviniścaya*, to which the title *abhidharma* applies, because one finds in it the definition of laws or, in a more general way, the definition of everything that the very vast term *dharma* designates, namely conditions, parallels, laws, or beings who present themselves under such-and-such conditions, who support among themselves such-and-such parallels, and who are governed by such-and-such laws.[28] The Abhidharma must

27. *Abhidharmakośavyākyā*, fol. 427b of my manuscript.

28. It is not useless to assemble here the ideas that Mr. Hodgson gives us about this important word in several places in his writings on Northern Buddhism. *Dharma*, derived from *dhṛ* (to contain), in this manner, *dhāraṇātmika iti dharmaḥ* means "nature, proper constitution"; it is in this sense that one of the great schools of the North could regard this term as a synonym of *prajñā*, the supreme wisdom, that is to say, the wisdom of nature grasping the foundation and the cause of all existences. The term *dharma* also signifies: 1. morality, virtue, 2. law or moral code, 3. material effects or the phenomenal world (Hodgson, "European Speculations on Buddhism," in *Journal of the Asiatic Society of Bengal*, vol. 3, p. 502). According to the same author, this word designates in an even broader manner sentient beings and external things or phenomena (Hodgson, "Further Note on the Inscription from Sārnāth," in *Journal of the Asiatic Society of Bengal*, vol. 4, pp. 213 and 214). Ordinarily I translate this term as "condition," other times as "laws"; but none of these translations is perfectly complete; we must understand by *dharma* that which makes something what it is, that which constitutes its own nature, as Lassen has shown so well on the occasion of the celebrated formula *ye dharmā hetuprabhavā* (Lassen, *Zeitschrift für die Kunde des Morgenlandes*, vol. 1, pp. 228 and 229). There are even a good many cases in which one need not press much on the signification of this word, because it is very vague and almost imperceptible, notably at the end of a compound. Thus I constantly find in the legends of the *Avadānaśataka* the term *deyadharma*, which must be translated, not as "duty or merit of what must be given," but as "charity, offering"; that is to say, one must see in it the fact of offering and alms, and not the duty of performing it or the merit attached to it. This meaning is placed beyond doubt by the expression *deyadharma parityāga*, which has no other meaning than "abandoning of an offering" (*Mahāvastu*, fol. 193b of my manuscript). One understands without difficulty how from the idea of duty or the merit of charity, one passes to the general idea of charity and from there to the particular fact of a special charity; our French word itself has all of this extended acceptation. This expression is, moreover, one of the most authentic and the most ancient in Buddhism, for it belongs to all schools. Clough, in his *Sinhalese Dictionary* (2:283, col. 2), expressly gives it with the meaning of "offerings, gifts, charity"; and I believe I have discovered it among the inscriptions of the caves of Saiṃhādri, in the north of Junīra, in the west of India. Prinsep ("Note on Syke's Inscription," in *Journal of the Asiatic Society of Bengal*, vol. 6, p. 1042 and pl. 53), who has deciphered these short legends so successfully, reads there *dayādhama*, which he translates as "compassion and piety"; shifting the vowels, I find 𑀤𑁂𑀬𑀥𑀫𑁆𑀫 *deya dhamma* (gift, offering).

have been a part of the teaching of Śākya, adds the commentator, since in a sūtra there is the matter of a monk to whom is attributed knowledge of the three piṭakas.[29] I will examine soon what we must think about the presence of this title "the three piṭakas" in a treatise considered to emanate directly from the preaching of Śākya; what is important to note at the moment is that, according to our author, the treatises on metaphysics are composed of axioms that are found dispersed throughout the teaching of Śākya, that they were detached from it, and for which a separate corpus was made under the name *abhidharma*.

But if this is so, we can say that the Abhidharma is included, by its origin, in the category of the Sūtras, and that the section of metaphysical works owes its existence as a distinct section above all to a work of compilation that extracted it from the teaching of the Buddha; and in pursuing these consequences, we can affirm, with the Buddhists of Nepal, that the sūtras are truly the word of the Buddha, *buddhavacana*, and the fundamental text, *mūlagrantha*. The section of the Vinaya still remains next to the Sūtras; but we have seen which analogies the books forming these two categories offer, at least as far as the form is concerned, since several treatises arranged by the Nepalese among the Sūtras are placed, according to the Tibetans, among the sources of the Vinaya. It is, moreover, easily understandable that the points of *vinaya,* or discipline, regarded as having been established by Śākya himself could only have been so in his discourses or, in a more general way, in his preaching; and since the sūtras contain this preaching, it is permissible to say that the Vinaya is just a part of the Sūtras, a section composed of those discourses of Śākyamuni that deal especially with discipline.

In the course of the observations to which the most general classification of Buddhist books has just given rise, I have attributed the origin of these books to Śākyamuni, that is to say, to the last of the seven human buddhas whose memory the tradition has preserved.[30] On this point I have only reproduced the opinion of the Nepalese, who attribute the composition or the redaction of their sacred books to the last of the buddhas they recognize. The date of these books is thus placed in historical time and is shielded from all uncertainties and all doubts that could arise if the tradition had linked it to the existence of this or that of the ancient buddhas who, if they ever existed, will escape the grasp of the historical critic for a long time to come. There doubtless does not yet result from this testimony a sufficiently rigorous precision for the determination of a fact that would be so important to fix in the most exact manner, since the epoch of the last buddha is a contested point among the different Buddhist schools. Nevertheless, it is already an advantage to be spared from having to examine, at the beginning of an investigation of literary history, the question of knowing when the six buddhas

29. *Abhidharmakośavyākhyā*, fol. 8b of my manuscript.
30. Hodgson, "Notices," etc., in *Asiatic Researches*, vol. 16, p. 422.

who, so to speak, preceded Śākyamuni existed, or from having to demonstrate, as capable critics think, that these buddhas owe their existence to the desire that the last one would have had to ensure for his doctrine the merit of a tradition consecrated by a long series of ancient sages. Thanks to the good faith of the Nepalese, this question of the buddhas prior to Śākya is quite distinct from that which concerns the date of the Buddhist books, and it will not be their fault if Western critics complicate the difficulties of the second by occupying themselves with the first before the appropriate time. Indeed, it would be a premature endeavor to classify these ancient buddhas chronologically before having taken note of and appraised the authenticity of the books that make them known to us. It would even place the realistic elements contained in these books into peril to present them to skeptical minds as carrying the origin of Buddhism back to an entirely mythological antiquity. I do not wish to say by this that we have to reject without examination, as if they were purely fabulous notions, everything that the Buddhist books recount about these buddhas previous to Śākya; and although I expect few positive results from this research, I do not believe that I have the right to condemn it in advance without having made the attempt. I wish solely to establish that the question of the origin of the Buddhist books must remain separate from that of the ancient buddhas; and I wish to record, in the name of the critic, the testimony of the Nepalese, which does not permit tracing back beyond the last buddha any of the works that have preserved the Buddhist doctrines for us.

The Nepalese tradition goes even further, and asserts that it was Śākya who wrote the first of these works and was for Buddhism almost what Vyāsa was for Brahmanism.[31] Mr. Hodgson, it is true, while reporting this opinion, cautions us that he is not able to cite the testimony of any text in its favor, and indeed I add that none of the works we have in Paris is regarded as having been written by Śākya himself. I do not believe that this second part of the Nepalese tradition merits as much confidence as the first. I will note at the outset that it is contradicted formally by the assertions of other Buddhist schools, and to confine ourselves to those that are the closest to the primitive source, I will only mention the books of Tibet and those of Ceylon. The Tibetans, like the Sinhalese, assert that it was three of the principal disciples of Śākya who collected the doctrines established by his preaching into a corpus of works: it was Ānanda who collected the Sūtras, Upāli the Vinaya, and Kāśyapa the Abhidharma.[32] The Sinhalese books have even preserved for us, touching on this first compilation of the Buddhist scriptures, a multitude of rather interesting details that we will recall elsewhere. It suffices for me at the moment to oppose this double testimony to

31. Hodgson, "Notices," etc., in *Asiatic Researches*, vol. 16, p. 422.

32. Csoma, "Analysis of the Dul-va," in *Asiatic Researches*, vol. 20, p. 42. Turnour, *Mahāvamso*, p. 12ff.

the opinion of the Nepalese, which is no easier to justify through the form of the Buddhist books. As we have already said, this form is that of a discourse or a dialogue in which Śākya seems to be conversing with his disciples; and those of his books which, according to the Nepalese, are regarded as authentic books, that is to say the sūtras, all commence with this formula: "Thus it was heard by me." If this sufficiently significant phrase was placed at the beginning of the books attributed to Śākya, it is because it was not possible, without contradicting the best established tradition, to dispense with marking the interval that existed between Śākya, from whose teaching these books emanated, and the monks who collected them after him. Everything leads us to believe that Śākya, similar in that way to other founders of religions, contented himself with establishing his doctrine through oral teaching, and that it is only after him that the need was felt to fix it through scripture in order to assure its preservation. This opinion will receive new confirmation from the account of the first attempts at redaction made in the council that assembled after the death of Śākya. But I must postpone the examination of these facts until the moment I collect what the tradition and the texts teach us about the destinies of the Buddhist collection from the moment when it was assembled into a corpus of works for the first time.

In setting forth what we know, according to the Nepalese tradition, about the triple division of the Buddhist scriptures, I have said that this division had for itself the testimony of texts enjoying some authority; I have reported, among others, several passages from the *Abhidharmakośavyākhyā*, and I could cite a much greater number, since this work constantly recalls the titles *sūtra*, *vinaya*, and *abhidharma*. But this treatise is not a canonical book; it is the work of two authors of whom neither concealed his name, a work whose date is unknown, but which is probably modern. Whatever its age, this compilation is far later than the canonical books to which it always refers. It is thus not surprising that one sees mentioned in it the general titles under which these books are classified. But what is surprising is that one can already read these titles in the canonical books themselves, books that the tradition nevertheless does not trace back beyond the last buddha. Before seeking to explain this fact, it is important to set it forth clearly.

I have put forward above, from the author of the *Abhidharmakośa*, the testimony of a sūtra (that is to say, from one of the books that everything leads us to regard as the most ancient) in which a monk, a contemporary of Śākya, is mentioned, who was regarded as knowing the *tripiṭaka*, or the three collections of the sacred scriptures.[33] This testimony is not isolated, and several treatises belonging to the great anthology entitled *Divyāvadāna* repeat this title *tripiṭaka*, as if it were perfectly known and in use from the time of Śākya; I believe it suf-

33. *Abhidharmakośavyākhyā*, fol. 8b of my manuscript.

ficient to consign these indications to a note.[34] Not only are these three great categories thus mentioned in a collective manner, they also are enumerated more than once, each one with its special title, and the third one with a remarkable name. It is indispensable to cite here the passages themselves where these titles appear: *pariprcchanti sūtrasya vinayasya mātṛkāyāḥ*, that is to say, "They ask questions about the Sūtra, the Vinaya, the Mātṛkā";[35] *sūtram mātṛkā ca devamanuṣyeṣu pratiṣṭhitam*, that is to say, "The Sūtra and the Mātṛkā are established among humans";[36] *āyuṣmatā mahākātyāyanena pravrājitaḥ tena pravrajya mātṛkā adhītā*, that is to say, "The respectable Mahākātyāyana made him embrace the religious life; when he had embraced it, he read the Matṛkā."[37]

What can we conclude about these texts? Shall we say that the triple division of the Buddhist scriptures already existed at the time of Śākyamuni? But it must be one of two things: either it was prior to him, or it came from him. If it was prior to him, that is to say, if it derived from the buddhas who are said to have preceded him, the tradition is mistaken when it attributes the books we possess today to the last buddha, Śākyamuni himself; if, on the other hand, it came from him, the tradition is again mistaken in attributing the division of the sacred scriptures to the three principal disciples of Śākyamuni and in placing this division after his death. But, I hasten to say, it is impossible that the tradition is in error on these two points at the same time, and I cannot accept that the quite rare mention that the works reputed to be sacred make of the triple division of the Buddhist scriptures must prevail over the testimony of the Nepalese tradition, which is confirmed, as we will see later, by that of the tradition of Ceylon.

The quotations I just reported appear to me to be those interpolations that are introduced naturally into books that have passed from the oral form to the written form. In collecting, after the death of Śākyamuni, the teaching of their master, the disciples classified the still-living memories of this teaching under three general titles, which the names *morality*, *discipline*, and *metaphysics* represent only imperfectly. Occupied as they were with this division, it was quite difficult for them not to let some sign of it penetrate the very works they include within it. That is the case for the ancient times. But if, since this first redaction, there was a second, then a third; if the books, preserved for a long time by the oral tradition, have been reshaped several times, is it not natural that the titles of the three great categories, which continued to be respected because of the antiquity of their origin, slipped into some of the books comprised under these

34. *Pūrṇa*, in *Divyāvadāna*, fol. 26b of the MS of the Société Asiatique: *tripiṭakaḥ saṃghaḥ* (assembly that knows the three collections). *Koṭikarṇa*, *ibid.*, fol. 9b: *tena tritīyapiṭakaṃ adhītaṃ* (the third collection was read by him).

35. *Koṭikarṇa*, *ibid.*, fol. 9b.

36. *Saṃgharakṣita*, *ibid.*, fol. 166a.

37. *Koṭikarṇa*, *ibid.*, fol. 9a.

very categories? It is in this manner that I explain how it happened that the titles recalled above appear in the very corpus of the books attributed to the last buddha, that is to say, in an epoch when, according to the tradition, these titles were still not invented. I see here nothing premeditated, and the matter seems to me very simple. It is possible if one supposes that there was only one redaction of the sacred books, but it became inevitable at the moment when these books were redacted more than one time; because at the time of the second redaction, and still more at the time of the third, the division of the Buddhist scriptures into three categories was a fait accompli, an almost sacred fact, that the compilers could easily confound with the other facts preserved in the scriptures for which they offered a new redaction.

I shall not insist any further on this point because, when summarizing what we know about the Nepalese collection, I must speak of the different redactions made in different epochs. I will only indicate the curious expression *mātṛkā* with which the three aforementioned passages from the *Divyāvadāna* designate, it appears, the third part of the tripiṭaka. It recalls the title *yum* or *ma mo*, "mother," that the Tibetans give to this same class.[38] Nothing indicates the origin of this designation; we only know from the texts of Nepal that it is familiar to the Buddhists of this country, as it is to those of Tibet, who undoubtedly borrowed it from the Sanskrit texts.[39] It must be considered ancient, since it is accepted by all schools, that of the South as well as that of the North. Indeed, I note in one of the most highly regarded Pāli suttas (sūtras) of the Sinhalese that some monks are called "possessors of the law, of the discipline, and of the *mātṛkā*";[40] and this expression is repeated in another collection that is no less celebrated.[41] I must nevertheless caution that Mr. Turnour makes the *mātṛkā* a portion of the Vinaya.

Finally, and to omit nothing that touches on the most general divisions of the Buddhist scriptures, I shall set forth another classification about which the Nepalese tradition maintains, to my knowledge, complete silence and which nevertheless is often indicated in the texts, more often even than the divisions into the three categories examined. I wish to speak of the four āgamas, or anthologies of the law, of which the *Divyāvadāna* makes mention several times. These are the texts in which I find their indication: *sa āyuṣmatā śāriputreṇa pravrājita upasaṃpādita āgamacatuṣṭayaṃ ca grāhitaḥ*, that is to say, "When he had been introduced into the religious life by the respectable Śāriputra,[42] he re-

38. Csoma, "Analysis of the Dul-va," in *Asiatic Researches*, vol. 20, p. 43.

39. Csoma, "Notices of the Life of Shakya," in *Asiatic Researches*, vol. 20, p. 317.

40. *Parinibbāna Sutta*, in *Dīgha nikāya*, fol. 92a of my manuscript.

41. *Anguttara Nikāya*, fol. *khi* b, MS of the Bibliothèque du Roi.

42. Śāriputra is, with Maudgalyāyana, about whom I will speak later, the foremost of the disciples of Śākyamuni. One can see in the *Foe koue ki*, as much in the text of Faxian as in the notes of Mr. Rémusat and Mr. Klaproth, details as interesting as they are accurate about this celebrated personage. The passages referring

ceived investiture and the knowledge of the four āgamas."[43] *āgamacatuṣṭayam adhītam*, "The four āgamas have been read."[44] *ihāpy āgamacatuṣṭayaṃ sthāpayet*, "May the four āgamas be established in this very place."[45] Finally, the titles of these four āgamas are provided to us in the following passage: *tvaṃ tāvat saṃyuktakam adhīṣva tvam api madhyamaṃ tvam api dīrghāmam . . . aham api tām evaikottarikāṃ vimṛṣṭarūpām prajvālayāmi*, "So read, you the short āgama, you the medium one, you the long one; as for me, I gave myself the task of clarifying the supplementary collection, whose subject I have clearly considered."[46] It is possible that some doubt still remains concerning the title of the fourth āgama, which is rather obscure. Be this point of detail as it may, we have here four collections or anthologies about which the Nepalese tradition informs us nothing. What makes this classification interesting, however, is that we find it again, as I will explain later, among the Sinhalese with exactly the same titles, except for the fourth one, which is read *anguttara*.[47] It is no less familiar to the Chinese, and among the original Buddhist works which their authors use, there are few that are more frequently cited than the āgamas. I have already mentioned the general title of these four anthologies when I was discussing the Indian books that must have been translated in China. I add here that the four āgamas are mentioned by name according to a great Chinese compilation, in a substantial note of Mr. Landresse on the *Foe koue ki*.[48] The fourth āgama bears there the title it has among the Sinhalese, *anguttara*, which would lead one to think that for the Chinese it is a matter of the āgamas from the South and not those from the North, if, however, some difference exists between the two schools regarding

to his birth and his death are all indicated in the table of this work. The only point that is subject to contestation is the note in which it is said that Śāriputra was instructed in *prajñā*, or in wisdom, by the celebrated Avalokiteśvara (*Foe koue ki*, p. 107). This assertion is most probably borrowed from some developed sūtra; I find not the slightest trace of it in the books I examine at the present time. Śāriputra was called Upatiṣya; it is the name that the Tibetans translate as *Nye rgyal* and which Klaproth mentions (*Foe koue ki*, p. 264. Csoma, *Asiatic Researches*, vol. 20, p. 49). He was named for his father, who was called Tiṣya, whereas the name Śāriputra came from his mother Śārikā (Csoma, *Asiatic Researches*, vol. 20, p. 49). Faxian informs us that he was born in the village of Naluo, near Rājagṛha. It is remarkable that Klaproth has not related this name to that of Nalantuo, which Chinese authors discuss between 780 and 804 of our era (*Foe koue ki*, p. 256). The first name is just an abbreviation of the second *Nalantuo*, and this latter reproduces exactly the orthography *Nalada* or *Nalanda*, as Csoma gives it (*Asiatic Researches*, vol. 20, p. 48), or more rigorously still *Nālanda*, as it is written in the Sanskrit texts of the North and the Pāli books of the South. The *Mahāvastu* calls this place Nālandagrāma and locates it half a yojana from Rājagṛha, the ancient capital of Magadha (*Mahāvastu*, fol. 264a of my manuscript). The work I cite at the moment reports in great detail the story of the youth and conversion of Upatiṣya or Śāriputra and almost in the same terms as the Tibetan Dul-va analyzed by Csoma (*Asiatic Researches*, vol. 20, p. 48ff.).

43. *Saṃgharakṣita*, in *Divyāvadāna*, fol. 165a.

44. *Koṭikarṇa*, in *Divyāvadāna*, fol. 166a.

45. *Saṃgharakṣita*, in *Divyāvadāna*, fol. 166a.

46. *Id. ibid.*

47. Turnour, *Mahāvamso*, Appendix, p. 75.

48. *Foe koue ki*, p. 327.

these books. I suspect nevertheless that the Buddhists of China equally know the Nepalese designation, *ekottara*; because it is doubtless this title that Mr. Rémusat already translated, perhaps a little obscurely, as "the āgama augmented by one."[49] It is probable that for the Buddhists of the North as for those of the South, this division, far from encompassing the whole of the Buddhist scriptures, refers only to the category of the Sūtras. But since the Sanskrit texts in which I find it do not settle this point, I have believed that I must indicate it here, although I may return to it when I compare the Pāli books of Ceylon to the Sanskrit books of Nepal.

The division into three great categories, which I have set forth first, shows us Buddhism established as a religion and a philosophy; for it encompasses discipline, morality, and metaphysics, and so responds to all the needs that the preaching of Śākyamuni aimed to satisfy. But it is not the only one known in Nepal, and Mr. Hodgson has given us, as I have said above, two lists of Buddhist books, drawn up following a different system. These two lists, which have been published, one in European characters with some details on the works that compose it, the other one in devanāgari characters, but without any clarification, have been equally arranged without regard to the triple division into Sūtra, Vinaya, and Abhidharma. One sees there, it is true, that the name *sūtra* appears quite often; but the titles *vinaya* and *abhidharma* are absolutely missing; moreover, that of *sūtra* is not as conspicuous as would be necessary if the compilers of these lists wished to indicate that the sūtras themselves alone formed one of the three great categories of the sacred scriptures. The classification of the list published in devanāgari characters is, according to Mr. Hodgson, the work of the Buddhist religious whom he employed; and this scholar, who from the beginning of his research has taken so many precautions in order to arrive at the truth, cautions us that it is doubtful that this classification can be justified by the testimony of the books themselves.[50] This observation saves me from pausing over it for a long time, and it will suffice for me to say that this division into *purāṇa*, or ancient books, *kāvya*, or poems, *vyākaraṇa*, or grammars, *kośa*, or dictionaries, *tantra*, or ascetic rituals, *dhāraṇī*, or charms and formulas, not only mingles the profane with the sacred, but confuses, under a vague denomination of ancient books, works of the most diverse characteristics and titles.

The much more detailed classification that Mr. Hodgson has appended to his first memorandum on Buddhism has a greater importance and merits a high degree of attention from the critic for the amount and the diversity of the information it contains and, in addition, because it is accepted almost equally by the Buddhists of Ceylon. We have to examine it in detail here, because the illumina-

49. *Journal des Savans*, 1831, pp. 605 and 728.
50. *Transactions of the Royal Asiatic Society*, vol. 2, p. 229.

tion we will find in it must serve to orient us in the obscure labyrinth of the sacred literature of the Buddhists. We have, furthermore, the advantage of finding it again among the Chinese, where it is commented on and justified with interesting observations;[51] and so we are in the position to compensate, in some cases, for the silence of the Nepalese Buddhists. Like the list given to Mr. Hodgson by his religious, the one we indicate at the moment is drawn up without regard to the triple division of the Buddhist scriptures. The works are assembled there, according to their content, under twelve principal headings, or to avail ourselves of the very words of Mr. Hodgson, the Buddhist scriptures are of twelve types, each known by a different name.[52]

1. "*Sūtra.* They are the fundamental scriptures (*mūlagrantha*), such as the *Rakṣabhāgavatī* and the *Aṣṭasāhasrikā Prajñāpāramitā.* They are equivalent to the Vedas of the Brahmins."

I note at the outset that we see the already mentioned opinion reappear here, that the sūtras are the fundamental scriptures of the Buddhists; but the books mentioned as specimens of the category of the Sūtras give rise to a difficulty that impedes a reader without access to the manuscripts of the works themselves. We have seen that the *Prajñāpāramitā* (and I add now the *Rakṣabhāgavatī*, which is only another title) was dedicated to metaphysics, and by virtue of that, this work was placed by the Tibetan translators among the books that form the *abhidharma piṭaka.* If the *Prajñāpāramitā* belongs to the Abhidharma, how can it be cited as a model of the category of Sūtras? This occurs, I believe, not solely from the high importance of the *Prajñā*, which is a fundamental collection for metaphysics among the Buddhists of the North, but also because this treatise, as with the various redactions of it that we have, is a true sūtra as far as its form is concerned. What I have said above about the possibility of including the section of the Abhidharma in that of the Sūtras is verified here. This possibility, which I deduced from the testimony of the *Abhidharmakośa*, must be accepted as an actual fact, now that we see the treatises dedicated to metaphysics presented in the form of true sūtras, and that it is observed that the Tibetan translators are able to form the section of the Abhidharma only from books that present themselves as sūtras, that is to say, as discourses of the Buddha.

2. "*Geya.* They are works in honor of the buddhas and bodhisattvas written in modulated language. The *Gītagovinda* of the Brahmins is equivalent to our *Gītapustaka*, which belongs to the category of the *geya*s."

I add to this description that the *Gītapustaka*, otherwise called the *Gītapustakasaṃgraha*, or "Summary of the Book of Songs," is described by Mr. Hodgson as a collection of songs on religious subjects, composed by various au-

51. Landresse in the *Foe koue ki*, p. 321ff.

52. "Notices," etc., in *Asiatic Researches*, vol. 16, pp. 426 and 427.

thors.[53] That leads me to think that this book is not part of the original collection of Buddhist scriptures. Mr. Hodgson's list does not mention any other geya. This title means "made to be sung," and if there are geyas in the books that are regarded as inspired, these geyas must be only fragments or pieces of greater or lesser length, composed in verses, and which can be sung. But I do not find that the geyas form a category of books recognized by the commentators I have been able to consult, and I can explain the existence of this title in Mr. Hodgson's list in only two ways: either the geyas are verses or songs that are part of the original books and, as I just said, extracted from these books, or these are works subsequent to the division of the Buddhist scriptures into three categories. I add that geyas of these two types can exist, in other words, that one must find songs or only verses called *geyas* in Buddhist texts, just as it is possible that modern authors composed songs of this kind in honor of buddhas and bodhisattvas. The testimony of the Chinese Buddhists confirms the first of these two suppositions. "This word, they say, means *corresponding song* or *reiterated song,* that is to say, that it responds to a previous text and that it repeats it to show the meaning. It has six, four, three or two phrases."[54] This definition applies exactly to these stanzas found dispersed through all the books emanating from the preaching of Śākya and whose object is to summarize and to present, in a precise form, the meaning of a discourse or of an account. In the developed sūtras (*vaipulya sūtra*)—I will speak of them below—these verses or stanzas sometimes occupy a significant place and their numbers exceed by far the proportions fixed by the Chinese definition; but their object is always the same, and there is nothing important in the poetic part of these books that is not already in the prose exposition. I will note, nevertheless, that in the sūtras I have just mentioned, and of which the *Lotus of the Good Law* provides a model, these stanzas are preceded by a formula of this kind: "At that moment, the Bhagavat (Śākyamuni) pronounced the following stanzas," and that these stanzas are called *gāthā.* It seems to me that, according to the Chinese definition, we should find here *geya* instead of *gāthā*; but this slight difficulty explains itself if we accept that *geya* is the generic name for everything which, due to its form, is susceptible to being sung, and that the word *gāthā* designates each of the stanzas themselves of which the geya is composed. In short, a geya can be formed by a single gāthā, or it can contain several of them. We will see below the word *gāthā* employed to designate a special category of books, and I will then have occasion to state this conjecture, that the definition of the term *geya* given in the Nepalese list applies better to that of *gāthā.* But whatever the nuance that distinguishes one from the other, I can say for the present that the word *geya* would be badly understood if one saw in it only the

53. "Notices," etc., in *Asiatic Researches*, vol. 16, p. 431.
54. Landresse, *Foe koue ki*, pp. 321 and 322.

title of a category of books, like that of *sūtra*. This can be the case, if we envisage collectively everything that is geya, exclusive of the texts in which the geyas are found. But this title designates, properly speaking, one of the elements that enter into the composition of the Buddhist books; and this observation, which we will see repeat itself in the greatest number of the articles of the Nepalese list, is, if I am not mistaken, the only one that shows this list in its true light.

3. "*Vyākaraṇa*. These are narrative works that contain the history of the various births of Śākya before he became nirvāṇa (or rather he entered into nirvāṇa), the various actions of the other buddhas and bodhisattvas, and formulas of prayers and of praises."

There are several observations to make concerning this definition. Mr. Hodgson's list presents a great number of works that are qualified as *vyākaraṇa śāstra*: These are, among others, the *Gaṇḍavyūha*, the *Samādhirāja*, and the *Saddharmapuṇḍarīka*. But the title *vyākaraṇa* does not appear in any of these works; these books are sūtras of the type called *mahāyāna*, or "serving as a great vehicle," and several, notably the *Saddharmapuṇḍarīka*, bear the special title *mahāvaipulya sūtra*, or "sūtra of great development." Thus, whence comes this title *vyākaraṇa* that the Nepalese tradition has preserved for us, and is it possible to find in the works that bear it the reason for its application to them? It is necessary to observe at the outset that this title must have rather great importance in the eyes of the Buddhists of Nepal, since Mr. Hodgson says at one point that it contains three other subdivisions of the Buddhist scriptures—I will speak of them later; and in another passage, he informs us that the *vyākaraṇa* is considered, although erroneously, the equivalent of *smṛti*, or the traditional science of the brahmans.[55] But these various opinions lose much of their value if we cannot discover the title *vyākaraṇa* in any of the books that, according to the tradition preserved in the list we are examining, should bear it. The explanation of this difficulty is found, if I am not mistaken, in the specific value that the Sanskrit texts of Nepal, like the Pāli books of Ceylon, assign to the word *vyākaraṇa*. This value, confirmed by a very great number of passages and by the testimony of the Tibetan versions,[56] is that of *explanation* of the future destinies of a personage whom Śākyamuni addresses; in a word, a *prediction*. These kinds of predictions, by which Śākyamuni announces to his disciples that the dignity of buddha will one day be the reward for their merits, are very frequent in the Sanskrit texts of Nepal, and there is hardly any sūtra of some length that does not contain one or several; but, as they have a considerable importance for the Buddhists in that they promise to their belief a future without limits and representatives without

55. *Asiatic Researches*, vol. 16, pp. 422 and 423.

56. Csoma, "Analysis of the Sher-chin," etc., in *Asiatic Researches*, vol. 20, pp. 400, 410, 453, 454, 480, 484.

end, it is possible that they furnished an element of sufficient value for a classification that is at least as literary as it is religious. I thus imagine that when in Nepal one says of a book renowned to be sacred (and this is said of several sūtras) that it is a *vyākaraṇa*, this means that this book contains a more or less lengthy section dedicated to the predictions Śākyamuni addresses to his disciples, or perhaps simply a chapter of predictions, as one sees in the *Lotus of the Good Law.* The explanation of the Chinese Buddhists is here again in accord with the etymological interpretation. "This Sanskrit word, they say, means *explanation.* It is when the Tathāgata, speaking to the bodhisattvas, to the pratyekas, to the śrāvakas, tells them the history of the buddhas, as in the *Fahua jing,* in which he says: 'You Ayiduo (*Maitreya*), in the coming century, you will achieve the intelligence of the buddha, and you will be called Maitreya.'"[57] The beginning of this definition is a bit vague; and perhaps instead of "tells them the history of the buddhas," we must say "tells them that they will become buddhas"; but the end of the Chinese explanation is more noteworthy in that it suggests to me a parallel of some interest. I cannot affirm whether *Fahua jing,* or the "Book of the Flower of the Law,"[58] is the abbreviated title either of the first Chinese version, *Zheng fahua jing,* or of the third, *Miaofa,* the knowledge of which, as I have said above, I owe to Mr. Stanislas Julien; but if these titles do not belong to the same work, it is at least permissible to suppose that the *Fahua jing* has many analogies with the *Lotus of the Good Law* that we have in Sanskrit; thus the *Ayiduo* of the aforementioned quotation is the Sanskrit *Ajita,* "invincible," a title, in the *Lotus,* that Mañjuśrī addresses each time to the bodhisattva Maitreya. I do not find in the *Lotus* the very sentence that the Chinese definition cites; but the sixty-fourth stanza of the first chapter of this work expresses the same idea, although in slightly different terms.

The result of the preceding is that the term *vyākaraṇa* designates not a category of Buddhist scriptures, but one of the elements that figure in these scriptures. There are vyākaraṇas in the books reputed to be inspired, in the sūtras for example; but there are no sūtras in the vyākaraṇas; in short, the predictions are contained in the books, as are the songs or *geyas* of the preceding article; but the books are no more in the predictions than they are in the songs.

4. "*Gāthā.* These are narrative works containing moral tales, *anekadharma-*

57. Landresse, *Foe koue ki,* p. 323.

58. The *Fahua jing* is a book very frequently mentioned in the notes of the *Foe koue ki,* either by Mr. A. Rémusat or by the editors of his work. But the translation I propose of this title is not found in the *Foe koue ki*; and I signal this for fear that my error, if I have committed one, will be attributed to the learned editors. By translating *fa* by *dharma* (law), I base myself on the meaning that this monosyllable *fa* has in the formula *fo fa seng,* which represents, as Mr. Landresse has established, the Sanskrit terms of the celebrated triad, *Buddha, dharma, saṃgha,* of which I shall speak later.

kathā (that is to say, various expositions of the law), related to the buddhas. The *Lalitavistara* is a *vyākaraṇa* of the type called *gāthā.*"

The observations I have just made concerning the geyas and the vyākaraṇas apply no less rigorously to the gāthas. This word designates a stanza, and I do not know of any work in Mr. Hodgson's collection that bears this title. The term *gātha*, however, is encountered more than once in a great number of these books; but, as I have said on the occasion of the geyas, it never designates anything other than the poetic portions of most variable length, which are frequently introduced into the texts written in prose. We do not have to attach any importance, it seems to me, to this observation that the *Lalitavistara* is a *vyākaraṇa* of the type called *gāthā*; it tends to give to the title *vyākaraṇa* a characteristic of generality that makes it the name of a category of some extent; and it is in this way that Mr. Hodgson could say, according to his Nepalese authorities, that the gāthas are regarded as a subdivision of the vyākaraṇas.[59] But the remarks on this title, which has been the subject of the previous paragraph, have informed us of what it designates properly speaking; and the unimpeachable authority of the texts shows us that it offers, with that of *gāthā*, no other analogy than that to be found in the same works. As for the term *gāthā* itself, the Chinese Buddhists define it in this way: "This word means sung verses; it is a direct and long-winded speech in verses, like the *Kong pin* in the *Jin guangming jing* or the 'Book of the Splendor of the Brightness of Gold.'"[60] This definition, by distinguishing the gāthās from the geyas by length, returns us to what the Nepalese list gives for the geyas, and which seems to apply to works of a certain length and written entirely in verse. I do not know the Sanskrit term corresponding to the Chinese words *Kong pin*, but the "Book of the Splendor of the Brightness of Gold" is very likely the *Suvarṇaprabhāsa* of the Nepalese collection; indeed, this book contains an extended piece, entirely written in verse. But whatever use one might make of the gāthās in the texts reputed as sacred, I cannot refrain from noting how much the Chinese definition confirms what I have said above touching on the relation of the gāthās to the geyas. Without returning to this point, I content myself with repeating that here we must again see, not the title of a special category of books, but the indication of one of the elements that enter into the composition of the books themselves.

5. "*Udān* (read *Udāna*). Treatises on the nature and the attributes of the buddhas, in the form of a dialogue between a *buddhaguru* and a *cela.*"

I note first that we must read *cailaka* rather than *cela*, a word that is the name of a sort of robe. The title *cailaka* designates, according to the Nepalese, the fourth of the five categories that together compose the body of Buddhist reli-

59. *Asiatic Researches*, vol. 16, p. 422.
60. Landresse, *Foe koue ki*, p. 322.

gious. The *cailaka* is one who contents himself with a piece of cloth sufficient to cover his nakedness, and who rejects all other robes as superfluous.[61] According to the definition of *udāna*, to constitute a book of this genre, there must be a religious who is a listener, and a buddha who is a guru, that is to say, a spiritual preceptor; but Mr. Hodgson's list does not offer any example of a book bearing the title *udāna*, and I have not found this title on any of the volumes we have in Paris. We do not therefore know of any specimen of this category of works, and it is more prudent thus far to see in it one of the parts or one of the elements of the Buddhist scriptures, in accordance with the explanation I have proposed for the three previous titles. Now, I often encounter in the legends that are part of the *Divyāvadāna*, for example, as well as in the *Lalitavistara*, the expression *udānam udānayati*, which, according to the entire context, seems to me to offer this meaning: "he grandiloquently pronounces praise or words of joy."[62] This particular signification of the word *udāna* which is, at least to my knowledge, foreign to classical Sanskrit, is also as easily justifiable by the Pāli texts of Ceylon as by the Sanskrit books of Nepal; and whatever uncertainty can remain over the choice to make between the two translations "words of joy" and "words of praise," it is my conviction that I am not very far from grasping the true meaning. The Tibetan interpreters favor the second translation; for the expression with which they replace *udāna* means, according to the dictionary of Schröter, "to praise, to exalt, to uplift";[63] while Mr. Turnour renders the Pāli word *udāna* as "hymn of joy."[64] Whatever it may be, I believe I have the right to say that the term *udāna*, otherwise rather vaguely defined in the Nepalese list, cannot form a category of original works, as this list seems to indicate. We must find the udānas in the Buddhist books, as we find the other elements I have reviewed above; but it is only in this sense that this term can serve as a title. Now, that these udānas take place in a dialogue between a buddha and one of his disciples, this is quite possible, although this is not absolutely necessary; that the words of joy or the giving of thanks that I believe they express refer to the nature and the attributes of the Buddha, it is this that is also easily supposable, as it is hardly contrary to the interpretation I propose for this term; finally, that a certain number were gathered to form a special category, this is also possible, and

61. Hodgson, "Sketch of Buddhism," in *Transactions of the Royal Asiatic Society*, vol. 2, p. 245.

62. *Koṭikarṇa*, in *Divyāvadāna*, fol. 1a. *Pūrṇa*, ibid., fols. 17b, 23a, and 25b. *Supriya*, ibid., fols. 47a and 58a. *Lalitavistara*, fol. 60a of my manuscript and passim.

63. See Csoma, "Analysis of the Sher-chin," etc., in *Asiatic Researches*, vol. 20, p. 477, in which the Sanskrit term *udāna* is rendered in Tibetan by the words *ched du brjod pa*, which one finds explained in this way: "to praise, to commend, to exalt, to extol, to laud," in Schröter, *A Dictionary of the Bhotanta or Boutan Language*, p. 98, col. 1. Mr. Schmidt (*Tibetisch-deutsches Wörterbuch*, p. 161, col. 2) translates this term as "to accept, to approve of, to praise."

64. "Examination of the Pāli Buddhistical Annals," in *Journal of the Asiatic Society of Bengal*, vol. 6, p. 526 and vol. 7, p. 793.

it is only in this manner that the use of the term as a title of a book is rigorously explicable.

I do not have to conceal, however, that the interpretation of the Chinese Buddhists does not accord here with the one I propose, and that it seems to come closer to that of the Nepalese. "The word *udāna*, they say, means to *speak about oneself*; understood as when, without being questioned by anyone, the Tathāgata, through the prudence that divines the thought of others, contemplates the motives of all living beings and, by his own volition teaches them through preaching; as in the *Lengyan*, where, before the assembly, he speaks about what is related to the fifty kinds of demons, without waiting for Anan (Ānanda) to beseech and ask him; just as in the *Mituo jing* where he speaks about himself to Shelifo (Śāriputra) without anything providing the occasion to do so."[65] We again find here some traces of the Nepalese explanation; but I do not know what the definition of the Chinese Buddhists is based on; and that which I have just proposed is the only one I have seen justified by the Sanskrit texts up to now.

6. "*Nidān* (read *Nidāna*). These are treatises in which the causes of events are shown; for example, how did Śākya become a buddha? Reason or cause, he fulfills Dān (*dāna*) and other Parmitas (*pāramitās*)"; and in a note: "*Pāramitā* here means virtue, the moral merit by which we succeed in freeing ourselves from the mortal condition. *Dāna*, or alms, is the first of the ten cardinal virtues of the Buddhists; the words *and the others* refer to the other nine virtues."

I also cannot see the title of a special category of works in the term *nidāna*. One finds nidānas in the Buddhist books we have; but I do not encounter this title on any of these books, nor does the Nepalese list I am analyzing at the moment offer any examples. Thus, it is again in the specific signification of the word *nidāna* that one must seek the reason for its application to this or that part of the Buddhist scriptures. This term, which is frequently employed in the Sanskrit texts of Nepal, means literally "cause, origin, motive," and it designates in particular a category of causes called "the twelve causes"—I will speak of them later—that can always be characterized in a general manner in this way: "the chain of the successive causes of existence." If it is because a work is occupied with this subject, so familiar to the Buddhists, that it is called a *nidāna*, it will be by virtue of a kind of extension similar to the one I have noted in examining the previous articles; but the texts do not authorize this explanation, and they suggest another that seems to me much more probable; it is that the *nidānas*, or the causes and motives, are a part that one finds or can find in the inspired books. And indeed, the *Lotus of the Good Law* offers us an example of the use made of this term to designate the subject or the cause of the miraculous apparitions that astonish Śākya's listeners; here it is even the title of the first chapter of

65. Landresse, *Foe koue ki*, pp. 322 and 323.

this book. So I think that when the Nepalese list says that the nidānas belong to the Buddhist scriptures, what it wishes to say is that one of the elements which enter into the composition of the books that form the corpus of these scriptures is the *nidāna*, or the indication of the reasons and motives. The definition of the Chinese Buddhists confirms my explanation point by point. "The word *nidāna*, they say, means *cause, reason for which*, as when in the *jing* there is someone who asks about the cause, and one says: this is such a thing; as for the precepts, when someone transgresses what they prescribe, one draws a consequence from it for the future. That is the way the Tathāgata gives the reason why this or that thing happens. All of this is called *cause, reason for which*, as in the sacred book *Huajing yupin*, where the cause of an event is explained by what has taken place in previous generations."[66] I believe this explanation leaves no doubt as to the true value of the word *nidāna*; we will see it confirmed by the testimony of the Buddhists of Ceylon.

7. "*Ityukta*. It is whatever is said in relation to (something) or in conclusion. The explanation of some prior discourse is an *ityukta*."

This not very clear definition gives only an imperfect idea about the category of books that it designates. The Nepalese list does not provide us any example of the application of the title *ityukta* to a specific work. To comprehend the value, we thus have no other assistance than the analysis of the word itself. This term means: "so it is said, said as above," and it is used to indicate and to close a quotation that it clearly separates from everything that follows. We see now what we must understand by the Nepalese definition; it is permissible to suppose that if there exists a category of books that bears the title *ityukta*, these books must be composed of quotations, of accounts, either borrowed from other books or collected by the tradition; for the formula "so it is said" supposes a narrator who only reports the words of another. But the explanation I have proposed for the previous articles is equally applicable here, and we must find in the Buddhist books some pieces for which the title *ityukta* is suitable, whether these pieces are placed in the mouth of the Buddha, or one of his disciples is reputed to be the author. In short, the ityukta must be one of the constituent elements of the Buddhist books, but it is not necessarily a category of these books. The definition of the Chinese Buddhists supports this explanation. "This word, they say, means *primitive affair*, when one recounts what is related to the acts of the disciples of the bodhisattva, during their sojourn on earth, as in the *Benshi pin* of the *Fahua jing*, where there is a question about the bodhisattva Yaowang, who rejoiced in virtue, brilliant and pure as the sun and the moon, and in the law obtained by the Buddha, who with his body and his arm practiced ceremonies, and who devoted himself to all kinds of austerities in order to obtain the supreme intelli-

66. Landresse, *Foe koue ki*, p. 322.

gence."[67] The expression *primitive affair* is rather vague; but the clarifications that follow show that the Chinese understand *ityukta* as an account. There is in our *Lotus of the Good Law* a chapter that offers some analogy to the sacrifice cited by the Chinese commentator; it is that in which the bodhisattva Sarvasattvapriyadarśana makes an offering of his arm and his body before the monument of a buddha.[68]

8. "*Jātaka* (pronounced *djātaka*). These books deal with the deeds of previous births."

This definition, which agrees with the meaning of the Sanskrit term, makes the books to which it applies exactly recognizable. I say the books, although there is only one in the Nepalese list and in the collection of Mr. Hodgson that bears and merits the title *jātaka* (birth); it is the volume entitled *Jātakamālā*, or the "Garland of Births," which is regarded as an account of the various meritorious acts of Śākya, prior to the epoch when he became a buddha. The definition of the Chinese Buddhists is no less exact. "This word, they say, means *primitive* or *previous births.* It is when one recounts the adventures the buddhas and bodhisattvas have experienced in the epoch of their existence in another world, etc."[69] One can very well imagine that the numerous accounts through which Śākya makes known his births prior to his last mortal existence were gathered separately, and that a category of books called *births* was made. We will see later what the Buddhists of Ceylon did. We thus have to accept that *jātaka* can be the title of a more or less numerous category of treatises dedicated to the account of the previous lives of Śākyamuni, and there is no reason to make the objections I have set forth about the preceding articles against the use of this term so defined. It is not less true, however, that this term must have designated a category of books, only because there were, in the works renowned as inspired, accounts related to the ancient existences of the Buddha. It is thus necessary to repeat again here what I have said on the occasion of the geyas, the gāthās, and the other divisions of the Nepalese classification. The births are one of the elements that enter into the composition of the books reputed to be inspired. I add that in even admitting the existence of a special category of jātakas, this category will not have an importance equal to that of the sūtras, because there are accounts of ancient existences in the sūtras whereas we still do not know of sūtras in the jātakas.

9. "*Vaipulya.* These books deal with the several sorts of Dharma and Artha, that is to say, of the several means of acquiring the goods of this world (*artha*) and of the world to come (*dharma*)."

Here again we have a category of books of which Mr. Hodgson's list does

67. Landresse, *Foe koue ki*, p. 322.

68. *Le Lotus de la bonne loi*, chap. 22, fol. 212a ff. of the text and p. 243 of the translation.

69. Landresse, *Foe koue ki*, p. 322.

not furnish us with any specimen. This division is no less real, and one notes its name on some of the volumes we have in Paris. Thus the *Lotus of the Good Law* is a mahāvaipulya sūtra if we are to believe a stanza that, it is true, is not part of this work and is like a kind of copyist's preface. The existence of the title *vaipulya sūtra* is, moreover, proved by a passage in the *Lotus of the Good Law*, where it is said that a Buddha sets forth vaipulya sūtras.[70] It is placed beyond doubt by the titles of several Sanskrit works collected in the Tibetan library of the Kah-gyur and that Csoma de Kőrös has translated as "sūtra of great extent."[71] I do not hesitate to render the term *vaipulya* as "development," and I say that the *vaipulya* sūtras, or the sūtras of development, form a subdivision of the category of sūtras, a subdivision whose title accords well, as we will see below, with the nature and form of the books it embraces. I have never seen this title on works other than sūtras; from which I conclude that the division called *vaipulya* does not constitute, properly speaking, a separate category, and that it is included in that of sūtras. Here again the definition of the Chinese Buddhists accords with the explanation I propose. "This word, they say, means *grandeur of the law*. These are the books of the law, of the great conveyance, whose doctrine and meaning are as extensive as the space of vacuity."[72] The words *great conveyance*[73] represent the Sanskrit term *mahāyāna*, and indeed the sūtras called developed are of the order of those called *mahāyāna*, or great vehicle. Furthermore, we find the specific meaning of the term *vaipulya* in the Chinese explanation.

10. "*Adbhutadharma.* [This division deals with] supernatural events."

I do not find, either in Mr. Hodgson's list or in the collection we have in Paris, any work that bears the title *adbhuta*. Thus I do not believe that it is, strictly speaking, the name of an actually existent division of the Buddhist scriptures, and I think this article is like most of those I have examined to this point. There are *adbhutas*, or miracles, set forth in the religious books, and the sūtras pro-

70. *Le Lotus de la bonne loi*, fol. 15a of the text and p. 15 of the translation.

71. "Analysis of the Sher-chin," etc., in *Asiatic Researches*, vol. 20, pp. 401 and 465.

72. Landresse, *Foe koue ki*, p. 323.

73. Mr. Schmidt has justly criticized (*Mémoires de l'Académie des sciences de Saint Pétersbourg*, 2:10ff) the translation that Mr. A. Rémusat has given of the term *yāna*, which he renders as "conveyance" (*Foe koue ki*, p. 9, note). More recently, Lassen has proposed to substitute it with *path*. The *triyāna*, says this scholar, designates the three paths that the mind can take, according to the different degrees of their intelligence and virtue; and the Buddhist works receive this title *yāna*, according to whether their content corresponds to one or another of these three paths (*Zeitschrift für die Kunde des Morgenlandes*, vol. 4, p. 494). I regard this observation as well founded; nevertheless, because *yāna* means even more commonly "vehicle, means of transportation," I prefer this latter translation, all the more so because several parables, among others, those of the *Lotus of the Good Law*, compare the different yānas to carts hitched to animals of different species (*Le lotus de la bonne loi*, p. 47ff.; compare A. Rémusat, *Foe koue ki*, p. 10). I add that the Tibetans understand the word *yāna* exactly in the same way, and that the term *theg pa*, with which they replace it, means "vehicle," as the uniform testimony of Csoma and Mr. Schmidt informs us. It is this notion of "vehicle, means of transportation" that Wilson develops very well, following the analysis of the Kah-gyur by Csoma ("Analysis of the Kah-gyur," in *Journal of the Asiatic Society of Bengal*, vol. 1, p. 380).

vide frequent examples of them. We thus here again have one of the elements that enters into the composition of the Buddhist scriptures, where the belief in the supernatural power of the buddhas and their disciples certainly occupies a considerable place. These miracles must have, because of this same belief, a great importance in the eyes of the Buddhists, and we find them mentioned in a passage of the *Lotus of the Good Law*;[74] but I repeat, this does not suffice to elevate this title to the height of that of *sūtra*, since the account of the miracles is part of the sūtras, and what we cannot say is that the sūtras are contained in the miracles. I add, to conclude, that the explanation of the Chinese Buddhists conforms on all points with that of the Nepalese list, if not for the fact that it brings out more clearly the specific value of the word *adbhuta*, which means "what is wonderful, what did not happen already . . . What the four groups hear that has never been heard, what they believe that has never been believed, is so called."[75]

11. "*Avadāna* [This division deals with] the fruit of works."

It is as easy to criticize the use the Nepalese list makes of the titles examined in the nine preceding articles, as it is impossible to contest that that of *avadāna* is found in a great number of treatises, as much in Mr. Hodgson's list as in the collection of the Bibliothèque royale. In examining the second category of the Buddhist scriptures, that of the Discipline, I have already had occasion to signal the existence of these treatises, which are more numerous even than the sūtras. They are concerned, indeed, as the Nepalese list says, with the fruit of works; but this definition does not give the true meaning of the word *avadāna*, which means "legend, legendary account," as Csoma de Kőrös understands it, following the Tibetan interpreters of the Kah-gyur.[76] These legends ordinarily turn on these two subjects: the explanation of present actions by past actions and the announcement of the rewards or punishments reserved to present actions in the future. This double object is, as we see, clearly summarized in the definition of the Nepalese list, to which only the literal translation of the Sanskrit word is missing. It is not as easy for me to account for the explanation of the Chinese Buddhists, who define this term in this way: "this word means *comparison*. It is when the Tathāgata, explaining the law, borrows metaphors and comparisons in order to clarify and make it more easily understood as, in the *Fahua jing*, the house of fire, the medicinal plants, etc."[77] I do not find, on the one hand, that the Sanskrit texts of Nepal justify the meaning of "comparison" given to the word *avadāna*, and on the other, that the legends, a considerable number of which I have been able to read, make more use of comparison or parable than the other Buddhist works in

74. *Le lotus de la bonne loi*, chap. 2, fol. 28b of the text, and p. 29, stanza 44 of the translation.

75. Landresse, *Foe koue ki*, p. 322.

76. "Analysis of the Sher-chin," in *Asiatic Researches*, vol. 20, pp. 481–84.

77. Landresse, *Foe koue ki*, p. 322.

which this figure certainly plays the leading role. The note from which I borrow the opinion of the Chinese Buddhists transcribes the Indian term in two ways: *botuo* and *abotuona* (*avadāna*). The first transcription is, to all appearances, the representation of the Sanskrit *vāda*, the proper meaning of which is "discussion, controversy, reply." But here again the signification "comparison" does not appear. Without pausing further on this definition, I shall content myself with observing that the examples put forward to sustain it could be borrowed from the *Lotus of the Good Law*, where the parable of the burning house and that of the medicinal plants are indeed found. It is one more proof in favor of the conjecture I have set forth above touching on the more or less great analogy that must exist between the Chinese *Fahua jing* and the *Lotus of the Good Law* of the Nepalese.

12. "*Upadeśa.* These books deal with esoteric doctrines."

Mr. Hodgson has already contested the accuracy of this definition, remarking that the terms *upadeśa* and *vyākaraṇa*, which are familiar to the Buddhists of Nepal, express the distinction that must exist between esoteric doctrine and exoteric doctrine no more clearly than those of *tantra* and *purāṇa.*[78] This critic informs us that the term *upadeśa* is synonymous with that of *tantra*; and indeed several of the works cited in Mr. Hodgson's list with the title *tantra* are related to the category of *upadeśa*s. However, I have never seen this name on any of the tantras I have examined, and I believe that we must recognize in it, as with the greatest number of the articles just analyzed, one of the elements of the Buddhist scriptures rather than a distinct category of these scriptures. The definition of the Chinese authors confirms, it seems to me, this supposition. "This word, they say, means *instruction, advice.* It is, in all the sacred books, the requests and the responses, the discourses that serve to discuss all points of the law, as in the *Fahua jing* the chapter *Tipodaduo*, where the bodhisattva Zhiji discourses with Wenshu shili on the excellent law."[79] We see thereby that the Chinese Buddhists understand the word *upadeśa* in its specific sense, and that if this term has a special application to a particular portion of the Buddhist books, it is by a kind of extension that its signification of "advice" and "instruction" sufficiently justifies. As for the tantras, to which this title *upadeśa* is connected, according to Mr. Hodgson's list, they form a distinct portion of Buddhist literature, to which I will return later.

It is now necessary to summarize in a few words the results of the analysis to which I have just devoted myself.

1. Of the twelve articles that form the Nepalese list, the same as that of the Chinese, two names, that of *sūtra* and that of *avadāna*, designate two categories of books or treatises; only one, that of *upadeśa*, is synonymous with another

78. "Notices," etc., in *Asiatic Researches*, vol. 16, p. 422.
79. Landresse, *Foe koue ki*, p. 322.

category, that of the tantras; and since the legends, as well as the sūtras, report discourses of the Buddha, and since the first differ from the second only in rather unimportant circumstances of form, it is permissible, in research related to ancient sources of Buddhist literature, to include the category of legends in that of sūtras. We see that this result accords with what we arrived at when we examined the triple division of the Buddhist scriptures.

2. The nine other articles are not divisions of the Nepalese collection, but names of elements which enter into the composition of books that this collection encompasses. This result, however, can be adopted only with the following distinctions: although true when we speak of the *geyas*, the *vyākaraṇas*, the *udānas*, the *nidānas*, and the *adbhutas*, it applies less rigorously to the other articles, which it is necessary to envisage under a double point of view. For example, if it is demonstrated that one can find in the Buddhist books some parts for which the names *gāthā*, *jātaka*, *vaipulya*, and *ityukta* are suitable, it is no less true that these names can also designate more or less considerable categories of books. This observation applies in particular to the title *vaipulya*, which we find connected to that of *sūtra* to designate sūtras of great development.

3. Finally, regarding the distinction between two categories of sūtras, which arise from the addition of the term *vaipulya*, namely that of the simple sūtras and that of the developed sūtras, it is necessary to add another category, that of the Mahāyāna sūtras, or sūtras which serve as the great vehicle, and whose titles in the Tibetan library provide numerous examples.[80] The two qualifications can sometimes come together in the same sūtra, which thus will be at once a developed sūtra and a sūtra serving as the great vehicle; but it is easy to imagine that each in its own way can be attached to distinct sūtras.

This would be the place to examine in detail some of the books comprised under the three great divisions set forth above, if it was not necessary to exhaust beforehand what remains to be said in general about the Sanskrit collection of Nepal. Therefore, we find, in the oft-quoted memorandum of Mr. Hodgson, two other divisions that are important to recall here, adding an indication of a type analogous to that with which Csoma de Kőrös furnishes us in his analysis of the Tibetan collection. The Buddhist books, according to Mr. Hodgson, "are known collectively and individually by the name of *sūtra* and that of *dharma*. We read in the *Pūjākhaṇḍa* the following stanza: 'All that the buddhas have said is contained in the Mahāyāna sūtras, and the rest of the sūtras are *dharmaratna*.'"[81] I confess that I do not understand very well the significance of this distinction between

80. Csoma, "Analysis of the Sher-chin," in *Asiatic Researches*, vol. 20, p. 407ff.

81. "Notices," etc., in *Asiatic Researches*, vol. 16, p. 422. In "Quotations from Original Sanscrit Authorities," Mr. Hodgson gives this passage as borrowed from the *Guṇakaraṇḍavyūha* (*Journal of the Asiatic Society of Bengal*, vol. 5, p. 87). It is possible that the *Pūjākhaṇḍa* is a modern book.

the Mahāyāna sūtras and the sūtras collectively called *dharmaratna*. This latter title literally means "jewel of the law," and we know that the word *ratna*, placed after another term, designates for the Buddhists what is most eminent among the beings or the things defined by this term. Do we have to search here for a most vague allusion, it is true, to a division accepted by the Tibetan interpreters of the Kah-gyur, and which consists in making two parts of the books contained in this collection, one called *mdo*, or sūtra, the other *rgyud*, or tantra?[82] I confess that I cannot assert anything definitive in this regard, and it is because the division that the aforementioned text indicates does not seem to me sufficiently precise that I have not spoken about it at the beginning of my research, although it was the most general of those we owe to Mr. Hodgson. But it is necessary to recognize as well that it is the least instructive, and that it little advances the knowledge of the most diverse books that it encompasses.

The one indicated by Csoma de Kőrös is certainly more interesting in that it distinguishes clearly the tantras, or rituals in which Buddhism is mingled with Śivaist practices, from all the other Buddhist scriptures, whatever they are. In putting on one side, under the name *sūtra*, everything that is not tantra, it places this second category of books in a perspective from which we will recognize that it must be envisaged. This is, at present, everything that I have to say about this distinction; later we will see the advantage that it is possible to draw from it. I only note that this distinction, as a result of which the tantras are placed outside the collection of the sūtras, was not unknown to Mr. Rémusat, who expresses himself in this way: "In general, the *prajñāpāramitā* and the *dhāraṇīs* are not included among the collections of sacred books, the whole of which are designated by the words *the three collections.*"[83]

Finally, and it is with this that I shall bring an end to this general description of the Buddhist collection, the Nepalese, according to Mr. Hodgson, separate from this collection nine books, which they call the *nine dharmas*, or the nine volumes of the law par excellence;[84] they worship these works constantly; but Mr. Hodgson does not know the reasons for this preference. These books are the following: 1. *Prajñāpāramitā*, 2. *Gaṇḍavyūha*, 3. *Daśabhumīśvāra*, 4. *Samādhirāja*, 5. *Laṅkāvatāra*, 6. *Saddharmapuṇḍarīka*, 7. *Tathāgathaguhyaka*, 8. *Lalitavistara*, 9. *Subaranaprabhā* (undoubtedly *Suvarṇaprabhāsa*).

The examination of the content of these works, all of which we have in Paris, does not completely explain the reasons for the choice made by the Nepalese. One understands easily their preference touching on numbers 1, 5, 6, and 8; because the *Prajñāpāramitā*, or Perfection of Wisdom, is a type of philosophi-

82. Csoma, "Analysis of the Sher-chin," etc., in *Asiatic Researches*, vol. 20, p. 412.
83. *Foe koue ki*, p. 109.
84. "Notices," etc., in *Asiatic Researches*, vol. 16, pp. 423 and 424.

cal compendium in which the highest speculative part of Buddhism is contained. The *Laṅkāvatāra*, and more exactly the *Saddharmalaṅkāvatāra*, or the "Instruction of the Good Law Given on the Island of Lanka or Ceylon," is a treatise of the same genre, with a more marked tendency toward polemics. The *Saddharmapuṇḍarīka*, or the "White Lotus of the Good Law," in addition to the parables it contains, deals with a most important point of doctrine, that of the fundamental unity of the three means a buddha employs to save humanity from the conditions of the present existence. Finally, the *Lalitavistara*, or the "Development of Games," is the human and divine history of the last buddha, Śākyamuni. But numbers 2, 3, and 4, where the philosophical subjects perhaps do not occupy as much space, have much less merit to my eyes; repetitions, endless enumerations, and scholastic divisions dominate there almost exclusively. As for numbers 7 and 9, the *Tathāgathaguhyaka* and the *Suvarṇaprabhāsa* are tantras of a rather mediocre value. But it would doubtless be a waste of effort to search for the motives of a preference that may perhaps have no other reason than superstitious ideas, alien to the content of the books themselves. It is time to pass on to the examination of some of the volumes of the collection of Nepal to which we have access, in order to discover there, if this is possible, the main features of the history of Indian Buddhism.

I say if this is possible, not with the puerile desire to exaggerate the difficulties of this research, but with the just sentiment of diffidence that I feel in undertaking it. It is not a matter here of concentrating on an obscure but isolated text the strength that the rigorous and patient use of analysis gives to the mind, even less to draw from monuments already well known consequences that are new and worthy to take their place in history. The task I impose upon myself, although different, is equally arduous. It is necessary to browse through almost one hundred volumes, all manuscripts, written in four languages still little known, for whose study we have only lexicons, I could say of imperfect vocabularies, one of which has given birth to popular dialects even whose names are almost unknown. To these difficulties of form, add those of content: an entirely new subject, innumerable schools, an immense metaphysical apparatus, a mythology without boundaries; everywhere disorder and a dispiriting vagueness on questions of time and place; then, outside and among the small number of scholars whom a laudable curiosity attracts toward the results promised to this research, ready-made solutions, opinions that are immovable and ready to resist the authority of the texts, because they pride themselves in resting on an authority superior to all others, that of common sense. Do I need to recall that, for some people, all the questions related to Buddhism were already decided, when no one had read a single line of the books I shall analyze shortly, when the existence of these books was not even suspected by anyone? For some, Buddhism was a venerable cult born in Central Asia, and whose origin was lost in the mists of time; for others it was a miserable counterfeit of Nestorianism; the Buddha has been made a Negro, because he had frizzy hair; a Mongol, because he had slanted eyes; a Scythe, because he was called Śākya. He has even been made a planet; and I do not know whether some scholars do not still delight today in recognizing this peaceful sage in the traits of the bellicose Odin. Certainly, it is permissible to hesitate, when to such vast solutions one promises only to substitute doubts, or only explanations that are simple and almost vulgar. The hesitation can even lead to discouragement, when one retraces one's steps and compares the results obtained to the time they have cost. I would like, nevertheless, to rely on the indulgence of serious persons to whom these studies are addressed; and while they leave me with the feeling of my insufficiency, with which I am affected more than ever, the hope for their benevolent consideration has given me the courage to produce these rough drafts, destined to open the way to research, which, while still not having a numerous public, is nonetheless in itself of incontestable value for the history of the human spirit.

SECTION 2

Sūtras, or Discourses of Śākya

The general description of the collection of the Buddhist scriptures that I have just given clearly traces the course I must follow in the examination that remains to be done of the principal works contained in this collection.

I have shown that all the information accords in presenting the sūtras as the treatises connected most closely to the preaching of Śākya.[1] The sūtras are dis-

1. Here I must recall, once and for all, the observation that has been made on more than one occasion by Messrs. A. Rémusat and Schmidt, that Śākya is the name of the race (branch of the military caste) to which the young prince Siddhārtha of Kapilavastu belonged, who having renounced the world, was called Śākyamuni, "the recluse of the Śākyas," and who having reached the perfection of science he had set as his ideal, took the title *buddha*, "the enlightened one, the savant." In the course of these memoranda I sometimes call him Śākya, that is to say, the Śākya, sometimes Śākyamuni, that is to say, the recluse of the Śākyas; but I never use the term *Buddha* alone, without preceding it with the article, because this term is, properly speaking, a title. We must expect to find this title explained in more than one way in the Buddhist books; and indeed, the commentator of the *Abhidharmakośa*, a work I will speak about later, interprets it in as many ways as it is possible to give meanings to the suffix *ta*, the characteristic of the past participle *buddha*, from *budh* (to know). Thus, it is explained by similarities of this type: *blossomed* like a lotus (*buddha vibuddha*), the one in whom the science of a buddha has blossomed, which is basically to explain the same by the same; *awakened*, like a man who is emerging from sleep (*buddha prabuddha*). It is taken also in a reflexive sense: he is buddha, because he instructs himself (*budhyate*). Finally, one can even see a passive in it: he is buddha, that is to say, *known*, either by the buddhas or by others, for being endowed with the perfection of all qualities, to be free of all imperfections (*Abhidharmakośavyākhyā*, fol. 2b of the MS of the Société Asiatique). This latter explanation, which is the worst of all, is precisely the one that the aforementioned commentator prefers. It seems to me that *buddha* means "the savant, the enlightened one," and it is exactly in this way that a Sinhalese commentator of the *Jinālaṃkāra*, a Pāli poem on the perfections of Śākya, understands it: *pāliyam pana buddhoti kenatthena buddho bujjhi tā saccāniti buddhoti ādinā vuttam*, that is to say: "In what sense does one say in the text, buddha? The Buddha has known the truths, this is why he is called buddha, etc." (fol. 13a of my manuscript). This

courses of a most variable length in which the Buddha converses with one or several of his disciples on various points of the law, which ordinarily are mentioned rather than treated in depth. If we are to believe the tradition preserved in a passage of the *Mahākaruṇapuṇḍarīka*, a book translated into Tibetan, it is Śākyamuni himself who determined the form of the sūtras, when he recommended to his disciples that they respond to religious who come to question them: "This is what has been heard by me, one day when the Bhagavat (the Blessed One)[2] was in such-and-such a place, when his listeners were such and such"; adding at the conclusion "that when he had completed his discourse, all those present greatly rejoiced and approved of his doctrine."[3] In Paris we only have the *Karuṇapuṇḍarīka*, a different treatise from the *Mahākaruṇapuṇḍarīka*, in which the passage I have just cited is found. I have no doubt, however, concerning the authenticity of this passage, which we will find in almost the same form in the Pāli books. If, as I think, it does not belong to the teaching of Śākya, it nonetheless must not be much later than him, and it is one of these details that can surely be connected to the epoch of the first redaction of the Buddhist scriptures.

---

commentary is, as we see, only the beginning of a longer gloss, where we could find other explanations of the word *buddha*. We can content ourselves with this one; it seems to me preferable to the explanation of the *Lalitavistara*: "he teaches ignorant beings this wheel called the wheel of law, this is why he is called buddha" (fol. 228b of my manuscript). The translation of the Tibetans, "perfect saint" (*sangs rgyas*), is taken from the idea one has of the perfections of a buddha; it is not a translation, and the mutilated transcription of the Chinese, *fo* (for *fotuo*), is perhaps even preferable. I must add that it is from this title *buddha* that the followers of Śākya are called by the brahmans *bauddhas*, that is to say, Buddhists. The *Viṣṇu Purāṇa*, instead of taking this derivation from the word already formed *buddha*, explains it by deducing it immediately from the root *budh*: "'Know' (*budhyadhvam*), exclaimed the Buddha to the demons he wished to mislead. 'This is known' (*budhyate*) answered his listeners" (*Viṣṇu Purāṇa*, pp. 339 and 340).

2. The term *Blessed One* renders only a portion of the ideas expressed by the term *bhagavat*, by which Śākyamuni is usually designated in the sūtras, and in general in all the Sanskrit books of Nepal. It is a title which is not accorded to anyone but the Buddha or to the being who must soon become one. I find in the commentary on a treatise on metaphysics called *Abhidharmakośavyākhyā* details that teach us the true value of this title, which is used as frequently by the Buddhists as by the brahmans. On the occasion of the title *bhagavat*, which is found connected by a text to that of *buddha*, the aforementioned commentator recalls a gloss from the books called *vinaya*, or on the discipline, to prove that the addition of this title is neither arbitrary nor superfluous. A pratyekabuddha (a kind of individual buddha about which I will speak below) is *buddha*, and not *bhagavat*. Since he instructs himself through his individual efforts (*svayaṃbhūtvāt*), he can be called *buddha*, enlightened; but he has no right to the title *bhagavat*, because he has not fulfilled the duties of almsgiving and of the other higher perfections. Indeed, only one who possesses magnanimity (*mahātmyavān*) can be called *bhagavat*. The bodhisattva (or future buddha) who has arrived at his last existence is *bhagavat* and not *buddha*, because he has fulfilled the duties of a sublime devotion; but he is still not completely enlightened (*anabhisaṃbuddhatvāt*). The perfect buddha is at once *buddha* and *bhagavat* (*Abhidharmakośavyākhyā*, fol. 3a of the MS of the Société Asiatique). One finds, nevertheless, exceptions to the principles set out by these definitions; so, in a sūtra whose translation I will give below, one sees a pratyekabuddha known as Bhagavat, the Blessed One; but it is doubtless because this personage, who was represented as a bodhisattva, that is to say, as a future buddha, does not feel that he has the courage to complete the course of his ordeals on behalf of mankind, and he contents himself with becoming a pratyekabuddha; it is perhaps that he receives the title *bhagavat* only in memory of his first aim, that of bodhisattva.

3. Csoma, "Analysis of the Sher-chin," etc., in *Asiatic Researches*, vol. 20, p. 435.

We have seen, furthermore, in what I have said concerning the category of sūtras in general, that there existed several types of treatises designated by this title, some of which are called simply *sūtras*, and the others *mahāvaipulya sūtras*, or sūtras of great development; and I have conjectured that it was chiefly to these latter that the epithet *mahāyāna*, "great vehicle," which is attached to several sūtras, must have applied. It is important at the moment to investigate the point at which the examination of the sūtras, characterized by these different titles, explains and justifies these titles themselves. We will soon possess an ample specimen of the *vaipulya* sūtras, or of great development: it is the *Lotus of the Good Law* of which I have already spoken; in addition to that, I shall return below, in this very memorandum, to these kinds of treatises. But until now, still not a single ordinary sūtra has been published, with the exception of the *Vajracchedikā* that Mr. I. J. Schmidt has translated from the Tibetan text,[4] a text which is only the translation of a Sanskrit treatise of which Mr. Schilling von Canstadt possessed a very faulty Tibetan edition, printed in characters called *ranjā* and in ordinary letters. This treatise, which belongs to the category of books of metaphysics, is doubtless enough to allow one to recognize the exterior form of the sūtra; nothing, however, proves to us that it is not a modern summary of one of the redactions of the *Prajñāpāramitā*, and this single doubt prevents us from admitting it into the category of sūtras properly speaking. It has seemed to me that it was necessary to do for this category of books what I have carried out for the sūtras of great development, and that it was convenient to translate some portions of it in order to put before the eyes of the reader the differences that distinguish these two types of treatises, and to support with the authority of the texts the conclusions to which these differences seem to lead me.

I thus have chosen from the great Nepalese collection, known by the title *Divyāvadāna*, two fragments in which I have recognized all the characteristics of the real sūtras, focusing, in order to make this choice, on the subject itself rather than on the title these fragments bear in the aforementioned collection. The first is related to the epoch of Śākyamuni Buddha, and causes one to recognize some of the methods of his teaching. The second is a legend of purely mythological character, which Śākya recounts in order to make the advantages of almsgiving understandable, and to show the great rewards connected to the practice of this duty. My translation is as literal as it has been possible to make it; I have taken care to preserve the repetitions of ideas and words, which are one of the most striking characteristics of the style of these treatises. One will notice without any difficulty that the first fragment bears a title that has no relation to the subject that the passage itself deals with; I shall discuss below the reason for this disagreement between the title and the content of the sūtra as I give it here.

4. *Mémoires de l'Académie des sciences de Saint-Pétersbourg*, 4:126ff.

SŪTRA OF MĀNDHĀTṚ[5]

This is what I have heard. One day, the Bhagavat was at Vaiśālī, on the edge of the pond Markaṭahrada (Pond of the Monkey), in a hall called Kūṭāgāra (the hall situated at the top of the building). So, the Bhagavat, having dressed before noon, after having taken his robe and his bowl, entered Vaiśālī in order to collect alms, and after having gone through the city for this purpose, he took his repast. When he had eaten, he ceased gathering alms; and having arranged his bowl and his robe, he went to the place where the Cāpāla caitya[6] was located, and after having arrived there, he sought the trunk of a tree and sat under it to pass the day. Here he addressed the respectable Ānanda in this way: "Beautiful, O Ānanda, is the city of Vaiśālī, the land of the Vṛjis; beautiful is the Cāpāla caitya, that of the seven mango trees, that of the many boys, the fig tree of Gautama, the grove of the śālas, the place where one lays down his burden, the caitya where the Mallas crown themselves.[7] Varied is Jambudvīpa;[8] life is pleasant there for people. O Ānanda, the being, whoever he is, who has searched for, understood, and disseminated the four principles of supernatural power can live, if so requested, either for a full kalpa, or until the end of the kalpa.[9] Now, Ānanda, the

5. *Divyāvadāna*, fol. 98b of the MS of the Société Asiatique; fol. 125a of my manuscript. It is important to compare this piece with the one Mr. Schmidt has translated from the Mongol (*Mémoires de l'Académie des Sciences de Saint-Pétersbourg*, 2:15) with the legend of the king Da-od (*Candraprabha*), as Mr. Schmidt offers it in his recently published anthology (*Der Weise un der Thor*, p. 165, German trans.), and with the passage translated not very accurately, I suspect, by Klaproth in the *Foe koue ki*, pp. 246 and 247. Later, I will compare the present sūtra with the *Parinibbāṇa Sutta* of the Sinhalese, of which Mr. Turnour has already given some fragments of the highest interest and translated with a rare exactitude (*Journal of the Asiatic Society of Bengal*, vol. 7, p. 991ff.). One will find that the Pāli sutta is longer and richer in interesting detail; but one should not conclude from that that the Buddhists of the North have lost memory of the events that form the subject of this piece. If we had in Sanskrit the volumes of the Tibetan library entitled *Mahaparinirvāṇa Sūtra* (Csoma, *Asiatic Researches*, vol. 20, p. 487) we would find there, without any doubt, all the circumstances recounted in the Pāli sutta. We can already see how the Tibetan books contain precious details on the death of Śākyamuni, by reading the long and beautiful fragment extracted by Csoma de Kőrös from volume 11 of the Dul-va, and translated with the care he has brought to all his work (*Asiatic Researches*, vol. 20, p. 309ff.). I could not find the original of this passage in Mr. Hodgson's collection; but I do not remain less deeply convinced that the Tibetan account in the Dul-va is the literal version of a text originally written in Sanskrit.

6. The word *caitya* is a term with such a wide meaning that I have believed I had to retain it. It designates all places consecrated to a cult and to sacrifices, like a temple, a monument, a covered site, a tree where one comes to worship the divinity. In this sūtra, in which the elements are contemporary with the establishment of Buddhism, there is certainly no question of these being purely Buddhist caityas or these monuments called in Ceylon *dhātu gabbhas* (dāgabs), erected over the relics of a buddha or of some other illustrious personage. This is why the ancient commentator of the *Parinibbāṇa Sutta* cautions that the caityas of the *Vajjis* (Vṛjis) are not Buddhist edifices (Turnour, *Journal of the Asiatic Society of Bengal*, vol. 7, p. 994).

7. This place is mentioned in the Pāli sutta just referred to, and Mr. Turnour designates it as the coronation hall of the Mallas (*Journal of the Asiatic Society of Bengal*, vol. 7, p. 1010).

8. We know that Jambudvīpa is one of the four continents in the form of islands of which the Buddhists, here imitating the brahmans, believe that the earth is composed; for them it is the Indian continent (A. Rémusat, *Foe koue ki*, p. 80ff.).

9. This word, which means "the duration of a period of the world," is also a notion common to Buddhists

four principles of supernatural power belong to the Tathāgata; these are: 1. the faculty to produce such conceptions in order to destroy the idea of desire; 2. the supernatural power of mind; 3. that of strength; 4. that which is accompanied by the appropriate conception to destroy the idea of all exercise of thought.[10] The four principles of supernatural power, O Ānanda, have been searched for, understood, and disseminated by the Tathāgata.[11] So he can live, if so requested, either for a full kalpa, or until the end of the kalpa." This said, the respectable Ānanda remained silent. Two times and three times, the Bhagavat addressed the respectable Ānanda in this way.[12] "Beautiful, O Ānanda, is the city of Vaiśālī, the

---

and brahmans. On the different types of kalpas and their duration, one can see a special memorandum of Mr. A. Rémusat (*Journal des Savans*, 1831, p. 716ff.) and particularly the exposition Mr. Schmidt has made about the theory of kalpas (*Mémoires de l'Académie des sciences de Saint-Pétersbourg*, 2:58ff.).

10. I cannot, in the absence of a commentary, flatter myself to have rendered these formulae well, which are summaries of notions I have not seen elsewhere. See the additions at the end of the volume.

11. The title *tathāgata* is one of the most elevated of those given to a buddha. The unanimous testimony of the sūtras and of the legends claims that Śākyamuni bestowed it on himself in the course of his teaching. We can see the explanations that the scholars involved with Mongol and Chinese Buddhism have proposed for it, notably Mr. Schmidt (*Mémoires de l'Académie des sciences de Saint-Pétersbourg*, 1:108) and Mr. A. Rémusat (*Foe koue ki*, p. 191). According to our plan, which is to first of all consult the Indian sources, the interpretations we have to place at the first rank are those we find in the books from Nepal, or that we know from Mr. Hodgson, and those that Mr. Turnour has extracted from the books of Ceylon. The explanations we owe to the two authors just named are rather numerous, and I believe it sufficient to refer the reader to them; one will see there the more or less subtle methods by which the Buddhists have tried to recover from this title the ideal of perfection they grant to a buddha (Hodgson, "European Speculations on Buddhism," in *Journal of the Asiatic Society of Bengal*, vol. 3, p. 384. Turnour, *Mahāvamso*, introduction, p. lvi). Csoma, following the Tibetan books, is of the opinion that *tathāgata* means "the one who has gone through his religious career in the same manner as his predecessors" (Csoma, *Asiatic Researches*, vol. 20, p. 424). This meaning is as satisfactory with regard to the content as it is to the form; in the term *tathāgata* it shows us a title by which Śākya wished to authorize his innovations by the example of ancient sages whose conduct he claimed to imitate. The texts that Mr. Hodgson relies on give this title a more philosophical meaning; I only mention the first one: "gone in this way," that is to say, gone in such a way that he will not reappear again in the world. The difference that distinguishes these two interpretations is easy to grasp; the second is philosophical, the first is historical, if we may express it in that way: this is a reason to believe that the first is the more ancient. According to the Buddhists of the South, *tathāgata* (*tathā āgata*) means "the one who has come, in the same way, as have the other buddhas, his predecessors," but also *tathāgata* amounts to *tathā gata*, "the one who has walked or has gone like them." One sees that, without doing violence to the terms, one can recognize the interpretation of the Tibetans in the second of those Mr. Turnour has borrowed from the Sinhalese. Thus, if one accepts the principle of criticism, numerous applications of which I will make later, namely that one has to search for the truly ancient elements of Buddhism in that which the school of the North and that of the South hold in common, there will be good reason to regard the version given by Csoma as the first and the more authentic. See the additions at the end of the volume.

12. Ānanda was the first cousin of Śākyamuni and his beloved servant; he had as his brother Devadatta, the mortal enemy of Śākya, his cousin (Csoma, *Asiatic Researches*, vol. 20, p. 308, note 21). Among the interesting information given by the *Foe koue ki* on this personage, it is necessary to consult a very detailed note of Mr. A. Rémusat (*Foe koue ki*, pp. 78 and 79). The purely accidental resemblance of this name, which means "joy," to the adjective *ananta* (infinite) had misled Mr. Schmidt, who had believed these two words to be synonyms, and who regarded the Mongol translation of the title *āyuṣmat* (endowed with a venerable age) as a repetition of the word *Ānanda* (*Grammatik der Mongolische Sprache*, p. 157). Later, in translating the Tibetan texts, Mr. Schmidt himself has clearly recognized the true value of the honorific title *āyuṣmat* (*Mémoires de l'Académie des sciences de Saint-Pétersbourg*, 4:186). So, I make this remark only for readers who would hold to the statement in the Mongol Grammar without comparing it to the translation the same author has given of the Tibetan *Vajracchedikā*.

land of the Vṛjis [etc., as above, until:] The Tathāgata can now, if so requested, live either for a full kalpa, or until the end of the kalpa."

Two times and three times, the respectable Ānanda remained silent. So, the Bhagavat had this reflection: "It seems that Māra the sinner[13] has cast his light on the monk Ānanda, because today, at the moment when he is instructed as many as three times by means of this noble manifestation, he is not able to comprehend the subject. It seems that Māra has cast his light on him."

So, the Bhagavat addressed the respectable Ānanda in this way: "Go, O Ānanda, seek the trunk of another tree to sit under; it is too confined here for us to remain together." "Yes, Venerable One," the respectable Ānanda responded to the Bhagavat; and having sought the trunk of another tree, he sat down to spend the day.

Meanwhile, Māra the sinner went to the place where the Bhagavat was and having arrived there, he spoke to him in these terms: "May the Bhagavat enter into complete annihilation; for the Sugata,[14] the time for complete annihilation has come." "But why, O Sinner, do you say so: 'May the Bhagavat enter into complete annihilation; for the Sugata, the time of complete annihilation has come'?" "This is, O Blessed One, the very time [as was fixed by] the Bhagavat, while in Uruvilvā,[15] on the bank of the river Nairañjanā, seated under the Bodhi tree, at the moment when he had just attained the state of a perfect buddha. As for me, I went to the place where the Bhagavat was and having arrived, I spoke to him in this way: 'May the Bhagavat enter into complete annihilation; for the Sugata,

13. Māra is the demon of love, of sin, and of death; he is the tempter and enemy of the Buddha. He often figures in the legends related to the preaching of Śākyamuni when he became an ascetic (Klaproth, *Foe koue ki*, p. 247. Schmidt, *Geschichte der Ost-Mongolen*, p. 311. *Mémoires de l'Académie des sciences de Saint-Pétersbourg*, 2:24, 25, and 26). He notably plays a large role in the last battles Śākyamuni endured to reach the supreme state of a perfectly accomplished buddha (Csoma, "Life of Shakya," in *Asiatic Researches*, vol. 20, p. 301, note 15). The *Lalitavistara* gives some interesting details about his supposed conversations with Śākyamuni (*Lalitavistara*, chap. 18, fol. 138a of my manuscript).

14. Here is a new title of the Buddha. It seems to me that here *gata* can only mean one of these two things: "who is arrived" or "who has gone." The first explanation is the more likely, although it accords less well than the second with the one I have just accepted, following Csoma, for *tathāgata*. I think thus that the word *sugata* means "the one who has come well or fortunately." Mr. Turnour is of the opinion that this title means either happy arrival, or happy departure of the Buddha (*Mahāvamso*, index, p. 24). See the additions at the end of this volume.

15. Uruvilvā is one of the most frequently mentioned places in the Buddhist legends, because it is here that for six years, Śākyamuni submitted himself to the harshest ordeals, in order to reach the supreme state of *buddha*. It is a village situated near the river Nairañjanā, which Klaproth recovers in the *Nilajan*, a stream that is the most important tributary of the Phalgu. One knows that the Phalgu is a river that crosses through Magadha, or Eastern Bihar, before flowing into the Ganges (Klaproth, *Foe koue ki*, p. 224. Francis Hamilton, *The History, Antiquities, Topography, and Statistics of Eastern India*, 1:14). The arrival of Śākyamuni in Uruvilvā, once he had left the mountain of Gayāśirṣa, is one of the most interesting pieces of the *Lalitavistara* (*Lalitavistara*, fol. 131a of my manuscript). The word *bodhi* is the name the Buddhists gave to the fig tree (*ficus religiosa*) under which Śākya attained *bodhi*, or intelligence, and in a more general way, the state of a perfectly accomplished buddha. I think that this name *bodhi* has been given to the fig tree only in commemoration of this event, and to my eyes, it is a Buddhist denomination more than a Brahmanical one.

the time of complete annihilation has come.' But the Bhagavat responded: 'I shall not enter, Sinner, into complete annihilation as long as my listeners are not instructed, wise, disciplined, capable; as long as they do not know how to reduce with the law all adversaries who will rise up against them; as long as they are not able to have all their reasonings adopted by others; as long as the monks and the devotees[16] of the two sexes do not fulfill the precepts of my law, by propagating it, by having it accepted by many people; by disseminating it everywhere until its precepts have been explained completely to devas and humans.'—But today, O Respectable One, the listeners of the Bhagavat are instructed, wise, disciplined, capable; they know how to reduce with the law all adversaries who rise up against them; they are able to have all their reasonings adopted by others. The monks and the devotees of the two sexes fulfill the precepts of the law, which is propagated, accepted by many people, until it has been explained completely to devas and humans. This is why I say: 'May the Bhagavat enter into complete annihilation; for the Sugata, the moment of complete annihilation has come.'"—"Do not be hasty, O Sinner, you do not have a long time to wait now. In three months, this very year, there will be the annihilation [of the Tathāgata] into the element of nirvāṇa where nothing that constitutes existence remains."[17] Then, Māra the Sinner had this reflection: "He thus will enter into complete annihilation, the śramaṇa Gautama!"[18] And having learned that, content, satisfied, joyous, enraptured, filled with pleasure and satisfaction, he disappeared on that very spot.

Then, the Bhagavat had this reflection: "Who must be converted by the Bhagavat? It is Supriya, the king of the gandharvas[19] and the mendicant Subhadra.[20] Their senses will come to full maturity at the end of three months, this

16. The terms that the text uses are *bhikṣu* (mendicant or monk) and *upāsaka* (devotee). I will return to these terms in the section of this memorandum related to the Discipline.

17. Related to this expression, see a note whose length compels me to move it to the end of the volume, Appendix no. 1.

18. The title *śramaṇa* means "the ascetic who masters his senses." It is at once Brahmanical and Buddhist. I will return to it in the section on the Discipline.

19. The gandharvas are the geniis and the musicians of the court of Indra, who are well known in Brahmanical mythology; they have been adopted and preserved in the ancient pantheon of the Buddhists.

20. Subhadra is the last monk to have been ordained by Śākyamuni himself. He often appears in the suttas and in the Pāli books of the Sinhalese (Turnour, *Journal of the Asiatic Society of Bengal*, 7:1007 and 1011. *Mahāvamso*, p. 11). I think that it is this proper name that the Chinese transcribe in this way: *Xubatuoluo* (Landresse, *Foe koue ki*, p. 385). Xuanzang tells us that in the seventh century, there was a stūpa near Kuśinagara that bore his name. Two centuries before him, Faxian called this sage Xuba (*Foe koue ki*, p. 235), and Klaproth affirms, according to the Chinese books, that he was a brahman who lived for one hundred twenty years (*ibid.*, p. 239). I suspect that there are some inaccuracies in the translation Mr. A. Rémusat has given of the passage of Faxian related to this brahman, and which he expressed in this way: "There, where Xuba, long after, obtained the law." It is not long after the nirvāṇa of Śākya that Subhadra was converted to Buddhism, but in Śākya's own lifetime. I will thus dare to urge persons who have access to the Chinese text of the *Foe koue ki* to verify whether it is not possible to translate it: "There where Xuba, at an advanced age, obtained the law." The Sanskrit books of the North agree with the Pāli texts of the South in representing Subhadra as a very old man when he received ordination from Śākyamuni.

very year." It is easy to understand that the man who is able to be converted by a śrāvaka[21] can also be by the Tathāgata, and that one who is able to be converted by the Tathāgata cannot be by a śrāvaka.

Then, the Bhagavat had this reflection: "Why would I not enter into a meditation such that by applying my mind to it, after having mastered the elements of my life, I renounce existence?"[22] Then, the Bhagavat entered into a meditation such that by applying his mind, after having mastered the elements of his life, he abandoned existence. As soon as he had mastered the elements of his life, a great trembling of the earth was felt; meteors fell [from the sky], the horizon appeared to be on fire. The kettledrums of the devas resounded through the air. As soon as he had renounced existence, six prodigies appeared among the Kāmāvacara devas.[23] The flower-trees, the diamond-trees, the ornament-trees were broken; the thousand palaces of the gods were shaken; the peaks of Meru fell in ruins; the musical instruments of the devatās were struck [and made sounds].

Then the Bhagavat, having emerged from this meditation, pronounced at that moment the following stanza: "The recluse has renounced existence, which is similar to and different from the elements of which life is composed. Focused in mind, meditative, like a bird born from an egg, he has broken his shell."

As soon as he had renounced existence, several hundred thousand Kāmāvacara devas, having performed their ceremonies, advanced into the presence of the Bhagavat, in order to see and adore him. The Bhagavat gave such a teaching of the law that the truths were seen by several hundred thousand devatās, and when they had seen them, they returned to their palaces.

As soon as he had renounced existence, from the caverns of the mountains and the retreats in the hills came several hundred thousand ṛṣis. These sages were introduced into the religious life by the Bhagavat, who told them: "Follow this conduct, O monks." By applying themselves to it, by devoting their efforts to it, they saw face to face the state of arhat[24] through the annihilation of all corruptions.

21. The word *śrāvaka* means "listener"; I will return to it in the section on the Discipline.

22. The expression the text uses here, *jīvitasaṃskārān adhiṣṭhāya*, is not clear; I have translated it tentatively. The root *sthā*, preceded by *adhi* in Buddhist Sanskrit, has the sense of *to bless*; this is proved abundantly by the Tibetan versions (Csoma, *Asiatic Researches*, vol. 20, p. 425 and passim). If such was the meaning of this term here, we should translate it: "After having blessed the elements of my life, I renounce existence."

23. I looked in vain in the Sanskrit books of Nepal at my disposal for the meaning of this name, which designates the gods of the realm of desire. The Sinhalese translate this word as "sensual, indulging in the desires of the senses," and they derive it, with good reason, from *kāma*, "desire," and *avacara*, "who goes" (Clough, *Singhalese Dictionary*, 2:828, col. 2, compare to p. 51, col. 1). The orthography *kāmāvacāra* must then be abandoned, because it does not yield any meaning (Schmidt, *Mémoires de l'Académie des sciences de Saint-Pétersbourg*, 2:24). For the numerous subdivisions of the celestial stages, see the memoranda of Mr. Schmidt (*Mémoires de l'Académie des sciences de Saint-Pétersbourg*, 1:89ff.; 2:21 ff.) and of A. Rémusat ("Essai sur la cosmographie et la cosmogonie des bouddhistes," in *Journal des Savans*, 1831, p. 597ff.).

24. The title *arhat* is one of the most elevated degrees of the moral and scientific hierarchy of Buddhism. I will return to it in the section on the Discipline.

As soon as he had renounced existence, nāgas, yakṣas, gandharvas, kinnaras, mahoragas gathered in a multitude in the presence of the Bhagavat, in order to see him. The Bhagavat made such an exposition of the law that this multitude of nāgas, yakṣas, gandharvas, kinnaras, mahoragas received the refuge formula[25] and the axioms of the teaching, until at last they returned to their abodes.

Then, the respectable Ānanda, having emerged at nightfall from his deep meditation, went to the place where Bhagavat was, and having arrived there, after having saluted the feet of the Bhagavat by touching them with his head, he stood close to him. There, standing, the respectable Ānanda spoke to the Bhagavat in this way: "What is the cause, O Venerable One, what is the reason for this great trembling of the earth?" "There are eight causes, O Ānanda, there are eight reasons for a great trembling of the earth. And what are these eight causes?[26] The great earth, O Ānanda, rests on the waters; the waters rest on the wind; the wind on the ether. When, O Ānanda, it happens that opposing winds blow over the ether, they stir the waters; the roiling waters make the earth move. This, O Ānanda, is the first cause, the first reason for a great trembling of the earth.

"Still one more thing, O Ānanda. When a religious endowed with a great supernatural power, with a great strength, concentrates his thought on a limited point of the earth and encircles it with the limitless expanse of water; if he wishes, he makes the earth move. When a divinity endowed with a great supernatural power, with a great strength, concentrates her thought on a limited point of the earth and encircles it with the limitless expanse of water; if she wishes, she makes the earth move. This, O Ānanda, is the second cause, the second reason for a great trembling of the earth.

"Still one more thing, O Ānanda. At the time when a bodhisattva,[27] having departed from the abode of the Tuṣita devas, descends into the womb of his mother, then, at this very moment, there is a great trembling of the earth. And this entire world is illuminated by a noble splendor. And the beings who live beyond the boundaries of this world,[28] these blind beings plunged into the deep obscurity of darkness, where the two celestial bodies of the sun and the moon, so powerful, so forceful, could not efface by their light this [miraculous] radiance,

25. These formulas, called *śaraṇagamana*, are three in number: *buddhaṃ śaraṇaṃ gacchāmi, dharmaṃ śaraṇaṃ gacchāmi, saṃghaṃ śaraṇaṃ gacchāmi*, that is to say: "I go for refuge to the Buddha, to the law, to the assembly."

26. Compare this text with a note of Klaproth related to the same subject, *Foe koue ki*, p. 217ff.

27. The being who has only one human existence to pass through before becoming a buddha is referred to in this way. This title will appear several times in the course of this memorandum.

28. The word *lokāntarika* designates the beings who inhabit the intermediate region between the world where we live and the neighboring worlds, the union of which forms what is called the great thousand of the three thousand worlds (Schmidt, *Mémoires de l'Académie des sciences de Saint-Pétersbourg*, 2:54). This region is that in which the hells that the Sinhalese call *Lokāntara* are located (Clough, *Singhalese Dictionary*, 2:611, col. 2, cf. *Journal Asiatique*, vol. 8, p. 80).

these beings themselves are, at that moment, illuminated by a noble splendor. Then, the creatures who were born in these regions, seeing themselves in this light have cognizance of each other and say to themselves: 'Ah! There are other beings born here! There are other beings born among us!' This, O Ānanda, is the third cause, the third reason for a great trembling of the earth.

"Still one more thing, O Ānanda. At the time when a bodhisattva emerges from the womb of his mother, then, at this very moment, there is a great trembling of the earth. And this entire world is illuminated by a noble splendor. And the beings who live beyond the boundaries of this world [etc., as above, until:] say to themselves: 'Ah! There are other beings born among us!' This, O Ānanda, is the fourth cause, the fourth reason for a great trembling of the earth.

"Still one more thing, O Ānanda. At the time when a bodhisattva attains the supreme science, then, at this very moment, there is a great trembling of the earth. And this entire world is illuminated by a noble splendor. And the beings who live beyond the boundaries of this world [etc., as above, until:] say to themselves: 'Ah! There are other beings born among us!' This, O Ānanda, is the fifth cause, the fifth reason for a great trembling of the earth.

"Still one more thing, O Ānanda. At the time when the Tathāgata turns the wheel of the law, which in three turnings appears in twelve different ways,[29] then at this very moment, there is a great trembling of the earth. And this entire world is illuminated by a noble splendor. And the beings who live beyond the boundaries of this world [etc., as above, until:] say to themselves: 'Ah! There are other beings born among us!' This, O Ānanda, is the sixth cause, the sixth reason for a great trembling of the earth.

"Still one more thing, O Ānanda. At the time when the Tathāgata, having mastered the elements of his life, renounces existence, then, at this very moment,

29. I find related to this manner of turning the wheel of the law, that is to say, of disseminating the doctrine, a passage in the memorandum of Des Hautesrayes entitled: "Recherches sur la religion de Fo," which refers directly to it: "That those who are ignorant of the four holy distinctions, that is to say, the four distinct degrees of contemplation, could not be delivered from the miseries of the world; that in order to be saved it was necessary to turn the religious wheel of these four distinctions three times, or of the twelve meritorious deeds" (*Journal Asiatique*, vol. 7, p. 167). That amounts to saying, if I am not mistaken, that the four distinctions, viewed under three different aspects, provide the sum of twelve points of view of these four distinctions. The holy distinctions of Des Hautesrayes are probably the four sublime truths (*āryasatyāni*), of which I will speak below; and it is often mentioned in the texts on the three turnings that it is necessary that they be given to these four truths, without which it is not possible to reach the supreme state of a perfectly accomplished buddha. I suppose that the three aspects or turnings are: 1. the determination of the very term that we investigate, the term which is one of the four truths; 2. that of its origin; 3. that of its cessation. One will find very precise details on the expression *to turn the wheel of the law* in a note of Mr. A. Rémusat (*Foe koue ki*, p. 28). The only point that I believe is contestable is this scholar's opinion that this expression derives from the use the disciples of Śākya made of prayer wheels, so well known among the Buddhists of the North. On the contrary, I think that these wheels, which are completely unknown among the Buddhists of the South, have been invented in order to reproduce in a material way the figurative sense of this Sanskrit expression that is, as is known, borrowed from the military arts of the Indians.

there is a great trembling of the earth. Meteors fall [from the sky]; the horizon appears to be on fire; the kettledrums of the devas resound in the air. And this entire world is illuminated by a noble splendor. And the beings who live beyond the boundaries of this world [etc., as above, until:] say to themselves: 'Ah! There are other beings born among us!' This, O Ānanda, is the seventh cause, the seventh reason for a great trembling of the earth.

"Still one more thing, O Ānanda. The moment is not so distant when the complete annihilation of the Tathāgata into the midst of nirvāṇa will occur, when nothing remains of that which constitutes existence. Thus, at such a moment, there is a great trembling of the earth. The meteors fall [from the sky]; the horizon appears to be on fire; the kettledrums of the devas resound in the air. And this entire world is illuminated by a noble splendor. And the beings who live beyond the boundaries of this world [etc., as above, until:] say to themselves: 'Ah! There are other beings born among us!' This, O Ānanda, is the eighth cause, the eighth reason for a great trembling of the earth."

Then, the respectable Ānanda spoke to the Bhagavat in this way: "If I understand well, O Venerable One, the meaning of the language of the Bhagavat, in this very place, the Bhagavat, after having mastered the elements of his life, has renounced existence." The Bhagavat said: "This is so, Ānanda, this is just so. Now, O Ānanda, the Bhagavat, after having mastered the elements of his life, has renounced existence."—"I have heard from the lips of the Bhagavat, while in his presence, I have gathered from his lips these words: 'The being, whoever he may be, who has searched for, understood, disseminated the four principles of supernatural power can live, if so requested, either for an entire kalpa, or until the end of the kalpa.' The four principles of supernatural power, O Venerable One, have been searched for, understood, disseminated by the Bhagavat. The Tathāgata can live, if so requested, for either an entire kalpa, or until the end of the kalpa. Therefore, may the Bhagavat consent to remain during this kalpa; may the Sugata remain until the end of this kalpa."—"It is a mistake on your part, O Ānanda, it is an evil deed that at the moment when the noble manifestation of the thought of the Tathāgata is produced as many as three times, you could not understand the purpose of it and that you had to have Māra the Sinner cast his light on you. What do you think about that, O Ānanda? Is the Tathāgata capable of pronouncing a word that is duplicitous?"—"No, Venerable One."—"Good, good, Ānanda. It is not in his nature, Ānanda, it is impossible that the Tathāgata pronounces a word that is duplicitous. Go away, O Ānanda, and bring to the assembly hall all the monks that you will find near the Cāpāla caitya."[30]—"Yes,

30. The text uses the word *upasthānaśālā*, which I translate with the dictionary of Wilson, giving *upasthāna* the meaning of "assembly." Mr. Turnour, following the Sinhalese authorities in his possession, explains this term in this way: "The hall or apartment which, in each Vihāra or monastery, was reserved

Venerable One." And having responded to the Bhagavat in this way, Ānanda brought together and had seated in the assembly hall all the monks he found gathered near the Cāpāla caitya. [He then made known to] the Bhagavat that the moment to carry out his intention had come.

Thus the Bhagavat went to the place where the assembly hall stood, and having arrived, he sat in front of the monks on the seat intended for him; and when he was seated on it, he addressed the monks in this way: "All compounds, O monks, are perishable; they do not endure; one cannot rely on them with confidence; their condition is change, so that it is not fitting to conceive anything about what is compounded nor is it fitting to take pleasure in it.[31] This is why, O monks, here or elsewhere, when I shall be no more, the laws that exist for the use of the temporal world, for the happiness of the temporal world, as well as for its future use and happiness, it is necessary that after having collected them, understood them, that the monks cause them to be preserved, preached, and understood in such a way that the religious law long endures, that it be accepted by many people, that it be disseminated everywhere, until it is completely explained to devas and humans. Now, O monks, there exists for the use of the temporal world, for the happiness of the temporal world, as well as for its future use and happiness, laws that the monks, after having collected them, understood them, must cause to be preserved, preached, and understood in such a way that the religious law long endures, that it be accepted by many people, that it be disseminated everywhere, until it is completely explained to devas and humans. These laws are the four supports of memory,[32] the four complete abandonments, the four principles of supernatural power, the five senses, the five forces, the seven elements constituting the state of bodhi, the sublime path composed of eight parts.[33] These are the laws, O monks, that exist for the use of the temporal world, for the happiness of the temporal world, as well as for its future use and happiness, that the monks, after having collected them, understood them, must cause to be preserved, preached, and understood in such a way that the religious law long endures, that it be accepted by many people, that it be disseminated everywhere, until it is completely explained to devas and humans."—"Let us go, O

for the personal use of the Buddha" (*Journal of the Asiatic Society of Bengal*, vol. 7, p. 996). This meaning is equally legitimate and it is justified very well by the well-known signification of the prefix *upa* with the roots *sthā* and *as*.

31. The text uses here the difficult term *saṃskāra*, which has several acceptations, among others, *conception* and *compound*. I will return to it below in the section of this memorandum dedicated to Metaphysics.

32. See the additions at the end of this volume.

33. I believe that the eight parts of which this path or this sublime conduct (*āryamārga*) is composed are the eight qualities whose enumeration I find in the *Mahāvastu*: the right or just and regular view, will, effort, action, life, language, thought, meditation (*Mahāvastu*, fol. 357a of my manuscript). These qualities are all expressed with a term in whose formation the adjective *samyac* figures. This enumeration belongs to all the Buddhist schools.

Ānanda, toward Kuśigrāmaka."[34]—"Yes, Venerable One"; thus did the respectable Ānanda respond to the Bhagavat.

The Bhagavat, making his way toward the grove of Vaiśālī, turned his body fully to the right and looked in the way that elephants look.[35] Thus, the respectable Ānanda spoke in this way to the Bhagavat: "It is not without cause, it is not without reason, O Venerable One, that the venerable tathāgatas, perfectly and completely buddhas, look to the right in the way that elephants look. What, O Venerable One, is the cause, what is the motive for this kind of look?" "This is so, O Ānanda, this is just so. It is not without cause, it is not without motive that the tathāgatas, perfectly and completely buddhas, turning their body fully to the right, look in the way that elephants look. It is the last time, O Ānanda, that the Tathāgata looks upon Vaiśālī.[36] The Tathāgata, O Ānanda, will go no more to

34. Kuśigrāmaka is the city that the Pāli texts of Ceylon call Kusinārā and the one that Xuanzang, in the seventh century of our era, calls in Chinese *Jushina jieluo*, a transcription that implies an original Sanskrit *Kuśinagara*; we will see it elsewhere called Kuśinagarī. The difference, moreover, is of little importance, since it turns solely on the word *grāma*, which designates a town or a city located in an agricultural country but which is not fortified, and on *nagara*, a name generally given to a city defended by some earthworks or by a fort. What was at the time of Śākya only a large town could later become an enclosed city. The Pāli term *Kusinārā* means, I believe, "the water of Kuśi" or "of the town rich in Kuśa" (*poa cynosuroides*). This designation doubtless comes from the fact that this place was not very far from the river Hiraṇyavatī, whose waters fertilized the fields. Csoma de Kőrös, who had been alerted by the Tibetan word *tsa can* about the real meaning of *kuśi*, which he translated well with the English *grassy*, "rich in lawns," has believed wrongly that Kuśinagarī was a city in Assam (*Asiatic Researches*, vol. 20, p. 91); but Klaproth has noticed this error, showing that this place should be located on the eastern bank of the Gaṇḍakī (*Foe koue ki*, p. 236), and Wilson believes he has recognized the location in the small city of Kesia (*Journal of the Royal Asiatic Society*, vol. 5, p. 126), where a colossal image of Śākya was discovered (Liston, *Journal of the Asiatic Society of Bengal*, vol. 6, p. 477). Francis Hamilton has provided a drawing with an incomplete inscription (*The History, Antiquities, Topography, and Statistics of Eastern India*, 2:357).

35. Mr. Turnour informs us that, according to the Buddhists of the South, a buddha, like a sovereign king, has a neck formed of a single bone, so that he is obliged to turn his body entirely in order to see objects that are not directly in front of him (*Journal of the Asiatic Society of Bengal*, vol. 7, p. 1003, note).

36. Regarding this name, here I provide some details that the lack of space has prevented me from inserting the first time it appeared. Vaiśālī is a city anciently celebrated for its wealth and its political importance, whose name often appears in the preachings and legends of Śākya. It was located in central India, to the north of Pātaliputra, and on the river Hiraṇyavatī, the *Gaṇḍakī* of the moderns (Klaproth, *Foe koue ki*, p. 244). Xuanzang has informed us that it was in ruins at the beginning of the seventh century of our era. Wilson has rightly seen that this city should be the *Viśālā* of the *Rāmāyaṇa* (ed. Schlegel, text, bk. 1, canto 47, st. 13; Latin trans., 1:150); but the Gauḍa recension, as Gorresio gives it, writes this name *Vaiśālī* (bk. I, canto 48, st. 14), as do Carey and Marshmann (*Rāmāyaṇa*, 1:427), exactly like the Buddhist books I have before me. Between these two orthographies, I do not hesitate in preferring that of *Vaiśālī*, which has for itself the already ancient Pāli transcription *Veśālī* (Clough, *Pali Grammar and Vocabulary*, p. 24, chap. 2). It is clear that if at the time of the redaction of the Pāli books, this name was pronounced *Viśālī* and not *Veśālī* (for *Vaiśālī*), it would have been transcribed *Visālī* in these books. The adoption of the Buddhist orthography that two editions of the *Rāmāyaṇa* offer us, and that the *Viṣṇu Purāṇa* and the *Bhāvagata* (bk. 9, canto 2, st. 33) also confirm, has, moreover, the advantage of bringing an end to the confusion Wilson indicates (*Vishṇu Purāna*, p. 353, note) between the *Viśālā* that is the same as Ujjayanī and the *Viśālā* (for *Vaiśālī*) of the *Rāmāyana*. Long before one could make use of the Buddhist books to clarify the geography of this part of India, Hamilton had rightly seen that Vaiśālī (which he writes *Besala*) should be found in the country located to the north of the Ganges, almost across from Patna and bordering on Mithila (*Genealogy of the Hindu Gods*, Introduction, p. 38). This

Vaiśālī; he will go, in order to enter into complete nirvāṇa, to the country of the Mallas,[37] in the grove of the two śālas."[38]

Then, one of the monks at that moment pronounced the following stanza: "Lord, it is here that you last look upon Vaiśālī; the Sugata Buddha will go no more to Vaiśālī; in order to enter into annihilation, he will go to the country of the Mallas, in the grove of the two śālas."

At the moment when the Bhagavat pronounced these words: "It is the last time that the Tathāgata looks upon Vaiśālī," the numerous divinities who inhabited the grove near this city shed tears. Ānanda the sthavira[39] then said: "There must be a cloud, O Bhagavat, to produce this abundant rain." The Bhagavat responded: "These are the divine inhabitants of the grove of Vāiśālī who, because of my departure, shed tears." These divinities also made this news known in Vaiśālī: "The Bhagavat is going to enter into complete annihilation; the Bhagavat will go no more to Vaiśālī." After having heard the voice of these divinities, several hundred thousand inhabitants of Vaiśālī came to gather in the presence of the Bhagavat. This one, knowing their mind, their disposition, their character, and their nature, made such an exposition of the law to them that these numerous hundreds of thousands of living beings received the formulas of refuge and the axioms of the teaching. Some obtained the reward of the state of śrotāpatti;[40] others that of the state of sakṛdāgāmin; others acquired that of the state of anāgāmin; some, who became mendicants, after having entered the religious life, obtained the state of arhat. Some understood that which is the intelligence (*bodhi*) of the śrāvakas; others that which is the intelligence of the

---

is sufficient, I think, to refute the opinion of Csoma, who looked for Vaiśālī on the site of Allahabad, formerly *Prayāga* (*Asiatic Researches*, vol. 20, pp. 62 and 86). Near this city was a garden that a woman called Anpoluo by Faxian and Anmoluo by Xuanzang (*Foe koue ki*, pp. 242 and 245) donated to Śākyamuni. Wilson, through a comparison that I do not allow myself to judge, has proposed in the name of this woman to see Ahalyā, the virtuous spouse of Gautama (*Journal of the Royal Asiatic Society*, vol. 5, pp. 128 and 129). I think, for my part, that the Chinese syllables *Anpoluo* or *Anmoluo* are the transcription of the name Ambapāli, a celebrated courtesan from Vaiśālī who is mentioned in the legends and about whom Mr. Turnour has given us very interesting details (*Journal of the Asiatic Society of Bengal*, vol. 7, p. 999). The *Parinibbāṇa Sutta* of the Sinhalese gives an extremely interesting account of this donation. I add here that Faxian, to whom the tradition of Śākyamuni's last sojourn in Vaiśālī was well known, since he reports it almost in the same terms as our text, says, with his usual accuracy, that Śākya, at the point of entering into nirvāṇa, departed from Vaiśāli by the western gate. This is perfectly true, since he was going toward the west, toward Kuśigrāmaka, which I believe to be the same city as the *Kusinārā* of the Pāli books.

37. The Mallas were the inhabitants of the country where Kuśigrāmaka was located, in the land watered by the Gaṇḍakī. It is probably they who are mentioned by the Digvijaya of the *Mahābhārata* (1:347, st. 176), and who are placed at the foot of the Himalayas, in the eastern part of Hindustan (Wilson, *Vishṇu Purāṇa*, p. 188, notes 38 and 52). It is known that this country, notably the districts of Gorakhpur, Bettiah, and Bakhra, still retain to the present day very precious traces of the ancient predominance of Buddhism.

38. *Shorea robusta*.

39. This word means "old man"; I will speak of it below, in the section on the Discipline.

40. This term, like the following, *sakṛdāgamin*, *anāgāmin*, *bodhi*, etc., will be explained below in the section on the Discipline.

pratyekabuddhas; others that which is the supreme intelligence of a perfectly accomplished buddha; others received the formulas of refuge and the axioms of the teaching in such a way that this entire gathering of humans was absorbed into the Buddha, plunged into the law, drawn into the assembly.

Ānanda the sthavira, holding his hands joined as a sign of respect, spoke to the Bhagavat in this way: "See, O Venerable One, how the Bhagavat, at the moment when he has departed in order to arrive at complete annihilation, has established hundreds of thousands of gods in the truths! Several thousand ṛṣis, emerging from caves in the mountains and from retreats in the hills, have gathered here. These monks have been introduced into the religious life by the Bhagavat. Following their application, their efforts, and the difficulties they have undertaken, they have seen face to face the state of arhat through the annihilation of all corruptions. Numerous devas, nāgas, yakṣas, gandharvas, kinnaras, mahoragas have received the formulas of refuge and the axioms of the teaching. Several hundred thousand inhabitants of Vaiśālī have been established in the reward of the state of śrotāpatti; some have been in that of the state of sakṛdāgamin; others in that of the state of anāgāmin. Some, who became mendicants, after having entered into the religious life, have obtained the state of arhat; some others have been established in the formulas of refuge and in the axioms of the teaching."

"Thus, why it is astonishing, O Ānanda [replied the Bhagavat], that today I have fulfilled this duty of teaching, I who now know everything, I who possess science in all its forms, who have acquired the free disposition of what must be known by the supreme science, who am without desire, who am in search of nothing, who am exempt from all feeling of egoism, of selfishness, of pride, of obstinacy, of enmity? In a time past, I have been spiteful, passionate, given to error, in no way free, slave to the conditions of birth, old age, sickness, death, grief, pain, distress, disquiet, misfortune. Being prey to the suffering that precedes death, I made this prayer: 'May several thousand creatures, after having abandoned the condition of householders, and embraced the religious life under the direction of the ṛṣis, after having meditated on the four fortunate abodes of the Brahmās, and renounced the passion that draws man to pleasure, may, I say, these thousands of creatures be reborn in the participation of the world of Brahmā and become its numerous inhabitants!'"

As soon as he had recalled his vow, Śākya recounts to his disciple Ānanda the story of a king named Māndhātṛ, which he gives as one of his previous existences. It will be better if this account, which is a little too long to be reproduced at the moment, finds its place elsewhere. It is replete with quite fabulous circumstances and has, in this respect, too great a similarity to the sūtra I will translate. Suffice it to say that the name Māndhātṛ, well known in the heroic story of the brahmans, became the title of the sūtra, a fragment of which we have just read, doubtless because the compilers of the Buddhist books attached more importance to the fabulous legend than to the traditional account of the final conversations of Śākya. Perhaps also the preference that they accorded here to legend over history comes from the fact that the last years of the life of the Buddha are recounted in detail in other books. Whatever the case, the fragment that we have just read has for us the kind of interest associated with a tradition whose elements are contemporary with the epoch of Śākya. Despite the place that the belief in the supernatural power of the Master occupies, several circumstances of his human life can still be perceived in it. This is the reason why I placed it before the purely fabulous sūtra of Kanakavarṇa. It is worth remarking that this latter piece, which is a real sūtra as far as the form is concerned, bears, according to the Sanskrit text and the Tibetan translation, the title *avadāna,* or legend; it is one more argument in favor of the analogy that I have already noted between the category of the avadānas and that of the sūtras.

SŪTRA OF KANAKAVARṆA[41]

This is what I have heard. One day the Bhagavat was at Śrāvastī, at Jetavana, in the garden of Anāthapiṇḍika, with a great assembly of monks, with twelve hundred fifty monks. He was respected, honored, venerated, and adored by monks and by devotees of both sexes, by kings and by the counselors of kings, by persons of the various sects, by śramaṇas, by brahmans, by ascetics, by mendicants, by devas, nāgas, asuras, garuḍas, gandharvas, kinnaras, and mahoragas. After having collected numerous and excellent provisions, divine and human, in clothing, food, beds, seats, and medicines for the sick, the Bhagavat was no more attached to all these things than the drop of water to the lotus leaf. Therefore, the glory and renown of his immense virtue thus spread to the limits of the horizon and in the intermediate points of space: There he is, this blessed tathāgata, venerable, perfectly and completely buddha, endowed with science and good conduct, well come, knowing the world, without a superior, leading humans like a young bull, preceptor of humans and devas, Buddha, Bhagavat! There he is, he, who by virtue of himself alone and immediately[42] recognized, saw face to face, and penetrated this universe with its devas, its Māras, and its Brahmās, as well as the gathering of creatures, śramaṇas, brahmans, devas, and humans, makes known [all this and] teaches the good law! He sets forth the religious conduct that is

41. *Divyāvadāna*, fol. 144b of the MS of the Sociéte Asiatique; fol. 182a of my manuscript. *bKa' 'gyur,* sec. *Mdo*, vol. *a*, or 30, fol. 76b. Csoma, "Analysis of the Sher-chin," etc., in *Asiatic Researches* vol. 20, p. 483.

42. The expression I translate here is *dṛṣṭaiva dharme*: these words seem to me to mean "the condition or object being only seen, as soon as the object is seen, under the very view of the object." However, I do not assert that this must be the only signification of these two words. When *dṛṣta* is opposed to its opposite *adṛṣta*, it can mean the visible world, the actual world, as opposed to the other world, the invisible world.

virtuous in the beginning, in the middle, and in the end, whose meaning is good, whose every syllable is good, which is absolute, which is accomplished, which is perfectly pure and beautiful!

Then, the Bhagavat addressed the monks in this way: "If beings, O monks, understood the fruit of alms, the fruit and results of the distribution of alms as I myself understand the fruit and results, certainly, even if they were reduced at present to their smallest, their last mouthful of food, they would not eat it without having given some away, without having distributed something. And if they would encounter a man worthy to receive their alms, the thought of egoism that might have been born in their mind to obscure it would certainly not remain there. But because beings, O monks, do not know the fruit of alms, the fruit and results of the distribution of alms in the way that I myself know the fruit and results, they eat with an utterly selfish sentiment, without having given anything away, distributing anything, and the thought of egoism that is born in their mind certainly remains there to obscure it. Why is that? [It is this]."

Long ago, O monks, in times past, there was a king called Kanakavarṇa, beautiful, pleasant to look at, amiable, endowed with the supreme perfection of radiance and beauty. The king Kanakavarṇa, O monks, was wealthy, the possessor of great riches, of great opulence, of boundless authority, of a fortune and immense properties, of an abundant collection of precious things, of grains, gold, suvarṇas, jewels, pearls, lapis lazuli, śangkhaśila,[43] coral, silver, precious metals, elephants, horses, cows, and numerous herds; lastly, he was the master of a treasury and a granary that were perfectly full. The king, Kanakavarṇa, O monks, had a capital city called Kanakavatī that was twelve yojanas long from east to west and seven yojanas wide from south to north. It was wealthy, prosperous, fortunate, abundant in all goods, agreeable, and filled with a great number of men and people. The king Kanakavarṇa owned eighty thousand cities and eighteen thousand koṭis[44] of towns, fifty-seven koṭis of villages, and sixty thousand district county seats, all wealthy, prosperous, fortunate, abundant in all goods, agreeable, and filled with a great number of men and people. The king Kanakavarṇa had eighty thousand counselors; his inner apartments kept twenty thousand women. The king Kanakavarṇa, O monks, was just and he exercised his reign with justice.

One day when king Kanakavarṇa was alone, retired to a secret place and reclining in the posture of meditation, the following thought and reflection came to his mind: "What if I exempted all the merchants from duties and taxes? What if I freed all the people of Jambudvīpa from all taxes and all imposts?" Having thus called the tax collectors, the great counselors, the ministers, the guardians of

43. I do not find anything that explains this word *śaṅkhaśilā* (stone of conch); it may designate the mother-of-pearl that covers shells.

44. One *koṭi* is equal to ten million.

the gates, and the members of the various councils, he spoke to them in this way: "From this day, lords, I exempt the merchants from all duties and all taxes; I free the people of Jambudvīpa from all taxes and all imposts."

He governed in this way for many years, when one day there appeared a baneful constellation which announced that the god Indra would refuse to give rain for twelve years. Then the brahmans, understanding the signs, knowing how to interpret the omens, experts in the formulas that affect the earth and the air, having recognized the announcement of this event in the movements of the constellations, of Śukra (Venus) and the planets, went to the place where king Kanakavarṇa was, and when they had arrived, they addressed him with these words: "Know, O king, that there has just appeared a baneful constellation which announces that the god Indra will refuse to give rain for twelve years." Having heard these words, the king began to shed tears while he exclaimed: "Ah! people of my Jambudvīpa! Ah! my Jambudvīpa, so wealthy, so prosperous, so fortunate, so abundant in all goods, so agreeable, so filled with men and people, soon it will become deserted and deprived of inhabitants." After he had lamented in that way, the king had the following reflection: "Those who are wealthy and possessors of great fortune and great opulence will certainly be able to continue to live; but the poor, but those who are of little wealth, little food, drink, and other goods, how will they be able to survive?" Then, this reflection came to his mind: "What if I collected all of the rice and other means of subsistence in Jambudvīpa; had it all counted and measured; once this process was completed, then establishing a single granary for all of the villages, cities, towns, district county seats, capitals in Jambudvīpa, I had an equal portion distributed to each of the people of Jambudvīpa?" Immediately, the king called the tax collectors, the great counselors, the ministers, the guardians of the gates, and the members of the various councils, and he spoke to them in this way: "Go, lords, collect all of the rice and other means of subsistence in Jambudvīpa; count and measure it all; and once this process is completed, establish a single granary for all of the villages, cities, towns, district county seats, and capitals in Jambudvīpa." "Yes, Lord," responded all those whom the king had summoned, and they immediately carried out what they were ordered to do. Then, they went to the place where king Kanakavarṇa was, and when they had arrived near him, they spoke to him in this way: "Know, O king, that all of the rice and other means of subsistence in Jambudvīpa have been collected, counted, measured, and deposited in a single granary for all of the villages, cities, towns, district county seats, and capitals in Jambudvīpa. The moment set for the king to do what he wishes has now come." Thus Kanakavarṇa, having called all those who knew how to count, calculate, and keep records, spoke to them in this way: "Go, lords, count all the people of Jambudvīpa and when you have counted them, give to each an equal portion of food." "Yes, Lord," responded those who had been summoned by the king; and they immediately started to count the people of Jambudvīpa, and acting on the authority of the king's will, they assigned to each of the inhabitants of Jambudvīpa an equal portion of food. The people lived in this way for eleven years, but there was nothing more to live on in the twelfth year. Hardly one month of the twelfth year had passed that a great number of men, women, and children of both sexes died from hunger and thirst. At that moment, all of the rice and other means of subsistence in the country were exhausted, save for only one small measure of food left to king Kanakavarṇa.

Meanwhile, there came at that time in the Saha[45] universe a bodhisattva who had reached this rank forty aeons before. This bodhisattva saw in the depths of a dense forest a son committing incest with his mother, and at this sight, he had this reflection: "Ah! What corruption! How corrupted are beings! Should a man act in such a way with the one in whose womb he lived for nine months, the one whose milk he suckled? I have had enough of these creatures, hostile to justice, passionate for illicit pleasures, indulging in false doctrines, inflamed by sinful desires, who do not know their mother, who do not love śramaṇas or brahmans, who do not respect the elders of each family. Who would have the courage to accomplish the duties of a bodhisattva in the interest of such beings? Why would I not content myself in fulfilling these duties in my own interests?" The bodhisattva thus sought the trunk of a tree, and when he had found one, he sat near it, his legs crossed, keeping his body in a perpendicular position; then calling his memory to mind, he started to reflect by contemplating successively the five aggregates of conception, from the perspective of their production and their destruction, in this way: this is form, this is the production of form, this is the destruction of form; this is perception, this is notion; these are the concepts, this is consciousness, this is the production of consciousness, this is the destruction of consciousness. Having in this way contemplated successively the five aggregates of conception, from the perspective of their production and their destruction, it was not long until he recognized that everything that has production as its law has destruction as its law; and reaching this point, he obtained the state of pratyekabuddha, or individual buddha.[46] Then, the blessed pratyekabuddha, having contemplated the laws that he had just attained, pronounced the following stanza at this time:

45. See, regarding this expression, a note whose length has forced me to place it at the end of the volume, Appendix no. 2.

46. The word *pratyekabuddha* is the most elevated title after that of buddha. The pratyekabuddha is a being who, alone and by his own efforts, has reached bodhi, or the superior intelligence of a buddha, but who, according to Mr. A. Rémusat's expression, "can bring about only his personal welfare and who is not given to being moved to these great gestures of compassion that benefit all living beings" (*Foe koue ki*, p. 165). Our legend completely confirms the elements of this definition. I refer to the note of Mr. A. Rémusat for the complete explanation of this term, which we will see again more than once; and I only add that the Tibetans render this title as: "he who is buddha by himself."

"From seeking, attachment is born, from attachment, suffering is born in this world: may he who has recognized that suffering comes from attachment retire to solitude, like the rhinoceros."

Then, the blessed pratyekabuddha had this reflection: "I have accomplished, in the interest of a great number of creatures, difficult deeds and I still have not benefited any being whatsoever. Today, to whom will I show compassion? From whom will I beg for the alms of some food to nourish me?" Then, the blessed pratyekabuddha with his divine, pure vision, superior to that of man, encompassing the totality of Jambudvīpa, saw that all the rice and all the other means of subsistence of this continent were exhausted, save for a small measure of food left to king Kanakarvarṇa. And immediately he had this reflection: "Why would I not show my compassion to king Kanakavarṇa? Why would I not go to his palace in search of the alms of some food to nourish me?" The pratyekabuddha, soaring miraculously through the air, by virtue of his supernatural power, letting his body be seen, like a bird, made his way toward the place where the capital city Kanakavatī was located.

At that moment, king Kanakavarṇa had climbed to the terrace of his palace, surrounded by five thousand counselors. One of the great officers perceived the blessed pratyekabuddha advancing from a distance, and, at this sight, he addressed the other ministers in this way: "Look, look, lords, this bird with red wings comes this way." But a second counselor replied in this way: "It is not a bird with red wings, lords, it is the rākṣasa, the demon ravisher of the energy of humans who hastens here; it comes to devour us." But king Kanakavarṇa, passing his two hands over his face, addressed his great counselors in this way: "This is not, lords, a bird with red wings or the rākṣasa, ravisher of the energy of humans; it is a ṛṣi who comes here through compassion for us." At that moment, the blessed pratyekabuddha landed on the terrace of the palace of Kanakavarṇa. Immediately, the king, having risen from his seat to go and meet the pratyekabuddha, saluted his feet by touching them with his head, and made him sit on the seat intended for him; then, he addressed these words to him: "For what reason, O ṛṣi, have you come here?"—"In search of food, great king." At these words, king Kanakavarṇa began to cry and he exclaimed amid a torrent of tears: "Ah! misery, ah! what misery is mine! How can it be that I, monarch and supreme master of Jambudvīpa, am incapable of giving a portion of food to a single ṛṣi?" Then, the divinity who resided in the capital city of Kanakavartī recited, in the presence of king Kanakavarṇa, the following stanza:

"What is suffering? It is misery. What is worse than suffering? Again, it is misery: misery is equal to death."

Then, king Kanakavarṇa summoned the guardian of the granary. "Is there something to eat in my palace, so that I can give it to this ṛṣi?" The guard responded: "Know, O king, that all the rice and other means of subsistence in

Jambudvīpa are exhausted, save for a single small portion of food that belongs to the king." Kanakavarṇa then had this reflection: "If I eat it, I will save my life; if I do not eat it, I will die." Then, he said to himself: "Whether I eat it or do not eat it, it will be obligatory, necessary, that I die; I have had enough of this life. Indeed, how could such a ṛṣi, a sage full of morality and endowed with the conditions of virtue, depart from my palace today with his bowl as clean as when he arrived here?" Immediately, king Kanakavarṇa, having gathered the tax collectors, the great counselors, the guardians of the gates, and the members of the various councils, spoke to them in these terms: "Listen with satisfaction, lords: this is the last alms of a portion of food that king Kanakavarṇa gives. By the effect of this root of virtue, may the misery of all the inhabitants of Jambudvīpa cease!" Immediately, the king, taking the bowl of the great ṛṣi, put into it the single measure of food that remained for him; then lifting up the bowl in his two hands and falling to his knees, he placed it in the right hand of the pratyekabuddha. It is a rule that the pratyekabuddhas teach the law through the actions of their body and not through their words. As a consequence, the blessed pratyekabuddha, after having received his portion of food from king Kanakavarṇa, soared miraculously into the air, from the very place where he was. And king Kanakavarṇa, his hands joined in a sign of respect, remained immobile looking at him, without closing his eyes until he could no longer see him.

Then, the king addressed the tax collectors, the great counselors, the ministers, the guardians of the gates, and the members of the various councils in this way: "Lords, each of you retire to your houses; do not remain in this palace, you will all die from thirst and hunger." But they responded: "When the king lived in the midst of prosperity, happiness, and opulence, then we indulged in joy and pleasure with him. Today, when the king reaches the term of his existence, at the end of his life, how could we abandon him?" But the king started to cry and shed a torrent of tears. Then, wiping his eyes, he [again] addressed the tax collectors, the great counselors, the ministers, the guardians of the gates, and the members of the various councils in this way: "Lords, each of you retire to your houses; do not remain in this palace, you will all die from thirst and hunger." Listening to these words, the ministers and all the counselors started to cry and shed a torrent of tears. Then, wiping their eyes, they approached the king; and when they were close to him, saluting his feet by touching them with their head, their hands joined in a sign of respect, they spoke to him in this way: "Forgive us, Lord, if we have committed some fault; today, we see the king for the last time."

Meanwhile, the blessed pratyekabuddha had hardly eaten his portion of food when, from the four points of the horizon, there rose four curtains of clouds. Cold winds began to blow and drove from Jambudvīpa the corruption that infected it; and the clouds, letting the rain fall, settled the dust. That very day, in the second half of the day, there fell a rain of food and dishes of various kinds. These foods were cooked rice, flour of roasted grains, husked grains of rice, fish, meat; these dishes were preparations of roots, stalks, leaves, flowers, fruits, oil, sugar, sugar candy, molasses, and finally of flour. Then, king Kanakavarṇa, content, joyous, delighted, enraptured, filled with joy, satisfaction, and pleasure, addressed the tax collectors, the great counselors, the ministers, the guardians of the gates, and the members of the various councils in this way: "Look, lords, at this moment this is the bud, the first result, of the alms just made of a single portion of food; soon another fruit will appear." On the second day, there fell a rain of grains, namely: sesame, rice, beans, māchas,[47] barley, wheat, lentils, white rice. This rain lasted for seven days, as did a rain of clarified butter, sesame oil, and a rain of cotton, various kinds of precious materials, a rain of the seven priceless substances, namely: gold, silver, lapis lazuli, crystal, red pearls, diamonds, emeralds. Finally, thanks to the power of king Kanakavarṇa, the misery of the inhabitants of Jambudvīpa ceased entirely.

Now, O monks, if in your minds some doubt arose, some uncertainty that made you say: "At this time and at this epoch it was someone other [than the Bhagavat] who was the king Kanakavarṇa," this subject should not be envisaged in this way. Why is that? Because it is I who was king Kanakavarṇa at that time and at that epoch. This O monks, is the way in which the subject must be envisaged. If beings, O monks, knew the fruit of alms, the fruit and results of the distribution of alms as I myself know the fruit and results, certainly, if they were reduced at the present time to their smallest, their last portion of food, they would not eat it without having given some away, without having distributed something. And if they would encounter a man worthy to receive their alms, the thought of egoism that might have been born in their mind to obscure it would certainly not remain there. But because beings, O monks, do not know the fruit of alms, the fruit and results of the distribution of alms in the way that I myself know the fruit and results, they eat with an entirely selfish sentiment, without having given anything away, distributing anything, and the thought of egoism that is born in their mind certainly remains there to obscure it.

A previous action does not perish; it does not perish whether it is good or bad; the society of sages is not lost; what one says, what one does for the āryas,[48] for these grateful personages, never perishes.

A good deed well accomplished, a bad deed maliciously done, when they have reached their maturity, equally bear an unavoidable fruit.

This is how the Bhagavat spoke; and enraptured with joy, the monks, the nuns, the devotees of both sexes, the devas, nāgas, yakṣas, gandharvas, asuras,

47. *Phaseolus radiatus.*
48. I will discuss this title in the section on the Discipline.

garuḍas, kinnaras, mahoragas, and the entire assembly approved of what the Bhagavat had said.

I have cited this piece because its object is to extol the merit of the first of the five transcendent virtues that a man must practice in order to attain supreme perfection, a virtue that is called *dānapāramitā*, or the perfection of almsgiving. It is one of the subjects that recurs most often in the texts; indeed, we possess a great number of legends in which almsgiving is recommended, and in which it is even established that one who practices it must take it as far as the sacrifice of his life; I will have the opportunity to return to it later. At the moment, what is important for us is to study the form of the sūtras by comparing them to some other analogous treatises of the Nepalese collection. And at the outset, I must remark that most of the other treatises that have the same title do not differ from that of Kanakavarṇa except in the virtues celebrated there. As in our sūtra, Śākya recommends the practice of duties, the object of his teaching, and he shows its importance by recounting the merits that those who conform to it are assured to possess. Most often, he supports his doctrine by recounting events that happened, to him or to his disciples, in a previous life, accepting, like the brahmans, that all beings are condemned by the law of transmigration to pass successively through a long series of existences where they collect the fruit of their good or evil deeds. Sūtras of this kind very much resemble the legends properly speaking, and they differ from them only in external characteristics of little importance. A sūtra always begins with this formula: "This is what has been heard by me," while this formula is lacking in all the avadānas I know. One must then say that the legend forms the content and material proper of the avadāna, while it is nothing more than an accessory of the sūtra, and that it figures there only to confirm, by the authority of the example, the teaching of the Buddha, a teaching that is in itself independent of the account given to support it. Apart from these differences, whose number it would be possible to increase if we possessed more sūtras, I believe I must repeat here what I have advanced above regarding the analogy of these two kinds of treatises; and I do not hesitate to add that the observations to which the following analyses give rise apply almost as exactly to the legends as they do to the sūtras.

Before passing to the comparative examination of the books that bear the title *sūtra*, I believe it is indispensable to make known through a rapid analysis one of the treatises of this genre that is specifically called *mahāyāna sūtras*, or sūtras serving as the great vehicle. It would have been easy for me to choose a longer one, but I could hardly find one more celebrated and that dealt with a subject more familiar to the Buddhists of Nepal. I suppose that, when one has read the extract, one will not reproach me for not having reproduced the text in its entirety.

The Mahāyāna sūtra of which I will speak has as its title *Sukhavatīvyūha*, that is to say, the "Constitution of Sukhavatī," the fabulous land inhabited by the divine buddha Amitābha. The setting of the scene of the sūtra is Rājagṛha,[49] in Magadha; the dialogue occurs between Śākyamuni and Ānanda. It opens with the expression of the admiration the disciple experiences in viewing the calmness of the senses and the perfection of the physical beauty of the buddha Śākya. The latter responds to him that even if the Buddha should live for a countless number of kalpas, or ages of the world, this calmness and this perfection would remain without ever decaying. To explain this marvelous ability, Śākya recounts that long before a great number of buddhas, whom he enumerates, there was a tathāgata named Lokeśvararāja, who had among his listeners a monk named Dharmākara. One day, this monk asked his master to instruct him in order that he could attain the supreme state of a perfectly accomplished buddha, and that he could picture all of the qualities that distinguish a buddha land. The master invites his disciple to imagine them himself, but the monk responds that he cannot succeed alone if the Tathāgata does not enumerate them to him. Lokeśvararāja, knowing the dispositions of his disciple, sets forth to him the perfections that distinguish the lands inhabited by eighty-one times one hundred thousand myriads of koṭis of buddhas. The monk retires and after some time, he returns to say to his master that he has comprehended the perfection of a buddha land. The Tathāgata then invites him to expound it himself before the assembly. The monk responds by enumerating the perfections with which he wishes the land he will inhabit to be endowed, if ever he reaches the supreme state of a perfectly accomplished buddha. This exposition is made in a negative manner; all the perfections are indicated there by their opposite, as here, for example: "if in the buddha land to which I am destined, there must be a distinction between gods and humans other than that of name, may I not reach the state of a buddha!" These unselfish vows are expressed again in verses; and when the stanzas have ended, the Bhagavat resumes his speech in order to elucidate the perfections of virtue and merit that the bodhisattva Dharmākara has attained. Ānanda then asks Śākya if so perfect a bodhisattva has passed away or is to come or if he exists at the moment in which he speaks; to which the Bhagavat responds that he exists at that very moment

49. This is the name of the ancient capital of Magadha where Bimbisāra, father of Ajātaśatru, reigned, and also that of the new city that this latter prince built to the north of the first (Klaproth, *Foe koue ki*, pp. 266 and 267). It is necessary to read the interesting remarks, of which this celebrated city was the subject, on the part of Wilson (*Journal of the Royal Asiatic Society*, vol. 5, pp. 130 and 131). While reminding us that Rājagṛha was the capital of Jarāsandha, one of the ancient kings of Magadha, a contemporary of Kṛṣṇa, he refers to the description of the ruins of this city given by a Jaina in the service of Colonel Mackenzie, and included in two accounts, only one of which I can consult (*Quarterly Oriental Magazine*, July 1823, p. 71ff.). This description, which is very detailed, proves what an intelligent traveler could make of curious discoveries in the provinces where Buddhism reigned. See also *The History, Antiquities, Topography, and Statistics of Eastern India*, 1:86, and Lassen, *Indische Alterthumskunde*, 1:136, note.

in the West, that he inhabits the buddha land named Sukhavatī,[50] and bears the name of Amitābha. Then comes the description of the splendor of this buddha, the splendor to which he owes his name Amitābha, "the one whose radiance is without measure." The Bhagavat resorts to various comparisons to express how it is impossible to imagine the perfections of this buddha. He then describes at length the land that he occupies and the felicity of the inhabitants of this land; it is because of this marvelous abundance of benefits that this world merits the name Sukhavatī, "the fortunate land." The Bhagavat then returns to the same subject in verse. He next enumerates in prose the advantages assured to one who pronounces the name of this buddha, who thinks of him, who experiences some desire for the land he inhabits. This subject then reappears in verse. The Bhagavat goes on to describe the Bodhi tree under which Amitābha is seated, and the innumerable bodhisattvas who form the assembly of this buddha. Two of these bodhisattvas, Avalokiteśvara and Mahāsthānaprāpta,[51] have left their fortunate abode to come to live in the world inhabited by Śākya. When the praise of the bodhisattvas of Amitābha has concluded, Ānanda expresses the desire to see this tathāgata himself, and hardly has he expressed it when Amitābha immediately releases from the palm of his hand a ray that illuminates the land he inhabits with such splendor that the beings who populate the world of Śākya are able to see the tathāgata Amitābha. Śākyamuni then addresses the bodhisattva Ajita (The Invincible), who, in our *Lotus*, is Maitreya,[52] to ask him if he sees all these marvels. The latter, who has answered affirmatively to all the questions of the Bhagavat, asks him in turn if there are, in the world they inhabit, bodhisattvas destined to be reborn in that of Sukhavatī. The Bhagavat assures him that there are a considerable number of them, as there are in the world of the buddha Ratnākara located in the East, in that of Jyotiṣprabha, of Lokapradīpa, of Nāgābhibhu, of Virajaprabha, and of many other buddhas. The work ends with

50. The name Sukhavatī means "the fortunate land." Mr. Schmidt, according to authorities unknown to me, identifies this land with the most elevated of the celestial stages, called *Akaniṣṭha* (*Geschichte der Ost-Mongolen*, p. 323). The books I have at my disposal do not say anything at all about this comparison, the accuracy of which I am unable to verify.

51. I do not possess any particular detail on this bodhisattva, who is cited in the Chinese Vocabulaire Pentaglotte (sec. 9, art. 3), in a legend translated by A. Rémusat (*Foe koue ki*, p. 120), and in the *Lotus of the Good Law*, where, as here, he immediately follows Avalokiteśvara and where his name is written *Mahāsthāmaprāpta* (*Le lotus de la bonne loi*, p. 2).

52. Mr. A. Rémusat thinks, according to the Chinese authorities, that Ajita (in Chinese *Ayiduo*) was one of the disciples of Śākyamuni during his human existence, from which one must conclude that he will not take this name Maitreya until he appears in the capacity of the successor of Śākya (*Foe koue ki*, p. 33); but Mr. Landresse has, I believe, better recognized the true value of the word *Ajita*, which he takes as a simple title of Maitreya (*Foe koue ki*, p. 323, note). I will examine below at which point one can believe that one or several bodhisattvas appeared in India at the same time as Śākya. At present, I content myself with remarking that if Ajita was the human name of Maitreya, there would be good reason to ask why this name is not the only one that appears in the developed sūtras when this personage figures as one of the listeners of Śākyamuni. It obviously follows from the *Lotus of the Good Law* that *Ajita* is only an epithet.

the enumeration of the merits promised to one who will listen to such an exposition of the law. This enumeration is made in prose and in verse. I must add that the hero of this treatise, Amitābha, is sometimes called Amitāyus in it. As for the style, the prose is Sanskrit; the verses are filled with Pāli, Prakrit, and barbarous forms, like those of the *Lotus of the Good Law.*[53]

We are at present in a position not only to compare the sūtras properly speaking with those of the Mahāyāna, but to appreciate as well the nature of these resemblances and these differences that bring together or separate these treatises from those called *mahāvaipulya*, or of great development. It is true that I could not place here, before the eyes of the reader, a developed sūtra in its entirety, and that I will often be compelled in the discussion that follows to refer to the still unpublished *Lotus of the Good Law*; but I can affirm that this lacuna is almost completely filled by the analysis I have just made of the *Sukhāvatīvyūha.* Nothing indeed resembles a Mahāyāna more than a mahāvaipulya, and the difference between these two kinds of treatises is, to be truthful, only a difference of volume.

The common title that exists among all these treatises, the sūtras, the Mahāyāna sūtras, and the mahāvaipulya sūtras, announces, at least one must believe, great similarities. Nevertheless, the examination of the texts themselves does not entirely confirm this presumption. A sūtra of great development is, as far as its form is concerned, certainly a true sūtra; it begins and ends with the same formula; it is, like the sūtra I will call simple, written in prose, with a mixture of versified passages of greater or lesser number. It is also dedicated to the exposition of some point of doctrine, and the legends there serve as example and authority in the same way. But compared to these traits of resemblance, the value of which cannot be ignored, one finds numerous differences, whose importance seems to me far superior to those characteristics by which the vaipulya sūtras are classified in the category of sūtras.

Let us take first that which is the most external in a book, the manner in which it is written, and we will be struck immediately by the difference that distinguishes the simple sūtra from the developed one. The first of these treatises is written in prose; the second is in prose mixed with verse, somewhat like the Brahmanical compositions called *campū*, which I referred to above.[54] But the analogy goes no further; because the poetic part of a great sūtra is only the repetition in another form of the part written in prose, save for some details that the poetic exposition naturally introduces, there is not much more in the versified passages than in the prosaic passages, and one could, with very few exceptions,

53. Csoma de Kőrös has already given a short analysis of this sūtra (*Asiatic Researches*, vol. 20, pp. 439 and 440).

54. Above, First Memorandum, p. 65.

omit the former without mutilating the work in which they are found. This arrangement, particular to all great sūtras, merits comparison to the definition the Chinese Buddhists give for the term *geya*, which means, according to them, "reiterated song, that is to say, which responds to a previous text and which repeats it to show the meaning; it is of six, of four, of three, or of two phrases."[55] I refer to what I have said previously about this definition. It suffices for me to remark here that it in some way confirms the introduction of a small number of poetic stanzas into the body of the sūtras. The proportion of these stanzas to the text written in prose as it is fixed by the Chinese Buddhists proves to us that they did not have the developed sūtras in view, since the versified parts of the sūtras equal the parts written in prose, when they do not exceed them. On the contrary, the Chinese definition applies exactly to the simple sūtras, where one indeed encounters few stanzas that have no other object than to reproduce a part of the text in either a more precise or a more ornate form. But there is a rather great distance between these stanzas, which appear only at long intervals, and the great poetic developments of the developed sūtras, which recur regularly after each part written in prose, and which have the effect of introducing in fragments a kind of poem in the midst of a work of which this poem is only the repetition. In this regard, the vaipulya sūtras composed in this way merit their title "developed." I do not hesitate to believe that on this point they are later than those which fit the definition best, that is to say, the ordinary sūtras. They are applying, it seems to me, in a more general manner, a principle already in place in the sequence of a sūtra like that of Kanakavarṇa. The development is here a sure indication of posteriority; and without attaching an exaggerated value to the Chinese definition, one can say that between the two kinds of sūtras with which we are concerned, the more authentic and consequently the more ancient are those in which the simplicity of the form has the merit of being in perfect accord with this definition.

If these observations are well founded, they furnish us from the outset with a definite characteristic with whose aid one can divide the sūtras into two categories: the first formed of the sūtras properly speaking, these are the more simple and very likely the more ancient; the second comprising the sūtras of great development, these are the more complicated and hence the more modern. As a consequence, if the sūtras called *fundamental texts* by the Buddhists of the North are considered to preserve the repository of the word of the Buddha with more fidelity than the other books, it is to the redaction of it, doubtless by various hands and at successive periods, that we must attribute the existence of the two categories of sūtras I have just indicated.

To this sometimes exaggerated characteristic of development just mentioned, another is to be added that completes the separation, as far as the form is con-

55. Above, Second Memorandum, section 1, p. 98ff.

cerned, of the simple sūtras from the great sūtras. The stanzas introduced in the first of these treatises do not distinguish themselves, with regard to language, from the body of the treatise written in prose. The verses and the prose are equally Sanskrit; but it is entirely otherwise in the developed sūtras; the poetic parts of these treatises are written in an almost barbaric Sanskrit, where forms of every age, Sanskrit, Pāli, and Prakrit, seem to be confused. I have already indicated this fact when I compared the value of the translations executed in Tibet, Mongolia, and China with that of the Sanskrit original from Nepal. This fact indicates another redaction in the most clear manner, and it accords with the development of poetic pieces, where one observes it as testimony that these pieces at least do not derive from the same hand as the simple sūtras. Nothing in the books characterized by this difference of language provides the slightest light on its origin. Should we see in it the use of a popular style that would have developed after the teaching of Śākya, and that would be in an intermediate position between regular Sanskrit and Pāli, a dialect entirely derived from and manifestly subsequent to Sanskrit; or should we recognize in it only the crude compositions of writers to whom Sanskrit was no longer familiar and who forced themselves to write in the scholarly language that they knew poorly, with the liberties that the habitual use of an unfixed popular dialect provides? It will be for history to decide between these two solutions, of which it is my sense that the second is much more probable than the first; but we lack its direct testimony, and we are here reduced to inductions furnished to us by the rather rare facts known to us at present. Yet we do not find all these facts in the collection of Nepal: it is indispensable to encompass the question as a whole, to consult for a moment the Sinhalese collection and the traditions of the Buddhists of the South. What we learn is that the sacred texts there are written in Pāli, that is to say, in a dialect derived at the first degree from the scholarly idiom of the brahmans, and which differs very little from the dialect one finds on the most ancient Buddhist monuments of India. Is it in this dialect that the poetic portions of the great sūtras are composed? By no means; the style of these portions is an unspeakable mixture in which an incorrect Sanskrit is bristling with forms, some of which are entirely Pāli and others that are popular in the most general sense of this term. There is no geographical name to give to such a language; but one understands at the same time that such a mixture could be produced in places where Sanskrit was not studied in a scholarly manner, and among populations who had never spoken it or who only knew dialects derived at degrees more or less distant from the primitive root. I am thus inclined to believe that this part of the great sūtras must have been written outside India or, to express myself in a more precise manner, in the countries situated beyond the Indus or in Kashmir, for example, a country where the scholarly language of Brahmanism and Buddhism must have been cultivated with less success than in central India. It seems to me rather difficult, not to say impossible, that the gibberish of this poetry could have occurred in a epoch when Buddhism flourished in Hindustan. At that time, indeed, the monks could choose between only these two idioms: either Sanskrit, the language that dominates in the compositions collected in Nepal; or Pāli, the dialect one finds in the ancient Buddhist inscriptions of India and that has been adopted by the Sinhalese Buddhists.

I have just said that Sanskrit dominates the Buddhist compositions of the North: this is a fact that the discovery of the Nepalese collection leaves beyond doubt, but which, although entirely incontestable as it is, cannot be advanced without some restrictions. In which Sanskrit are these books written? Is it in the epic style, this style at once noble and simple of the *Rāmāyaṇa* and the *Mahābhārata*? Is it in the rich and vivid language of the dramatic compositions? Is it in the monotonous and slightly dull idiom of the Purāṇas? Or, finally, is it in the compact but obscure prose of the commentators? One understands easily what use the historical critic would make of an affirmative response, if it were possible to give one to this or that of these four questions. But the response cannot be affirmative on any of these points, because the Buddhist books are not written in any of these styles. They are composed with Sanskrit words often taken in new acceptations and above all are joined by virtue of unusual combinations that astonish a reader familiar with works of literature of the brahmans. Language, among the Buddhists, has followed the movement of ideas; and since their conceptions differ appreciably from those of the brahmans, their style has become very different from the scholarly style of the latter. This observation applies rigorously to the canonical collection in its entirety; the sole exceptions that are encountered are found in books that appear with a more modern character or that are attributed to more or less well-known authors. These books either very much resemble the Brahmanical Purāṇas, or they are written in the style of the commentators and in a rather correct Sanskrit. The result of this is that the more the Buddhist compositions move away from the times when the books marked with the character of inspiration were written, the more they approach the classical style of the brahmans; while the more they go back to these times, the less they resemble the various models that the orthodox literature has preserved for us.[56]

56. In calling the literature of the brahmans orthodox, I take the Indian perspective, and I think there is nothing in the use of this expression that is contrary to history, since from its origin Buddhism was heterodox in that it denies the authority of the Brahmanical Vedas. I would wish that this observation could shield me from the severe judgment that Mr. Schmidt has passed on this opinion when, stressing the immense extension that Buddhism gained and maintained, he declares the use of these expressions *orthodox* and *heterodox* "which the English use with much gravity and which French and German scholars repeat with such naïveté" to be "completely contrary to philosophy and almost laughable." Mr. Schmidt has no more indulgence for the designation *sectarian,* which has sometimes been applied to the Buddhists and which he declares to be no less absurd (*Mémoires de l'Académie des sciences de Saint-Pétersbourg*, 2:45, note).

It is in the category of inspired books that the sūtras take their place, the only books with which we have to occupy ourselves at the moment, and it is also their style that offers the greatest number of these features peculiar to the Sanskrit of Buddhism. They are written in a very simple prose in which the sentences have in general little development. From time to time one sees some stanzas dedicated to moral or philosophical maxims, stanzas probably very ancient, but which are not in a better style than the works in which they are found. These books have a popular color that is striking at first sight, and the dialogue form that is ordinarily dominant in them gives them the appearance of conversations that have really taken place between a master and his disciples. There is, in this respect, hardly any distinction to be made between the simple sūtras and the developed sūtras, at least in regard to the comparable parts of these two categories of books, that is to say, the dialogue and the account written in prose. But the developed sūtras have a more ample and more diffuse style; propositions are always recurring and the periods are often immense, which is very rare in the simple sūtras.

Without going into technical details, I could not give a more rigorous precision to the description I have just provided of the Sanskrit style of the sūtras. I do not, however, believe that I am exempt from producing proofs of my opinion, but I find that these proofs would not have a place here. The study of Buddhist Sanskrit will certainly be more interesting when it is possible to compare it to the Pāli of the books of Ceylon. I have already assembled numerous materials for this comparison, and I hope to be able to gather an even greater number. It will suffice for me to set forth here the more general result of this study; it is that the same features that distinguish Buddhist Sanskrit from Brahmanical Sanskrit are all found in the Pāli of the Buddhists of the South; that these features, which are conveyed in the meaning of the words but above all in the syntax, amount to idioms and popular turns of phrase, and it is in this way that the books of the North, although composed in the scholarly idiom of the brahmans, are linked in the most intimate manner to the books of the South, written, as one knows, in a popular dialect derived from Sanskrit. This conclusion will, I hope, be accepted without difficulty when one recognizes that these analogies of style are noticed principally in passages dedicated to the expression of beliefs and traditions common to the Buddhists of the North and to those of Ceylon.

The external form of these two kinds of sūtras, whose existence has just been noted, furnishes us with still other characteristics, all of which deserve attention. Thus, that which, in regard to form, distinguishes a sūtra of the great development, like the *Lotus of the Good Law*, from a simple sūtra, like that of Kanakavarṇa translated above, is development and diffusion. The ordinary sūtras, compared to books such as the *Lotus*, are written with a remarkable moderation. The principal features of the developed sūtras are in general found; but these features are only sketched there and always in a concise manner. Usually, the Buddha is in a city in the middle of India, among an assembly of monks who listen to him; this assembly, composed generally of a not particularly significant number of listeners, increases sometimes with the multitude of the gods with whom Śākya converses, by virtue of his supernatural power. But one does not find in this indication of the scene and the framework of the simple sūtras anything that recalls the ample and tedious developments that open a great number of developed sūtras, an example of which can be seen in the *Lotus of the Good Law*. Indeed, let us compare it to the beginning of this last work, that of the *Sūtra of Kanakavarṇa*, and one will understand on what the difference I intend to indicate turns. In the long sūtras, like the *Saddharmapuṇḍarīka*, the *Samādhirāja*, the *Saddharmalaṅkāvatāra*, the *Lalitavistara*, the *Gaṇḍavyūha*, the Buddha does not gather an assembly other than one composed of a usually exaggerated number of monks and nuns, of devas of all orders, and above all of bodhisattvas, personages whose merits are no less innumerable than their names are complicated.[57] The presence of bodhisattvas in the preamble of the great sūtras is notably a very characteristic particularity, which separates them in a most definite manner from the simple sūtras. It is not said in any of the simple sūtras or avadānas I know that a single bodhisattva ever attended an assembly where Śākya was teaching the law; and the bodhisattva one finds most frequently mentioned there, Maitreya, that is to say, he who must succeed Śākyamuni[58] as buddha, never appears, to my knowledge, except where he must be in the system of all Buddhists, namely among the Tuṣita gods,[59] the abode from which he will descend to earth one day in order to complete his final mortal existence, ascend to the rank of a buddha, savior of the world, and then enter into the complete annihilation of nirvāṇa. If I have understood the Sanskrit sūtras and avadānas at my disposal well, a buddha and a bodhisattva cannot exist on earth at the same time; because a bodhisattva is a potential buddha, the coexistence of these two personages will produce the coexistence of two buddhas living at the same time in the same world; this appears not to be something that is accepted by the Buddhists, among whom the oneness of a living buddha is a dogma as solidly established as the oneness of God was among the Jews. This at least is what appears to me to result from this maxim I find in the *Saddharmalaṅkāvatāra*: "It is impossible, it cannot happen, the Bhagavat has said, that several tathāgatas are born at the same time in the same

57. Mr. Schmidt has given, according to the Mongol books, a very good description of the preamble of a developed sūtra ("Über einige Grundlehren des Buddhismus," in *Mémoires de l'Académie des sciences de Saint-Pétersbourg*, 1:242 and 243).

58. One can see in a note of the *Foe koue ki* (pp. 33 and 34) the brief summary of the legend regarding the future coming of Maitreya in his capacity as a buddha.

59. The Tuṣita, or *joyful* gods, are also known by the brahmans, from whom the Buddhists have probably borrowed the name. In the Buddhist cosmogony, they inhabit the fourth of the six heavens superposed above the earth, which together form the world of desire (A. Rémusat, "Essai sur la cosmogonie buddhique," in *Journal des Savans*, 1831, p. 610).

universe."[60] The name *bodhisattva*, which literally means "one who possesses the essence of bodhi or the intelligence of a buddha," is the title of the man in whom, according to all Buddhist schools, the practice of all virtues and the exercise of meditation have matured for the acquisition of the supreme state of a perfectly accomplished buddha. The man who feels the desire to reach this state cannot attain it by the efforts of his will alone; he must have merited, during numerous existences, the favor of one or several of these ancient and colossal buddhas, the reality of whom the Buddhists believe in; and it is only when he is in possession of their favor that, in one of the heavens that rise above the earth, he will, with the title *bodhisattva*, await the moment of his coming into the world. Descending to earth, he is still a bodhisattva and is not yet a buddha; and it is when he has passed through all the ordeals, accomplished the highest duties, penetrated the most sublime truths with science, that he becomes a buddha. Then, he is capable of delivering humans from the conditions of transmigration, by teaching them charity and by showing them that one who practices the duties of morality and strives to attain to science during this life can one day reach the supreme state of a buddha. Then, when he has taught the law in this way, he enters nirvāṇa, that is to say, complete annihilation where, according to the most ancient school, the definitive destruction of the body and soul occurs.

One could nonetheless suppose (and it is with this that I will conclude what I have to say on the subject) that the presence of the bodhisattva Maitreya in the assemblies of Śākya is but momentary, and that there is nothing in it that is contradictory to the dogma of the oneness of the Buddha, in that it is the result of a miracle. It is evidently through this kind of *ultima ratio* of the Oriental religions that we must explain it; and indeed, if the gods descend from heaven to make themselves visible to Śākya, as the Buddhists believe, Maitreya is equally able to appear among the number of listeners of this sage, just as the *Lotus of the Good Law* has it.[61] Let us then acknowledge that it is by virtue of his supernatural power that he sometimes leaves the heaven of the Tuṣita gods, which another passage of the *Lotus* also depicts as his habitual dwelling place,[62] in order to come to earth. Nevertheless, the simple sūtras, which, like the developed sūtras, attribute a superhuman power to the bodhisattvas, do not say, as I remarked before, that Maitreya ever attended the assemblies of Śākya. If they thus left the future heir of the sage in heaven, it is doubtless not that they recoil from a miracle, but rather that they reproduce a tradition different from that of the developed sūtras. Here, at least I think, the difference is all the more worthy of attention, in that the point it conveys is in itself of less value.

60. *Saddharmalaṅkāvatāra*, fol. 59b.

61. Chap. 1, p. 2 and passim.

62. Chap. 26, fol. 245a text, and p. 279 of the translation.

I will say the same about the presence of these myriads of bodhisattvas whose miraculous arrival occupies so much space in the later chapters of the *Lotus of the Good Law*. Just as the Buddhists of the North conceive of infinities of universes situated at the ten points of space, so they increase to infinity the number of buddhas and bodhisattvas who coexist at the same time; and in order that these bodhisattvas can hear the preachings of this or that of these innumerable buddhas, the most simple act of their supernatural power is sufficient. But here also I indicate a difference between the simple sūtras and the developed sūtras. These myriads of worlds with which the great sūtras populate space, these numerical exaggerations in which, despite their aridity, one finds a vague feeling of the infinite grandeur of the universe, are completely foreign to those of the simple sūtras I have read. That is why these latter treatises do not show us, as the *Lotus of the Good Law* does, buddhas and especially bodhisattvas arriving in multitudes from all points of space in order to attend the preachings of Śākyamuni. The redactors of these treatises, apart from their penchant to believe in miracles, had, however, more than one occasion to recount scenes of this kind, and the tradition furnished them with all the elements of accounts analogous to those that we read in the later chapters of the *Lotus*. And to cite just one example, the preamble of the simple *Sūtra of Kanakavarṇa*, a preamble in which are enumerated all the beings from whom Śākya receives homage, does not mention any of the names of the bodhisattvas introduced at the beginning of the *Lotus*, any more than it speaks about this multitude of similar personages who figure in some chapters of this latter treatise. This remark applies equally to the formula that ends this same simple sūtra; one does not see there, any more than in the preamble, the slightest trace of the presence of these personages who appear so frequently on the scene of the developed sūtras.

The observations to which the supernatural listeners who miraculously attend the assemblies of Śākya just gave rise touch at the same time on the form and the content of the developed sūtras. These bodhisattvas in fact do not appear solely in the framing of these treatises, a framing one could conceive, if absolutely necessary, as having been added afterward, but rather they take part in the events of the preaching of the Buddha. Their presence or their absence thus affects the very content of the books in which one notes it, and it is most evident that this single point draws a deep line of demarcation between the ordinary sūtras and the developed sūtras. The comparative examination of these two categories of books will enable us to indicate several other differences that must, if I am not mistaken, cast daylight on the history of the sūtras and at the same time on that of the Buddhism of the North in general. But since I have spoken about the bodhisattvas, permit me to indicate here two of these personages who appear in the first rank, not only in the *Lotus of the Good Law*, but in the greatest number of developed sūtras.

I have already expressed myself sufficiently concerning Maitreya, whose presence in the assemblies of Śākya was certainly something unknown to the compilers of the vast collection of simple sūtras that bears the name *Divyāvādana*. Nevertheless, the name of Maitreya appears in these treatises; he is, I have said above, a personage of the mythology of the time to come, the future buddha. The names of the two sages of whom I shall speak are on the contrary completely foreign to the sūtras of the *Divyāvadāna*; they do not appear there even once. These names are those of Mañjuśrī and Avalokiteśvara, who are both bodhisattvas. In our *Lotus of the Good Law*, Mañjuśrī is one of the listeners of Śākya; he is the first mentioned among the bodhisattvas who sit in the assembly described in the first chapter; he is the one to whom Maitreya requests the explanation of the difficulties that impede him. The *Lotus of the Good Law* portrays Mañjuśrī as a bodhisattva eminent in science and in virtue, who has fulfilled all the duties imposed to his condition under innumerable buddhas prior to Śākyamuni; but apart from this, this book does not indicate anything else to us that makes him more particularly recognizable, and it is clear, moreover, that it speaks about him as a celebrated personage.

And indeed, few names are so often mentioned among the Buddhists of the North as that of Mañjuśrī, after, however, the name of Śākya, and perhaps also that of the second bodhisattva I will discuss later. Thus, the Chinese, who, as I have already intimated, in general follow the tradition of the North, have a most special veneration for Mañjuśrī, which is equally shared by the Tibetans and Mongols. The account by Faxian also furnishes us with information of some interest about this personage: first, in that it traces the cult of which Mañjuśrī was the object back at least to the fourth century of our era; second, in that it causes us to think that the existence of Mañjuśrī is connected, in ways still unknown to us, to a considerable portion of the collection of the North, the *Prajñāpāramitā*, which will be discussed shortly. This is the very passage that it is important to cite. After having reported the homage that he had seen paid to the towers, that is to say, to the stūpas of Śāriputra, of Maudgalyāyana, and of Ānanda, which still remained in his time in Madhyadeśa, that is to say, in central India, Faxian adds: "Those who have Apitan as their master pay their homage to Apitan; those who have precepts as their master honor the precepts. Each year, there is a service of this kind, and each of them in its turn. The devotees of Moheyan (Mahāyāna) pay homage to Banruo boluomi (Prajñāpāramitā), to Wenshu shili (Mañjuśrī) and to Guanshiyin (Avalokiteśvara)."[63] I do not doubt that by the term *Apitan*, one must understand Abhidharma, as Mr. Rémusat has seen well, and that the precepts designate the sūtras, a distinction that belongs to the first ages of Buddhism, and which was perpetuated while the different philosophical

63. *Foe koue ki*, p. 101.

schools born in the midst of this cult developed, some connected particularly to the sūtras, or to the precepts that emanated from the lips of Śākya himself; others following the Abhidharma, or the collections of metaphysics extracted from the sūtras or, in a more general way, from the very preaching of the Buddha. Next to these two categories of texts that I have discussed amply in my description of the Buddhist collection in general, Faxian places Buddhists who followed the Mahāyāna, or the books serving as the great vehicle, and who worshipped the perfection of wisdom. I have already indicated briefly, and I will show later in detail, that the title *prajñāpāramitā* is the generic denomination of the books dedicated to high metaphysics, and it suffices for me at the moment to say that the treatises assembled under this title are, indeed, as Faxian thought, works serving as the great vehicle. But what is important to recall is that the developed sūtras are also called *mahāyāna*, and that this title applies, to my knowledge, to but one of the simple sūtras of the collection of the *Divyāvadāna*; this sūtra is the *Dānādhikāra*, a small treatise of one page concerning the thirty-seven ways one must practice almsgiving, which has a most mediocre value and has only the title of a simple sūtra.[64] Thus, is it not a fact worthy of attention to see the name Mañjuśrī, whom Faxian presents to us as somehow the patron of the Mahāyāna followers, cited in books, in sūtras, to which, according to the double testimony of the tradition and of the monuments, this title *mahāyāna* is applied? And does this comparison not explain up to a certain point the opinion of Csoma de Kőrös, for whom Mañjuśrī is a mythological personage, the model and beautiful ideal of wisdom?[65] Everything thus leads us to recognize that there is some relation between this personage and the part of the Buddhist collection known under the title *prajñāpāramitā*, to which must be added those of the developed sūtras in which his name is mentioned, not to say that he is the author of these books, but simply to establish that they have been written since the epoch when a role, either real or imaginary, began to be attributed to this personage. This is not the place to investigate what this role might have been; this point will find its place in the sketch I will draw of the history of Indian Buddhism. It suffices at this moment to have shown that the simple sūtras never speak of a bodhisattva named Mañjuśrī, a bodhisattva who, on the contrary, plays a very important role in the developed sūtras, and to have added this new feature to the already numerous features that distinguish the vaipulya sūtras from those that other indices lead me to regard as earlier.

What I have just said about Mañjuśrī applies no less rigorously to the second of

64. *Divyāvadāna*, fol. 275b of the MS of the Société Asiatique.

65. *Tibetan Grammar*, p. 193. Mr. Schmidt, prior to Csoma, already regarded Mañjuśrī as the source of divine inspiration (*Geschichte der Ost-Mongolen*, p. 310). Since then, he has shown even more clearly his role in the metaphysical cosmogony of Northern Buddhism ("Über einige Grundlehren des Buddhismus," in *Mémoires de l'Académie des sciences de Saint-Pétersbourg*, 1:100).

the bodhisattvas I wished to speak of, the one called Avalokiteśvara. This name is not cited a single time in the sūtras, or in the legends of the *Avadānaśataka* or in those of the *Divyāvadāna*, whereas it figures in the first rank in our *Lotus of the Good Law.* He is named second, immediately after Mañjuśrī, in the enumeration of the bodhisattvas that serves as an introduction to this work; and, moreover, an entire chapter, the twenty-fifth, having the title: "The Perfectly Happy Account," is dedicated in its entirety to the glory of this holy personage. One must acknowledge that this account seems quite mediocre, even among the mediocrities that fill the later chapters of the *Lotus of the Good Law*; and the presence of such a piece in a book where nothing announces it is not itself a fact that is easy to explain. Everything becomes clear if one considers the elevated role that the Buddhists of the North assign to this bodhisattva. The Tibetans regard him as the patron of their country, the Mongols have adopted the legends that celebrate his supernatural faculties, and the Chinese equally offer a special worship to him. Mr. Schmidt has learnedly insisted on the role that this bodhisattva plays in the history of Northern Buddhism, notably among the Tibetans and the Mongols.[66] Mr. A. Rémusat has written, based on various Chinese texts, an interesting note on this great bodhisattva, and he has shown the influence that he exercises, according to the Buddhists of the North, on the preservation and perpetuation of their faith.[67] I will have occasion, in my Historical Sketch, to return to this celebrated personage; I only remark here that, by representing him to us as associated with Mañjuśrī in the worship that the followers of the Abhidharma render to him, Faxian allows us to draw from the presence of his name in the developed sūtras the same consequences as those just set forth with regard to Mañjuśrī.

The names of these two bodhisattvas, in legends dominated by elements almost exclusively fabulous, lead me naturally to indicate another set of conceptions of an analogous order, whose absence is equally noted in the most simple sūtras, but whose numerous traces strike one in the developed sūtras. I wish to speak about this system of superhuman buddhas and bodhisattvas called *dhyāni buddhas* and *dhyāni bodhisattvas*, which was not very generally known before the research of Mr. Hodgson.[68] I could refer to the first memorandum of this scholar as regards this part of Northern Buddhism; it is in this memorandum,

66. See the observations of this author at the end of his *History of the Eastern Mongols* (p. 424) and especially those he has recorded in his first memorandum on some fundamental points of Buddhism (*Mémoires de l'Académie des sciences de Saint-Pétersbourg*, 1:110ff.). The only point on which I would distance myself from his view is his opinion that Avalokiteśvara must have been one of the listeners of Śākyamuni (*ibid.*, 1:244; 2:13). The remarks developed in my text tend to prove that this name is completely foreign to the sūtras that appear to me to have issued most directly from the preaching of Śākya and that I believe to be the most ancient.

67. *Foe koue ki*, p. 117.

68. Mr. Schmidt establishes that they are very often mentioned by the Mongol Buddhists, and in fact, Pallas (*Sammlungen historischer Nachrichten über die mongolischen Völkerschaften*, 2:86 and 87) and Mr. Schmidt (*Geschichte der Ost-Mongolen und Ihres Fürstenhauses verfasst von Ssagang Ssetsen Chungtaidschi der Ordus*,

still so new, in spite of everything that has been assembled since, that the reader will find the most precise clarifications of the theory of the celestial buddhas and bodhisattvas, as the Nepalese understand it.[69] It is nevertheless indispensable that I present here the principal features of this system, in order to place the reader in the position to appreciate the difference, to my mind very deep, that distinguishes the books in which it shows itself from those in which it does not appear.

In the memorandum I have just mentioned, after having asked himself at which point the four great sects, into which the Buddhism of Nepal is divided at the present time and which will be discussed later, adopted the numerous divisions of the popular pantheon, Mr. Hodgson establishes that the practical religion of this country clearly distinguishes the sages of human origin, who acquired the rank of buddha through their efforts and virtues, from another more exalted category of buddhas whose nature and origin are purely immaterial. The first, who are called *manuṣi buddhas*, or human buddhas, are seven in number; they are those personages, celebrated in legends, of whom Śākyamuni is the latest.[70] The second are called *anupapādakas*, that is to say, "without parents"; and *dhyāni buddhas*, that is to say, "buddhas of contemplation." The theistic school of Nepal presumes that an *ādibuddha*, or primordial buddha, existing by himself, infinite and omniscient, created these five buddhas, called collectively *pañca dhyāni buddhas*, through five acts of his contemplative power. Each of these divine buddhas at birth received the double energy of science and contemplation to which he owed his existence; and by this double strength, each one gave birth to a dhyāni bodhisattva, who is to the progenitor buddha like a son to his father. These bodhisattvas are considered the true authors of the created world; but the works they produce are perishable. Three of these creations have already ceased to exist; the one to which we belong is the fourth, that is to say, that which is the work of the fourth bodhisattva, named Avalokiteśvara or Padmapāṇi.[71] This is

p. 473) have cited, although with some alterations, the names of the five superhuman buddhas (*Mémoires de l'Académie des sciences de Saint-Pétersbourg*, 1:95, note 7).

69. *Asiatic Researches*, vol. 16, p. 440ff. It is by design that I so limit this summary; one knows that Mr. Schmidt has set forth a different opinion concerning the dhyāni buddhas, to which I shall return later.

70. Among the seven buddhas, the first three belong to ages prior to the one in which we live; the following four appeared in our present system; Śākyamuni is the fourth and Maitreya must be his successor ("Sapta Buddha Stotra," in *Asiatic Researches*, vol. 16, p. 453ff. compare to Schmidt, *Mémoires de l'Académie des sciences de Saint-Pétersbourg*, 1:105 and 106). Mr. Schmidt is of the opinion that these three buddhas could have appeared in a period of expansion of this system. (*ibid.*, 2:65). Wilson has shown (*Asiatic Researches*, vol. 16, p. 455) that the special worship rendered to the seven buddhas from among the innumerable multitude of ancient personages of this name was not unique to Nepalese Buddhism. I add that we will find it also in the Buddhism of the South; but I must defer what I have to say on this point until the moment I occupy myself with the predecessors of Śākya, in the Historical Sketch of Buddhism.

71. "Notices of the Languages, Literature and Religion of the Bauddhas of Nepal and Bhot," in *Asiatic Researches*, vol. 26, p. 440ff.

what explains the particular worship of which this bodhisattva is the object on the part of the Nepalese and the Tibetans, who sometimes regard him almost as the supreme and only god. In conclusion, and to summarize, this is the double list of these divine buddhas and bodhisattvas, fruits of the contemplation of a primitive and ideal ādibuddha.

BUDDHAS	BODHISATTVAS
1. Vairocana	Samantabhadra
2. Akṣobhya	Vajrapāṇi
3. Ratnasambhava	Ratnapāṇi
4. Amitābha	Padmapāṇi
5. Amoghasiddha	Viśvapāṇi[72]

From the succinct presentation I have just made of this system, it follows that the theistic school of Nepal links this double series of divine buddhas and bodhisattvas to a superior buddha who plays exactly the same role in this school as Brahma, the absolute and impersonal being among the brahmans. However, an observation by Mr. Hodgson leads us to believe that this system of ideal buddhas is susceptible to a materialistic interpretation;[73] and this author expressly says so in another place, when he attributes the belief in the existence of dhyāni buddhas to the Svābhāvikas, or naturalists, true atheists, who say that all things, gods as well as humans, are born from *svabhāva*, or from their own nature.[74] Moreover, this opinion is placed beyond doubt by a passage of utmost importance by a Buddhist author that Mr. Hodgson cites elsewhere, and according to which the five dhyāni buddhas correspond to the five elements, to the five sensible qualities, and to the five senses, that is to say, they are pure personifications of natural phenomena of the sensible world.[75] The testimony of this text is,

72. *Ibid.*, p. 442.

73. *Ibid.*, p. 441.

74. Hodgson, "European Speculations on Buddhism," in *Journal of the Asiatic Society of Bengal*, vol. 3, p. 503. See the additions at the end of this volume.

75. Hodgson, "Quotations from Original Sanscrit Authorities," in *Journal of the Asiatic Society of Bengal*, vol. 5, p. 76, note. See also *Quarterly Oriental Magazine*, 1827, vol. 9, p. 221, note. Such is the relation that the Buddhists of Nepal establish between the five dhyāni buddhas and the present world. That which Mr. Schmidt accepts and which he sets forth with as much talent as science in his first two memoranda on some fundamental dogmas of Buddhism (*Mémoires de l'Académie des sciences de Saint-Pétersbourg*, 1:104ff. and 223ff.) is completely unknown to the Buddhists of Nepal. According to this theory, each buddha has three distinct natures, each of which belongs to its distinct world. The first nature is that of abstraction, of the absolute state, of being in itself; it only exists as such in the first world, in that of emptiness: it is the Buddha in nirvāṇa. The second nature is the manifestation of the Buddha amid power and holiness; it appears in the second world: it is the dhyāni buddha. The third is his manifestation in a human form; it appears in the third world: it is the manuṣi buddha. In this way, the Buddha belongs at once to the three worlds because he is essentially limitless. Mr. Schmidt supports this theory with a remarkable passage from the *Suvarṇaprabhāsa*, the text of which I

to my eyes, decisive, and I do not hesitate to believe that the system just set forth can exist rather well with the conception of nature as well as with that of God, especially when one gives to the first a portion of the attributes one recognizes in the other. The *Lotus of the Good Law* furnished more than one argument of great weight in favor of this opinion. One must admit at the outset that it is a book that contains nothing that the naturalistic school, as the extracts and the analyses of Mr. Hodgson represent it, cannot avow.[76] One does not find there the least trace of the idea of God, or of any buddha superior to the last of the human buddhas, to Śākyamuni. Here, as in the simple sūtras, it is Śākya who is the most important, the first of beings; and although the imagination of the compiler endowed him with all the perfections of science and virtue accepted among the Buddhists; although Śākya already takes on a mythological character, when he declares that it has been a long time since he fulfilled the duties of a buddha, and that he must still fulfill them for a long time despite his imminent death, which does not destroy his eternity; although in the end he is depicted creating buddhas from his body who are like ideal images and reproductions of his mortal person, nowhere is Śākyamuni called God; nowhere does he receive the title *ādibuddha*; nowhere do his work and his acts of heroism, as one calls them, have the slightest relation to these evolutions by which, according to the theistical school, the five buddhas called *dhyāni* come from an eternal and absolute buddha.

Well, this book in which the idea of God and, to speak like the Buddhists of Nepal, the idea of an ādibuddha, is so unknown[77] offers obvious traces of the system of the superhuman buddhas in this passage of the twenty-second chap-

unfortunately do not have but which must have been, I do not doubt, composed originally in Sanskrit. Thus far, I have not encountered in the books at my disposal any text that has a direct relation to this doctrine, to which I shall return when I discuss the buddhas prior to Śākya. I can, nevertheless, say at this point that, in my opinion, it is going a little too far to present this theory as the expression of pure Buddhism and as belonging to all schools, except that of Nepal. I am not afraid to advance that it is unknown, as are all the buddhas it deals with, to the Buddhists of Ceylon, and to the most ancient form of Northern Buddhism.

76. "Quotations from Original Sanscrit Authorities," in *Journal of the Asiatic Society of Bengal*, vol. 5, p. 71ff.

77. Mr. Schmidt informs us, in more than one passage of his memoranda, that as much can be said of the Mongol books, where the existence of the five superhuman buddhas is frequently referred to, whereas that of the ādibuddha of the Nepalese is not mentioned anywhere (*Mémoires de l'Académie des sciences de Saint-Pétersbourg*, 1:97ff. and 222ff.). This author saw well that the notion of a supreme God represented by Ādibuddha was foreign to primitive Buddhism; and he has refuted with success, although slightly severely, the theory Mr. A. Rémusat had established on the existence of this notion borrowed from the theistical Buddhism of Nepal ("Über einige Grundlehren des Buddhismus," in *Mémoires de l'Académie des sciences de Saint-Pétersbourg*, 2:3ff.). I think that doubt can no longer exist on this point since Csoma de Kőrös has established, through the authority of the Tibetan books, that the belief in an ādibuddha had not been introduced into central India before the tenth century of our era ("Note on the Kāla chakra," in *Journal of the Asiatic Society of Bengal*, vol. 2, p. 57ff. "Analysis of the Sher-chin," etc., in *Asiatic Researches*, vol. 20, p. 488).

ter, where we learn that the buddha Amitābha, that is to say, the fourth of the buddhas of contemplation, is contemporary, although in another universe, with Śākyamuni, the sole and unique buddha of our world.[78] And complementing the notion that this passage expresses, a couplet of the twenty-fourth chapter shows us Avalokiteśvara, the bodhisattva renowned as the son of this Amitābha, standing next to the buddha, his father, who is the sovereign of a world in the West that is as ideal as he is.[79]

I also recognize another trace of it at the beginning of the twenty-fourth chapter, where the bodhisattva Samantabhadra miraculously comes to attend the assembly presided over by Śākyamuni, to show him his satisfaction. For Samantabhadra is none other than the first of the bodhisattvas or the son of the first of the divine buddhas of the list cited above. These texts, I repeat, support this opinion, that the theory of the five superhuman buddhas can belong to a sect other than that of the theists—in other words, that this theory is not necessarily linked to the conception of an ādibuddha, as the latter assert it. But whatever this opinion may be, which I do not hesitate to dwell on, the principal point of the present discussion is no less solidly established; and this point is that one of the developed sūtras, the most esteemed of Nepal, bears the obvious imprint of ideas connected with this system.

Now, it is a good time to say that nothing of what I have just described exists in the simple sūtras or the *Divyāvādana.* The idea of one or several superhuman buddhas, and that of bodhisattvas created by them, are conceptions as foreign to these books as that of an ādibuddha or a God. Mr. Hodgson, it is true, has cited two very curious pieces extracted from the *Divyāvadāna*, which expressly establish the existence of Ādibuddha, supreme and ideal form of the human buddha Śākyamuni,[80] and which would thus trace back to the sūtras and the avadānas that I examine, conceptions which, to my eyes, appear only in other works that I shall discuss later. But I have searched in vain for these two passages in the two copies of the *Divyāvadāna* at my disposal. I conclude from that either that the manuscripts consulted by Mr. Hodgson are more complete than ours, and that they possibly contain some works of a different character from those that occupy the largest place there, or that the title *Divyāvadāna* of the extract has been applied to these two fragments, through one of these typographical transpositions that Mr. Hodgson has already complained about on the occasion of the same memorandum in which he included them. In whatever way one explains this difficulty, I persist in saying that the conceptions just indicated are completely for-

78. *Le lotus de la bonne loi*, chap. 22, fol. 220a of the text; p. 251 of the translation.

79. *Le lotus de la bonne loi*, chap. 24, fols. 223b and 234a of the text; p. 267 of the translation.

80. "Quotations from Original Sanscrit Authorities," in *Journal of the Asiatic Society of Bengal*, vol. 5, pp. 72 and 82.

eign to the sūtras of the aforementioned collection. Whatever attention I have brought to the reading of these treatises, I could not discover the slightest trace of this vast mythological apparatus in which the imagination frolics through infinite spaces, amid gigantic forms and numbers. I have never encountered any but the buddhas renowned as human, of whom Śākyamuni is the last; nor did I see anyplace where this qualification of human buddhas was given to them, since the conception of a buddha that would not be a man who has reached the highest degree of holiness is outside the circle of ideas which constitute the very core of the simple sūtras. In short, the buddhas prior to Śākya have in no way the divine character of the buddhas of contemplation; like him, they are men, sons of brahmans or kings; and the accounts where they appear have such a resemblance to those in which Śākya plays the leading role that by hearing them, if this latter ever recounted them, his disciples could have said to him, like the Latin poet, *mutato nomine de te fabula narratur.*

Among all the features that I have indicated in the course of this discussion, the one I just elaborated on is, without objection, the most important, because it touches on the very core of the doctrine. Whatever interpretation one gives to it, it distinguishes the developed sūtras from the other sūtras in the most definite manner, and it adds to the various indices that have authorized me to make of the second a category of books that is quite different from the category of the first, despite the commonality of titles. Other details could doubtless be assembled here in favor of the distinction on which I insist; but none would be of such great value as those I have just set forth. I shall content myself with indicating a single one, to which I do not attach a very great importance, because it can be, as I will say, the result of an interpolation. I want to speak of the magical formulas or charms called *mantras* or *dhāraṇīs*, which belong properly to the part of Buddhist literature called *tantra*, which I will discuss in a special section. These formulas, where some signifying words are lost among a multitude of unintelligible syllables, have found a place in the developed sūtras, and the *Lotus of the Good Law* notably has a chapter dedicated to the charms that the bodhisattvas promise to one who possesses the *Lotus* itself.[81] One can imagine without difficulty that once the belief in the efficacy of such formulas is accepted, they could have been introduced afterward into such respected books as the developed sūtras of the Mahāyāna. But it is permissible to ask oneself why these formulas do not equally slip into the sūtras I call simple. Therefore, I have examined with very great attention all the treatises of the two anthologies of the *Divyāvadāna* and the *Avadānaśataka*; and the most striking trace of *dhāraṇī* or magical formula I have encountered in them is found in the legend of Śārdūlakarṇa, a legend from which I will borrow some passages related to the castes, and that I suspect

81. *Le lotus de la bonne loi*, chap. 21, fol. 207b of the text; p. 238ff. of the translation.

to be more modern than several other legends of these two collections.[82] One must thus regard as established that mantras and dhāraṇīs are quite foreign to the simple sūtras, while one finds more or less numerous traces of them in the developed sūtras. Whatever the cause of this fact might be, it constitutes in itself a notable difference that it is important to add to the other characteristics I have assembled above. So, and to summarize, the sūtras that I regard as primitive, that is to say, as closest to the preaching of Śākya, remain shielded from the double influence that the system of celestial buddhas and bodhisattvas and the category of tantras or most especially of dhāraṇīs, that is to say, the formulas that belong to this category of books, exercised on the developed sūtras.

How is it now possible to understand the existence of these two categories of sūtras? It seems to me that the aforementioned passage of Faxian and the results of my research on the ancient schools into which the Buddhism of the North is divided furnish a very satisfying explanation of this difficulty. Faxian attests in twenty places of his account that in his time numerous schools existed, living peacefully in proximity with one another, under distinct masters and ordinarily in separate monasteries. The Mahāyāna followers are, among others, frequently mentioned, and distinguished by this very fact from monks engaged in the study of the sūtras, or, as it is translated according to Faxian, of the precepts. Indeed, nothing is easier to understand than the simultaneous existence of several Buddhist schools, and the testimony of the Chinese traveler is here fully confirmed by that of the philosophical texts we will discuss below in the section dedicated to the metaphysics of Buddhism, and where we will see a sect of Sautrāntikas, or followers of the sūtras. But once one recognizes this point, that the simple sūtras belonged to one school and the developed sūtras to another, for example, to the school of the Mahāyāna, so numerous in the fourth century of our era, it still remains to be investigated whether these two schools are equally ancient, that is to say, if they are due to the sole fact of the redaction of the Buddhist scriptures in three great categories, a fact which, I shall explain later, belongs to the first period of the history of Buddhism. That is, one sees, the true point of the question, the truly historical point. For, either one succeeds in establishing that the developed sūtras are contemporary with the simple sūtras, and then it will be necessary to place the one and the other at the same rank among the sources from which one may draw knowledge of primitive Buddhism. Or, if it only becomes possible, on the contrary, to show that these two categories of books belong to different epochs, it is hardly necessary to say that one of them should be placed at a greater distance than the other from the epoch when the doctrine of Śākya was committed to writing for the first time. If, among the books of Nepal that are in France today, there was a history of Buddhism to be found, or only

82. *Śārdūlakarṇa*, in *Divyāvadāna*, fol. 218a of the MS of the Société Asiatique.

a chronological summary of the principal events that marked its origin and development, the question I have just posed could doubtless be resolved in a direct manner. But up to now we lack the history of Buddhism almost completely; and when it is a question of determining, as is the case here, the relative epochs of two works or of two schools, one places oneself in a kind of vicious circle, searching to deduce some historical elements from the analysis of works of whose history one is ignorant. The study of the texts themselves is, however, the sole guide we must follow in order to depart from these obscurities; and one knows what light has been cast on facts totally unknown to history through the comparative examination of ancient texts. Also, despite the silence that the Buddhist works I have consulted maintain on the differences that distinguish the developed sūtras from the more simple sūtras and on the question of whether one and the other have been written in the same epoch, even despite the presumption that this silence creates in favor of the opinion that presents these two kinds of books as belonging equally to the first epoch of the redaction of the Buddhist scriptures, I do not hesitate to believe that the vaipulya sūtras are subsequent to the others, or in other words, that the simple sūtras are closer to the preaching of Śākyamuni than the developed sūtras.

The reasons I can give in favor of this opinion are of two kinds: one, which is intrinsic, results from the very study of the ordinary sūtras compared to the developed sūtras; the other, which is extrinsic, is furnished to me by some facts belonging to the general history of Indian Buddhism; I refer for the presentation of the second to the history of the Nepalese collection and to the comparison I will make with that of Ceylon, and I focus here exclusively on the first. I shall commence by responding to an objection that one would perhaps wish to draw from the oft-cited classification of the Buddhist scriptures into three great categories: the Sūtras, or precepts; the Vinaya, or discipline; and the Abhidharma, or metaphysics. Why, one could say, would the developed sūtras, which already bear the title *mahāyāna* (great vehicle) by universal acknowledgment, not belong to the category of books dedicated to metaphysics? Why would one not make the most simple sūtras into the category of the true sūtras, the first category of the inspired scriptures? In short, what reason prevents one from regarding these books as emanating from the preaching of the last buddha to the same degree, and, equally, as written at the same time? This reason, I am not afraid to advance, is that which, in the silence of history, would prevent one from placing the Letters of St. Augustine and the Epistles of St. Paul at the same rank; in order to rule out this comparison that is concerned only with form, one would be warranted in saying that because Saint Augustine cites Saint Paul at every instant, and because he never leaves us in doubt for a single moment on the fact of the apostle's anteriority to him, I would say that the Christianity of Saint Augustine is much more the Christianity of Saint Paul than the Buddhism of the developed sūtras is that of the ordinary sūtras. Moreover, I beg the reader to weigh carefully the proper value of this title *vaipulya sūtra*, or developed sūtra, in opposition to that of *sūtra* properly speaking, of *sūtra*, in other words, without any epithet. If the sūtras of this latter species were somewhere called *abridged sūtras*, I would imagine that one could maintain that they imply an earlier category of similar books, of which they are only the extracts. But who would ever dare to assert, after having read the sūtras of the *Divyāvadāna* and one of the developed sūtras, that one will decide that a single simple sūtra is the extract of a vaipulya sūtra? It seems to me much more natural to conclude from this very qualification *developed* that the treatises that bear it distinguish themselves from the other sūtras through the development of the matters contained in them. There is nothing more accurate, indeed, than this title; nothing better conveys the true nature of these works, which are in some way doubled by this poetic exposition, or rather by this paraphrase in verse that expands its content. I have already recognized in this case an obvious sign of posteriority; I refer to what I said above, in discussing the exterior form of our two categories of sūtras. I only repeat here that this characteristic seems to me to give a great weight to my opinion on the posteriority of the developed sūtras in relation to the ordinary sūtras.

But the fact of a poetic paraphrase that is the simple repetition of the text is not the only indication of development that it is possible to note in the vaipulya sūtras. I leave aside the various editions of the *Prajñāpāramitā*, these almost monstrous sūtras, where it seems that it takes on itself the task of realizing the ideal of diffusion; I will return to it later. I choose another developed sūtra, the *Gaṇḍavyūha*, which belongs to the nine dharmas, that is to say, to these books that are the object of particular veneration in Nepal. Next, I propose to a reader versed in the knowledge of Sanskrit and endowed, moreover, with a robust patience to read the first fifty leaves of this treatise, and then to say whether it seems to him that such a work is a primitive book, an ancient book, one of these books on which religions are founded, a sacred code, in short, if he recognizes in it the character of a doctrine still in its first beginnings; if he apprehends the trace of the efforts of proselytism; if he encounters the struggles of a new belief against an order of previous ideas; if he discovers in it the society in whose milieu the preaching is tested. Either I am gravely mistaken or, after such a reading, the one whose testimony I invoke will find in this book nothing other than the developments of a complete doctrine, triumphant, which believes itself to be without rival; nothing other than the peaceful and monotonous conceptions of the life of the cloisters; nothing other than vague images of an ideal existence that calmly slips away into regions of absolute perfection, far from the noisy and passionate agitation of the world. Thus, what I say about the *Gaṇḍavyūha* applies almost as rigorously to the other great sūtras, to the *Samādhirāja*, the *Daśabhūmīśvara*, for example. And in the other developed sūtras, such as the *Lalitavistara* and the *Lotus of the Good Law*, where something more distinguishable and more real than the ideal virtues of bodhisattvas appears, where the life of Śākyamuni is related and where beautiful parables are recounted that give such a high idea of the preaching of the last buddha, in these sūtras, I say, the traces of development let themselves be so often recognized that we are constantly led to suppose that these books are but working at their leisure on an already existent theme.

Well, it is here that the difference and the anteriority of the simple sūtras relative to the vaipulya sūtras appears clearly; everything lacking in the second is found in the first. The ordinary sūtras show us Śākyamuni Buddha preaching his doctrine in the midst of a society that, judging from the legends in which he plays a role, was profoundly corrupt. His teaching is above all moral; and although metaphysics is not forgotten, it certainly occupies a less grand position than the theory of virtues imposed by the law of the Buddha, virtues among which charity, patience, and chastity are without objection at the first rank. The law, as Śākya calls it, is not set forth dogmatically in these books; it is only mentioned there, most often in a vague manner, and presented in its applications rather than in its principles. In order to deduce from such works a systematic exposition of the belief of the Buddhists, it would be necessary to have a very great number of them; still, it is not certain that one would be able to succeed in drawing a complete picture of Buddhist morality and philosophy by this means; for the beliefs appear there, so to speak, in action, and certain points of doctrine recur there on each page, while others are hardly mentioned, or not mentioned at all. But this circumstance, which for us is a true imperfection, also has its advantages from the historical perspective. It is a certain index of the authenticity of these books, and it proves that no systematic effort attempted to complete them afterward, or to place them, through later additions, at the level of progress that Buddhism certainly reached in the course of time. The developed sūtras have, as far as doctrine is concerned, a marked advantage over the simple sūtras, for the theory there proves to be more advanced from the dual perspective of dogma and metaphysics; but it is precisely this particularity which makes me believe that the vaipulya sūtras are later than the simple sūtras. These latter make us witness to the birth and the first developments of Buddhism; and if they are not contemporary with Śākya himself, they at least have preserved for us the tradition of his teaching very faithfully. Treatises of this kind could doubtless have been imitated and composed afterward in the silence of the monasteries; but even in accepting that we have only imitations of the original books, all readers of good faith who study them in the Sanskrit manuscripts of Nepal will be forced to agree that they are still closer to the preaching of Śākya than the developed sūtras. This is the very point I desire to establish at present, it is the one that it is important to shield from all contestation; at whatever date subsequent research must one day place the most simple sūtras, whether they go back to the time of the first disciples of Śākya or they come as far as the epoch of the last council of the North, is of little importance; the relation that seems to me to exist between them and the developed sūtras will not change; only the distance that separates one from the other could increase or decrease.

If, as I have every reason to believe, the preceding observations are well founded, I am entitled to say that what there is in common between the developed sūtras and the simple sūtras is the framing, the action, the theory of moral virtues, that of transmigration, of rewards and pains, of causes and effects, subjects that belong equally to all schools; but these various points are treated, in the one and the other, with differences of proportion that are quite characteristic. I have shown how the framing of the developed sūtras was more vast than that of the simple sūtras; that of the first is almost boundless; that of the second is restricted to the limits of plausibility. The action, although the same on both sides, is not performed for the same listeners in the developed sūtras as in the simple sūtras; it is always Śākyamuni who teaches; but instead of these brahmans and merchants whom he converts in the simple sūtras, in the developed sūtras it is bodhisattvas, as fabulous as the worlds from which they depart, who come to attend his teaching. The scene of the first is India, the actors are humans and some inferior divinities; and save for the power to make miracles that Śākya and his foremost disciples possess, what occurs there seems natural and plausible. On the contrary, everything that the imagination can conceive as immense in space and time is still too confining for the scene of the developed sūtras. The actors there are these imaginary bodhisattvas, with infinite virtues, with endless names one cannot pronounce, with bizarre and almost ridiculous titles, where the oceans, the rivers, the waves, the rays, the suns are coupled with qualities of unmerited perfection in a manner most puerile and least instructive, because it is without effort. No one is left to convert; everyone believes, and each is quite sure to become a buddha one day, in a world of diamonds or lapis lazuli. The consequence of all this is that the more developed the sūtras are, the poorer they are in historical details; and the farther they penetrate into metaphysical doctrine, the more they distance themselves from society and become estranged from what occurs there. Is it not enough to make us believe that these books were written in countries and in periods in which Buddhism had reached its full development, and to assure all desirable likelihood to the opinion I sought to establish, namely the anteriority of the ordinary sūtras, which takes us back to times and countries where Buddhism encountered its adversaries at every moment, and was obliged by preaching and by the practice of moral virtues to do battle with them?

I acknowledge that in order to share this opinion knowingly, the reader would need to compare a certain number of simple sūtras to other developed sūtras such as the *Lotus of the Good Law*; but perhaps the time is not far off when these interesting monuments will come to light. While waiting, I have believed that I must set forth the results that a careful reading of the six hundred sixty-four pages of the *Divyāvadāna* has provided me. I do not believe that I go too far in saying that if one does not find in them a quite complete exposition of Buddhism, one will see in them at least the faithful history of its first efforts and something like the exact picture of its establishment amid Brahmanical society. It is this, if I am not mistaken, that gives the sūtras and the legends an interest that books in which beliefs are more fixed and more dogmatically set forth would not have. Such sūtras illuminate a very important point in the history of Buddhism, namely, its relation with Brahmanism, a point on which the purely speculative treatises maintain an almost complete silence. And this circumstance suffices in itself to establish that these sūtras were written when these two cults were living close to each other, just as the presence of some Buddhist monks in several Brahmanical dramas proves that these dramas were written in an epoch when followers of the Buddha still existed in India. One sees that the study of the sūtras envisaged from this particular point of view provides a new confirmation in favor of the opinion that makes me regard them as the monuments closest to the preaching of Śākyamuni.

It settles, moreover, in a definitive way, a question which has been recently revived, that of knowing whether Brahmanism or Buddhism is the more ancient, and which someone has wished to decide in favor of this latter cult, on the grounds that the most ancient epigraphic monuments one finds in India belong to Buddhism and not to Brahmanism. Without entering at this hour into the examination of each of these monuments, which have still not been studied, in my view, with sufficient attention or critique, I will say that from the existence of ancient Buddhist inscriptions written in Pāli, and even from the anteriority of these inscriptions with regard to Brahmanical monuments of the same order written in Sanskrit, one should have to conclude not that Pāli is prior to Sanskrit, which is impossible, not that Buddhism is prior to Brahmanism, which is just as impossible, but that the sense and the processes of history were produced and applied among the Buddhists rather than among the brahmans. Still, one should recognize that these processes did not undergo truly great developments among them, since we possess no more coherent history of Buddhist India than of Brahmanical India. But what should be said now in the presence of the formal testimony of the sacred texts of Nepal, where Brahmanical society appears completely, with its religion, its castes, and its laws? Will one maintain that the society to whose existence the books testify was originally Buddhist, and that the brahmans, who later became its masters, borrowed certain elements from it, to which they gave the form in which one finds them in the *Law of Manu* and in the epics of the *Rāmāyaṇa* and the *Mahābhārata*? Or will one imagine that the names of divinities and the Brahmanical castes, with which the sūtras of the North are replete, were introduced into them afterward? And by whom? By the

Buddhists, no doubt, in order to be credited with the honors of a superiority, or at least of an equality they would not have been able to preserve in India with regard to the brahmans; or by the brahmans, perhaps, in order to date their existence back to a more ancient epoch than that in which they actually appear? As if, on the one hand, the redactors of the Buddhist books would have had an interest in showing Buddhism detaching itself from Brahmanism, if Brahmanism had not, indeed, existed in their time; and as if, on the other, they would have permitted the brahmans to come in afterward in order to slip their odious name among the names of Śākya and his disciples. Indeed, it is not possible to depart from this alternative: the sūtras that attest to the existence of Brahmanical society were either written around the time of Śākya, or a very long time after him. If they are contemporary with Śākya, the society they describe existed then, because one could not imagine why they would have spoken in such detail of a society that was not the one in which Śākya appeared. If they were written a very long time after Śākya, one does not understand any better how the Brahmanical gods and personages occupy so vast a place there, because long after the Buddha, Brahmanism was profoundly separated from Buddhism, and because these two cults had but a single ground on which they could meet, that of polemic and war. It is sufficient, I think, to raise these simple hypotheses, especially because the monuments that give rise to these different suppositions will soon be the object of a special examination on my part. With a small number of facts and a great use of dialectic, it is easy to arrive at consequences that are most bizarre and most contrary to common sense; and if I could convince myself that polemic serves in general to bring to light something other than the passions or vanity of one who indulges in them, I would find material for long and laborious argumentation on the subject I am considering at this moment. But the reader will doubtless prefer that I show him, by way of some features, the point of view from which the sūtras, and I add the legends, lead us to envisage the society within which Buddhism was born and propagated.

In the plan of my work, I cannot note all the indications, one by one, attesting that at the time when Śākyamuni traveled through India to teach his law, Brahmanical society had reached its highest degree of development. One might as well translate the *Divyāvadāna* in its entirety and the hundred legends of the *Avadānaśataka*, so numerous are the proofs of the fact I put forward, so many times are they repeated in the sūtras and legends of these voluminous collections. But it is always possible, and it is here necessary, to indicate some of the characteristic features of the society in which Śākya appears, fulfilling his mission. Thus, I will focus on two points in particular, which, as one knows, are closely related in India, religion and political organization; and I shall show through some extracts what the redactors of the sūtras and Buddhist legends of the North teach us about these two great elements of society as it existed in India at the time of Śākya.

The divinities whose names appear in the sūtras of the Nepalese collection are: Nārāyaṇa,[83] Śiva, Varuṇa, Kuvera, Brahmā[84] or Pitāmahā,[85] Śakra or Vāsava,[86] Hari[87] or Janārdana,[88] Śaṃkara,[89] which is only another name for Śiva, and Viśvakarman.[90] After these gods, well known in the Brahmanical pantheon, come the multitude of inferior divinities such as the devas, the nāgas, the asuras, the yakṣas, the garuḍas, the kinnaras, the mahoragas, the gandharvas, the piśācas, the dānavas, and other good or evil genii whose names are encountered at every moment in the legends and in the preachings of Śākyamuni.[91] At the head of these secondary divinities appears Indra, ordinarily called Śakra or Śacīpati, the husband of Śacī.[92] Among all the gods, it is he whose name occurs most often in the sūtras and the legends. There, he ordinarily appears to Śākyamuni, with whom he has frequent conversations, and he receives the title *Kauśika,* a title he bears in the Upaniṣads of the Brahmanical Vedas. His name appears with that of Upendra, one of the most ancient epithets of Viṣṇu, in the very formula by which the legends express that a monk has reached the degree said to be that of the arhats, a formula composed in this way: "He becomes one of those who deserve that the devas, with Indra and Upendra, respect them, honor them, and salute them."[93]

All these divinities are those of the people among whom Śākyamuni lives with his monks. They are, on the part of all the castes, the object of a continuous and exclusive worship: one requests children from them;[94] sailors in fear of perishing implore them to be delivered from danger.[95] But their power is not regarded as absolute by the Buddhists, and it is inferior to that of the Buddha. Śākya, indeed, is depicted saving from shipwreck merchants who have invoked these gods in vain;[96] and as for the power to bestow children that the people attribute to them,

83. *Avadānaśataka*, fol. 53a.

84. *Koṭikarṇa*, in *Divyāvadāna*, fol. 1. *Purṇa, ibid.*, fol. 20b. *Maitrakanyaka*, fol. 327b. *Paṃśupradāna*, fol. 178a. *Avadānaśataka*, fols. 6b, 31b, 49b, 55b, 80b, 112b, 169b, 242b.

85. *Maitrakanyaka*, in *Divyāvadāna*, fol. 327b.

86. *Avadānaśataka*, fol. 31b.

87. *Pūrṇa*, in *Divyāvadāna*, fol. 20b.

88. *Maitrakanyaka, ibid.*, fol. 327b.

89. *Pūrṇa, ibid.*, fol. 20b. *Maitrakanyaka, ibid.*, fol. 327b.

90. *Maitreya, ibid.*, fol. 28b.

91. *Pūrṇa, ibid.*, fol. 20b. *Aśoka, ibid.*, fol. 66a. *Prātihārya, ibid.*, fol. 69b and passim.

92. *Pūrṇa, ibid.*, fol. 20b.

93. *Supriya*, in *Divyāvadāna*, fol. 46a. *Avadānaśataka*, fols. 39b, 148b, 150a.

94. *Koṭikarṇa, ibid.*, fol. 1a. *Maitrakanyaka, ibid.*, fol. 327b.

95. *Pūrṇa, ibid.*, fol. 20b. *Dharmaruci, ibid.*, fol. 114a. *Samudra*, in *Avadānaśataka*, fol. 190b.

96. *Dharmaruci, ibid.*, fol. 114b.

this is how the redactors of the sūtras contest its existence: "This is a maxim accepted in the world, that these are prayers addressed to gods who bring about the birth of sons and daughters; but this is not so; for otherwise each would have a hundred sons, all sovereign monarchs."[97] The subordination of gods to the Buddha is expressed and somehow regularized in the following passage: "It is a rule that when the blessed buddhas conceive a mundane thought, at the same instant Śakra, Brahmā, and the other devas have knowledge of the thought of the blessed ones."[98] So we see, in more than one passage, Śakra, the Indra of the devas, as he is ordinarily called, coming to assist Śākyamuni in his undertakings.[99] The legend of Śākyamuni, found embedded among the diffuse developments of the *Lalitavistara*, recounts that when the young son of king Śuddhodana, who had not yet taken on the religious character, was conducted to the temple of the gods at Kapilavastu, the inanimate statues of Śiva, Skanda, Nārāyaṇa, Kuvera, Candra, Sūrya, Vaiśravaṇa, Śakra, and those of the lokapālas all rose from their seat to bow before the young man.[100]

And it is not solely to the superiority of the Buddha that the gods are compelled to render homage: a simple monk, Pūrṇa, also makes his power felt by a yakṣa, who watched over a forest of sandalwood.[101] Another monk, Upagupta, a contemporary of king Aśoka,[102] triumphs by his irresistible power over Māra, sin incarnate, who finds refuge in Brahmā to implore his help; Brahmā responds to him: "Unquestionably, my strength is immense, but it is not equal to that of a son of the Tathāgata"; and the god counsels Māra to make an act of faith in the Buddha.[103] Finally, to worship the gods is less meritorious in the eyes of Śākya than the practice of moral virtue. I find, on this subject, in an avadāna, a passage that places the accomplishment of the duties that morality imposes above the most venerated objects of the brahmans and the people, namely Brahmā,

97. *Koṭikarṇa*, *ibid.*, fol. 1. *Avadānaśataka*, fols. 6b, 49b.

98. *Maitreya*, *ibid.*, fol. 30b.

99. *Aśoka*, *ibid.*, fol. 67a. *Prātihārya*, *ibid.*, fols. 79a and b. *Avadānaśataka*, fols. 14b. *Kapphina*, in *Avadānaśataka*, fol. 211a.

100. *Lalitavistara*, chap. 8, fol. 68b of my manuscript.

101. *Pūrṇa*, in *Divyāvadāna*, fol. 20a ff.

102. I say Aśoka, without distinguishing whether it is Kālāśoka or Dharmāśoka, not wishing to give to the tradition of the North more precision than it actually has. Indeed, I will establish in my Historical Sketch that the texts of the North generally confuse into a single personage the two Aśokas whom the Pāli texts of the South distinguish. See, meanwhile, a proof of this fact in the anthology of Mr. Schmidt (*Der Weise und der Thor*, trans. p. 218). I only add here that, for the Sinhalese, the Aśoka in question in the text would be Kālāśoka.

103. *Paṃśupradāna*, in *Divyāvadāna*, fol. 178a and b. The same fact is recounted, although in slightly different terms, in a legend of the *Uligerün Dalai*, which is identical in its content to that of this passage I extract and that Mr. Schmidt has translated (*Mémoires de l'Académie des sciences de Saint-Pétersbourg*, 2:28). This legend is found in a more complete form and with more details in the anthology of Tibetan legends (*Der Weise und der Thor*, p. 386ff.), which is, as Mr. Schmidt conveyed to us long ago, the Tibetan original of the *Uligerün Dalai* (*Forschungen im Gebiete der älteren religiösen, politischen und literärischen Bildungsgeschichte der Völker Mittel-Asiens, vorzüglich der Mongolen und Tibeter*, p. 175).

sacrifice, fire, and the household gods, and which shows at the same time the nature of the attacks of which the gods of India were the object on the part of Śākya.

One day when the Bhagavat was in Śrāvastī, at Jetavana, in the garden of Anāthapiṇḍika, he addressed the monks in this way: "Brahmā, O monks, is with families in which the father and the mother are perfectly honored, perfectly venerated, served with a perfect happiness. Why is that? It is that, for a son of good family, a father and a mother are, according to the law, Brahmā himself. The preceptor, O monks, is with families in which the father and the mother are perfectly honored [etc., as above]. Why is that? It is that, for a son of good family, a father and a mother are, according to the law, the preceptor himself. The fire of sacrifice, O monks, is with families in which the father and the mother are perfectly honored [etc., as above]. Why is that? It is that, for a son of good family, a father and a mother are, according to the law, the fire of sacrifice itself. The [domestic] fire, O monks, is with families in which the father and the mother are perfectly honored [etc., as above]. Why is that? It is that, for a son of good family, a father and a mother are, according to the law, the domestic fire itself. The deva [doubtless Indra], O monks, is with families in which the father and the mother are perfectly honored [etc., as above]. Why is that? It is that, for a son of good family, a father and a mother are, according to the law, the deva himself."[104]

The testimonies I have just summarized clearly mark the relation of the popular gods of India to the founder of Buddhism. It is evident that Śākyamuni found their cult already existing, and that he did not invent it. He could say, and the authors of the legends could believe, that a buddha was superior, in this very life, to the greatest gods recognized in his time in India, to Brahmā and to Indra; but he did not create these gods, or Śiva and the others for the pleasure of making them the ministers of his will. The supernatural power with which he claimed to have been endowed was certainly enough for the execution of everything that he made Indra and the other inferior divinities accomplish; and I have the deep conviction that if Śākya did not find a pantheon around him entirely populated with the gods whose names I have provided, he did not have any need to invent it to ensure to his mission the authority that the people could refuse to a man. For, this is important to note, Śākya does not come, like the Brahmanical incarnations of Viṣṇu, to show the people an eternal and infinite god, descending to earth and preserving, in the mortal condition, the irresistible power of the divinity. He is the son of a king who becomes a monk and who has only the superiority of his virtue and his science to recommend him to the people.

The universally accepted belief in India that a great saintliness is necessarily accompanied by supernatural faculties is the only support he had to find in

104. *Avadānaśataka*, fol. 79b.

their mind;[105] but that was an immense help, and that gave him the means to build a past of ordeals and virtues to justify his mission. This past, however, was not exclusively divine; the Buddha had revolved, like all beings, in the eternally moving circle of transmigration; he had passed several existences in the bodies of animals, of the damned, of humans, and gods, in turn virtuous and criminal, rewarded and punished, but accumulating little by little the merits that would make him pleasing to the buddhas under whom he was living and assure him their blessing. In this system, one sees, Śākya is not dependent on any god; he has everything himself and by the grace of a previous buddha, whose origin is no more divine than his. The gods do nothing here; they do not create the Buddha, nor do they prevent him from taking form, since it is to the practice of virtue and to his personal efforts that he owes his character, which is more than divine. Far from it, the gods are only beings endowed with a power infinitely superior to that of man, but like him, subject to the fatal law of transmigration; and their existence does not seem to have any other reason than the need of the imagination to try to explain the creation of the universe, and to populate the infinite spaces it conceives beyond the visible world.

There is no reason, therefore, to pose the question of whether the gods mentioned in the sūtras and legends of Nepal are prior to Buddhism, or whether they were invented by the founder of this doctrine. For whoever reads just one of these treatises will not form the slightest doubt that the Indian pantheon existed at the time of Śākya. It will no longer be permissible to say that the brahmans borrowed their divinities from the Buddhists and that, excluding the Buddha alone, they accepted all the other personages who compose the Buddhist pantheon, for it is contrary to the truth. It is Śākyamuni, or if one wishes, it is these redactors of the legends who found and accepted, almost entirely, the Brahmanical gods, with this sole difference (a major difference, it is true), that they made them submissive to their Buddha, that is to say, the wisest of men. It is, I repeat, a point that can no longer be contested. What still remains to be studied is, first, the extent and the nature of the borrowings made by the Buddhists from the brahmans; second, the relation of these Brahmanical gods to those who belong in particular to the followers of Śākya, whom one sees somehow arrayed in the various worlds inhabited by intelligences superior to man. It will be necessary to note through attentive reading of all the Buddhist documents of the North whether the legends related to Śiva and to Viṣṇu, for example, were all equally widespread at the time of the first establishment or at least during the first centuries of Buddhism. One understands, without my insisting further, the importance of this research; it must cast a new light on the historical succession of Brahmanical beliefs, at the same time that it must be used to fix, in a more precise manner, the epoch

105. Benfey, "Indien," pp. 200 and 201, extract of the *Encyclopédie* of Ersch and Gruber.

when the Buddhist legends from which one draws its elements were written. As an example of the results one must expect from the study of the sūtras envisaged from this point of view, I will mention only one fact, which would merit being verified with texts more numerous than those we possess; it is that nowhere in the treatises of the *Divyāvadāna* have I found the name of Kṛṣṇa. Is this to say that the legends related to this personage, so celebrated at present in India, were not yet spread among the people, or that his name had not yet taken its place next to the other Brahmanical gods? I certainly would not venture to assert it, but the subject is most worthy of all the attention of the critic; for it is one of two things: either Kṛṣṇa was venerated in India with the almost divine character that the *Mahābhārata* ascribes to him when Śākyamuni appeared and when his preachings were written down; or his divinity was still not universally recognized at the time of Śākya and the first apostles of Buddhism. In the first case, one will have to explain the silence that the Buddhists maintain with regard to him; in the second, it will be necessary to recognize that the literary monuments of the brahmans in which Kṛṣṇa plays so great a role are subsequent to the preaching of Śākya and to the redaction of the books one has the right to regard as the most ancient written authorities of Buddhism.[106] But in one case as in the other, one must have acquired the certainty that none of the Buddhist works mention Kṛṣṇa among the divinities, according to me Brahmanical, who are accepted by Śākya himself.

Whatever the general solution might be to the problem just indicated, this circumstance that the name of Kṛṣṇa is absent in all the sūtras I have read accords with other indices to present Indian religion to us, just as these treatises offer it to us, in a slightly different light than that in which the Brahmanical Purāṇas show it to us. I do not hesitate to say that Brahmanism bears there a more ancient and more simple character than in the collections I just mentioned. Must this difference be attributed to the action of Buddhism, which would have made a choice among the divinities adored by the brahmans? Or does it come from the fact that the sūtras reproduce a tradition prior to that of the Purāṇas? I confess that between these two suppositions, it is the second that seems to me by far the more plausible. The sūtras appear to me to be contemporary with an epoch when the Vedas and the legends related to them constituted the core of Indian beliefs. I do not rely solely on these mentions of the Vedas that one notices on

106. I do not have any means to express myself more precisely on this interesting question. I will only recall that the superior judgment of Colebrooke had already raised doubts for him concerning the antiquity of the cult of Kṛṣṇa, and that this scholar was at the point of declaring that the development of the fables and legends that have made the son of Devakī into a god was subsequent to the establishment of Buddhism (*Miscellaneous Essays*, 2:197). One will perhaps find later that the considerable extension that the cult of Kṛṣṇa achieved was only a popular reaction against that of the Buddha, a reaction that was directed or entirely accepted by the brahmans.

almost every page of the simple sūtras; for this fact proves only the anteriority of one with regard to the other. I am much more struck by the role played in the Buddhist sūtras by a divinity equally celebrated in the Vedas and the Purāṇas, but who certainly encounters fewer rivals in the first than in the second. I wish to speak of Indra or Śakra, as he is called, of this god, hero of the Vedas, who appears more often in the sūtras than all the other gods combined. I do not wish to conclude from this that the Buddhist sūtras are contemporary with the Brahmanical Vedas; on the contrary, there is, for me, an immense distance between these two categories of books. I only wish to say that Brahmanism, as it appears in the sūtras, certainly offers an intermediate state of Indian religion, a state that more closely approaches the slightly naked simplicity of the Vedic beliefs than the exuberance of the developments that overburden the Purāṇas. I cannot help but think that at the time when the sūtras were written down, or to express myself in a less exclusive manner, at the time whose memory the sūtras preserve, Indian mythology was not yet enriched with this luxury of fables that sometimes have their point of departure in the Vedas, but which however are until now found in their entirety only in the Purāṇas.

The details that the sūtras provide us on the state of Indian society at the time of the preaching of Śākya are much more numerous and more important than those concerning the religion, and this difference is easy to understand. Indeed, the redactors of these treatises only had to discuss popular beliefs occasionally, and always more to refute them than to set them forth; whereas they could not pass in silence over the society in which Śākyamuni appeared, and which he encountered at every step. In this respect, the sūtras are almost all of a remarkable interest, and it would be impossible to extract everything that the most fascinating of these treatises contain of this kind without translating them entirely. I will, however, report here the most characteristic features, those that best express the true form of a society.

India was subject to the regime of the castes, and these castes were those of the brahmans, the kṣatriyas, the vaiśyas, the śūdras, and the cāṇḍālas, without discussing several other subdivisions of the lower classes. This is a point that, according to the remark of Mr. Hodgson, no Buddhist author ever contested.[107] The names of these castes are mentioned at every instant, and their existence is so well established that it is accepted by Śākya himself, as well as by his disciples, and becomes the object of special observations only when it creates an obstacle to the preaching of the Buddha. The brahmans are those whose name occurs most of-

107. "Quotations from Original Sanscrit Authorities," in *Journal of the Asiatic Society of Bengal*, vol. 5, p. 31. As early as 1830, Mr. Schmidt had established this point, according to the Mongol writers, as a fact beyond all contestation henceforth (*Mémoires de l'Académie des sciences de Saint-Pétersbourg*, 1:119).

ten; they figure in almost all the sūtras, and their superiority over the other castes is always uncontested.[108] They distinguish themselves by their knowledge and by their love of virtue. One sees some of them who, having reached the rank of ṛṣis or sages, live in the middle of the forest,[109] or in the caves of the mountains.[110] There, they devote themselves to harsh penances, some lying on beds bristling with sharp points or on ashes; others holding their arms raised above their head for their entire life; some sitting in the full sun, in the middle of four blazing fires.[111] They recite the Brahmanical mantras and teach them to their disciples.[112] That is their most noble function, which belongs exclusively to their caste. The sūtras offer us several examples of brahmans educated in the Indian sciences, and so they teach us what these sciences were. I shall cite only one of these passages, because it is the most characteristic of all. A brahman from Śrāvastī had raised his older son in the Brahmanical knowledge and practices. He had taught him the four Vedas, the Ṛc, the Yajus, the Sāman, and the Atharvan;[113] he had taught him the practice of the sacrifices, which one celebrates for oneself or which one makes others celebrate, like the reading of the Vedas, which one studies for oneself or which one makes a disciple study; and thanks to this teaching, the young man had become an accomplished brahman. The father wanted to do as much with his second son; but the child could not learn to read or to write. His father, abandoning the idea of giving him these primary elements of any instruction, put him in the hands of a brahman, charged with teaching him the Veda by heart.

But the child did not succeed any further under this new master. When one told him *om*, he forgot *bhūḥ*; when one told him *bhūḥ*, he forgot *om*. The master thus said to the father: "I have many children to instruct; I cannot occupy myself exclusively with your son Panthaka. When I tell him *om*, he forgets *bhūḥ* and when I tell him *bhūḥ*, he forgets *om*." The father then had this reflection: "Brah-

108. Among others, I will cite the sūtras and avadānas entitled: *Śārdūlakarṇa*, *Brāhmaṇadārikā*, *Stutibrāhmaṇa*, *Indrabrāhmaṇa*, *Dharmaruci*, *Jyotiṣka*, *Sahasodgata*, *Candraprabha*, *Saṃgharakṣita*, *Nāgakumāra*, *Paṃśupradāna*, *Rūpavatī*, *Mākandika*, *Candra*, and in the *Avadānaśataka*, *Upoṣadha*, *Soma*, *Raṣṭrapala*, *Subhuti*.

109. *Pūrṇa*, in *Divyāvadāna*, fols. 23a and 24a. *Rūpavatī*, *ibid.*, fol. 215a. *Subhuti*, in *Avadānaśataka*, fol. 221a.

110. *Prātihārya*, in *Divyāvadāna*, fol. 74a.

111. *Paṃśupradāna*, *ibid.*, fol. 174a. *Vītāśoka*, *ibid.*, fol. 205a. *Rūpavatī*, *ibid.*, fol. 215a.

112. *Maitreya*, *ibid.*, fol. 29a. This is expressly asserted by Śāriputra, son of Tiṣya, a brahman living in Nālanda, near Rājagṛha: *gurukule vedamantrān adhīyati*, "he reads the mantras of the Vedas in the house of his spiritual preceptor" (*Mahāvastu*, fol. 264a of my manuscript). One sees by this example (and I could cite many others that are similar) that it is not accurate to say, as Mr. Schmidt has done, that the ancient Buddhist sūtras do not mention the Vedas, and do not even allude to them (*Mémoires de l'Académie des sciences de Saint-Pétersbourg*, 2:43). But this assertion can be true when one speaks of the developed sūtras, which, according to the remarks set forth above, are much more devoid of historical details. See also another mention of the Vedas in the analysis of the Tibetan translation of the Vinaya by Csoma (*Asiatic Researches*, vol. 20, p. 85).

113. *Cūḍāpakṣa*, in *Divyāvadāna*, fol. 276b.

mans do not all know the Veda by heart, no more than they all know how to read and write; hence, my son will be a simple brahman by birth."[114]

These last words are very remarkable; the text uses the expression *jāti brāhmaṇa*, "brahman by birth," opposed to that of *veda brāhmaṇa*, "brahman of the Veda": and this expression is all the more worthy of attention in that it indicates the true role of the brahmans in Indian society; it was really a caste that perpetuated itself by birth, and that birth was enough to place it above all the others. The sūtras thus show us the brahmans in the same light as do the monuments of Brahmanical literature; and the accuracy of the Buddhist treatises on this important point extends even to apparently minute details, even to the costume itself; for in a legend one sees the god Indra disguised as a tall brahman who carries in his hands the religious staff and the bowl to draw water.[115] At the time when the Buddha, who still is only a bodhisattva, is descending to earth in order to take birth in the family of king Śuddhodana, the legend tells us that "sons of devas, from the troop of the śuddhāvāsas, went to Jambudvīpa and, hiding their divine form, they took on the guise of brahmans and started to study the Brahmanical mantras."[116]

One finds in the sūtras, as in Indian poems foreign to Buddhism, brahmans who perform the functions of *purohitas*, or household priests for kings, as the brahman Brahmāyus for the king Śaṅka.[117] Others work as panegyrists and praise kings in order to obtain gifts in return.

"There was in Benares, during the reign of Brahmadatta, a brahman who was a poet. The brāhmaṇī, his wife, told him one day: 'The cold weather has arrived; go say something pleasing to the king in order to obtain enough to protect us against the cold.' The brahman departed, indeed, for this purpose, and found the king going out, mounted on his elephant. The poet said to himself: 'Whom, between the two, shall I extol, the king or his elephant?' Then, he added: 'This elephant is dear and pleasing to the people; leaving aside the king, I will sing the praises of the elephant.'"[118]

And he pronounces a stanza in honor of this dignified animal, which so satisfies the king that he grants the brahman ownership of five villages. Some work as astrologers and predict the future of children according to their birth chart;[119] it is these very brahmans who attend the birth of Siddhārtha, son of Śuddhodana,[120] and it is a great ṛṣi, named Asita, who predicts to the king that

114. *Cūḍāpakṣa*, in *Divyāvadāna*, fol. 277a.
115. *Rūpavatī*, in *Divyāvadāna*, fol. 213a.
116. *Lalitavistara*, fol. 9b of my manuscript.
117. *Maitreya*, in *Divyāvadāna*, fol. 29a.
118. *Stutibrāhmaṇa*, *ibid.*, fol. 35.
119. *Rūpavatī*, *ibid.*, fol. 214a. *Lekuṇcika*, in *Avadānaśataka*, fol. 234a.
120. *Lalitavistara*, fols. 56a and 57a of my manuscript. *Divyāvadāna*, fol. 193a.

his son will become either a sovereign monarch or a blessed buddha;[121] so it is true that the Buddhists recognize in the most formal manner the anteriority of the Brahmanical caste with respect to the very founder of their belief, Śākyamuni Buddha. Some brahmans, in times of distress, engage in agriculture and guide the plow.[122] Finally, one sees a great number of them who, like Buddhist monks and other mendicants, sustain their life by means of alms distributed to them by householders.[123] It is impossible not to recognize in these features the Brahmanical caste as the law of Manu describes it; but these features, which, in the summary I have just made, are spare and without life, form a lively picture of the first of the Indian castes with the various details that accompany them in the sūtras. It is not permissible to doubt, by the Buddhists' own admission, that this caste was not constituted with its prerogatives and its power before Śākyamuni began to disseminate his doctrines of reform in India. To the testimonies just put forward in favor of this assertion, some others will be added accordingly as we advance in our research; I intentionally omit them at this moment.

There is, however, one that I cannot pass over in silence, because it seems to me to be one of the most convincing proofs of the anteriority of the brahmans with regard to the Buddhists. It is the use that all the Sanskrit texts of Nepal make, and notably the sūtras (that is to say, those which I have reason to say are the most ancient), of the word *brahmacarya*, in order to designate in a general manner the duties of the religious life of a Buddhist, and in particular chastity. If this term was rarely used, it still would not be easy to explain its presence in Buddhist texts, where one would expect in its place *buddhacarya*, an expression that also exists, but which means exactly Buddhism, and which is almost synonymous with *buddhamārga*, "the path of the Buddha." But no term is as common in the sūtras; it figures even in the most important of the formulas, in the sentence that one who feels disposed to become a Buddhist utters, before Śākya or before one of his disciples, the vow to enter into the religious life: "'Enable us, O Bhagavat, under the discipline of the well-renowned law, to enter into the religious life, to receive investiture and to become monks! Enable us, Lord, under the Bhagavat to accomplish the duties of brahmacarya!' Then, the Bhagavat responded

121. *Lalitavistara*, fol. 58a ff. of my manuscript. I do not doubt that this Asita is the wise brahman Faxian speaks about and calls Ayi (*Foe koue ki*, p. 198 and Klaproth, *ibid.*, p. 208ff.). Without the *Lalitavistara*, it would have been very difficult to find the Sanskrit Asita in the Chinese transcription Ayi. One knows, in the lists of the ancient Brahmanical sages, of a ṛṣi by the name Asita, but apart from that I have not found information that positively identifies him for us, I am not in a position to assert whether he is the same as the one that the Buddhists speak about. I only find his name in the *Bhāgavata Purana* (bk. 6, chap. 15, st. 12a). It is not likely that the Asita mentioned in the *Lalitavistara* is the genii who, according to the brahmans, presides over the planet Saturn.

122. *Indrabrāhmaṇa*, in *Divyāvadāna*, fol. 36a.

123. *Koṭikarṇa*, *ibid.*, fol. 7a.

to them with his voice of Brahmā: 'Come, children, accomplish the duties of brahmacarya.'"[124]

This term doubtless receives a slightly broader meaning in sentences like the following: "They will disseminate my religious law (*brahmacarya*)," says the Buddha; to which his adversary, who is sin, responds with the same formula: "Your religious law is disseminated, it is accepted by many people, it has become immense." *vaistārikaṃ te brahmacaryam, bāhujanyam, pṛthubhūtam.*[125] I will say as much about this formula: "In the way that the religious law (*brahmacarya*) survives for a long time."[126] In all these passages, and in many other similar ones that I could cite here, it is evident that the term *brahmacarya* is taken in a special sense, in that of "life" or "religious law," a sense that does not exclude, I confess, that of "chastity," but which is more comprehensive. Now, for the Buddhists to allow this acceptation, it would have been necessary that it had lost its primitive signification, that which it has in the Brahmanical monuments, "the state of *brahmacārin*, or of a brahman fulfilling his novitiate"; it would have been necessary that the Buddhists had forgotten the value of this title *brahmacārin*, which means and only can mean "one who walks in the Veda." That a brahman designates his son or his student with this title, that the law of Manu dedicates this denomination and traces at length the duties of novitiate, the first and the most severe of them being indeed the vow of chastity, nothing is easier to understand. But, in order for the founders of Buddhism to adopt this term, it would have been necessary that they no longer paid attention to its first signification, that of brahman novice, and that the word could have been used with impunity with the sense of "one who undertakes a religious novitiate." It would have been necessary, in the end, that it was almost popular with this acceptation before Śākyamuni, in order that this latter could, without fear of confusing his law with that of the brahmans, make the extensive and quite remarkable use of it that I have just indicated.

Let us go on to the second caste, that of the kṣatriyas. It also existed at the time of Śākyamuni, and it was from it that the kings came. In the sūtras, in accordance with the Brahmanical authorities, a kṣatriya on whose forehead the royal consecration has been performed is called "king."[127] Śākyamuni was himself a

124. *Supriya*, in *Divyāvadāna*, fol. 46a. *Prātihārya*, *ibid.*, fols. 77 and 78a. *Jyotiṣka*, *ibid.*, fol. 140b. *Kanakavarṇa*, *ibid.*, fol. 149a, and *Sahasodgata*, *ibid.*, fol. 151a. *Saṃgharakṣita*, *ibid.*, fols. 169a and b. *Nāgakumāra*, *ibid.*, fol. 172a, and *Vītāśoka*, *ibid.*, fol. 207a. *Śārdūlakarṇa*, *ibid.*, fol. 119a. *Cūḍāpakṣa*, *ibid.*, fol. 277b. One sees in our text the sound of the voice of Śākyamuni designated by the term *voice of Brahmā*, which is a new proof of the fact I intend to establish. To this proof must be added that which the word *brahmapathakovida* furnishes, "skilled in the Brahmā path," which the *Lalitavistara* gives to Śākyamuni when he was still only a bodhisattva (*Lalitavistara*, fol. 6a of my manuscript).

125. *Māndhātṛ*, in *Divyāvadāna*, fol. 99b.

126. *Id. ibid.*, fol. 102a.

127. *Lalitavistara*, fol. 10ff. of my manuscript.

kṣatriya, for he was the son of Śuddhodana, king of Kapilavastu.[128] When the future Buddha, while still only a bodhisattva, examines with the gods at which time, in which world, in which country, and in which family it is appropriate for him to descend to earth to accomplish his last mortal existence, the author of the legend of Śākyamuni succinctly sets forth the reasons for his choice, and here is what he tells us concerning the family.

"Why, O monks, does the bodhisattva examine the family in which he must be born? It is that bodhisattvas are not born into the womb of abject families, like those of the cāṇḍālas, of flute players, of cart makers, and of the puṣkasas. There are only two races into which they are born, the race of the brahmans and that of the kṣatriyas. When it is principally to the brahmans that the world shows respect, it is in a family of brahmans that bodhisattvas descend to earth. When, on the contrary, it is principally to the kṣatriyas that the world shows respect, then they are born into a family of kṣatriyas. Today, O monks, the kṣatriyas obtain all the respect of the people: it is for this that bodhisattvas are born among the kṣatriyas."[129]

Here, one sees, the existence and the superiority of the two first castes is quite clearly acknowledged, and in which work? In one of the nine canonical books of the North, in the very life of Śākyamuni Buddha. And this kind of theme, in which the limits between which the choice of a bodhisattva must be contained are determined in advance, is applied with rigor to all the fabulous or real buddhas who preceded Śākyamuni, since there are very few of them whom the legends say were born in a caste other than the brahmans and the kṣatriyas. I insist at the moment only on the most general consequences which result from this text, that of the existence of the two first castes and notably that of the kṣatriyas; I will return to it shortly when I examine the political influence of Śākya's preaching on the organization of Indian society.

128. This city is certainly the most celebrated of all those mentioned in the sūtras of the North, and in general, in the Buddhist books of all the schools. It was the residence of Śuddhodana, king of the Śākyas; and it is in one of its pleasure gardens that Siddhārtha, later Śākyamuni, came into the world. Klaproth, in a very substantial and most interesting note, has established that it must have been situated on the banks of the Rohiṇī River, one of the tributaries of the Raptī, and not far from the mountains that separate Nepal from the district of Gorakhpur (*Foe koue ki*, p. 199ff. Wilson, *Journal of the Royal Asiatic Society*, vol. 5, p. 123). When our legends (and this is rather rare) speak of the position of this city, they do so in vague terms; thus, the legend of Rudrāyaṇa says of Śākyamuni "that he was born on the slope of the Himavat, on the bank of the river Bhāgīrathī, not far from the hermitage of the ṛṣi Kapila" (*Divyāvadāna*, fol. 411b of my manuscript). The Bhāgīrathī being the Ganges in the longest part of its course, Kapilavastu should be sought much more to the west or more to the south than the itineraries of the Chinese travelers place it: the terms of the legend must therefore be taken only as an approximate indication. Faxian informs us that at the time of his travels in India, this city was deserted and had only about ten houses (*Foe koue ki*, p. 198).

129. *Lalitavistara*, fol. 13b of my manuscript. In the Historical Sketch I will note the names of the kings contemporary with Śākyamuni, adding details found accompanying these names in the legends. The assemblage of these details forms a picture unique in the history of ancient India, around the seventh or the sixth century before our era.

The sūtras give us fewer details on the kṣatriyas than on the brahmans for a double reason. The first is that the brahmans are the real adversaries of the Buddhists, and it is to their conversion that Śākyamuni applies himself; the second is that the kṣatriyas seem to have favored an ascetic who came from their same caste in a special way. The sūtras and the legends are replete with the tokens of benevolence that Śākyamuni received from Bimbisāra,[130] king of Magadha, from Prasenajit, king of Kośala, and from Rudrāyaṇa, king of Roruka. One day when Śākya was going to a cemetery to miraculously save the offspring of a woman who had been put to death by her husband at the brahmans' instigation, "he met in Rājagṛha two young men, one the son of a brahman, the other the son of a kṣatriya, who had gone outside to play together. The young kṣatriya had a deep faith, but it was not the same for the young brahman."[131]

All the kings of central India were, however, not equally favorable to Śākyamuni, and that of Rājagṛha, Ajātaśatru, persecuted the monk for a long time and made every effort to drive him from his realm, forbidding his subjects from having any relation with him.[132] Moreover, whatever the reasons for the kṣatriyas appearing less often than the brahmans in the Nepalese sūtras, these books at least preserve for us some features appropriate not only for establishing the existence of the second caste, but for making known some of its prejudices and its habits.

Kings, who came from the caste of the kṣatriyas, were in possession of an unlimited power, and it does not seem that their will encounters any obstacles other than the privileges of the castes. One sees some whose ministers encouraged despotism with the most violent counsel. The king of Roruka[133] needed money; his two prime ministers told him one day: "A country is like a grain of sesame, which

130. It is not easy to determine, according to our manuscripts, what the spelling should be of this proper noun, which plays a great role in the legends related to the life and preaching of Śākya. One could gather as many authorities for the spelling *Bimbasāra* as for that of *Bimbisāra*. I have consulted, in order to escape this small difficulty, the Tibetan versions of the Kah-gyur, and they seem to me able to settle the question in favor of the spelling *Bimbisāra*. This name is translated there as *gzugs can snying po*, "the essence of the being who has a body." This title, hardly clear in itself, was given to the young prince by his father Mahāpadma in memory of that moment when the child came into the world and the body of his mother the queen shone like the disk of the sun when it rises (*'Dul ba*, vol. *ka* or 1, fol. 5a). The use of the suffix *can* after *gzugs* indicates a possessive; it is thus *Bimbi* and not *Bimba* that the Tibetan interpreters had before their eyes. I add that the spelling *Bimbisāra* is that adopted by the Buddhists of the South, as one can see it in the *Mahāvaṃsa* of Mr. Turnour.

131. *Jyotiṣka*, in *Divyāvadāna*, fol. 134a.

132. *Avadānaśataka*, fol. 36a.

133. I have thus far not found any precise information on the location of this city. The legend of Rudrāyaṇa, who was converted to Buddhism by the influence of Bimbisāra, king of Rājagṛha, informs us that Roruka was to the east of this latter city, and that it rivaled in riches the famous Pāṭaliputra, the *Palibothra* of the Greeks, after the invasion of Alexander (*Divyāvadāna*, fol. 306a). It cannot have been too far from Rājagṛha, and one would probably have to look for it in the eastern part of Bihar; but today I find on our maps only Row, whose name offers some analogy to that of Roruka. I do not have any further information on this locality.

does not give its oil unless one squeezes it, cuts it, burns it, or grinds it."[134] I will cite below, in speaking about the struggles of Śākyamuni against the brahmans, an act of this violent despotism, of which the king of Kośala is the author. It is the order he gives, based on a mere suspicion, to mutilate his own brother, having his feet and hands cut off.[135] We can assume that kings had the power of life and death over their subjects, or at least that their decision was sufficient for the guilty to be executed in an instant. I shall mention on that occasion an example which proves that even in the case of a crime justly punishable, their will alone was consulted. The following text will also have the advantage of making us appreciate the true character of the Buddhist legends.

There was in Mathurā[136] a courtesan named Vāsavadattā. One day, her servant went to Upagupta in order to buy perfume. Vāsavadattā told her upon her return: "It seems, my dear, that you like this perfume merchant, since you always buy from him." The servant responded: "Daughter of my master, Upagupta, the son of the merchant, who is endowed with beauty, talent, and gentleness, passes his life observing the law." Upon hearing these words, Vāsavadattā fell in love with Upagupta, and at last she sent her servant to him to tell him: "My intention is to go to find you; I want to give myself over to pleasure with you." The servant carried the message to Upagupta; but the young man instructed her to answer her mistress: "My sister, it is not the time for you to see me." Now, to obtain the favors of Vāsavadattā it was necessary to give five hundred purāṇas.[137] So, the courtesan thought that [if he refused her, it was because] he could not give the five hundred purāṇas. This is why she again sent her servant to him in order to tell him: "I do not demand from the son of my master even one kārṣāpaṇa; I desire only to give myself over to pleasure with him." Again, the servant carried the new message, and Upagupta responded in the same way to her: "My sister, it is not the time for you to see me."

In the meantime, the son of a chief of artisans had come to live in Vāsavadattā's house; when a merchant, who brought five hundred horses from the north that he wanted to sell, entered the city of Mathurā and asked who was the most beautiful courtesan, he was told that it was Vāsavadattā. Immediately, taking five hundred purāṇas and a great quantity of presents, he went to the courtesan's house. Then Vāsavadattā, possessed by cupidity, murdered the son of the chief of artisans who

134. *Rudrāyaṇa*, in *Divyāvadāna*, fol. 315a.

135. *Prātihārya*, in *Divyāvadāna*, fol. 75a.

136. Mathurā is almost as celebrated in the Buddhist legends as it is in the books of the brahmans. This city, situated on the right bank of the Yamunā, was visited at the beginning of the fifth century by Faxian, who found Buddhism flourishing there (*Foe koue ki*, pp. 99 and 102).

137. See on this word and on that of *kārṣāpaṇa*, which comes below, a note placed at the end of the book, Appendix no. 3.

was in her house, threw his body into the rubbish, and gave herself over to the merchant. After some days, the young man was pulled from beneath the rubbish by his parents, who denounced the murder. The king immediately gave the order to the executioners to go and cut off the hands, the feet, the ears, and the nose of Vāsavadattā and to leave her in the cemetery. The torturers carried out the order of the king and abandoned the courtesan in the appointed place.

In the meantime, Upagupta heard talk of the torture inflicted on Vāsavadattā, and immediately this reflection came to his mind: "This woman once desired to see me with a sensual purpose [and I did not consent for her to see me]. But today her hands, her feet, her nose, and her ears having been cut off, it is time for her to see me," and he pronounced these stanzas:

"When her body was covered with beautiful finery, when she sparkled with various kinds of ornaments, it was best that those who aspire to deliverance and who wish to escape from the law of rebirth not go to see this woman.

"Today when she has lost her pride, her love, and her joy, when she has been mutilated by the edge of the blade, when her body is reduced to its true nature, it is time to see her."

Then, sheltered under a parasol carried by a young man who accompanied him in his capacity as servant, he went to the cemetery at a meditative pace. The servant of Vāsavadattā had stayed by her mistress out of attachment to her old kindnesses, and she prevented the crows from approaching her body. [Seeing Upagupta] she said to her: "Daughter of my master, the one to whom you sent me several times, Upagupta, advances in this direction. He doubtless comes drawn by the love of pleasure." But Vāsavadattā, hearing these words, responded to her:

"When he sees me, deprived of my beauty, lacerated by suffering, thrown on the ground, defiled with blood, how will he be able to feel the love of pleasure?"

Then, she said to her servant: "Friend, pick up the limbs that were severed from my body." The servant immediately gathered them and hid them under a piece of cloth. At that moment, Upagupta appeared, and he stood in front of Vāsavadattā. The courtesan, seeing him standing in front of her so, said to him: "Son of my master, when my body was whole, when it was made for pleasure, I sent my servant to you several times, and you answered me: 'My sister, it is not time for you to see me.' Today when the blade has deprived me of my hands, my feet, my nose, and my ears, when I am thrown in the mud and the blood, why do you come?" And she pronounced the following stanzas:

"When my body was as sweet as a lotus flower, when it was adorned with precious jewels and clothes, when it had everything to catch the eye, I was so unhappy not to be able to see you.

"Today, why do you come to gaze here at a body the eyes cannot bear to see, that was abandoned by games, pleasure, joy, and beauty, that inspires terror and that is defiled with blood and mud?"

Upagupta responded to her: "I did not come to you, my sister, attracted by the love of pleasure; but I came to see the true nature of the miserable objects of man's enjoyment."[138]

Then Upagupta adds some other maxims on the vanity of pleasures and the corruption of the body; his discourse brings calm to the soul of Vāsavadattā, who dies after having made an act of faith in the Buddha and is immediately reborn among the gods.

I cited this piece in its entirety, although it is related to the present discussion only by one feature, the punishment of Vāsavadattā sentenced by the sovereign will of the king. I will only add here that the legend is not contemporary with Śākyamuni; for it is found in a text that, as I will show elsewhere, is certainly later than the time of Aśoka (Kālāśoka).

To the features that I have just mentioned, I will add two others to go somewhat further into the habits of the royal caste.

A brahman from Campā[139] had a very beautiful daughter. The astrologers predicted to him that she would give birth to two sons, one of whom would become a sovereign monarch, the other a monk eminent in his saintliness. Emboldened by this prediction, the brahman went to present his daughter to Bindusāra, the king of Pāṭaliputra, who accepted her and had her enter the apartment of the women. At the sight of the young woman, the wives of the king, fearing the mastery that her beauty could have over the mind of Bindusāra, decided to make her pass for a woman from the abject caste of barbers, and taught her to attend to the beard and the hair of the king.

The young woman soon became skilled in this work, and each time that she commenced to carry out her duties for the king, the latter laid down. One day, the king, who was pleased with her, offered to grant her whatever favor she wished and asked her: "Which favor do you wish?" "Lord," the young woman responded, "that the king consent to unite with me." "You are of the caste of barbers," Bindusāra told her, "and I am a king from the race of kṣatriyas who has received royal anointing; how is it possible that you have intercourse with me?" "I do not belong to the caste of barbers," she replied, "I am the daughter of a brahman who has given me to the king in order that he make me his wife." "Then who has taught you the profession of barber?" said the king. "It is the women of the inner apartments." "Henceforth," said Bindusāra, "I do not want you to do

138. *Pāṃśupradāna*, in *Divyāvadāna*, fol. 175b. The anthology of Tibetan legends recently published by Mr. Schmidt reproduces the gist of this account, but in abridging it considerably, he removes part of its interest (*Der Weise und der Thor*, p. 385, German trans.).

139. Campā is a city celebrated in ancient times that already played an important role in the traditions of the *Mahābhārata*. Faxian visited it at the beginning of the fifth century (*Foe koue ki*, pp. 328 and 329). It is probable that it was situated, if not on the site of Champapur or Champanagar, a city next to Bhagalpur, then at least not far from there (Wilson, *Journal of the Royal Asiatic Society*, vol. 5, p. 134).

this work anymore." And the king declared the young woman to be the first of his wives.[140]

Another legend, that of Aśoka, son and successor of Bindusāra, offers us a no less interesting example of the power of the prejudices created by the castes. Tiṣyarakṣitā, one of the wives of the king, had developed an incestuous passion for Kunāla, son of the king and another of his wives, but she was rejected. Deciding to avenge herself, she takes advantage of a grave and reputedly incurable malady that threatened the life of the king to completely seize possession of his mind and obtain the exclusive use of royal power for several days. I extract that which touches on our subject from this legend now.

Aśoka, seeing that his illness was incurable, gave the following order: "Summon Kunāla; I wish to place him on the throne; what need is there for me to live?" But Tiṣyarakṣitā, having heard the words of the king, had this reflection: "If Kunāla ascends to the throne, I am lost." She then said to king Aśoka: "I take it on myself to restore you to health, but you must forbid the doctors entry to the palace." The king denied all doctors from being allowed to enter. On her side, the queen said to them all: "If a man or a woman who is stricken by the same illness as the king comes to you, be certain to show him to me."

Now, it happened that a man from the caste of the abhīras (shepherds) was struck by this same malady. His wife went to report the condition of her husband to a doctor, who responded to her: "Have the sick man come to see me; when I recognize his condition, I will tell him the appropriate remedy." The abhīra went accordingly to the doctor, who conducted him into the presence of Tiṣyarakṣitā. The queen ushered him into a secret place and put him to death. When the abhīra had been slain, she had his belly opened, looked in, and saw an enormous worm in his stomach. When the worm moved up, the excrement of the sick man came out of his mouth; when it moved down, the impure substances followed their course through the lower parts. The queen had ground pepper offered to the worm, and it did not die from it; she also had long pepper and ginger given to it without any success. Finally, it was touched with an onion; the worm immediately died and moved down through the lower tracts. The queen then went to the king and said: "Lord, eat onions and you will recover." "Queen," the king responded to her, "I am a kṣatriya, how could I eat onions?" "Lord," the queen then said, "it is as medicine that you must take this substance in order to save your life." The king ate the onion and the worm died and it went out through the lower tracts.[141]

I do not need to remark that the scruple which prevented king Aśoka from eating onions, although prevalent also among the Buddhists, has its source in the

140. *Pāṃśupradāna*, in *Divyāvadāna*, fol. 183b.
141. *Kunāla*, in *Divyāvadāna*, fol. 200b.

Brahmanical prohibition formulated by the law of Manu.[142] But it is important to note that the event just recounted occurred, according to the legend, in a period when king Aśoka was already entirely converted to Buddhism; and nonetheless the prejudice based on the existence of caste still exerted such a powerful control over his mind!

The passages I have just reported suffice to make known the true position of the first two classes in Indian society, that of the brahmans and that of the kṣatriyas. Other texts fix, with almost equal precision, the position of the lower castes, which one sees given over to commerce, agriculture, and finally to the servile professions. I shall not stop here to report the names of all the castes mentioned in the sūtras; the political organization of Indian society at the time of Śākyamuni is sufficiently determined by the names of those that have appeared in the passages cited above. I content myself with recalling here, according to the sūtras, the double principle on which the existence and the perpetuity of the castes rests. The first of these principles was the obligation in which each could marry only a woman of his own caste. This rule was so universally accepted at the time of Śākya's preaching that one sees it applied at every instant in the sūtras and legends of the *Divyāvadāna*. Each time that a marriage is mentioned, the text adds the usual formula: "he took a wife in a family equal to his own."[143] The story of Śākyamuni provides us with a very interesting example of it. The young prince, who was urged to marry, had declared that he would not be stopped by the consideration of caste, and that he would indiscriminately take a wife from among the brahmans, the kṣatriyas, the vaiśyas, or the śūdras, if he found one who corresponded to the type of perfection he conceived. The brahman who performed the functions of family priest for king Śuddhodana was charged with seeking the woman who fulfilled what the prince desired, and he found her in the house of an artisan of Kapilavastu called Daṇḍapāṇi. As a consequence, king Śuddhodana asked for his daughter for the young Śākya. But what did Daṇḍapāṇi respond? "Lord, the prince was raised in his house amid happiness; and moreover it is family law among us that our daughters are given in marriage only to one who knows a trade and not to another. But the prince does not know any trade; he does not know how to wield the sword, or the bow, or the quiver, etc."[144] The king stops in the face of this objection, and Śākya is obliged to show the knowledge he possesses in all the arts, knowledge among which are included those connected with the liberal arts, like the study of ancient vocabularies (*nighaṇṭu*); the reading of the sacred books, the Vedas, the Purāṇas, the itihāsas; the trea-

142. *Mānavadharmaśāstra*, bk. 1, chap. 5, st. 5.

143. *Cūḍāpakṣa*, in *Divyāvadāna*, fol. 281b and passim.

144. *Lalitavistara*, chap. 12, fols. 79b and 80a of my manuscript. An analogous circumstance is recounted in one of the Tibetan legends recently published by Mr. Schmidt (*Der Weise und der Thor*, pp. 334 and 335, German trans.).

tises on grammar; the explanation of obsolete terms; reading; metrics; ritual; astronomy.[145]

The second principle for the preservation of the castes was the heredity of the professions, and this principle was no less generally respected than the first. The son of the merchant followed the profession of his father;[146] the son of the butcher was a butcher because his father and his ancestors had been before him.[147] Respected by all classes, from the brahman to the cāṇḍāla, the two principles I have just recalled formed the base on which rested the edifice of the society whose plan and picture the *Mānavadharmaśāstra* has preserved for us.

It is into the milieu of a society so constituted that was born, in a family of kṣatriyas, that of the Śākyas of Kapilavastu, who claimed descent from the ancient solar race of India, a young prince who, renouncing the world at the age of twenty-nine, became a monk under the name of Śākyamuni or also śramaṇa Gautama. His doctrine, which according to the sūtras was more moral than metaphysical, at least in its principle,[148] rested on an opinion accepted as a fact and on a hope presented as a certitude. This opinion is that the visible world is in perpetual change; that death succeeds life and life death; that man, like all that surrounds him, revolves in the eternal circle of transmigration; that he successively passes through all forms of life from the most elementary to the most perfect; that the place he occupies on the vast scale of living beings depends on the merit of the actions he performs in this world; and thus the virtuous man must, after this life, be reborn with a divine body, and the guilty with a body of the damned; that the rewards of heaven and the punishments of hell have only a limited duration, like everything in the world; that time exhausts the merit of virtuous actions as it effaces the faults of evil actions; and that the fatal law of change brings the god as well as the damned back to earth, in order to again put both to the test and make them pass through a new series of transformations. The hope that Śākyamuni brought to humanity was the possibility to escape from the law of transmigration, entering what he calls *nirvāṇa*, that is to say, annihilation. The definitive sign of this annihilation was death; but a precursory sign in this life announced the man predestined for this supreme liberation; it was the possession of an unlimited science, which gave him a clear view of the world as it is, that is to say, the knowledge of physical and moral laws; and in short, it was the practice of the six transcendent perfections: that of alms-giving, morality, science, energy, patience, and charity. The authority on which the monk of the Śākya race supported his teaching was entirely personal; it was formed of two elements, one

145. *Lalitavistara*, chap. 12, fol. 87a.

146. *Koṭikarṇa*, in *Divyāvadāna*, fol. 1 and passim.

147. *Id. ibid.*, fol. 5b.

148. This fact has not escaped Mr. Benfey ("Indien," p. 201, extract of the *Encyclopédie* of Ersch and Gruber).

real and the other ideal. The first was the consistency and the saintliness of his conduct, of which chastity, patience, and charity formed the principal features. The second was the claim he made to be buddha, that is to say, enlightened, and as such to possess superhuman science and power. With his power, he performed miracles; with his science, he perceived, in a form clear and complete, the past and the future. Thereby, he could recount everything that each man had done in his previous existences; and so he asserted that an infinite number of beings had long ago attained like him, through the practice of the same virtues, the dignity of buddha, before entering into complete annihilation. In the end, he presented himself to humanity as its saviour, and he promised that his death would not annihilate his doctrine; but that this doctrine would endure for a great number of centuries after him, and that when his salutary action ceased, there would come into the world a new buddha, whom he announced by name and whom, before descending to earth, the legends say, he himself had crowned in heaven, with the title *future buddha.*[149]

That is what the sūtras teach us about the position and the intentions of Śākyamuni in the milieu of Indian society; and that is, if I am not mistaken, the most simple and the most primitive form in which his doctrine appears, as long as it still is, as it is in these treatises, only in a state of preaching. It must not surprise us that other books of Nepal, such as the various editions of the *Prajñāpāramitā*, offer us a more regular system, encompassing a rather greater number of matters than those indicated in the sūtras; but this is not the place to compare the developed Buddhism of the *Prajñā* with that of the sūtras; the important thing for us at the moment is to fix, according to this latter category of treatises, the position of Śākyamuni among the brahmans, the kṣatriyas, and the other castes. It is clear that he presented himself as one of those ascetics who since the most ancient times travel through India preaching morality: the more respected by society, the more they pretend to scorn it; it is even by placing himself under the tutelage of brahmans that he had entered the religious life. The *Lalitavistara* shows him, indeed, upon leaving the paternal house, going to the most celebrated brahmans, in order to draw from their school the science he seeks.[150] When he has obtained from these masters what they are able to teach him, when the most skilled has even shared with him the exercise of his function as preceptor, Śākya, like all the ascetics, gives himself over to severe mortifications, to a long and rigorous abstinence; and the *Lalitavistara*, which recounts all the details of this part of his life, naively ends its account with this instructive remark: "It was to show to the

149. *Lalitavistara*, fol. 25a of my manuscript. Csoma, "Life of Shakya," in *Asiatic Researches*, vol. 20, p. 287.

150. *Lalitavistara*, chap. 16, fol. 125b ff. of my manuscript. He put himself at the outset under the discipline of Ārāḍa Kālāma and then under that of Rudraka, son of Rāma, who resided near Rājagṛha. The Pāli books called the first of these brahmans Alāra Kālāma (Turnour, *Journal of the Asiatic Society of Bengal*, vol. 7, p. 1004).

world the spectacle of astonishing actions."[151] Śākyamuni, or the recluse of the Śākya race, is originally not distinguished from other recluses of the Brahmanical race; and one will see later, when I assemble the proofs of the battles he was compelled to wage against other ascetics, his rivals, that the people, astonished by the persecutions he was subjected to, sometimes demanded of his adversaries the reasons they had to hate him so, since he was but a mendicant like them.

It is no less evident that the philosophical opinion by which he justified his mission was shared by all classes of society: brahmans, kṣatriyas, vaiśyas, and śūdras; all believe equally in the fate of transmigration, in the distribution of rewards and punishments, in the necessity and at the same time the difficulty of escaping in a definitive manner from the perpetually changing conditions of a completely relative existence. To that point, the recluse of the Śākya race was not in opposition to Brahmanical society. Kṣatriya by birth, he had become an ascetic, like some others, and notably Viśvāmitra, had done before him.[152] He even preserved, in one of the names he bore, the trace of the essentially religious link that connected his family to the Brahmanical caste; he called himself the *śramaṇa Gautama*, or the Gautamid ascetic, doubtless because Gautama was the sacerdotal family name of the military race of the Śākyas, who in the capacity of kṣatriyas did not have an ancestor or tutelary saint in the way the brahmans did, but who could take, as Indian law allowed, the name of the ancient sage of the race to which their spiritual director belonged.[153] Philosopher and moralist, he believed in most of the truths accepted by the brahmans; but he separated himself from them when it became a question of drawing out the consequence of these truths and of determining the conditions of salvation, the aim of the efforts of man, since he substituted annihilation and emptiness for the unique Brahma into whose substance his adversaries had the world and man return.

I will now extract from the sūtras the passages that have appeared to me liable

151. *Lalitavistara*, fol. 135b of my manuscript.

152. Besides Viśvāmitra, whose legend is well known from the *Rāmāyaṇa*, the ancient Itihāsas cited by the commentators of the Vedas, or the treatises forming a kind of appendix to these ancient books, speak of a warrior of the race of the Kurus who became a brahman (*Commentary on the Nirukta*, 1st part, p. 49b of my manuscript).

153. See in the *Foe koue ki*, p. 309, a note in which I tried to explain this difficulty. The analyses of Csoma inform us that Maudgalyāyana, in addressing the Śākyas of Kapilavstu, called them "Gautamāḥ" or "Gautamides" (*Asiatic Researches*, vol. 20, p. 74, and *Journal of the Asiatic Society of Bengal*, vol. 2, p. 386ff.). But this only proves that the Śākyas took the name Gautama. The origin of this title remains unknown, and the explanation I propose is still only a conjecture. A curious fact, although it does not advance our knowledge very much on the question of origin, is that even today, there exists in the district of Gorakhpur, that is to say, in the very country where Śākyamuni was born, a branch of the race of the Rajputs, who take the name of Gautamides (*The History, Antiquities, Topography, and Statistics of Eastern India*, 2:458). Francis Hamilton, to whom we owe the knowledge of this fact, has gathered some slightly confused details touching on these Gautamides Rajputs. He does not explain how a family of kṣatriyas can say they are descended from a Brahmanical saint.

to cast the most daylight on the following points: the position that Śākya and his disciples had with regard to the brahmans and to other ascetics in general; the aim that Śākya and his monks had in common; the battles that the leader waged against his adversaries; the means of conversion he employed; and the effect his teaching at long last must have had on the Brahmanical system of castes. These diverse subjects are often intermingled in the same passage, and one doubtless does not expect to find here a methodical classification; the point that is important to establish is the impression that results, for all impartial readers, from the study of the sūtras, considered from these diverse points of view.

One of the facts that the reading of the sūtras and legends of the *Divyāvadāna* best brings to light is that within Indian society Śākyamuni and his monks were placed at the same rank as the ascetics of another origin. This assertion, although not expressed in such an affirmative manner, is no less the fact which, at bottom, the study of the sūtras most obviously demonstrates. I have just recalled the disciplines to which Śākyamuni submits himself in order to penetrate the most secret mysteries of Brahmanical science. None of the masters under whose teaching he successively places himself finds his claims unusual, and the legend of the *Lalitavistara* even teaches us that one of these brahmans shared his title of preceptor with him.[154] Five of the disciples of this brahman are so struck by the progress of Śākya that they leave their old master to follow the new ascetic.[155] It is true that when Śākya, exhausted by an excessive abstinence, is compelled to take some food and to renounce excessively prolonged fasts, the five disciples, shocked by this infraction of the rule, abandon him to go alone to Benares to continue their life of mortifications;[156] but Śākya finds them later, and the sight

154. *Lalitavistara*, fols. 129a and b of my manuscript.

155. *Lalitavistara*, fol. 139b of my manuscript. The *Mahāvastu* mentions the names of these five first disciples, who are called "of good caste." It is not without interest to compare them with the transcriptions given by the Chinese (*Foe koue ki*, p. 310). The first mentioned is Ājñāta Kauṇḍinya: the Chinese call him *Aruo jiaochenru* and say very well that *Aruo* (Ājñāta) means "knowing" and that *Kauṇḍinya* is the family name of this brahman; one knows indeed a Brahmanical family of the Kauṇḍinyas. The second one is Aśvajit, for the Chinese *Ebi* or, according to Xuanzang, *Axifoshi* (*Foe koue ki*, p. 267). His name is exactly rendered by "master of the horse." This monk belonged to the Śākya family. The third one is Bhadraka or Bhadrika; for the Chinese *Poti*. However distant this transcription appears to be from the original, it is certainly because it goes through the medium of Pāli; it is nonetheless rendered very probably by the translation "little sage" given by the Chinese. The notion of *little* is indeed in the suffix *ka* of *Bhadraka*. It is said that this personage also belonged to the Śākya family, and one finds the legend of his conversion to Buddhism in the *Avadānaśataka* (fol. 214b). The fourth one is Vāṣpa, whom the Chinese know under the name of *Daśabala Kāśyapa*; but they also give him the name of *Pofo*, which cannot be anything other than *Vāṣpa*, especially since *Pofo* is translated in Tibetan by *Rlangs pa*, which is exactly the meaning of the Sanskrit *vāṣpa* (vapor); this monk was related to Śākya through his maternal uncles. The fifth is Mahārāta, or rather Mahānāma, as Csoma writes it (*Asiatic Researches*, vol. 20, p. 293). The Chinese transcribe this name exactly as *Mohenan* (*Foe koue ki*, p. 203); they give him also that of *Julitaizi*, "the royal prince Juli." Mahānāma was the elder son of the king Amitodana and the first cousin of Śākya (*Mahāvastu*, fol. 356a of my manuscript. Csoma, *Asiatic Researches*, vol. 20, p. 293).

156. *Lalitavistara*, fol. 139b of my manuscript.

of his physical and moral perfections moves them again and converts them forever to his law.[157]

There is nothing in all this that could not have also happened to a Brahmanical ascetic, and Śākya, although a kṣatriya, is placed by the legend exactly on the same footing as a brahman. Other texts show us his disciples hardly distinguished from those who later became their violent adversaries. Among several passages I could refer to, I will cite only one, which shows us one of the most zealous partisans of Śākyamuni distributing his alms equally to Buddhists and brahmans and telling the doorkeeper of his house: "Do not open the door to the tīrthyas[158] (they are Brahmanical ascetics) during the time that the assembly of monks, with the Buddha at its head, is occupied with eating its meal; my intention is not to receive the tīrthyas until after the assembly."[159] And the difference that exists between these two types of ascetics, the brahman and the Buddhist, is indefinite enough that at the sight of Kāśyapa, that is to say, one of the foremost and the most fervent disciples of Śākya, the keeper takes him for a Brahmanical mendicant and closes the door to him.[160] This almost complete

157. *Mahāvastu*, fol. 356a of my manuscript. The place where Śākya encountered his first five disciples again is very famous in the legends; it is called Ṛṣipatana Mṛgadāva, "the place where the ṛṣis fell into the Grove of the Antelopes." This is how the *Lalitavistara* set forth the origin of this denomination: "At this time, there was in Vārāṇasī, in the Grove of the Antelopes, in the place called Ṛṣipatana, five hundred pratyekabuddhas who lived there. Having learned the news, they rose into the air to the height of five spans and, entering in the element of light, they vanished like meteors. Whatever bile, phlegm, flesh, bones, muscles, and blood was in their bodies, all of that was consumed by fire, and their pure bodies fell to earth. Thus, one says: the ṛṣis have fallen here; hence this place came to have the name of "Ṛṣipatana, the falling of the ṛṣis" (*Lalitavistara*, fols. 12b and 13a). The same text gives a poor explanation of the name Mṛgadāva, "Grove of the Antelopes." This is it: *abhayadattāśca tasmin mṛgāḥ prativasanti*, "the gazelles live there, in possession of a sense of security," as if *mṛgadāva* was formed from the elements found in *datta*, namely *dā*, and in *vasanti*, namely *va*. Faxian, at the beginning of the fifth century of our era, visited this celebrated place; he calls it in his account "The Park of the Stags of the Immortal" (*Foe koue ki*, p. 304). By *Immortal*, one has to understand a pratyekabuddha who, learning that the son of king Śuddhodana was at the point of becoming a buddha, entered nirvāṇa himself. It is, as one sees, our legend slightly transformed.

158. The term of *tīrthya* or *tīrthika* or also *tīrthakara* literally means "one who performs a pilgrimage to sacred ponds." It is the title by which the Buddhist books designate ascetics and Brahmanical monks in a general manner. I fear that Mr. Schmidt confused this word with that of *tārkika*, "logician, sophist," when he believed he could assert that the Sanskrit word *tārkika* was written *tirtika* by the Mongols (*Mémoires de l'Académie des sciences de Saint-Pétersbourg*, 2:44 and note). I do not see why the Mongol *tirtika* would not simply be the transcription of the Sanskrit *tīrthika*. Mr. Schmidt, I believe, is more fortunate when he reduces the Mongol word *tars* or *ters* to only an alteration of these two Sanskrit words; but it is from *tīrthika* that one must draw it. This remark seems to me to reduce to nothing all the hypotheses by which someone has wished to recognize the Parsis in the Ters of the Mongol authors.

159. *Nāgarāvalambikā*, in *Divyāvadāna*, fol. 38a. *Svāgata*, *ibid*., fol. 86b.

160. *Nāgarāvalambikā*, in *Divyāvadāna*, fol. 38b. Klaproth already has noticed that at the time of Śākyamuni there were several brahmans with the name Kāśyapa, who are often mentioned in the legends, namely Mahākāśyapa, Uruvilvākāśyapa, Gayākāśyapa, and Nadīkāśyapa. According to the texts consulted by Klaproth, the last three Kāśyapa were brothers, and one must distinguish them from Mahākāśyapa (*Foe koue ki*, p. 292). One has to add to them the Daśabalakāśyapa, otherwise known as *Vāṣpa*, of whom I just spoke while listing the first five disciples of Śākya, to whom he belonged. Upon the death of Śākya, this last Kāśyapa was one of the greatest listeners of Śākya who existed in India (Csoma, *Asiatic Researches*, vol. 20, p. 315).

equality of the two orders is expressed in the most clear manner by the formula that reappears at each line of the primitive sūtras: *śramaṇabrāhmaṇa*, that is to say, the śramaṇas and the brahmans, a formula according to which the only advantage that the Buddhists give themselves is to be stated first.[161] Śākya is often depicted traveling through the country, surrounded by the assembly of monks, and followed by a multitude of brahmans, merchants, and householders.[162] An often-repeated formula, whose object is to express the extent of the science of the Buddha, contains these words: "Knowing creatures, including śramaṇas and brahmans."[163] These facts and others that are similar prove that Buddhists and brahmans lived together in the same country; they belong as such to the history of Indian Buddhism, and are certainly previous by a good many centuries to the violent separation that expelled from Hindustan the beliefs related to the preaching of Śākyamuni.

The aim that the recluse of the Śākya race intended is no less clearly established by the sūtras. He wanted to save humans, detaching them from the world and teaching them the practice of virtue. To that end, he sought to convert them to his doctrine, and to make them his disciples, able to disseminate it and perpetuate it after him. Encouraged by the example of his virtues and by the memory of the ordeals he said he had gone through during his previous existences, his disciples took upon themselves the harshest sacrifices in order to reach, like him, the perfection of sanctitude. It is not rare to see them renouncing life with the desire and firm hope of reaching the supreme state of a perfectly accomplished buddha one day. Their dedication, however, is more disinterested than that of the brahmans, who indulge in harsh penances, in order to share the abode of Indra or that of Brahmā in another life; for the perfection to which the Buddhist ascetic aspires must not elevate him alone, and it is to share the benefit of it with other people that he seeks it among the most difficult ordeals. The sūtras and the legends offer us more than one example of this tendency of Buddhist conversions, a tendency that places almost at the same rank, save for the aim, the followers of the Buddha and the worshippers of Brahmā. When Aśoka, dying, leaves the empire of the earth, of which he believes he was the master, to the assembly of the monks of the Buddha, he exclaims that he does not perform this act of generosity to collect its fruit, either in the heaven of Indra, or in the world of Brahmā, but to obtain the reward his faith in the Bhagavat merits.[164] A young brahman who has retired into the depths of a forest to give himself over, in the

161. *Supriya*, in *Divyāvadāna*, fol. 44a. *Prātihārya*, *ibid.*, fol. 74a. *Dharmaruci*, *ibid.*, fol. 113a. *Jyotiṣka*, *ibid.*, fol. 137a.

162. *Supriya*, in *Divyāvadāna*, fol. 44a. *Kanakavarṇa*, *ibid.*, fol. 146b. *Avadānaśataka*, fols. 81b, 101a, 106b, 120b, 122a, 127b.

163. *Rūpavatī*, in *Divyāvadāna*, fol. 212a.

164. *Aśoka*, in *Divyāvadāna*, fol. 211a.

interest of living beings, to an extraordinary penance, gives his body as food to a starving tigress that just gave birth to cubs. At the moment of commiting this heroic sacrifice, he exclaims: "How true it is that I do not abandon life for kingship, or for the enjoyments of pleasure, or for the rank of Śakra, or for that of sovereign monarch, but rather to reach the supreme state of a perfectly accomplished buddha."[165] One finds in another sūtra, that of Candraprabha, an allusion to a similar legend, that of the female tiger, whose double translation, carried out according to two Mongol works, the *Uligerün dalai* and the *Altan gerel*,[166] we owe to Mr. Schmidt. In this same sūtra, the king, at the moment of abandoning his life, calls the gods to witness that he performs such a great sacrifice, not to obtain the rewards one usually expects from it, rewards that are the state of Brahmā, Śakra, or a sovereign monarch, but one day to become a perfect buddha.

Here, as in many other texts, there appears at once similarity and difference of Buddhism compared with Brahmanism. The belief in the sanctity of suicide with a religious aim in mind is the same on both sides, because it is based on this ancient sentence of reprobation, brought against the body by Oriental asceticism. And indeed, if life is a state of suffering and sin, if the body is a prison where the captive and miserable soul languishes, what better use can one make of it than to extricate oneself from it? And with what ardor must the ascetic not turn to this sacrifice, if he believes that in this way he more quickly draws near to the high aim promised to his efforts? This is, one cannot doubt, the meaning of these voluntary immolations that are still perpetrated these days under the Jagannātha chariot. The Buddhist legends in which I find examples of it refer, it is true, to epochs that are quite mythological; and it is permissible to suppose that they were placed in these distant times only because it would have been difficult to find their equal during the first centuries of the establishment of Buddhism. Nevertheless, whatever the facts may be in themselves, the tendency of legends of this kind is no less identical to those of ideas that drive fanatical sectarians to torture and kill themselves for Viṣṇu the Benevolent, or for the implacable Devī. In our legends, the aim is different; it must even be said that this difference is entirely to the advantage of the Buddhists, since the sacrifice the ascetic takes upon himself is always in the interest of all humanity.[167] But this difference could easily disappear in the eyes of the people in the face of similarity of mind and means; and the zeal with which the Buddhist monks exalt such sacrifices sufficed to make them share the respect of the masses with other ascetics who also practiced them.

That which seems to support this supposition is the nature of the reproaches

165. *Rūpavatī*, in *Divyāvadāna*, fol. 115b.

166. *Grammatik der Mongolischen Sprache*, p. 192ff. The story of the *Uligerün dalai* is naturally found reproduced in the German translation of the original Tibetan anthology published by Mr. Schmidt (*Der Weise und der Thor*, p. 21ff.).

167. This distinction has not escaped Mr. Benfey ("Indien," p. 199, col. 2).

that, according to our sūtras, the brahmans addressed to Śākyamuni and his disciples. I know that these reproaches are reported by Buddhists, who were able to choose among those to which it was most easy for them to respond, while they had to remain silent on purely philosophical objections, objections otherwise more serious, that the commentators of the Brahmanical systems of Sāṃkhya and Nyāya raise for the followers of Śākyamuni. But, I repeat again, here it is a matter of the legends related to the first preachings of Śākya, and not of a fixed system that defends itself with weapons similar to those with which it is attacked. Thus, even when the redactors of the sūtras would have deliberately passed over in silence the polemic of which the opinions of Śākyamuni must have been the object on the part of the brahmans, the less serious reproaches that they place in the mouths of their adversaries could always have been made to them, however philosophically small the motive might be.

One of the grievances that ordinarily animated the Brahmanical caste against the Buddhists was that these latter, giving themselves over, as they did, to an ascetic life and attracting the respect of the people by the steadiness of their conduct, deprived the monks of other sects of a portion of the homages and profits that before were due to them. We will see later six brahmans who wanted to test their supernatural power against that of Śākya, complaining openly about the wrong he did to them since he embraced the religious life. Another legend, that of Dharmaruci, reproduces these complaints, but it carries the subject and the authors back to a quite mythological epoch, under Kṣemaṃkara, one of the fabulous buddhas prior to Śākyamuni. A merchant, who had amassed vast wealth in a sea voyage, wished to enlarge and adorn the stūpa, or the monument of this buddha. "But the brahmans who lived in the city, having all gathered, came to the great merchant and told him: 'You know, merchant, that at the time when the buddha Kṣemaṃkara had not yet appeared in the world, we were then an object of respect for the people; and when he was born, it is he who received the homages of the masses. Now that he has entered into complete annihilation, it is to us that the world must pay respect; this gold is by rights due to us.'"[168]

Such words must have been pronounced since the death of Śākyamuni; and it is because they indeed were that the legend reports them, placing them in a past prior to historical times. They also show, in our view, one of the perspectives from which ascetics of all orders envisaged the appearance and development of the new sect, which came to contend with them for the material advantages of so lucrative a profession in India. Another more serious reproach, doubtless because it came from the most respectable classes of society, was the blame with which the majority of the conversions carried out by Śākyamuni were received. He was reproached for admitting among his disciples persons spurned by all for

168. *Dharmaruci*, in *Divyāvadāna*, fols. 120a and b.

their crimes or for their misery; but I must content myself with noting this kind of blame here; I will have occasion to speak about it in detail later, when I examine the nature of the conversions carried out by Śākya and the effects produced by the conversions themselves.

If the objections with which, according to the sūtras, the brahmans opposed Śākya and his disciples were not very philosophical, neither was the battle they waged against him; for the legends show them to us disputing with him about who would perform the most convincing miracles. I believe it is necessary to translate the greater part of a sūtra related to this subject, which will make understandable, better than anything I could say, on which terrain the brahmans, according to the Buddhist tradition, were doing battle with Śākyamuni and his first followers.

At that time, there resided in the city of Rājagṛha six masters who did not know everything, but thought that they knew everything. They were: Pūraṇa Kāśyapa, Maskarin, son of Gośāli, Saṃjayin, son of Vairaṭṭī, Ajita Keśakambala, Kakuda Kātyāyana, Nirgrantha, son of Jñāti.[169] Now, these six tīrthyas, gathered and seated in a hall for recreation, had the following conversation and discussion together: "You certainly know, lords, that when the śramaṇa Gautama had not yet appeared in the world, we were honored, respected, venerated, adored by kings, the ministers of kings, by brahmans, by householders, by the inhabitants

169. This interesting piece is found reproduced with some variants in the Tibetan anthology Mr. Schmidt has just published in a German translation (*Der Weise und der Thor*, p. 71ff.). See also the names of these six brahman ascetics mentioned by Csoma de Kőrös in his notes on the life of Śākya (*Asiatic Researches*, vol. 20, pp. 298 and 299). It is most interesting to compare what Mr. Rémusat explains to us about these heretics; we will see thereby how the Chinese Buddhist texts contain precious documents and the care with which this eminent Orientalist studied them (*Foe koue ki*, p. 149). The first one is named, according to the Chinese, *Fulanna jiashe*; it is exactly Pūraṇa Kāśyapa; from his mother he took his second name, which means "the descendant of Kāśyapa." The second brahman is *Mojiali jushelizi*; it is Maskarin, son of Gośāli; it is probable that this name had passed through a Pāli form; otherwise one could not explain the absence of an *s* in the Chinese transcription. The third is *Shansheye biluozhi*; it is Saṃjayin, son of Vairaṭṭī: Mr. Rémusat came very close to these two names. The fourth is *Ajiduo chishe qinpoluo*; it is Ajita Keśakambala or Ajita, who had only his hair as clothes. Mr. Rémusat has rightly guessed *Kambala*. The fifth is *Jialuojiutuo jiazhanyan*; it is Kakuda of the Kātyāyana family. The sixth is *Nijiantuo ruotizi*; it is Nirgrantha, son of Jñāti: here again I find a trace of a Pāli origin in the absence of the two *r*'s. Mr. Rémusat explains this proper noun perfectly: "*Nijiantuo* means *exempt from bonds*: it is the common title of heterodox monks; this one took the name *ruoti* from his mother." This legend is celebrated in all the Buddhist schools, and one finds an extract of it in the presentation on Burmese religion given by Francis Buchanan, according to San Germano (*Asiatic Researches*, vol. 6, p. 267ff.).
Mr. Schmidt believes that it is beyond doubt that these six masters represent the six principal philosophical schools of the brahmans (*Mémoires de l'Académie des sciences de Saint-Pétersbourg*, 2:44). But nothing proves that this coincidence between the number of the six masters and the existence of the six Indian sects is something other than an accidental correspondence. I must only add before closing that the memory of Pūraṇa and of the other masters has left some traces in the Buddhist tradition; for on the occasion of the word *preceptor*, the *Dharmakośavyākhyā* expresses itself in this way: "There are two kinds of masters, the false and the true; the false, like Pūraṇa and the others, the true, that is to say, the Tathāgata" (*Dharmakośavyākhyā*, fol. 6b of the MS of the Société Asiatique).

of the city and by those of the countryside, by the chiefs of the guilds and by merchants; and that we received from them various assistance, such as clothes, food, beds, seats, medicines for the sick, and other things. But since the śramaṇa Gautama has appeared in the world, it is he who is honored, respected, venerated, adored by kings, by brahmans, by the ministers of kings, by the householders, by the inhabitants of the city and of the countryside, by the wealthy, by the chiefs of the guilds and by the foremost merchants; it is the śramaṇa Gautama who, with the assembly of his listeners, receives various assistance, such as clothes, food, beds, seats, medicines for the sick, and other things as well; our profits and our honors are entirely and completely taken from us. However, we are endowed with a supernatural power, we know how to debate about science. The śramaṇa Gautama also claims to be endowed with a supernatural power; he claims to know how to debate about science. It is fitting that one who knows how to debate do battle with one who knows as much as he does, performing, by means of his supernatural power, miracles superior to what man can do.[170] If the śramaṇa Gautama performs, by means of his supernatural power, a single miracle superior to what man can do, we will do two; if he performs two, we will do four; if he performs four, we will do eight; if he performs eight, we will do sixteen; if he performs sixteen, we will do thirty-two. In the end, we will do two times, three times as many miracles as the śramaṇa Gautama will have performed by means of his supernatural power. Should the śramaṇa Gautama advance only halfway, we will advance no more than halfway. Thus, let us go do battle with the śramaṇa Gautama in the art of performing, by means of supernatural power, miracles superior to what man can do."

170. The expression the text uses here is peculiar to Buddhist Sanskrit; the manuscripts give it with some variants: *uttare manuṣyadharme ṛddhiprātihāryaṃ vidarśayitum* or *uttarimanuṣyadharme*, etc., or also *anuttarimanuṣya* . . . etc. If one reads *uttare*, it will be necessary to translate word by word: "to make a supernatural transformation appear in the law superior to man"; if one reads *uttari* (an otherwise unusual form), one will say: "to make a supernatural transformation appear in the law of a superior man," and I add that the reading *anuttari* will little change this last meaning; it will only be that one will have to say "a man without superior." The most common reading in our manuscripts is that of *uttari*; it is also the one that the Pali texts of Ceylon follow. The first of these two translations I have just proposed appears to me to be confirmed by the Tibetan words of the version of this text: *mi'i chos bla ma'i rdzu 'phrul*, "miracles of the law superior to man." This meaning is expressed in other terms in the legend published by Mr. Schmidt: *mi'i bla ma'i chos kyi cho 'phrul la 'jug go*, according to Mr. Schmidt; *in der magischen Verwandlungskunst aus der Lehre des Lama* (*Oberhauptes*) *der Menschen* (*Der Weise und der Thor*, Tibetan text, p. 58; and German trans., p. 71.) This translation appears to me to wrongly introduce the term *lama*, which is a rather modern conception peculiar to the Tibetans. It is true that the word *lama* (*bla ma*) means "superior," like the Sanskrit *uttari* that it replaces; this is a point I do not contest; I only ask whether in a legend whose elements are contemporary with Śākyamuni, one does not replace the word *superior* with that of *lama*. The Tibetan expression, literally interpreted, seems to me to give this meaning: "entered in a metamophorsis of the law of the superior of man," the meaning of which doubtless comes down to this: "entered in a legal metamorphosis (that is to say, which is the condition) of that which is superior to man." I have followed the latter meaning, however vague it still is, because it is the closest to the original expression; but I allow myself some liberty in my translation in order to render the thought clearer (cf. Spiegel, *Kammavākya*, p. 38).

Meanwhile, Māra the sinner had the following reflection: "More than once, more than once, I attacked the śramaṇa Gautama but never could I destroy him.[171] Why would I not use the tīrthyas as a weapon?" Having made this resolution, he took on the form of Pūraṇa and soaring into the air, he produced magical apparitions of flames, light, rain, and lightning; and he spoke in this way to Maskarin, son of Gośāli: "Know, O Maskarin, that I am endowed with a supernatural power, that I know how to debate about science. The śramaṇa Gautama claims to be endowed with a supernatural power, to know how to debate about science. It is fitting that one who knows how to debate about science do battle with one who knows as much as him [etc., as above, until:] Thus, let us go do battle with the śramaṇa Gautama in the art of performing, by means of a supernatural power, miracles superior to what man can do."

Then, Māra the Sinner took on the form of Maskarin and used the same language with Saṃjayin, son of Vairaṭṭī.[172] This is how they were deceived, one by the other.

This is why each of them said to himself: "I have obtained supernatural power." Pūraṇa and the other five masters who thought they knew everything went before Bimbisāra, called Śreṇya,[173] king of Magadha, and having approached him, they spoke to him in this way: "Know, O king, that we are endowed with a supernatural power, that we know how to debate about science. The śramaṇa Gautama also claims that he is endowed with a supernatural power and that he knows how to debate about science. It is fitting that one who knows how to debate about science do battle with one who knows as much as him [etc., as above, until:] Thus, let us go do battle with the śramaṇa Gautama in the art of performing, by means of a supernatural power, miracles superior to what man can do."

This being said, Bimbisāra Śreṇya, king of Magadha, spoke in this way to the tīrthyas: "If you wish to become cadavers, you need only have a battle of supernatural power with the Bhagavat." [Some time later] Pūraṇa and the other five masters, who, not knowing everything, thought that they knew everything, having met Bimbisāra Śreṇya, king of Magadha, on the path, repeated to him what they had already told him; but Bimbisāra responded in these terms to the tīrthya mendicants: "If you repeat the same thing to me a third time, I will drive you from the country." The tīrthyas then had this reflection: "King Bimbisāra is

171. The text says: *na kadācid avatāro labdaḥ*; this can also be translated as: "I never could find the occasion." The first meaning seems preferable to me; it is the one that the *Prajñāpāramitā* gives to the terms *avatāra* and *avatāraṇa*: we could easily justify it with Brahmanical authorities.

172. I abridged this passage, which in the text is the literal reproduction of the previous paragraph, except for the proper names.

173. The Tibetan translation of the legends related to the Discipline indicate that king Bimbisāra received the title of *Śreṇya* or *Śreṇika* because he was expert in all arts (Csoma, "Analysis of the Dul-va," in *Asiatic Researches*, vol. 20, p. 46).

a listener of the śramaṇa Gautama, let us leave Bimbisāra; but Prasenajit, king of Kośala, is impartial; when the śramaṇa Gautama goes to the city of Śrāvastī, we will go there, and we will challenge him to perform, by means of his supernatural power, miracles superior to what man can do." Having said these words, they withdrew.

Then, Bimbisāra said to one of his people: "Go and promptly harness a good chariot; I will climb into it, because I wish to go see the Bhagavat in order to honor him." "Yes, Lord," responded the servant, and having promptly harnessed a good chariot, he brought it before Bimbisāra, and having approached him, he said to him: "The good chariot of the king is harnessed; the appointed moment for that which the king wishes to do is arrived." Then, Bimbisāra, having climbed into the good chariot, left Rājagṛha and made his way toward the Bhagavat, with the intention to see him, in order to honor him. As long as the terrain allowed him to make use of his chariot, he advanced in this way; then having stepped down from it, he entered the hermitage on foot and saw the Bhagavat there. As soon as he had laid aside his five insignia of royal power, that is to say, the turban, the parasol, the dagger, the flyswatter made from the tail of a yak, and the shoes of various colors, he moved toward the Bhagavat, and having approached him, he saluted his feet by touching them with his head and sat to the side. The Bhagavat, seeing the king seated to the side, started to instruct him with a discourse on the law; he caused him to receive it, he aroused his zeal, he filled him with joy; and after having in more than one way instructed him with discourses on the law, after having caused him to receive it, after having aroused his zeal and overwhelmed him with joy, he remained silent. Then, Bimbisāra, after having praised the Bhagavat and having shown his assent, saluted his feet by touching them with his head and retired from his presence.

Then, this reflection came to the mind of the Bhagavat: "In which place did the perfectly accomplished buddhas of the past perform great miracles for the well-being of creatures?" The divinities responded to the Bhagavat in this way: "Long ago, Lord, the perfectly accomplished buddhas of the past performed great miracles for the well-being of creatures. The Bhagavat possesses the insight of science. It is at Śrāvastī that the perfectly accomplished buddhas of the past performed great miracles for the well-being of creatures." Then, the Bhagavat spoke in this way to the respectable Ānanda: "Go, O Ānanda, and announce the following to the monks: 'The Tathāgata must go and travel through the countryside of Kośala; if there is one who wishes to go there with the Tathāgata, he should wash, sew, and dye his robes.'" "Yes, Venerable One!" So the respectable Ānanda responded to the Bhagavat; and he announced to the monks what the Bhagavat had told him, and in the same terms. The monks promised the respectable Ānanda to do it.

Then, the Bhagavat, master of himself, calm, free, consoled, disciplined, venerable, exempt from passion, benevolent, was surrounded by a retinue of sages who shared with him these same merits; he was like the bull surrounded by a herd of cows; like the elephant among his young; like the lion among the animals of the woods; like the *rājahaṃsa* among the swans; like Suparṇa (Garuḍa) among the birds; like a brahman among his disciples; like a good doctor among his patients; like a brave man among his soldiers; like the guide among the voyagers; like the leader of the caravan among the merchants; like a chief of the guilds among the inhabitants of a city; like the king of a fortress among his counselors; like a sovereign monarch among his thousand children; like the moon among the nakṣatras (lunar mansions); like the sun surrounded by his thousands of rays; like Virūḍhaka[174] among the kumbhāṇḍas; like Virūpākṣa[175] among the nāgas; like Dhanada[176] among the yakṣas; like Dhṛtarāṣṭra[177] among the gandharvas; like Vemacitra among the asuras; like Śakra among the gods; like Brahmā among the brahmakāyikas; he resembled the moving ocean, a lake filled with water, the king of the elephants who would be peaceful; the Bhagavat, I say, advancing with a gait in which his senses, well mastered, did not disturb his calm,[178]

174. It is the god whose name is transcribed by the Chinese in this way: *Piloulecha* or *Piliuli*; they rightly see in it the meaning of "increased grandeur," but it is probably a matter of physical grandeur here; for one knows that the kumbhāṇḍas are deformed gods. This god resides in the fourth heaven arrayed on Mount Meru on the southern side (Rémusat, *Foe koue ki*, pp. 139 and 140).

175. The Chinese transcribe this name in this way: *Piliubocha*; but the note of Mr. A. Rémusat that furnishes me with these transcriptions does not give the true meaning of them. The word *virūpākṣa* means "he who has deformed eyes." This god resides in the fourth heaven of Mount Meru, on the western side (Rémusat, *Foe koue ki*, p. 140).

176. Dhanada, or the god of wealth, also has another name, Vaiśravaṇa, which often appears in the Buddhist legends, and which the Chinese transcribe as *Pishamen*, "the glorious." This god resides in the fourth heaven of Mount Meru, on the northern side (Rémusat, *Foe koue ki*, p. 139).

177. This name is transcribed in this way by the Chinese: *Titou laizha* or *Tiduo luozha*, "the protector of the realm." It seems that the Chinese transcription comes from a Pāli original and not Sanskrit. This god resides in the fourth heaven arrayed on Mount Meru, on the eastern side (Rémusat, *Foe koue ki*, p. 139).

178. The expression the text uses here is again particular to Buddhist Sanskrit: *sudāntair indriyair asaṃkṣobhiteryāpathapracāraḥ*, literally "advancing on the path with a gait unmoved by his well-mastered senses." Wilson, however, gives *īryā* with the meaning of "wandering about" in speaking of a religious mendicant; but this term certainly has a broader signification in Buddhist Sanskrit, for example that of "manner of being, posture." We will indeed see below that four *īryāpatha*, or manners of being, are counted, and that these manners are walking, the act of standing, of being seated, and of being reclined. They were made a particular merit of Śākyamuni in the legends, and the word *īryā* forms the principal element of two epithets that figure in the series of titles of the Tathāgata: *praśānteryāpatha*, "who has the way of a calm gait," and *sarvairyāpatha caryāviśeṣa samanvāgata*, "endowed with the practice of various kinds of postures" (*Lalitavistara*, fol. 222a of my manuscript). The Chinese also know the value of this term, which, if not transcribed, is at least defined in a passage of a note of Mr. A. Rémusat regarding the discipline (*Foe koue ki*, p. 60). The Sinhalese also know this expression, and Clough defines it in this way: "A general term expressing existence, either sitting, standing, reclining or walking" (*Singhalese Dictionary*, 2:70, col. 2). The Pāli texts teach us that Ānanda reached the perfection of an arhat at a moment when he did not practice any of the four *īryāpatha*, that is to say, he was not reclining, or sitting, or standing, or walking (Turnour, "Examination of the Pāli Buddhistical Annals," in *Journal of the Asiatic Society of Bengal*, vol. 6, p. 517). The translation I give here does not prejudge in any way the meaning that this term, of which the present note sufficiently fixes the general signification, can have in other passages. I find an example of it in the *Mahāvastu* (fol. 265a of my manuscript), which proves that it is

and with the numerous attributes of a buddha that are not confused with one another,[179] made his way toward the city of Śrāvastī, followed by a great assembly of monks. Accompanied by several hundred thousand divinities, he reached the end of his journey to Śrāvastī, where he settled, taking up residence at Jetavana, in the garden of Anāthapiṇḍika.

The tīrthyas learned that the śramaṇa Gautama had gone to Śrāvastī, and at this news, they also went to this city. When they had arrived there, they spoke in this way to Prasenajit, king of Kośala: "Know, O king, that we possess a supernatural power, that we know how to debate about science. The śramaṇa Gautama also claims to be endowed with a supernatural power, he claims to know how to debate about science. It is fitting that one who knows how to debate do battle with one who knows as much as he does, performing, by means of his supernatural power, miracles superior to what man can do [etc., as above, until:] Thus, permit us to do battle with the śramaṇa Gautama in the art of performing, by means of a supernatural power, miracles superior to what man can do."

This being said, Prasenajit, king of Kośala, spoke in this way to the tīrthyas: "Go and wait until I have seen the Bhagavat." Then, Prasenajit said to one of his people: "Go and promptly harness a good chariot; I will climb into it to go see the Bhagavat to honor him this very day." "Yes, Lord," responded the servant, and having promptly harnessed a good chariot, he went to Prasenajit, and having approached him, he said to him: "The good chariot of the king is harnessed; the appointed moment for that which the king wishes to do is arrived." Then, Prasenajit, king of Kośala, having climbed into this good chariot, left Śrāvastī, and made his way toward the Bhagavat, with the intention to see him, in order to honor him. As long as the terrain allowed him to make use of his chariot, he advanced in this way; then having stepped down from it, he entered the hermitage on foot. Making his way then in the direction where the Bhagavat was, he ap-

applied to personages other than the Buddha, and that it is used frequently. The first time that Śāriputra, who was not yet converted to Buddhism, meets a monk, he exclaims: *kalyāṇā punar iyam pravrajitasya iryā*, "Beautiful, indeed, is the gait of the monk." Since the monk in question is presented going through Rājagṛha, the translation of this word as "gait" is certainly the more accurate here. See the additions at the end of this volume.

179. We have here again a difficult expression quite peculiar to the Buddhists; it is the term *āveṇika*, which one ordinarily finds connected to *dharma*. Thus far, I have not encountered the explanation of this adjective anywhere, and it is by conjecture that I translate it as I do, taking it as a derivative of the word *aveṇi*, "which does not form a braid or which does not mingle in the manner of several rivers uniting into one." What suggests this interpretation to me is a passage in the *Avadānaśataka* (fol. 4a), where it is a matter of three memory aids that are not confused with one another. These aids are probably the superior means that the Buddha possesses to remember the past, to know the present, and to predict the future, and by *smṛti* (memory) one must undoubtedly understand the mind in general, as the Buddhists ordinarily do. The Buddha, indeed, possesses a distinct knowledge of the three parts of the duration of time, the spectacle of which is not confused in his mind. In another place of the *Avadānaśataka* (fol. 7a), one speaks of the five distinct conditions (*āveṇika*), which are found in a woman of an enlightened nature; this second passage does not present anything that contradicts the meaning that I believe I can deduce from the first.

proached him, and having saluted his feet by touching them with his head, he sat to the side. There, Prasenajit, king of Kośala, spoke in this way to the Bhagavat: "The tīrthyas, Lord, challenge the Bhagavat to perform, by means of his supernatural power, miracles superior to what man can do. May the Bhagavat consent to manifest, by means of his supernatural power, miracles superior to what man can do, in the interest of creatures; may the Bhagavat confound the tīrthyas; may he satisfy devas and humans; may he delight the hearts and souls of virtuous people."

This being said, the Bhagavat spoke in this way to Prasenajit, king of Kośala: "Great king, I do not teach the law to my listeners by telling them: 'Go, O monks, and, with the aid of a supernatural power, perform miracles superior to what man can do before brahmans and householders that you meet'; but this is how I teach the law to my listeners: 'Live, O monks, hiding your good deeds and revealing your sins.'"

Two times and three times, Prasenajit, king of Kośala, made the same entreaty to the Bhagavat, addressing it to him in the same terms. Now, it is a law that the blessed buddhas must perform ten indispensable acts while they live, they exist, they are, and they find themselves in this life. The blessed Buddha does not enter into complete annihilation as long as another does not learn from his lips that he must one day become a buddha; as long as he has not inspired in another being a thought incapable of ever turning away from the supreme state of a perfectly accomplished buddha; as long as all those who must be converted by him have not been; as long as he has not exceeded three-quarters of the duration of his existence; as long as he has not entrusted [to others] the repository of duties; as long as he has not appointed two of his listeners as the foremost of all; as long as he has not shown himself descending from the heaven of the devas in the city of Sāṃkāśya;[180] as long as, gathered with his listeners by the great lake Anavatapta,[181] he has not expounded the sequence of his previous actions; as long as he has not

180. The Chinese traveler Faxian recounts in detail the legend to which an allusion is made here, and A. Rémusat expands on it in excellent notes (*Foe koue ki*, p. 124ff.). Sāṃkāśya is a city formerly known from the Brahmanical authors. The *Rāmāyaṇa* (bl. 1, chap. 70, st. 3b, Schlegel; and chap. 72, st. 3b, Gorresio) mentions this name as it is written here, and Wilson thinks that it has to be restored in the *Viṣṇu Purāṇa* (p. 390, note 5). The Buddhists from Ceylon call this city Saṃkassa, due to a distortion peculiar to Pāli (Clough, *Pāli Grammar and Vocabulary*, p. 24, st. 4b). At the beginning of the fifth century of our era, Faxian extended this name to the realm, or more exactly to the district, of which Sāṃkāśya was the capital; but in the seventh century, this district, according to Xuanzang, had already changed its name. A. Rémusat places Sāṃkāśya near Farrukhabad, and Wilson near Manpuri (*Journal of the Royal Asiatic Society*, vol. 5, p. 121). The ruins of this formerly celebrated city were found in 1842 by Mr. A. Cunningham on the site of the village of Saṃkassa, which is situated on the northern bank of the Kālīnadī (*Journal of the Royal Asiatic Society*, vol. 7, p. 241). The name and the geographical conditions agree here.

181. This lake, as was established by Klaproth, is the same as the Rāvaṇahrada (*Foe koue ki*, p. 37), and the name that our legends give to it confirms the explanation that I have already proposed of the name it bears in Pāli, Anavatatta, and among the Chinese, *Anouda*. The legend of the miraculous journey of Śākya is recounted in detail in the Tibetan Dul-va analyzed by Csoma de Kőrös (*Asiatic Researches*, vol. 20, p. 65).

established his father and mother in the truths;[182] as long as he has not made a great miracle in Śrāvastī. Then, the Bhagavat had this reflection: "This is an action that the Tathāgata must necessarily accomplish." Convinced by this truth, he spoke in this way to Prasenajit, king of Kośala: "Go, O great king; seven days from now, in the presence of a great multitude of people, the Tathāgata will perform, by means of his supernatural power, miracles superior to what man can do, and this in the interest of creatures."

Then, king Prasenajit spoke in this way to the Bhagavat: "If the Bhagavat consents, I will have a building constructed so that the Blessed One can perform his miracles there." However, the Bhagavat had this reflection: "In what place have the perfectly accomplished buddhas done great miracles for the good of creatures?" The divinities responded to the Bhagavat: "Between Śrāvastī and Jetavana; it is at a site located between these two places that the perfectly accomplished buddhas of the past performed great miracles for the good of creatures." The Bhagavat thus received the proposition of Prasenajit, king of Kośala, by remaining silent. Then, the king seeing that the Bhagavat granted him his consent, spoke to him in this way: "In which place, Lord, shall I have the building of the miracles constructed?" "Between Śrāvastī and Jetavana, O great king." Then, Prasenajit, king of Kośala, having praised and approved the words of the Bhagavat, saluted his feet by touching them with his head and withdrew.

Then, king Prasenajit spoke in this way to the tīrthyas: "Know, lords, that seven days from now the śramaṇa Gautama is to perform miracles, by means of his supernatual power, superior to what man can do." Then, the tīrthyas had this reflection: "In seven days is the śramaṇa Gautama capable of acquiring faculties that he does not possess? Or else will he run away? Or else does he want to attempt to make a following for himself?" Then, this thought came to their mind: "Certainly the śramaṇa Gautama will not run away, and certainly also he will not acquire faculties that he still does not possess; the śramaṇa Gautama wants to attempt to make a following for himself; and we, on our side, we will try to make one." Having decided in this way, they sent for the mendicant named Raktākṣa, who was skilled in magic, and recounted the matter to him in detail, telling him: "Know, O Raktākṣa, that we have challenged the śramaṇa Gautama to make use of his supernatural power; now he says that seven days from now he will perform, by means of his supernatural power, miracles superior to what man can do. Certainly the śramaṇa Gautama wants to attempt to make a following for himself. You, however, seek to make followers for us among those who follow the same religious rule as we do." The mendicant promised to do what they asked

182. Faxian makes an allusion to this fabulous legend (*Foe koue ki*, pp. 124 and 171. A. Rémusat, *ibid.*, p. 129). One can find it also reported in substance by the Mongol historian Sagang Secen (Schmidt, *Geschichte der Ost-Mongolen*, p. 15).

of him. He thus went to a place where there were many tīrthikas, śramaṇas, brahmans, ascetics, and mendicants, and when he had arrived there he recounted the matter to them in detail, telling them: "Know, lords, that we have challenged the śramaṇa Gautama to make use of his supernatural power. Now, he said that seven days from now he will perform, by means of his supernatural power, miracles superior to what man can do. The śramaṇa Gautama certainly wants to attempt to make a following for himself. You, however, you must also make an alliance with those who follow the same religious rule as you do; it is necessary that seven days from now, you leave Śrāvastī." The assembly promised him to do what he asked.

Now, there were five hundred ṛṣis who resided on a certain mountain. The mendicant Raktākṣa went to the place where these ṛṣis were and when he had arrived there, he recounted the matter to them in detail [etc., as in the previous paragraph, until:] "It is necessary that seven days from now, you go to Śrāvastī." The ṛṣis promised him to do what he asked of them.

There was at that time a religious, named Subhadra, who possessed the five supernatural knowledges; he lived in the city of Kuśinagarī, and passed the day by the great lake Anavatapta.[183] The mendicant Raktākṣa went to the place where Subhadra was; and when he had arrived there, he recounted the matter to him in detail [etc., as above, until:] "It is necessary that seven days from now, you go to Śrāvastī." But Subhadra responded: "It is not good for you to have challenged the śramaṇa Gautama to make use of his supernatural power. Why is that? It is this: my residence is in Kuśinagarī, and I pass the day by the great lake Anavatapta. Now, the śramaṇa Gautama has a disciple, named Śāriputra, who has a novice named Cunda,[184] and this Śāriputra also passes the day by the great lake Anavatapta. But the divinities themselves who live in this lake do not believe that they must show as much respect [to me] as to this monk. Here is an example: when I have traveled through Kuśinagarī in order to collect alms, and when I have received something to make my repast, I go by the great lake Anavatapta. But the divinities of the lake do not go to draw water from it for me and do not come to offer it to me. Cunda, obeying the orders of his master, takes the rags with which he covers himself, and goes by the great lake Anavatapta. Then, the divinities who live in it, after having washed these rags, sprinkle their body with the water supplied for this use. This sage, whose disciple has a disciple of whom we are not even the equals, is the one you have challenged to perform miracles superior to what man can do. You did not do well when you challenged him to display his supernatural power; for I know well that the śramaṇa Gautama is endowed with

183. This could happen only by virtue of a miracle, if the lake Anavatapta is in reality Rāvaṇahrada.

184. The word I translate as "novice" is *śrāmaṇera*; I will return to this title in the section on the Discipline. Cunda was one of the foremost disciples of Śākya; at the time of his death, he was considered one of his four most learned listeners (Csoma, *Asiatic Researches*, vol. 20, p. 315). One finds his name cited by the Vocabulaire Pentaglotte in the list of the respectable personages of the past, sec. 21.

great superhuman faculties and has a great power." Raktākṣa responded to him: "Thus, you take the side of the śramaṇa Gautama; you must not come." "And so," replied Subhadra, "I do not plan to go to Śrāvastī."

Prasenajit, king of Kośala, had a brother named Kāla, handsome, pleasant to behold, gracious, full of faith [in the Buddha], a good man endowed with a virtuous heart. One day as he went out through the door of the palace of Prasenajit, one of the women confined in the royal residence, who was on the terrace, having seen the young prince, threw down a garland of flowers, which fell on him. The world is composed of friends, enemies, and the indifferent. Someone then went to say to Prasenajit: "Know, O king, that Kāla just seduced a woman of the inner apartments." The king of Kośala was violent, hot-tempered, cruel; without fuller investigation, he immediately gave the following order to his guards: "Go quickly, cut off the feet and the hands of Kāla." "The king will be obeyed," responded the guards; and soon after they cut off the feet and the hands of the prince, right in the middle of the street. Kāla cried out violently, and he experienced a cruel, sharp, excruciating, and terrible suffering. Seeing Kāla, the brother of the king, so ill-treated, the crowd of people started to cry. Pūraṇa and the other ascetics also came to this place, and the friends of the young man told them: "This is the time to act, lords, call on the truth of your belief, in order to restore Kāla, the brother of the king, to his original state." But Pūraṇa responded: "This one is a listener of the śramaṇa Gautama; by virtue of the law of the śramaṇas, it is for Gautama to restore him as he was before." Then Kāla, the brother of the king, had this reflection: "In the unhappiness and the cruel distress that has befallen me, the Bhagavat must succor me." Then he pronounced the following stanza:

"Why does the master of the worlds not know the miserable state that has befallen me? Adoration to this being free from passion, who is full of mercy for all creatures!"

Nothing escapes the knowledge of the blessed buddhas;[185] this is why the Bhagavat addressed the respectable Ānanda in these terms: "Go, O Ānanda, take your robe, and having made a monk accompany you in the capacity of servant, go to the place where Kāla, the brother of the king, is; then, putting the feet and the hands of the young man back in their place, pronounce these words: 'Among all beings, those who have no feet as well as those who have two or several, those who have a form as well as those who have none, those who have consciousness as well as those who have none, or who have neither consciousness nor the absence of consciousness, the venerable Tathāgata, perfectly and completely Buddha, is called the foremost being. Among all the laws, those that are fulfilled as well as

185. The text here uses an expression peculiar to Buddhist Sanskrit: *asaṃmoṣadharmāṇo buddhāḥ*. It is only by conjecture that I provide this translation.

those that are not, detachment is called the foremost law. Among all assemblies, troops, multitudes, meetings, the assembly of the listeners of the Tathāgata is called the foremost assembly. Now, may your body, by the effect of this truth, this declaration of the truth, return to what it was before.'" The respectable Ānanda having responded: "Lord, it will be so done," took his robe and having made a monk accompany him in the capacity of servant, he went to the place where Kāla, the brother of the king, was; then, when he had arrived there, he put the feet and the hands of the young prince back in their place, and pronounced these words: "Among all beings [etc., as above, until:] the venerable Tathāgata, perfectly and completely Buddha, is called the foremost being. Among all laws [etc., as above, until:] detachment is called the foremost law. Among all assemblies [etc., as above, until:] the assembly of the listeners of the Tathāgata is called the foremost assembly. Now, may your body, by the effect of this truth, this declaration of the truth, return to what it was before." These words had hardly been pronounced when the body of the prince returned to its original form; and this was done in such a way that by the power unique to the Buddha and by the divine power of the devas, the young Kāla saw at the same instant the reward of the state of *anāgāmin*, and manifested supernatural faculties. Then, he retired to the hermitage of the Bhagavat and he started to perform the duties of domestic service for him. And since his body had been torn to pieces, his name was changed to Gaṇḍaka, the servant of the hermitage. Prasenajit, king of Kośala, sought by all possible means to make him return; but Kāla told him: "You do not need me; I only wish to serve the Bhagavat."

Meanwhile, king Prasenajit had a building constructed between Śrāvastī and Jetavana so that the Bhagavat could make his miracles in it; it was a maṇḍapa, the four sides of which were a hundred thousand cubits in length; a throne had been prepared in it for the Bhagavat. The listeners of the tīrthyas also had a building constructed for each of the other ascetics. When the seventh day had come, the king had the ground separating Jetavana from the building dedicated to the Bhagavat cleaned by taking away the stones, the gravel, and the rubbish. A cloud of incense and perfumed powders was spread there; parasols, flags, standards were raised; the ground was sprinkled with scented water; various flowers were scattered; and resting places made of flowers were erected here and there.

Now, on the seventh day, the Bhagavat, having gotten dressed around the beginning of the day, took his mantle and his bowl and entered Śrāvastī to collect alms. When, traveling through the city, he had collected food, he made his repast; then having ceased the gathering of alms, he arranged his bowl and his mantle; having then washed his feet outside the vihāra, he entered it to recline there.

Then king Prasenajit, accompanied by a retinue of several hundred, several thousand, several hundred thousands of people, went to the place where the building dedicated to the Bhagavat had been constructed; and when he had arrived there, he sat on the seat intended for him. The tīrthyas, also accompanied by a great multitude of people, made their way toward their building, and when they had arrived there, each one sat on his seat, and spoke to Prasenajit, king of Kośala, in this way. "Know, O king, that we just arrived; where is the śramaṇa Gautama now?" "Wait a moment," responded the king, "the Bhagavat will come soon." Then, Prasenajit called a young man who was named Uttara: "Go find the Bhagavat," he said to him, "and when you have approached him, salute the feet of the Bhagavat in our name by touching them with the head. Wish him little pain, few maladies; wish him facility in effort, means, strength, pleasure, the absence of all reproach, and agreeable relations, and speak to him in this way: 'This is, Lord, what Prasenajit, king of Kośala, has said: The tīrthyas, Lord, have arrived; the appointed time for what the Bhagavat wishes to do has come.'" Uttara promised to obey the king, and having gone to the place where the Bhagavat was, he approached him, and after having exchanged pleasant and benevolent words of conversation with him, he sat to the side; then, from his place, he spoke in this way to the Bhagavat. "Prasenajit, king of Kośala, salutes the feet of the Bhagavat by touching them with the head. He wishes him little pain, few maladies; he wishes him facililty in effort, means, strength, pleasure, the absence of all reproach, and agreeable relations." "May king Prasenajit be happy, O young man, and be so also yourself!" "This is, Lord, what Prasenajit, king of Kośala, said: 'The tīrthyas, Lord, have arrived; the appointed time for what the Bhagavat wishes to do has come.'"

This having been said, the Bhagavat responded in this way to the young Uttara: "Young man, I go there at once." And he blessed Uttara in such a way that the young man, rising up from the very place where he was, set off through the air, making his way toward Prasenajit. The king saw the young Uttara, who arrived through the air; and as soon as he had seen him, he addressed the tīrthyas in this way: "Here is the Bhagavat, who has just performed a miracle superior to what man can do; thus, it is your turn to perform one." But the tīrthyas responded: "Great king, there is an immense multitude of people here; how will you know if the miracle is performed by us or by the śramaṇa Gautama?"

Then, the Bhagavat entered into a meditation such that, as soon as he turned his mind to it, one saw, going out through the hole where the lock [of the door] is placed, a flame that fell on the building dedicated to the Bhagavat and set it completely on fire. The tīrthyas saw the building of the Bhagavat claimed by the flames, and at this sight they said to Prasenajit, king of Kośala: "The building where the Bhagavat must make miracles, O great king, is completely claimed by the flames; go then to extinguish it." But before water touched it, the fire extinguished itself without burning the building; and this took place by the Buddha's own power and by the divine power of the devas. At that moment, king

Prasenajit said to the tīrthyas: "The Bhagavat just performed, with the aid of his supernatural power, a miracle superior to what man can do; thus, it is your turn to perform one." But the tīrthyas responded: "Great king, there is an immense multitude of people here; how will you know if the miracle is performed by us or by the śramaṇa Gautama?"

Then, the Bhagavat made a light as bright as gold appear, which filled the entire world with a noble splendor. Prasenajit, king of Kośala, saw the entire universe illuminated by this noble splendor, and at this sight, he said once again to the tīrthyas: "The Bhagavat just performed, with the aid of his supernatural power, a miracle superior to what man can do; thus, it is your turn to perform one." But the tīrthyas responded: "Great king, there is a great multitude of people here; how will you know if the miracle is performed by us or by the śramaṇa Gautama?"

Gaṇḍaka, the servant of the hermitage, having brought a karṇikāra stalk[186] from the continent named Uttarakuru, came to place it in front of the building where the Bhagavat would make his miracles. Ratnaka, the servant of the hermitage, having brought an aśoka stalk[187] from Gandhamādana, came to put it behind the building where the Bhagavat would make his miracles. Then, Prasenajit, king of Kośala, spoke in this way to the tīrthyas: "The Bhagavat just performed, with the aid of his supernatural power, a miracle superior to what man can do; thus, it is your turn to perform one." But the tīrthyas gave him the same response that they had already given.

Then, the Bhagavat put his two feet on the earth with intention; and immediately a great trembling of the earth took place. This great thousand of three thousand worlds,[188] this great earth was shaken in six differents ways: it moved and trembled, it was agitated and tossed, it bounced and jumped. The eastern part sank, and the western rose; the south rose and the north sank; then the opposite movement occurred. The center rose, the ends sank; the center sank, the ends rose. The sun and the moon blazed, glittered, shined. Varied and marvelous apparitions were seen. The divinities of the atmosphere spread on the Bhagavat divine lotuses of blue, red, as well as powders of aguru,[189] sandalwood, tagara,[190]

186. *Pterospermum acerifolium.* This is again a miraculous journey, as is that of Ratnaka. One knows that Uttarakuru is one of the four dvīpas, or continents in the shape of islands, that the Buddhists recognize; Uttarakuru lies to the north. The Buddhists certainly borrowed it from the mythical geography of the brahmans (Lassen, *Indische Altertumskunde*, 1:511).

187. *Jonesia Aśoka.* Gandhamādana is a mountain located to the south of Meru, or else one of the seven ranges of Bhāratavarṣa. One can see in the table of the *Viṣṇu Purāṇa* of Wilson the various applications of this ethnic term. It is again a borrowing the Buddhists made from the brahmans.

188. See on this expression, and on the world system among the Buddhists, the learned clarifications by Mr. Schmidt (*Mémoires de l'Académie des sciences de Saint-Pétersbourg*, 2:53ff.) and the special memorandum by Mr. A. Rémusat (*Journal des Savans*, 1831, p. 670ff.).

189. *Aquilaria agallocha.*

190. *Tabernœmontana coronaria.*

tamāla leaves,[191] and divine flowers of mandārava.[192] They made their celestial instruments resound and made a rain of robes fall.

Then, the ṛṣis had this reflection: "Why did a great trembling of the earth take place?" This idea came to their mind: "Undoubtedly, those who follow the same religious rule as we do must have challenged the śramaṇa Gautama to make use of his supernatural power." Convinced of that, the five hundred ṛṣis departed for Śrāvastī. When they set out on the journey, the Bhagavat blessed the route in such a way that at the same instant, they completed their journey.[193] They saw from afar the Bhagavat adorned with the thirty-two characteristics of a great man, who looked like the law arrayed in a body; the sacrificial fire sprinkled with butter; the wick of a lamp put in a vase of gold; a mountain of gold that walks; a pillar of gold enhanced with various jewels; they saw, in short, the blessed Buddha, whose great and high intelligence, pure and without stain, manifested itself externally; and having seen it, they were filled with joy. Indeed, the possession of quietude does not cause so perfect a happiness for the man who practices yoga for twelve years, the possession of a child does not give as much to one who has no son, the sight of treasure does not provide as much to a poor person, royal anointing does not give as much to one who desires the throne, as the first sight of a buddha assures to those beings whose roots of virtue previous buddhas have made to grow. Then these ṛṣis went to the place where the Bhagavat was, and when they had arrived there, having saluted the feet of the Bhagavat by touching them with the head, they stood to the side; and from the place where they stood, they spoke to him in this way: "Enable us, Lord, under the discipline of the well-renowned law, to embrace the religious life and receive the investiture and the rank of a monk! Enable us, having become mendicants in the presence of the Bhagavat, to fulfill the duties of the religious life!" The Bhagavat then said to them, with his voice that has the sound of that of Brahmā: "Approach, O monks, fulfill the duties of the religious life!" And hardly had he pronounced these words than they found themselves shaved, covered in the religious robes, holding in the hand the pitcher that ends in the beak of a bird, having a beard and hair of seven days, and with the decent aspect of monks who would have received investiture a hundred years ago. "Approach," the Tathāgata said [again] to them; and shaved, the body covered with the religious robes, feeling the truths bringing calm to all their senses, they stood, then sat with the permission of the Buddha.[194]

191. *Xanthocymus pictorius.*

192. *Erythrina fulgens*? This name is given to the Mandāra.

193. I am not certain to have grasped the meaning of this expression: *ekāyano mārgo' dhiṣṭhitaḥ.* Do we have to translate it more simply: "The Bhagavat blessed the road on which they advanced together"?

194. I am not certain that I have understood this passage, where one finds a negation that is not in the Tibetan version, as it is given in a passage of the story of Pūrṇa, which will be translated below: *naiva sthitā*

Then the Bhagavat, honored, respected, venerated, adored with homages such as those rendered by humans and gods; surrounded by personages as venerable as him, followed by seven kinds of troops and by a great multitude of people; the Bhagavat, I say, went to the place where the building erected for him was; and when he arrived there, he sat in front of the assembly of monks, on the seat intended for him. Immediately, rays emanated from the body of the Bhagavat, which illuminated all of the building with a light the color of gold. At that moment, Lūhasudatta, the householder, having risen from his seat, having pushed his upper robe back over his shoulder, and placing his right knee on the ground, pointed his joined hands toward the Bhagavat as a sign of respect, and spoke to him in this way: "May the Bhagavat moderate his ardor; I will do battle with the tīrthyas in the art of performing, with the aid of a supernatural power, miracles superior to what man can do; I will confound the tīrthyas with the law; I will satisfy devas and humans; I will fill the hearts and souls of virtuous people with joy."—"It is not you, householder, who has been challenged by them to make miracles, but I myself who has been. It is I who must, with the aid of my supernatural power, perform miracles superior to what man can do; it would not be fitting that the tīrthyas could say: 'The śramaṇa Gautama does not have the supernatural power to perform miracles superior to what man can do, which one of his listeners, a householder who wears white robes, possesses.'[195] Go take your seat, householder!" Lūhasudatta indeed sat down again on his seat. The request that he had expressed was made also by Kāla, the brother of the king; by Rambhaka, the servant of the hermitage; by the mother of Ṛddhila,[196] a devotee who served a śramaṇa; by Cunda, the servant of a śramaṇa; and by the nun Utpalavarṇā.[197]

---

buddhamanorathena, which seems to mean: "They did not remain standing in accordance with the wish of the Buddha." The Tibetan version expresses itself in this way: *sangs rgyas dgongs pas lus gzugs bkab par gyur*, which seems to mean: "With the permission of the Buddha, they covered their body."

195. This is a quite characteristic expression, which can only be understood well if one recalls that Buddhist monks had to wear robes dyed in yellow by means of an ocherous earth. This detail is set forth with a good deal of interest in the famous drama *Mṛcchakaṭī* (act 8, pp. 213 and 216, Calcutta ed.). The text designates the color in question with the word *kaṣāya*, "brown-yellow," the very same that our Buddhist legends use. One sees from our sūtra that white was the color of the robe of laypersons, compared to that of monks, which was yellow; and this passage casts daylight on an account in the Sinhalese history, according to which a king who wants to degrade some guilty monks strips them of their yellow mantle and orders them to dress in white clothes (Turnour, *Journal of the Royal Asiatic Society of Bengal*, vol. 6, p. 737. Upham, *The Mahāvansi*, etc., 2:91). Mr. W. von Humboldt had already made the same remark on the occasion of some monuments of Javanese Buddhism; and he had very judiciously conjectured that white should be the color of the laypeople, as opposed to the yellow color, which is that of monks (*Über die Kawi-Sprache*, 1:250).

196. I have not encountered this name elsewhere; my two manuscripts are so defective that I would be tempted to assume that Ṛddhila is a faulty spelling of Rāhula, the son of Yaśodharā. One knows indeed that she was one of the first women who embraced the religious life (*Asiatic Researches* vol. 20, p. 308, note 21). I did not believe, however, that I needed to change the text.

197. This name means: "she who has the color of the blue lotus." She is probably the same as the nun whom Faxian speaks about, and whom he calls *Youboluo*. Mr. A. Rémusat had recognized well the Sanskrit

Then, the respectable Mahāmaudgalyāyana,[198] having risen from his seat, having pushed his upper robe back over his shoulder and placing his right knee on the ground, pointed his joined hands toward the Bhagavat as a sign of respect, and spoke to him in this way: "May the Bhagavat moderate his ardor; I will do battle with the tīrthyas in the art of performing, by means of a supernatural power, miracles superior to what man can do; I will confound the tīrthyas with the law; I will satisfy devas and humans; I will fill the hearts and souls of virtuous people with joy." "You are able, O Maudgalyāyana, to confound the tīrthyas by the law; but it is not you who has been challenged by them to make miracles, it is I myself who has been. It is I who must, by means of my supernatural power, perform miracles superior to what man can do, and this in the interest of creatures;

---

utpala in this transcription (*Foe koue ki*, pp. 124 and 131). The anthology recently published by Mr. Schmidt contains an interesting legend about this nun (*Der Weise und der Thor*, p. 206ff.). It would seem, according to a note of Csoma (*Asiatic Researches*, vol. 20, p. 308, note 21), that Utpalavarṇā, before becoming a nun, had been the third wife of Śākyamuni. But, in another part of the Life of Śākya, Csoma designates his third wife with a Tibetan name that means "born from the gazelle" (*ibid.*, p. 290). The Sinhalese also know this nun, and the *Dīpavaṃsa* mentions two with this name among the first women who converted to Buddhism (Turnour, *Journal of the Royal Asiatic Society of Bengal*, vol. 7, p. 933). One of these two women could have been the wife of Śākya when he still had not left the world.

198. This monk is, with Śāriputra, the foremost of the disciples of Śākyamuni. I write his name *Maudgalyāyana*, contrary to the authority of the Tibetan version of the *Saddharmapuṇḍarīka*, which reads this word with *nga* instead of a *dga*, and contrary also to the opinion of Csoma, who believes, I know not on what basis, that this term means "the Mongol," thus dating the existence of the name of this people back at least to the sixth century before our era (*Asiatic Researches*, vol. 20, p. 49). Lassen has already sufficiently refuted this singular hypothesis (*Zeitschrift für die Kunde des Morgenlandes*, 3:158). The authority of the Tibetan version of the *Saddharma* and the opinion of Csoma de Kőrös are already contradicted by this single fact, that in the Tibetan version of the *Vinayavastu*, I find this proper name written in Tibetan in the following way: *Mohu dgal gyi bu*, "the son of Mohudgal," which is a sufficiently exact transcription of *Mudgala* (*'Dul ba*, vol. *kha*, or 2, fol. 64; vol. *da*, or 11, fol. 55). I find an even better spelling of it in the Tibetan legends published by Mr. Schmidt: *Mau dgal ya na* (*Der Weise und der Thor*, text p. 92). Let me add that the spelling of the Pāli texts supports the one I prefer. Indeed, the Pāli name of Moggallāna results from the contraction of *dga* into *gga*. If the original had had *nga*, the Pāli would have had nothing to change, and would be written *Mongallāna*. It is, however, fair to say that the confusion of *dga* and *nga* is extremely easy, for pronunciation as much as for writing. Buchanan Hamilton has already remarked that the present name of the city of Monghyr, which he transcribes, according to the natives, *Mungger*, is written *Mudga giri* in an ancient inscription found at the site (*The History, Antiquities, Topography, and Statistics of Eastern India*, 2:45). Our monk is the same sage that the Chinese call *Mujianlian*, according to the spelling of Mr. A. Rémusat (*Foe koue ki*, p. 32). He is regarded as the disciple of Śākya who had acquired the greatest supernatural power (*Sumāgadhāvadāna*, fol. 6a). Ritter, the great geographer, has made an artisan of him and has called him "the Daedalus of high Indian antiquity." I cannot believe that this comparison is serious (*Die Erdkunde von Asien*, 5:821). Klaproth, like Csoma, is mistaken when he advances that the Sanskrit form of this proper name is Manggalyam; but he has the merit, with the help of the Chinese, of approaching the true meaning of the name that the brahman, author of the race from which Maudgalyāyana issued, bore (*Foe koue ki*, p. 68, note a). This patronymic derives, indeed, from *Mudgala*, in which one recognizes *mugda*, the *phaseolus Mungo*; here too, in this popular name, *nga* replaces the Sanskrit *dga*. The *Harivaṃśa* mentions a Mudgala, son of Viśvāmitra, who could have been the head of the family to which Maudgalyāyana belonged (Langlois, *Harivamsa*, 1:123 and 148); and in the list of the twenty-four *gotras*, or Brahmanical families, which the great dictionary of Rādhākānta-deva provides, one finds the name of Maudgalya, that is to say: "the descendant of Mudgala" (*Śabdakalpadruma*, 1:813 and 814). When the legends speak of this personage, they always have his name preceded by the honorific epithet of *mahā*, "great"; but when it is Śākyamuni who addresses him, he never makes use of this title. I have noticed the same distinction with regard to the name Kāśyapa.

it is I who must challenge the tīrthyas, satisfy devas and humans, fill the hearts and souls of virtuous people with joy. Go, Maudgalyāyana, and take your seat again!" And Mahāmaudgalyāyana indeed went to take his seat again.

Then, the Bhagavat addressed the king of Kośala, Prasenajit, and told him: "Who asks, O great king, that the Tathāgata perform miracles superior to what man can do, and this in the interest of creatures?" Immediately, Prasenajit, king of Kośala, having risen from his seat, having pushed his upper robe back over his shoulder and placing his right knee on the ground, pointed his joined hands toward the Bhagavat as a sign of respect, and spoke to him in this way: "It is I, Lord, who beseeches the Bhagavat to perform, by means of his supernatural power, miracles superior to what man can do; may the Bhagavat perform miracles in the interest of creatures; may he challenge the tīrthyas; may he satisfy devas and humans; may he fill the hearts and the souls of virtuous people with joy!"

Then, the Bhagavat entered into a meditation such that, as soon as he turned his mind to it, he disappeared from the place where he was seated, and soaring into the air in the western direction, he appeared in the four attitudes of decorum, that is to say, he walked, he stood, he sat, he lay down. Then, he reached the region of light; and as soon as he united with it, various glows emanated from his body, blue, yellow, red, white glows and others having the most beautiful shades of crystal. He made numerous miracles appear besides; from the lower part of his body, flames shot out and from the upper came a shower of cold water. What he had done in the west, he performed also in the south; he repeated it in the four points of space; and when, by these four miracles, he had displayed his supernatural power, he returned to sit on his seat; and as soon as he sat on it, he addressed Prasenajit, king of Kośala, in this way: "This supernatural power, O great king, is common to all the listeners of the Tathāgata."

Again, a second time, the Bhagavat addressed Prasenajit, king of Kośala, in this way: "Who asks, O great king, that the Tathāgata perform, by means of his own supernatural power, miracles superior to what man can do, and this in the interest of creatures?" Then, king Prasenajit, having risen from his seat, [etc., as above, until:] spoke to him in this way: "It is I, Lord, who beseeches the Bhagavat to perform, by means of his own supernatural power, miracles superior to what man can do, and this in the interest of creatures; may the Bhagavat confound the tīrthyas; may he satisfy devas and humans; may he fill the hearts and the souls of virtuous people with joy!"

At that moment, the Bhagavat conceived a mundane thought. Now, it is a rule that when the blessed buddhas conceive a mundane thought, all beings down to the ants and other insects know the thought of the Blessed One with their mind; but when they conceive a thought superior to the world, this thought is inaccessible to the pratekyabuddhas themselves, all the more reason is it to the śrāvakas. Now, Śakra, Brahmā, and the other gods then had this reflection: "With what intention did the Bhagavat conceive a mundane thought?" And immediately, this idea came to their mind: "It is that he desires to perform great miracles in Śrāvastī, in the interest of creatures." Then, Śakra, Brahmā, and the other gods, as well as several hundred thousand divinities, knowing the thought of the Bhagavat with their mind, disappeared from the world of the devas with as much ease as a strong man would extend his closed arm or close his extended arm and came to take their place before the Bhagavat. There, having circled around the Tathāgata three times, keeping him on their right, Brahmā and other gods saluted his feet by touching them with the head; and having taken their place on his right, they sat there. Śakra and other gods, after having shown the same respect, took their place on his left and sat there. The two kings of the nāgas, Nanda and Upananda, created a one-thousand-petal lotus, the size of the wheel of a chariot, entirely of gold, whose stem was of diamonds, and they came to present it to the Bhagavat. And the Bhagavat sat on the pericarp of this lotus, legs crossed, body straight, placing his memory before his mind. Above this lotus, he created another one; and on this lotus, the Bhagavat also appeared seated. And likewise in front of him, behind him, around him appeared masses of blessed buddhas, created by him who, rising up to the heaven of Akaniṣṭha,[199] formed an assembly of buddhas, all created by the Blessed One. Some of these magical buddhas walked, others stood; those were seated, these lay down; some reached the region of light, and produced miraculous apparitions of flames, light, rain, and lightning; several asked questions, others answered them and repeated these two stanzas:

"Begin, go forth [from the house], apply yourself to the law of the Buddha; annihilate the army of death, as an elephant knocks down a hut of reeds.

"He who walks without distraction under the discipline of this law, escaping from birth and the cycle of the world, will put an end to suffering."[200]

The Bhagavat arranged everything in such a way that the entire world could see this crown of buddhas without veils, the entire world from the heaven of Akaniṣṭha to small children; and this took place by the Buddha's own power and by the divine power of the devas.

199. This is the name of the eighth of the superposed heavens of the fourth contemplation. This word, which must be read in this way and not Aghaniṣta, as it has been written according to the Vocabularaire Pentaglotte, literally means "the one that is not the smallest," that is to say, "the largest" (*Foe koue ki*, p. 146. Schmidt, *Mémoires de l'Académie des sciences de Saint-Pétersbourg*, 2:28, 1:103).

200. These two maxims are celebrated in all the Buddhist schools, and we will find them again word for word in that of the South among the Sinhalese at that time. I will in that case seek to establish that they have been originally conceived in Pāli and from there translated into Sanskrit. Csoma gave a translation of it according to a Tibetan version, which differs from mine in the second verse: *dhunīta mṛtyunaḥ sainyam naḍāgāram iva kuñjaraḥ*, "Triumph over the army of the master of death (the passions), who resembles an elephant in this residence of mud (the body)." Or else: "Tame your passions as an elephant tramples everything under his feet in a muddy lake." I do not think that the Sanskrit original yields either of these two translations, and I even believe that it would be possible to retrieve the one I propose in the Tibetan version (Csoma, *Asiatic Researches*, vol. 20, p. 79).

At that moment, the Bhagavat addressed the monks in this way: "Be convinced, O monks, the miracle of this mass of buddhas who rise up in order one above the others will disappear in an instant." And indeed, the buddhas immediately disappeared. After having shown his supernatural power in this way, he appeared again on the seat that he occupied previously, and immediately he pronounced the following stanzas:

"The insect shines as long as the sun does not appear; but as soon as the sun has risen, the insect is confounded by its rays and shines no more.[201]

"In the same way, these sophists spoke while the Tathāgata said nothing; now that the perfect Buddha has spoken, the sophist says nothing in the world, and his listener is as silent as he is."

Then, Prasenajit, king of Kośala, spoke in this way to the tīrthyas: "The Bhagavat just performed, by means of his supernatural power, miracles superior to what man can do; it is your turn to perform them." But the tīrthyas remained silent at these words, only thinking about leaving. Two times, king Prasenajit said the same thing. Then, the tīrthyas, pushing each other, said among themselves: "Get up, it is you who must get up"; but none of them got up.

Now at this time in this assembly there was Pāñcika,[202] the great general of the yakṣas. This reflection came to his mind: "These are impostors who will continue to torment the Bhagavat and the assembly of monks for a long time." Filled with this idea, he created a great storm accompanied by wind and rain, which made the building intended for the tīrthyas disappear. Struck by the thunder and the rain, they started to run away in all directions. Several hundred thousands of living beings, driven away by this violent rain, went to the place where Bhagavat was; and when they arrived there, having saluted his feet by touching them with the head, they sat to the side. But the Bhagavat arranged everything in such a way that not even a single drop of water fell on this assembly. Then, these numerous hundreds of thousands of living beings made these words of praise be heard: "Ah the Buddha! Ah the law! Ah the assembly! Ah how well-renowned is the law!" And Pāñcika, the general of the yakṣas, said to the tīrthyas: "And you, impostors, take thus refuge in the Bhagavat, in the law, in the assembly of monks!" But they exclaimed, running away: "We take refuge in the mountains; we seek a sanctuary near the trees, the walls, and the hermitages."

Then, the Bhagavat pronounced the following stanzas on this occasion:

"Many people, driven by fear, seek sanctuary in the mountains and the woods, in the hermitages and near the consecrated trees.

"But it is not the best of sanctuaries, it is not the best of refuges, and it is not in this sanctuary that one is delivered from all sufferings.

201. My two manuscripts are here very defective; I have sought the more plausible meaning.

202. See the additions at the end of the volume.

"He, on the contrary, who seeks refuge in the Buddha, the law, and the assembly, when he sees with wisdom the four sublime truths,

"Which are suffering, the production of suffering, the annihilation of suffering, and the way that leads to it; and the path formed of eight parts, the sublime, salutary path, which leads to nirvāṇa,

"It is he who knows the best of sanctuaries, the best refuge; as soon as he has reached it, he is delivered from all sufferings."

Then, Pūraṇa had the following reflection: "The śramaṇa Gautama is going to steal my listeners from me." Filled with this idea, he ran away, saying: "I will set forth to you the essence of the law," and he started to repeat these heterodox propositions: the world is perishable; it is eternal; it is at once perishable and eternal; it is neither perishable nor eternal; the soul is the body; the soul is something else, the body is something else. Such were, in a word, the heterodox propositions that he communicated [to his disciples]. So one began saying: the world is perishable. A second one replied: it is eternal and perishable; the soul is the body; the soul is something else, the body is something else. It is in this way that, given over to discussions, to quarrels, divided by opinions, they started to debate among themselves. Pūraṇa himself was afraid and he ran away. At the moment he was going, he was met by a eunuch, who, seeing him, recited this stanza:

"Where do you come from, hands hanging down like that, looking like a black ram whose horn has been broken? Ignorant of the law promulgated by the Jina, you bray like the ass of Kola (Kalinga?)." Pūraṇa responded to him: "The moment to depart has come for me; my body has no more strength or vigor. I have known beings; they partake of pleasure and pain. The science of the arhats [alone] in this world is without veils; I am quite distant from it. The obscurity is profound; the one who dispels it falls into desire.[203] Thus tell me, vile being, where is the pond with cold waters?" The eunuch replied in turn: "This, O last of the śramaṇas, is the cold pond, filled with water and covered with lotuses; do you not see it, malevolent man?" "You, you are not a man or a woman," replied Puraṇa. "You have no beard or breasts, your voice is staccato like that of a young cakravāka; so you are called *vātahata* ('beaten by the wind')."[204]

Then the mendicant Pūraṇa, having tied a jar filled with sand around his neck, plunged into the cold lake and found death there. However, the other mendi-

203. This last sentence is certainly altered; I have attempted to translate it quite literally. This fortunately does not affect the general meaning of the words that Pūraṇa pronounces at the moment he decides to give up his life. I think that the pond with cold waters is an expression analogous to that of *cold forest*, which one always sees mentioned in the legends, when one speaks of carrying a dead person to the cemetery. This pond is that in which Pūraṇa wants to drown, a project he indeed carries out.

204. I confess that I do not understand this allusion; is the word *vātahata* an epithet of the cakravāka, the name of the *Anas casarca*?

cants who were looking for him, having met a courtesan on the path, addressed this question to her: "Woman, have you seen a certain Pūraṇa coming this way, dressed with the belt of the law and carrying a bowl, like the one used by those who keep to cemeteries?" The courtesan responded: "Condemned to the abode of torments, condemned to hell, your Pūraṇa who runs, hands hanging down, perishes with his white hands and feet."[205] "Woman," said the mendicants, "do not speak like this. This is not well said by you: he fulfills the law, the recluse who is dressed with the belt of the law." "How can he be wise," replied the courtesan, "who, displaying the signs of virility, promenaded naked in the villages, before the eyes of the people? One who follows the law covers the front of his body with a robe; [if not,] the king must cut off his ears with a two-edged sword."[206]

Then, the mendicants went toward the pond of cold waters; and there, they saw Pūraṇa Kāśyapa dead and having finished his time. They pulled him from it, and having put him in another place, they went away.

Meanwhile, the Bhagavat produced a magical figure of the Buddha who bore the thirty-two marks characteristic of a great man, who was shaved and dressed with the religious robes. Now it is a rule that the blessed buddhas converse with the magical figures they have created. But if it is a śrāvaka who produces a magical figure, this figure speaks when the śrāvaka speaks, and it is silent when he is silent. When only one speaks, all the magical figures created by him speak at the same time. When only one remains silent, all also remain silent. The Bhagavat, on the contrary, poses a question to his magical figure and this figure gives its solution; for it is a rule for the tathāgatas, venerable, perfectly, and completely buddhas.

When this great multitude of people had been so favorably disposed, the Bhagavat, who knew the mind, the dispositions, the character, and the nature of all those who surrounded him, made an exposition to them of the law appropriate for them to penetrate the four sublime truths, so that among these numerous hundreds of thousands of living beings, some avidly received and understood the formulas of refuge and the precepts of the teaching,[207] others saw face to face the reward of the state of śrotāpatti, that of the sakṛāgamins and that of the anāgāmins. Some, having entered the religious life, obtained the state of arhats, through the annihilation of all corruptions; others increased the seeds that would one day produce in them the intelligence of śrāvakas or pratyekabuddhas. In the end, this entire gathering was absorbed in the Buddha, plunged into the law, drawn into the assembly. When the Bhagavat had so disposed this gathering of humans, he rose from his seat and retired.

205. Is this an allusion to the paleness of these limbs in death?

206. Pūraṇa was thus a naked mendicant, and the words "dressed with the belt of the law" were a mystical expression indicating his nakedness.

207. Here there are four words that I have omitted, because they obviously break the sentence, where they seem to be introduced as a gloss in a text; these are: *mūrdhānaḥ kṣāntayo laukikā agradharmāḥ*.

"Happy are the humans who, in the world, seek refuge in the Buddha; they will reach nirvāṇa in return for the respect they will have shown to him.

"Those who will render at least some honor to the Jina,[208] chief of humans, after having lived in the various heavens, will obtain the immortal abode."[209]

The successes of Śākya, however, aroused the jealousy of his adversaries, and in the *Divyāvadāna* one encounters more than one trace of the sentiments of joy with which the brahmans received the hope of seeing him vanquished. A legend already mentioned furnishes me with an example of that to which I have alluded above, but only in passing. Śākya had predicted to a merchant that he would have a son who would become a Buddhist monk. A brahman whom the merchant consults interprets this prediction in an insidious way; and the merchant, frightened of the future, wants to give his wife an abortion, and she dies as a result of his attempts. When the brahmans of Rājagṛha learn that this woman is dead, they pour out into the city and go into the streets and into the public squares, recalling the prediction made by Śākya, accusing him of lies and powerlessness, and ending their speeches in this way: "Now, this woman is dead; she is carried to the cemetery of the cold forest; how could he who does not even have the root of the tree have branches, leaves, and flowers?"[210] This does not prevent the Buddha from saving the child that the mother carried in her womb; but for us, such details are proof of the kind of hostility with which the brahmans and in general the religious of the other sects received the claims of Śākyamuni.

I believe it useful to add to this text another that shows us how far the resentment against the recluse of the Śākya race sometimes went.

When, says the legend of Meṇḍhaka, the Bhagavat had accomplished great miracles in the city of Śrāvastī, the devas and the humans were full of joy, the hearts of virtuous people were filled with satisfaction. Then the tīrthyas, whose power was broken, withdrew to the neighboring countries [of central India]; some went to the city of Bhadraṃkara[211] and settled there. These religious learned

208. See the additions at the end of the volume.

209. *Prātihārya Sūtra*, in *Divyāvadāna*, fol. 69b ff. of the MS of the Société Asiatique, fol. 88a ff. of my manuscript. *Bka' 'gyur*, sec. *'Dul ba*, vol. *da*, or 11, p. 230ff. Csoma, *Asiatic Researches*, vol. 20, p. 90. The Tibetan version differs notably from the Sanskrit text, and, moreover, the copy of the Kah-gyur that contains it is very badly printed and almost illegible here. This difficulty, combined with the Tibetan, which is less familiar to me than the Sanskrit, deprived me of the use of this version. The end of this piece is obviously altered in our two manuscripts; moreover, it contains allusions to ideas that do not reappear elsewhere; it is, among all the sūtras, the most difficult that I have ever encountered.

210. *Jyotiṣka*, in *Divyāvadāna*, fol. 131a.

211. Thus far, I have not found anything in the legends that indicates in which part of India one should look for this city; it is probably to the north or the west of Kośala. I do not know definitively the ancient form of the present name of Bahraich, which is that of a district or city to the north of Awadh and to the east of the river Devha (*Dvivāha*); perhaps it is none other than *Bhadraṃkara* or *Bhadrakara*, of which Bahraich

that the śramaṇa Gautama was making his way toward the city; and troubled by this news, they said one to the other: "In the past, we have been driven from Madhyadeśa by the śramaṇa Gautama; if he comes here now, he will certainly likewise drive us away; let us thus seek a means to avoid this misfortune." Having gone to the hall where the people come to ask for help, they started to cry out: "Justice! Justice!" Immediately, the people said: "What is that? Let us go to see what is happening," and they said to the tīrthyas: "Why these cries? We see that you are perfectly happy, and we do not perceive what misfortune you can complain about." "Lords," responded the tīrthyas, "it is a matter of a misfortune that will swoop down upon us. The śramaṇa Gautama is approaching, striking with the sharpness of lightning and depriving fathers of their children and wives of their husbands. Thus, lords, if he comes here, we will have to leave the place, at the very moment he settles there." "Stay," cried the people, "you must not go away." But the tīrthyas responded: "No, we will not stay, because you will not want to listen to us." "Speak," replied the people, "we will listen." "It is necessary," the tīrthyas then said, "after having made all the people leave the country of Bhadraṃkara, that the city be abandoned, the pastures plowed, the boundary stones of the fields knocked down, the fruit trees and the flowering trees cut down, and the fountains poisoned." "Lords," cried the people, "stay, we will carry out all that you order." The tīrthyas withdrew and immediately, all the people of the country of Bhadraṃkara were made to leave; the city was abandoned; the plow was pulled through the pastures, the boundary stones knocked down, the fruit trees and the flowering trees cut down, and the waters poisoned.

At this moment, Śakra, the Indra of the devas, had this reflection: "It would not be fitting for me to permit that one not render the duties of hospitality to the Bhagavat, to him who during three asaṃkhyeyas of kalpas has known, by means of a hundred thousand difficult deeds, how to fulfill the duties of the six perfections, and who has reached the supreme science. The Bhagavat, who is superior to all the worlds, who is the universal conqueror, will thus travel in this way through a deserted country! Why would I not display my zeal, in order that the Bhagavat, accompanied by the assembly of his disciples, meets with happiness?" Immediately, he gave to the sons of the devas, masters of the winds, the following order: "Go to the country where the city of Bhadraṃkara is found and dry up the poisoned waters there." He then gave to the sons of the devas, masters of the rain, the following order: "Fill the springs with a refreshing water." He said to the devas who form the retinue of the four great kings [of heaven]:

---

can well be a provincial alteration. Besides, the name Bhadrakara is already well known in the geographical nomenclature of India; Wilford has extracted it from a list of names of peoples who belong to the *Brahmāṇḍa Purāṇa*. The Bhadrakāras are included in it among the tribes inhabiting Madhyadeśa, or central India (*Asiatic Researches*, vol. 8, p. 336, Calcutta ed.).

"Go and settle in the countryside of Bhadraṃkara." Immediately, the sons of the devas, masters of the winds, dried up the poisoned waters; the sons of the devas, masters of the rain, filled the hollows, the fountains, the wells, the ponds, and the lakes with a refreshing water. The devas who form the retinue of the four great kings [of heaven] settled throughout the country where the city of Bhadraṃkara is located, and the countryside became rich and prosperous. Meanwhile, the tīrthyas, united with the inhabitants of the city, sent spies into the country. "Go," they said, "and see what is the state of the countryside." Arriving near Bhadraṃkara, the spies saw the countryside extraordinarily prosperous, and when they returned, they said to the tīrthyas: "Lords, we have never seen the countryside so rich or so prosperous." The tīrthyas then said to the people: "Lords, the one who changes material objects in this way for you will also change your dispositions. Why is that? Be totally devoted to us, or see us for the last time, we are leaving." The people responded to them: "Stay, lords, what then is the śramaṇa Gautama doing to you? He is a mendicant religious, and you also are religious who live on alms. Will he deprive you of the alms intended for you?" The tīrthyas responded: "We will stay on the condition that it will be agreed that no one will go to see the śramaṇa Gautama, and that one who goes to the śramaṇa will be sentenced to a fine of sixty kārṣāpaṇas."[212] The people consented to it and accepted the pact. Some time later, the Bhagavat, having crossed through the countryside, entered the city of Bhadraṃkara, and settled there in the southern pavilion.

Now there was at that time in Bhadraṃkara the daughter of a brahman of Kapilavastu who was married to a man of the country. From the top of the wall [that surrounds the city], she saw the Bhagavat in the darkness; and she had this reflection: "Here is this Blessed One, the joy of the Śākya family who, after having abandoned his house and the monarchy, entered into the religious life; there he is today in the gloom! If there was a ladder here, I would take a lamp and descend." In that moment, the Bhagavat, knowing the thought that rose in the mind of this woman, miraculously created a ladder. Immediately, the woman, content, joyous, delighted, having taken a lamp and having descended on the ladder, went to the place where the Bhagavat was. When she had arrived there, having placed her lamp in front of the Bhagavat and having saluted his feet by touching them with her head, she sat down to listen to the law. Then, the Bhagavat, knowing what were the mind, the dispositions, the character, and the nature of this woman, gave her the exposition of the law appropriate to penetrate the four sublime truths, in such a way that she felt faith in the formula by which one seeks refuge in the Buddha. Then, the Bhagavat added: "Go, young woman,

212. According to the observations made in the note placed in Appendix 3, one can evaluate this sum to be about sixty sous weighing 11.375 grams each, that is to say, about 3 francs 40 centimes, with a slight fraction more.

go to the place where Meṇḍhaka, the householder, lives; and when you have found him, announce to him that you come on my behalf and report to him these words: 'Householder, it is for your sake that I have come here; and you, you close the door of your house! Is it fitting to receive a guest as you do?' And if he responds to you: 'It is the pact made among the people of the country that constrains me,' you will say to him: 'Your son carries, hung on his back, a purse containing a hundred gold pieces; if he takes a hundred or a thousand pieces, the purse will always be full; it never runs out, and you cannot give sixty kārṣāpaṇas to come to see me!'"

The young woman, having responded to the Bhagavat that she would do what he ordered, immediately started and went to the place where someone had pointed out to her that Meṇḍhaka lived. When she was in his presence, she spoke to him in this way: "The Bhagavat sends me to you." The merchant immediately responded: "I salute the blessed Buddha." "Householder," replied the young woman, "this is what the Bhagavat says: 'It is for your sake that I have come here; and you, you close the door of your house! Is it fitting to receive a guest as you do?'" "Young woman," replied the householder, "the people are agreed that no one will go to see the śramaṇa Gautama; that one who goes to him will be sentenced to a fine of sixty kārṣāpaṇas." "Householder," responded the young woman, "this is what the Bhagavat said: 'Your son carries, hung on his back, a purse containing a hundred gold pieces; if he takes a hundred or a thousand pieces, the purse will always be full; it never runs out, and you cannot give sixty kārṣāpaṇas to come to see me!'" The householder then said to himself: "No one will know, for only the Bhagavat knows everything! I will go to see him." Having thus left sixty kārṣāpaṇas at the door of his house, he descended on the ladder that the daughter of the brahman had pointed out to him, and he made his way toward the place where the Bhagavat was. When he had arrived there, having saluted his feet by touching them with his head, he sat in front of him to listen to the law. Then, the Bhagavat, knowing what were the mind, the dispositions, the character, and the nature of Meṇḍhaka, the householder, gave him the exposition of the law appropriate to penetrate the four sublime truths, in such a way that after having heard it, the householder saw face to face the reward of the state of śrotāpatti. When he had seen the truth, he said to Bhagavat: "Lord, will the people who live in the city of Bhadraṃkara receive laws like those that I just heard?" "Householder," responded the Bhagavat, "all the people, after having gathered around you in a multitude, will receive them." Then, Meṇḍhaka the householder left the Bhagavat, after having saluted his feet by touching them with his head, and he returned to his house. Then, having made a pile of kārṣāpaṇas in the middle of the city, he recited this stanza:

"May the one who wishes to see the Jina, conqueror of passion and of sin, free from all bonds, incomparable, merciful, and pure, hasten quickly with a steadfast and strong heart; I will give him the necessary money."

With these words, the people cried: "Householder, the sight of the śramaṇa Gautama is thus a delight?" "Yes, a delight," responded Meṇḍhaka. "If it is," replied the multitude, "the people alone have made a pact, let the people break it now: who can prevent them from doing it?" Having thus declared the pact void, the inhabitants began to depart [from the city]. But as they pressed against one another, they could not depart. Then, the yakṣa who carries the thunderbolt, taking pity on this multitude intent on being converted, threw the thunderbolt and knocked down a portion of the rampart. Several hundred thousand inhabitants then went out, some pushed by a natural eagerness, others excited by the ancient roots of virtue within them. Having come to the Bhagavat, they saluted his feet and sat in front of him.[213]

The passage I have just quoted leads me naturally to speak about the means Śākya employed to convert the people to his doctrine. These means were the teaching and, according to the legends, the miracles. Let us leave the miracles aside for the moment, which are no more worthy than those with which the brahmans opposed him. But the teaching is a means quite worthy of attention and which, if I am not mistaken, was unheard of in India before the coming of Śākya. I have already emphasized, in the first section of this memorandum, the difference between the Buddhist teaching and that of the brahmans. This difference is entirely in the teaching, which had the effect of bringing truths, which previously were the share of the privileged castes, within the reach of all. It gives Buddhism a character of simplicity and, from the literary point of view, of mediocrity, that distinguishes it in the most profound manner from Brahmanism. It explains how Śākyamuni was led to receive among his listeners persons whom the highest classes of society rejected. It accounts for his successes, that is to say, of the facility with which his doctrine spread and his disciples multiplied. Finally, it provides the secret of the fundamental modifications that the propagation of Buddhism must have brought to the Brahmanical constitution, and of the persecutions that the fear of change could not fail to attract to the Buddhists from the day they became strong enough to place in peril a political system founded principally on the existence and perpetuation of the castes. These facts are so intimately linked with one another that it is sufficient that once the first took place, the others, with time, developed in an almost necessary way. But exterior circumstances could have favored this development; minds could have been more or less successfully prepared; the moral state of India, in a word, could have

213. *Meṇḍhaka*, in *Divyāvadāna*, fol. 61a ff.

promoted the eagerness of the people to listen to the teachings of Śākya. This is what the sūtras, which make us present at the first times of the teaching of Buddhism, can alone teach us, and it is the subject on which it is important to fix our attention at this moment.

I just said that the means employed by Śākya to convert the people to his doctrine were, besides the superiority of his teaching, the magnificence of his miracles. The proofs of this assertion are found on each page of the sūtras, and I often see repeated this kind of maxim: "miracles performed by a supernatural power attract ordinary people quickly."[214] To this means, feelings of benevolence and faith, awakened in those who come to listen or only to see the Buddha, always respond through the influence of virtuous actions they have performed in previous existences. It is one of the favorite themes of the authors of legends; there is not, to be truthful, a single conversion that is not prepared by the benevolence that the listener of the Buddha feels for him and his doctrine; and Śākya enjoys recounting to his disciples at length the actions they have done long ago to have merited being reborn in his time, to be present at his teaching, and to feel themselves moved by benevolence toward him. This benevolence, or to say it more clearly, this kind of grace, is, moreover, the great motive for the most inexplicable conversions; it is the link by which Śākya connects the new present introduced by his doctrine to an unknown past that he explains in the interest of his teaching. One understands easily the effect such a means would have exerted on the mind of a people among whom the belief in the law of transmigration was so generally accepted. Starting from this belief, on which he relied to authorize his mission, Śākya appeared to explain the past rather than to change the present; and one cannot doubt that he uses it to justify conversions that the prejudices of the high castes, to which he belonged by birth, condemned. But this motive of grace is essentially religious, and it is one of those whose use the authors of the legends could and doubtless would exaggerate afterward, when Buddhism had acquired an importance it certainly still did not have at the time of Śākya. More human motivations probably acted on minds, and have favored the propagation of a belief whose beginnings announce only one of these sects that have always been so numerous in India and whose existence Brahmanism tolerates by scorning them. These motivations are individual or general; I will report some borrowed from the sūtras and from the legends of the collection so often cited in this research.

I have spoken above about the son of a brahman whom his father had wished, in vain, to give an education in accordance with his birth, and who was not even able to read or write. This young brahman, remarkably enough, proved to be an excellent Buddhist, and he learns very quickly from a monastic follower of Śākya

214. *Sahasodgata*, in *Divyāvadāna*, fol. 156a.

what the paths of virtuous actions are, as well as the theory of the origin and annihilation of the successive causes of existence. This teaching suffices to inspire in him the desire to embrace the religious life, a desire that he expresses with the formula reported above. The only precaution the young man takes is not to wear the dress of the Buddhists in the same city where he is known as a brahman; but he asks his master to retire to the countryside, and it is there that he gives himself to the double spiritual exercise that must give him the science of the law, namely meditation and reading.[215] A conversion of this kind is perfectly natural, and in India it appears to have always been easier to embrace the convenient and independent role of the ascetic than to remain in society, where the heavy yoke of caste enchains man during every instant of his life. Thus, I regard the admission of the legend as very precious for the history of the first times of Buddhism; it confirms for us that the doctrine of Śākya became, probably quickly enough, a kind of easy devotion that recruited those frightened by the difficulties of Brahmanical science.

At the same time that Buddhism attracted ignorant brahmans to itself, it welcomed with an equal eagerness the poor and unhappy of all conditions. The interesting legend of Pūrṇa that we will consider below furnishes an example. Pūrṇa, son of a merchant and of a slave, returns from his seventh sea voyage; he has amassed great wealth, and his elder brother, wanting him to settle down, spoke to him in this way: "My brother, show me a rich man or a merchant from whom I can ask the daughter for you." Pūrṇa responded to him: "I do not desire the happiness of the senses, but if you will give me your permission, I will embrace the religious life." "What?" replies his brother, "when we had no means of existence in the house, you never dreamed of embracing the religious life; why would you enter it today?"[216] It was thus accepted that the poor and those who had no means of existence could become mendicants, and Buddhism, in order to increase the number of its adepts, had only to profit from this frame of mind. Here is yet another proof of this fact. An ascetic from the Brahmanical caste, explaining in his own way the prediction Śākya made about a child not yet born, expresses himself in this way: "When Gautama has told you, 'The child will embrace the religious life under my law,' he has spoken the truth; for when your son will no longer have anything to eat or to wear, he will come before the śramaṇa Gautama in order to become a mendicant."[217] Does this passage not remind us of the unfortunate gambler in the Indian comedy who, disgusted by gaming due to the bad luck that pursues him, makes up his mind to renounce the world in order to become a Buddhist monk, and who exclaims: "So, I will walk with my head

215. *Cūḍapakṣa*, in *Divyāvadāna*, fol. 277a.
216. *Pūrṇa*, in *Divyāvadāna*, fol. 17b.
217. *Jyotiṣka*, *ibid.*, fol. 13a.

held high along the great road"?[218] This kind of predestination of poor people to the adoption of the new doctrine presents itself at each instant in the sūtras and the legends. One of the Tibetan stories translated into German by Mr. Schmidt, but originally composed from Sanskrit originals, shows us a god who aspires to become a Buddhist monk, and who complains that his elevated condition makes it difficult for him to fulfill his desires. "I wish to become a monk," he says, "and to practice the holy doctrine, but it is difficult to embrace the religious life if one is reborn in a high and illustrious race; it is easier, on the contrary, when one is from a poor and base extraction."[219]

A great and sudden misfortune, for the one who undergoes it, is also often a decisive motivation to quit the world and become a Buddhist monk. When the young Kāla, brother of Prasenajit, king of Kośala, is mutilated on the orders of the king, and is miraculously healed by Ānanda, he retires to the hermitage of the Bhagavat and intends to serve him.[220] We have a legend dedicated entirely to the story of the misfortunes of Svāgata, the son of a merchant, who, after having fallen to the last degree of degradation and misery, is converted to Buddhism in the presence of Śākyamuni.[221] The ease with which the latter admitted persons rejected by the first classes of Indian society among his disciples was, for the brahmans and the other ascetics, a frequent subject of reproach; and in the same legend I have just mentioned, one sees the tīrthyas bitterly mocking the Bhagavat about the conversion of Svāgata. But Śākya contents himself with responding: *samantaprāsādikam me śāsanam.* "My law is a law of grace for all;[222] and what is a law of grace for all? It

218. *Mṛcchakaṭī*, act 2, p. 83 of the text of Calcutta. Wilson, *Hindu Theater*, 1:56.

219. *Der Weise und der Thor*, pp. 40 and 41, German trans.

220. *Prātihārya*, in *Divyāvadāna*, fol. 75b.

221. *Svāgata*, *ibid.*, fol. 88b.

222. I believe I am able to translate the word *prasāda* as "grace" because the idea of *grace* is that which corresponds best to one of the most ordinary uses of the Sanskrit *prasāda* and its derivatives. In general, this term means: "favor, benevolence, approval"; the Tibetans ordinarily render it by a word that means "faith." I would not have hesitated to preserve this interpretation if it did not leave in the dark the very remarkable meaning that I assign to *prasāda*, according to a great number of texts. To express the idea of *faith*, the Buddhist books have, in addition, a specific word, *śraddhā*. The term *prasāda* seems to me to have a double acceptation, according to the subject to which it applies. Absolutely speaking, it means "benevolence, favor." Relatively and considered among the people who come to meet the Buddha, *prasāda* expresses this feeling of benevolence they feel for him; in this case, it seems to me necessary to preserve the word *benevolence*; for it is not yet faith, it is only its beginning. Viewed in the Buddha, *prasāda* is the favor with which he welcomes those who come to him, and from that the Buddha is called *prāsādika*, "gracious, favorable." The remarkable formula that gave rise to this note should thus be translated in this way: "My law is favorable, gracious for all," which is exactly the meaning given by my version. This particular sense of the word *prasāda* is expressed, if I am not mistaken, in a perfectly clear manner in the following passage: "The king, while walking in the garden, saw the blessed Prabodhana, this perfectly accomplished buddha, favorable and suitable for one to seek his favor," etc. (*Avadānaśataka*, fol. 41b). The words of the text are *prāsādikam, prasādanīyam*, to which would correspond the two Latin words *propitium, propitiandum*, and of which my translation gives only a rather feeble commentary compared to the beautiful concision of the original. I believe that the Tibetan translation *mdzes shing, dga' bar mdzad*, that is to say, "gracious, made to delight," only renders in an imperfect manner the meaning that results from the bringing together of the two derivatives of this single term *prasāda* (*Bka' 'gyur*, sec. *Mdo*, vol. *ha*, or 29, fol. 68b). Would

is the law under which such destitute mendicants as Durāgata and others become monks."[223] Remarkable words, whose spirit has sustained and propagated Buddhism, which still animated it in Ceylon at the beginning of our century, when a monk, disgraced by the king for having preached to the destitute and scorned caste of the Rhodias, responded to him almost as the buddha Śākyamuni himself would have: "The religion should be the common good of all."[224]

One can again count the despotism of kings and the fear their violence inspired among the causes that must have brought numerous proselytes to Śākya. The legend of Jyotiṣka furnishes a striking example. Jyotiṣka was a wealthy personage whom a supernatural power showered with inexhaustible prosperity. The king Ajātaśatru made several attempts to take possession of his goods, but none succeeded. There were so many warnings for Jyotiṣka that he, from that time on, conceived the plan to become a monk following the Buddha, a plan that he executed by distributing all his goods to the poor.[225]

In the end, if we are to believe the legends, the grandeur of the rewards that Śākya promised for the future to those who embraced his doctrine was the powerful cause of the most numerous and most rapid conversions. The collection entitled *Avadānaśataka,* from which I have already borrowed several pieces, is composed exclusively of legends written according to a single model, and whose object is to promise the dignity of a perfectly accomplished buddha to persons who had shown Śākya only the most ordinary respect. I shall cite one, which will be enough to judge the others.

The blessed Buddha was the object of respect, homage, adoration, and worship from kings, the ministers of kings, wealthy men, the inhabitants of the city, the chiefs of the guilds, the chiefs of merchants, devas, nāgas, yakṣas, asuras, garuḍas, gandharvas, kinnaras, and mahoragas. Honored by the devas and by the other beings just enumerated, the blessed Buddha, full of wisdom, endowed with great

it not seem that the Tibetan translator has derived *prasādanīya* from *prasādana*, "the action of testifying in his favor"? But this derivation seems to me less regular than that which draws *prasādanīya* from the causal form of *pra-sad*.

223. *Svāgata*, in *Divyāvadāna*, fol. 89a. The text here plays on the term *Svāgata*, "the welcome," which is the name of the hero of the legend, by changing it into that of *Durāgata*, "the unwelcome," the name given him frequently in the course of the story, each time he comes to share his misfortune with those among whom he finds himself. The term I translate as "destitute mendicants" is *kroḍamallaka*; I do not find other meanings for this compound than that of "who carry a pouch at the side," from *kroḍa* (side) and *malla*, which in the Sanskrit of Ceylon means "bag, pouch" (Clough, *Singhalese Dictionary*, 2:524, col. 1), or also from the Sanskrit *mallaka* (pot, bowl.) The more ordinary senses of pork (*kroḍa*) and wrestler (*malla*) do not provide me with any satisfactory translation. In another legend of the *Avadānaśataka*, that of Bhadrika, this term is written *koṭṭamallika* (fol. 216a), which perhaps means "mendicant of the city." The Tibetan translates it with *sprang po* (mendicant). This version, without giving us the meaning of *kroḍa*, justifies my interpretation (*Mdo*, vol. *ha*, or 29, fol. 363b).

224. Davy, *Account of the Interior of Ceylon*, p. 131, and Forbes, *Eleven Years in Ceylon*, 1:75, note.

225. *Jyotiṣka*, in *Divyāvadāna*, fol. 140b.

virtues, who received the religious robes, the alms bowl, the bedding, the seat, the medicines intended for the sick, and the other things necessary for life, who was to henceforth in a perfect way teach humans and devas who, taking advantage of the recent appearance of the Buddha, seized the opportunity of drinking the essence of the commandments; the Blessed One, I say, was with the assembly of his listeners at Śrāvastī, in Jetavana, in the garden of Anāthapiṇḍika. At the time when the Bhagavat had not yet appeared in the world, king Prasenajit honored the devas by offering them flowers, incense, garlands, perfumes, and unctuous substances. But when the Bhagavat had appeared in the world, king Prasenajit, converted by the teaching of the sūtra entitled *Dahara sūtra,*[226] had faith in the teaching of the Bhagavat. So, his heart full of joy and contentment, having approached the Bhagavat three times, he honored him by offering him lamps, incense, perfumes, garlands, and unctuous substances.

Now one day it happened that the gardener of the hermitage, having taken a lotus that had just opened, came into Śrāvastī to bring it to king Prasenajit. A man who followed the opinions of the tīrthikas saw him and said to him: "Hello! Is this lotus for sale?" "Yes," responded the gardener. This response inspired in the passerby the desire to buy it; but at that moment Anāthapiṇḍika, the householder, arrived unexpectedly in this place and offered double the price of what was asked for the lotus. The two buyers started to bid against each other until at last they went up to a hundred thousand coins. Then, the gardener had this reflection: the householder Anāthapiṇḍika is not a fickle man; he is a serious personage: there must be a motive [in order for him to insist so much]. This is why, feeling a doubt arise in his mind, he asked the man who followed the opinion of the tīrthikas: "For whom do you thus bid in such a way?" "For the blessed Nārāyaṇa," responded the passerby. "And me, I bid for the blessed Buddha," replied the householder. "Who is the one you call Buddha?" said the gardener. The householder then started to set forth to him in detail the qualities of the Buddha. The gardener then said to him: "Householder, I, also, I will go to address my homage to the Bhagavat." The householder, thus taking the gardener with him, went to the place where the Bhagavat was. The gardener saw the blessed Buddha, adorned with the thirty-two signs characteristic of a great man, whose limbs were ornamented with the eighty secondary marks, surrounded by a splendor which spread to the distance of one fathom, shedding a radiance which surpassed that of a thousand suns, similar to a mountain of jewels that moves, entirely perfect; and hardly had he seen him than he threw his lotus in front of the Bhagavat. No sooner had the lotus been thrown than immediately assum-

226. The term *Dahara Sūtra*, which I believe it is necessary to preserve, seems to mean "The Sūtra of the Child." Would it not be a mistake for *Dahra Sūtra*, "the Sūtra of the Fire"? See the additions at the end of the volume.

ing the size of the wheel of a chariot, it stopped above the Bhagavat. Upon seeing this prodigy, the gardener, like a tree whose root has been cut, fell at the feet of the Bhagavat; then, joining his hands as a sign of respect, after having reflected attentively, he began to pronounce this prayer: "May I, by the effect of this principle of virtue, of the conception of this thought, of the offering that I have made of this gift, may I, in the world of the blind deprived of a leader and guide, become one day a buddha, become the one who causes to pass beyond [the world] beings who have not crossed beyond it, who delivers those who have not been delivered, who consoles the afflicted, who leads to complete nirvāṇa those who have not reached it!" Then the Bhagavat, knowing the succession of deeds and motivations that led the gardener to him, let a smile be seen.

Now it is a rule that when the blessed buddhas smile, then blue, yellow, red, and white rays of light escape from their mouth; some descend below, others rise on high. These which descend below, flowing to the bottom of the hells Saṃjīva, Kālasūtra, Saṃghāta, Raurava, Mahāraurava, Tapana, Pratāpana, Avīci, Arbuda, Nirarbuda, Aṭata, Hahava, Huhava, Utpala, Padma, Mahāpadma,[227] fall cold into those of these hells that are burning and hot into those that are cold. Thereby, the various kinds of pains that the inhabitants of these places of misery suffer are calmed. They thus have these following reflections: "Would it be, friends, that we are departing from the hells to be reborn elsewhere?" In order to engender grace in them, the Bhagavat performs a miracle; and at the sight of this miracle, the inhabitants of the hells say to each other: "No, friends, we are not departing from these places to be reborn elsewhere: but this is a being we have not seen before; it is by his power that the various kinds of suffering that tormented us are pacified." Feeling calm reborn in their soul at the sight of this prodigy, these beings, completing the expiation of the action for which they had to be punished in the hells, are metamorphosed into devas and humans, conditions in which they become vessels capable of receiving the truths. Those of these rays that rise on high, flowing to the devas of Cāturmahārājika, Trayastriṃśa, Yāma, Tuṣita, Nirmāṇarati, Paranirmitavaśavartin, Brahmakāyika, Brahmapurohita, Mahābrahmā, Parīttābha, Apramāṇābha, Ābhāsvara, Parīttaśubha, Apramāṇaśubha, Śubhakṛtsna, Anabhraka, Puṇyaprasava, Vṛhatphala, Avṛha,

227. One must compare this list of the sixteen hells, of which the first eight are burning and the last eight are freezing, with the list given by Mr. Landresse according to the Chinese. The names of the first eight are very likely translated, and not transcribed; at least, it is according to the definition accompanying each of these names that I believe I am able to propose the following synonymy: Saṃjīva is the *Xiang diyu*, Kālasūtra is *Heisheng diyu*, Saṃghata is *Duiya diyu*, Raurava is *Jiaohuan diyu*, Mahāraurava is *Da jiaohuan diyu*, Tapana is *Shaozhi diyu*, Pratāpana is *Da Shaozi diyu*, Avīci is *Wujian diyu*. The eight following names are transcriptions; here, I complete the synonymy started in the note of the *Foe koue ki* to which I refer. Arbuda is *Efutuo*, Nirarbuda is *Nilafutuo*, Aṭata is *Ezhazha*, Hahava is *Hepopo*, Huhava is *Huhupo*, Utpala is *Youboluo*, Padma is *Botoumo*, Mahāpadma corresponds to *Fentuoli*, the transcription of *puṇḍarīka*, "great white lotus" (*Foe koue ki*, pp. 298 and 299).

Atapa, Sudṛśa, Sudarśana, Akaniṣṭha,[228] made these words resonate: "This is passing; this is misery; this is empty; and they made these two stanzas to be heard:

"Begin, go forth [from the house], apply yourself to the law of the Buddha; annihilate the army of death, as an elephant knocks down a hut of reeds.

"He who walks without distraction under the discipline of this law, escaping from birth and the cycle of the world, will put an end to suffering."

Then these rays, after having enveloped the universe formed by the great thousand of three thousand worlds, returned behind the Bhagavat. If the Buddha desires to explain an action accomplished in a past time, the rays disappear into his back. If it is a future action that he wishes to predict, they disappear into his chest. If he wishes to predict a birth in hell, they disappear under the sole of his feet; if it is a birth among the animals, they disappear into his heel; if it is a birth among the pretas (the souls of the dead), they disappear into the big toe of his foot; if it is a birth among humans, they disappear into his knee; if he wishes to predict a monarchy of a balacakravartin, they disappear into the palm of his left hand; if it is a monarchy of a cakravartin, they disappear into the palm of his right hand; if it is a birth among the devas, they disappear into his navel. If he wishes to predict to someone that he will have the intelligence of a śrāvaka, they disappear into his mouth; if it is the intelligence of a pratyekabuddha, they disappear into his ears; if it is the supreme science of a perfectly accomplished buddha, they disappear into the protuberance that crowns his head.

Now, the rays [that had just appeared], after having turned three times around the Bhagavat, disappeared in the protuberance that crowns his head. Then, the respectable Ānanda, joining his hands as a mark of respect, spoke to the Bhagavat in this way:

"A mass of various rays, mixed with a thousand colors, just came from the

228. On the twenty-three orders of divinities inhabiting the celestial levels that, starting from the four great kings and the gods who submit to them, rise above the earth, see the research by Messrs. Schmidt and A. Rémusat (*Mémoires de l'Académie des sciences de Saint-Pétersbourg*, 2:24ff. A. Rémusat, "Essai sur la cosmographie et la cosmogonie des boudhistes d'après les auteurs chinois," in *Journal des Savans*, 1831, pp. 609 and 610 and p. 668ff.). But it is especially interesting to compare this list to that which Mr. Hodgson had set forth a long time ago, according to the Buddhists of Nepal ("Sketch of Buddhism," in *Transactions of the Royal Asiatic Society*, vol. 2, pp. 233 and 234). The list of Mr. Hodgson places, between Akaniṣṭha, that is to say, the highest of all gods, and Sudarśana, ten, or according to others, thirteen levels, of which I have not found the slighest trace in the sūtras I regard as the most ancient. These are the heavens of the bodhisattvas, which appear to me a modern invention analogous to that of the Ādibuddha or perhaps even a special product of Nepalese Buddhism. What is certain is that the list of the Vocabulaire Pentaglotte does not know anything about this addition of ten or thirteen heavens, and that it encompasses, from section 49 up to and including section 53, the same series that our sūtra provides, except for the last article (the abode of Maheśvara), which the Vocabulaire adds. It is necessary to submit the majority of articles of these five sections to very considerable corrections, the Sanskrit words being, as usual, reproduced with extreme inaccuracy. What serves to completely ensure the desirable authenticity to the list of our sūtra is that it is found, except for some differences in the names, and save for only one article, in the Sinhalese list as Upham gives it, according to mainly oral authorities (*The Mahâvansi*, etc., 3:135ff.). See a special note on the names of these gods, Appendix no. 4.

mouth of the Bhagavat and it has completely illuminated all points of space, as the sun when it rises."

Then he added the following stanzas:

"No, it is not without motivation that the jinas, who have triumphed over the enemy, who are exempt from frivilousness, who have renounced pride and discouragement, and who are the cause of the happiness of the world, let a smile like the yellow filaments of a lotus be seen.

"O hero! O you who, with your intelligence, knows the suitable moment, be so good, O śramaṇa, O you Indra of the jinas, be so good as to dispel, with the firm, excellent, and beautiful words of the hero of recluses, the doubts aroused in the mind of your listeners given to uncertainty.

"No, it is not without motivation that the perfect buddhas, these leaders of the world, who are as full of steadfastness as the ocean or as the king of mountains, let a smile be seen. But for what reason do these sages full of constancy let this smile be seen? This is what this great multitude of creatures wishes to hear from your mouth."

The Bhagavat then said to Ānanda: "It is that, it is just that; it is not without motivation, O Ānanda, that the venerable tathāgatas, perfectly and completely buddhas, let a smile be seen. Do you see, O Ānanda, the homage this gardener full of benevolence just addressed to me?"—"Yes, Lord."—"Good! O Ānanda, this gardener, through the effect of this principle of virtue, of the conception of this thought, of the offering he has made of this gift, after having practiced the intelligence of bodhi, in which he must train himself during three asaṃkhyeyas of kalpas, after having entirely fulfilled the six perfections manifested through great mercy, this gardener, I say, will become in the world a perfectly accomplished buddha with the name of Padmottama, a buddha endowed with the ten strengths, the four intrepidities, the three supports of memory that do not mix with each other, and finally with great mercy. Thus, the offering of a gift here is the benevolence this gardener has felt for me."

This is how the Bhagavat spoke, and the monks, enraptured with joy, approved of what the Bhagavat had said.[229]

The subject that the previous extracts have made known touches quite closely on the question of the influence that the teaching of Śākya exerted on the caste system; we have already seen the Brahmanical disposition to reproach Śākyamuni for seeking for his disciples those who are too base. A similar reproach was inspired, without any doubt, by a feeling of wounded pride; it pained the first caste to see men of base extraction elevated to the rank of ascetics, a rank that, legally speaking, it had the almost exclusive privilege to hold up for the homage and

229. *Avadānaśataka*, fol. 16a ff.

admiration of the masses. The expression of this sentiment would prove, if there was still a need to do so, how the division of people into permanently separated castes had plunged deep roots into India at the moment when Śākya appeared. For us, who have never questioned for an instant the historical precedence of Brahmanism with respect to Buddhism, the reproaches that the brahmans address to Śākya inform us simultaneously about how he conducted himself in the face of the absolute principle of the castes as well as how his adversaries received his usurpations. This double instruction is found, in a perfectly clear form, in a legend I shall analyze and whose most characteristic parts I shall translate.

One day, Ānanda, the servant of Śākyamuni, after having traveled through the countryside for a long time, meets a young mātaṅgī girl, that is to say, from the cāṇḍāla tribe, who was drawing water, and he asks her for a drink. But the young girl, fearing that she would defile him with her touch, warns him that she was born into the mātanga caste, and that she is not permitted to approach a monk. Ānanda then responds to her: "My sister, I do not ask you about your caste or your family; I only ask you about water, and whether you can give me some."[230] Prakṛti—this is the name of the young girl—who according to the legend was destined to be converted to the doctrine of the Buddha, immediately falls in love with Ānanda, and she tells her mother of her desire to become his wife. The mother foresees the obstacle that the difference in castes must cause for this union (for Ānanda was of the military race of the Śākyas and was the cousin of the Buddha). The mother, I say, resorts to magic to lure the monk to her house where Prakṛti awaits him, dressed in her most beautiful clothes. Ānanda, drawn by the powers of the charms that the mātangī puts to use, indeed goes into this house, but recognizing the danger that threatens him, he remembers the Bhagavat and calls out to him, weeping. Immediately the Buddha, whose science is irresistible, destroys the charms of the cāṇḍālī with opposing charms, and Ānanda is freed from the hands of the two women and leaves. Yet Prakṛti does not become disheartened; she decides to appeal to Śākyamuni himself and goes to wait for him under a tree, near one of the gates of the city through which he must leave after begging for his meal. Śākyamuni appears, and he learns from the mouth of the young girl of the love she feels for Ānanda and the determination she has to follow him. Taking advantage of this passion, in order to convert Prakṛti, the Buddha, through a series of questions that Prakṛti can understand in the sense of her love but that he intentionally asks in a completely religious sense, succeeds in opening the eyes of the young girl to the light and inspiring in her the desire to embrace the ascetic life. Thus, he asks her if she consents to follow Ānanda, that is to say, to imitate him in his conduct; if she wants to wear the same clothes that he does, that is to say, the clothes of monks; if she has the permission of her par-

230. *Śārdūlakarṇa*, in *Divyāvadāna*, fol. 217a.

ents. These are questions that the law of the discipline requires to be addressed to those who wish to become Buddhist mendicants. The young girl responds to all in the affirmative. Śākyamuni requires in addition the formal consent of the father and mother, who, indeed, come to affirm to him that they approve of all that she desires. And then, discerning the true object of her love, the young girl recognizes her initial error and declares that she has decided to enter into the religious life. At that time, Śākya, in order to prepare her to receive the law, uses the magical formula (*dhāraṇī*) that purifies a human being of all the sins and defilements acquired in the miserable existences to which the law of transmigration has condemned him.[231] Now, I will let the legend speak.

"The brahmans and the householders of Śrāvastī learned that a young girl of the cāṇḍāla caste had just been admitted by the Bhagavat into the religious life, and they began to make the following remarks among themselves: 'How will this cāṇḍāla girl be able to fulfill the duties imposed on nuns and on those who follow them? How will the daughter of a cāṇḍāla be able to enter the houses of brahmans, kṣatriyas, the heads of families, and wealthy men?'[232] Prasenajit, king of Kośala, also received this news, and having had the same reflections as the inhabitants of Śrāvastī, he had a good chariot harnessed, which he mounted; and surrounded by a great number of brahmans and householders, all inhabitants of Śrāvastī, he departed from the city and made his way toward Jetavana, where the hermitage of Anāthapiṇḍika is located."[233] The text next depicts for us the king entering into the hermitage with the brahmans, the kṣatriyas, the householders, and going to the Bhagavat. Each one, approaching him, told him his name and the family of his father and mother. Then the Bhagavat, knowing the thoughts that had arisen in the mind of the king and his retinue, convened the assembly of his monks and began to recount to them one of the past existences of the daughter of the cāṇḍāla. He then sets forth the story of a king of this caste called Triśaṅku,[234] who lived in a thick forest situated on the bank of the Ganges. "This king, O monks, remembered the Vedas, which in a previous existence he had

231. *Śārdūlakarṇa*, in *Divyāvadāna*, fol. 219a.

232. The Tibetan anthology of Mr. Schmidt contains an extremely interesting legend in which reproaches of the same kind are made by the upper castes on the occasion of the investiture that Śākyamuni grants to destitute mendicants (*Der Weise und der Thor*, p. 283, German trans.)

233. *Divyāvadāna*, fol. 220a.

234. The name Triśaṅku is already known to us through the Brahmanical traditions, and notably through the beautiful episode of the *Rāmāṇaya* (Schlegel ed., vol. 1, bk. 1, chap. 56ff.; Latin trans., 1:175 ff.; Gorresio ed., chap. 59ff., 1:231ff.). The legend of this prince is also recounted in the *Viṣṇu Purāṇa* (Wilson, p. 371, note 7) and in the *Bhāgavata Purāṇa* (bk. 9, chap. VII). In spite of the noticeable differences among these three accounts, a common tradition serves as their basis; this tradition is that Triśaṅku, who belonged to the family of the Ikṣvakides, was deprived of royal dignity by the malediction of the Vasiṣṭhides or of their father, and changed into a cāṇḍāla. It is also the only point in which the Buddhist legend is related to the account of the brahmans. The Buddhists made Triśaṅku a king of the cāṇḍālas; this is also a borrowing from the Brahmanical tradition.

read with the aṅgas, the upāṅgas, the rahasyas, with the nighaṇṭus, the kaitabhas, with the differences that distinguish the letters from each other, finally with the itihāsas that form a fifth Veda."[235] This king had a son called Śārdūlakarṇa, to whom he taught everything that he himself had learned in a previous existence. When he saw him perfectly skilled in all the ceremonies, master of the mantras of the Veda, which he had read in its entirety, he dreamed about marrying him to a virtuous, learned, and beautiful young girl. There was then at Utkaṭā, capital of a district in the north of the forest of Triśangku, a brahman named Puṣkarasārin, who enjoyed the revenue of this district, which had been granted to him by king Agnidatta. He was from a noble family of brahmans, and could say the name of his father and mother back to the seventh generation. He had mastered the mantras and had read the three Vedas with everything that depends on them, and the itihāsas that form a fifth Veda. This brahman had a daughter called Prakṛti. Triśangku made up his mind to ask for her for his son Śārdūlakarṇa, and he went into the wood in order to await the brahman, who had to come there to recite the Brahmanical mantras. "Triśangku, king of the cāṇḍālas, soon saw the brahman Puṣkarasārin, who resembled the rising sun, who shone with a splendor like fire, who was like a sacrifice that the brahmans surround, like Dakṣa encircled by his daughters, like Śakra in the middle of the multitude of devas, like the Himavat with its medicinal plants, like the ocean with its jewels, like the moon with its nakṣatras, like Vaiśravaṇa among the troops of yakṣas, like Brahmā, finally, in the middle of devas and devarṣis."[236] Immediately, he went to meet him and said: "It is I, Lord Puṣkarasārin; be welcome; I will tell you what brings me, listen." At these words, the brahman Puṣkarasārin responded in this way to Triśangku, king of the cāṇḍālas: "You are not permitted, O Triśangku, to employ the salutation of lord with a brahman." "Lord Puṣkarasārin," replied Triśangku, "I can employ this kind of salutation with a brahman." Then, he asked Puṣkarasārin for his daughter Prakṛti for the young Śārdūlakarṇa. As soon as the brahman heard this proposal, overcome with fury, his brow wrinkled, his neck swelled with rage, his eyes popping out of his head, he responded to Triśangku: "Get out of here, miserable cāṇḍāla. How does one who eats dog, like you, dare to speak in such a way to a brahman who has read the Veda? Insane! You do not know Prakṛti, and you have a rather high opinion of yourself! Do not stay here long, if you do not wish to bring misfortune on yourself. You are only a cāṇḍāla and I, I am from the caste of the dvijas. How dare you, miserable one, request the union of the most noble with the most vile being? In this world, the good join in marriage with the good, the brahmans with brahmans. You request the impossible in wishing to become allied with us, you who are scorned in the world, you the

235. *Divyāvadāna*, fol. 220b.
236. *Śārdūlakarṇa*, in *Divyāvadāna*, fol. 221b.

lowest of men. Here below, the cāṇḍālas join in marriage with the cāṇḍālas, the puṣkasas with the puṣkasas, and so do the brahmans, the kṣatriyas, the vaiśyas, and the śūdras, each in his caste; but nowhere does one see brahmans join in marriage with cāṇḍālas." To this speech, which is in verse in the original, and which I have abridged slightly, Triśangku responded in this way: "Between a brahman and a man of another caste, there is not the difference that exists between stone and gold, between darkness and light. The brahman, indeed, has not emerged from the ether or the wind; he has not split the earth to appear in the light, like the fire that escapes from the wood of the araṇi.[237] The brahman is born from the womb of a woman, like the cāṇḍāla. Where then do you see the cause that one must be noble and the other vile? The brahman himself, when he is dead, is abandoned like a vile and impure object; it is for him as for the other castes; where then is the difference?"

Triśangku then continues, reproaching brahmans for their vices and their passions; he forcefully blames them for the means they employ in order to satisfy them, and among other things, for the hypocrisy with which they dare to pretend to be pure while committing the blackest deeds. "When they want to eat meat, this is the means they employ: they kill the animals pronouncing mantras, because, they say, the ewes so immolated go straight to heaven. But if this is the path to heaven, why thus do these brahmans not also immolate themselves and their wives with mantras, their father and their mother, their brothers and their sisters, their sons and their daughters?[238] . . . No, it is not true that lustral water and mantras make goats and ewes go up to heaven; all these inventions are means employed by these wicked brahmans to satisfy their desire to eat meat."[239]

The brāhman seeks to defend himself by recounting the myth of origin of the four castes, which the tradition says are born from the four parts of the body of Brahmā; and when the cāṇḍāla has responded to him, Puṣkarasārin asks him if he is versed in the Brahmanical sciences. Then, king Triśangku satisfies him on this point with a detailed enumeration of the Vedas, their divisions, the sacrifices, and the other objects whose knowledge is ordinarily reserved for brahmans alone. All of this piece is of a great interest, and it proves that the Buddhists were not unaware of anything that formed the foundation of Indian education. Yet to extract some historical consequences, it would be necessary to know exactly the epoch during which it was written; for if it is later than the events that forced the Buddhists to leave India, it is all the more surprising that it contains so varied and precise details touching on Brahmanical literature and sciences.

237. *Premna spinosa.*

238. This argument seems familiar to the adversaries of the brahmans, because one can find it quoted in the *Viṣṇu Purāṇa*, in the chapter related to the heresy of the Jainas (Wilson, *Viṣṇu Purāṇa*, p. 340).

239. *Divyāvadāna*, fol. 122b.

But at the moment, it is not a question of assembling the lights that the legend, from which I have just given some extracts, can cast on this particular object; it is important to show how Śākyamuni freed himself from the obstacles that the division of Indian society, split into hierarchically arranged castes, raised in front of him. His avowed aim was to save human beings from the miserable conditions of existence that they drag along in this world and to remove them from the fatal law of transmigration. It was acknowledged that the practice of virtue assured the good person a sojourn in heaven and the pleasure of a better existence in the future. But this happiness was not regarded by anyone to be definitive; to become a god was to be reborn in order to die one day; and it was from the necessity of rebirth and death that one had to escape forever. As for the distinction of the castes, in the eyes of Śākyamuni, it was an accident of the existence of humanity here below, an accident that he acknowledged, but that he could not stop. This is why the castes appear, in all the sūtras and all the legends I have read, as an established fact against which Śākya does not make a single political objection. This is so true that when a man attached to the service of a prince wished to embrace the religious life, Śākya received him only after the prince had given his consent. A legend from the *Avadānaśataka* furnishes us with a quite characteristic example: "Go, O Ānanda," said Śākya to his servant, "and say to king Prasenajit: 'Grant me this man who is in your service; I will let him embrace the religious life.'" Ānanda consequently went to the place where Prasenajit, king of Kośala, was and when he had arrived, he spoke to him in the name of the Bhagavat in this way: "Grant, Lord, the Bhagavat permission to receive this man into the religious life!" When the king knew that it concerned Bhavyarūpa, he granted the monk what he requested of him.[240] This respect of Śākya for royal power has even left its traces in modern Buddhism; and one of the fundamental rules of the ordination of a monk is to respond in the negative to this question: "Are you in the service of the king?"[241] In another legend, one sees king Prasenajit of Kośala sending a messenger to Rājagṛha, in order to invite the Bhagavat to come among his people, to Śrāvastī. This is the response that Śākyamuni gives to the messenger: "If king Bimbisāra permits me, I will go to Prasenajit."[242]

Śākya thus accepted the hierarchy of castes; he even explained it, as the brahmans did, by the theory of sorrows and rewards; and each time that he instructed a man of vile condition, he did not fail to attribute the baseness of his birth to the reprehensible acts this man had commited in a previous life. To convert a man, whomever he was, was thus for Śākya to give him the means to escape from the

240. *Avadānaśataka*, fol. 42b.
241. *Kammavākya*, pp. 6 and 17, Spiegel ed.
242. *Avadānaśataka*, fol. 135a.

law of transmigration; it was to relieve him of the vice of his birth, absolutely and relatively; absolutely, by putting him on the path that leads one day to definitive annihilation where, as the texts say, the law of rebirth ceases; relatively, by making him a monk, like Śākyamuni himself, who came to take his place, according to his age, in the assembly of the listeners of the Buddha. Śākya thus opened to all castes without distinction the path of salvation that before was closed by birth to the greatest number; and he rendered them equal among themselves and before him by conferring on them investiture with the rank of monk. In this latter respect, he was going further than the philosophers Kapila and Patañjali, who had begun work that was almost the same as that which the Buddhists later accomplished. In attacking the works prescribed by the Veda as useless, and in substituting the practice of an entirely individual asceticism, Kapila had brought within the reach of all, at least in principle if not in reality, the title *ascetic*, which until then was the complement and almost exclusive privilege of the life of the brahman. Śākya did more: he knew how to give isolated philosophers the organization of a monastic body. One finds here the explanation of these two facts: the ease with which Buddhism must have spread in principle and the opposition Brahmanism naturally made to its progress. The brahmans had no objection to address to him as long as he contented himself with working as a philosopher for the future deliverance of man, to assure him the freedom I called absolute before. But they could not accept the possibility of this actual deliverance, of this relative freedom, which aimed at nothing less than destroying, in a given time, the subordination of castes, as far as it touches on religion. This is how Śākyamuni attacked the Indian system at its base, and why a moment had to arrive when the brahmans, placed at the head of this system, would feel the need to proscribe a doctrine whose consequences could not escape them.

I do not believe that this moment had already arrived in the epoch when the sūtras I have analyzed above were redacted; or rather, I think that these sūtras, whatever the epoch in which they were written down, preserve for us a tradition previous to the violent separation of the Buddhists from the brahmans. These treatises show us Śākyamuni exclusively occupied with forming disciples, adepts, finally imitators of his moral and exemplary life. What he is seeking above all is to be surrounded with disciples who disseminate his doctrine and who convert people to the religious life, just as he himself converted them. He takes, or rather he receives these disciples from all castes: brahmans, warriors, merchants, slaves, all are equally admissible in his eyes, and birth ceases to be a sign of merit as well as a title of exclusion.

We now see, if I am not mistaken, how this celebrated axiom of Oriental history, that Buddhism has erased all distinction of caste, must be understood. The writers who have repeated this assertion have seen it verified by the political constitution of the peoples among whom Buddhism reigns today. This verification, however, encounters a capital exception, which has not been paid sufficient attention; for if the distinction of castes is unknown to the Buddhist nations of Tibet, Burma, and Siam, it is nonetheless very firmly established among the people who have first adopted Buddhism, among the Sinhalese. I refer for this point to the testimony of travelers, so unanimous as to be irrevocable.[243] This does not mean that there are Buddhist castes divided into brahmans, kṣatriyas, vaiśyas, and śūdras; the number of classes of Indian origin is notably reduced in Ceylon; the highest are almost unknown, and there, as in India, one is either *brāhmaṇa* or *bauddha*; it is not possible to be one and the other at the same time. It is nevertheless true that the existence of castes among a Buddhist people is a very remarkable fact, one of those that, as Tolfrey has rightly indicated,[244] shows most obviously that Buddhism and Brahmanism have a common origin, in other words, that the doctrine of Śākya was born in a society whose political principle was the distinction of castes. But how is this principle reconciled with the spirit of the doctrine of the Buddha, that is to say, what concession has one made to the other? This is how things must have occurred, judging at least by the effects. The priesthood ceased to be hereditary, and the monopoly on religious matters left the hands of a privileged caste. The body charged with teaching the law ceased to be perpetuated by birth; it was replaced by an assembly of monks dedicated to celibacy, who were recruited indiscriminately from all classes. Finally, the Buddhist monk, who receives everything from the teaching and from a kind of investiture, replaced the brahman, who owed it only to birth, that is to say, to the nobility of his origin. This is without question a fundamental change, and it is enough to explain the opposition the brahmans made to the propagation and application of the principles of Buddhism. Indeed, the brahmans disappeared in the new order of things created by Śākya. From the moment when birth was no longer sufficient to place them above the other castes, from the moment when in order to perform a religious function for the people, it was necessary for them to submit themselves to a novitiate, to receive an investiture that did not give them more rights than the lowest of slaves, and to take their place in a hierarchy based on age and knowledge, beside the most scorned of humans, the brahmans in fact no longer existed. The existence of the other castes, on the contrary, was not at all compromised by Buddhism. Founded on a division of work, which birth perpetuated, they could survive under the protection of the Buddhist priesthood, to which they all indiscriminately supplied monks and ascetics. As much as brahmans should feel aversion for the doctrine of Śākya, so

243. Valentia, *Voyages and Travels*, 1:488, ed. in –4°. Davy, *Account of the Interior of Ceylon*, p. 111. Forbes, *Eleven Years in Ceylon*, 1:70 and 72. Upham, *Mahāvansi*, etc., 3:331. One finds in these authors lists of castes still in existence in Ceylon.

244. Valentia, *Voyages and Travels*, 1:496.

much should persons of lower castes welcome it with eagerness and favor; for if this doctrine abased the first, it uplifted the second, and it assured to the poor and the slave in this life what Brahmanism did not even promise in the next: the advantage to see himself, from the religious point of view, as the equal of his master.

The preceding observations sufficiently explain the remarkable fact of the coexistence of Indian castes and Buddhism on the soil of Ceylon. It is not necessary to assume, as the illustrious W. von Humboldt has, that the distinction of castes has exercised a less profound action on the character of the Sinhalese than on that of the Indians of the continent;[245] for proofs are not lacking to establish that the military caste is as jealous of privileges owed to birth in Ceylon as elsewhere, and the Sinhalese kings have shown, on more than one occasion, that they understood rather poorly the principles of equality to which the Buddhist priesthood owes its existence and whose repository it endeavors to preserve. There is more: the military caste, that of the kṣatriyas, is always named first in the Sinhalese lists, even before that of the brahmans. Here one recognizes the influence of Buddhism, which, in seizing the superiority the Brahmanical caste had from birth, naturally left an open field to the military caste. But this influence, which could have promoted the displacement of the great divisions of society, as organized by the brahmans, did not annihilate these divisions, nor did it entirely destroy the spirit on which they rest. The castes have continued to survive; but the divisions that are their effect have become purely political rather than religious, as they were before.

The example of the island of Ceylon permits one to suppose that the phenomenon of the coexistence of Buddhism with the castes also took place in India in ancient times, and the reading of the sūtras fully confims this supposition. In order to give substance to his doctrine, Śākyamuni did not need to resort to a principle of equality, in general little understood by the Asiatic peoples. The germ of an immense change was in the constitution of this assembly of monks, coming from all castes, who, renouncing the world, had to live in monasteries under the direction of a spiritual leader and under the dominion of a hierarchy based on age and knowledge. People received a most moral instruction from their mouth, and there no longer existed a single human being condemned forever by his birth, never to know the truths disseminated by the teaching of the most enlightened of all beings, the perfectly accomplished Buddha.[246]

Thus in carefully rereading the previously analyzed legend of Triśangku, I see, in the polemical form of this piece, some reasons to suspect that it need not be ranked among the most ancient productions of Northern Buddhism. The part of

245. *Über die Kawi-Sprache*, 1:87.

246. On this subject, see the excellent observations of Mr. Schmidt (*Mémoires de l'Académie des sciences de Saint-Pétersbourg*, 1:252).

this legend related to the monk Ānanda reminds us of a tradition that is certainly ancient. The story of Triśangku, on the other hand, must have been added, or at least expanded, afterward. The great number of pieces written in verse of which the legend is composed is still to my eyes a sign of posteriority; in this respect, this treatise resembles a developed sūtra much more than an ordinary legend. I will thus be inclined to believe that it does not belong, at least entirely, to the teaching of Śākyamuni, but to the number of those books redacted in the repose of the cloister, at the time when the Buddhists enjoyed enough leisure to collect and comment on their religious traditions.

Whatever the value of these observations might be, I believe at least that our legend is prior to the *Vajraśuci*, a treatise of pure polemic, directed against the institution of the castes and composed by a Buddhist scholar called Aśvaghoṣa. We owe to Messrs. Wilkinson and Hodgson the publication and translation of the text of this small book, to which is added a defense of the castes by a brahman who was still living in 1839.[247] Is Aśvaghoṣa the celebrated monk whose name is translated in Chinese by *Maming* (horse voice) and who, according to the list of the Japanese encyclopedia, was the twelfth Buddhist patriarch since the death of Śākyamuni,[248] or is he but a more modern ascetic who bears the same name? This is what I would not be able to decide. All that Mr. Hodgson informs us about him is that in Nepal he is cited as a mahāpaṇḍita, and that he is the author of two very valuable works, the *Buddhacaritakāvya* and the *Nandimukhasughoṣāvadāna*.[249] It suffices for us that the polemical treatise of which he is said to be the author is attributed to a known monk, in order for it to leave the category of canonical books, to which the legend analyzed above belongs, and to take its place in the class of works bearing authors' names, a more modern class in general than that of the treatises supposed to have emanated from the very teaching of Śākya. As such, I could have avoided speaking about it here, since I have to occupy myself later with the treatises whose authors are known. I believed, however, that the advantage of encompassing at a glance what one knows about the objections that the Buddhists address to the brahmans against the system of castes compensated for the flaw in order, in reality not very grave, that I permit myself here.

247. *The Wujra soochi or Refutation of the arguments upon which the Brahmanical institution of caste is founded, by the learned Boodhist Ashwa Ghochu; also the Tunku by Soobojee Bapoo being a Reply to the Wujra soochi*, 1839, ed. in -8°, printed in India, but without the name of the place. The translation and the foreword occupy one hundred pages; the text, lithographed in relatively large devanāgari characters, has sixty. The translation of the treatise of Aśvaghoṣa had already appeared in vol. 3 of the *Transactions of the Royal Asiatic Society*, p. 160. The use of the word *vajra* leads me to think that this treatise is modern.

248. A. Rémusat, *Mélanges Asiatiques*, 1:120ff. Everything that has been said in *Essai sur le pali* (p. 55) on the possible identity of the Chinese name *Maming* with the Sinhalese name of the prince Mahindu Kumāra can no longer be sustained today, in that we know so definitively that the word *bodhisattva* is not a proper noun, but the title of a living buddha.

249. *Transactions of the Royal Asiatic Society*, vol. 3, p. 161, and *Wujra soochi*, p. 6, note.

The objections of Aśvaghoṣa are of two kinds: the first are borrowed from the most revered texts of the brahmans themselves; the others rely on the principle of the natural equality of all humans. The author shows through quotations drawn from the Veda, from Manu, and the *Mahābhārata* that the quality of brahman is inherent not in the principle that lives within us or in the body where this principle resides, and that it is not the result of birth, or of science, or of religious practices, or of the observation of moral duties, or of knowledge of the Vedas. Since this quality is neither inherent nor acquired, it does not exist; or rather all humans are able to possess it: for to him, the quality of brahman is a state of purity similar to the dazzling whiteness of the jasmine flower. He emphasizes the absurdity of the law that refuses the śūdra the right to embrace the religious life, under the pretext that his religion is to serve the brahmans. In the end, his philosophical arguments are mainly directed against the myth that presents the four castes emerging successively from the four parts of the body of Brahmā, from his head, his arms, his belly, and his feet. "The udumbara[250] and the panasa,"[251] he says, "produce fruit born from the branches, from the trunk, from the joints, and from the roots; and yet these fruit are not distinct from one another, and it is not possible to say: this is the brahman fruit, that is the kṣatriya fruit, this the vaiśya, that the śūdra, for all are born from the same tree. Thus, there are not four classes, there is but one alone."[252] Between the legend of Triśangku and the treatise of Aśvaghoṣa, there is, we see, a notable difference. In the second, the subject is envisaged from a point of view as philosophical as a man from the Orient can conceive; in the first, it is indicated in a general manner rather than a dogmatic one. In each, however, the capital point is the appeal made to all classes by Buddhism, which admits all equally into the religious life, or, in more general terms, to the highest culture of the mind, and which thus breaks the true barrier that, in the Brahmanical system, kept them all under the yoke of the caste to which the privilege of birth assured that of knowledge and teaching.

I have sought through the previous observations to appraise the true character of the sūtras I believe to be most ancient. After having given some likelihood to this opinion, that those treatises bearing the title *vaipulya* are later than those that do not bear it, that is to say, than the very sūtras I have just analyzed, I have tried to establish the antiquity and the authenticity of the simple sūtras through the examination of various facts by which they reveal to us the state of the Indian society in which they were written. Still ignorant of the dates of the various parts of the Nepalese collection, this method is the only one able to give us some approximate notions touching on the relative age of these numerous works. It is

250. *Ficus glomerata.*
251. *Artocarpus integrifolia.*
252. *Wujra soochi*, pp. 11 and 12 of the translation, p. 10 of the text.

now a matter of applying it to the particular category of the simple sūtras, which is, in my view, prior to the developed sūtras, and trying to investigate whether the treatises contained in that category all belong to the same period.

I have said in the first section of this memorandum that all the sūtras were considered to emanate directly from the preaching of Śākyamuni: the result of this is that, if we hold to the testimony of the tradition and to the very form of these treatises, which is that of a conversation between the Buddha and his disciples, we should regard all of them as equally ancient. The examination of the sūtras and of the legends of the two great collections of the *Divyāvadāna* and the *Avadānasataka*, which comprise more than one hundred fifty different treatises, does not justify this supposition. We have seen above that Śākyamuni boasted of knowledge of the past and the future as well as the present, and that he took advantage of this supernatural science to instruct his listeners on what they had done in their previous existences and on the fate that awaited them in the existences to which the future still condemns them. As long as he contents himself with predicting to them that they will become eminent monks through their saintliness or even buddhas as perfect as he, his predictions are not very instructive for us, and they do not furnish us any help in the critique and examination of the tradition that indistinctly attributes all the sūtras to the founder of Buddhism. But when he speaks about personages who are really historical, when he fixes the date of their future appearance, his predictions acquire a new value, and they prove to us that the sūtras where we find them are subsequent, in content as well as form, to the events announced there in advance, in a divination whose authority the critic does not recognize. This remark applies to several treatises of the collection of Nepal, notably to one sūtra that will be a topic later, and in which the name of a king celebrated in the history of Buddhism appears. This king is Aśoka, of whom Śākyamuni, in more than one place and notably in some avadānas, speaks as if he were to be born long after him. I repeat, such predictions impart at least two incontestable facts to us: that the book in which we find them is subsequent not solely to Śākyamuni, but also to the events and to the personages whose future existence Śākya predicts. Thus, without prejudging anything about the epoch in which the sūtras have been redacted, and by confining ourselves to a general description of this category of books, it is evident that we have to divide it into sūtras where it is only a matter of personages contemporary with Śākya, and into sūtras that speak of personages who have appeared at a more or less long time after him, whether the date can be fixed with precision, or whether one arrives at the knowledge of only this single point, namely that they are subsequent to Śākya. It is a historical element whose importance one will appreciate when I have assembled everything that my readings have furnished me on the history of the collection of Nepal. Let us note now, however, that indications of this type are foreign to the developed sūtras, which in no way proves that these sūtras were redacted before the period of the personages recalled by the references to them I have just spoken about, but which belong exclusively to the character of the great sūtras, where it is no longer a matter of any human event, and which are filled with the fabulous history of these gigantic and marvelous bodhisattvas, in the contemplation and description of whom the primitive simplicity and the good practical sense of ancient Buddhism are lost.

But this is still not all, and it remains to be examined if, when a work bears the title *sūtra,* the result is that it must be classified rightfully into one of these categories whose existence the previous research has demonstrated: 1. that of the sūtras in which the events are contemporany with Śākyamuni; 2. that of the sūtras which speak of personages subsequent to him; 3. lastly, that of the sūtras of great development in which it is almost no longer a matter of human events. It is obvious *a priori* that the sole title of a work is not, in the eyes of the critic, a sufficient guarantee of its authenticity; for one understands easily that a forger could have imitated the form of the canonical books, in order to cloak the fruit of his personal conceptions. Here I do not intend, however, to discuss these falsifications, which the critics, in my opinion, are too disposed to presume, although they often have no other proof than the possibility of their existence. I am only considering, at the moment, books into which modifications, brought by the course of time to all things human, could have successively crept. It would be to deny all probabilities to maintain that Buddhism remained sheltered from modifications of this kind. Much to the contrary, I dare to assert that the detailed and comparative study of this belief, as it exists among the diverse peoples of Asia who adopted it, will prove that it passed, like all religions, through revolutions that modified and sometimes altered the primitive character. Thus, if Buddhism (and here I intend to designate in particular that of the North) developed, expanded, became regularized; if it even admitted into it ideas and beliefs that one has the right to regard as foreign to its primitive institution, it is permissible to believe that some of the works placed nowadays among the canonical books bear the more or less recognizable trace of the changes whose possibility I just presumed. From the beginning of this study, and when Mr. Hodgson had at his disposal only oral and traditional information that he did not yet have the opportunity to compare with the original texts, the so trustworthy judgment that guided him in his research indicated to him the precautions that critics should take in order to arrive at the complete and just appreciation of such an ancient and vast belief. Such wise warnings cannot be lost on the critic, and they must put him on guard against the consequences one would be tempted to draw from the existence of an ancient title, found on a book that could be modern. I repeat, the title indicates absolutely nothing to the reader regarding the authenticity of the work that bears it; for it must be one of two things: either the work was intended to bring to light some of these ideas that submit a system only to modifications of little importance; or the beliefs it served to express were likely to seriously change the character of the system. Thus, in either case, the author had to give his work the form of the books whose authority was universally and long recognized.

These reflections, which it suffices for me to mention briefly, apply in a rigorous manner to some of the books of the Nepalese collection. I have good reason to believe that the reading and, I should say, the exact translation of this entire collection would provide the means to extend them to a more considerable number of works than those I will mention. But it will take many years and also a great fund of patience to properly carry out an examination of this type. Thus, rather than a rapid and necessarily superficial review of several volumes, I have preferred the exact and sufficiently detailed analysis of a limited number of treatises that appeared suspicious to me at first sight.

Among the treatises I have just designated, there are two to which the title *sūtra* has probably been applied only afterward or which amounts to the same thing, that in spite of their title of *mahayana sūtra*, or sūtra serving as a great vehicle, they cannot pretend to be classified among the primitive sūtras, or even the developed sūtras. Both bear the title *Guṇakaraṇḍavyūha* or *Kāraṇḍavyūha*, that is to say, "Construction of the Basket of the Qualities" of the saint Avalokiteśvara; but one is written in prose and the other in verse. The version composed in prose forms a manuscript of sixty-seven folios, or one hundred thirty-four pages; the poem has one hundred ninety-five folios, or three hundred ninety pages of a smaller size than that of the other manuscript.[253] It seems evident to me that, in spite of the differences that exist between the two books, one is only the development and the paraphrase of the other, and I think that the more ancient of the two is the version in prose. This is what the first of the lists on the literature of Nepal reported by Mr. Hodgson in his memorandum already indicated to us. This list defines these two treatises as follows: "*Karaṇḍavyūha*, of the gāthās type, history of Lokeśvara Padmapāṇi in prose; and *Guṇakaraṇḍavyūhagāthā*, development of the previous treatise in verse."[254] I will provide the analysis of the longer one, that is to say, the poem; then, I will mention the passages where it differs from the other treatise. Since, with some exceptions, there is nothing in the prose sūtra that is not in the poem, the analysis of one necessarily comprises that of the other. Besides, the manuscript of the prose *Karaṇḍa* is so incorrect, that it would have been a good deal more difficult for me to provide a perfectly accurate extract than it would be to translate the poem in full.

The work opens with a dialogue between a Buddhist scholar, Jayaśrī, and the

253. The manuscript of the *Guṇakaraṇḍavyūha* written in prose belongs to the Bibliothèque royale; that in poetry is a part of the library of the Société Asiatique.

254. Hodgson, "Notices of the Languages, Literature and Religion of the Bauddhas of Nepal and Bhot," in *Asiatic Researches*, vol. 16, p. 428.

king, Jinaśrī, who questions him. Jayaśrī announces that what he is going to set forth has been taught to him by his master, the monk Upagupta. He says that the great king Aśoka, having gone to the hermitage of Kukkuṭārāma, asked the sage Upagupata what should be understood as the *triratna*, or the three precious objects. Upagupta answers, setting forth to him the perfection of the *mahābuddha*, or the great buddha, who is born from a portion of each of the five dhyāni buddhas;[255] that of *prajñā*, called the mother of all the buddhas, and called *dharma*, or the law; and lastly that of the *saṃgha*, or the assembly, considered from a completely mythological point of view and called the true son of the buddha. These are called the three precious objects, objects that merit a special worship, explained at length. Upagupta then recounts that long ago the blessed Śākyamuni taught the two bodhisattvas Maitreya and Sarvanivaraṇaviṣkambhin the perfections of the saint Avalokiteśvara, beginning with the miracles the latter performed when he descended to the hells to convert sinners, causing them to depart from there and transporting them to the universe of Sukhāvatī, of which Amitābha is the buddha. Śākyamuni explains that long ago he had been born as a merchant, under the dominion of the ancient buddha Vipaśyin, and he heard from the mouth of this blessed one the account of the qualities of Avalokiteśvara. He tells how, at the origin of things, there appeared in the form of a flame Ādibuddha, the primordial buddha, called *svayaṃbhū*, "the being existing by himself," and *ādinātha*, "the first sovereign." He is depicted engaging in the meditation called the *creation of the universe*. From his mind Avalokiteśvara is born, who also becomes absorbed in a similar meditation and who creates the moon and the sun from his two eyes, Maheśvara from his forehead, Brahmā from his shoulders, Nārāyaṇa from his heart, and Sarasvatī from his teeth.

Then, Avalokiteśvara traces for each of the gods he has created the limits of his authority, and in particular entrusts to them the defense and protection of the Buddhist faith. The narrator infers from this account the great superiority of Avalokiteśvara; he makes him the foremost of all beings, save Ādibuddha, and even goes as far as to say that "all the buddhas themselves take refuge in him with faith."

Śākyamuni then recounts that he was a bodhisattva named Dānaśūra under the ancient buddha Śikhin, and that he learned the merits of Avalokiteśvara from the mouth of the blessed one. The long enumeration of his virtues introduces some passages analogous to those contained in chapter 24 of the *Lotus of the Good Law*, notably those in which the various roles that Avalokiteśvara

255. In this passage, the great Buddha is represented as being born from the gathering of the five buddhas, who here can only be those of contemplation; it is at least the only manner in which I can understand the stanza in which this supreme buddha is defined as follows: *tat yathādisamudbhūto dharmadhātusvarūpakaḥ pañcabuddhāṃśasaṃjāto jagadīśas tathāgataḥ* (*Guṇakāraṇḍavyūha*, fol. 3b of the MS of the Société Asiatique).

takes on with the intention of converting beings are mentioned, appearing for some in the shape of the sun, for others in that of the moon, and so on of the main deities.[256] The saint is depicted teaching the law to the asuras in a cave of Jambudvīpa named Vajrakukṣi, and recommending to them the reading and study of the *Karaṇḍavyūha*, whose efficacy he exalts.

Śākyamuni continues with his account, saying that under the ancient buddha Viśvabhu, he was a ṛṣi bearing the name Kṣāntivādin, and that he heard from the mouth of this buddha everything he is asked about today. One finds inserted into this account the story of Bali, the powerful king who was relegated to the hells by Viṣṇu, and who repented having followed the law of the brahmans. Avalokiteśvara enumerates for him the advantages assured to one who has faith in the three precious objects; he makes known to him the rewards promised to the faithful and the pains that await one who does not believe. A dialogue is established between him and Bali, in which the saint endeavors to clarify and guide his new faith; he announces to him in the end that he will become a buddha one day. Avalokiteśvara then extends his teachings to the rākṣasas, and he is depicted going to the isle of Siṃhala (Ceylon), where he preaches the necessity of fasting and of confession to the female demons who inhabit this island. Once the rākṣasīs are converted to Buddhism, he betakes himself to Benares to render the same service to beings whose evil actions have reduced them to the miserable condition of insects and worms. He then goes to Magadha, where he miraculously saves the inhabitants from a terrible famine. Then he comes to assist the assembly of the listeners of Viśvabhū, gathered at Jetārāma, and teaches them the means to reach the knowledge of the state of a perfectly accomplished buddha.

Śākyamuni thus explains that Avalokiteśvara owes the faculty of accomplishing such great things to his meditations, and that he himself in particular long ago was saved from imminent danger by the saint bodhisattva. On that subject, he recounts the story of Siṃhala, son of the merchant Siṃha who, having embarked in search of precious stones on a remote island, is assailed as he approached Tāmradvīpa (the same as Tāmraparṇa, the Taprobane of the ancients) by a tempest that the rākṣasīs, malevolent deities who inhabit this island, raise. He is shipwrecked with his companions and swims ashore, where the rākṣasīs, who appear in the form of beautiful women, lead the merchants away to indulge in pleasure with them. Siṃhala, after having spent the night in the arms of one of these women, learns from the lamp that illuminates them that he has fallen into the hands of an ogress at whose pleasure he serves and who will devour him. He is warned that other merchants shipwrecked like him have, since his arrival, been thrown into a prison from which the rākṣasīs take them out each day to

256. *Le lotus de la bonne loi*, chap. 25, fol. 230b ff., p. 263ff.

feed on their flesh. Instructed by the revelations of the lamp, he goes to the shore with his companions, where a miraculous horse appears to him, which will carry him away from the island. But he must beware of looking back; he who, letting himself be moved by the tears of the rākṣasīs, casts a single glance at the shore, is condemned to fall into the ocean, where ogresses await to put him to death. The companions of Siṃha consent wholeheartedly to leave the island with him; but unfaithful to their promise, they lend an ear to the pleas of the women they abandon, and disappear one after the other, devoured by the rākṣasīs. Siṃhala alone escapes; and despite the pursuit of the woman he has left on the island, the marvelous horse carries him to India.

This part of the work, of which I provided but a very succinct analysis, is far superior to the rest, but the core belongs to other Buddhist legends; and I do not need to call the attention of readers familiar with Oriental stories to the ogresses and the marvelous horse, fables already known in Europe and very frequently recounted by the redactors of the legends of Nepal.[257]

The rākṣasī from whose hands Siṃhala just escaped seduces king Siṃhakeśarin and enters his inner apartments. Assisted by the other demons whom she calls from the island of Tāmradvīpa, she devours the king and his family. Siṃhala, who alone knows how to explain this disaster, is proclaimed king; and he resolves to go annihilate the rākṣasīs of the island, in order to spread the worship of the three precious objects. The demons withdraw into a forest; and since this event, the country named Tāmradvīpa in the past takes the name of Siṃhaladvīpa. Then Śākyamuni, connecting this story to the personages who are his contemporaries, explains to his listeners that he was king Siṃhala and that the miraculous horse that saved him was the saint Avalokiteśvara.

Śākyamuni continues by making a presentation of the physical qualities of the bodhisattva, a presentation that is purely mythological. In each of his pores rise mountains and woods where gods and sages live, exclusively engaged in the practice of religion. It is for this reason, says Śākya, that he is called *dharmakāya*, "who has the law for his body." The bodhisattva Viṣkambhin, with whom Śākyamuni converses, expresses the desire to see this marvelous spectacle of the body of Avalokita. But Śākya responds that all that is invisible, and that he himself could succeed in contemplating the saint in this way only after infinitely prolonged efforts. This lord of the world, he says, is like a magical apparition; his form is subtle; he does not even really have attributes, or form; but when he assumes one, it is an immense form, multiple and most grand of all; thus, he shows himself with eleven heads, a hundred thousand hands, a hundred times ten million

257. The legend analyzed in my text is found also in Xuanzang, from which it has been extracted by Mr. Landresse (*Foe koue ki*, pp. 338 and 339).

eyes, etc. Viṣkambhin then expresses the desire to know the magical formula in six letters, *vidyā ṣaḍakṣarī*, whose marvelous efficacy Śākya exalts.[258] Śākya sends Viṣkambhin to Benares, where Avalokiteśvara miraculously appears to him in the air, enjoining the preceptor he has chosen to communicate the formula in six letters to his student. Avalokiteśvara next causes him to see in a supernatural way the assembly of Śākyamuni in Jetavana; then, after having conversed with the Buddha on various religious subjects, he goes to Sukhavatī to visit Amitābha, the buddha of this universe. The sage Viṣkambhin, who thus has had the opportunity to contemplate Avalokiteśvara, returns again to his favorite subject, the enumeration of the qualities of this divine being. Śākyamuni then recounts to him that in the time of the ancient buddha Krakuchanda, he was born, he Śākya, as a bodhisattva, with the name of Dānaśūra, and at that time, Avalokiteśvara gained possession of the highest modes of meditation. Śākya then teaches Viṣkambhin about the existence of two tīrthas, or sacred ponds, located on the southern side of Mount Meru, which have the property of retrieving all objects thrown into their waters; and he compares their virtue to that of the *Karaṇḍavyūha*, the very sūtra he sets forth.

One of the principal interlocutors of the dialogue changes at that point; and it is Ānanda, one of the foremost disciples of Śākya, who converses with his master on various points of the discipline. Śākyamuni predicts, on the occasion of this conversation, that three hundred years after his passage into complete nirvāṇa, that is to say, after his death, there will appear in Buddhist monasteries monks who will violate the rules imposed by him on his listeners, and who will bring the conduct of men indulging in the world into the ascetic life. Śākya uses this occasion to set forth the principles of morality and the rules of conduct that the monks must observe, and it is with this exposition that he concludes his conversation with Ānanda.

The work ends there, strictly speaking; but it is necessary that the various narrators in whose mouths this account has been successively placed reappear in turn. Thus, Upagupta, who has set it forth to king Aśoka, continues the speech recommending to him the worship of the three precious objects. Aśoka responds

258. It is the famous formula "oṃ maṇi padme hūṃ," of which the saint Avalokiteśvara is supposed to be the author. Thus, one does not encounter it in the works or among the peoples to whom Avalokiteśvara is unknown, that is to say, in the simples sūtras of the North, or in those of Ceylon. Mr. Schmidt has indeed seen that it must not have belonged to primitive Buddhism, since it has the bodhisattva Avalokiteśvara as its author (*Geschichte der Ost-Mongolen*, p. 319). But later, he seems to have wished to attribute to this saint, at least by conjecture, some influence on the Buddhism of Ceylon and of transgangetic India (*Mémoires de l'Académie des sciences de Saint-Pétersbourg*, 1:110). I will show later, in examining the books of the Buddhists of the South, that none of those at my disposal speak even once of Avalokiteśvara or of his formula. One must see on this prayer the works of scholars most occupied with Buddhism, and in particular of Klaproth (*Nouveau Journal Asiatique*, 7:185ff.), of Schmidt (*Mémoires de l'Académie des sciences de Saint-Pétersbourg*, 1:112ff.), of Rémusat (*Foe koue ki*, p. 118), of Hodgson (*Journal of the Royal Asiatic Society of Bengal*, 4:196ff.).

in turn, asking him the reason why the bodhisattva whose supreme merits he has just celebrated is named Avalokiteśvara. Upagupta responds that it is because he looks with compassion on the beings suffering from the ills of existence.[259] He adds to this explanation new advice on the worship it is necessary to render to the saint Avalokiteśvara, and on the advantages this worship assures to those who practice it. The first of all the narrators, Jayaśrī, after bringing an end to this exposition he received from his master, still adds some stanzas on the advantages that await one who reads or who listens to the recitation of this sūtra of *Karaṇḍavyūha*, and king Jinaśrī expresses his approval of everything he has just heard. The volume ends on folio 195, with the title conceived in this way: "End of the king of sūtras called the Composition of the Basket of the Qualities of Avalokiteśvara, set forth by Jayaśrī to king Jinaśrī who questioned him."

This rather mediocre subject is set forth in verses of anuṣṭubh meter, and in a Sanskrit that is striking in its extreme similarity to that of the Brahmanical Purāṇas. The language is correct, and I have noticed only two words that attest to the presence of a vulgar dialect derived from Sanskrit. These words, which I mention in the note,[260] are such that they could have been borrowed from other works, from which they would have passed into the *Karaṇḍavyūha*; they are not sufficient to characterize the language of this poem and to make it a dialect, or at least a mixture of Sanskrit and Prakrit, similar to that which one notices in the developed sūtras. They are simple borrowings, explained by the extremely frequent use made of these words in the books regarded as canonical. One can consider it certain that the *Karaṇḍavyūha* is a composition that must be called classical, as far as the language is concerned, in contrast to the other books with which it shares the title *sūtra*; and it is not the least of the differences that distinguish this work from the other developed sūtras. I would not dare to be as

259. One sees thereby that the Buddhists of the North consider the name Avalokiteśvara as composed of two words, a participle and a noun, namely *īśvara*, "the lord," and *avalokita*, "who has looked down." It is evident that they give to the participle not the passive sense (looked) but the active sense (who has looked). I do not believe that this use of the participle in *ta*, which is explicitly authorized by Pāṇini when it is a case of an action commencing (vol. 1, bk. 3, chap. 4, p. 71 and 72), can be accepted in classical Sanskrit for the root *lok*. But it would not be the first time that the language of the Buddhist books would deviate from Brahmanical compositions. There is no doubt that the Oriental peoples who have known the name Avalokiteśvara and who have had to translate it into their idioms have assigned the active sense that I indicate here to the first part of which it is composed. In a special dissertation, Klaproth has put the fact beyond doubt in relation to the Tibetans and the Mongols (*Nouveau Journal Asiatique*, vol. 7, p. 190), and Mr. Rémusat has also established it more than one time with regard to the Chinese (*Foe koue ki*, pp. 56, 117, and 119).

260. These words are the following forms of the adjective *tāyin* (protector) for the Sanskrit *trāyin*, which has lost its *r*, according to the principle of Pāli; namely, *tāyine*, dative singular fol. 19a; *tāyinām*, genitive plural fols. 80a and 179a; then the term *poṣadha* for *uposatha*, a most Pāli term, which designates at once the fast imposed on Buddhist monks and the six days that follow the new moon. This term, which recalls the Sanskrit *upoṣaṇa* (fast), is even more altered than the Pāli, since it has lost its initial vowel, which is always preserved, as far as I know, in the Pāli of Ceylon. The frequent repetition of this term is sufficient to explain how it could have been subjected to such a strong modification.

explicit with regard to the version in prose; the manuscript is so incorrect that I am not able to say if the shocking errors that disfigure it do not hide some Pāli or Prakrit forms. The truth is that I recognized at most four of them, which I report in a note.[261] But these forms are quite characteristic, and they belong to the same influence as those one can notice, for example, in the *Lotus of the Good Law.* They do not appear to me, however, to be sufficiently numerous or sufficiently important to assign a place to the *Karaṇḍavyūha* among the Buddhist works to which the mixture of Pāli and Sanskrit gives such a recognizable character. If, as other indices that will be taken up later allow us to believe, the *Karaṇḍa* in prose does not belong to the preaching of Śākya himself, these forms, not numerous in any case, lose much of their importance; and if they appear in a book that other characteristics distance from the category of the primitive sūtras, it is only due to the influence that must have been exercised on the author by reading treatises in which similar forms are employed in almost every line.

At the same time that the style of the poetic *Karaṇḍa* is that of the Purāṇas, the exterior form and the framing of the work also recall the Indian compilations I have just mentioned. Here, as in the Purāṇas, the account does not present itself to the reader directly and without preamble; it arrives, on the contrary, only through the intermediary of numerous narrators, who receive it one from the other, and it is not until after having gone through these intermediaries that one reaches Śākyamuni, the primitive narrator, or rather the sacred revealer. That is one of the most important features that distinguish the poem from the version in prose. The latter begins like all the sūtras: "This is what I heard: One day, the Bhagavat was in the great city of Śrāvastī, at Jetavana, in the garden of Anāthapiṇḍika, with a great assembly of monks, with one thousand two hundred fifty monks and many bodhisattvas, etc." I conclude from this difference that the poem is later than the prose sūtra; for whereas nothing informs us about the motives that have induced the narrator to precede the sūtra proper with these two dialogues between Aśoka and Upagupta on the one hand and Jayaśrī and Jinaśrī on the other, the addition of all this apparatus copied from the tradition is even easier to understand than the elimination of these dialogues would be if they had had a real existence. We still know nothing, it is true, about Jayaśrī or Jinaśrī, the final narrators of the poem; but we have already noted that king Aśoka and the sage Upagupta, who are very celebrated in the tradition of the North, lived long after Śākyamuni. I also add that in announcing the future appearance of perverse monks who, three hundred years after Śākya, will alter the purity of the law, our poem is making a prediction whose effect is to carry it back to a time in which

261. These are the only traces of Pāli forms that I have come across in the *Karaṇḍavyūha* in prose: *sāntaḥpura parivārehi* instead of *parivāraiḥ*, fol. 20a; *paramāṇurajasya* instead of *rajasaḥ*, fol. 23a; *jīvanta* for *jīvan*, fol. 25b; *viṣkaṃbhim* (proper noun) instead of *viṣkaṃbhinaṃ*, fol. 44b.

Buddhism was in decline. Moreover, the redaction is not sufficiently simple, or sufficiently disentagled from all mythological development, to be ranked among the repository books of the most ancient tradition. The saint Avalokiteśvara, in whose praise it was written, is, as I have shown above, entirely unknown to the redactors of the sūtras and the primitive legends. It is necessary to say as much about the magical formula in six letters, which is none other than the sentence so often quoted, *oṃ maṇi padme hūṃ*! This formula, which is not given in our poem, but which is read two times in the prose version, is quite foreign to the primitive sūtras. The presence of this singular phrase, whose existence is so intimately related, according to the Tibetans, to that of their saint Avalokiteśvara, is an index of the same order as the development of this mythological system, based on the supposition of an immaterial and primordial buddha, of whom I have spoken above. All this clearly distinguishes the *Karaṇḍavyūha*, not only from the primitive sūtras but even from the developed sūtras; and yet the argument that I draw today from these various elements in order to establish the posteriority of this poem with regard to the monuments of Buddhist literature examined to this point does not present itself at the moment with all the force it will receive later from the comparison I intend to make of the Sanskrit collection of the North with the Pāli collection of the South.

The manner in which the author of the *Karaṇḍavyūha* appropriated the legend related to the first settlement of Indians on the island of Siṃhala, previously named Tāmradvīpa or Tāmraparṇa, is also an index that the prose version itself is modern. The Sinhalese legend of the *Mahāvaṃsa* is modified there for a purely particular and rather ridiculous purpose, that of making the leader of the Indian emigrants, Siṃhala, pass for an ancient form of Śākyamuni, and to exalt the supernatural power of Avalokiteśvara, who hid in the guise of a horse in order to save him. If this puerile legend were ancient and common to all the schools of Buddhism, it would be found without any doubt in the *Mahāvaṃsa*, this precious chronicle of the Sinhalese traditions. But although the details of the arrival of the Indian Siṃhala on the coast of Tāmpavarṇa are, in the previously mentioned Sinhalese chronicle, mingled with some fables, their ensemble nonetheless still shows more characteristics of probability to the eyes of an impartial reader than the account of the *Karaṇḍavyūha*.

Moreover, whatever the age of this composition, its anteriority with regard to the poem appears to me sufficiently established. The form of these two works suffices in itself to settle the question; but unfortunately that is a kind of proof addressed only to the small number of persons to whom the two original texts are accessible. In comparing these two works, one remains intimately convinced that the *Karaṇḍavyūha* in prose is the germ of the *Karaṇḍavyūha* in verse. I could also produce, in favor of my sentiment, the argument furnished by the mention that the poem makes of Ādibuddha, this supreme buddha, invention of the theist school, whose traces are found only in treatises that other indices compel us to assign a modern date, and that Csoma de Kőrös had reason to believe to be later than the tenth century of our era.[262] Since the prose version does not speak of Ādibuddha, whereas he is expressly named in the verse version, one could say that the first is anterior to the other. But perhaps it would be to attach too much value to a negative argument; and, moreover, the description of the body of Avalokiteśvara, which the prose version gives in the same terms as the poem, is a characteristic so mythological as to make one presume that the notion of a divine and supreme buddha, indispensable complement of the theist pantheon of the Buddhists, was as much in the mind of the author of the *Karaṇḍa* in prose as in that of the author of the *Karaṇḍa* in verse.

I will add again in favor of my opinion on the anteriority of the prose version that it is, as far as I know, the only one of the two that has been translated by the Tibetan interpreters to whom we owe the Kah-gyur. The Tibetan version, which it would be indispensable to consult if the translation of the *Karaṇḍa* became necessary, is found in the same volume that contains the translation of the *Lotus of the Good Law*.[263] The names of the translators indicated at the end of this version are Śākyaprabha and Ratnarakṣita; but nothing informs us of the precise date of these two authors; and since the translations of the Kah-gyur were carried out, according to Csoma, from the seventh to the thirteenth century,[264] the prose version of the *Karaṇḍavyūha* must be placed in the interval between the year 600 and the year 1200 of our era. The Sanskrit text is necessarily anterior to this latter limit; but we can neither affirm nor deny that it is to the former. As far as the verse version is concerned, either it existed prior to the seventh century, or it was composed after the thirteenth. If one wants it to have existed before the year 600, it will be necessary to recognize that it did not have enough authority to be admitted into the collection of the Kah-gyur, where a good many works whose antiquity can be justly contested have nonetheless found a place. If it was composed only after the thirteenth century, it goes without saying that it could not have been included in a collection considered to have been fixed in great part around this time. I confess that if the presence of a translation of the prose *Karaṇḍavyūha* in the Kah-gyur is certain proof that the Sanskrit original existed before the thirteenth century, and even a rather strong presumption that it was written before the seventh, this fact that the Kah-gyur does not contain the version of the poetic *Karaṇḍa* is for me definitive proof of the posteriority of this version with regard to the former, and a presumption of great weight in favor of the opinion that tends to portray the *Karaṇḍa* in verse as more modern than the

262. "Analysis of the Sher-chin," etc., in *Asiatic Researches*, vol. 20, p. 448.
263. Csoma, "Analysis of the Sher-chin," etc., in *Asiatic Researches*, vol. 20, p. 440.
264. "Analysis of the Dul-va," in *Asiatic Researches*, vol. 20, p. 42.

thirteenth century. I add, in conclusion, that in the opinion of Mr. Hodgson,[265] the *Karaṇḍavyūha* is one of the books that belong exclusively to Nepal. This author does not have an explanation, it is true, on the question of whether we are to understand here the work in prose or the work in verse, but the quotations he gives from it allow me to believe that he has the poem in mind. The assertion of Mr. Hodgson accords perfectly with the inductions set forth in the preceding discussion. I am strongly inclined to regard it as well founded; and from that point the difficulties created by the origin and the existence of such a modern book among the Nepalese sources of Buddhism, and the absence of a Tibetan translation of this poem, disappear. The *Karaṇḍavyūha* in verse is not a canonical book; it is on the contrary a work written outside India, after the epoch when Buddhism was driven from its native soil. I have believed that this point merits being discussed with some attention, not because of the value of the book in itself, but to show the indices with whose aid one can recognize whether a given work is ancient and authentic or not.

It is important now to summarize in few words the results of this long discussion.

Starting with the description of the sūtras, as the tradition has preserved it for us and as is possible according to the two sūtras I have translated as specimens of this kind of treatise, I have tried to establish:

1. That there are two kinds of sūtras that differ from each other in form as well as in content, namely: the sūtras that I call simple and the sūtras that the Nepalese themselves, in accord with our manuscripts, call developed;

2. That this difference, marked by important modifications in doctrine, announces that these two kinds of sūtras were written at different periods;

3. That the simple sūtras are more ancient than the developed sūtras, also sometimes called sūtras used as a great vehicle; that is to say, they are closer to the preaching of Śākyamuni;

4. That among the simple sūtras, it is also necessary to distinguish those that recall events contemporary with Śākyamuni, and those that recount facts or mention personages manifestly subsequent to the epoch of the founder of Buddhism;

5. Finally, that all the works that bear the title *sūtra* must not, by that alone, be ranked rightfully in one of the three preceding categories, namely in the two categories of the simple sūtras, and in the category of the developed sūtras; but that there are sūtras even more modern, notably sūtras in verse, which are only a kind of amplification of other more or less ancient prose sūtras.

265. "Sketch of Buddhism," in *Transactions of the Royal Asiatic Society*, vol. 2, p. 250.

SECTION 3

Vinaya, or Discipline

In giving the general description of the Nepalese collection at the beginning of this memorandum, I said that one did not find a category of books bearing the general title *vinaya*, or discipline, as one finds one bearing that of *sūtra*; and I showed that it was the *avadānas*, or legends, that represented the Vinaya, or second category of the Buddhist scriptures. Then, I showed the striking analogy that exists between the sūtras and the avadānas, treatises that differ from one another only due to a formula of little importance; and this analogy seemed to me strong enough even to authorize me to draw my examples indiscriminately from avadānas and from sūtras, when I had to describe the state of the society within which Śākyamuni appeared. What I have said about the sūtras in the previous section thus applies exactly to the avadānas; there are avadānas that speak only of Śākyamuni and his first disciples; these are incontestably the most ancient of all, at least in their core; there are some that mix into the account of events related to the Buddha the names of personages who lived a long time after him, like that of Aśoka, for example, and even kings a good deal later than this monarch. There are, finally, some that are written in verse and that, like the *Guṇakaraṇḍavyūha*, which I just analyzed, are rather modern amplifications of works or only of more or less ancient traditions.

Another analogy that draws the avadānas to the sūtras is that the discipline is no more dogmatically set forth in them than morality and metaphysics are in the sūtras. That is, I hardly need to say, a natural consequence of the analogies I have just indicated. If morality and metaphysics are not presented systematically in the sūtras, it is because these treatises date back to an epoch in which these two elements of all religions still had not acquired their full and entire development, or to put it in a more general way, it is that they reproduce the free and varied teaching of Śākya, who preached but did not profess. And if the discipline is not more regularly formulated in the avadānas, it is because these treatises are of the same time as the sūtras, and Śākya, in order to establish a point of discipline, did not impose on himself the strict progression of a didactic exposition, any more than he did for morality and metaphysics. It would thus be as difficult to sketch the complete picture of Buddhist discipline from reading the avadānas as it is to extract from the sūtras an absolutely regular system of philosophy and morality. Buddhist monks were able to engage themselves successfully in a work of this kind not only because they possessed a good many texts that we lack, but also because the discipline that they had to formulate was alive among them; and that practice, which is also an authority, made up for the silence or the obscurity of the words of the master. But we, who do not have the same resources, have to content ourselves with ascertaining, as they appear, the most important points of the system that formed a regularly organized body from the monastic followers of Śākya. This is what I have attempted to do in the course of the readings, whose summary I will present here, by assembling the most general features of the organization to which the monks were subject at the time of Śākya and of his first disciples.

In order to become a Buddhist monk, it sufficed, as I have said above, to feel faith in the Buddha and to declare to him the firm will one had to follow him. Then, the Buddha had the hair and the beard of the neophyte shaved off; he took a kind of tunic and a mantle made of patched rags dyed yellow for his clothes; and he ordinarily was placed under the direction of an older monk who was charged with his education. But at the beginning of the preaching of Śākya, and when the number of his disciples was hardly considerable, it is he who directly instructed the neophyte; and the legends are full of accounts in which brahmans and merchants figure, who present themselves to the Buddha, make their religious declaration to him, and receive from him the knowledge of the very few moral and metaphysical truths that form the essential part of the doctrine. This teaching ordinarily fructified rather quickly, such that those to whom it had been addressed immediately cross the degrees that separate the ordinary man from the most accomplished monks. In sects animated by the spirit of proselytism, it is necessary to proceed quickly; thus on each page the legends offer us proof that faith affected the first disciples of the Buddha even more forcefully than his teaching.

Next to these conversions performed directly by Śākyamuni, one sees others that are only accomplished with the aid of an intermediary, who is a monk or simply a man known for his favorable disposition toward the Buddha. These various methods are set forth in the legend of Pūrṇa; and I prefer to portray them here in their real form, rather than to perform a dry analysis of this legend. I shall thus translate this account, to which I have already made more than one allusion, and which seems to me to offer a good specimen of an avadāna.

LEGEND OF PŪRṆA[1]

The Bhagavat was in Śrāvastī, in Jetavana, in the garden of Anāthapiṇḍika. Now, at that time, in the city of Sūrpāraka,[2] there lived a householder named Bhava, fortunate, having great wealth, enjoying a great fortune, having a vast and large entourage, capable of contending with the opulence of Vaiśravaṇa.[3] He chose a wife in a family equal to his own; then he enjoyed himself with her, he indulged in pleasure and sensual delight with her. When he had enjoyed himself with her, his wife became pregnant after a certain time. She delivered after eight or nine months and gave birth to a son. Three times seven or twenty-one days after the delivery, they celebrated the festival of birth in a splendid manner, and they occupied themselves with giving him a name. "What name will the child have?" [said the father]. The relatives answered: "This child is the son of the householder Bhava; may he be called Bhavila." Thus, Bhavila was the name he received.

The householder again enjoyed himself with his wife; with her he indulged in pleasure and sensual delight and had a second son with her, to whom the name Bhavatrāta was given. He also had a third son with her, who received the name of Bhavanandin.

Meanwhile, after several years, the householder Bhava fell ill. Since he let himself fly off into extremely violent words, he began to be neglected by his own

1. MS of the Société Asiatique, fol. 12a; my manuscript, fol. 14a. *Bka' 'gyur*, sec. *'Dul ba*, vol. *kha*, or 2, pp. 37–69. *Asiatic Researches*, vol. 20, p. 61.

2. The legend does not determine the location of this city in a precise manner; it only informs us that it was a seaport, since one embarked from there for expeditions to distant lands, probably as far as the islands of the Indian Archipelago. It places it at a distance of more than one hundred yojanas from Śrāvastī, which with Wilson we look for not far from Faizabad. This information does not tell us anything very certain; one knows that there are several estimates of the yojana, one will give nine hundred English miles and the other five hundred English miles for one hundred Indian yojanas. The Buddhist books of the Sinhalese also know this city; the *Mahāvaṃsa* calls it Suppārakapaṭana and mentions it as a point where Vijaya, the founder of Sinhalese civilization, landed during his voyage to Ceylon (*Mahāvamso*, chap. 6, p. 46. Turnour, *ibid.*, index, p. 25). Vijaya came from the country of Banga (Bengal), from which he had been banished; it is thus in the Bay of Bengal that one must look for the city of Sūrpāraka, in Pāli Suppāraka. I do not hesitate to identify this name with the Σιππάρα of Ptolemy, which Mr. Gosselin has, thanks to most ingenious calculations, believed to be able to recognize in the modern Sipeler at one of the mouths of the Kṛṣṇa (*Recherches sur la géographie des anciens*, 3:253). Perhaps this puts the city called Sippāra by Ptolemy a little below; but the designations agree very well, and if one has no objections to the identification of Sippāra and Sipeler, one must not have any further objections against the connections I propose between the Greek Sippāra and the Pāli Suppāra; the final *ka* does not have enough importance to be taken into account here. It is not useless to note that the itineraries from which Ptolemy borrowed his materials transcribed this name in its popular form.

3. It is one of the Brahmanical names of Kuvera, the god of wealth.

wife and children. He had a young slave; this girl had the following reflection: "My master has, through a hundred kinds of means, amassed abundant wealth; today he is sick, and he is neglected by his own wife and children; it would not be suitable were I also to abandon my master." She thus went to a doctor and told him: "Lord, do you know Bhava the householder?" "I know him. What needs to be done for him?" "A sickness of such a kind has stricken him, and he is neglected by his own wife and children; tell me what the medicine is for his illness." The doctor replied: "Young girl, you tell me that he is neglected by his own wife and children; who then will care for him?" The young girl responded: "It is I who will treat him. But enough; indicate to me which medicines are not too expensive."[4] The doctor indicated to her what was necessary, saying: "This is the medicine that is good for the sick man." The young girl, taking something from her personal provisions and pilfering others from the house of her master, began to treat him. Bhava returned to health and had this reflection: "I have been neglected by my own wife and children; if I live, I owe it to this young girl; I have to show my gratitude to my slave for this service." He thus said to her: "Young girl, I have been abandoned by my own wife and children; all the life I have, I owe to your care; I want to offer you a gift." The young girl responded: "Master, if you are satisfied, agree to have intercourse with me." "Why," said the master, "do you wish to have intercourse with me? I will give you five hundred kārṣāpaṇas and free you."[5] The young girl responded: "Son of my master, even if I should still live a long time,[6] I would never be anything but a slave; but if the son of my master has intercourse with me, I immediately cease being a slave." Seeing that the determination of the young girl was irrevocable, the householder responded to her: "When you are in the suitable season, inform me." After some time, the young girl, having had her period, informed her master that she was in the suitable season. Bhava the householder thus had intercourse with her and she became pregnant. Now, from the day she became pregnant, all of the enterprises and all of the affairs of Bhava the householder succeeded perfectly.

After eight or nine months, the slave gave birth to a son, beautiful, pleasant

4. I translate in this way the reading whose Tibetan version allows one to suppose: *alpamūlyāni bhaiṣajyāni*, for this version renders this passage in this way: "inexpensive medicines." Our two manuscripts read *asya mūlyāni bhaiṣajyāni vyapadiśa*, which means "indicate to me precious medicines for him." I do not hesitate to prefer the Tibetan version, all the more so because अल्प *alpa* could have been very easily confused with अस्य *asya*.

5. The five hundred kārṣāpaṇas, at the rate of 11 grams 375 milligrams of the copper kārṣāpaṇa, represent about 28 francs 45 centimes.

6. The manuscript of the Société Asiatique says in a few more words: *dūram api param api gatvā dāsyevāham*, "Even if I go far away, even somewhere else, I am nothing but a slave." My manuscript only reads *dūram api gatvā*, "even if I should go quite far away." The Tibetan version derives perhaps from an original where one reads *dūram api pāraṃ gatvā*, these last two words having the meaning of: "having crossed to the shore" because this version conceived in this way: *bdag rgyangs bkum par mchis*, seems to mean: "although I should not die for a long time from now." I have translated in this sense, but following the reading of my manuscript.

to see, delightful, having a white complexion and skin the color of gold; his head had the shape of a parasol; his arms were long, his forehead large, his eyebrows joined together, his nose prominent. The day this child came into the world, the enterprises and the affairs of Bhava the householder succeeded in an extraordinary manner. The relatives, having gathered after three times seven or twenty-one days, celebrated the festival of the birth of the child in a splendid manner and gave him the name of Pūrṇa (the accomplished one). The small Pūrṇa was entrusted to the care of eight nurses, who were charged with giving him particular attention two by two, so that he grew rapidly, like a lotus in the middle of a lake. When he was older, he was taught writing, arithmetic, calculation, palmistry; what is concerned with shares, wages, and deposits; the art of judging fabrics, lands, precious stones, trees, elephants, horses, young men, young girls; the eight objects, in short, in whose valuation he became skillful, eloquent, wise, and an experienced practitioner.

Then, Bhava the householder successively married Bhavila and his two other sons. These young men, smitten with an excessive passion for their wives, indulged themselves in inactivity and dreamed of nothing but adorning their person. This is why Bhava the householder, holding his head in his hands, was constantly absorbed in his thoughts. His sons noticed it and said to him: "Why, dear father, do you remain so, with your head in your hands, absorbed in your thoughts?" Bhava responded: "My children, I did not marry before having amassed one lak of suvarṇas;[7] but you who scorn work, you have excessive passion for your wives, and you dream of nothing but adorning yourselves. When I am dead, the house will be filled with misery; how thus could I not be absorbed in my thoughts?"

Bhavila wore diamond earrings; he took them off, and replacing them with wooden rings, he pronounced this vow: "I will no longer wear diamond earrings until I have earned one lak of suvarṇas." The second son, doing the same, took lacquer earrings and the third took lead ones. The names they bore of Bhavila, Bhavatrāta, and Bhavanandin stopped being used and were replaced by those of Dārukarṇin, Stavakarṇin, and Trapukarṇin.[8] Having assembled merchandise, they departed for the great ocean. Pūrṇa then said: "O my father, I also wish to go on the great ocean!" But Bhava responded to him: "You are still only a

7. The observations I have made in a special note on the value of the silver purāṇa apply equally to the gold currency called *suvarṇa*, literally "gold." This is the evaluation according to Colebrooke. Five kṛṣṇalas or black grains of the *arbrus precatorius* are necessary to make one māṣa of gold, and sixteen māṣas to make one suvarṇa (*Asiatic Researches*, vol. 5, p. 93, ed. in -8°). Now, the kṛṣṇala being worth 2 3/16 English troy grains, the māṣa of gold, which is equal to five kṛṣṇalas, is worth exactly 10 15/16 troy grains. Sixteen māṣas making one suvarṇa, this latter currency is equal to 175 English troy grains, that is to say, 11.375 grams, which is 35 francs 26 centimes and a very slight fraction. As one lak (*lakṣa* in Sanskrit) is equal to one hundred thousand, the lak of suvarṇas amounts nowadays to 3,526,200 francs. In the Buddhist legends, it amounts to an immense fortune. See also other evaluations according to Wilson (*Hindu Theatre*, 1:47, note *).

8. These three names respectively mean: "who has wood, lacquer, and lead earrings."

child, O my son, stay here; take over the affairs of the shop." Pūrṇa thus stayed at home.

Meanwhile, his brothers returned, bringing their ship back safe and sound. After having rested from the fatigue of the voyage, they said to Bhava: "Evaluate our merchandise, dear father." The father made the evaluation, and it happened that one lak came to each. Pūrṇa also had conducted the affairs of the house with orderliness and probity; so, he had amassed more than one lak of suvarṇas. Having thus prostrated at the feet of his father, he said to him: "Evaluate, O my father, the amount I have earned in the shop." Bhava responded: "You have stayed here, my son, what is there to evaluate for you?" Pūrṇa responded: "Evaluate nevertheless, O my father, it will thus be known what there is." The father made the evaluation, and besides the value in suvarṇas from the proceeds of ordinary earnings, more than one lak was also found. Bhava, the householder, filled with satisfaction and joy, began to reflect: "He is virtuous," he said to himself, "and possesses greatness,[9] the being who, without having left here, has earned so much gold."

However, there arrived a time when Bhava came to grow weak; he thus had this reflection: "When I am dead, my children will be divided; it is necessary to find some way [to prevent their disunity]." So he said to them: "My children, bring some wood." When the wood was brought: "Set it on fire," he said to them; and they set fire to it. Then, Bhava said: "Each of you take out the firebrands"; they took them all out and the fire went out. Bhava then said to them: "Do you understand, my children?" "Yes, dear father, we have understood." Immediately, Bhava recited the following stanza:

"United the coals burn; in the same way, the union of brothers makes their strength; and like the coals as well, it is by separating them that men die out."

"When I am dead, O my children, you must not listen to your wives; indeed, the family is divided by women; confused things are divided (distinguish themselves) by words; a spell wrongly cast is destroyed; pleasure is destroyed by cupidity."

The sons withdrew; Bhavila alone stayed with Bhava, who told him: "O my

9. The expression that the text uses here is, as far as I know, especially peculiar to Buddhist Sanskrit. It is *puṇyamaheśākhya*, a term formed from the union of *puṇya* and *maheśākhya*, which is often found alone, and which is the opposite of *alpeśākhya*. This latter term is explained in the following manner in the commentary to the *Abhidharmakośa*: *alpeśākhya anudaro hīnajātīya ity arthaḥ; iṣṭa itīśaḥ; alpa īśo alpeśaḥ; alpeśa ity ākhyā yasya, so 'lpeśākhyaḥ, viparyayāt maheśākhyaḥ* (fol. 202b of my manuscript), that is to say: "*Alpeśākhya* means *who is not noble, who is from base extraction*; *īśa* is synonymous with *iṣṭa* (desirable); joined to the adjective *alpa*, it means *not very desirable* and with *ākhyā* (noun) it forms the compound *alpeśākhya*, that is to say, *one whose name is not very desirable*. One says in the opposite sense *maheśākhya*, or *one whose name is highly desirable*." One would perhaps arrive at the real meaning more directly and more quickly by retaining for *īśa* the meaning of *master* and by explaining these two words in this way: "one who has the name of a minor master, or of a great master."

son, never abandon Pūrṇa, for he is a man who is known to be virtuous and possesses greatness."

"All that is amassed is eventually destroyed; what is lofty falls in the end; what is united eventually dissolves; what is living ends in death."

After having thus spoken, Bhava succumbed to the law of time. His sons, adorning a litter with blue, yellow, red, and white cloth, carried him to the cemetery with great pomp, and cremated his body on the pyre there. When their sorrow afterward began to dissipate, they said to one another: "At the time when our father was living, we were subjected to his authority; but if now we give up the business, the house will fall into decline; it will no longer flourish. Why would we not take merchandise and go to a foreign country?" Pūrṇa then told them: "If it is so, I will also go with you." His brothers responded to him: "Stay here instead for the affairs of the shop; we will depart alone." They thus gathered merchandise and departed for another country. Pūrṇa, to whom all the affairs had been entrusted, looked after the house. It is a rule that in the houses of wealthy people, what is necessary for the expenditures of the day is distributed [each morning]. The wives of the brothers [who had gone] sent their servants to seek the silver to spend. But Pūrṇa was surrounded by wealthy persons, the chiefs of guilds, the chiefs of merchants, and by other people who made their living from commerce; so the servants could not find the moment [to approach him]. When those who surrounded him stood up and departed, Pūrṇa gave the servants the silver necessary for the day. They did not return until very late to their mistresses, who reproached them. But the girls recounted to them in detail[10] what had happened, and added: "This is what happens to those in the family where the son of a slave exercises control as he pleases." Bhavila's wife said to her servant: "You must watch for the right moment to go [to look for what is due to me]." This one, having watched for the right time, went to Pūrṇa and received quite quickly [what was due to her]. The other girls still spent their time waiting; they questioned the first servant, who told them how she did it. They thus went with her and then received what was due to them as quickly as the first. So their mistresses asked them: "How is it that now you return so quickly?" The servants responded: "You owe this happiness to your elder sister-in-law. Her servant re-

10. The word that I translate as *in detail* is *vistareṇa* in the text. This term is used in Buddhist Sanskrit each time that a discourse or an enumeration, whose terms are known by what precedes it, is abridged. In order to understand its use, it would be necessary, then, instead of the literal translation "with extension," to use a form like this: "to say it in a word." Basically this locution means: "one repeats here what is said elsewhere in detail." The Tibetan version fills the ellipsis and resumes the account, adding to it some expressions that are missing in my two manuscripts. "Pūrṇa, surrounded by wealthy persons, the chiefs of guilds, the chiefs of merchants, and other people who made their living from commerce, is seated, shining with a luster equal to the light of the sun. It is when those who surrounded him had stood up and had departed that he has given us what was due to us." In addition, the Tibetan version also contains other additions that did not appear to me to have enough importance to be introduced into the account.

ceived what is due to her as soon as she arrived; so, we always leave with her." The two sisters said with a feeling of jealousy: "This is what happens to those in the family where the son of a slave exercises control as he pleases."

Meanwhile, when a certain time had passed, Bhavila, Bhavatrāta, and Bhavanandin, still united and being on perfect terms with one another, returned from the great ocean, bringing their ship back safe and sound. Bhavila asked his wife: "Have you been treated honorably by Pūrṇa?" She responded: "As by a brother or by a son." The other women, questioned by their husbands, responded to them: "This is what happens to those in the family where the son of a slave exercises control as he pleases." The two brothers had this reflection: "Women sow division between friends."

After some time, cloth from Benares was displayed in the shop; this cloth had just been put on display when the son of Bhavila came in. Pūrṇa gave this child a couple of pieces of this cloth for him to wrap himself. The other women saw him; they sent their children [to the shop]. Now, cloth from Benares and cloth of coarse material were on display. As luck would have it, when these children arrived, Pūrṇa dressed them in the latter. The two mothers told their husbands: "Look! Cloth from Benares was given to some; that of coarse material was given to the others." The two brothers responded with this observation: "How could this have been done? Cloth from Benares and cloth of coarse material certainly had been displayed in the shop."[11]

Another time, sugar was displayed in the shop. The son of Bhavila came in and took a bowl full of it. The two other mothers, having seen him, sent their children there. As luck would have it, they came at a time when molasses was on display in the shop; so, they took molasses. Their mothers noticed it, and they pestered their husbands so much that they began to think about dividing up the establishment. The two brothers had discussions on the subject between themselves: "One does harm to us in every way," they said to themselves. "We have to divide everything." One of them said: "Let us warn our elder brother"; the other responded: "Still, let us examine how we will divide [everything]." So they divided the establishment at their pleasure; to one what the house holds and what the lands produce; to the other what the shop contains and the goods located abroad; to the third Pūrṇa. "If our elder brother takes the house and the lands, we will be able to subsist with the shop and the goods located abroad. If on the contrary he takes the shop and the goods located abroad, we still will be able to subsist with the house and the lands, and keep Pūrṇa [to make him work]."[12]

11. The Tibetan version adds: "It cannot be an oversight."

12. I tentatively translate in this way the sentence of the text that appears obscure to me: *pūrṇakasya ca maryādābandhanaṃ kartum*, "et Pūrṇam intra limites cohibere." The Tibetan translates: "and to make Pūrṇa suffer."

After having engaged in such discussions, they went to Bhavila. "Brother," they said to him, "one does harm to us; let us carry out the division of the house." Bhavila told them: "We have to act only after having given it much thought; women create divisions in families." The two brothers responded: "We have thought about it enough; let us make the division." Bhavila replied: "If it is so, let us call the people from our caste [as arbiters]."[13] "We have already made the division ourselves," his two brothers said to him; "we have assigned to one what the house holds and what the lands produce; to the other the shop and the goods located abroad; to the third Pūrṇa." "You do not make a share for Pūrṇa?" said Bhavila. "He is the son of a slave," replied the two brothers; "who could give him a share? Quite to the contrary, we have made him an object to be shared; if this is convenient for you, you can take him." Bhavila then had this reflection: "My father told me: 'Abandon, if you must, all your goods, and take Pūrṇa'"; then, having resolved to keep this latter, he said to his brothers: "Let it be so; I take Pūrṇa for myself." The one who had the house and the lands returned in all haste to the house and said: "Wife of my elder brother, leave here." She left, and the brother added: "You shall come here no more. And why? Because we made the division." The one who had the shop and the goods located abroad went in all haste to the shop and said: "Pūrṇa, get down." Pūrṇa got down, and the brother added: "You shall come up here no more. Why? Because we made the division of our goods."

Meanwhile, the wife of Bhavila withdrew, as did Pūrṇa, to the house of a relative. Her children, who were hungry, started to cry. Then, the mother said to Pūrṇa: "Give these children their first meal." "Give me one kārṣāpaṇa," replied Pūrṇa. "What?" said the mother, "you who have known how to earn so many laks of suvarṇas, you do not even have a first meal to give to these children!" "Did I know," replied Pūrṇa, "that your house would be divided like this? If I had known it, I would not have failed to take several laks of suvarṇas." It is the custom that the women tie bronze kārṣāpaṇas[14] to the end of their garment. The mother handed Pūrṇa a bronze māṣaka and told him: "Go look for something to make the first meal." Pūrṇa, taking the coin, went to the market. There was a

13. I tentatively translate *āhvayantāṃ kulāni* in this way; the Tibetan uses the expression *gzo ba mi lta*, which may mean "the meeting of the artisans." Here the artisans must be the caste of merchants to which the sons of Bhava belong. The most general sense of *kula* is that of "family, troops"; but this sense can be determined only by context. Thus, in the *Mṛcchakaṭī*, one sees a Buddhist monk promoted to the rank of chief of the monasteries of Ujjain; and this rank is called that of the *kulapati*, that is to say, "chief of the troop of monks" (*Mṛcchakaṭī*, p. 342, Calcutta ed., Wilson, *Hindu Theatre*, 1:179, note ‡).

14. There is a divergence here between the Sanskrit text and the Tibetan version that must be noted; instead of "bronze kārṣāpaṇas," the Tibetan says: "fake māṣakas." This version has the advantage of being more logical; for if it is māṣakas that the women tie to the end of their garment, it is natural that the mother hands one of these coins to Pūrṇa; nevertheless, I would not change anything in the wording of the Sanskrit text, because it indicates the coarse metal the coin was made of.

man there who, carrying a load of wood that had been washed up by the sea at the edge of the shore, had been seized by the cold and was going away, shivering badly. Pūrṇa saw him and asked: "Hey! Friend, why do you shiver?" The man replied: "I do not know; hardly had I loaded this burden on my shoulders, than I felt myself in this state." Pūrṇa, who was expert in recognizing wood, began to examine what the man carried, and recognized that it was sandalwood of the kind called *gośīrṣa.*[15] So he said to the porter: "Friend, for what price would you give me this piece of wood?" "For five hundred kārṣāpaṇas," he replied.[16] Pūrṇa took his load for this price; and having carried it away, he went to the market and cut it into four pieces with a saw. Then, he sold them for one thousand kārṣāpaṇas[17] to a buyer who wanted to make fragant powder from them. Of these thousand kārṣāpaṇas, he gave five hundred of them to the porter and told him: "The wife of Bhavila resides in such a house; go and bring her this piece of wood and tell her: 'This is what Pūrṇa sends you.'" The man went to the wife of Bhavila, and told her what had happened. Then, beating her breast, she exclaimed: "After having lost his fortune, did he lose his mind? I told him to bring something cooked and he sends me something to make a fire; but what he does not provide is something to cook." Meanwhile, with what remained of the kārṣāpaṇas, Pūrṇa acquired two slaves of each sex, a bull and a cow, clothing, and other means of subsistence; then taking cooked rice, he went to the house, and served it to his brother and his wife. The family was overwhelmed with joy.

Some time after that, the king of Sūrpāraka felt ill with a high fever. The doctors prescribed to him sandalwood of the species called *gośīrṣa* as medicine. The ministers of the king thus undertook to collect sandalwood of this species. They gradually learned what had happened in the market. Having gone to Pūrṇa's home, they said to him: "You have sandalwood of the species called *gośīrṣa.*" "Yes," he responded. "At what price would you give it?" "For one thousand kārṣāpaṇas." The ministers took it for this amount. It was given to the king in form of an ointment and he regained his health.[18] The king then had this re-

15. Literally "cow's head." On this denomination, see a note at the end of this volume. Appendix no. 5.

16. That is to say, for about 28 francs 45 centimes.

17. About 56 francs 90 centimes.

18. The opinion expressed here touching on the refrigerant properties of sandalwood was very widespread in the early times of Buddhism, and legends offer frequent testimony to it. When king Ajātaśatru fainted at the news of the death of Śākyamuni, he was brought back to consciousness with sandalwood (Csoma, *Asiatic Researches*, vol. 20, p. 310). A Tibetan legend translated from the Mongol by Mr. Schmidt, and related to the discovery of a statue of Avalokiteśvara, expresses the same belief in this way: "The places where there are sandalwood trees are marked by their coolness; elephants look for them and come there to take refuge from the burning heat of the sun" (Schmidt, *Geschichte der Ost-Mongolen*, p. 332). Ancient authors who have dealt with Indian botany also mention this belief, which survives to the present day (Rumphius, *Herbarium Amboinense*, 2:45, Burmese ed. Garcias ab Horto, *Aromatum*, vol. 1, bk. 1, chap. 17). Lastly, one knows that the refreshing quality of sandalwood is a subject of comparison frequently employed by Brahmanical poets; it suffices for me to recall here some well-known verses of the *Gītagovinda*.

flection: "What kind of king has no sandalwood of the species gośīrṣa in his house?" Then, he asked: "Where does this come from?" "From Pūrṇa's house." "Summon this Pūrṇa." A messenger was dispatched to the merchant and told him: "Pūrṇa, the king is asking for you." Pūrṇa then started to reflect: "Why," he said to himself, "does the king summon me? It is probably because he owes his recovery to the gośīrṣa sandalwood that he has summoned me; I must go to see him, carrying all my sandalwood with me." Thus, wrapping three pieces of sandalwood in his clothes, and holding one in his hand, he went into the presence of the king. He asked him: "Pūrṇa, do you still have sandalwood?" "Yes, Lord, here you are." What price do you want for it?" "One lak of suvarṇas." "Do you still have another?" "Yes, Lord," replied Pūrṇa, and he showed him the three other pieces. The king ordered his ministers to count out four laks of suvarṇas to Pūrṇa. Pūrṇa replied: "Have them give me only three, Lord; one of these four pieces is offered as a present to the king." Only three laks were thus given to him; but the king said to him: "Pūrṇa, I am pleased; tell me, which favor can I bestow on you?" "If the king is pleased with me," replied Pūrṇa, "may he promise me that I will live in his domain shielded from all insult." The king immediately charged his ministers as follows: "From this day on, you will give your orders to all young men, except Pūrṇa."

Meanwhile, five hundred merchants arrived in Sūrpāraka, returning from a voyage on the great ocean and bringing their ship back safe and sound. The body of traders [of the city] agreed on this regulation: it is necessary to remain always united, and none of us may separate from the others to go alone to find the [newly arrived] merchants. If someone goes there, he will pay [as a fine] sixty kārṣāpaṇas and the united body of traders will seize the merchandise. Some said: "Let us inform Pūrṇa [about this arrangement]." Others said: "What is the use of informing that wretch?"

At that time, Pūrṇa was away from his house. He learned that five hundred merchants had arrived at Sūrpāraka, returned from a voyage on the great ocean, bringing their ship back safe and sound. Without returning to the city, he went to them and said: "Lords, what is this object?" The merchants responded to him: "This is such-and-such a thing." "What is its price?" The merchants responded to him: "Chief of merchants, it is to you, who has been far away and in foreign countries, that one must ask the price." "This may be; however, state your price." The merchants set the price at eighteen laks of suvarṇas. Pūrṇa replied: "Lords, take these three laks as a deposit and give me this merchandise. I will pay you the rest [when I am back in the city]." "It is so agreed," said the foreigners. He thus gave the three laks that he had brought; and after having left the imprint of his seal [on the merchandise], he went away.

The body of traders of the city then sent servants, charged with identifying the merchandise [of the foreigners]. These men, having gone to them, said to them:

"What is this object?" "It is such-and-such a thing." "We also have granaries and warehouses full [of merchandise]." "Whether they are full or empty, this is sold." "To whom?" "To Pūrṇa." "You will lose a great deal with Pūrṇa; we bid higher than he." The merchants replied: "You would not even give as the full price what he has given as a deposit." "What then did he give?" "Three laks of suvarṇas." The two brothers [hearing these words] were filled with envy. They went to the body of traders and apprised them of what had happened. "The merchandise is sold." "To whom?" "To Pūrṇa." "They will lose a great deal with Pūrṇa; we bid higher than he." "You would not even give as the full price what he has given as the deposit." "What then did he give?" "Three laks of suvarṇas." Upon hearing this account, everyone was filled with envy. They had Pūrṇa summoned and said to him: "The body of traders agreed on this regulation: No one may go alone to buy the merchandise; otherwise, the body of traders will seize the purchased object. Why then have you gone to buy alone?" "Lords," responded Pūrṇa, "when you made this regulation, did you inform me about it, me or my brother? You made this order among yourselves alone, so also observe it alone." But the traders, filled with envy, kept him exposed to the heat of the sun, in order to force him to pay sixty kārṣāpaṇas. The people of the king saw what happened and went to him to repeat it to him. "Have these traders come," said the king. When they had arrived, the king said to them: "For what reason do you keep Pūrṇa exposed to the heat of the sun?" "Lord," they responded, "the body of traders agreed on the following regulation: No one may go alone to buy the merchandise; however, this one has gone alone." Pūrṇa then said: "O king, be so good as to ask them if, when they made this regulation, they informed me or my brother about it." "No, they were not informed," replied the traders. The king then said: "Pūrṇa speaks well." So, the merchants, filled with shame, released him.

Some time after that, it happened that the king had need of a certain object. He summoned the body of traders and said to them: "Merchants, I have need of this object; procure it for me." "It is Pūrṇa who possesses it," said the traders. "I cannot command Pūrṇa," replied the king. "It is you who must buy this object from him, and then furnish it to me." Consequently, they sent a messenger to Pūrṇa to say to him: "Pūrṇa, the body of traders wishes to speak to you." Pūrṇa responded: "I will not go." The traders, having all gathered together as a group, went to the house of Pūrṇa, and standing at his door, they sent a messenger to say to him: "Come out, Pūrṇa, the body of traders is at your door." So Pūrṇa, who felt arrogant, went out, haughty to do only what he wanted. The body of traders then said to him: "Chief of merchants, give us your merchandise at the price you have paid for it." "I would be a skilled merchant," replied Pūrṇa, "if I gave my merchandise for the price it cost me!" "Give it to us for double," said the merchants. "The body of traders is respected." Pūrṇa reflected: "The body of traders is honorable; I will give it to them for this price." Pūrṇa thus turned over his merchandise to them for double what he had bought it for. Then, bringing fifteen laks to the foreigners, he put away the rest in his house. He then had this reflection: "Is it possible to fill a bowl with a dewdrop? I must embark on the great ocean." At the sound of a bell, he thus had the following proclaimed in the city of Sūrpāraka: "Listen, merchants of Sūrpāraka. Pūrṇa, chief of merchants, is going to embark on the great ocean. May he among you who wants to embark with Pūrṇa, under the guarantee of a complete exemption from taxes, the import tax, and the price of passage for his merchandise, prepare what he intends for this travel on the great ocean." At this news, five hundred traders gathered the merchandise they intended for this travel. Then, Pūrṇa, the chief of merchants, after having called on the benedictions and the favors of the heavens for his enterprise, embarked on the great ocean with this retinue of five hundred traders. He then returned, bringing his ship back safe and sound, and started out again on his voyages six times. So this news spread from all sides: "This is Pūrṇa, who has embarked six times on the great ocean, and who each time has brought his ship back safe and sound."

Merchants from Śrāvastī, having assembled a cargo, came one day to Sūrpāraka. When they had rested from the fatigue of the voyage, they went to the place where Pūrṇa, chief of merchants, was, and having arrived there, they said to him: "Chief of merchants, embark with us on the great ocean." Pūrṇa said to them: "Have you ever seen, lords, or have you heard mention of a man who, after returning from the great ocean six times, bringing his ship back safe and sound, embarked a seventh time?" "It is for you, Pūrṇa," they replied, "that we have come from a distant country. If you do not embark, only you are responsible for that."

Pūrṇa then had this reflection: "I have no need for wealth for myself; however, I will embark in the interest of these people." He thus departed with them on the great ocean. These merchants, in the night and at dawn, read hymns with uplifted voices, the prayers that lead to the other shore, the texts that disclose the truth, the stanzas of the sthaviras, those related to the various sciences, those of the recluses, as well as the sūtras containing sections related to temporal interests. Pūrṇa, who heard them, said to them: "Lords, what are these beautiful poems that you sing?" "These are not poems, chief of merchants; these are the very words of the Buddha." Pūrṇa, who had never heard this name Buddha pronounced until then, felt the hairs over his entire body stand on end, and he asked, filled with respect: "Lords, who is he whom you call Buddha?" The merchants responded: "The śramaṇa Gautama, issued from the family of the Śākyas, who after having shaven his hair and beard, after having dressed in robes of yellow color, left his house with a perfect faith in order to enter into the religious life, and who reached the supreme state of a perfectly accomplished buddha; it is he, O chief of merchants, who is the one called the Buddha." "In which place, lords, is he now?" "At Śrāvastī, chief of merchants, in the wood of Jetavana, in the garden of Anāthapiṇḍika."

Pūrṇa, having engraved these words on his heart, navigated on the great ocean with these men of Śrāvastī, and returned, bringing his ship back safe and sound. His brother Bhavila then had this reflection: "Pūrṇa is fatigued from traveling on the great ocean; he must get married." He thus said to him: "Tell me, my brother, from which wealthy man, or from which chief of merchants will I ask the daughter for you?" "I do not desire the pleasures of the senses," replied Pūrṇa; "but if you give me your permission, I will embrace the religious life." "What?" replied Bhavila. "When there was nothing in the house, you never dreamed of embracing the religious life; why would you enter it today [when we are wealthy]?" "That was not suitable for me then," said Pūrṇa. "Now this seems good to me." Bhavila, seeing thereby that his resolution was unshakable, gave him his permission. Pūrṇa then said to him: "My brother, the great ocean has much misery and little sweetness; many embark on it but few return from it; never embark on it, under any pretext; you have great wealth that has been honestly earned; but the fortune of your brothers are goods unjustly acquired. If they ever come to say to you: 'Let us live together,' you must respond: 'No.'"

After having given him these counsels, he took a servant and departed for Śrāvastī. When he had arrived there, he stopped in the garden and sent his messenger to Anāthapiṇḍika the householder. The messenger, having presented himself before the householder, said to him: "Pūrṇa, chief of merchants, is in the garden, desirous of seeing the householder." Anāthapiṇḍika had this reflection: "It is doubtless because he is fatigued from his maritime expeditions that he now travels by land." Then, he asked the messenger: "How considerable is the cargo he has brought?" "It is hardly a question of merchandise! He came alone with me, who is his servant." Anāthapiṇḍika then had this reflection: "It would not be good for me not to receive in my house, with the honors of hospitality, a man of this importance." Pūrṇa was thus introduced with great pomp; he was perfumed, he was given a bath, he was offered a meal. While they were conversing with pleasant words, Anāthapiṇḍika asked the following question to Pūrṇa: "Chief of merchants, what is the purpose of your journey?" "I suddenly desired, O householder, to embrace the religious life under the discipline of the well-renowned law; I desire investiture and the rank of monk." Then, Anāthapiṇḍika the householder, straightening the upper part of his body, extending his right arm, pronounced these words with a tone of joy: "Ah Buddha! Ah the law! Ah the assembly! How your fame is well spread, that today a man of this importance, leaving the large crowd of his friends and his people, as well as his rich warehouses, desires to embrace the religious life under the discipline of the well-renowned law, and asks for the investiture and the rank of monk." Then,

Anāthapiṇḍika the householder, taking Pūrṇa with him, went to the place where the Bhagavat was.

Now, at that time the Bhagavat, seated in the presence of an assembly composed of several hundred monks, taught the law. He saw Anāthapiṇḍika the householder, who came forward with the present [which he intended for him]; and when he had seen him, he spoke again in these words to the monks: "Here, O monks, is Anāthapiṇḍika the householder, who comes forward with a present. For the Tathāgata, there is no present as pleasing as that made by bringing him a man to convert." Then, Anāthapiṇḍika the householder, having saluted the feet of the Bhagavat by touching them with his head, stood on the side with Pūrṇa, chief of merchants; then, from the place where he was, he addressed the Bhagavat in this way: "Here is Pūrṇa, chief of merchants, who desires to embrace the religious life under the discipline of the well-renowned law, and who asks for investiture and the rank of monk. May you, through compassion for him, O Bhagavat, admit and receive him as a monk." The Bhagavat received the words of Anāthapiṇḍika the householder with silence.[19] Then, he addressed Pūrṇa, chief of merchants, in this way: "Approach, O monk, embrace the religious life." No sooner had the Bhagavat pronounced these words than Pūrṇa found himself shaved, dressed in the religious mantle, and provided with the begging bowl and the pitcher that ends in the beak of a bird; having a beard and hair of seven days, he appeared with the decent aspect of a monk who would have received investiture one hundred years ago. "Approach," said the Tathāgata again; and Pūrṇa, shaved, covered with the religious mantle, feeling the truths bringing calm to all his senses, stood, then sat, with the permission of the Buddha.

After some time, the respectable Pūrṇa went to the place where the Bhagavat was; and when he had arrived there, having saluted the feet of the Blessed One by touching them with his head, he stood on the side and addressed him in this way: "May the Bhagavat consent to teach me the law in brief, in order for me to be able, after having heard it from the mouth of the Bhagavat, to live alone, retired to a deserted place, sheltered from all distraction, attentive, assiduous, and with a meditative mind. When I have lived retired in solitude, sheltered from all distraction, attentive, assiduous, and with a meditative mind, enable me, after having recognized it immediately for myself, after having seen face to face this supreme goal of the religious life, for which sons of good family, having shaved

19. The text uses a Buddhist expression here: *adhivāsayati bhagavān anāthapiṇḍadasya gṛhapates tūṣṇībhāvena*, following the Tibetan: "No one word was granted by the Bhagavat to the householder Anāthapiṇḍada." This expression is no less familiar to the Buddhists of the South, who use Pāli (Turnour, *Mahāvanso*, p. 6, line 9 and passim).

their hair and beard and dresssed in yellow-colored robes, leave the house with a perfect faith and embrace the life of mendicants; enable me, I say, after having received investiture, to make others embrace the religious life! Birth is annihilated for me; I have fulfilled the duties of the religious life; I have accomplished what I had to do; I do not know another state than the one in which I find myself."

That being said, the Bhagavat spoke in this way to the respectable Pūrṇa: "Good, good, Pūrṇa; it is good that you have spoken as you just did: 'May the Bhagavat consent to teach me the law in brief [etc., as above, until:] I do not know another state than the one in which I find myself.' Thus listen, O Pūrṇa, and engrave well and completely in your mind what I tell you. There exist, O Pūrṇa, forms made in order to be perceived by sight, forms which are desired, looked for, loved, which are ravishing, which arouse passion, which excite the desires. If a monk, at the sight of these forms, is satisfied by them, if he looks for them, if he feels an inclination for them, if he revels in them, then, the result of these various movements is that he finds pleasure. When pleasure exists, immediately with pleasure satisfaction of the heart appears. When, with pleasure, there exists satisfaction of the heart, passion immediately appears. When, with pleasure, there exists passion, enjoyment immediately appears with them. The monk, O Pūrṇa, who feels pleasure, passion, and enjoyment is said to be very far from nirvāṇa. There exist, O Pūrṇa, sounds made to be perceived by hearing, smells made to be perceived by the sense of smell, flavors made to be perceived by taste, things to touch made to be perceived by the body, laws (or conditions) made to be perceived by the manas (the heart or internal organ), all attributes which are desired, looked for, loved, which are ravishing, which arouse passion, which excite the desires. If a monk, seeing these attributes, is satisfied by them and so on as above, he is very far from nirvāṇa. On the other hand, O Pūrṇa, there exist forms made to be perceived by sight, forms which are desired, looked for, loved, which are ravishing, which arouse passion, which excite the desires. If a monk, at the sight of these forms, is not satisfied by them, if he does not look for them, if he does not feel inclination for them, if he does not revel in them, then, the result is that he has no pleasure. When pleasure does not exist, then neither contentment nor satisfaction of the heart exists. When neither contentment nor satisfaction of the heart exists, passion does not exist. When passion does not exist, enjoyment does not exist. When enjoyment does not exist, the monk, O Pūrṇa, who does not feel pleasure, or passion, or enjoyment, is said to be very close to nirvāṇa. There exist, O Pūrṇa, sounds made to be perceived by hearing, smells made to be perceived by the sense of smell, flavors made to be perceived by taste, things to touch made to be perceived by the body, laws made to be perceived by the manas, all attributes which are desired, looked for, loved, which are ravishing, which arouse passion, which excite the desires. If a monk, seeing these attributes, is not satisfied with them and so on as above, he is said to be very close to nirvāṇa."[20]

"With this exposition, O Pūrṇa, I have just instructed you in a brief way. Where do you want to settle now? Where do you want to establish your abode?" "Lord," responded Pūrṇa, "with this exposition the Bhagavat has just instructed me in a brief way; I want to live, I want to establish my abode in the country of the Śroṇāparāntakas."[21] "They are violent, O Pūrṇa, the men of Śroṇāparānta; they are hot-headed, cruel, choleric, furious, insolent. When the men of Śroṇāparānta, O Pūrṇa, address you to your face with spiteful, rude, and insolent words, when they fly into a rage against you and abuse you, what will you think about that?" "If the men of Śroṇāparānta, O Lord, address me to my face with spiteful, rude, and insolent words, if they fly into a rage against me and abuse me, this is what I will think about that: 'These are certainly good men, the Śroṇāparāntakas, these are gentle men, those who address me to my face with spiteful, rude, and insolent words, those who fly into a rage against me and who abuse me, but who do not strike me with their hand or throw stones at me.'" "They are violent, O Pūrṇa, the men of Śroṇāparānta [etc., as above, until:]; they are insolent. If the men of Śroṇāparānta strike you with their hand or throw stones at you, what will you think about that?" "If the men of Śroṇāparānta, O Lord, strike me with their hand or throw stones at me, this is what I will think about that: 'These are certainly good men, the Śroṇāparāntakas, these are gentle men, those who strike me with their hand or throw stones at me, but who do not strike me with a stick or with a sword.'" "They are violent, O Pūrṇa, the men of Śroṇāparānta [etc., as above, until:]; they are insolent. If the men of Śroṇāparānta strike you with a stick or with a sword, what will you think about that?" "If the men of Śroṇāparānta, O Lord, strike me with a stick or with a sword, this is what I will think about that: 'These are certainly good men, the Śroṇāparāntakas, these are gentle men, those who strike me with a stick or with a sword, but who do not

20. I have completed the translation of this passage following the Tibetan version. The Sanskrit text of the two manuscripts that I have before my eyes just says: *pūrvavat śuklapakṣe*, which means: "as above, on the favorable hypothesis."

21. This name of a people is formed from two words: one is *aparānta*, which means "country located on this side of the border," as opposed to *parānta*, "country located on the other side of the border." This meaning has been perfectly established by Wilson (*Viṣṇu Purāṇa*, p. 189, note 60). Wilford mentions, following the *Varāha Saṃhitā*, Aparāntikas, who are located to the west without a more precise designation (*Asiatic Researches*, vol. 8, p. 339, Calcutta ed.). The other word, forming the ethnic group of our text, is *śroṇa*, which I do not recall having seen mentioned until here as the name of a people. I only find *śroṇī*, given for a river whose course is not indicated (*Viṣṇu Purāṇa*, p. 185, note 80). One finds the term *aparānta* mentioned in the most ancient Buddhist monuments, notably in the inscriptions said to be of Aśoka (*Journal of the Asiatic Society of Bengal*, vol. 7, pp. 247 and 267), and in the *Mahāvaṃsa* (chap. 12, p. 73, ed. in -4°). Mr. Wilson has connected the name *aparānta* with the *Aparitæ* of Herodotus, whose position, moreover, is not quite precisely determined. The term *Sunāparānta* exists in Burmese geography, but it is a name copied from India.

deprive me completely of my life.'" "They are violent, O Pūrṇa, the men of Śroṇāparānta [etc., as above, until:]; they are insolent. If the men of Śroṇāparānta deprive you completely of your life, what will you think about that?" "If the men of Śroṇāparānta, O Lord, deprive me completely of my life, this is what I will think about that: 'There are listeners of the Bhagavat who, because of this body filled with ordure, are tormented, covered with confusion, scorned, struck with swords, who take poison, who die from the punishment of the rope, who are thrown off precipices. These are certainly good men, the Śroṇāparāntakas, these are gentle men, those who deliver me with so little pain from this body filled with ordure.'" "Good, good, Pūrṇa, with the perfection of patience you are endowed with you can, yes, you can live, establish your abode in the country of the Śroṇāparāntakas. Go, Pūrṇa, being delivered, deliver; having arrived at the other shore, let others arrive there; being consoled, console; having reached complete nirvāṇa, let others arrive there."

Then, the respectable Pūrṇa, having received with agreement and pleasure the words of the Bhagavat, saluted his feet by touching them with his head and left the place where he was; then when the night was at its end, Pūrṇa, having dressed at the beginning of the day and having taken his bowl and his mantle, entered Śrāvastī to receive alms. When he had gone through Śrāvastī for this purpose, he took his repast; then afterward he finished eating and receiving alms in his bowl. Having then put in order what he owned, his bed and his seat, and having taken his alms bowl with his robes, he set out toward the country of the Śroṇāparāntakas and in the end arrived there. Having dressed at the beginning of the day and having taken his bowl, he entered Śroṇāparānta to receive alms.

Now a hunter holding his bow in his hand went out at that moment to hunt antelope. He saw Pūrṇa and had this reflection: "It is a bad omen that I just saw this shaved śramaṇa." Then, having reflected in this way, he bent his bow with all his might, and ran to the place where Pūrṇa was. As soon as the respectable Pūrṇa saw him, he threw back his upper robe and said to him: "You whose face shows kindness, I come to accomplish this difficult sacrifice; strike here." And he recited this stanza:

"This end for which birds travel through the air, for which wild animals fall into traps, for which men perish incessantly in combat, struck by the arrow or by the lance, for which unfortunate starving fish devour the iron hook: this end, it is for it that amid this multitude of sins that the belly produces, I have come here from afar."

The hunter, hearing these words, had this reflection: "This is a mendicant endowed with a great perfection of patience; why would I kill him?" This thought inspired feelings of benevolence in him. This is why Pūrṇa taught him the law; he taught him the formulas of refuge and the precepts of teaching. And in addition he trained five hundred novices of each sex; he had five hundred vihāras erected, and placed in them beds, seats, carpets, cushions decorated with figures, and square pedestals. Finally, after three months, the hunter saw the collection that contains the three sciences face to face, and he became an arhat. Then, receiving the name "he who is freed from the passions of the three worlds," he became one of those that the devas, accompanied by Indra and Upendra, respect, honor, and salute.

Meanwhile, little time had passed, and the fortune of the two brothers of Dārukarṇin had diminished, had grown less, had been dissipated. They thus both went to say [to their older brother]: "Now that the one who looks like Kālakarṇin[22] has left our house, come, let us all live together." "Who is this," responded Bhavila, "he who looks like Kālakarṇin?" "It is Pūrṇa," they replied. "It is prosperity itself that has left my house," said Bhavila. "It is not a man who looks like Kālakarṇin." "Whether it is prosperity or Kālakarṇin, it is of little importance; come and let us live together." Bhavila responded: "Your fortune has been unjustly earned; mine has been honestly; no, I will not live with you." "It is this son of a slave," replied the brothers, "who by dint of sailing on the great ocean has earned a fortune that you take pride in enjoying. Where would you have found the courage to embark on the great ocean yourself?"

These words stung the self-respect of Bhavila and inspired this reflection in him: "I shall also embark on the great ocean." Things happened as has been said above until finally he embarked on the great ocean, and his ship was pushed by the wind toward the forest that produces the sandalwood of the kind called gośīrṣa.[23] The pilot then said: "Here, lords, is the place known by the name Forest of Sandalwood, of the kind called gośīrṣa; go there to look for the product one finds there."

Now at that time, the grove of gośīrṣa sandalwood was the possession of Maheśvara the yakṣa.[24] The yakṣas had left it at that time to go to their assem-

22. This name Kālakarṇin is a contemptuous epithet given by the last two sons of Bhava to Pūrṇa, the son of the slave. Since the brothers were named according to their earrings, which were wood, lead, and lacquer, in order to inflict an ominous name on Pūrṇa, they call him "he who has death as an earring." This is why the elder brother, who defends him, responds that, on the contrary, Pūrṇa is prosperity itself.

23. It is possible that this place is the island designated on English maps with the name Sandalwood Island, situated at 10° north latitude and 120° east longitude of Greenwich, or even better, Timor, an island known for the great quantity of sandalwood exported at the present time to Java and to China (Ritter, *Die Erdkunde von Asien*, 5:816). It is, however, important to remark that, since the sandalwood in question here is certainly the best, and that the premier quality of this wood is found only in the mountains of Malaya, as the legends of the North inform us (Schmidt, *Geschichte der Ost-Mongolen*, p. 332) and which on this point the testimonies of the naturalists agree, it would perhaps be necessary not to search so far for the place where our seafarers stop to collect the *gośīrṣacandana*. Who knows whether here it is nothing more than a case of a voyage along the Malabar Coast and of an expedition to the lands of Wyand or Coduga?

24. The yakṣas, under whose protection the legend places the forest of sandalwood, are perhaps the savages inhabiting Sandalwood Island. These islanders have always treated the seafarers whom trade or chance brought to their coasts as enemies, and Walter Hamilton informs us that the Dutch, at about the beginning of our century, lost possession of this island because they chopped down the sandalwood trees. The inhabitants,

bly. This is why the merchants began to cut down the forest with five hundred axes. The yakṣa named Apriya saw these axes cutting down the grove; and having recognized the fact, he went to the place where the yakṣa Maheśvara was; and when he had arrived there, he spoke to him in these terms: "This is what the chief must know. Five hundred axes cut down the forest of gośīrṣa sandalwood; do now what you must do, or what is convenient for you to do." Then, the yakṣa Maheśvara, after having dismissed the assembly, raised a black and terrible hurricane and departed for the place where the forest of sandalwood was. "Listen," exclaimed the pilot, "O you merchants of Jambudvīpa, this is what is called a black and terrible hurricane. What do you say about that?" At these words, the merchants, afraid, terror-stricken, struck by dread, feeling their hairs bristling on their entire body, began to invoke the gods: "O you, Śiva, Varuṇa, Kuvera, Śakra, Brahmā, and you chiefs of the asuras, mahoragas, yakṣas, dānavas, here we have fallen into most terrible danger; Ah! May those who are safe from danger today be our protectors!"

Some invoked the spouse of Śacī, others Brahmā, others Hari and Śaṃkara, throwing themselves on the earth, taking refuge near trees and in the forest; these unfortunate ones, carried away by the wind and by the piśacas, implored the aid [of the gods].

However, Dārukarṇin was motionless with discouragement; the passengers asked him: "Chief of merchants, here we have fallen into terrible danger that is difficult to escape. Why do you remain plunged so in discouragement?" "Lords," he replied, "my brother warned me, saying: 'The great ocean has few enjoyments and many miseries; a good many people, blinded by cupidity, embark on it but few return from it; take care not to embark, under any pretext whatsoever, on the great ocean.' Without taking account of his words, I told myself: 'I must embark,' and indeed I have embarked; thus what can I do now?" "Who is your brother?" said the merchants. "Pūrṇa," replied their chief. "Lords," exclaimed the merchants, "this is this same Pūrṇa, the ārya, the one who possesses greatness and virtue; let us hasten to implore his aid." Immediately, all, in a single voice, made this prayer to be heard at the same time: "Adoration to Pūrṇa the ārya! Adoration, adoration to Pūrṇa the ārya!" Then, the divinities who were favorable to the respectable Pūrṇa went to the place where he was; and when they had arrived there, they addressed him in these terms: "O ārya, your brother has fallen into terrible danger from which it is difficult to escape; think about it." Pūrṇa started to reflect; and he engaged in a meditation such that as soon as his thought was immersed in it, he disappeared from the country of the Śroṇāparāntakas and found

convinced that each of these trees was related to the existence of one of them, rose up against the Dutch traders and drove them from the island (*East Indian Gazetteer*, 2:500).

himself in the middle of the great ocean, seated with crossed legs on the edge of the ship. Immediately the black tempest subsided, as if it had been stopped by Sumeru. Then, Maheśvara the yakṣa started to reflect: "In former times, a ship, whatever it was, that was assailed by a black tempest was flung and destroyed like a cotton wick; but today, what is the cause for which the tempest subsides, as if it was stopped by Sumeru?" He thus began to look here and there until at last he caught sight of the respectable Pūrṇa seated with crossed legs on the edge of the vessel; and when he had seen him, he cried out to him: "Oh! Pūrṇa the ārya, why do you defy me?" "O you who have submitted to the condition of old age," replied Pūrṇa, "is it I who defy you? It is rather you who insults me. If I had not acquired the multitude of qualities that I possess, nothing would remain of my brother, than a hollow name, thanks to you." Maheśvara the yakṣa responded to him: "This forest of gośīrṣa sandalwood, O respectable one, is reserved for a cakravartin king." "Whom do you believe is worth more," replied Pūrṇa, "a cakravartin king or a tathāgata perfectly and completely buddha?" "Would it be, O ārya, that the Bhagavat is born in the world? If it is so, may what was not accomplished, be so!" Then, the merchants recovering the life that was at the point of abandoning them, after having directed their thoughts with faith to the respectable Pūrṇa, filled their vessel with sandalwood of the gośīrṣa kind, and resumed their voyage. They returned finally to the city of Sūrpāraka.

There the respectable Pūrṇa said to his brother: "All of this must be returned to him in whose name your vessel was brought back safe and sound: thus divide these jewels among the merchants; with this sandalwood, I will have a palace built for the use of the Bhagavat, adorned with garlands of sandalwood." The elder brother consequently divided his jewels among the merchants; then the respectable Pūrṇa began to have a vihāra of sandalwood built. Having thus summoned the architects, he said to them: "Which do you prefer, lords, to receive each day: five hundred kārṣāpaṇas or one karṣa of gośīrṣa sandalwood powder?"[25] "We prefer one karṣa of sandalwood powder," replied the architects. The palace adorned with garlands of sandalwood was completed in a very short time. The king then said [to the architects]: "This is a beautiful palace."[26] The building was

25. Instead of one *karṣa*, the Tibetan says *pho sum khang*, "full three *pho*"; but the name of this latter measure is not in Csoma or in Schmidt. Would it be the abbreviation of the word *phon*, "package"? Be this as it may, since a karṣa equals sixteen māṣas, each of which is worth five kṛṣṇalas or 10 15/16 English troy grains, the karṣa represents 175 troy grains, that is to say, 11.375 French grams. One can see thereby what price one attached to the sandalwood, since the architects preferred to receive a little more than eleven grams than a sum that was equivalent to about 28 francs 45 centimes. Assuming the two payments were almost equal, the gram of sandalwood would have cost 2 francs 50 centimes.

26. This sentence is missing in the Tibetan version, and it could be that it is an interpolation owed to the copyist, who would have taken the words *rājā kathayati bhavantaḥ śobhanam* some lines further down. Nevertheless, since this sentence is in my two manuscripts, I do not believe I should omit it.

cleaned in all its parts. The splinters of sandalwood[27] [that were not used] and what was left of the powder [which had been made] was ground up and given to the vihāra, to be used as ointment.

Meanwhile, in the end the three brothers asked forgiveness from one another. [Pūrṇa told them]: "You must have your meal after having invited the Buddha, the assembly of monks, and other persons [worthy of respect]." "Where is the Blessed One, O ārya?" "In Śrāvastī." "How far is Śrāvastī from here?" "A little more than one hundred yojanas." "In that case, let us invite the king." "Yes, do so." The brothers went thus into the presence of the king; and after having bowed their head before him, they spoke to him in these terms: "Lord, we wish to have our meal after having invited the Buddha, the assembly of monks, and other persons [worthy of respect]. May the king deign to honor us with his presence." "It is good," said the king, "let it be so; I will be with you."

Then, the respectable Pūrṇa, having climbed to the top of the building, his face turned toward Jetavana, placed his two knees on the ground; and after having thrown flowers and burned incense, he had his servant hold the golden pitcher that ends in the beak of a bird, and he began to pronounce the following prayer:

"O you, whose conduct is perfectly pure, whose intelligence is also perfectly pure; you who, at the time of taking your meal never has anything other than necessity in sight, casting a glance on these beings deprived of a protector, may you show them your compassion, O excellent being, and come here."

Immediately, thanks to the Buddha's own power and to that of the divinities, these flowers, transforming themselves into a canopy, were carried to Jetavana and took their place in a row; the offered incense appeared there in the form of a great cloud, and the water that escaped from the clouds formed needles of lapis lazuli. The respectable Ānanda, who was skilled in recognizing prodigies, joining his hands in a sign of respect, addressed this question to the Bhagavat: "From which place, O Bhagavat, does this invitation come?" "From the city of Sūrpāraka, O Ānanda." "How far from here, Lord, is the city of Sūrpāraka?" "A little more than one hundred yojanas, O Ānanda." "Let us go," replied the latter. "Thus announce to the monks the following: 'May anyone among you who desires to go tomorrow to the city of Sūrpāraka to have his meal there, take his stick.'"[28] "Yes, Lord," replied Ānanda to express his agreement to the Bhagavat;

27. The text uses a word that I did not see elsewhere, *yat tatra saṃkalikā*. The meaning of this term is expressed in this way in the Tibetan version: *de na zhogs ma*, which perhaps means "the rubbish that was there."

28. The text uses the word *śalākā*, "splinter of thin wood." The Tibetan version translates this word with *tshul cing*, which I do not find in our lexicons but which, by substituting *shing* for *cing*, would mean "the tree of the rule." There is nothing to indicate what we should understand by the stick distributed to the monks here; but a passage that the legend places in the mouth of Śākya shows us that it is also called the *caitya stick*; but in this passage the expression *caityaśalākā* (stick of the monument) perhaps must be translated "stick taken from

and having taken a stick, he stood in front of him. The Bhagavat and the monks who were sthaviras among the sthaviras each took one as well.

At this moment, the respectable Pūrṇa, the sthavira of Kuṇḍopadhāna,[29] who was freed by science, was seated in the assembly. He was ready to take a stick also; but the respectable Ānanda addressed this stanza to him:

"It is not, O respectable one, in the abode of the king Kośala, or in the house of Sujāta, or in the palace of Mṛgāra that we have to take the meal. The city of Sūrpāraka is more than one hundred yojanas away from here; it is by supernatural means that we must go there; thus remain silent, O Pūrṇa."

Pūrṇa, who was freed by science, had not up to then performed any miracle that attested to his supernatural power. So, this reflection came to his mind: "I who have completely rejected, repelled, abandoned, dispelled the entire multitude of corruptions, would I thus be incapable of using a supernatural power common among the tīrthikas?" Developing his energy accordingly and deploying his supernatural power, he extended his arm like the trunk of an elephant to reach the place of the third sthavira [seated in front of him], to whom Ānanda did not give a stick, and he took one himself; then he pronounced this stanza:

"It is not by fame, or by knowledge, or by the qualities of greatness, or by forceful desires that one obtains in this world, O Gautama, possession of the six supernatural knowledges. Beings like me, perfect beings, in whom age has consumed youth, obtain these knowledges by the energies of quietude, morality, wisdom, and by the various energies of contemplation."

Then, the Bhagavat addressed himself to the monks in this way: "He who is chief among my monks is the first to take the caitya[30] stick that belongs to my listeners. This is why, among those who take it, it is the sthavira Pūrṇa of Kuṇḍopadhāna who is the first." Then, the Bhagavat addressed himself to the respectable Ānanda in this way: "Go, Ānanda, and say to the monks: 'Have I not told you, O monks, that you must live hiding your good deeds and showing

a consecrated tree" or even more generally "religious stick." Happily, the Buddhists of the South come to our aid here, and Messrs. Turnour and Clough inform us that something called *śalākā*, or small splinters of bamboo, were serving as tickets for those to whom alms should be distributed. The names of the monks were inscribed on these small sticks, which were then thrown into a bowl and drawn as lots; the one whose stick was the first to come out received the first alms (Turnour, *Mahāvanso*, index, p. 22. Clough, *Sinhalese Dictionary*, 2:719.)

29. I consider the word *kuṇḍopadhānīyaka*, an epithet of this Pūrṇa (who is not the one of the legend), as an ethnic term intended to distinguish him from the other Pūrṇa. I do not know where this so-called place is; the elements of this proper noun are *kuṇḍa* (spring) and *upadhāna* (or *upadhānīya*), which usually means "cushion, pillow," and which, according to the etymology, must express in a very general manner everything that sustains and supports. If, as I believe, *kuṇḍopadhāna* is the name of a place, it must mean "the country that contains springs." The Tibetan version favors this interpretation, since it translates the epithet *kuṇḍopadhānīyaka* with *yul chu mig can na gnas pa*; which means, if I am not mistaken, "residing in the country that contains springs." In the Tibetan version of the story of Sumāgadhā, this word is simply transcribed in this manner: *kun da ud pa da na*.

30. See above, p. 266, note 28.

your sins? As for you, O tīrthikas, dwell in this city; but let each of you, O monks, using the kind of supernatural means you possess, transport yourselves to the city of Sūrpāraka in order to take your meal there.'" "Yes, Lord," responded the respectable Ānanda to express his agreement with the Bhagavat. Then, he said to the monks: "Here, O respectable ones, is what the Bhagavat has said: 'Have I not told you, O monks, that you must live hiding your good deeds [etc., as above, until:] let each of you transport yourselves to the city of Sūrpāraka in order to take your meal there.'"

Meanwhile, the king of Sūrpāraka had the stones, gravel, and rubbish carried away from the city; he had sandalwood water spread there, placed various kinds of bowls in which exquisite perfumes burned, arranged rows of garlands made from silk cloth, planted various flowers; in the end, he made it into a charming city. Sūrpāraka had eighteen gates and the king had seventeen sons. He placed one of his sons with a magnificient train at each of these gates. At the main gate was the king of Sūrpāraka, amid the trappings of royal power, accompanied by the respectable Pūrṇa, by Dārukarṇin, and his two other brothers.

Meanwhile, one saw monks approaching with the aid of supernatural means: some used wings, others were carried by lions, and others in bowls.[31] Catching sight of them, the king said: "Respectable Pūrṇa, is it the Bhagavat who approaches?" "Great king," responded Pūrṇa, "these are monks, some of whom use wings, others are carried by lions, and others in bowls; it is still not the Bhagavat." Then, there was seen approaching, with the aid of the numerous and various perfections of the contemplation with which they were endowed, the monks who were sthaviras among the sthaviras. The king again repeated his question: "Respectable Pūrṇa, is it the Bhagavat who approaches?" "Great king," answered Pūrṇa, "it is not the Bhagavat, but these are the monks who are sthaviras among the sthaviras." Then, a certain devotee [to the Buddha] pronounced the following stanzas at that time:

"Some approach, riding on the beautiful forms of lions, tigers, elephants, horses, snakes, buffaloes; others carried on divine palaces of gems, on mountains, on trees, on chariots painted with various colors and resplendent. Some approach through the atmosphere like clouds ornamented with a trail of lightning. They are eager to arrive, with the aid of their supernatural power, filled with joy, as if they were going to the city of the devas.

"Some surge up from the bowels of the open earth; others descend from the

31. I translate these obscure terms of the text solely based on the etymology: *patratcārika*, *haritacārika*, and *bhājanacārika*. The Tibetan replaces them in this way: *lo ma 'dri ma, shing tshe 'dri ma, snang spyad 'dri ma*, "who questions the leaves, the *tshe* tree, the lamps?" It is possible that the monosyllable *ma* that ends each of these expressions is intended to designate nuns; that, however, is not credible according to the text as a whole.

atmosphere on high; others finally are departing miraculously from their seat; behold the energy of beings endowed with a supernatural power."

Meanwhile, the Bhagavat, having washed his feet outside the monastery, entered the vihāra; then, having sat on the seat intended for him, he held his body perfectly upright and brought his memory before his mind. Then, the Bhagavat placed his foot in the hall of perfumes[32] with intention, and immediately the earth trembled in six different ways. The great earth moved and trembled, it was agitated and tossed, it bounced and jumped. The east rose; the west sank; the west rose, the east sank; the south rose, the north sank; the north rose, the south sank; the ends rose, the center sank; the center rose, the ends sank.

The king consequently asked the respectable Pūrṇa: "O Pūrṇa the ārya, what is this?" "Great king," replied Pūrṇa, "the Bhagavat just intentionally placed his foot in the hall of perfumes; this is why the earth trembled in six different ways." Then, the Bhagavat produced a splendor that had the color of a golden light, and the effect of which was to give Jambudvīpa the radiance of melted gold. Opening his eyes in surprise, the king again asked Pūrṇa: "What is this, O Pūrṇa the ārya?" "Great king," replied Pūrṇa, "it is the Bhagavat who produces a splendor that has the color of a golden mirage."

Then, the Bhagavat, disciplined, with a retinue of personages as disciplined as he; calm, with a retinue of personages as calm as he, accompanied by a group of five hundred arhats, departed with his face turned toward Sūrpāraka. Then, the divinity who lived in the wood of Jetavana, taking a bough of vakula,[33] began walking behind him in order to shelter him with it. The Bhagavat, knowing the mind, the dispositions, the character, and the nature of this divinity, set forth the teaching of the law made to bestow the intelligence of the four sublime truths, such that this divinity, as soon as she had heard him, splitting with the thunderbolt of science the mountain from which one believes in the view that the body exists, a mountain that rises with twenty peaks,[34] saw the reward of the state of *śrotāpatti* face to face.

32. I translate the compound *gandhakūṭī* literally; the Tibetan version replaces this word by *dri gtsang khang*, an expression that, according to Csoma, means "a holy place, a chapel" and which is translated literally as "the pure house of odors." It is probable that it is the chapel where perfumes are burned in honor of the Buddha, as has happened since long ago in China (A. Rémusat, *Foe koue ki*, p. 41). But what is true of the times posterior to the establishment of the cult of Śākyamuni Buddha is perhaps less accurate for the epoch in which he lived. I thus presume that the hall called *gandhakūṭī* in the vihāras was, when Śākya was living, the one in which he took his lodging; and I am confirmed in this opinion by the translation given by Clough of this term: "the residence of the Buddha" (*Sinhalese Dictionary*, 2:165, col. 2). After the death of Śākya, in the room where he usually stayed, there had to be placed a statue representing him and before which perfumes were burned. It is this hall that is the topic here.

33. *Mimusops elenghi*.

34. I have translated as literally, and I should say as vaguely, as has been possible for me this obscure expression in the text, which I have ruminated on in many senses before discovering the little light that I perceive

There dwelled in a certain place five hundred widows; they saw the blessed Buddha adorned with the thirty-two signs that characterize a great man and whose limbs were embellished with the eighty secondary marks, surrounded by a splendor that extended to a distance of a fathom, spreading a radiance that surpassed that of one thousand suns, like a mountain of jewels which would be in motion, and having a perfectly beautiful aspect. Hardly had they seen him than they felt in themselves a great benevolence born for the Bhagavat. Indeed, and it is a known rule, the possession of quietude does not cause so perfect a happiness for the man who practices yoga for twelve years, the possession of a child does not give as much to one who has no son, the sight of treasure does not provide as much to a poor person, royal anointing does not give as much to one who desires the throne, as the first sight of a buddha assures to the being in whom exists the cause of the accumulation of the roots of virtue. This is why the Bhagavat, recognizing that the time of their conversion had come, sat on the seat intended for him, in the presence of the assembly of monks. The widows, after having adored the feet of the Bhagavat by touching them with their heads, sat on the side. The Bhagavat, knowing the mind, the dispositions, the character, and the nature of these women, set forth the teaching of the law to them as it has been said above, in such a manner that they saw the reward of the state of śrotāpatti face to face. As soon as they had seen the truth, they sang three times these thanksgivings.

"No, Lord, neither from our mother, nor father, nor king, nor from the multitude of our relatives or from those beloved to us, nor from divinities, nor from those who have been dead for a long time, nor from śramaṇas, nor from brahmans, from none of those, we say, have we received anything to equal what the Bhagavat has done for us.

"The oceans of blood and of tears are dried up; the mountains of bones are overcome; the gates of the bad paths are shut;[35] we are established among devas and humans; we have reached eminence, superiority.

---

there. This is the original, which I give to readers who will want or will be able to find something better: *viṃśatiśikharasamudgataṃ satkāyadṛṣṭiśailaṃ jñānavajreṇa bhittvā*. The truly difficult term is *satkāyadṛṣṭi*; by the word *dṛṣṭi* (view), one generally understands, in the Buddhist style, an erroneous opinion: this must be the proper meaning here, since it is a case of an opinion that the divinity, instructed by Śākya, splits with the thunderbolt of science. This opinion is that of the *satkāya*, a term that must have the meaning of "existing body," or "the union of what exists." A passage in the *Abhidharmakośavyākhyā* (fol. 474b of my manuscript) related to the I, which the Buddhists call *pudgala,* or the person who transmigrates, and whom they distinguish from the five immaterial attributes of existence (*skandha*), leads me to believe that *satkāya* means "existing body," and that the compound *satkāyadṛṣṭi* comes to this: "the opinion that the body is what exists," that is to say, that it is the I alone which exists, since it transmigrates in bodies that successively perish. According to this passage, there are four ways in which to envisage the I, by identifying it more or less completely with one of the five attributes of existence. Thus, one says: "Form is the I or the I has a form or form is the essence of the I or the essence of the I is in form." What one says about form can be repeated for the four other attributes of existence, which will be a topic below, in such a way that these four points of view attributed to the five attributes of existence form twenty erroneous opinions, the sum of which is compared to a mountain that rises with twenty peaks.

35. The Tibetan version adds: "the gates of freedom and of heaven are opened."

"We seek an asylum in the Bhagavat, in the law, in the assembly of monks, in the faithful; may the Bhagavat receive us as disciples."

Then, having risen from their seat and pointing their hands joined as a sign of respect toward the Bhagavat, they spoke to him in this way: "Ah! May the Bhagavat deign to give us something, whatever it is, in order to render to his gift the homage due to it!" Then, the Bhagavat through his supernatural power cut his hair and his nails and gave them to them. And immediately the widows erected a stūpa for the hair and the nails of the Bhagavat. Then, the divinity who lived in the wood of Jetavana planted in the manner of a post, near this stūpa,[36] the branch of vakula that she held in her hand and said to the Bhagavat: "And I, Bhagavat, I will render to this stūpa the homage due to it"; so she stopped in this place. Hence, the names "the stūpa of the widows" and "the stūpa of the post of vakula" were given to this monument that monks who honor edifices erected to the Bhagavat still venerate today.

The Bhagavat then left this place. He soon encountered another hermitage in which five hundred ṛṣis lived. This hermitage was abundant with flowers, with fruits, and with water. Intoxicated by the well-being they enjoyed there, these ṛṣis did not think about anything. So the Bhagavat, recognizing that the time to convert them had come, went toward the hermitage; and when he was nearby, with his supernatural power he destroyed the flowers and fruits there; he dried up the water; he made the green and fresh lawn black and overturned the seats there. So, the ṛṣis, holding their heads in their hands, remained absorbed in their reflections. But the Bhagavat said to them: "Why, O great ṛṣis, do you remain so, absorbed in your thoughts?" "O Bhagavat, you had no sooner set foot here, on this earth of purity, than we have fallen into the state in which you see us." "Why?" said the Bhagavat. "This hermitage," they responded, "which abounded in flowers, fruits, and in water, is destroyed; may it become again as it was formerly!" "May it be as it was before," said the Bhagavat; and after he had deployed his supernatural powers, the hermitage returned to what it had been formerly. So, the ṛṣis were struck by an extreme astonishment, and they experienced feelings of benevolence for the Bhagavat. The Bhagavat, knowing the mind, the dispositions, the character, and the nature of these five hundred ṛṣis, set forth the teaching of the law made to bestow the intelligence of the four sublime truths, in such a way that as soon as they had heard it, they saw the reward of the state of anāgāmin face to face, and acquired a supernatural power. Then, pointing their hands joined as a sign of respect toward the Bhagavat, they spoke to him in these

36. I translate *yaṣṭyām* literally; but the Tibetan replaces it with two words: *'khor sa*, to which Schröter gives the meaning of "courtyard" and which literally mean "the surrounding earth." According to this interpretation, it would be necessary to translate: "planted in the enclosure that surrounded the stūpa." One still finds traces of enclosures near some stūpas.

terms: "Enable us, Lord, to gain entry into the religious life, under the discipline of the law that is well-renowned, and to become monks! Enable us to accomplish, in the presence of the Bhagavat, the duties of the religious life!" Then, the Bhagavat said to them: "Approach, monks, embrace the religious life." No sooner had the Bhagavat pronounced these words than they found themselves shaved, covered in the religious mantle, and provided with the bowl of alms and the pitcher that ends in the beak of a bird; having beard and hair of seven days, they appeared with the decent aspect of monks who would have received investiture a hundred years ago. "Approach," the Tathāgata said again to them; and shaved, covered with the religious mantle, feeling calm immediately descending in all their senses, they stood, then sat with the permission of the Buddha. After prolonged efforts, after deep studies and application, these ṛṣis [having recognized what the wheel of transmigration is], which bears five marks [which is at once mobile and immobile; having triumphed over all the paths of existence by smashing them, by overturning them, by dissipating them, by destroying them], became those who are worthy of respect.[37] The ṛṣi who had been their master then said: "In this costume, O Bhagavat, I have led a great many people astray; I will begin by making them conceive benevolence for you, then I will enter into the religious life."

Then, the Bhagavat, surrounded by his five hundred ṛṣis and by the first five hundred monks [who deployed themselves around him] like the two points of a crescent moon, set out through the path of the atmosphere, by virtue of his supernatural power, and soon reached the mountain of Musalaka. Now at that time there resided on this mountain a ṛṣi named Vakkalin.[38] This ṛṣi saw the Bhagavat from afar, adorned with the thirty-two marks that characterize a great man, [etc., as above, until:] having a perfectly beautiful aspect. Hardly had he perceived him than he felt feelings of benevolence for the Bhagavat born in his heart. Under the influence of this benevolence, he had the following reflection: "What if I descend from the heights of this mountain and what if I go to the Bhagavat to see him? The Bhagavat, doubtless, will have come here for the purpose of converting me.

37. This passage is expressed only briefly in our two manuscripts of the *Divyāvadāna* in this manner: *idam eva pañcagaṇḍakam pūrvacad yāvad abhivādyāśca saṃvṛttāḥ*. It is clear that the words "as above, until" announce an elision. I have filled the gap, at least for the most part, with the aid of the *Avadānaśataka* (fol. 21b). I say for the most part, because the principal proposition that ends this phrase, "they became those, etc." is more developed elsewhere, notably in a passage of the same anthology that I have quoted previously, section 2, p. 163. I am not very sure about what one is to understand by the expression "who bears five marks," for in Buddhism there are many categories designated by the number five. It is a matter here of either the five corruptions of evil, *pañcakleśa*, which are the lot of all men entering the circle of transmigration; or the five senses with whose aid man perceives sensations and performs actions that condemn him to rebirth; or perhaps the five objects of the senses or the five sensations that man reaps during his travels in the world.

38. This name means: "one who wears cloth made of bark." It is the well-known Sanskrit term *valkalin*, modified by the popular influence of Pāli.

And why would I not rush from the heights of this mountain? Nothing escapes the knowledge of the blessed buddhas." The Bhagavat received the ṛṣi with the aid of his supernatural power; then, knowing the mind, the dispositions, the character, and the nature of this ṛṣi, he set forth the teaching of the law to him, in such a way that after having heard it, Vakkalin saw the reward of the state of anāgāmin face to face and acquired a supernatural power. Then, the ṛṣi said to the Blessed One: "Enable me, O Bhagavat, to enter into the religious life, under the discipline of the well-renowned Law! Enable me to become a monk!" [etc., as above, until:] The Bhagavat told him: "Approach, monk," and he entered into the religious life, as it has been said above; and he sat with the permission of the Bhagavat. Then, the Bhagavat addressed the monks in these terms: "The foremost of my monks who have faith and confidence in me[39] is the monk Vakkalin."

Then, the Bhagavat, surrounded by his thousand monks, reached the city of Sūrpāraka, making prodigies of various kinds. This reflection then came to his mind: "If I enter through a door, the others will feel differently [from the one whose door I chose]; why would I not enter in a miraculous manner?" Immediately rising up into the air by means of his supernatural power, he descended from the sky in the middle of the city of Sūrpāraka. Then, the king, chief of the city, the respectable Pūrṇa, Dārukarṇin, his two brothers, and the seventeen sons of the king, each with his retinue, went to the place where the Bhagavat was, as did several hundreds of thousands of creatures. Then, the Bhagavat, escorted by numerous hundreds of thousands of living beings, went toward the place where the palace adorned with garlands of sandalwood had been erected; and when he had arrived there, he sat before the assembly of monks, on the seat intended for him; but the immense multitude of people who could not see the Bhagavat tried to knock down the palace adorned with sandalwood. The Bhagavat then had this reflection: "If the palace is destroyed, those who have provided it will see their good deed perish; why would I not transform it into a palace of rock crystal?" The Bhagavat consequently made it into a palace of crystal.[40] Then, knowing the mind, the dispositions, the character, and the nature of this assembly, the Bhagavat set forth the teaching of the law, such that after having heard it, several hundreds of thousands of living beings understood the great distinction; there were among them some who produced roots of virtue, which will become, among some, degrees of freedom, among others degrees of the science that distinguishes clearly. These saw the rewards of the state of śrotāpatti, or sakṛdāgāmin, or anāgāmin face to face; those reached the state of arhat through the

39. The Tibetan version translates: "who are completely freed by faith," *śraddhāvimukta*; but our two manuscripts read *śraddhādhimukta*: but *adhimukti* is ordinarily translated in Tibetan as "inclination, confidence."

40. The Tibetan version adds: "in order that the multitude of people could clearly see the body of the Buddha."

annihilation of all corruptions of evil. There were some who understood that which is the intelligence of the śrāvakas, or that of the pratyekabuddhas, or that of a perfectly accomplished buddha. In the end, this entire gathering of men was absorbed in the Buddha, plunged in the law, transported into the assembly.

Then, Dārukarṇin and his two brothers, having prepared pleasing foods and dishes in a pure manner, and having arranged seats,[41] announced by a message to the Bhagavat the time [of the repast]. "It is the time [of noon], O Bhagavat; the repast is prepared; may the Bhagavat deign to consider that the appropriate moment has come."

At that time, Kṛṣṇa and Gautamaka, kings of the nāgas, resided in the great ocean. Both had the following reflection: "The Bhagavat teaches the law in the city of Sūrpāraka; let us go listen to it. Immediately, accompanied by five hundred nāgas, they gave birth to five hundred rivers and went toward the city of Sūrpāraka. Nothing escapes the knowledge of the blessed buddhas; so the Bhagavat had the following reflection: "If these two kings of the nāgas, Kṛṣṇa and Gautamaka, enter the city, they will destroy it from top to bottom." He thus addressed the respectable Mahāmaudgalyāyana in these terms: "Receive for the Tathāgata the quickly collected alms.[42] Why is that? It is, O Mahāmaudgalyāyana, that there are five quickly collected alms. And what are they? These are the alms of one who arrives unexpectedly, the alms of the traveler, the alms of the sick, the alms of one who cures the sick, the alms of the keeper [of the vihāra]."[43] Now, in this circumstance, the Bhagavat was thinking of the keeper of the vihāra. Then, accompanied by Mahāmaudgalyāyana, he went to the place where the two kings of the nāgas were; and when he had arrived there, he spoke to them in this way: "Take care, O kings of the nāgas, that the city of Sūrpāraka not be knocked down from top to bottom." "We have come, Lord, with such dispositions of benevolence," responded the nāgas, "that it is impossible for us to commit evil to any living being, even to an insect or an ant, all the more reason to the multitude of people who live in the city of Sūrpāraka." Then, the Bhagavat set forth to the two kings of the nāgas, Kṛṣṇa and Gautamaka, the teaching of the law, in such a way that after having heard it, taking refuge in the Buddha, in the law, and in the assembly, they grasped the precepts of the teaching.

Then, the Bhagavat started to take his repast. Each of the nāgas had this reflection: "Ah! if the Bhagavat drank my water!" The Bhagavat then said to himself: "If I drink the water of one of them, the others will feel differently [from the one I chose]. It is necessary that I resort to some other means." Then, the Bhagavat ad-

41. The Tibetan version adds: "having placed a pitcher made from one precious stone."

42. The expression of the text is *atyayika piṇḍapāta*, which is translated in the Tibetan version in this way: *rings pa'i bsod snyoms*, "quick alms." (See the additions at the end of the volume.)

43. The word used in the original is *upayi-cārika*; according to the Tibetan, "verger, keeper of the vihāra."

dressed the respectable Mahāmaudgalyāyana in this way: "Go, Maudgalyāyana, to the place where the five hundred rivers gather, and bring back from there my pitcher filled with water." "Yes," responded the respectable Mahāmaudgalyāyana to show his assent to the Bhagavat; then, having gone to the place where the five hundred rivers gather, he drew water from there into the pitcher; returning then to the place where the Bhagavat was, he presented the pitcher filled with water to him. The Bhagavat took it and drank it.

The respectable Mahāmaudgalyāyana then had this reflection: "The Blessed One previously said: 'They do, O monks, something rather difficult for their child, the father and the mother who feed him, who raise him, who make him grow, who give him their milk to drink, who make him see the various spectacles of Jambudvīpa. Let us suppose, on one side, a son who spends a full hundred years carrying his mother on his shoulders, or who provides her with the pleasures that power and domination procure by giving her all kinds of goods, for example, everything that the great earth contains of jewels, pearls, lapis lazuli, conches, crystal, coral, silver, gold, emeralds, diamonds, rubies, stones collected in the Dakṣiṇāvarta;[44] this son will thus have done nothing, will have given back nothing to his father and mother. But on the other side, suppose that a son, initiated, disciplined, introduces, establishes his father and his mother who have no faith in the perfection of faith; that he gives the perfection of morality to parents who have bad morals, that of generosity to greedy parents, that of science to ignorant parents; this son will have thus done good to his father and his mother; he will have given back to them what he owed them.' This is what the Bhagavat has said. And I, I have not rendered any service to my mother; I must reflect in order to discover the place where she has taken a new existence."

Consequently, he then engaged in this search, and he saw that she was reborn in the Marīcika universe. He then had this reflection: "By whom must she be converted?" He recognized that it was through the Bhagavat, and this idea came to his mind: "Here, we are quite far from this universe. Why would I not make this matter known to the Bhagavat?" Consequently, he spoke to him in these terms: "The Bhagavat has said in the past: 'They do something rather difficult, the father and mother who feed their child.' Now my mother has taken a new existence in the Marīcika universe, and it is through the Bhagavat that she must be converted. May the Blessed One, out of compassion for her, thus consent to convert her." The Bhagavat responded to him: "Through whose power will we go [to this universe], O Maudgalyāyana?" "Through mine," responded the latter. Then, the Bhagavat and the respectable Mahāmaudgalyāyana, placing their foot on the

44. This is an obvious allusion to the mines of gems and precious metals that made the province of Golkonda celebrated for centuries, which has always been included in the vast country called Deccan, that is to say, "the country of the South."

summit of Sumeru, set out; after the seventh day, they reached the Marīcika universe. Bhadrakanyā[45] saw the respectable Mahāmaudgalyāyana; and seeing him from afar, she ran eagerly to meet him and exclaimed: "Ah! Here is my son who comes from quite far away." But the multitude of beings [forming this universe] said to themselves: "This mendicant is old and this woman is young; how can she be his mother?" The respectable Mahāmaudgalyāyana then said to them: "The elements that compose my body were produced by this woman; this is why she is my mother." Then the Bhagavat, knowing the mind, the dispositions, the character, and the nature of Bhadrakanyā, set forth the teaching of the law made to give the intelligence of the four sublime truths such that as soon as Bhadrakanyā had heard it, splitting with the thunderbolt of science the mountain from which one believes in the view that the body exists, a mountain that rises with twenty peaks, she saw the reward of the state of śrotāpatti face to face. As soon as she had seen the truth, she sang three times the thanksgiving [reported above, until]: "we are established among devas and men." And she added:

"The fearsome path of bad existences, filled with numerous miseries, is closed through your power. The pure path of heaven is opened, and I have entered on the way of nirvāṇa.

"Rid of my sins, O you whose view is so pure, because I have taken refuge in you, today I acquire purity; I have obtained the desirable rank that the āryas seek; I have reached the other shore of the ocean of sufferings.

"O you who in the world is the object of homage from daityas, from men, and from immortals; you who are free from birth, old age, sickness, and death; you the sight of whom is difficult to obtain even after a thousand births, O recluse! The happiness of seeing you bears its fruits today.

"I have attained eminence, O Lord; I have attained superiority; I take refuge in the Bhagavat, in the law, and in the assembly of monks; receive me thus among your faithful, I who from today, as long as I live, as long as I keep the breath of life, will seek asylum in you, and will have feelings of benevolence for you. May the Bhagavat grant me the favor today of accepting the repast of alms, with the ārya Mahāmaudgalyāyana!" The Bhagavat received the words of Bhadrakanyā with his silence. Then, seeing that the Bhagavat and Mahāmaudgalyāyana were comfortably seated, she satisfied them by presenting pleasant food and dishes to them with her own hands, purely prepared, the qualities of which she enumerated. When she saw that the Bhagavat had eaten, that he had washed his hands and that his bowl was wiped clean, she took a very low seat and sat before the Bhagavat to listen to the law. Consequently, the Bhagavat taught it to her. The respectable Mahāmaudgalyāyana, who had taken the bowl of the Blessed One, began to wash it. Then, the Bhagavat told him: "Let us go, Mahāmaudgalyāyana."

45. This is the new name of Maudgalyāyana's mother.

"Let us go, Bhagavat," replied the monk. "And through whose power?" said the Bhagavat. "Through that of the blessed Tathāgata," said the monk. "If this is so, reflect on the place where Jetavana is," said the Bhagavat; and at that same instant the monk exclaimed: "Bhagavat, have we arrived?" Overwhelmed with surprise, he immediately said: "What then is the name, O Bhagavat, of this supernatural power?" "It is called, O Maudgalyāyana, 'rapid as thought.'" "I myself do not know it clearly, so profound are the laws of the buddhas. If that was known [to me], my thought would never turn away from the supreme state of a perfectly accomplished buddha, even if my body were ground as small as a sesame seed. Today, what could I do, now that the wood is burned."[46]

But the monks in whose mind doubts had been raised, addressed the blessed Buddha, who settles all uncertainties, in this way: "Which action had the respectable Pūrṇa thus performed, O Lord, to be born in a wealthy, fortunate family, enjoying great riches? Which action did he also perform to be born in the womb of a slave and then to obtain, when he had entered into the religious life, to see the state of arhat face to face, after having annihilated all corruptions of evil?" The Bhagavat responded to them: "Pūrṇa, O monks, in the capacity of a monk, has performed and accumulated actions that have attained their completion, whose causes have reached their maturity, which have accompanied him like light [accompanies the body that produces it], which must necessarily have an end. Who other [than I] will distinctly know the actions performed and accumulated by Pūrṇa? Actions performed and accumulated, O monks, do not reach their maturity in the external elements, neither of earth, nor water, nor fire, nor wind; but it is only in the [five] intellectual attributes, in the [six] constituent parts of the body, and in the [five] sense organs, the true elements of all individuals,[47] that the actions performed and accumulated, the good as well as the bad, reach their full maturity.

"Deeds are not destroyed, even by hundreds of kalpas; but when they have attained their perfection and their time, they bear fruit for creatures endowed with a body.

"Long ago, O monks, in this very bhadrakalpa in which we are, when creatures had an existence of twenty thousand years, there appeared in the world a venerable tathāgata, perfect and complete buddha, called Kāśyapa, endowed with science and good conduct, well come, knowing the world, without superior, leading men like a young bull, preceptor of men and gods, blessed one, buddha. This tathāgata, having withdrawn near the city of Benares, settled there. Pūrṇa, who had entered into the religious life under his teaching, possessed the three

46. I have translated these words literally, whose enigmatic meaning I do not grasp well.

47. Here the text reads *api bhūpānteṣveva*, with which I can do nothing, and which I replace with *api bhūtānteṣveva*, "which only end in an individual being," that is to say, "which constitute him."

sacred collections, and fulfilled for the assembly the duties of servant of the law.[48] One day, there appeared the domestic of a certain arhat, who started to sweep the vihāra; but the wind drove the dirt from one side to the other. He then had this reflection: 'Let us wait a while for the wind to calm.' The servant of the law happened to arrive and saw that the vihāra still had not been swept. Blinded by a violent anger, he pronounced these rude words: 'He is the domestic of some son of a slave.' The arhat heard him and had this reflection: 'This man is blinded by his anger; let us wait a while; I will reprimand him later.' When the anger of the servant of the law had calmed, the arhat appeared before him and spoke to him in these terms: 'Do you know who I am?' 'I know you,' responded the servant of the law; 'you and I, we entered into the religious life under the teaching of Kāśyapa, the perfectly accomplished Buddha.' 'This may be,' answered the arhat. 'As for me, I have fulfilled all the duties imposed on one who has entered into the religious life, and I am delivered from all bonds; but you, you have pronounced rude words. Because of this fault, confess that you have sinned, and thereby this action will be diminished, it will be destroyed, it will be forgiven.'

"Consequently, the servant of the law confessed that he had sinned; and since he should have taken a new existence in hell and then be reborn as the son of a slave, he did not come back to life in hell, but he was reborn, for five hundred generations, in the womb of a slave. Finally he reappeared in this world also, in his last existence, as the son of a slave woman. Because he had served the assembly, he was born in the midst of a wealthy, fortunate family, enjoying great wealth; because while serving it, he had read, he had studied, he had acquired skill in the knowledge of the accumulation [of the constituent elements of existence], he obtained the happiness of entering into the religious life under my teaching, and of seeing the state of arhat face to face, after having annihilated all corruptions of evil. This is so, O monks, for completely black actions is reserved a reward that is also completely black; for completely white actions is reserved a reward that is also completely white; for mixed actions is reserved a result as mixed as they are. This is why, O monks, it is necessary in this world to avoid completely black actions as well as completely mixed actions, and to have in view only completely white actions. This is, O monks, what you have to learn."

This is how the Bhagavat spoke, and the monks, transported in joy, praised what the Bhagavat had said.

One has been able to see, through the preceding legend, that the rather expeditious investiture by which Śākyamuni created disciples for himself gave the char-

48. The text uses the expression *dharmavaiyāvṛtyaṃ karoti*, which I have seen only in this style; the Tibetan renders it with *zhal ta pa byed do*. One must probably understand thereby one who serves the assembly of monks as a domestic of the monastery.

acter of mendicant monks to those who received it; for such is the meaning of the word *bhikṣu*, which means exactly "he who lives on alms."[49] After the obligation to observe the rules of chastity (*brahmacarya*), there was nothing more pressing for the monk than to live only on the help he received from public charity. As he stopped belonging to the world, the resources that society offers for work were prohibited to him, and he had no other means of existence than begging.

The life of privation to which the monks condemned themselves caused them to also receive the name *śramaṇas*, "ascetics who tame their senses."[50] They had taken this title in imitation of their master Śākyamuni, who called himself *śramaṇa Gautama*, the Gautamid ascetic. But this title, in regard to monks, is much less frequent in the legends than that of *bhikṣu*, just as this latter never applies, as far as I know, to Śākyamuni, without being preceded by the epithet of *mahā*, "the great monk." Like the term *bhikṣu*, that of *śramaṇa* belongs to the Brahmanical language; but the Buddhists apply it in a very special way to the ascetics of their belief, and the Indian dramas prove to us with more than one example that the brahmans themselves recognized the legitimacy of this application.[51]

It sometimes happened that the conversions were not as rapid as that of Pūrṇa; then, he who desired to embrace the ascetic life, and who did not satisfy the various required conditions, was not for that reason driven from the gathering of monks he wished to enter. Without yet being part of the assembly of bhikṣus, he was placed under the direction of a monk and took the title *śrāmaṇera*, that is to say, little *śrāmaṇa* or novice ascetic. As soon as he had received investiture, he substituted this title with that of *śramaṇa* or *bhikṣu*. These

49. I believe I can translate this title with the slightly more general term *monk*, in order to avoid the confusion that the use of the word *mendicant* entails, which it is necessary to retain for *parivrājaka* and for some other similar terms.

50. I have kept this name without translating it, in the same way that we keep that of *brahman*, because it is the title that Śākyamuni himself bore from the moment he withdrew from the world. The Chinese were not unaware of the true meaning of this term, as one can see in a note of Mr. Rémusat (*Foe koue ki*, p. 13). I recall that in my text this title belongs as much to Brahmanism as to Buddhism; but, since in all the books I have had the occasion to read or translate, the title *śramaṇa* is constantly distinguished from that of *brāhman*, which it regularly precedes, "the śramaṇas and the brahmans," it certainly designates not an Indian ascetic in general, but a Buddhist in particular, and it is taken there in the special acceptation that Clough gives it, "a Buddhist ascetic, a mendicant, a religious mendicant, a Buddhist priest" (*Sinhalese Dictionary*, 2:778). Colebrooke (*Miscellaneous Essays*, 2:203) and Rémusat (*Foe koue ki*, p. 13) have already observed that the name *śramaṇa* was formerly known by the Greeks; but it is still a question whether, for the ancients, this name designated Indian ascetics in general or Buddhists in particular. We have to come down to Porphyrus to find the name Samanéen applied to a sect that one can conjecture to be that of the Buddhists.

51. I could cite here the words of this gambler of the *Mṛcchakaṭī* who, prosecuted for debts, has no other recourse than to make himself a disciple of Śākya; for the Prakrit term he uses, *śakka śavaṇake*, is certainly the transcription of the Sanskrit *śākya śramaṇaka*, the diminutive of *śākya śramaṇa*, which is found in the commentary of the edition of Calcutta (*Mṛcchakaṭī*, p. 82, Calcutta ed.; Wilson, *Hindu Theatre*, 1:56, 2nd ed). What leaves no doubt on this subject is that this same monk is designated elsewhere by his true title *śamaṇaka* for *śramaṇaka* (*Mṛcchakaṭī*, pp. 213 and 329).

two degrees of monks appear in the texts of the North; that of *śramaṇera* is, however, used there less often than that of *śramaṇa.* I am not afraid to say that this comes from the fact that at the time to which these texts take us, the novitiate was a much more rare state than that of monk. The facility with which the conversions took place gave those who desired to follow Śākya the means to rapidly pass over the first degrees of the initiation.

I just spoke about the conditions imposed by Śākyamuni on those who wanted to become his disciples; this point requires some clarification. The first of all conditions was faith, and one can believe that those who satisfied it would be exempted from all others. But it is equally easy to understand that Śākya or his first successors soon recognized the necessity to join it to some other obligations that were somewhat less easy to carry out. This necessity must have been all the more promptly sensed as the new belief found more favor among the people. The legends that have found a place in the section on Discipline give us the most instructive information on this subject. There one sees that Śākya receives all those who present themselves to him, but that as soon as an admission gives rise to some difficulty, he hastens to rescind it with a decision that would become a rule for his successors. It is in this way that the investiture conferred on men affected by certain maladies reputed to be incurable,[52] or having some serious deformity,[53] such as the leper or the hermaphrodite,[54] or on great criminals such as the parricide,[55] the murderer of his mother[56] and of an arhat,[57] the man who has caused dissension among the monks,[58] one who is guilty of one of the four great crimes condemned by the brahmans,[59] is declared not valid, and that Śākya excludes from the assembly one who is affected by these moral and physical vices. Rules no less natural and no less easy to understand prevented the admission of one less than twenty years old,[60] and of one who cannot provide proof of the authorization of his father and mother.[61] The slave whom his master has the right to reclaim[62] and the debtor prosecuted for debt[63] are also excluded. Lastly, no one can be admitted by a single monk, and it is necessary, in order to take one's place in the assembly of the disciples of Śākya, to have been examined and received in

52. Csoma, "Analysis of the Dul-va," in *Asiatic Researches*, vol. 20, p. 53.
53. *Ibid.*, pp. 57 and 58.
54. *Ibid.*, p. 55.
55. *Ibid.*, p. 57.
56. *Ibid.*, p. 56.
57. *Ibid.*, p. 57.
58. *Ibid.*, p. 57.
59. *Ibid.*, p. 57.
60. *Ibid.*, p. 53.
61. *Ibid.*, p. 54.
62. *Ibid.*, p. 53.
63. *Ibid.*, p. 53.

the eyes of all.[64] The legends even inform us that Śākyamuni conferred on the assembled body of monks the right to receive novices and to give investiture to those who would be recognized as capable.[65] Thus, he is shown to us establishing two chiefs of the assembly.[66] Nothing is indeed more easy to understand: all the monks received by Śākya are received at the moment when he speaks in the presence of a more or less numerous gathering of the already converted, or those aspiring to be; the institution of one or two chiefs of the assembly manifestly has the aim to continue, after the master, a state of things that could disappear at his death. If it does not belong to him, historically speaking, it is certainly the work of his first successors.

Before passing on to something else, it is important to enumerate the different classes of persons who, along with the monks who were his listeners, attended the assembly of which he was the chief; this is indispensable if one wishes to follow the history of this institution and to understand its import. To the body of mendicant monks there corresponded that of mendicant nuns, for whose admission the same rules were observed as that of monks; they were called *bhikṣunīs.*[67] It does not seem that the institution of a body of nuns had originally been in Śākya's mind. The first woman to obtain permission from him to embrace the ascetic life is Mahāprajāpatī, his aunt, the Gautamid, the very one who raised him.[68] Even then she succeeded only after long entreaties, and the master yielded only to the request of his cousin Ānanda.[69] This legend asserts that this conversion led to that of five hundred other women of the Śākya race;[70] legends like round numbers, and its account could well be a pure invention of the compilers of the Vinaya. Whatever it is, the same authority informs us that soon the three wives of Śākya, whom Csoma names as Gopā, Yaśodharā, and Utpalavarṇā,[71] joined Mahāprajāpatī. The law of the discipline imposed the same general obligations on the women as on the monks, namely the observation of perpetual chastity and the need to beg in order to live; so they are given the generic title *bhikṣunī.* The Brahmanical monuments show us that when speaking of a nun, a bhikṣu called her "sister in the law," *dharmabhaginī.*[72] One finds in

64. *Ibid.*, p. 54.

65. *Ibid.*, p. 52.

66. *Ibid.*, p. 52.

67. Csoma, *Asiatic Researches*, vol. 20, p. 84.

68. *Lalitavistara*, fol. 58a of my manuscript. Csoma, *Asiatic Researches*, vol. 20, p. 308, note 21. A. Rémusat, *Foe koue ki*, p. 111.

69. Csoma, *Asiatic Researches*, vol. 20, p. 90. Rémusat, *Foe koue ki*, p. 111.

70. Csoma, *Asiatic Researches*, vol. 20, p. 90.

71. *Asiatic Researches*, vol. 20, p. 308, note 21. The two first names are indeed those of two wives of Śākya; as for the third, see what has been said above about her, section 2, p. 202, note 197. Georgi only mentions two wives of Śākya, the one he calls *Grags 'dzon ma* (read *Grags 'dzin ma*) is Yaśodharā; the other whom he calls *Sa tsho ma*: if one read *Ba tsho ma*, it would be Gopā (*Alphabetum Tibetanum*, p. 34).

72. *Mṛcchakaṭī*, p. 258, Calcutta ed.; Wilson, *Hindu Theater*, 1:142, note †.

the legends of the North several examples of women converted to Buddhism. We have seen several of them mentioned in the legend of Śākya's battle with the brahmans; it is necessary to add to them the young girl of the cāṇḍāla caste of whom I spoke at the end of the previous section, and with more texts than those we have, we would find still others.

Next to the monks and nuns, or to speak more accurately, below these two orders that constitute the core of the assembly of Śākya, the legends place the upāsakas and the upāsikās, that is to say, the male and female devotees, and in a more general manner, the faithful who profess belief in the truths revealed by Śākya, without however adopting the ascetic life. The legends nowhere explain the term *upāsaka*, and it is in itself vague enough to allow us to doubt if it would not be preferable to translate it as "servant," and to see in it a name of the novice placed under the direction of a monk, for whom he renders the duties of domestic service in some way. This interpretation would greatly facilitate the idea one would have about the composition of the assembly of Śākya, which one would thus picture as formed of monks and nuns and novices of both sexes, in short, by the four gatherings of which our Sanskrit texts speak.[73] Let us add that the manner in which the authors of our Tibetan dictionaries translate *dge bsnyen* (which replaces the Sanskrit *upāsaka*)[74] would favor this interpretation, since according to Csoma this word means "catechumen," and according to Mr. Schmidt, "pupil, novice, layman fulfilling religious duties." But the careful reading of the texts, and some authorities no less respectable to my eyes than those I have just cited, have caused me to decide in favor of the meaning of "devotee" or "faithful."

I remark at the outset that classical Sanskrit takes the word *upāsaka* in the sense of *worshipper* as often as that of *servant*; this is because the elements themselves of which this word is composed mean "to be seated by or below." Second, the Buddhists of the South, that is to say, those of Ceylon and Ava, do not understand it in another way; and one of the most imposing authorities when it is a question of the proper meaning of Buddhist terms, Mr. Turnour, translates it entirely in this sense; for him, *upāsaka* means "devotee, one who lives near the Buddha or with the Buddha."[75] Judson, the author of the Burmese dictionary, goes even slightly farther, perhaps a bit too far, when he translates this word as "layman";[76] but it is necessary to recall that he speaks of a people entirely converted to Buddhism, and in which one who is not a monk cannot be other than a layman, especially in the eyes of a European. Lastly, the Chinese, who, as I have

73. *Catasṛṇām parṣadām*, in *Avadānaśataka*, fols. 77b, 88a, 101b.

74. *Avadānaśataka*, fol. 121a, compared to the *Bka' 'gyur*, sec. *Mdo*, vol. *ha*, or 29, fol. 207b.

75. *Mahāvanso*, index, p. 27, ed. in -4°.

76. *Burman Dictionary*, see *Upāsaka*, p. 45.

often remarked, in general follow the tradition of the North, have exactly the same idea about the word *upāsaka* as the Buddhists of the South. "The term *Youposai*," according to Mr. A. Rémusat, "means pure ones, and indicates that despite the fact that those who bear it remain in their house, that is to say, lead a lay life, they observe the five precepts and maintain a pure behavior. One renders their name also as 'men who come near' duty, in order to expresss that they render themselves appropriate to receive the law of the buddhas by fulfilling the precepts."[77] In an enumeration of the several types of religious that the same scholar has borrowed from Chinese sources, the upāsakas of both sexes are designated as *remaining in the house*, in opposition to the other categories, which, according to the Buddhist expression, departed from it to enter into the religious life.[78] And the learned author to whom we owe these interesting extracts ends his note with this summary: "The word *upāsaka* applies properly to Buddhists who lead the lay life, while they observe the precepts of the religion and maintain a regular and stainless behavior."[79]

To these authorities, I will now add several expressions that needed to be preceded by the clarifications I have just given in order to be understood as I propose. I find, for example, the term *buddhopāsaka*, "devotee of the Buddha,"[80] opposed to that of *tīrthikopāsaka*, "devotee of the tīrthikas," that is to say, Brahmanical ascetics.[81] This term *buddhopāsaka* is taken exactly in the same sense by a Brahmanical text of an incontestable authority, the drama of *Mṛcchakaṭī*. A Buddhist monk addressed a prince with the title *upāsaka*; this title, which gives rise to a play on words because of its double meaning of "devotee" and "barber," is explained by another person as being synonymous with *buddhopāsaka*, "devotee of the Buddha."[82] In another passage, the heroine of the play, who is a courtesan, is called *buddhopāsikā*, that is to say, "devotee of the Buddha,"[83] which demonstrates sufficiently that the title *upāsikā* (feminine of *upāsaka*) expresses nothing similar to *novice* or *catechumen*. One legend of the *Avadānaśataka* says of an upāsaka that he is skilled in the law of the Buddha;[84] of another, that he has understood the formulas of refuge and the precepts of the teaching;[85] of still

77. *Foe koue ki*, p. 180.

78. *Foe koue ki*, p. 181. The standard expression is *agārād anagārikām pravrajitaḥ* (*Divyāvadāna*, fol. 411b of my manuscript).

79. *Foe koue ki*, pp. 182 and 183.

80. *Avadānaśataka*, fol. 140b.

81. *Avadānaśataka*, fol. 16b, 20b, 21a and b.

82. *Mṛcchakaṭī*, p. 214, Calcutta ed. The translation of Wilson perhaps does not sufficiently bring out the proper meaning of this term (*Hindu Theater*, 1:123).

83. *Mṛcchakaṭī*, p. 255ff., 322ff., and 329. Here Wilson has perfectly rendered this title as "the devotee worshipper of Buddha" (*Hindu Theater*, 1:141).

84. *Avadānaśataka*, fols. 29b, 31b.

85. *Ibid.*, fol. 121a.

others, that they know the truths.[86] And when it is a case of designating a servant, it is the word *upasthāyaka* that is used, for example in this text: "For us, who are the servants of the Bhagavat, we desire to be constantly employed to sweep Jetavana."[87] Lastly, the two titles *bhikṣu*, mendicant monk, and *upāsaka*, devotee, are opposed in this passage: "'What is to be done in the mendicant state?' 'One must observe the rules of chastity (*brahmacarya*) during one's entire life.' 'That is not possible, is there no other way?' 'There is another, friend, it is to be a devotee (*upāsaka*).' 'What is to be done in that state?' 'One must abstain, during one's entire life, from every inclination to murder, theft, pleasure, lying, and the use of intoxicating liquors.'"[88]

I do not hide the fact that Mr. Hodgson has, in a memoradum filled with precious information,[89] contested the legitimacy of the distinction that is established in this way between bhikṣus, or monks, and upāsakas, or devotees. Relying on considerations borrowed from the history of the beginnings of the Christian church, he is unable to acknowledge that a body of faithful separate from the monks existed from the early times of Buddhism. I do not believe that it is possible to oppose anything in the remarks of Mr. Hodgson in principle; and if it is a question of the first attempts made by Śākya to have disciples, I recognize, with this ingenious author, that in India there were not originally Buddhists other than those who, renouncing the world, made a vow to follow Śākya and to practice the duties of the ascetic life by his example. But if one believes the legends, this state did not last long, and the moment that Śākyamuni began to preach to the masses, those who, without being his disciples, nevertheless came to listen to him were upāsakas, that is to say, bystanders. It is but one step from the title of *bystander* to that of *devotee*, because these men and these women seated in a crowd near the recognized disciples of Śākya were doubtless not in general animated by feelings of malevolence toward the new ascetic. I am thus rather far from believing that Śākyamuni, from the commencement of his preaching, constituted an assembly of religious divided into bhikṣus and upāsakas of each of the sexes. Far from it, the external organization of Buddhism, like its metaphysics, passed through numerous stages, before arriving at the state that the peoples whom Buddhism converted long ago show us that it reached. The books of Nepal even make us witness to the progress of this organization, which starts with the most feeble beginnings, as one sees there Śākya followed first by five disciples, who abandon him rather quickly, because their master, exhausted by long fasts,

86. *Ibid.*, fol. 36a.

87. *Id. ibid.*

88. *Sahasodgata*, in *Divyāvadāna*, fol. 151a.

89. "Quotations from Original Sanscrit Authorities," in *Journal of the Asiatic Society of Bengal*, vol. 5, p. 33ff.

has broken the vow of abstinence by which he had linked himself to them. Little by little, the number of his adepts increased; kings, brahmans, merchants join them to listen to the word of the master. These are the upāsakas, bystanders, and later true devotees, if they take from the preaching of Śākya the seeds of the virtues that it is the aim of his teaching to propagate. So natural an explanation in addition has facts of a great value in its favor; we will see soon that the views of Śākya, or perhaps of his first successors, moved beyond the circle of his disciples, and in promising rewards of different orders in the future to those who, without being his adepts, were imbued more or less intimately with his word, supporters and real devotees were created among those of his listeners who could not or would not become monks.

But monks alone formed the assembly of the listeners of Śākya, as I have already indicated; this is why in the texts one finds this assembly called *bhikṣusaṃgha*, "the gathering of mendicants."[90] In the sūtras and in the legends of Nepal, the term *saṃgha* has no other acceptation, and it is also the one it retains in the formula *Buddha, dharma, saṃgha*, "the Buddha, the law, the assembly," as Mr. Hodgson has shown quite well;[91] the more or less philosophical

90. No doubt can now remain as to the spelling of this term; inscriptions like that of Amarāvatī and Sancī (*Journal of the Asiatic Society of Bengal*, vol. 6, pp. 222 and 455) and our manuscripts represent it always as I do: *saṃgha* (or सङ्घ), a word that has the meaning of "masses, multitude of people." This signification accords perfectly with the nature of the assembly of the monks of Śākya, which was composed of men coming from all castes. I do not believe that the spelling *saṃga* is very frequent, if it is ever used in our manuscripts. Mr. W. von Humboldt preferred that of *sanga* (सङ्ग), which Hodgson and Rémusat had adopted, to that of *sangha* (सङ्घ) given by Schmidt and Wilson (*Über die Kawi-Sprache*, 1:273, note 1); but at the time when this scholar wrote, one still did not possess in Europe the manuscripts that are in my hands. We will sufficiently see through my text why I cannot accept the philosophical explanations with which this scholar accompanies the term *saṃgha*: "The gathering called *sanga*," he says, "is not in principle at all terrestrial, and it is composed of bodhisattvas, pratyekas, and śrāvakas who have already left the world. This gathering, however, following the ordinary application of celestial things to terrestrial things, became the basis of the Buddhist hierarchy. . . . Lastly, this term was clearly applied to the gathering of the followers of the Buddha, living together and with their master in the cloisters called *vihāras*" (*Über die Kawi-Sprache*, 1:273). I think, for my part, that things must have happened in reverse order: that the primitive signification of the word *saṃgha* was that of "gathering of listeners"; that this gathering was perfectly real and human, as human as any other assembly of disciples following a master; that when the mystical ideas of triad, of sexes, and other things, which I regard as inspired in the Buddhists of the North by the proximity of the brahmans, were introduced into the originally very simple system founded by Śākya, an ideal application was made of this perfectly historical term to the celestial gathering of the highest personages in the philosophical and moral hierarchy of Buddhism. This at least is what the reading of the sūtras and the legends allows me to believe; but I fear that this opinion finds little favor among persons who have ideas on the origin and development of religious beliefs in general and of Buddhism in particular, whose meaning I humbly confess I do not completely grasp. Moreover, this observation, which is suggested to me by the feeling of distrust I experience each time I deviate from the opinions of a man like Mr. von Humboldt, applies to many other ideas and many other terms than that which occupies us. The present volume is dedicated in its entirety to put in relief the purely human character of Buddhism; I am thus not able to believe here, any more than elsewhere, that this belief is the expression of I do not know which divine types that I find nowhere, at least in the texts that I take to be the closest to the preaching of Śākya.

91. "Quotations from Original Sanscrit Authorities," in *Journal of the Asiatic Society of Bengal*, vol. 5, p. 37.

senses that have been sought in this formula certainly do not belong to primitive Buddhism.[92] The term *saṃgha* expresses a double relation, first that of all the monks to the Buddha, then that of the monks among themselves. In principle, the only link that binds them to the master and joins them together is, according to the legends, a common submission to his word. Moreover, coming from different classes of society in order to devote themselves to the religious life, when they have received the knowledge of the fundamental truths and the title of monk from Śākya, they go to live, some in the solitude of the forests and mountains, others in abandoned houses, in the woods near villages and cities; and they leave only to procure food by begging. I have cited a short while ago the legend of Pūrṇa, where we see this monk, hardly having converted to Buddhism, asking Śākya for permission to withdraw to a barbarian country; and I could report here a great number of similar examples borrowed from the sūtras and the legends. It is sufficient for me to recall one, which shows what importance Śākyamuni attached to the solitary life. By his preaching, he had attracted a young merchant, who had embraced the religious life, or to speak more exactly, who had taken the title of monk; but the young man continued to live in the paternal house. Śākyamuni showed him how life in the world was inferior to retreat, whose advantages he glorified. The exhortations of the master were not unfruitful; the merchant abandoned the world to go to live in solitude, where, taking Śākya as his "friend of virtue," that is to say, his spiritual director, he attained the highest degree of perfection through complete knowledge of the world.[93]

92. A. Rémusat ("Observations sur trois Mémoires de de Guignes," in *Nouveau Journal Asiatique*, vol. 7, p. 264ff.) and Schmidt (*Mémoires de l'Académie des sciences de Saint-Pétersbourg*, 1:114ff.) are the authorities to consult for the exalted meanings that this formula has taken in the relatively modern schools of Buddhism. It is necessary to add to them Hodgson as far as Nepal is concerned, whose religion is treated in depth in a special memorandum ("Sketch of Buddhism," in *Transactions of the Royal Asiatic Society*, vol. 2, pp. 246 and 247); and Benfey ("Indien," p. 201), who thought that the Buddhist triad of *Buddha, dharma*, and *saṃgha* was an imitation of Brahmanism. In my opinion, it is quite essential to distinguish the formula itself from the more or less varied applications made of it. The formula seems to me to be ancient and the meaning it had in principle must have been very simple; but nothing proves that the applications are not modern or at least invented afterward, in different epochs.

93. *Avadānaśataka*, fols. 85 and 86b. The expression "friend of virtue," *kalyāṇamitra*, is one of the most remarkable in Buddhism; I do not doubt that it belongs to the first ages of this belief. The friend of virtue is the one who introduces the future disciple to the master; it is also the accomplished monk who gives the novice the instruction that he still lacks; it is also, for a monk, all respectable ascetics whose company he must seek. One finds this title mentioned frequently in the legends with this last acceptation (*Avadānaśataka*, fols. 34b, 87a and b); one even sees it opposed to that of *pāpamitra*, "friend of sin" (*Ibid*., fol. 87a and b *Bka' 'gyur*, sec. *Mdo*, vol. *ha*, or 29, fol. 155a). This term furnishes a new example of the inconvenience there would sometimes be in confining oneself to the statements of the Tibetan versions, without going back to the Sanskrit originals. The Tibetans translate exactly *kalyāṇamitra* by *dge ba'i bshes gnyen*, according to Csoma, "a friend of virtue, a priest"; it is exactly the translation also given by Schmidt, "ein Freund der Tugend, ein Priester." Csoma translates it also as "doctor, a learned priest," and Mr. Schmidt as "ein geistlicher Rath." I do not hesitate to prefer this latter translation to all the others; the friend of virtue is certainly a true spiritual director, but he is not for that reason a priest; on the contrary, all priests (if, however, this term is exact) can be a virtuous friend; in short, there does not exist in the Buddhist hierarchy an order of kalyāṇamitras, as there is of bhikṣus.

One sees, at the origin, the disciples of Śākya are only isolated ascetics; and one still does not suspect, if one confines oneself to the text of the most ancient legends, the possibility of an organization that must have joined all these monks, who assembled only to hear the word of the master, with a lasting link.

Various circumstances, reported in the legends and the sūtras, allow us, however, to grasp the beginnings of this organization. As long as Śākya lived, it was natural that those who were converted by him attached themselves to his person in order to profit from his teaching. All the monks did not settle in solitude forever; and even those who had chosen this kind of life abandoned it from time to time in order to come to listen to the Buddha. Thus, the legends show us Śākya always followed by a more or less considerable number of monks, who accompanied him and begged following him. When the rainy season came, that is to say, when communications between the countryside and the cities were, if not completely interrupted, at least more difficult, the monks could stop the vagabond life of mendicants. They were permitted to withdraw into fixed residences; and then, they dispersed and each went their own way, to reside with the brahmans or householders who they knew to be favorable to them. There, they occupied themselves by disseminating through their speech the knowledge of the truths that constituted their belief, or else by meditating and by studying the points of the doctrine that were least known to them. This was called "to sojourn during the varṣa," *varṣavasana,* that is to say, during the four months that the rainy season lasts in India.[94] When the *varṣa* had expired, they had to gather again; and then, forming a true monastic assembly, they questioned one another on the various points of the doctrine they had meditated on during this kind of retreat. Everything leads us to believe that this custom was introduced by Śākya himself, or very certainly by his first disciples; but even if it was not practiced in the master's lifetime, it is nonetheless mentioned so frequently in the legends related exclusively to Śākya that I do not hesitate to take it to be very ancient.

This, if I am not mistaken, is one of the circumstances that must have most favored the organization of the monks into a regular body. One of the first results that it must have produced was the establishment of vihāras, kinds of monasteries, located in woods or gardens, where monks gathered to attend the

94. This institution of *varṣa* is certainly one of the most ancient in Buddhism; for one finds it among all the peoples who have adopted this belief, among those of the South as among those of the North. Mr. Turnour defines the word *vassa* (Pāli for *varṣa*) in this way: "the four months of the rainy season, from the full moon of July until that of November." During this part of the year, the monks should stop their pilgrimages, and devote themselves to religious practices in fixed places (*Mahāvanso*, index, p. 28. *Journal of the Asiatic Society of Bengal*, vol. 7, p. 1000. Clough, *Sinhalese Dictionary*, 2:632, col. 2). But this institution has become modified with the progress of Buddhism; and, for example, today among the Buddhists of Ava, it is in their monasteries and not in individuals' houses that the monks pass the time of the rainy season (Sangermano, *Description of the Burmese Empire*, p. 92, Tandy ed.). See the additions at the end of the volume.

teaching of the master. We should not believe, however, that the vihāras were, in principle, establishments where monks secluded themselves for their whole life; they were so little obliged to settle in them forever that they left them, as I have just said, at the time of the rainy season, that is to say, at the time of the year when it seems that they must have come and gathered, as the custom was later established among the peoples converted to Buddhism. Thus, the vihāras were, at the beginning, only places of temporary abode; they were, according to the etymology of the word, the places where they were; and the origin of the term reveals itself in the very formula that opens each sūtra: "One day, Śākya was (*vihārati sma*) in such a place."[95] The first purpose of vihāras, after that of serving as asylum for the monks, was to be open to traveling ascetics and to foreigners who came to the country. "Is there not in your homeland," the Buddha says to an anchorite, "some vihāra in which monks who travel find someplace to stay upon their arrival?"[96] When the monks had stayed for a rather long time in a country, they left their vihāra to go to another province, where they chose a new domicile for themselves to which they were not more attached than to the first. All of this is easy to understand, when one thinks about this easy life of India, where ascetics passed the day under the trees and the night in huts of foliage, or under the shelters, covered but not closed, that the beneficence of the wealthy have erected from time immemorial on all the roads.

It is doubtless a long way from this almost nomadic state of Buddhism to the flourishing situation in which it existed in the fourth century of our era, amid the wealthy vihāras and prosperous hermitages described by the author of the *Foe koue ki*; but between the epoch in which Faxian visited India and that which the avadānas and sūtras make known to us, more than nine centuries had passed, following the Sinhalese reckoning for the death of Śākya. Nevertheless, whatever difference exists between these two states of Buddhism, taken from epochs so distant one from the other, one sees clearly that the second must result

95. One can see in Georgi (*Alphabetum Tibetanum*, p. 407) the illustration and description of a complete vihāra, as it could be constructed in the most flourishing epochs of Buddhism, and as they are still constructed in Tibet. I think it would not be impossible to find today in India more or less perfect models of these edifices, which the celebrated caves of Gujarat and the Marathi country have preserved for us. So, I cannot prevent myself from believing that the cave of Magathani described by Salt is a vihāra hollowed out in the rock (*Transactions of the Literary Society of Bombay*, vol. 1, p. 44). Erskine has not hesitated to express the same opinion (*Transactions of the Literary Society of Bombay*, vol. 3, p. 527). This judicious author has long remarked, in the context of the caves of Elephanta, that one must ordinarily find attached to the Buddhist temples hollowed out of the mountains a more or less considerable number of cells intended to be used as residences for the monks who lived there together (Erskine, *ibid.*, 1:202). These cells are the most characteristic feature of a vihāra. It is necessary to say as much about the beautiful caves of Bagh on the road of Ujjain, whose exclusively Buddhist character the same author has perfectly indicated (*ibid.*, 2:202). This observation would doubtless apply exactly to several other caves of India, if we had more exact descriptions of them, and above all less mixed with mythological and historical interpretations than those given by some travelers. See also, on the word *vihāra*, the *Foe koue ki*, pp. 19 and 352.

96. *Avadānaśataka*, fol. 35b.

rather rapidly from the first. Indeed, once the monks had fixed places where they could live together, the link that bound them to one another must have tightened further; and the single effect of this gathering was to constitute them into a much more organized body, and consequently more durable than that which could be formed by the ascetics, usually isolated, who belonged exclusively to the Brahmanical caste.

To this entirely material fact there came to be added the influence that the necessity confronting them to resist the attacks of their adversaries must have exerted at an early point on the organization of Buddhist monks. This necessity made them feel the need to unite together and to form an association that could very easily be changed into a monastic institution. There, as a judicious author has remarked, one finds the true difference that distinguishes the Buddhist monks from the more ancient ascetics, such as the sannyāsins and the vanaprasthas.[97] These latter, who, far from being in opposition to the popular religion, were on the contrary authorized by the law of Manu, had no need to create regularly organized religious associations. If they gathered some disciples around them, accidental encounters resulted that did not survive the master. But the isolation in which the Buddhists had placed themselves, in the midst of Indian society, could not fail to make them sense the advantages of communal life; and once these advantages were appreciated, it was not difficult to ensure their conservation, in giving to the chief of the association a successor who continued the work of him who had founded it.

Once the assembly of monks formed by gathering all the bhikṣus ordained by Śākyamuni, a hierarchy capable of maintaining the order must have been established rather quickly. Thus we see, in all the legends, the bhikṣus ranked according to their age and according to their merit. It is in accordance with their age that they took their rank in the assembly, and the first received the name of *sthaviras,* old men or elders. The sthaviras, in turn, distinguish themselves into elders of the elders, *sthavirāḥ sthavirāṇām;*[98] but I have never found in the texts an appellation like *young* or *new* corresponding to that of *old man.* In the assembly, the sthaviras occupied the first rank after Śākya; and this explains the remarkable translation that the Tibetan interpreters give to their name. The word *sthavira* is regularly replaced in their versions by the two monosyllables *gnas brtan*, which our Tibetan dictionaries all render as "vicar, substitute," except for Schröter, who gives it the meaning of "very good priest, very excellent monk."[99] The etymology of the word *sthavira* (*sthā*, to remain) on the one hand, and on the other the role usually played in the legends by the sthaviras, whom Śākyamuni entrusts with

97. Bochinger, *La vie contemplative chez les Hindous*, p. 166.
98. *Pūrṇa*, in *Divyāvadāna*, fol. 22a. *Sumāgadhāvadāna*, fol. 4a, MS of the Bibliothèque royale.
99. *Bhotanta Dictionary*, p. 38, col. 1.

the care of teaching the law when he does not speak himself, doubtless justify the version of the Tibetan interpreters. Would it not, however, give the reader a singular idea of the original, to translate a sentence that appears on every page of the *Prajñāpāramitā* in this way: "Then, the vicar Subhuti spoke in this way to the Bhagavat"? I do not hesitate to maintain that it would be to translate too much; thus, I have believed that I must keep the term itself *sthavira* in my French translation of the *Lotus of the Good Law.* Mr. Turnour has also kept the title *thera*, the Pāli form of *sthavira*, in the English translation he has given of the Pāli *Mahāvaṃsa*; and nevertheless the Sinhalese theras, who, over all the other monks, have the privilege to teach the law, are clearly, for the Sinhalese as for the Tibetans, in reality types of vicars, who replace their master today as they sometimes replaced him during his life.

Merit also served to mark the ranks, and I even think that it must be linked with the privilege of seniority to assure an incontestable superiority for a monk. We have seen, in the legend of Pūrṇa, proof that a monk is able, through his personal qualities, to rise to a more elevated rank than that which he has by age. It is good, still, to remark that there it is a case of supernatural power; from which it follows that the principle of seniority must be in general superior to that of merit, since it yielded only in the face of superhuman faculties. One cannot believe, however, that knowledge and virtue have not sometimes served to mark the ranks, especially in the early times of Buddhism. It is certain, according to the legends, that the teaching of Śākya acted in a more or less rapid manner, depending on whether those who received it were more or less prepared; such that a monk could in a short time acquire a science more profound and a holiness more perfect than another among those who had preceded him in the assembly by a long time. The knowledge of the truths taught by Śākya had, moreover, its degrees, and doubtless one who had crossed over all of them was regarded as superior to one who had stopped in his progress. These various degrees occur so often in our legends that I believe it necessary to cite a text in which they are indicated according to their relative position. This text will have the advantage of presenting in brief the entirety of what the avadānas indicate to us related to the distinctions established among the listeners of Śākya with regard to merit and science.

"The Bhagavat, knowing the mind, the dispositions, the character, and the nature of the ferrymen who listened to him, set forth the teaching of the law intended to make them penetrate the four sublime truths such that after having heard them, some obtained the fruits of the state of śrotāpanna, others those of the state of sakṛdāgāmin, still others those of the state of anāgāmin. Some, having embraced the religious life, succeeded in seeing, through the annihilation of all corruptions of evil, the state of arhat face to face. These understood the intelligence (*bodhi*) that the śrāvakas reach; those understood that of the pratyekabuddhas; others that of a perfectly accomplished buddha. In the end, the entire gathering was absorbed in the Buddha, plunged into the law, drawn into the assembly."[100]

Let us now examine the various terms of this enumeration; they designate, as we will see, various degrees in the hierarchy, which I will call moral and scientific, of the listeners of Śākya. First, the four sublime truths are the fundamental axioms that serve as the basis of Buddhist doctrine: namely that suffering exists, that it is the lot of all who come into the world, that it is important to free oneself from it, lastly that it is through science alone that one can do so in such a way as to obtain deliverance.[101] Those who understand these truths and model their conduct on them are called āryas, or venerable ones, in contrast to ordinary men (*pṛthagjana*), who still have not reflected on these important subjects. One would, however, have only a feeble idea of the value of this title, if one saw it only as an epithet whose meaning is the opposite of that of common man. The quality of ārya appears to me, on the contrary, to be one of the highest that one who is not a buddha can reach; it even ordinarily supposes, in addition to the knowledge of the truths just enunciated, the possession of supernatural faculties. It is given to the first and most eminent disciples of the Buddha; divine personages, like Avalokiteśvara and Mañjuśrī, receive it in all the books, and the copyists of Nepal apply it even to the works supposed to have emanated from the teaching of Śākyamuni; in this latter use, this term comes down to almost that of *saint*.[102] These āryas, or venerable ones, are not so called according to their age, like the sthaviras; they owe this title to their virtues, to their superior faculties, and to the perfections that free them more or less completely from the conditions of the existence to which common men remain subject. Following the Burmese, whose testimony I borrow here, because the titles of the enumeration with which we are occupied are encountered in the Buddhism of the South as well as in that of the North, the title *ārya* applies to the four orders that appear first in the text cited above: the śrotāpannas, the sakṛdāgāmins, the anāgāmins, and the arhats.[103] Each of these orders is in turn subdivided into two categories, depending on whether the one who belongs to it has or has not reached the rewards that his order comprises. Thus, one distinguishes the *śrotāpattimārgasthāna* from the *śrotāpattiphalasthāna*, that is to say, the action of being on the

100. *Avadānaśataka*, fol. 126b. Pūrṇa, in *Divyāvadāna*, fol. 24b. *Sumāgadhāvadāna*, fol. 18a.

101. I will return below to these axioms, otherwise already known, which I will present in the same form they have in the Sanskrit texts of the North. See the additions at the end of the volume.

102. On the use of the word *ārya*, and on the different translations that the Buddhists of Central Asia give of it, see Mr. Schmidt, *Geschichte der Ost-Mongolen*, p. 395.

103. Judson, *Burman Dictionary*, p. 27.

path of śrotāpatti[104] from that of being in the reward of this same state; and it is in this way that these expressions and others similar that one encounters at every moment in the legends of Nepal are explained: "He obtains the reward of such-and-such state." Thus, there are, strictly speaking, eight categories of personages to whom, according to the Burmese, the title *ārya* is suitable, although these eight categories are reduced basically to four, which the titles we will analyze distinguish. All of that, I repeat, is known as commonly to the Sinhalese as to the Nepalese; it is the common patrimony of the Buddhists of all countries.

The titles that follow, although so frequently employed by the redactors of the sūtras and the legends, are not at first sight so easy, and up to now I could not find a definitive interpretation in any text of Nepal. The works that I can consult speak of them as something perfectly known and which do not need explication. It is not, indeed, a translation of these terms to say, as Judson and Clough do in their Burmese and Sinhalese dictionaries: "*Sotāpatti* (Pāli form of the Sanskrit, *śrotāpatti*), the first state reached by an *ārya*, the state of an *ārya*";[105] and so of *sakṛdāgāmin*, which is the second state; of *anāgāmin*, which is the third; and of *arhat*, which is the fourth. Fortunately, the analysis of these terms, brought together with the Tibetan, Chinese, and Sinhalese explanations, does not leave any doubt concerning their true meaning.

Let us begin with the Tibetans, who are the least distant from the Nepalese tradition. The first degree, that of *śrotāpatti*, is represented in their versions by the words *rgyun du zhugs pa*, which, according to their grammatical form, designate the man who has reached this degree. This term, which one encounters at the beginning of an anthology of legends published and translated with much care by Mr. Schmidt,[106] means, according to this scholar: "the man entered into the continuity," *der in die Fortdauer Eingegangene.*[107] In another passage the state of such a man is called: "the continual, perpetual entrance," *die beständige Einkehr.*[108] Lastly, in a third, the reward of this state is called: "that of those who constantly persist," *die Frucht der beständig Verbleibenden.*[109] These various interpretations do not offer a perfectly clear meaning; Mr. Schmidt seems to have adopted them in consideration of the words *rgyun du*, which Schröter, Csoma, and Mr. Schmidt himself translate as "always, perpetually existing." Schröter even gives the whole expresssion with which we are occupied and renders it in

104. The difference between these two forms *śrotāpatti* and *śrotāpanna* is that of abstract noun from adjective. *Āpatti* means "acquisition, obtainment"; it is the state. *Āpanna* means "one who has obtained, acquired"; it is the adjective.

105. Judson, *Burman Dictionary*, p. 400.

106. *Der Weise und der Thor*, p. 44.

107. *Ibid.*, p. 51, note.

108. *Ibid.*, p. 54.

109. *Ibid.*, p. 26, and trans. p. 31.

this way: "the disciples or followers of Śākya."[110] This, I believe, is going too far; and while I recognize that one can arrive at the state of śrotāpatti only after having listened to the word of the Buddha, I nonetheless think that this title is not synonymous with that of *listener* or *monk*. Schröter, moreover, effaces that which is figurative in this title; and even though it would be accurate, his version would be nonetheless incomplete. Georgi, more fortunate with this word than he ordinarily is when he speaks about Tibetan, translates this title as follows: "those who always advance."[111] But the Tibetan words lend themselves to an interpretation no less simple and more instructive; I see in them the meaning of "one who has entered into the current." This is exactly the interpretation of the Sinhalese that Mr. Turnour has transmitted to us in these terms: "this title comes from *sota*, torrent that flows; it is the first degree of sanctification, that which leads the man who has attained it to the other degrees."[112] The Chinese Buddhists are no less explicit, at the same time they are more detailed. According to them, the term *śrotāpanna*, which means "entered into the current," designates a being who has left the universal current of creatures to enter that which leads to deliverance. Such a being, if I understand well the so substantial and so interesting note of Mr. A. Rémusat, still must pass through eighty thousand kalpas, or ages of the world, at the end of which he must be reborn seven times among the devas and among humans, before obtaining the supreme perfection of the science of a buddha.[113] This notion has all desirable precision; one sees in it the necessary agreement between the elements of which the original expression is composed and the application that one makes of it in practice. It designates the first steps of man toward perfection, and does it with the aid of a simple and perfectly intelligible image: to arrive at the port of salvation, it is necessary that man enter the current that will lead him there.

The titles that follow are no less clear, and the aformentioned note of Mr. A. Rémusat explains them in a manner no less satisfactory. That of *sakṛdāgāmin*, which means "the man who must return one time," designates a being who must still cross over sixty thousand kalpas to be reborn one time among the devas and one time among humans, before attaining the absolute science. The word *anāgāmin*, which means "one who must not return," designates a being who does not have to traverse any more than forty thousand kalpas, at the end of which time he is exempted from rebirth in the world of desire and is ensured of reaching the perfect science.[114]

110. *Bhotanta Dictionary*, p. 328, col. 1.

111. *Alphabetum Tibetanum*, p. 278; however, he writes it in this faulty manner: *rgyan duzhu gas pa*.

112. Turnour, *Mahāvamso*, index, p. 24. "Examination of the Pāli Buddhistical Annals," in *Journal of the Asiatic Society of Bengal*, vol. 7, p. 816.

113. *Foe koue ki*, p. 94. This note contains other details to which I refer the reader.

114. A. Rémusat, *Foe koue ki*, p. 94.

It is to be noted that these great rewards, which are the fruits of the teaching of the Buddha, are promised for a fabulous future; nothing, as far as I can discover, attests to their presence in our current life, unless it is the title *ārya*, which is given, according to the Burmese, to these three first orders, as to the fourth. It is equally worthy of note that they do not necessarily accompany the title of *monk*, for in all the passages in which I have found an enumeration similar to that which I examine, the category of bhikṣus is invariably mentioned after the three degrees just analyzed. This observation has in itself great importance; indeed, if these advantages were assured through the teaching of Śākya to those other than monks, it would be necessary to recognize that the founder of Buddhism had by this single fact constituted a type of body of the faithful formed of all those who, without adopting the religious life, had nevertheless penetrated to a certain point into the knowledge of the truths he wanted to establish. I must say, however, that among one of the earliest peoples to adopt Buddhism, the three previous titles are, as those which follow, degrees of holiness that do not appear to be for the use of the simple faithful. This is what is established by a passage of the *Mahāvaṃsa*, in which personages endowed with these very titles are included among the monks who form the assembly.[115] In the same way, Buddhaghosa, in his commentary on the Pāli *Dīghanikāya*, informs us that a great number of monks who had still only attained the degrees of sotāpanna, sakadāgāmi, and anāgāmi were expelled by Kāśyapa from the first assembly, which was concerned with the redaction of the Buddhist scriptures.[116] It is nevertheless a point to which I take the liberty of calling the attention of persons who have access to the diverse sources from which one must draw knowledge of modern Buddhism; and I pose the question in this way: are the three degrees which precede that of arhat really, as I believe they are in the sūtras and in the avadānas of Nepal, three states promised to all who believe in the words of the Buddha and who understand them in a more or less complete manner, or are they three states to which only monks can ascend through efforts of virtue and intelligence?

The fourth degree, or that of *arhat*, does not raise the question I have just indicated; the text cited above leaves no doubt in this regard, since it says in definite terms that it is only after having adopted the religious life that one can, with the aid of a superior science, become an arhat. The arhat, or the venerable one, has, from the point of view of knowledge, reached the most elevated degree among monks; and the sūtras, as do the avadānas, attribute to him supernatural faculties, that is to say, the five *abhijñās*, or superior knowledges, which are: the

115. *Mahāvanso*, chap. 27, p. 164, 4° ed.

116. *Buddhaghosa*, in Turnour, "Examination of the Pāli Buddhistical Annals," in *Asiatic Journal of Bengal*, vol. 6, p. 513. The aforementioned titles are given here, following Mr. Turnour, in their Pāli form, which is sufficiently recognizable.

power to take on the form one desires; the faculty to hear all sounds, however faint; the knowledge of the thoughts of others; that of the past existences of all beings; lastly the faculty to see objects at whatever distance.[117] The note of Mr. Rémusat mentioned above informs us that the arhat must still traverse twenty thousand kalpas, after which he will obtain the supreme science.[118] Moreover, according to the texts of Nepal, it is through the annihilation of all corruptions of evil that one arrives, according to the Chinese author, at the rank of arhat; and it is probably necessary to look into this circumstance for the cause of the false etymology of the name *arhat* that the Buddhists of all schools, those of the North as well as those of the South, propose, and which consists in regarding *arhat* as synonymous with *ariṇāṃ hattā* (Pāli), "conqueror of enemies." We already have, Mr. Lassen and myself, indicated this erroneous interpretation,[119] and I add here that its presence among the Buddhists of all countries proves that it comes from a single and most certainly ancient source. The Jainas, who in India are the true heirs of the Buddhists, do not seem to have made the same mistake, however, if we might refer to the testimony of the *Viṣṇu Purāṇa*, which wisely derives the word *arhat* from *arh*, "to deserve, be worthy of."[120]

However elevated the knowledge of an arhat is, he still did not reach what the sūtras and the legends call *bodhi*, or the intelligence of a buddha. It is important not to confound the word *bodhi* with that of *buddhi*. This latter, which belongs to the language of the Buddhists as well as the brahmans, designates the intelligence or the faculty with which man knows. The former, which is rather rare in Brahmanical Sanskrit, even if it is used there, designates, according to Wilson, not only intelligence but also "the act of keeping his mind awakened for the knowledge of the true God";[121] it is a branch of sacred knowledge. In the Buddhist style, on the contrary, *bodhi* designates at once the state of a buddha and the intelligence of a buddha, which, moreover, comes to the same thing, since the proper state of a buddha, that is to say, of an *enlightened being*, is to be intelligent and omniscient. Nevertheless, since, in the texts of Nepal, one is concerned often with the science of the buddhas, *buddhajñāna*, which is only

117. Clough, *Sinhalese Dictionary*, 2:39, col. 2.

118. A. Rémusat, *Foe koue ki*, p. 95.

119. *Essai sur le Pāli*, p. 203. The Tibetans do not translate this word in another way.

120. Wilson, *Viṣṇu Purāṇa*, p. 339. Bohlen has ingeniously connected the word *arhat* to the Aritonians mentioned by Nicolas of Damascus (*Das alte Indien*, 1:320). Whatever the value of this connection, one can acknowledge with Lassen that the arhats were known to the Greeks. The Σεμνοί, or venerable ones, who, according to Clement of Alexandria, worshipped a pyramid raised above the relics of a god, are the *arhats*, whose name has been translated in this way by the Greeks (Lassen, "De nomibus, quibus a veteribus appellantur Indorum philosophi," in *Rheinisches Museum für Philologie*, 1:187 and 188). One can add that Clement speaks also of the Σεμναί, or venerable women; they are most probably the bhikṣunīs of our texts (*Stromata*, p. 539, Potter).

121. *Sanscrit Dictionary*, s.v. p. 606, 2nd ed.

the knowledge acquired with the aid of human means enlarged by the effect of a supernatural power, I have believed that the term *bodhi*, like *nirvāṇa*, was one of those words that we have to retain, except in the case where its signification is perfectly determined; and in the *Lotus of the Good Law* and in the present work, I have represented it either as "intelligence, or *bodhi*," or "the state of *bodhi*."

These translations here have the advantage of not prejudging anything in the application made of this term to the two categories of beings following the arhats, namely the śrāvakas and the pratyekabuddhas. The text we examine at the moment indeed shows us several of those present in the assembly where Śākya teaches conceiving the idea of the bodhi of the śrāvakas. Now, since the śrāvakas are the listeners of the Buddha, and since all the monks who are part of the assembly have the right to this title, at least apparently, it results from this that a simple monk, if he is well gifted, can reach the bodhi with which a buddha is also endowed. It is doubtless to the listeners who have reached this high degree of knowledge that the denomination *mahāśrāvakas*, or great listeners, is applied in the sūtras and the avadānas; and I add that this title sometimes coincides with that of *sthavira*, or old man, when these listeners are really the oldest in the assembly. But from the fact that these listeners privileged by grace or by their previous virtues attain the intelligence of a buddha, must one conclude that there is a category of buddhas that could be called *śrāvaka buddhas*? I do not think so, or at least the texts at my disposal do not authorize a supposition of this kind. In my opinion, the bodhi of a śrāvaka is the highest science that a listener can reach; but this listener does not depart for that reason from the category to which he belongs; he is always a disciple of the Buddha, an enlightened disciple, it is true, and the most enlightened of all, but who has still not attained all the perfections of a completely accomplished buddha.

This is so true, that the text I am analyzing places above such educated listeners the *pratyekabuddhas*, or private buddhas, who actually bear this title *buddha*, which does not seem to me to be accorded to the śrāvakas by our books. The pratyekabuddhas are, if I can express myself in this way, egoist buddhas, who possess all the perfections of a buddha, science, power, and charity, minus this character of saviors that belongs to the perfect buddhas alone. Mr. Schmidt expressed their role well when he indicated the difference the Mongol texts make between a true buddha and a pratyekabuddha.[122] When the sūtras and the legends speak of these high personages, they have the custom to repeat the following formula: "When no buddha is born in this world, pratyekabuddhas appear there."[123] These pratyekabuddhas, however, are nowhere represented accomplishing

122. "Über einige Grundlehren des Buddhismus," in *Mémoires de l'Académie des sciences de Saint-Pétersbourg*, 1:241. See also the observations made above, section 2, p. 133, note 46.

123. *Nāgara avalambikā*, in *Divyāvadāna*, fol. 41b; see also fol. 64b.

the deeds that mark the mission of a true buddha. But, I must hasten to say, here we depart from the hierarchy of categories that form the assembly of Śākyamuni, and we enter into this ideal world of beings superior to man, whose invention is perhaps not due entirely to the founder of Buddhism. To return to the special object of the present section, we do not have to go beyond the śrāvakas, the general title, as I have said, of the listeners of the Buddha, and which, with the addition of *mahā* (great), gives rise to the distinction between two categories of listeners, the *śrāvakas* and the *mahāśrāvakas.*

In summary, the assembly of Śākya or, it comes to the same thing, the body of monastic followers of his doctrine was composed of *bhikṣus*, or mendicants, who were also called *śramaṇas*, or ascetics, and among whom the elders took the title *sthaviras*, or old men. The first two titles were absolute designations somehow; but considered in relation to the other members of Indian society, the monks were sometimes called *āryas*, or honorable, and in relation to their master, *śrāvakas*, or listeners. Among the śrāvakas, there were distinguished the *mahāśrāvakas*, or great listeners; this qualification was certainly given to them in consideration of their merit. While acknowledging, as I have proposed, that the designations *śrotāpanna*, *sakṛdāgāmin*, and *anāgāmin* must be applied to the faithful, one must also believe that the advantages promised to those whom these titles designated were not refused to true monks; but these advantages, which were to be realized only beyond the present life, did not constitute grades designed to give a rank in the hierarchy. The only title of this kind is that of *arhat*, or venerable one, which designated a monk far superior to other bhikṣus by his knowledge as well as by his supernatural faculties. Such that, at bottom, and except for the synonyms and the slight nuances just indicated, there were only two orders in the assembly of the true listeners of Śākya: the *bhikṣus* or ordinary monks and the *arhats* or superior monks. The founder of Buddhism himself had two of these titles, that of simple ascetic, *śramaṇa*, which is almost a synonym of *bhikṣu*, and that of *arhat.*

It would not be easy to enter into greater detail concerning the treatises in which one finds some of the points of the religious discipline mentioned; I have shown that in this respect the Nepalese collection is not as rich as would be necessary in order to be able to present the complete picture of the discipline. The precepts of the vinaya are, indeed, mixed with the story of the actions of those whose conduct appears to Śākyamuni worthy of praise or blame; they occur only incidentally, often in a very concise manner, and in the form of allusions to regulations already in practice or at least known. They are concerned with robes, with food, with the hours and the number of meals, with the care to be taken of the vihāra, with the rules to follow for the admission of a monk, an important subject that, as one must expect, is treated in a detailed manner in many legends. I do not hesitate to abstain from more ample details on such diverse subjects, since the excellent analysis of the Dul-va that Csoma de Kőrös has provided makes known in general that which is most interesting in this part of the Tibetan collection, which is, as I could convince myself, composed of translations made of Sanskrit texts, some of which are in our hands.[124] I have already discussed the avadānas of Pūrṇa and of Saṃgharakṣita; I have given the greater part of the *Prātihārya Sūtra*, which is drawn from the collection of the ancient legends, entitled *Divyāvadāna*, and I am certain that if we possessed everything that exists or has existed of Sanskrit texts in Nepal, we would recover the translation in the Tibetan Dul-va. It is thus possible, as far as the discipline is concerned, to fill the lacunae that the collection of the religious books of Nepal offers with the aid of the first thirteen volumes of the Kah-gyur.

It is important, however, to indicate here a remarkable institution, which certainly belongs to the early times of Buddhism, and which is even contemporaneous with Śākya; it is that of confession. One sees it firmly established in the most ancient legends, and it is easy to recognize that it stems from the very foundations of Buddhist beliefs. The fatal law of transmigration attaches, as is known, rewards to good actions and penalties to bad; it even establishes the compensation for the one by the other in offering to the guilty person the means to recover through the practice of virtue. Hence, the origin of expiation, which occupies so much space in Brahmanical law; the sinner, indeed, besides the interest in his present rehabilitation, should desire to collect the fruits of his repentance in another life. This theory is passed into Buddhism, which received it ready-made, together with so many elements that constitute Indian society; but it took a peculiar form there, by which its practical application was perceptibly modified. The Buddhists continued to believe with the brahmans in the compensation of bad actions by good, for they accepted with them that the one was inevitably punished and the other inevitably rewarded. But since, on the other hand, they no longer believed in the moral efficacy of the tortures and torments through which, according to the brahmans, the guilty person could efface his crime, the expiation was naturally reduced to its principle, that is to say, to the sentiment of repentance, and the only form it received in practice was that of admission or confession.

Such is the institution that we find in the legends, and whose first beginnings these treatises recall for us. The legend of Pūrṇa gives an interesting example of it in the story of this monk, who, insulted by another, tells him: "Because of this fault, confess that you have sinned (*atyayam atyayato deśaya*); and thereby this action will be diminished, it will be destroyed, it will be forgiven." The admission of the fault, accompanied by repentance, was its true expiation, as much for

124. "Analysis of the Dul-va," in *Asiatic Researches*, vol. 20, p. 43ff., and in *Journal of the Asiatic Society of Bengal*, 1:1ff.

this life as for the other; and this expiation applied to the three kinds of faults it was possible to commit: the faults of thought, of words, and of actions. One understands that the transition must have been easy from this admission made to the one who had been injured,[125] from this purely individual confession to the public admission made before the assembly of bhikṣus, who are the repositories and the guardians of the law, and once this step was taken, the destiny of this institution was definitively established among the Buddhists. The Tibetan Dul-va informs us that public confession was practiced at the very time of Śākya, and that it took place in the presence of the assembly, on the day of the new and full moon.[126] The guilty person, questioned by Śākya about the action for which he was reproached, had to respond in a loud voice.[127] All of this is confirmed by the legends; I only do not find a trace of the institution of censure of which Csoma speaks.[128] At the time of Śākya, he himself must have been the censor; after his death, this high ministry must have passed into the hands of the chief of the assembly, just as it could have been delegated by him to another monk.

The institution of confession leads us directly to a subject related to it in the most intimate manner, and which has extreme importance in the eyes of Buddhists of all schools; it is the distinction and classification of various kinds of faults, or more generally, casuistry. But to penerate somewhat further into this interesting subject, we should possess the *Prātimokṣa Sūtra*, or the *Sūtra on Freedom*. This book is missing in the collection of Mr. Hodgson, and I only know about it from the very short analysis Csoma has given of the translation the Tibetans inserted into the Dul-va. According to Csoma, this translation comprises two hundred fifty-three rules divided under five headings based on the nature of the faults that these rules have the aim to condemn.[129] Csoma does not indicate the Sanskrit titles of these divisions, or the number of rules contained in each of them, except in two cases. It is nevertheless not impossible to reconstruct the greater part of the Sanskrit titles by comparing an interesting note of Mr. A. Rémusat on the Buddhist discipline among the Chinese[130] to the table of the chapters of the Pāli *pātimokkha*, as my friend Mr. Lassen and I published it long ago and as Mr. Spiegel has recently provided.[131]

The first section of the book, of which Mr. Rémusat reproduces a succinct analysis, has for its title *boluoyi*, which is translated as "corruption, extreme spite." It is composed of four articles, which embrace the four greatest crimes one can be

125. Csoma, "Analysis of the Dul-va," in *Asiatic Researches*, vol. 20, p. 73.
126. *Id. ibid.*, pp. 58 and 79.
127. Csoma, "Analysis of the Dul-va," in *Asiatic Researches*, vol. 20, p. 79.
128. *Id. ibid.*, p. 59.
129. *Id. ibid.*, p. 80.
130. *Foe koue ki*, pp. 104 and 105.
131. *Essai sur le Pāli*, p. 201 and particularly Spiegel, *Kammavakya*, p. 35ff.

guilty of: murder, theft, adultery, and lying. The title *boluoyi* is certainly the Pāli *phārājika* or *pārājika*, which Clough translates as "unpardonable, inexpiable."[132] I do not recall ever having encountered this word in the Sanskrit books of Nepal; it is, however, possible that one can find it there in this same form *pārājika*, an adjective derived from *parāja*, a term that I also do not know, but which I take from *parā* (*retro*) and *aj* (*abigere*), "crime that drives away, pushes behind" the one who was guilty of it. The *pārājikā dhammā* of the Pāli book forms four articles, a number equal to that in the rules of the Chinese *boluoyi*. The monk who had commited one of these crimes was degraded and excluded from the assembly.[133]

The second section has for its title *sengjia fa shisa*, which is translated as "ruin of the saṃgha"; it contains thirteen articles. This title, which corresponds to that of the second section of the *pātimokkha*, according to the list of Mr. Spiegel, is less clear than the previous one. I recognize in it *sengjia* for *saṃgha*, "the assembly"; but the other three syllables, *fa shisa*, are probably altered. In the title *saṃghādisesa*, which Clough makes the second category of faults enumerated in the moral code of monks[134] (which is in accordance with the tradition preserved in the commentary of Buddhaghosa),[135] the end of the word stands for *ādiśesa* and the whole term means: "that which must be declared to the saṃgha from beginning to end." This section contains exactly thirteen articles, like the *sengjia fa shisa* of the Chinese. Faults of this kind, according to Clough, must be confessed before a secret gathering of no less than five monks, which has the right to set the punishment. I have not found this title or that of the first section in the Sanskrit books of Nepal; I still do not know if the Buddhists of the North make regular use of it.

The third section is that of undetermined rules; the title as the Chinese transcribe it is not given. But it is probable that this section corresponds to the third of the *pātimokkha*, which has the title *aniyatā dhammā*;[136] this title indeed lends itself well to the meaning given in the list of Mr. Rémusat. What confirms me in this opinion is that it contains the same number of articles as the Pāli list, that is to say two.

The fourth is that of the rules of the *nisazhi*, a term translated as "to abandon"; these rules relate to love for wealth and are composed of thirty articles. This section corresponds to the fourth of the *pātimokkha*, which has the title

132. *Sinhalese Dictionary*, 2:388, col. 2. Cf. Turnour, "Examination of the Pāli Buddhistical Annals," in *Journal of the Asiatic Society of Bengal*, vol. 6, p. 519.

133. Csoma, "Analysis of the Dul-va," in *Asiatic Researches*, vol. 20, p. 80.

134. *Sinhalese Dictionary*, 2:688, col. 2.

135. Turnour, "Examination of the Pāli Buddhistical Annals," in *Journal of the Asiatic Society of Bengal*, vol. 6, p. 519.

136. Mr. Turnour gives the word *ariyatāni* as the title of this section; I do not doubt that it is a misprint for which he is not responsible.

nissaggiyā dhammā and which also contains thirty articles. The Chinese transcribe and translate this title *nissaggiya* very exactly, which means, "that which is to be renounced."[137]

The fifth section has the title *boyiti* and contains ninety articles; the term *boyiti* means "to fall"; and the title of this section, brought together with the previous one, implies that if one does not abandon the *nissaggiyā dhammā*, one falls into hell. This section corresponds to the fifth of the Pāli *pātimokkha*, which has the title *pācittiyā dhammā* and which contains ninety-two articles.[138] Csoma gives, like the Chinese, ninety articles to the fourth section of the Tibetan *prātimokṣa*. It is clear that the Chinese title *boyiti* is the transcription of *phācittiya* or *pācittiya*, a Pāli term translated by Clough as "sin" and which may be derived from the Sanskrit *prāyaścitta*, "that which one must repent." If this explanation is not erroneous, the translation of the Chinese list is hardly accurate.

The sixth section has the title *boluodi tisheni*; it contains four articles. The Chinese translate this title as "to repent to someone"; this derives from the fact that the faults it designates must be declared to the assembly. This section corresponds to the sixth of the Pāli *pātimokkha*, which has the title *pāṭidesanīyā dhammā* and also contains four articles.[139] This Pāli title is the alteration of the Sanskrit *pratideśanīya*, "declarable to"; I even conclude from the two first syllables of the Chinese transcription *boluo* that it derives from the original Sanskrit (*pra*), rather than from a Pāli form in which the *r* would be regularly omitted.

The seventh section has no title transcribed in Chinese; it contains in one hundred articles the rules prescribed to monks for study. It is obviously the seventh section of the Pāli *pātimokkha*, the title of which is *sekkhiyā dhammā* and which is composed of seventy-five articles.[140] The title *sekkhiyā* corresponds to the Sanskrit *śaikṣya*, which I regard as a derivation, either from *śaikṣa* (student), or from the substantive *śikṣā* (study). It must be translated as "related to students," or better as "related to study." This explanation fits well with the Chinese interpretation.

The eighth section has no title in Chinese either; it contains in seven articles rules for bringing an end to disputes. It is obviously the same section as the eighth of the Pāli *pātimokkha*, whose title is *sattādhikaraṇasamathā*.[141] We have here two words combined into one by the laws of orthography, namely *satta*, "the seven," and *adhikaraṇasamathā*, "pacification of discussions."[142] This title fits exactly, as one sees, with the Chinese definition.

137. Turnour, "Examination," etc., in *Journal of the Asiatic Society of Bengal*, vol. 6, p. 519.

138. *Id. ibid.*, p. 520.

139. *Id. ibid.*

140. *Id. ibid.*

141. *Id. ibid.*

142. The word *adhikaraṇa* means, properly speaking, "subject or matter for discussion." The sense of *discussion* leads right to that of *dispute* (Turnour, *Journal of the Asiatic Society of Bengal*, vol. 6, p. 736).

In summary, our two lists, that of the *Foe koue ki* and that of the Pāli *pātimokkha*, differ only with regard to the titles of some sections. A more important difference is that the Chinese treatise contains two hundred fifty rules, whereas the Pāli *pātimokkha* counts only two hundred fourteen, or more exactly, two hundred twenty-seven, by including in it the thirteen rules of the second section called *saṃghādisesa.* Be that as it may on this point, to which I intend to return later when I deal with the Sinhalese collection, it was not useless to glance quickly at the principal books of the discipline. The restoration of the Chinese transcriptions makes this supposition very likely: that there exists in the collection of the North a *prātimokṣa* that is not essentially different from the *pātimokkha* of the Sinhalese. This supposition becomes almost a certitude when one compares the expression *śikṣāpada*, that is to say, "precepts of the teaching," so frequently used in the texts of Nepal, with that of *sikkhāpada*, which is no less common in those of Ceylon. The interesting report, preserved by a Buddhist commentator, on the first council during which the canonical scriptures had been gathered, indicates to us that the generic name *sikkhāpada* was given to the majority of the rules of discipline.[143] Now the Pāli term *sikkhāpada* is the regular transformation of the Sanskrit *śikṣāpada*, which I do not find defined anywhere in the books of Nepal, but to which I do not hesitate to apply the meaning that the term *sikkhāpada* possesses among the Sinhalese. At present, since these precepts of the teaching encompass, according to the Buddhists of the South, the majority of the ordinances of the discipline, I conclude that the book named *prātimokṣa* in the North contains the same materials as that known in Ceylon under the title *pātimokkha.*

I must not leave this subject without offering some words on the extract Mr. A. Rémusat has given from an interesting book entitled *Shier toutuo jing*, (The Sacred Book of the Twelve Observances).[144] This book is, to all appearances, only a translation of a treatise written originally in Sanskrit; at least one finds in the words *toutuo* the exact transcription of the Sanskrit *dhūta*, that the Chinese derive well from a word meaning "to shake off."[145] But even though the original of this Chinese treatise might be in Pāli, we have a plausible reason to believe that a similar book existed in the North in a Sanskrit form; it is that

143. Mr. Turnour has the merit of having given an excellent translation of this major piece, to which I will return later when I discuss the Sinhalese collection ("Examination of the Pāli Buddhistical Annals," in *Journal of the Asiatic Society of Bengal*, vol. 6, pp. 519 and 520). When I translated the *Sūtra of Māndhātṛ* (above, section 2, p. 118 ff. and p. 123, note 25), I had not fixed the precise signification of the term *śikṣāpada*, which I rendered as "axioms of teaching," giving it a philosophical meaning. The connections set forth in my text tend to prove that this expression applies to the discipline, and this is my feeling today. I thus request the reader to substitute the word *precepts* for the word *axioms* in some passages of the aforementioned sūtra.

144. *Foe koue ki*, p. 60ff.

145. *Foe koue ki*, p. 60.

the titles of the twelve observances of the *Shier toutuo jing* are found enumerated in the Buddhist Vocabulaire Pentaglotte.[146] There they are for the most part clearly corrupt; the alteration, however, does not go so far as to make the characteristic features of the original language disappear. The enumeration in the Vocabulaire Pentaglotte also has another interest: it is possible to compare it with a similar list in current use among the Sinhalese.[147] The list I refer to has the title *teles dhūtaṅga*, in Pāli *terasa dhūtaṅga*, that is to say, "the thirteen rules through which one shakes off sin." We find here again the Chinese *toutuo* of which I have just spoken; it is just the transcription of the Sanskrit *dhūta*, which one must not translate with Clough as "messenger." These two lists, that of the Vocabulaire and that of Clough, certainly differ on some points, even apart from the difference of the two numbers, twelve in one and thirteen in the other. I will indicate these differences following the order of the list in the Vocabulaire, which accords better with that of the Sinhalese than with that of the Chinese treatise. It is a question here, moreover, of the Sanskrit sources of Buddhism, and it is only in passing that I can speak of the Pāli forms peculiar to the Buddhism of the South.

The first of the twelve articles of the Vocabulaire is written *sānpukulika*; it is an incorrect spelling of the term *pāṃśukūlikaḥ*, which in the language of the Buddhists means "wearing rags found in the dust." This term is regularly derived from *pāṃśukūla*, "dustheap"; it is indeed in the piles of rubbish, in the cemeteries, and in other abandoned places that the monks must collect the rags from which their robe is made. This prescription is the first according to the list of the Sinhalese, and it corresponds to the seventh article of the Chinese treatise, related to the rags from which the monks must make patched robes. The injunction that this article contains is certainly one of the most ancient among the Buddhists, and the legends make perpetual allusions to it; for example, when Śākya recommends that the monks sew and wash the pieces of their robes. I add that the Tibetan portion of the Vocabulaire Pentaglotte[148] justifies my reading and my interpretation; the article with which we are occupied is translated there *phyag dar khrod pa*, "what is among the rubbish," according to Shröter,[149] and more exactly, "pile of rubbish." It is, to be truthful, the translation of *pāṃśukūla*, without the adjectival form that this term takes in the list in the Vocabulaire

146. Vocabulaire Pentaglotte, sec. 45.

147. Clough, *Sinhalese Dictionary*, 2:242, col. 2.

148. I owe to the kindness of Mr. Foucaux the list of the Tibetan titles of the twelve sections that follow; he was kind enough to extract it for me from the Vocabulaire Pentaglotte, which was not at my disposal. I do not, however, wish to make him responsible for the interpretations I propose, which he has the means to rectify better than anyone.

149. *Bhotanta Dictionary*, p. 191, col. 1.

Pentaglotte. The name of the cloth made of rags found in the rubbish is *phyag dar khrod kyi gos* in Tibetan, literally "cloth of piles of rubbish."[150]

The second article is regularly written *traicīvarikaḥ*; it means "one who has three robes." It is, like the previous term, an adjective; it is derived from *tricīvara*, "the three robes." This article is also the second in the Sinhalese list: it is naturally written there in the Pāli form *tecīvarikaṅga*; this difference of orthography sufficiently shows that the Vocabulaire Pentaglotte was written from Sanskrit originals, as I have long tried to establish.[151] It corresponds to the eighth injunction of the Chinese treatise, which prescribes that monks possess only three robes at one time. Here again the Tibetan portion of the Vocabulaire Pentaglotte exactly translates the Sanskrit: *chos gos gsum pa*, "one who has the three religious robes."

The third article is written *nāmatikaḥ*; this title is certainly altered and, as it is here, it offers no meaning. In the Tibetan version I find *phying ba can*, which means "one who has a felt or wool blanket." To recognize this meaning in the Sanskrit title, it should be read *kāmbalikaḥ*; but I would not dare, without more proof, to substitute this reading for the orthography *nāmatikaḥ*, from which it is too distant. It is nonetheless true that Buddhist monks must wear a wool mantle, dark yellow in color, and it is evident that the Tibetan interpreters thought that this present article was related to this injunction. But I do not find the least trace of it in the Sinhalese list; there is nothing about this wool robe or the color it must have.

The fourth article is written *peṇḍapātikaḥ*; one must read *piṇḍapātikaḥ*; this term means "one who lives on alms," and it is just in this way that the second paragraph of the note of Mr. Abel Rémusat interpets it. It is the third in the Sinhalese list, where it is written *piṇḍapātikaṅga*. But the Sinhalese, or perhaps only their interpreter B. Clough, seem to have caused a confusion here that it is necessary to disentangle. They translate *piṇḍapāta* as "bowl of alms,"[152] as if *pāta* was synonymous with *patta*, the Pāli transformation of the Sanskrit *pātra* (bowl). I do not believe that this interpretation is admissible, and *piṇḍapāta* appears to me formed from *piṇḍa*, "rice ball" or some other food substance, and from *pāta*, "throwing": the throwing of a ball is here synonymous with the term *alms* of some food. The Tibetans are not of great help here in clarifying the etymology of the word for us; but in translating the term that occupies us as *bsod snyoms pa*, "one who lives on alms," they give us the general and perfectly accurate meaning of *piṇḍapātika*.

The fifth article is written *ekāpanikaḥ*. Mr. A. Rémusat placed it fourth on

150. I find a very clear example of the first three monosyllables of this compound in the Tibetan version of the *Prātihārya Sūtra*, translated above (section 2, p. 196), *De'i phyag dar khrod de dag bkrus nas*, which represents exactly the Sanskrit expression: *tasya pāṃśukūlān dhāvayitvā* (*Dul-va*, vol. *da*, or 11, fol. 35b).

151. In a note inserted in *Mélanges Asiatiques*, 1:452ff.

152. Clough, *Sinhalese Dictionary*, p. 394, col. 2.

his list, and he thought that it related to the injunction that the monks be satisfied with one meal only. I believe this is an error that comes from the apparent analogy of *pānika* with *pātika*. The comparison of the Sinhalese list to the Tibetan version of the Vocabulaire Pentaglotte furnishes us with the means to reconstruct this term, which must certainly be read *ekāsanikaḥ*. The Sinhalese write it *ekāsanikaṅga*, and translate it as "one who always uses the same seat to take his meal." The Tibetans represent our article with the words *stan gcig pa*, "one who has only one seat." The correction of *ekāsanika* for *ekāpanika* is further justified by the observation that in the Vocabulaire Pentaglotte the letter *p* is frequently substituted for *s*. But a doubt can remain on the question of knowing if the Buddhists have not played here on the double meaning this term yields, according to whether it is written with a *ś* or with an *s*: thus the orthography *ekāsanika* in Sanskrit can only have this meaning, "one who has only one seat"; the orthography *ekāśanika* in Sanskrit can only have this meaning, "one who takes one meal only." But in Pāli, since the difference between the *ś* and the *s* has disappeared, *ekāsanika* can have both the first and the second meaning at the same time. One sees that one would justify the interpretation of Mr. A. Rémusat in reading *ekāśanika*; but if the doubtful testimony of the Sinhalese does not oppose this translation, the express assertion of the Tibetans, who see here the meaning of "seat," formally contradicts it.

The sixth article is written *khalupaśvāddhaktiṃkaḥ*; it is the fifth of the list of Mr. A. Rémusat, and this scholar regards it as related to the injunction that forbids the monk from eating more than two-thirds of the portion of alms he has collected. This barbaric term is unintelligible, and if, in order to explain it, it was necessary to adhere to the proposed meaning, we would only find in the Sinhalese list the term *pattapiṇḍikaṅga*, which forbids the monks from eating more than one bowl, an injunction that certainly is included in the fifth article of Mr. Rémusat, but that is not rendered by the same term. Fortunately, the Sinhalese list has another article of which the one that occupies us is, to all appearances, only an alteration; it is *pacchābhattikaṅga*, or the rule that orders the monks to have but one meal a day and not to have it before or after midday. If indeed one restores the Pāli word to Sanskrit, one has *paścādbhaktika*, a term that will not appear too distant from *paśvāddhaktiṃka*, if one goes back to the so easy confusion of the ligatures श्च *śca* or श्व *śva*, and द्भ *dbha* or द्ध *ddha*. There remains *khalu*, which I confess not being able to explain; the meaning of this Sanskrit word ("indeed, namely") has no place here. I am thus still reduced to proposing a conjecture, and starting from the striking resemblance that the ligature स्व *sva* has with the aspirate consonant ख *kha*, I transform *khalu* into *svādu*; and combining this term with the one that follows, I read the whole *svādvapaścād-bhatika*, that is to say, "the one who does not eat sweets after his meal," or after the midday hour, which comes to the same thing. This correction, based in part on the study of the Sinhalese list, seems to me to be placed almost beyond doubt by the sixth article contained in the list of Mr. A. Rémusat, that "the juice of fruits, honey, and other things of the same kind may never be taken by the mendicant past midday." If even this was adopted, it would give us a much preferable expression to that of the Sinhalese list, which, in reality, means "one who eats after," that is to say, exactly the contrary of what the rule forbids. It seems to me completely confirmed by the Tibetan translation of our article: *zas byis mi len pa*, "one who does not take anything after his meal," by reading, as Mr. Foucaux proposed to me, *phyis* (after) instead of *byis*, which does not make any sense.

The seventh article is written *āraṇyakaḥ*; this orthography is accurate, and the word that it reproduces means "one who lives in the forest," as contained in the first paragraph of the list of Mr. A. Rémusat. Here as well, the Vocabulaire Pentaglotte starts obviously from a Sanskrit source; for in Pāli this injunction is expressed as *āraññakaṅga*. The Tibetan version is entirely in accord with this explanation; it represents our article with the words: *dgon pa pa*, "one who lives in solitude." In saying that the monk must live in an *alanruo* place, the Chinese are only transcribing the Sanskrit term *araṇya*.

The eighth article is written *vṛkṣamūlikaḥ*; it is the tenth of the list of Mr. A. Rémusat, that which enjoins the monk to sit under a tree and not to seek other shelter. The word *vṛkṣamūlika* indeed means "one who is near the root of a tree." Here as well the term of the Vocabulaire Pentaglotte is in Sanskrit, for in Pāli this article is written *rukkhamūlikaṅga*. The Tibetan version agrees here with our explanations; it replaces the term with which we are occupied with these words: *shing drung pa*, "one who is under a tree."

The ninth article is written *ābhyavakāśikaḥ*; it is the eleventh item of the list of Mr. A. Rémusat, which enjoins the monk to sit on the ground. The Vocabulaire Pentaglotte again follows the Sanskrit originals here; for in Pāli this article is written *abbhokāsikaṅga*. The Sinhalese give this term an accurate interpretation when they say that it expresses the injunction that the monk is made to live outdoors, without ever being sheltered under a roof or in a house. This explanation clearly results from the meaning *avakāśa*, "open space." It is important to relate this prohibition to the previous one, and one must conclude that the only shelter under which the monk could take refuge was the shade of trees, near the trunks of which he was permitted to sit. The Tibetan version here gives itself a little more latitude; indeed, the expression *bla gab med pa* means, if I understand it well, "one who is not at ease."

The tenth article is written *smāśānikaḥ*; it is the ninth article in the list of Mr. A. Rémusat, and it enjoins the monk to live among tombs. Here again, we have a purely Sanskrit term and one easy to distinguish from the Pāli form, which is *sosānikaṅga.* According to the Sinhalese, this article orders the monk to make only temporary visits to the places where the dead are left; he must go to a cemetery from time to time, in the middle of the night, to meditate on the instability of things human. The Tibetan version is here perfectly accurate: the words *dur khrod pa* indeed mean: "one who is in cemeteries."

The eleventh article is written *naiṣadikaḥ*; it is the twelth item in the list of Mr. A. Rémusat, one which enjoins the monk to be seated and not lie down. We have here again a perfectly recognizable Sanskrit term; the Pāli form in the Sinhalese list is *nesajjikaṅga.* According to Clough, this article enjoins the monk to sleep in the seated position and not to lie down. The Tibetans replace this term with the expression *tsog pu pa*, which our dictionaries translate in this way: "one who is seated with one leg tucked under his body."

The twelfth article is written *yāthāpaṃtari*; it corresponds to the third paragraph in the list of Mr. A. Rémusat, the one that enjoins the monk to keep his rank when he begs. The Sinhalese read and interpret this article slightly differently: according to Clough, it is written *yathāsanthatikaṅga*, and one sees in it the injunction that the monk is made not to change the position of the rug or the mattress on which he lies down, and to leave it as he has spread it out the first time. The Sinhalese interpretation rigorously conforms to the etymology, since if one subtracts the suffix *ika,* the word that remains, *yathāsanthat* for *yathāsanthata*, exactly represents the Sanskrit *yathāsaṃstṛta*, "as it is spread out"; such that the whole article should, in this hypothesis, be read in Sanskrit as *yāthāsamstṛtika*, "one who leaves his rug as it has been spread out the first time." But the examination of the orthography *yāthāpaṃtari*, most incorrect as it is, places us on the track of another reconstruction, which consists of reading *yāthāsaṃstarika*, the adjective formed of *yathāsaṃstara*, "as the rug is." The reading of the Vocabulaire Pentaglotte leads more directly to this correction than that which the orthography of the Sinhalese list suggests to me, and I even prefer it to the supposed reading *yāthāsaṃstṛtika.* But also, one sees, the first and the second take us away from the Chinese interpretation, which orders the monk to keep his rank when he begs. The Tibetan version does not seem to me to settle the question decisively, for the expression *gzhi ji bzhin pa* is so vague as to provide these two interpretations: "one who stays at the place where he is," or [the one who keeps his rug,] "as it has been placed the first time."

The preceding analysis has given us twelve Pāli articles, each of which corresponds to an article of the Vocabulaire Pentaglotte; but the Sinhalese count a thirteenth, which occupies the fourth place in their enumeration. Clough writes it *sapadānacārikaṅga* and translates it: "ordinance that enjoins the monk to live by begging for his food from house to house." One explains this term with *sa* (for *saha*), "with"; *padāna* (for *pradāna*), "gift, alms"; and *cārika*, "who walks," that is to say, "one who walks collecting alms." This rule is so naturally included in that of *piṇḍapātika* that it is not difficult to understand how it can be missing from the enumeration of the Vocabulaire Pentaglotte and from that of the Chinese treatise cited by Mr. A. Rémusat.

I would regret having paused for such a long time over these details if some interesting consequences touching on the habits and life of monks in the early times of Buddhism did not result from them. It is evident that the rules contained in the twelve items just explained belong to an epoch in which the organization of the monks into a body subject to a simple but strong hierarchy and living among wealthy monasteries was still just in its early stages. The obligation to retire to the solitude of the forest, to sit near the trunks of trees, to live outdoors far away from houses or any other shelter, are certainly three early rules. They are even contrary to the institution of vihāras, or monasteries, which are nevertheless rather ancient in Buddhism, and whose need began to be felt as soon as the body of adepts became more numerous. Another institution no less remarkable is the set of rules related to robes. The monk must make the pieces of fabric with which he covers himself from rags collected in cemeteries or among rubbish, and he cannot own more than three of these miserable patched robes. A rug to sit on, a bowl to beg with, this, with these three robes, is what constitutes all his wealth. The brahman, or more exactly the ascetic coming from the Brahmanical caste, certainly felt an even greater detachment, when he lived entirely naked, without thinking of covering this body which he believed to have subjugated; but he offended a sensibility that survives among all men at the inevitable loss of their first innocence. Śākyamuni, on the contrary, gave a great place to modesty in his morality; and it seems that he has wished to make it the safeguard of the chastity he imposed on his disciples. The legends are filled with reproaches he addresses to mendicants who go naked, and the revolting spectacle of their coarseness is compared more than once to the chaste picture of a decently dressed assembly of monks. One is even permitted to believe that the faculty accorded to women to enter into the religious life was not without influence on the rigor of the injunctions related to robes. Who would have been able to tolerate the sight of a naked nun?

Among many examples of the disgust that the Buddhists feel when they encounter naked ascetics, I choose one of the most characteristic: One day, naked mendicants had gathered to take their meal in the house of the mother-in-law of Sumāgadhā, daughter of Anāthapiṇḍika. The mother-in-law said to her daughter-in-law: "My daughter, come to see respectable personages." Sumāgadhā said to herself: "She has undoubtedly invited great listeners like the sthavira Śāradvatīputra (Śāriputra), Mahāmaudgalyāyana, and others." She thus left full of joy and satisfaction; but as soon as she had seen these mendicants wearing their hair in the shape of pigeons' wings, filthy, not having any other robes than the stains that covered them, emitting a bad smell, naked, and looking like demons, she was struck by a keen discontent. "Why are you so sad?" her mother-in-law said to her. Sumāgadhā responded: "O my mother, if respectable personages are like that, how then will sinners be?"[153]

These last words express very well the true feelings of the Buddhists: they make us understand how Śākyamuni could proscribe the practice of living naked while shifting the shame to the tīrthikas.[154] Let us add with Mr. Wilson that the obligation that the monks had to always be covered furnishes archaeology with a characteristic of the first order for the determination of statues or sculpted scenes, which one hesitates sometimes to declare to be Jaina or Buddhist. The scenes in which the religious personages are covered belong most certainly to Buddhism; but one cannot say as much for those where they appear naked. The ascetics or saints who do not wear any robes must be, in all likelihood, declared Jainas; they are personages who, as their name *digambara* indicates, had no other robe than space.[155]

To the details that I have just given concerning those rules of discipline that seem to me most ancient, I believe it useful to add a text that casts light on the life of monks in the vihāras, or monasteries. This text, which I borrow from the *Divyāvadāna*, doubtless contains some ridiculous details; but I did not want to omit anything, in order to see clearly how the compilers of the legends imagined the obligations imposed on the monks gathered in the vihāras. One will judge thereby the importance that these institutions had in the eyes of the Buddhists.

153. *Sumāgadhāvadāna*, fol. 2b.

154. Csoma, "Analysis of the Dul-va," in *Asiatic Researches*, vol. 20, p. 71.

155. Wilson, "Abstract of the Dul-va," in *Journal of the Asiatic Society of Bengal*, vol. 1, p. 4. Mr. Rémusat had already remarked on the fact; but he had not drawn the consequence as it touches on the comparison of Buddhist and Jaina statues (*Fo koue ki*, p. 62). I must not conceal from myself, however, that this distinction between the dressed images of the buddhas and the naked images of the Jainas is formally refuted by Mr. Hodgson, to whose opinion Mr. W. von Humboldt gives unreserved assent. Mr. Hodgson, taking the opportunity of an analysis of the memoirs of Mr. Erskine on the caves of Elephanta, an analysis in which the author (who is perhaps Mr. Wilson) endeavored to place in relief the characteristic indicated by Mr. Erskine (*Quarterly Oriental Magazine*, March 1824, pp. 15 and 16), has expressly denied that the images of the buddhas were always depicted covered with a robe, unlike the images of Jainas, which are ordinarily naked (*Transactions of the Royal Asiatic Society*, vol. 2, pp. 229 and 230). In support of this assertion, he has produced a drawing depicting a sage seated in the posture of a man who is teaching, and in a state of complete nakedness. This proof, as I just indicated, has seemed sufficient to Mr. von Humboldt (*Über die Kawi-Sprache*, 1:115). Despite the deference that moves me to testify to the opinions of two such eminent men, I find that the authenticity of the drawing produced by Mr. Hodgson is not sufficiently established, for it rests only on the authority of one Bhotiya, to whom the English scholar says he is indebted. The testimony of the texts seems to me far superior to that of one isolated drawing whose true date is unknown. The texts that condemn nakedness among the monks are overabundant in the legends. I content myself to add to those that are the subject of the present discussion a passage characteristic of a sūtra quoted above (section 2, p. 208) on the miracles of Śākya.

THE LEGEND OF SAṂGHARAKṢITA[156]

There was in Śrāvastī a householder named Buddharakṣita,[157] wealthy, fortunate, having great riches. This man took a wife in a family equal to his own; then he enjoyed himself with her, with her he indulged himself in pleasure and sensual delight. *When he had enjoyed himself with her, his wife after a certain time became pregnant.[158]* Meanwhile, the respectable Śāriputra entered the house of this man with the intention of converting him, and he taught him and his wife the formulas of refuge and the precepts of the teaching.

After a certain time, the wife of the householder became pregnant. The respectable Śāriputra, recognizing that the moment to convert the child had come, entered the house of Buddharakṣita without anyone following him. The householder said to him: "The venerable Śāriputra then has no śramaṇa behind him who follows him?"[159] "O householder," replied Śāriputra, "do you believe that the śramaṇas who follow us are born for us from the kāśa or kuśa plant?[160] It is the children that your fellow men beget who become the śramaṇas made to follow us." "O venerable one," said the householder Buddharakṣita, "my wife is pregnant; if she brings a son into the world, I will give you this child in order for him to become a śramaṇa and follow you." "Householder," replied Śāriputra, "this is a good idea."

The wife of Buddharakṣita after eight or nine months brought a son into the world, beautiful, pleasant to see, delightful, having a white complexion, skin the color of gold; his head had the shape of a parasol; his arms were long, his forehead large, his eyebrows joined together, his nose prominent. The relatives, having gathered after three times seven or twenty-one days, celebrated the festival of the birth of the child in a splendid manner and concerned themselves

156. *Divyāvadāna*, fol. 164b of the MS of the Société Asiatique, fol. 207a of my manuscript. *Bka' 'gyur*, sec. *Dul-va*, vol. *ka*, or 1, fol. 147. Csoma, *Asiatic Researches*, vol. 20, p. 55. This story is preceded by a preamble that is related to the legend of the two nāgas or fabulous serpents named Nanda and Upananda, which contains the prohibition that Śākya makes against the receiving of the teaching by a man whose existence is not well demonstrated. This prohibition is made on the occasion of a nāga who had taken on the appearance of a monk. The Buddhists imagine that nāgas can transform themselves into any being they desire and that they are only forced to take on their true form to accomplish some of the acts that constitute their own individuality.

157. We already know a similar name that has been preserved by Brahmanical literature; this is the Buddharakṣita who is one of the disciples of Kāmandakī, this Buddhist nun who appears in the *Mālatīmādhava*. With the words *buddha*, *dharma*, and *saṃgha*, the Buddhists form proper nouns that mean respectively: "protected by the Buddha, by the law, and by the assembly."

158. The sentence I have placed between two asterisks is found in my two Sanskrit manuscripts, but is missing in the Tibetan version; it appears almost evident to me that it is only an interpolation of the copyists.

159. This makes allusion to the rule that forbids a monk to enter into the house of a layman without being followed by another monk, either already ordained or simply a novice; such a monk is called *paścātśramaṇa*, "*śramaṇa* who comes behind." We have already seen a similar allusion to this profoundly moral custom in the sūtra related to the miracles of Śākya during his battle with the tīrthikas (above, section 2, p. 197).

160. The *kāśa* is the *saccharum spontaneum* and the *kuśa* is the *poa cynosuroides*.

with giving him a name. "What name will the child have?" [said some; others responded:] "This child is the son of the householder Buddharakṣita; let him thus receive the name Saṃgharakṣita." The day when Saṃgharakṣita was born, five hundred merchants each had a son who came into the world, and to whom they gave a name conforming to that of their family. The young Saṃgharakṣita was fed and raised with milk, with curds, with fresh butter, with clarified butter, with the froth of butter, and with other kinds of hot seasoning; and he grew rapidly, like a lotus in a pond. When he was grown, the respectable Śāriputra, recognizing that the time to convert him had come, entered the house of Buddharakṣita without being followed by anyone, and began to give a sign [of his presence]. The householder Buddharakṣita then said to Saṃgharakṣita: "O my son, you were not yet born when I had already given you to the venerable Śāriputra in order for you to become a śramaṇa and to follow him." This young man who had entered into his last existence attached himself to the respectable Śāriputra closely and followed him continuously. Introduced by Śāriputra into the religious life, he received from him investiture and the knowledge of the four collections of commandments (*āgamas*).

Some time after that, five hundred merchants, having gathered the merchandise intended for a sea voyage and desiring to embark on the great ocean, said to themselves: "Why, friends, would we not embark with an ārya with us, in order for him to teach us the law when we are in the middle of the great ocean?" Others responded to them: "Friends, here is the ārya Saṃgharakṣita, who is our age, who was born at the same time as us, who has played in the dust with us;[161] it is he who must embark with us." They thus went to him and said to him: "O Saṃgharakṣita, the ārya, you are our age, you were born at the same time as us, you have played in the dust with us. We are departing for the great ocean; come then to embark with us; when we are in the middle of the great ocean, you will teach us the law." "I am not my own master," replied Saṃgharakṣita. "Address my preceptor." The merchants thus went to the place where the respectable Śāriputra was, and when they arrived there, they said to him: "O Śāriputra the ārya! Here is the ārya Saṃgharakṣita, who is our age, who was born at the same time as us, who has played in the dust with us. We are departing for the great ocean; consent to his embarking with us; when we are on the great ocean, he will teach us the law." Śāriputra responded to them: "Address the Bhagavat." Consequently, they went to the Bhagavat and said to him: "O Bhagavat, we are departing for the great ocean; here is Saṃgharakṣita the ārya, who is our age, who was born at the same time as us, who has played in the dust with us; con-

161. The two Sanskrit manuscripts read *sahaprāṃśukṛḍanaka*, which, if need be, could be translated as "who has height and games in common." But I have followed the Tibetan, which comes from a text where one reads *pāṃśu*, "dust," instead of *prāṃśu*, "who is tall."

sent to his embarking with us; when we are on the great ocean, he will teach us the law."

The Bhagavat then had this reflection: "What are the roots of virtue, whatever they are, that these people possess? Does there exist one on whom these roots of virtue depend? Yes, it is the monk Saṃgharakṣita." Consequently, he addressed Saṃgharakṣita in this way: "Go, Saṃgharakṣita, you will have to go through redoubtable dangers and situations." The respectable Saṃgharakṣita testified his assent to the words of the Bhagavat with his silence.

Then, the five hundred merchants, after having invoked the blessings and the favor of heaven on their enterprise, loaded a great quantity of merchandise onto carts, onto yokes, on the backs of porters,[162] in baskets on camels, on oxen, on donkeys, and set out for the great ocean. After having traveled successively through a great number of villages, cities, districts, hamlets, walled cities, they finally arrived at the seashore, and having had a vessel constructed by a skilled worker, they embarked on the great ocean, taking their riches with them. When they had reached the middle of the great ocean, nāgas seized their vessel. Then, they began to implore the divinities: "May the divinity," they exclaimed, "who lives in the midst of the great ocean, whether a deva, a nāga, or a yakṣa, let us know what it desires." Immediately, a voice came from the middle of the great ocean: "Deliver to us the ārya Saṃgharakṣita." The merchants responded: "The ārya Saṃgharakṣita is our age, he was born at the same time as us, he has played in the dust with us; the respectable Śāriputra has entrusted him to us, and he was given by the Bhagavat. It would be better for us to perish with him than to abandon the ārya Saṃgharakṣita." The respectable Saṃgharakṣita, having heard these words, said to them: "Friends, what are you saying?" "O Saṃgharakṣita the ārya," responded the merchants, "a voice has come from the middle of the ocean that has said: 'Deliver to us the ārya Saṃgharakṣita.'" "Why then do you not deliver him?" said the ārya. "It is," replied the merchants, "because you are the same age as us, you were born at the same time as us, you have played in the dust with us; the respectable Śāriputra has entrusted you to us, and you are given by the Bhagavat. It would be better for us to perish with you than to abandon you."

The respectable Saṃgharakṣita had the following reflection: "This is the fulfillment of the words that the Bhagavat has said to me: 'You will have to go through redoubtable dangers and situations.'" Having thus taken his alms bowl and his robe, he proceeded to throw himself into the great ocean. He was seen by the merchants, who exclaimed: "What are you doing, O Saṃgharakṣita the ārya? What are you going to do?" But while they shouted, the ārya had already fallen into the great ocean.

162. I read *ūḍhaiḥ*, taken in an active sense, instead of *mūḍhaiḥ* (insane) that the Tibetan version translates as *sbyangs pa*, a word whose known meaning does not seem to fit here.

Immediately, the vessel was freed, and the ārya, taken by the nāgas, was led by them to their palace. "O Saṃgharakṣita," they told him, "here is the hall of perfumes[163] of the perfectly accomplished buddha Vipaśyin; here is that of Śikhin, that of Viśvabhū, that of Krakuchanda, that of Kanakamuni, that of Kāśyapa; here is that of the Bhagavat. O Saṃgharakṣita the ārya, the sūtras and the mātṛkā of the Bhagavat are placed among devas and among humans;[164] but we who are only nāgas, we have vile bodies. May the ārya Saṃgharakṣita thus establish here as well the four collections of commandments (*āgamas*)!" "May it be so," responded the ārya.

Consequently, he chose three nāgakumāras (princes of the nāgas); to one, he said: "You, read the short collection"; to the second: "You, read the medium collection"; to the third: "You, read the long collection." Another [Bhadramukha] said in his turn:[165] "As for me, I will clarify the supplemental collection whose form is pure." The nāgas thus began to study. The first received the teachings with closed eyes; the second received it with his back turned; the third received it from afar. Of these nāgas, only the fourth was respectful, filled with deference, and always ready to immediately fulfill his duties. "Rise, respectable one" [said the master to him]; "remove the stick for cleaning the teeth; sweep the circle that surrounds the Bhagavat and honor the monument of the Buddha; eat, prepare your bed."

After some time, all of the nāgas had read the collections of commandments. The [fourth] nāga said to Saṃgharakṣita: "Ārya, these nāgas have read the collections of commandments; will they remember them?" "Since they have memory," replied the ārya, "they will remember them; however, there is a fault in them." "And what fault, ārya?" "It is that they all have lacked respect and deference: the first has received the teachings with closed eyes; the second has received it with his back turned; and the third has received it from afar. You alone have been respectful, filled with deference and always ready to fulfill your duties immediately." "It is not," replied the nāga, "that they have lacked respect and deference. The one who has received the teaching with closed eyes has poison in his eyes.

163. That is to say, the hall where one burns perfumes in honor of a buddha and before his image. See above, p. 269, note 32.

164. This passage seems to me to prove that the mātṛkā corresponds to the Abhidharma, or metaphysics; for the Buddhists of Ceylon believe that the Abhidharma has been revealed to gods and the sūtra to humans.

165. The text simply says *sa kathayati*, "he said," which seems to refer to Saṃgharakṣita; it is in this way that I understood it at first reading, and that I translated it in speaking of the āgamas (above, section 1, p. 96). But the rest of the text seems to me to prove that it is a matter of another nāga, whose intervention is necessary for the understanding of the piece and who is called Bhadramukha a little later. Besides, nothing is more confused or more imperfect than the exposition of this legend. The compiler took no care to indicate the personages of the dialogue with precision; he calls all of them *he*, exactly as a man without any education does in France. It is not certain that among all these "he said," I am not sometimes led astray. Furthermore, there are perhaps some lacunae in the text.

The one who has received it with his back turned has poison in his breath. The one who has received the teaching from afar has poison in his touch. I alone have poison in my teeth." The ārya, frightened, became pale, his color changed, he grew weak, lost the use of his strength, fell into a swoon and fainted. The nāga said to him: "O ārya, why do you become pale? Why does your color change, you grow weak, lose the use of your strength, fall into a swoon and faint?" "O Bhadramukha," replied the ārya, "I see that I live among enemies. If it happens that one among you becomes angry at another, nothing will remain of me but a hollow name." "We will not harm the ārya," responded the nāga; "but do you desire to return to Jambudvīpa?" "Yes, I desire it," replied Saṃgharakṣita. Immediately, the vessel of the merchants appeared before the ārya, and he was thrown into it by the nāgas.

As soon as the merchants saw him, they told him: "Be welcome, O Saṃgharakṣita the ārya." "Rejoice, friends," exclaimed the latter. "I have established the four collections of commandments among the nāgas." "We rejoice, O Saṃgharakṣita," replied the merchants. Having thus set their vessel in motion, they continued their voyage. Reaching the seashore after some time, all the merchants lay down and fell asleep; but the respectable Saṃgharakṣita started to gaze at the great ocean. The Bhagavat has said: "There are five things, O monks, that one does not grow tired of looking at: they are an elephant, a nāga, a king, the ocean, and a high mountain; one also does not grow tired of seeing the Buddha, who is the best of the blessed ones." He stayed awake for a long time, engaged in looking at the great ocean; but at the last watch of the night he felt overwhelmed and fell into a deep sleep.

The merchants, for their part, having risen before the end of the night, reloaded their baggage and resumed their journey. In the morning, when it was daylight, they said to one another: "Where then is the ārya Saṃgharakṣita?" Some responded: "He walks ahead." Others said: "He comes behind"; finally others: "He is in the middle of the caravan." In the end, all exclaimed: "We are separated from the ārya Saṃgharakṣita: it is not a good deed that we have done; we must retrace our steps." Others then said: "Lords, the ārya Saṃgharakṣita is endowed with great supernatural faculties; he has great power; could one who, falling into the middle of the ocean and not dying, perish today? It is certain that he has gone ahead; come, let us go." Consequently, the merchants continued on their journey.

Meanwhile, the respectable Saṃgharakṣita was struck in the morning by the rays of the sun, which had just risen, and being awake, he did not see anyone. "The merchants have departed," [he said to himself]; and taking a narrow path, he set off on his way. He reached a forest of śālas, where he saw a vihāra furnished with platforms and high seats, balustrades, windows made of trellis, œils-de-bœuf; and he saw monks suitably dressed there, peaceful, and in calm and decent postures. The ārya made his way toward them and immediately they said to him: "Be welcome, respectable Saṃgharakṣita." Then, they provided him with the means to relax and when he was rested, they led him into the vihāra. There, he saw a beautiful seat and a beautiful bed intended for him, and food purely prepared, which was served. "Are you thirsty, are you hungry, Saṃgharakṣita?" the monks said to him. "I am thirsty and hungry," responded the ārya. "Thus, eat, respectable Saṃgharakṣita." "I will eat among the assembly," replied the ārya. "Eat, Saṃgharakṣita," said the monks; "[without that] there will be punishment." He thus ate, and when he had taken his meal, he withdrew to the side and sat there. After some time, the sound of the metal plate that is struck to [call] the monks having been heard, each of them came to sit in his row, holding his bowl in his hand. And immediately, the vihāra vanished; in place of bowls there appeared iron hammers, and with these hammers the monks smashed one another's skulls, shouting in pain. This lasted until the moment when the evening came. Then, the vihāra reappeared again, and with it the monks, calm and in decent postures. The respectable Saṃgharakṣita came before them and said to them: "Who thus are you, respectable monks, and following what action were you born here?" "Respectable Saṃgharakṣita," they responded, "the men of Jambudvīpa are difficult to persuade; you are not going to believe us." "I am an eyewitness," he responded. "Why would I not believe you?" "We were, O respectable Saṃgharakṣita, listeners of Kāśyapa, the perfectly accomplished Buddha. A fight broke out one day among us at the moment when we gathered for the meal. Because we then did battle, we were born here, in hells that recur every day.[166] It is established that when death has taken us from this world, we will have to be reborn in the infernal regions. This is why, O Saṃgharakṣita, it is good that when you have returned to Jambudvīpa, you announce to those who fulfill the duties of the religious life with you: 'Do not do battle in the assembly, for fear of experiencing pain and a despair like that to which the listeners of Kāśyapa are condemned.'"

Saṃgharakṣita left these monks and reached a second vihāra furnished with platforms and high seats, balustrades, windows made of trellis, œils-de-bœuf; and he saw monks suitably dressed there, disciplined, peaceful, and in calm and decent postures. The ārya made his way toward them and immediately they said to him: "Be welcome, respectable Saṃgharakṣita." Then, they provided him the means to relax and when he was rested, they led him into the vihāra. There, he saw a beautiful seat and a beautiful bed that were intended for him and food purely prepared that was served; and they said to him: "Eat, respectable

166. The hell where these monks suffer is probably the type of which Des Hautesrayes speaks, and which he defines as hells dispersed on the surface of the earth, at the shores, and in isolated places. They are naturally distinct from the places of suffering that belong to each system of creation, and which appear there at the same time as the sinners ("Recherches sur la Religion de Fo," in *Journal Asiatique*, vol. 8, p. 82).

Saṃgharakṣita." The ārya, having reflected, took his meal in order not to incur punishment; and when he had taken his meal, he withdrew to the side and sat. After some time, the sound of the metal plate that is struck to [call] the monks having been heard, each of them came to sit in his row, holding his bowl in his hand. And immediately, the vihāra vanished; in the place of the rice and the drink of the monks there appeared liquid iron, and with this iron the monks splashed one another, uttering cries of pain. This lasted until the moment when the evening came. Then, the vihāra reappeared again, and with it the peaceful monks in calm and decent postures. The respectable Saṃgharakṣita came before them and said to them: "Who thus are you, respectable monks, and following which action were you born here?" "Respectable Saṃgharakṣita," they responded, "the men of Jambudvīpa are difficult to persuade; you are not going to believe us." "I am an eyewitness," he responded. "Why would I not believe you?" "We were, O respectable Saṃgharakṣita, listeners of Kāśyapa, the perfectly accomplished Buddha. One day, it happened that the assembly having received oil, monks suddenly arrived as guests. Then, giving way to our avarice, we conceived the thought to eat only when these newcomers had departed, and we did as we had planned. After seven days, bad weather arrived that made our rice and our drink go bad. As for us, because we had put to our use that which we should have given with faith, we were born here, in hells that recur every day. It is established that when death has taken us from this world, we will have to be reborn in the infernal regions. This is why, respectable Saṃgharakṣita, it is good that when you have returned to Jambudvīpa, you announce to those who fulfill the duties of the religious life with you: 'Do not use for yourself that which you have to give with faith, for fear of experiencing pains and a despair like that to which the brahmans of Kāśyapa are condemned.'"

Saṃgharakṣita left these monks, and reached a third vihāra furnished with platforms and high seats, balustrades, windows made of trellis, œils-de-bœuf, in which things happened as in the two others. When the respectable Saṃgharakṣita had eaten, he withdrew to the side and sat. At the moment when the sound of the metal plate that is struck to [call] the monks was heard, the vihāra caught fire, appeared ablaze, fell prey to the flames, and was consumed. And the monks, crying out in pain, were devoured by the flames until the evening came. Then, the vihāra reappeared again, and with it the peaceful monks in calm and decent postures. The respectable Saṃgharakṣita came before them and said to them: "Who thus are you, respectable monks, and following which action were you born here?" "Respectable Saṃgharakṣita," they responded, "the men of Jambudvīpa are difficult to persuade; you will not believe us." "I am an eyewitness," he responded. "Why would I not believe you?" "We were, respectable Saṃgharakṣita, listeners of Kāśyapa, the perfectly accomplished Buddha. Since we had bad conduct, we were expelled by the monks who were good. We went to settle in a deserted vihāra. There, a monk came one day who had moral conduct; so we then conceived this idea: 'If this monk stays with us, he will be sufficient on his own to attract alms for us.' The monk thus stayed in our vihāra. The presence of this monk again attracted to the monastery a great number of monks endowed with moral conduct. These newcomers expelled us once more from this place. Led astray by resentment, we gathered wood, grass, and dried cow dung, and we set fire to the vihāra. There many people were burned, as many among the students as among the masters.[167] And we, for having made these people perish by fire, we were born here, in hells that recur every day. It is established that when death has taken us from this world, we will have to be reborn in the infernal regions. This is why, respectable Saṃgharakṣita, it is good that when you have returned to Jambudvīpa, you announce to those who fulfill the duties of the religious life with you: 'Do not conceive spiteful thoughts against those who fulfill religious duties with you, for fear of experiencing pains and a despair like that to which the brahmans of Kāśyapa are condemned.'"

The respectable Saṃgharakṣita left these monks. He soon saw beings whose form resembled that of a column, a wall, a tree, a leaf, a flower, a fruit, a rope, a broom, a bowl, a mortar, a cauldron. The respectable Saṃgharakṣita arrived in a district. There, in a hermitage, lived five hundred ṛṣis; seeing the respectable Saṃgharakṣita from afar, they said to one another: "Let us continue with our ordinary pursuits: these śramaṇas, sons of Śākya,[168] are great talkers; none among us should say one word to this one." Consequently, they continued engaging in their ordinary pursuits. The respectable Saṃgharakṣita, having come before them, started to ask them for hospitality; but no one said a single word.

There was in the hermitage a ṛṣi whose dispositions were virtuous. "Why," he said to the religious, "do you not give hospitality [to this ārya]? You thereby commit a sin; you are nothing but big talkers. Respectable monk, I will immediately give you asylum, unless you demand something else." "Ṛṣi," responded the respectable Saṃgharakṣita, "may it be so." Then, the ṛṣi started alone to survey the countryside, and he found there a small hut that was vacant. He said to

167. The text says *śaikṣāśaikṣa*. It is quite clear that it is a matter here at once of those who receive instruction and of those who give it; the etymology of the word *śaikṣa* and of its opposite *aśaikṣa* is sufficient to prove it. But the precise nuance that the first of these terms expresses is not perfectly known to me, because I have not encountered it in such a great number of passages. The vocabulary of Hemacandra, who in his capacity as a Jaina was more versed in Buddhist things than a brahman could be, places the term *śaikṣa* immediately after that of *śiṣya*, which is the proper word to designate a student, a disciple (*Hemacandrakośa*, chap. 1, st. 79a). The *śaikṣa* is distinguished from the *śiṣya* in that he is *prathamakalpika*, a title that probably means "one who receives the first instructions." The term *aśaikṣa* is easier to specify, thanks to the Pāli Vocabulary of Clough. The *Abhidhānappadīpikā* makes it a synonym of *arhat* (*Pāli Grammar and Vocabulary*, p. 2, line 2). This term means properly "one who is not *śaikṣa*." If it designates the arhat, it is doubtless as having crossed through all the degrees of the teaching.

168. It is again one of the names given to the followers of Śākya; it is familiar to all schools; but it does not appear very often in our legends of the North.

Saṃgharakṣita: "Lay down in this small hut." The respectable Saṃgharakṣita proceeded to water, to clean, to sweep his hut, and to cover the ground with fresh cow dung. The other religious saw it and said to one another: "These śramaṇas, sons of Śākya, like cleanliness." The respectable Saṃgharakṣita, after having washed his feet outside the hut, entered it and sat there with crossed legs, keeping his body straight, and placing his memory before his mind.

The divinity who resided in the hermitage went to the hut of Saṃgharakṣita around the first watch of the night, and when she had arrived, she said to him: "O Saṃgharakṣita, set forth the law." "You are happy, O goddess," Saṃgharakṣita said to her. "Do you not see that I have obtained an asylum only by making the ordinary preparations myself? Is it that you wish to chase me away?" The goddess reflected: "His body is fatigued, let him sleep; I will return at the middle watch." She thus returned at the second watch and said to him: "O Saṃgharakṣita the ārya, set forth the law." "You are happy, O goddess," Saṃgharakṣita responded to her. "Do you not see that I have obtained an asylum only by making the ordinary preparations myself? Is it that you wish to chase me away?" The goddess reflected: "His body is fatigued, let him sleep; I will return at the last watch." She thus returned at the last watch and said to him: "O Saṃgharakṣita the ārya, set forth the law." "You are happy, O goddess," Saṃgharakṣita responded to her. "Do you not see that I obtained an asylum only by making the ordinary preparations myself? Is it that you wish to chase me away?" "Ārya Saṃgharakṣita," replied the goddess, "it is now day. If you are chased away, you will leave. Did the Bhagavat not say to you: 'You will have to go through redoubtable dangers and situations.'" The respectable Saṃgharakṣita reflected: "She speaks well. If I am chased away, I will leave." Then, he reflected again: "These ṛṣis are brahmans; I will speak to them in a language suitable to brahmans."

Consequently, the respectable Saṃgharakṣita started to instruct this gathering of brahmans: "It is not the custom of going naked," he said to them, "or plaited hair, or the use of clay, or the choice of different types of food, or the habit of lying on the bare ground, or dust, or dirtiness, or the vigilance to flee the shelter of a roof,[169] which are capable of dispelling the trouble into which unsatisfied desires throw us; but should a man who is master of his senses, calm, meditative, chaste, avoiding harm to any creature, accomplish the law, he will be, though adorned with ornaments, a brahman, a śramaṇa, a monk." The brahmans heard him and had this reflection: "This language is congenial to the sentiments

169. I translate the term *utkuṭuka-prahāna* in this way; it is probable that the first is an alteration of the Sanskrit *kuṭungaka* (roof) or also of *kuṭūka* (parasol). The Tibetan translates this word by *rtsog bu'i spong*, which is missing in Csoma de Kőrös; but *rtsog* (derived from *rtseg*) can mean "floor" and *rtsog bu*, "house with floors."

of a brahman"; and consequently, first one brahman came to him, then two, then three, until at last they all came to him.

The goddess, however, pronounced a benediction whose effect was that they remained invisible to one another. Then, the respectable Saṃgharakṣita taught them the sūtra that is similar to a city,[170] and recited this stanza: "May all the beings who are gathered here, whether they are on earth or in the air, show charity to creatures without ceasing, and may they accomplish the law day and night!"[171] While he preached this exposition of the law, all these brahmans, at the moment they recognized the truths, obtained the fruits of the state of anāgāmin and acquired supernatural faculties. All in a unanimous voice caused to be heard this exclamation: "Well spoken, respectable Saṃgharakṣita." The miracle that the goddess had performed with the aid of her supernatural power was destroyed, and the brahmans started to see one another, and each one said to the other: "Thus, you too have arrived?" "Yes, I have come also." "This is good." As soon as they had seen the truths, they said: "Enable us to enter, O Saṃgharakṣita, into the religious life under the discipline of the well-renowned law! Enable us to obtain investiture and the rank of monk! Let us accomplish the duties of religious conduct in the presence of the Bhagavat."[172] Then, the respectable Saṃgharakṣita said to them: "Will it be before me that you will enter into the religious life or before the Bhagavat?" "Before the Bhagavat," they responded. "If this is so," replied the respectable Saṃgharakṣita, "come, let us find the Bhagavat." "By which means will we come to him?" said the brahmans. "Will it be with the aid of our supernatural faculties or with the aid of yours?" The respectable Saṃgharakṣita then had this reflection: "If these brahmans have acquired through my teaching this multitude of qualities, it must be that I myself have become like a vessel [to carry them to the other shore]"; then he said to the brahmans: "Wait an instant." Then, having withdrawn near the trunk of a tree, he sat with crossed legs, keeping his body straight, again placing his memory before his mind. The Bhagavat has said: "Five advantages are assured to one who has heard much: he is skilled in the knowledge of the elements, in that of the successive production of the causes, in that of what is established and what is not established; lastly his instruction and his teaching do not depend on another. After long efforts, after deep studies and application, he obtains, through the annihilation of all corruptions of evil, to see the state of arhat face to face. Having become an arhat, free from all at-

170. I have not found this sūtra or anything that resembles it in our collection of Nepal. This title comes perhaps from the fact that the core of this treatise was a simile or a parable taken from a city. There is in the *Lotus of the Good Law* a parable in which there figures a caravan that is searching for the city of diamonds.

171. The Tibetan version introduces here a piece of five and a half leaves or eleven pages, which is probably the sūtra entitled in the text "Similar to a City": this sūtra is put in the mouth of the Bhagavat.

172. The Tibetan version inserts a long piece here on the duties and rewards of the religious life.

tachment to the three worlds, he becomes, as it has been said elsewhere, worthy of being adored, venerated, saluted." The respectable Saṃgharakṣita then said to the brahmans: "Hold on to the end of my robe and let us go." The brahmans consequently clung to the end of the robe of Saṃgharakṣita. Then, this latter, like the king of swans with outstretched wings, soaring into the air with the aid of his supernatural power, left this place and departed.

At that moment the five hundred merchants [mentioned above] were occupied with unloading their merchandise. They saw a shadow that fell on them and caught sight of Saṃgharakṣita. "Here you are thus returned, Saṃgharakṣita the ārya!," they exclaimed. "Yes, here I am returned." "Where are you going now?" "These five hundred sons of good family," he responded, "desire to enter into the religious life in the presence of the Bhagavat, under the discipline of the well-renowned law; they ask for investiture and the rank of monk." "And we also, Saṃgharakṣita," replied the merchants. "We will enter into the religious life. Descend for a little while so we can unload our merchandise." The respectable Saṃgharakṣita descended, and the traders unloaded their merchandise. Then, the respectable Saṃgharakṣita, taking these one thousand sons of good family with him, went toward the place where the Bhagavat was.

At that moment, the Bhagavat, seated in the presence of an assembly formed by several hundred monks, taught the law. The Bhagavat caught sight of the respectable Saṃgharakṣita and seeing him from afar, he again addressed the monks: "Here is the monk Saṃgharakṣita, who comes with a present. For the Bhagavat there is no present more precious than the gift of a man to convert." The respectable Saṃgharakṣita arrived in that instant at the place where the Bhagavat was; and when he had arrived, having saluted the feet of the Bhagavat by touching them with his head, he went to sit on the side and spoke to him in these terms: "These thousand sons of good family, Lord, desire to enter into the religious life under the discipline of the well-renowned law; they ask for investiture and the rank of monk. May the Bhagavat, through compassion for them, consent to receive them into the religious life, to give them investiture." The Bhagavat then addressed the formula to them: "Approach, monks!" And as soon as he had pronounced the words: "Approach, monks, enter into the religious life," all found themselves shaved and dressed in the religious mantle, having hair and a beard of seven days, and provided with the begging bowl and the pitcher that ends in the beak of a bird; they appeared with the decent aspect of monks who would have received investiture a hundred years ago. "Approach," the Tathāgata said again to them; and then, shaved, covered with the religious mantle, immediately feeling calm descending in all their senses, they stood, then sat, with the permission of the Buddha. The Bhagavat then gave them the teaching; and after long effort, after deep studies and application, they obtained, through the annihilation of all corruptions of evil, to see the state of arhat face to face. Having become arhats, *free from all attachment to the three worlds, viewing gold and a lump of earth in the same way, looking on space and the palm of the hand as equal, having the same feelings for sandalwood and for the axe [that cuts it], having broken the eggshell by means of wisdom, having acquired the science, the supernatural knowledges, and the accomplished wisdom, turning their back on existence, on profit, on pleasure, and honor, they became those whom all the devas accompanied by Indra and Upendra* worship, honor, and salute.[173]

The respectable Saṃgharakṣita addressed the Blessed Buddha in this way: "I saw, Lord, in this world beings whose form resembles that of a wall, a column, a tree, a flower, a fruit, a rope, a broom, a bowl, a mortar, a cauldron; I saw those whose bodies, divided down the middle, walked supported only by muscles. What is the action, Lord, of which these metamorphoses are the consequence?" The Bhagavat responded to him: "Those whom you have seen, O Saṃgharakṣita, in the form of a wall, have been listeners of Kāśyapa, the perfectly accomplished Buddha. They soiled the wall of the assembly hall with their mucus and their saliva. The result of this action is that they have taken the form of a wall. Those whom you have seen in the form of columns have been changed in that way for the same reason. The beings that you have seen, O Saṃgharakṣita, in the form of a tree were listeners of Kāśyapa, the perfectly accomplished Buddha; they enjoyed flowers and fruits of the assembly out of entirely personal interest. The result of this action is that they have taken the form of a tree. Those whom you have seen in the form of leaves, flowers, fruits have been changed in that way for the same reason. The one you have seen, O Saṃgharakṣita, having the form of a rope has been one of the listeners of Kāśyapa, the perfectly accomplished Buddha; he used the rope of the assembly out of entirely personal interest. The result of this action is that he has taken the form of a rope. It is the same as the preceding for the one you have seen in the form of a broom. The one that you have seen, O Saṃgharakṣita, in the form of a cup has been one of the listeners in the order of novices under Kāśyapa, the perfectly accomplished Buddha. One day he was charged with cleaning the cups and when he had finished washing them, suddenly foreign monks arrived. They asked him: 'O novice, does the assembly still have something to drink?' 'There is nothing left,' he responded; and the monks, in despair, had to continue on their way; and meanwhile, the assembly still had something to drink. The result of this action is that he has been changed into a cup. The one you have seen, O Saṃgharakṣita, in the form of a mortar has been one of the listeners of Kāśyapa, the perfectly accomplished Buddha. One day when the moment to use his bowl had come, he approached a novice who had acquired the

173. The part of this sentence included between two asterisks is borrowed from the Tibetan version. The Sanskrit original abridges the text by means of the formula *pūrvavat*, "as above"; but it is found more or less complete in other legends.

merits of an arhat and said to him: 'Novice, crush a small piece of sesame cake and give it to me.' 'Sthavira,' responded the novice to him, 'wait an instant, I am busy; when I have finished, I will give you what you ask.' Filled with impatience by this answer, the sthavira replied: 'Do you know that if it pleased me, I would throw you in this mortar and crush you there? All the more reason I can do the same to a sesame cake.' Now because he had uttered words of violence against an arhat, the result of this action is that he has taken the form of a mortar.

"Those that you have seen, O Saṃgharakṣita, in the form of cauldrons have been servants [of monks] under Kāśyapa, the perfectly accomplished Buddha. One day when they made boiled medicines for the monks, they broke the cauldron, which did harm to these monks. The result of this action is that they have taken the form of a cauldron.

"The one you have seen, O Saṃgharakṣita, walking with a body divided down the middle, and supported only by muscles has been a man who entered into the religious life under the teaching of Kāśyapa, the perfectly accomplished Buddha. Greedy for profit, he was in the habit of transforming what he earned in the summer into supplies for winter, and what he earned in the winter into supplies for summer. The result of this action is that he walks with a body divided down the middle and supported only by his muscles."[174]

The monks, feeling doubts growing in their mind, addressed the following question to the Blessed Buddha who settles all doubts: "Where did the nāgakumāra [Bhadramukha] begin to experience faith?" The Bhagavat responded to them as follows: "Long ago, O monks, in this very bhadrakalpa[175] in which we are, when the length of the life of creatures was twenty thousand years, there appeared in the world a venerable tathāgata, perfectly and completely buddha, named Kāśyapa, endowed with the qualities enumerated above.[176] This blessed one taught the law to his listeners in this way: 'Deserted places, O monks, abandoned houses, crevices of rocks, mountain caves, thatched roofs, open places, cemeteries, forest retreats, slopes of mountains, beds, and seats, these are the places where you must engage in contemplation. Do not be inattentive, do not do something you will repent; this is the instruction I give you.' Consequently, some of the monks retired to a valley of Sumeru to meditate there; others settled near the pond of the Mandākinī, these near the great lake Anavatapta, those in

174. This part of the legend of Saṃgharakṣita is separated from the end, which one will read below, by the very short legend of the nāgakumāra. I did not believe that I should omit this latter, because it explains in the manner of the Buddhists how Bhadramukha, one of the nāgas to whom Saṃgharakṣita taught the doctrine, could so soon have faith in it. According to the present division of the *Divyāvadāna*, the piece that starts in this way: "The monk feeling doubts, etc." is entitled: "Legend of the Nāgakumara, or the Nāga Prince."

175. The *bhadrakalpa* is the *kalpa*, or the period of creation in which we live. The name of this period means "virtuous kalpa" because during this age of the world, one thousand buddhas will appear on earth (Klaproth, in the *Foe koue ki*, p. 245).

176. See the end of the legend of Pūrṇa above, p. 277.

the seven mountains of gold; others lastly settled in villages, towns, kingdoms, capitals, and engaged in meditation there.

"It happened that a nāgakumāra who was in the world for a long time was carried above the valley of Sumeru [inhabited by the monks] by Suparṇin, the king of birds. The nāga saw the monks engaged in contemplation, occupied with reading and meditating; and having seen them, he felt growing in himself feelings of benevolence for these monks. Filled with these feelings, he engaged in these reflections: 'These āryas are free from the miserable condition in which I find myself.' The nāga, his time finished, left the world where he lived, and took a new existence in a family of brahmans that was scrupulous in the performance of the six ceremonies. There, he was fed, raised, and he became grown. After a certain time, he entered into the religious life under the teaching of Kāśyapa, the perfectly accomplished Buddha. After quite many efforts, after deep studies and application, he succeeded through the annihilation of all corruptions of evil to see the state of arhat face to face. Being an arhat and having acquired the perfections that have been enumerated elsewhere, he became an object of adoration, worship, and respect for the devas.

"One day, he had the following reflections: 'From which condition did I depart [before my present existence]?' 'From that of animals.' 'Where was I reborn?' 'Among humans.' 'Where are my father and mother now?' And immediately, he saw them crying in the home of the nāgas. He thus went there and when he arrived, he asked them the following question: 'Why thus are you crying, O my father and my mother?' 'O ārya,' the two nāgas responded to him, 'our nāgakumāra who was in the world for a long time has been taken by Suparṇin, the king of birds.' 'I am myself this nāgakumāra,' replied the monk.[177] 'Ārya,' the two nāgas said to him, 'the nature of a nāga is so bad, that we do not comprehend how such a being could enter into the path of a happy existence, all the more reason how he could place himself in possession of a condition such [as that of arhat].' But having retrieved the memory through the care of their son, they threw themselves at his feet and told him: 'Is it possible, O ārya, that you have acquired such a gathering of qualities? If you have need of food, we, we have need of virtue; thus, come here each day to take your meal, and when you will have taken it, retire.' Consequently, the monk came each day to the home of the nāgas to eat divine ambrosia and then he withdrew.

"There was a novice who was living with him. The other monks said to the young man: 'Novice, where does your master go to take his meal, and from where

177. The Tibetan version adds: "After my death, I was born in the house of a brahman scrupulous in the performance of the six ceremonies; and having entered into the religious life under the teaching of Kāśyapa, the perfectly accomplished Buddha, I have obtained through the annihilation of all corruptions of evil to see the state of arhat face to face."

does he return after?' 'I do not know,' responded the novice. Then, the monks said to him: 'He goes each day to eat divine ambrosia in the home of the nāgas and then he returns. Why then are you not going with him?' 'My master,' replied the novice, 'has great supernatural faculties, great power; this is why he goes [where he wants]; how can I transport myself [where he goes]?' The monks responded to him: 'When, in order to go, he makes use of his supernatural power, hold on to the end of his mantle.' 'And will I not fall?' replied the novice. 'Bhadramukha,' the monks told him, 'even though Sumeru, this king of mountains, would be hung from the end of the mantle of your master, it would not fall; all the more reason why you will not fall yourself.'

"It was at the place where his master disappeared that the novice resolved to seize the moment [to accompany him]. Having thus gone to the place where the monk ceased to be visible, the novice sat there; and thinking that he was about to disappear, he seized the end of his robe. The two monks then set off across the sky, and soon they were seen by the nāgas; two circles were drawn, the interior of which were cleaned for them to be able to sit. The master then had this reflection: 'For whom then is this other seat prepared?' And immediately, turning his head, he saw the novice and told him: 'Bhadramukha, so you also came?' 'Yes, master, I came [with you].' 'It is good,' said the nāgas to themselves. 'This ārya possesses great supernatural faculties, he has great power; he has the right to have divine ambrosia served to him; but this other monk who accompanies him does not have this right; *so, it is necessary to serve him common food.'*[178] Consequently, the nāgas gave the master divine ambrosia and the disciple ordinary food.

"This latter carried the pot of his master; he took it and found there a small portion of food. He put it in his mouth; it had the flavor of divine ambrosia. The novice then had this reflection: 'These nāgas are greedy; we are both seated together, and they give one divine ambrosia and me common food.' Consequently, he started to pronounce the following prayer: 'If I fulfill the duties of the religious life under the blessed Kāśyapa, the perfectly accomplished Buddha, who has no superior and who is greatly worthy of homage, may I, by the effect of this root of virtue, make a nāga depart from the home of his fellow creatures through death, and be reborn myself [in his place].' And immediately, the novice started to spread water with his two hands [to destroy a nāga he had chosen]. This latter soon felt a pain in his head and he said [to the master]: 'O ārya, this novice has conceived an evil thought; deter him [from carrying it out].' 'Bhadramukha,' said the ārya to the novice, 'the existence of the nāgas is a life of misery; renounce your plan.' But the novice recited the following stanza: 'This thought has possessed me; I am no longer able to free myself from it; I pour water, Lord,

178. The phrase contained between two asterisks is borrowed from the Tibetan version; it is absolutely necessary to the account.

with my two hands during the time that I exist in this world.' When he had made the nāga depart from the home of his fellow creatures through death, he was reborn there himself [in his place]. This is where, O monks, the nāgakumāra [Bhadramukha] started to experience faith."[179]

The monks, feeling doubts arising in their mind, addressed the following question to the blessed Buddha who settles all doubts: "What action, Lord, had the respectable Saṃgharakṣita thus done so that the result of this action was that he was born in a wealthy, fortunate family, enjoying a great fortune; that he entered into the religious life in the presence of the Bhagavat; that through the annihilation of all corruptions of evil, he saw the state of arhat face to face, and that he accomplished in this way [that you have said] the work of conversion?" The Bhagavat responded: "Saṃgharakṣita, O monks, has performed and accumulated actions *that have attained their completion, whose causes have reached their maturity, which have accompanied him like light [accompanies the body that produces it], which must necessarily have an end. Who other [than I] will distinctly know the actions performed and accumulated by Saṃgharakṣita? Actions performed and accumulated, O monks, do not arrive at their maturity in the external elements, either of earth, or of water, or of fire, or of wind; but it is only in the [five] intellectual attributes, in the [six] constituent parts of the body, and in the [five] sense organs, the true elements of all individuals, that actions performed and accumulated, the good as well as the bad, reach their full maturity.

"Deeds are not destroyed, even by hundreds of kalpas; but when they have attained their perfection and their time, they bear fruit for creatures endowed with a body.[180]

"Long ago, O monks, in this very bhadrakalpa in which we are, when creatures had an existence of twenty thousand years, there appeared in the world a preceptor called Kāśyapa, and endowed with the qualities enumerated above. Saṃgharakṣita, who had entered into the religious life under the teaching of this buddha, fulfilled the duties of servant [of the law]. There lived with him at that time five hundred other monks, and the capital of the district was usually the residence of a great multitude of people. The servant of the law had a great benevolence for them all. In this way, he accomplished in this place, throughout the duration of his life, the duties of the religious life; but he did not acquire [through that] the slightest gathering of qualities. After some time, he fell ill. When he had been given medicines made of roots, stalks, leaves, flowers, and fruits, he was seen to be in despair. Then, at the time of his death, he started to pronounce the

179. Here ends the piece entitled: "Legend of the Nāgakumāra, or the Nāga Prince," as it is given by our manuscripts of the *Divyāvadāna*. That which follows is the end of the story of Saṃgharakṣita.

180. This piece, from the word marked by an asterisk, is borrowed from the end of the story of Pūrṇa above, p. 277; the Sanskrit text contents itself with recalling it with the ordinary formula *pūrvavat*, "as above"; the Tibetan version reproduces it entirely.

following prayer: 'Since I have fulfilled, during the entire duration of my life, the duties of the religious life under the blessed Kāśyapa, the perfectly accomplished Buddha, who is without superior and who is greatly worthy of homage, without having been able to acquire the slightest gathering of qualities, may I, by the effect of this root of virtue, enter into the religious life under the teaching of this young brahman named Uttara, to whom the blessed Kāśyapa, the perfectly accomplished Buddha, has predicted that in the future, when the duration of the existence of creatures will be one hundred years, he will certainly be a buddha![181] Under this buddha may I, through the annihilation of all corruptions of evil, arrive to see the state of arhat face to face!'

"Some time after, those who lived with him came to find him and said to him: 'Have you acquired, O master, a gathering of some qualities?' 'Not one,' responded the sick person. 'Which prayer thus have you made?' 'This one and that one.' 'And we also, O master,' replied the monks, 'may we, after having searched for the master in the capacity of virtuous friend, through the annihilation of all corruptions of evil, arrive to see the state of arhat face to face in the presence of the same blessed buddha!' The multitude of people who resided in the capital of the district learned that the ārya had fallen sick; consequently they all came to meet him and said to him: 'Has the ārya acquired a gathering of some qualities?' 'Not one,' responded the sick person. 'Which prayer thus has he made?' 'This one and that one.' 'And we also,' replied the inhabitants, 'may we, after having searched for the ārya in the capacity of virtuous friend, through the annihilation of all corruptions of evil, arrive to see the state of arhat face to face!'

"Now, O monks, do you understand that? The one who fulfilled the duties of servant, it was the monk Saṃgharakṣita himself. The five hundred people with whom he lived, these are the five hundred ṛṣis themselves. The multitude of people who resided in the capital of the district, these are the five hundred merchants. Because he fulfilled then the duties of the servant of the law, the result of this conduct has been that he was born into a wealthy, fortunate family, enjoying a great fortune. Because he pronounced at the moment of his death the prayer I have reported, the result of this action was that after having embraced the religious life in my presence, he, through the annihilation of all corruptions of evil, has arrived to see the state of arhat face to face, and that he has accomplished, as I have told it, the work of conversion.

"It is in this way, O monks, that for completely white actions is reserved a reward completely white, as it has been said elsewhere."[182]

181. This Uttara is none other than Śākyamuni himself in one of his previous existences; it is supposed that by virtue of his supernatural power, he had memory of his existence as a brahman at the time when Kāśyapa was the Buddha.

182. That is to say, that the end of the speech of Śākyamuni is given only in a shortened form and that it is necessary to complete it with the formula that ends the story of Pūrṇa, above p. 278.

The piece we have just read allows us to appreciate the sometimes meticulous detail of the treatises where the rules related to the discipline are put into practice. A complete collection of legends of this kind would probably not leave us unaware of anything about these rules; above all it would make known to us with exactitude the duties to which the regimen of communal life subjected the monks. Those duties that recur most often in the legends of Nepal are the obligation imposed on each monk to take his meal with those who live in the same monastery, and the prohibition against ever refusing a guest the help that he needs. This latter prescription rests on the Orientals' beautiful idea regarding the duties of hospitality; but the Buddhists, following their predilection for moral sentiments, made a special application of these ideas, and endeavored to make them enter into the practice of the religious life, which they always present as the ideal life of man in this world. The distinctive character of Buddhism appears here, a doctrine where moral practice dominates, and which is distinguished in this way from Brahmanism, where philosophical speculation on the one hand, and mythology on the other, certainly occupy a greater place.[183] In that as well, Buddhism testifies clearly to its posteriority to Brahmanism. If moral systems indeed are only born following ontological systems, which is established in the most definitive manner by the history of Greek philosophy, then Buddhism must necessarily, and if one can express oneself in this way, genetically, be posterior to Brahmanism. Certainly the elements of Brahmanical science are not exclusively ontological, and the study of moral man already appears there, but speculative research is nonetheless the dominant principle that gives a uniform direction to the whole of Brahmanism. One need not exaggerate, moreover, the importance of those among the Indian compositions, such as the Purāṇas, where morality plays a considerable role. For without being reminded that it would create an anachronism, or at least raise a very obscure historical question, to introduce the Purāṇas into a comparison of Buddhism with Brahmanism, one can say that the morality of the Purāṇas is too engaged in the exterior practices enjoined by these books to be placed at the level of Buddhism, which, with its principle of universal charity, has won the first rank among the ancient religions of Asia.

These considerations are not so foreign, as one might believe, to the subject that occupies us in the present section. In addition to signaling Buddhism to be an essentially moral doctrine, they call the attention of philosophers to one of the characteristics that distinguish it most clearly from Brahmanism, and they have a direct relation and an intimate connection with the matter of discipline. What indeed is discipline for a body of monks, if it is not the set of prescriptions

183. Erskine had already very judiciously recognized and expressed the not very moral character in general of Indian mythology, and to say it briefly, of Brahmanism regarded as a popular religion (*Transactions of the Literary Society of Bombay*, vol. 1, p. 205).

that ensure and regularize the practice of duties? And if these duties are in large part those that morality imposes, that is to say, those in which human conscience recognizes an obligatory character, does the discipline not become in some way the form of the morality whose judgments it expresses? It is all the more true, since religious systems accord a more significant part to morality and a lesser one to dogma. In such systems, discipline increases with the theory of the duties it safeguards, at the same time that worship decreases with the dogma whose conceptions it expresses in an exterior form. I do not have to develop here the general point of these remarks; but it was important to indicate them in passing, in order to say that they apply with full rigor to Buddhism. Indeed, there are few beliefs that rest on so small a number of dogmas, and that also impose fewer sacrifices to common sense. I speak here in particular of the Buddhism that appears to me to be the most ancient, the human Buddhism, if I dare to call it so, which consists almost entirely in very simple rules of morality, and where it is enough to believe that the Buddha was a man who reached a degree of intelligence and of virtue that each must take as the exemplar for his life. I distinguish it intentionally from this other Buddhism of buddhas and bodhisattvas of contemplation, and above all from that of the Ādibuddha, where theological inventions rival the most complicated that modern Brahmanism has conceived. In this second age of Buddhism dogma develops, and morality, without disappearing entirely, is no longer the principal object of the religion. The discipline loses a part of its strength at the same time, as in Nepal, to mention only one example, where a new class of married monks formed, an institution that was impossible at the time of Śākya and of his first disciples.[184]

We are here naturally led to deal with worship and the objects to which it addresses itself, or to speak in a general manner, with the practice of the religion; for without this practice Buddhism would be a simple moral philosophy. It is on this point above all that the accuracy of the remarks just indicated are verified. To a religion that has few dogmas, a simple worship suffices; and, effectively, nothing is more simple than that imposed on the people by the law of the Buddha. It is doubtless useful to distinguish here the epochs and the countries; but in confining ourselves to Indian Buddhism, I do not hesitate to say that the religion, as one sees it in the sūtras and the legends, expresses, no less faithfully than

184. I wish to speak of the vajrācāryas, who have wives and children and who are nonetheless dedicated to the practice of the external duties of Buddhism (*Transactions of the Royal Asiatic Society*, vol. 2, p. 245). It is to this singular class of religious that the Buddhist of Lalita Patan belonged, to whom Mr. Hodgson owed part of the first information on the doctrine of Śākya (*ibid.*, p. 231). Mr. Hodgson is the first to have well appreciated this bizarre order of priests, which he regards with good reason as a modern invention of a degenerate Buddhism. "From the gradual decadence of the monastic institutions fallen entirely into disuse in Nepal today, came the vajra ācārya, who is the sole minister of the altar, whose name, functions, and very existence, not only are not justified by the Buddhist scriptures, but also are in direct opposition to their spirit and their tendency" (*ibid.*, p. 256).

any other part of these books, the true spirit and the primitive character of the doctrine attributed to Śākya.

In the state in which the texts that serve as the foundation for my research have reached us, it is not easy to see if Śākyamuni concerned himself with worship and if he determined its forms. That about which the sūtras and legends inform us on the subject belongs, indeed, less to the master than to his first disciples; and in attributing to him the institution of a complete religion with a consistent worship, one exposes oneself to commiting a grave anachronism. It is obvious *a priori* that worship must have been an object of small importance for Śākya; the sūtras even give us direct proof that he placed the accomplishment of moral duties far above the practice of religious ceremonies. I have cited elsewhere a fragment where I believe to see the expression of his true thought. "Brahmā," he exclaimed, "lives in the houses where the sons venerate their father and their mother."[185] In truth, Brahmā is the god of the brahmans, whose authority Śākya claims to remove; and this axiom of morality can be regarded as an attack directed at Brahmanical religion in particular, and not against all religion in general. If, however, one reflects that Śākya could speak only of the worship that existed in his time, one will recognize in this maxim the clear declaration, and one can say courageous for an Indian, of the independence of morality with regard to religion. I do not hesitate, on my part, to believe that Śākya did not have the thought of substituting new objects of adoration and new forms of worship for the objects and the forms of popular cults. He lived, he taught, and he died as a philosopher; and his humanity remained a fact so incontestably recognized by all that the compilers of legends to whom miracles cost so little did not even have the thought of making him a god after his death. It was necessary that there be sectarians so indifferent to the truth as the Viṣṇuvites in order to transform Śākya into an incarnation of their hero.[186]

185. Above, section 2, p. 165.

186. *Bhāgavata Purāṇa*, bk. 1, chap. 3, st. 24. The most ancient authority one can cite at the present time in favor of this identification of the Buddha (Śākyamuni) with the Brahmanical god Viṣṇu is probably the inscription of 1005 of the Vikramāditya era, or 948 of our era, found at Buddha Gayā, and published, a long time ago, in *Asiatick Researches* by Charles Wilkins (*Recherches Asiatiques*, vol. 1, p. 308, French trans.). This inscription, if it is authentic, is certainly the result of this modern syncretism, examples of which abound in India. Since Brahmanism regained an uncontested ascendancy over Buddhism, the brahmans, well served in that by popular ignorance, have not neglected any occasion to link to their belief the monuments, still standing today, that attest to the ancient existence of Buddhism. The ruins of palaces, topes, caves, all have changed names, and the Brahmanical heroes of mythology as well as those of history have seen themselves honored day by day in places which originally had a less orthodox purpose. The interesting description of the eastern provinces of India, which has been extracted from the papers of an excellent observer, Buchanan Hamilton, is filled with facts of this kind that would be superflous to mention here. I content myself with pointing out that these facts are numerous in the first volume of this compilation. When I have supposed that the authenticity of the inscription could be disputed, it is from the Buddhist point of view that I have spoken; I believe no less in the solidity of the conclusions on this inscription that Mr. Wilson has already drawn in the scholarly preface to his Sanskrit Dictionary (*Sanscrit Dictionary*, preface, pp. xij and xiij, 1819 ed.). This inscription can

Worship is so small a thing in Buddhism that there is no inconvenience in discussing it before having enumerated the objects to which it is addressed, although to be truthful, it is to reverse the logical order there. Religious ceremonies consist of offerings of flowers and perfumes accompanied by the sound of instruments and the recitation of songs and pious prayers. Moreover, there is no trace of blood sacrifice or offerings transmitted to the divinity through the intermediary of fire; initially, because the first of the fundamental precepts of Buddhist morality is not to kill any living thing, then, because the theory of the Veda, according to which the gods live on what is offered to fire, which is their messenger on earth, is radically incompatible with Buddhist ideas. Worship among the Buddhists, indeed, is not addressed to a single god, or to a multitude of divine beings that the imagination of the brahman dimly perceives, the first hidden in the world, the second dispersed among the elements; it has only two objects: the figurative representation of Śākyamuni, the founder of the doctrine, and the edifices that contain a portion of his bones. An image and relics, that is all that the Buddhists adore; so among them worship is called *pūjā*, or honor, while among the Brahmans it is named *yajña*, or sacrifice.

So simple a worship is the only one that appears in the texts of Nepal; there is, in this connection, almost no distinction among the different categories of books that I have indicated in the second part of the present memorandum; only the developed sūtras justify their title on that point as on all the others. They recount verbosely the pomp and the wealth of the offerings; but save for the observations I will make below, they do not change anything in the nature of the objects of adoration that appear in the sūtras and in the legends with which we are occupied above all at the moment. There, as in the treatises that I believe to be the closest to the preaching of Śākya, what is worshipped is the image of the Buddha depicted seated, legs crossed, in the attitude of meditation or teaching; it is also the monument that contains a part of his relics.

It is quite interesting to see how the redactors of the legends try to make the origin of this worship, which certainly took birth only after him, go back to the

in no way be an authority for Buddhism; on the contrary, it is a proof evident to my eyes that from the middle of the tenth century, Brahmanism, at least momentarily, recaptured a marked ascendancy in this ancient and celebrated sanctuary of the cult of Śākya. Besides, Mr. Schmidt has already expounded very clearly himself against the theory that claims that the last buddha is an incarnation of Viṣṇu; he is a thousand times right when he says that there is not the slightest trace of it in ancient Buddhism (*Mémoires de l'Académie des sciences de Saint-Pétersbourg*, 1:118). Neither is the judicious Erskine mistaken, and nothing is more right and more striking than this remark, which appears to me worthy of being reproduced literally here: "The Brahminical Buddha will never be recognized by true Buddhists as the same as the sage who is the object of their cult; for he owes his origin to the principles of a mythology different from theirs" (*Transactions of the Literary Society of Bombay*, vol. 3, p. 501). One can see also the excellent remarks made by Mr. W. von Humboldt, on the inscription that I have just mentioned, in his great work on the Kawi language (*Über die Kawi-Sprache*, 1:175, note 1; pp. 263 and 264, note 1).

times of Śākya himself. The adoration of the visible person of Śākya is indicated nowhere; for Śākya, as long as he lives, is always only a man, even for his most fervent disciples; but that of his image already appears in legends that are quite characteristic and whose intention is manifest. I have already made allusion to the miraculous voyage that Śākyamuni made to heaven, and I add here that Udāyanavatsa, king of Kauśambhī, beseeched one of the first disciples of Śākya to reproduce for him the image of the master, who took too long to come down to earth again.[187] The disciple yielded to the desire of the king and, with the most precious sandalwood, made a statue that depicted the Buddha standing and with joined hands in the position of a man teaching. This legend, it is true, does not prove more than a miracle does, and it is probably in part the invention of the Mongols; but I can quote a fragment of an avadāna, whose testimony is more instructive.

Rūdrayaṇa, king of Roruka, had just sent armor endowed with marvelous virtues and all covered with jewels to Bimbisāra, king of Rājagṛha.

Upon seeing this present, king Bimbisāra was struck with surprise. He summoned men expert at judging precious stones and said to them: "Set the price of this armor." "O king," responded the jewelers, "each of these stones has an exorbitant price; it is a rule that when one cannot determine the price of a thing, the value is fixed at ten million [coins]." King Bimbisāra then said with chagrin: "What present will I be able to send to the king of Roruka in return?" Then, he had this reflection: "The blessed Buddha [is now in the kingdom]; he knows by his unequaled science what a generous king is; he possesses supernatural means; I will go [to him]; I will go to meet the blessed Buddha." Having thus taken the armor, he went to the place where the Bhagavat was; and when he had arrived, having saluted the feet of the Bhagavat by touching them with his head, king Bimbisāra spoke to him in this way: "In the city of Roruka, Lord, lives a king named Rudrāyana; he is my friend, although I have never seen him; he has sent me as a present armor formed with five parts. Which present will I make in return?" "Have the representation of the Tathāgata drawn on a piece of fabric," said the Bhagavat, "and send it to him as a present."

Bimbisāra had the painters summoned and said to them: "Paint the image of the Tathāgata on a piece of fabric." The blessed buddhas are not easy to approach; this is why the painters could not seize the opportunity [to paint] the Bhagavat. They thus said to Bimbisāra: "If the king gave a meal to the Bhagavat inside his palace, it would be possible for us to seize the opportunity [to paint] the Blessed One." King Bimbisāra, having thus invited the Bhagavat to come inside his palace, gave him a meal. The blessed buddhas are beings one never grows tired of looking at. Whatever limb the painters were looking at, they could not grow

187. *Geschichte der Ost-Mongolen*, p. 15.

tired of gazing at it. This is why they could not seize the moment to paint him. Then, the Bhagavat said to the king: "The painters will have difficulty, O great king; it is impossible for them to seize the moment [to paint] the Tathāgata, but bring the canvas." The king having brought it, the Bhagavat cast his shadow on it and said to the painters: "Fill this contour with colors; then it will be necessary to write below the formula of refuge as well as the precepts of the teaching; it will be necessary to delineate the production of the [successive] causes [of existence], composed of twelve terms, in forward order as well as reverse order; and these two stanzas will be written there:

'Begin, go forth [from the house]; apply yourself to the law of the Buddha: annihilate the army of death as an elephant knocks down a hut of reeds.

'He who walks without distraction under the discipline of this law, escaping from birth and from the turning of the world, will put an end to suffering.'

"If someone asks what these sentences are, one must answer: 'The first is the introduction, the second the teaching, the third the turning of the world, and the fourth, the effort.'"

The painters wrote down everything that the Bhagavat had dictated to them; then the Bhagavat said to king Bimbisāra: "Great king, address a letter to Rudrāyaṇa written in this way: 'Dear friend, I send you as a present that which is most precious in the three worlds. [To receive this gift] you must have the road adorned over a distance of two and a half yojanas; you must yourself go out with an army corps composed of four types of troops; you must place this present in a large and open place and unveil it only after having worshipped it and having rendered great honor to it. The observation of what I recommend to you will assure you the possession of a great amount of merit.'"

King Bimbisāra, having written the letter as it was dictated to him, sent it to king Rudrāyaṇa, to whom it was presented. Rudrāyaṇa, having read it, felt some impatience; and having summoned his counselors, he said to them: "What can the present thus be, lords, sent by Bimbisāra that I must pay such honor to it? Equip an army corps composed of four types of troops and let us go to ravage his kingdom." The counselors responded: "Great king, Bimbisāra is regarded to be a magnanimous prince; he cannot have sent you an ordinary present in return for your gifts. Carry out point by point what he recommends to you; if it happens that the king is not satisfied, we will certainly find the occasion [to avenge him]." "May it be so," responded Rudrāyaṇa. Consequently, they had the road adorned over a length of two and a half yojanas; the king himself went out with an army corps composed of four types of troops; the present, introduced in the city, was placed in a large and open place, and it was unveiled only after having worshipped it and having paid great honor to it.

There were at that moment [in the city] traders, who had come with their merchandise they had brought from Madhyadeśa. As soon as they saw the representation of the Buddha, they all exclaimed in a unanimous voice: "Adoration to the Buddha!" The king, hearing this name Buddha, which he had not heard spoken until then, felt his hairs bristle over all his body and said to the merchants: "Who thus is the one that you call Buddha?" The merchants responded: "Great king, it is the prince of the race of Śākyas, born on the slope of the Himavat, along the river Bhāgīrathī, not far from the hermitage of the ṛṣi Kapila. At his birth, brahmans who know the future made this prediction: 'If he stays in the house, as chief of the family, he will be a cakravartin king, who will be a vanquisher at the head of four types of troops, who will be just and king of the law, who will possess the seven jewels, the seven precious things which are: the jewel of chariots, the jewel of elephants, the jewel of horses, the jewel of women, the jewel of householders, the jewel of generals, which form the seventh of the precious things. He will have a hundred sons, brave, filled with beauty, destroyers of the armies of their enemies. Having conquered the totality of the great earth to the limits of the ocean, he will make all causes of tyranny and misery disappear; he will reign there without punishing, without using the sword, in a manner just and peaceful. If on the contrary, shaving his hair and his beard and covering himself in robes of yellow color, he goes out from the house to enter with a perfect faith into the religious life, he will be a venerable tathāgata, perfectly and completely buddha.' This is the one who is called the Buddha, and whose name resounds in the world; and this painting represents his image." "And what is this?" "This is the introduction." "And this?" "The precepts of the teaching." "And this?" "The turning of the world." "And this?" "The effort." The king understood well the production of the [successive] causes [of existence] that was set forth in forward order as well as reverse order.[188]

Then, Rudrāyaṇa, surrounded by his ministers, pushed aside all affairs and all other objects, sat with legs crossed in the morning, body straight; and placing his memory before his mind, he started to reflect on the production of the [successive] causes [of existence], composed of twelve terms, envisaging it in forward order as well as reverse order, in this manner: "That being, this is; from the production of that, this is produced," starting from "concepts have ignorance for their cause" until he arrived at the annihilation of what is only a great mass of ills. While he was reflecting in this way on the production of causes, composed of twelve terms, envisaging it in forward order, splitting with the thunder-

188. This enumeration of the successive causes of existence recalls the circle that surrounds the picture of heaven, earth, and the hells, which Georgi has reproduced following a Tibetan drawing (*Alphabetum Tibetanum*, p. 485). This author, whose compilation contains curious information that would merit being verified and extracts of hodgepodge in the middle of which he has embedded it, gives the Tibetan names corresponding to twelve sciences that compose the circle (*ibid.*, p. 499). These names are none other than the Tibetan translation of the Sanskrit terms by which the Buddhists designate the *nidānas*, or successive causes of existence, to which I will return below, in the section on Metaphysics.

bolt of science the mountain from which one believes in the view that the body exits, a mountain that rises with twenty peaks, he saw the rewards of the state of srottāpatti face to face; and when he had recognized the truths, he recited this stanza:

"The view of the science has been purified [in me] by the Buddha, who is the jewel of the world; adoration to this good doctor of which this cure is certainly the work!"[189]

I have reported this piece in its entirety because it makes known the beginnings of the worship addressed to Śākya. The legend gives us more than one precious piece of information here. I admit that it commits this ordinary and so easily explicable anachronism, which consists in placing at the time of Śākya that which is the act of his disciples; but once this point is granted, it is no less true that it reveals to us the origin and the purpose of the images of Śākya. It is on a canvas that the figure of the Buddha is painted, and this canvas is sent to a king as the most beautiful present that a friendly prince can make. This image is intended to awaken in him the desire to know the doctrine of the accomplished master whose features it represents. And so as not to leave any doubt concerning this purpose, Śākya orders that there be inscribed the sacramental formulas, the true act of faith of the Buddhists: the precepts of the teaching, which I have shown to be identical with the main rules of the discipline;[190] lastly, the highest part of the doctrine, namely the theory of the causes of existence, all accompanied by an appeal inspired by proselytism. One sees thereby what an intimate relation must have existed at the origin between the doctrine and the image of Śākya. This image had as its principal object to awaken the memory of the teaching of the master; and it could not fail to succeed when it was accompanied, as the legend says, by the summary of this teaching. This alliance of the doctrine with the principal object of worship continued during all the ages of Buddhism. One finds traces of it not only in India, but also in the countries in which proselytism transported this belief; and among the statuettes of Śākya that the research of English voyagers brings to light each day, a great number of them have already been collected that bear on their base the famous axiom of metaphysics cited several times, by which deep knowledge of the origin and the end of beings is attributed to the Buddha.[191]

189. *Rudrāyaṇa*, in *Divyāvadāna*, fol. 410a ff. of my manuscript.

190. See above p. 302. It is not probable that the totality of the rules of the discipline was written down; even if the legend rests on a basis of truth, the contrary is certain; for at the time of Śākya, the precepts of the teaching must not have been as numerous as they became since, and they were doubtless restricted to the five fundamental rules, which are: not to kill, not to steal, not to commit adultery, not to lie, not to drink intoxicating liquors (A. Rémusat, *Foe koue ki*, p. 104). See the additions at the end of the volume.

191. I refer to the *Journal of the Asiatic Society of Bengal* published by Prinsep for the proofs of this fact as it touches on India. And as far as the countries where Buddhism is not indigenous, I will cite only one example taken from Java, because it has the merit of showing from which point Buddhism began to reach this island. I

One understands thereby at the same time why the legends occupy themselves so often with the physical beauty of Śākya. Indeed, everyone knows that the Buddhists attribute to the founder of their doctrine the possession of thirty-two characteristics of beauty, and of eighty secondary signs, which have been known for a long time from an extract of the Vocabulaire Pentaglotte[192] and much more exactly by a memorandum of Mr. Hodgson.[193] It is frequently a topic in the Buddhist books of all the schools, and the compilers of the legends maintain that this perfect beauty was one of the means that spoke most powerfully in favor of the Buddha in the eyes of the people. This importance accorded to human beauty is explained in part by what I have just said about the representations of Śākya, and it allows us to penetrate far into the spirit of primitive Buddhism. The image of the Buddha does not, like those of Śiva and Viṣṇu, have an exaggerated number of attributes; it does not multiply itself with the aid of this wealth of incarnations, where the same god produces an infinity of persons all different from one another.[194] It is simply that of a man seated in the attitude of meditation or making the gesture of teaching. This image, save for the very slight differences in the position of the hands, differences that perhaps would even disappear in an attentive analysis, is always the same. Only the scenes that surround him sometimes add a wealth of decorations, completely external to the rather naked simplicity of the principal object. Now, where everything is so human, the legend is excused

---

wish to discuss the inscription in devanāgari characters, written on the back of a bronze statue representing a buddha, which has been found near Prambanan by Crawfurd (*History of the Indian Archipelago*, 2:212, pl. 31). This inscription is none other than the famous philosophical formula *ye dharmā hetuprabhavāḥ*, etc; which is read on the base and on the back of so great a number of Buddhist statuettes discovered in India. This formula is written in Sanskrit and not in Pāli, which proves that the statue or the model from which it was made comes from the Indian continent and not from Ceylon; if it was original to this island, the formula would indubitably be written in Pāli. From this inscription and from some other monuments of this kind, which he mentions but does not reproduce, Crawfurd believes to be able to conclude that the Indians who wrote it came from the provinces of western India. The form of the letters of his inscription do not appear to me to favor this conjecture; it is a modern devanāgari, which can hardly be earlier than the twelfth or thirteenth century of our era, and which affects the very easily recognizable Bengali forms. If this writing is not original to Bengal, it certainly comes from a neighboring province, for example from the cost of Orissa; it even offers a striking analogy with the alphabet in use at the moment on this coast.

192. Rémusat, *Mélanges Asiatiques*, 1:104 and 108.

193. "Quotations from the Original Sanscrit Authorities," in *Journal of the Asiatic Society of Bengal*, vol. 5, p. 91. At the end of the memorandum of Mr. Hodgson, these physical perfections are attributed to the supreme Ādibuddha; but this must be a modern invention, like that of this mythological buddha. In the sūtras and in the legends, where this Ādibuddha is not named a single time, the thirty-two characteristics of beauty and the eighty secondary signs nonetheless exist, and they refer to the mortal person of Śākyamuni. The Buddhists of all schools agree on that point, and we possess the titles of these perfections in both Sanskrit and Pāli.

194. This characteristic, particular to the representations of the sage honored by the Buddhists, has not escaped Erskine, who has understood to set it forth very clearly in his remarks, so worthy to be read, on the religions which in sequence or simultaneously have flourished in India (*Transactions of the Literary Society of Bombay*, vol. 1, p. 202). In another memorandum, full of the most judicious observations, he expresses himself in this way: "The saints of the Buddhists are men and have a human form; the gods of the brahmans are innumerable; they have all kinds of forms and figures. . . . The first system presents men who have become gods, the second gods who have made themselves men" (*ibid.*, vol. 3, p. 504).

for imagining the ideal of human beauty; and it is quite interesting to see with what scrupulousness it stopped at the limit that separates man from God, above all when one recalls how little it hesitates to cross over it each time it is a matter of the science and power of the Buddha.

We nevertheless have to take account here of the observations I have made more than once on the modifications that Buddhism must have been subjected to in the course of time. Worship changed little, because in religions, form has a duration that survives for a good many centuries at the very core of the beliefs. But new objects of adoration associated themselves with the image of Śākya. In ancient times, these objects must have been the statues of the four buddhas who preceded Śākyamuni, at the beginning of the present period. In more modern times, there were those of the five dhyāni buddhas and of the bodhisattvas, whose representations Mr. Hodgson has made known to us through accurate drawings. Nevertheless, despite some slight variants in dress and in the position of the hands, variants that, moreover, only the mythological buddhas of contemplation bear, the type remains always the same, and this type is that of a man who meditates or who teaches. I am convinced that there was never another; and one would say that the unity and the invariability of the principal object of adoration among the Buddhists are expressed by the multitude of statues that adorn the various tiers of Borobudur of Java, and which all reproduce the figure of a buddha, either meditating or teaching.[195] The image of Avalokiteśvara, which seems to be an exception to this principle, on the contrary confirms its truth. Avalokiteśvara, indeed, is an entirely mythological bodhisattva; and one could have appraised through the analysis I have given above of a modern sūtra[196] what influence the exaggerated conceptions of popular Brahmanism exercised over the development of his legend. Is it thus astonishing that he is represented in Tibet with eleven heads and eight arms?[197] Here, the art has followed the course of the legend; and just as the idea that they had of Avalokiteśvara took hold in large part in an order of beliefs foreign to primitive Buddhism, in the same way the image through which they wished to express this idea must have borrowed part of his attributes from a system of representations that intend to make gods from monstrous and gigantic men.

195. Mr. W. von Humboldt has described and explained this interesting monument in a piece written with a master's hand, like all that has come from the pen of this eminent man (*Über die Kawi-Sprache*, 1:120ff.). It is also necessary to see in the work of the same author the description of the differences found in the position of the hands of these numerous statues of the Buddha. Mr. von Humboldt has quite ingeniously related these differences to the dhyāni buddhas. I nevertheless confess that these variants of position can be prior to the invention and worship of these superhuman buddhas (*ibid.*, p. 124ff.).

196. Above, section 2, p. 234 ff.

197. Pallas, *Sammlungen historischer Nachrichten*; vol. 2, pl. 1, fig. 3, compared with Georgi, *Alphabetum Tibetanum*, p. 176ff.

This respect for human truth in Buddhism, which prevented the disciples of Śākya from transforming the man into God, is quite remarkable for a people like the Indians, among whom mythology has so easily taken the place of history. It shows itself with an equal conspicuousness in the choice of the second object of veneration recognized by Buddhists of all schools. I have said that, with the image of Śākya, what they venerate exclusively are his relics.[198] They give them the expressive name *śarīra*, which means exactly "body." The use they make of this term in the special meaning of "relics" is completely unknown to the Brahmans; it belongs to the language of the Buddhists just as the object it designates belongs to their cult. It is the very body of Śākya that is worshipped in the fragments which remain.[199] These fragments, collected on the pyre where his mortal remains had been consumed, were sealed, according to tradition, in eight cylinders or metal boxes above which were erected an equal number of monuments called *caityas*, or consecrated edifices.[200] The monuments that still remain in India today vindicate the tradition in the most satisfying manner. I do not want to say thereby that the eight mausoleums in which the remains of Śākyamuni were deposited have been recovered; that cannot be, since the Buddhists themselves inform us that some centuries after Śākya, these eight edifices were opened and

198. On this subject, it is necessary to see the highly accurate remarks made by the Rev. Hough, in the context of the great bell of Rangoon; he definitively asserts that there is no other object of worship among the Burmese than the statue of Śākyamuni and the monuments that contain his relics, monuments that are regarded as representatives of the Buddha (*Asiatic Researches*, vol. 16, p. 280). Although these remarks deal exclusively with the Buddhism of the South, I do not hesitate to refer to them here because they apply with an equal exactitude to the Buddhism of the North.

199. I must say, to be accurate, that it is to the plural of this word (*śarīrāṇi*) that the Buddhists give the meaning of "relics"; it is as if they said the *bodies*, designating in this way the whole for the parts. This word is classical in all schools, and its value is confirmed by the testimony of the monuments themselves, that is to say, stone urns and metal boxes that have been discovered in a great number of topes in the Punjab and in Afghanistan. I find this term very distinctly written *śarīrehi* (Pāli form of the instrumental plural) in the short inscription carved on the copper cylinder found at Hidda; it reappears two times (*Journal of the Asiatic Society of Bengal*, vol. 3, pl. 22. *Ariana antiqua*, Antiquities, pl. 2). Mr. Wilson has read *śatinikhi*, which does not make any sense (*Ariana antiqua*, p. 259).

200. *Asiatic Researches*, vol. 16, p. 316. The texts at my disposal do not furnish me with the means to mark with all desired clarity the nuance that distinguishes the word *caitya* from the word *stūpa*. Both apply to the same type of monuments; but one is more general than the other, and it is perhaps on this point that the principal difference that distinguishes them lies. Thus, *stūpa* designates the tope from the point of view of construction and of material form; it is an accumulation, as the etymology of the word says, made of stones connected by earth or cement; in a word, it is a *tumulus*. The word *caitya*, on the contrary, is the tope regarded as a religious monument, that is to say, as consecrated by the deposit it contains. Any *stūpa*, in that it contains the relics of a buddha or any of the objects that he used, or even only in that it was constructed above a place that his presence made famous, is thereby only a *caitya*, that is to say, a consecrated *tumulus*. But the converse is not equally true, and one cannot say that any *caitya* is a *stūpa*; for an edifice containing a statue of a buddha, or even a tree marked by the presence of this precious object, is called a *caitya*. I believe, moreover, to be able to add that the word *caitya* is much more frequently used in the ancient sūtras than in the developed sūtras. In these latter, the word *caitya* ordinarily means only "temple," and *stūpa* seems reserved to designate a tope. See the additions at the end of the volume.

the relics they contained were gathered and distributed to other places. I only recall that a very considerable number of these mausoleums called *stūpas*, whose form and internal disposition correspond point by point to what the legends inform us touching on these revered monuments, have been found in India and in the provinces located beyond the Indus where Buddhism was established in the ancient past.

From Clement of Alexandria, who spoke of these respectable sages who worshipped a pyramid below which rested the bones of their God, to Faxian, the Chinese traveler who, at the beginning of the fifth century of our era, identified a great number of these edifices, to lastly General Ventura, who in our times opened the first of these topes,[201] as the popular language calls them, and whose fortunate attempts were imitated and surpassed by Honigberger and above all by Masson, an uninterrupted tradition of some seventeen centuries establishes the existence, and one can say in general, the purpose, of these interesting edifices. Who has not read the descriptions given by the antiquarians whose names I recall? Who does not know what glory Prinsep, Lassen, Raoul-Rochette, Wilson, and still others secured, by explaining and by classifying the medallions found inside or in the vicinity of the stūpas? None of the subjects related to India has excited so lively a curiosity in Europe; none has been so rich in positive consequences for the ancient history of India from the third century before our era. The beautiful works to which I allude at the moment are known to all my readers, and it suffices for the design of the present work to recall them by indicating the true purpose of the monuments they describe.

This purpose is expressly marked in the legends that attempt to make the worship of the relics, like all the rest, date back not only to the time of Śākya, but to the epoch of the buddhas, mythological in my view, who preceded him billions of centuries ago. The books of Nepal are filled with accounts of the homage paid to the repository monuments of the relics of these buddhas; and among the sūtras, those that I regard as the most modern endlessly celebrate the apparition of these marvelous stūpas, which miraculously partly open and which allow the

201. The word *tope* is one example among thousands of what could be called the Italianism of Sanskrit; it certainly comes from the Sanskrit *stūpa*, which means "heap," and it has passed, by taking this altered form, through the Pāli *thūpa*, which has the same meaning. This word is popular in the Punjab and in Afghanistan, and it appeared for the first time in the work of Elphinstone on Kabul (Elphinstone, *Account of Kabul*, p. 78). Since then, it has not ceased being applied to Buddhist monuments in the form of a cupola; and this application is all the more irreproachable, since these monuments are called *stūpas* in the books of the North, and *thūpas* in those of the South. It is to Mr. Masson that we owe the most exact and the most detailed descriptions of the external form and the internal disposition of the topes ("Memoir on the Topes," in *Ariana antiqua*, p. 55ff.). These descriptions refer exclusively to the monuments erected to the west of the Indus, and in particular to those of Afghanistan; but Mr. Wilson has shown well that the topes of central India and the dagobs of Ceylon, of Pegu and Ava are, as far as the exterior and the interior are concerned, monuments of the same nature (*Ariana antiqua*, p. 38ff.).

surprised spectators to see either a precious relic or the entire person of the Buddha himself that they enclose. One sees here, as with everything touching on the image of Śākya, that worship expanded over a vaster stage, without changing the object; and the invasion of mythology into Buddhism gave the gigantic proportions of a fable to a simple and natural fact. According to the compilers of the legends, it would be Śākyamuni himself who would have ordered that homage be rendered to his remains similar to that to which a sovereign monarch has the right; and it is in conformity with his instructions that his body would have been burned, and that the fragments of his bones that escaped the flames would have been sealed in urns, whose fundamental proportions the stūpa destined to receive them reproduced on a much larger scale, namely a cylinder surmounted by a cover in the form of a dome or a cupola.[202] Csoma de Kőrös has even translated from Tibetan a most interesting description of the funeral ceremony[203] that accords, in most important circumstances, with that which Mr. Turnour has extracted from the Pāli books touching on the same subject[204] and with what I find in one Sinhalese work in my collection, the *Thūpavaṃsa*, or the history of the stūpas erected in either India or Ceylon. But this description, which, save for some miraculous circumstances, bears the stamp of truth, can be perfectly faithful, provided that we should not have to accept as historical fact the opinion of the compilers of the legends, who want Śākyamuni himself to have ordered that one renders to his mortal remains the honors due to those of a cakravartin monarch. For my part, as far as the accuracy of this assertion is concerned, I have doubts that I must briefly explain.

It is possible that Śākya ordered that his body be burned with magnificence, although this injunction is hardly in accord with the modesty and simplicity of his mendicant life; but what appears doubtful, if one reflects on the contempt he had for the body, is that he wished that the remains of his bones found in the cinders of the pyre be preserved. How can we believe that he in whose eyes the living body was really nothing had attached the slightest value to some bones consumed by fire? The assimilation that the legend makes of the funeral of Śākyamuni with that of a sovereign monarch is, moreover, a slightly obscure point. Undoubtedly, at the time of Śākya, the title *cakravartin king*[205] or of a monarch who united under a single scepter all the kingdoms known to the Indians must have been alive in the memory of the people. The glory of the Pāṇḍus and of the great monarchy of Indraprastha was doubtless already popular; and, moreover, the tradition had

202. *Asiatic Researches*, vol. 20, pp. 296 and 312.

203. *Ibid.*, p. 309ff.

204. "An Examination of the Pāli Buddhistical Annals," in *Journal of the Asiatic Society of Bengal*, vol. 7, p. 1009ff.

205. See the explanations that Mr. W. von Humboldt has given of this term (*Über die Kawi Sprache*, 1:276 and 277). It is sometimes preceded by the word *bala* (army).

already immortalized other monarchs no less glorious, whose names are found equally in the books of the brahmans and in those of the Buddhists. I thus do not have any difficulty in accepting that Śākya could have spoken of a funeral reserved for such a monarch; but I do not see anywhere in the books of the brahmans that the bones of these powerful sovereigns were preserved, that they were sealed in boxes of gold or of another metal, and that they were covered with a mass of stones that reproduces the form of the box on a grand scale.

The only Brahmanical use to which one can relate the existence and perhaps the origin of the stūpas is that which Colebrooke described a long time ago,[206] and which has left visible traces in various parts of India.[207] When funeral ceremonies took place too far from a holy river, in order to be able to cast bones and cinders collected on the pyre into it, one kept them in an earthen pot provided with a lid and tied with a rope.[208] This urn was deposited in a deep hole in which a tree was planted, or above which a tumulus of masonry was erected.[209] Prinsep has brought out well the features of resemblance that exist between these prescriptions of the funeral ritual among the brahmans and the form of the greatest number of stūpas opened thus far;[210] but these prescriptions themselves are not general, for they are specially applied when one is not near a river; nor are they peculiar to sovereign monarchs, for nothing is specified in this regard in the ritual. The word *stūpa*, which is perfectly Sanskrit with the meaning of "heap, pile," could without contradiction apply exactly to such a Brahmanical tumulus; but no orthodox text authorizes us to believe that the brahmans have ever made use of it to designate one of these masses of stones to which a masonry covering gives the recognized form of the purely Buddhist stūpas.[211] I also have some difficulty

206. *Asiatic Researches*, vol. 7, p. 256, Calcutta ed.

207. See notably the Pandoo Coolies described by Babington in the *Transactions of the Literary Society of Bombay*, vol. 3, p. 324ff.

208. Colebrooke, in a note related to this description, adds that a mausoleum in honor of a prince or an illustrious personage is quite often constructed, and that such a monument is called *chetrī* in Hindustani (*Asiatic Researches*, vol. 7, p. 256). It seems that this name *chetrī* refers to the parasols with several tiers with which the stūpas are usually surmounted in Buddhist countries.

209. *Asiatic Researches*, vol. 7, p. 256.

210. *Journal of the Asiatic Society of Bengal*, vol. 3, pp. 570 and 571.

211. In a time when the fundamental characteristics that distinguish Buddhist constructions from those of the brahmans were still not perfectly known, there was the wish to see the stūpas observed rather frequently in the hypogeous temples of western India to be liṅgams or Śivaist phalluses (*Transactions of the Literary Society of Bombay*, vol. 3, p. 310). It is especially the caves of Ellora that would need to be visited and described by travelers free from all systematic prejudice. How many liṅgams would disappear to make room for pious stūpas! Erskine, however, was not mistaken on this point any more than he had been in his other observations on Buddhism, and he expressly maintained that the stūpas cannot be in any way symbols of Śivaism (*Transactions of the Literary Society of Bombay*, vol. 3, p. 508). I cannot refuse myself the pleasure of citing the following reflections by this author on this subject: "If there exists a connection of some kind between the cult of the Dagod and that of the Lingam, there is no reason that could establish it. These two symbols are different in their origin as well as in their object. The Dagod is the tomb or the cenotaph of a divine man; it is the place where the relic

in comprehending how the brahmans would have permitted the veneration of remains so miserable in their eyes as the bones of a cadaver consumed on the pyre. One knows the invincible horror that they feel for anything that has been alive, and the care they take to purify themselves when they encounter one of these objects, the mere sight of which is a defilement for them. The idea of preserving relics and of honoring them with a special worship thus does not appear to me to be a Brahmanical conception;[212] and when the Buddhists inform us that this worship was rendered to the remains of sovereign monarchs, and by imitation to those of the Buddha, they intend probably to speak not of all monarchs in general, but of those who shared their beliefs.

The objections I have just made to the accounts of the authors of the legends fall away if, instead of attributing the idea of causing his relics to be honored to Śākya, one leaves it to his first disciples, in whom it was doubtless inspired by a most human sentiment of respect and regret.[213] To render to Śākya the honors worthy of a king, his disciples had only to remember that he belonged to the royal race of Śākyas; in order to religiously preserve his relics, they had only to recall that their master had been a man of whom nothing more remained henceforth but these poor fragments. Śākya, for them, had entered into complete annihilation (*parinirvṛta*); in whatever way this annihilation was understood, there had been an end to his mortal person, since he was to return no more to this world. It was thus a proof of being profoundly penetrated with thoughts of Śākya to piously collect all that remained of him, and the worship of his relics must have resulted naturally from the conviction that death annihilates the entire man.

As for the assimilation that the legends establish between Śākyamuni Buddha and a sovereign monarch, it had been already done, according to the same authorities, at the moment of his birth; and the Buddhist books repeat at each instant this prediction that the brahmans address to the father of each buddha:

---

rests. The Lingam is the symbol of the organ of generation, venerated in its capacity as the productive power of nature. The one is always supposed to refer to a Buddha or to a man who became a saint; the other signifies the boundless energy of divine power acting on external universe. The untrained eye cannot mistake their respective forms" (*ibid.*, p. 516). If one recalls that these excellent observations already date back more than twenty-three years, one must admire even more the acuity and good sense of the skilled man to whom we owe them.

212. It has already been a long time since, in his comparative observations on Buddhism and Brahmanism, Erskine said that the Buddhists venerate the relics of their buddhas and their saints, but that in the eyes of the brahmans, the mortal remains of a man are something impure (*Transactions of the Literary Society of Bombay*, vol. 3, p. 506). The existence of ancient tumuluses that are purely Indian, that is to say Brahmanical, is not contradictory to this assertion; for nothing says that there was a worship rendered to them; and it is precisely the worship that makes the Buddhist stūpas monuments of a very special character.

213. This is what the account of the death of Śākya translated from the Tibetan by Csoma de Kőrös expressly says; according to this account, it is Ānanda who counseled the Mallas of Kuśinagarī to render to the mortal remains of Śākya the honors due to those of a sovereign monarch (*Asiatic Researches*, vol. 20, p. 312).

If your son embraces the life of a householder, he will be a sovereign monarch; if he enters into the religious life, he will be a buddha.[214] The prediction was demanded by the high rank to which Śākya was born, son of a kṣatriya consecrated by royal unction; and the comparison of the sage most elevated in the religious order to a sovereign monarch, vanquisher and master of all kings, was but one of these inventions permitted to the pious faith of the disciples. I even believe to recognize here one of the elements of what I would gladly call the theme of a buddha, a theme whose invention I attribute to the first disciples of Śākyamuni. I add that if the idea of preserving and honoring the relics of the king is, as I have just supposed, exclusively Buddhist, it must have been introduced by imitating what had been done at the death of the master. Accept with me that stūpas were not ordinarily erected above the relics of the kings of Brahmanical belief, and it will be necessary to recognize that in recalling the honors rendered to the mortal remains of sovereign monarchs, the Buddhists were speaking from the memory of what had been left to them by the glory of a monarch, like Aśoka, for example, who had extended their belief over the greater part of India.

If this supposition is not too hazardous, we have to accept that in the legends related to this part of the cult there are details that cannot be prior to the third or fourth century after the death of Śākya. That will also prove to explain, at least in part, the great number of stūpas one finds still standing today in India and Afghanistan. Of these stūpas, some will have been erected above some true or false relic of Śākya, or only at the places his presence had made famous; the others above the tombs of his foremost disciples and the chiefs of the assembly who succeeded him in the direction of the body of monks;[215] the others lastly above the mortal remains of kings who had favored the Buddhist doctrine.[216] The written authorities indeed extend to all these personages the right to be entombed under a stūpa; but the legends also reveal to us another cause for the multiplic-

214. See above, p. 333.

215. The Tibetan Dul-va speaks of a caitya that was erected above the body of Śāriputra, who died before his master (*Asiatic Researches*, vol. 20, p. 88). Faxian places it in *Naluo* or Nālanda, near Rājagṛha (*Foe koue ki*, p. 262). He speaks also of two stūpas that contained the relics of Ānanda. These stūpas were located on each of the two banks of the Ganges, not far from the place where the Gandakī flows into this river (*ibid.*, p. 250).

216. Prinsep has already proposed an analogous reconciliation of two conflicting opinions, one of which wants the stūpas to be purely religious edifices, the other that they be uniquely the tombs of sovereigns. He thinks that the two purposes, that of a tomb and that of an edifice consecrated to the divinity, could have been the common object that the authors of these interesting monuments had in mind (*Journal of the Asiatic Society of Bengal*, vol. 3, p. 570). Mr. Wilson has given good reasons against this sentiment, and he believes, with Erskine and Hodgson, that the stūpas, like the dagobs of Ceylon, are intended to contain and protect some holy relic, attributed, probably without many reasons or much likelihood, to Śākyasiṃha, or to some one of the personages who represent him, like a bodhisattva or a great priest venerated in the country where the stūpa was erected (*Ariana antiqua*, p. 45). I permit myself to add to this list the kings favorable to Buddhism; and I believe, moreover, that one has to take into account the cenotaphs built for the sake of the buddhas. Mr. Masson thinks that stūpas could have been erected above the mortal remains of kings (*Ariana antiqua*, pp. 78 and 79) and of holy personages (*ibid.*, p. 84).

ity of these tumuluses: it is the expectation of the merits the faithful believe are assured to them by having stūpas built for the sake of a buddha. These constructions, a kind of solid cenotaph, must have been numerous, as much in India as in neighboring countries; and if the antiquarians, in opening some of the topes of Afghanistan, were not able to find any human fragments in them, it is probably that they addressed themselves to stūpas of the kind of which I speak, and of which a very great number exist among the Burmese. Mr. W. von Humboldt has conjectured with great reason that the stūpa of the temple of Bagh, in the west of India,[217] must be a solid construction in which nothing could be contained; and this profound thinker has shown with his customary superiority how the idea of the sanctity of the relics had to be naturally transferred, in the mind of the people, to the edifices intended to contain them, and to assure in this way to the stūpas lacking relics the respects that at the beginning were accorded only to those that contain them.[218] I add that it was quite necessary for the Buddhists to content themselves with these empty constructions in order to continue to erect stūpas to Śākya. Whatever was the facility with which the popular faith welcomed the multiplication of relics, the eight original boxes were nevertheless not inexhaustible. But he who constructed one of these empty stūpas for the sake of a buddha probably did not look deeply into things, any more than the people did, and the exterior form sufficed for his devotion.

Before concluding, I must respond to one objection that a Buddhist would not fail to raise in the name of his legends if, however, a Buddhist could be worried by the impious doubts of the European critic. Why, he would say, suspect the truth of legends that attribute to Śākyamuni the establishment of the worship of the relics, when one sees this sage during his own life distributing to faithful listeners mementos of his mortal person even more coarse than the cinders of his pyre? If Śākya gave two merchants a handful of his hair, to others the clippings of his nails, why would he not enjoin rendering religious honors to what remained of his bones?[219] The objection certainly has some value; but without resorting to this method of facile critique, which would consist in repudiating these bizarre distributions, the accounts of which are ordinarily mingled with fantastic circumstances, it seems to me that it is possible, if one wishes, to accept

217. *Transactions of the Literary Society of Bombay*, vol. 2, p. 198.

218. *Über die Kawi-Sprache*, 1:163.

219. The legend of the two merchants to whom Śākya gave eight of his hairs is well known throughout the Burmese nation; it is recounted in detail in a note of Rev. Hough on the inscription of the great bell of Rangoon. These merchants were from Pegu, and they were miraculously informed that Śākya had reached the state of perfect buddha (*Asiatic Researches*, vol. 16, p. 282). We will encounter them again below, in the legend of Aśoka. Nothing is more ordinary, moreover, in the legends than the account of such gifts; see among others the story of Pūrṇa (above, p. 271). A passage from the life of Śākyamuni recounts that the sage made a present to a man of the tribe of Śākyas, *in an illusory manner*, says Csoma, of some hair of his head, with clippings of his nails, and one of his teeth (*Asiatic Researches*, vol. 20, p. 88).

their reality,[220] and that one is not obliged therefore to draw from it the consequence that we oppose the logic of a fervent Buddhist. Who does not know what religious respect is capable of, and who does not understand that passionate worshippers could have themselves collected the hair of an almost divine master? The Buddhists of Tibet have gone as far in this way as was possible; and the stupid respect they have for their lamas has them prostrating before the most disgusting relics that human superstition has invented. Will one say that the pure and chaste Śākyamuni invented this ignoble cult, and is it not rather by a succession of pitiable analogies that the Tibetans have descended so low? The legends which report that the disciples of Śākyamuni collected his hair and even more impure fragments thus explain themselves by this fervor of adoration that has never been lacking in India. Either the facts are true, and one cannot conclude that Śākyamuni instigated them, even less that he used them to recommend the worship of his relics; or they were invented afterward, and one must draw from them only one conclusion: it is that Buddhism, like all human institutions, has been subjected over the course of time to modifications easy to understand, and that the books the tradition has preserved for us have followed this movement and have been modified under its influence.

This last remark brings me back naturally to the observation I made at the beginning of the present section. This observation is that the divisions I had previously established in the class of the sūtras apply equally to that of the avadānas; that is to say, that all the treatises bearing this title do not belong to the same epoch, or in a more general manner, they report events that took place in epochs very distant from one another. I take the liberty of sending the reader back to the remarks I made in the preceding section on the historical importance of the predictions contained in the books attributed to Śākya. These reflections apply rigorously to several treatises of the *Divyāvadāna* and the *Avadānaśataka*, where Śākyamuni announces to his listeners the birth of king Aśoka, whose law would one day rule over all of India and render to his relics a worship that became celebrated among all Buddhist peoples. These predictions, which ordinarily are intermingled with interesting details, form almost everything that is most precise that the Nepalese collection has preserved for us on this great monarch;

220. Although I do not have any difficulty in recognizing that at the very time of Śākya, fanatic disciples could have respectfully collected the hair that fell from his head, I still cannot share the hope that Mr. von Humboldt seems to conceive, when after having described the boxes in which these relics are contained, and which are themselves interred under enormous stūpas, he expresses himself in this way: "One sees clearly thereby that in that sense, it would not be impossible that one would recover under the gigantic mass of the [stūpa] Shoe Da gon, the eight true hairs of Gautama which, according to the tradition, are interred there" (*Über die Kawi Sprache*, 1:161. Cf. Crawfurd, *Embassy to Ava*, p. 348). I do not believe that after having read the account of the fantastic voyage of these invaluable hairs from India to Pegu, it is possible for anyone to see something really historical in it. One might as well believe in the existence of the stick, the pot, and the robe of some predecessor of Śākya that the Peguans also claim to possess.

for the voluminous compilation of the *Aśokāvadāna*, which is a kind of purāṇa, adds little to what the legends of the *Divyāvadāna* and of the *Avadānaśataka* inform us. This is not the place to discuss the facts and the dates furnished to us by the legends to which I allude at the moment; this examination will find its place in the section dedicated to the sketch of the history of Buddhism; but it seems to me indispensable to give a slightly extended specimen of these legends, which have some resemblance to those in which only the name of Śākya figures, and are, however, manifestly later than his epoch. I begin with the piece of the *Divyāvadāna* that has the title *Aśokāvadāna*, while observing that this treatise is not to be confused with the great *Aśokāvadāna* in verse, of which I just spoke. I chose this piece by design, because it opens with a list of the kings who reigned between Bimbisāra, the contemporary of Śākya, and Aśoka, the hero of the legend.

At that time there reigned in the city of Rājagṛha king Bimbisāra.[221] Bimbisāra had Ajātaśatru as his son; the latter had Ujāyin as his son;[222] Udayibhadra had Muṇḍa as his son; Muṇḍa had Kākavarṇin as his son; Kākavarṇin had Sahālin[223] as his son; Sahālin had Tulakuci as his son; Tulakuci had Mahāmaṇḍala as his son; Mahāmaṇḍala had Prasenajit as his son; Prasenajit had Nanda as his son; Nanda had Bindusāra as his son. King Bindusāra reigned in the city of Pāṭaliputra; he had a son to whom the name Susīma was given.[224]

Now in those times, in the city of Campa there was a brahman to whom was born a charming, beautiful, pleasant daughter, who was the delight of the country. Astrologers made this prediction [at the moment of her birth]: This girl will have a king as her spouse, and she will give birth to two jewels of sons: one will be a cakravartin king, master of the four quarters of the earth; the other, after having embraced the religious life, will see his good deeds succeed.

Having heard this prediction, the brahman was enraptured with extreme joy; for man always loves prosperity. Taking his daughter with him, he went to Pāṭaliputra. There, after having adorned her with all kinds of ornaments, he gave

221. *Aśokāvadāna*, in *Divyāvadāna*, fol. 183a of the MS of the Société Asiatique, fol. 230a of my manuscript.

222. We have here an example of the flagrant inaccuracy of our manuscripts: the king named Ujāyin here is the same as Udayibhadra; this latter name is the only one that is true; at least it is the one given by the Pāli books; *Ujāyin* is obviously an error of the copyist.

223. Our manuscripts read *Sapālin* the first time.

224. I will later compare this list with the historical documents preserved in the Pāli books of Ceylon, a summary of which has been given by Mr. Turnour in the preface to his *Mahāvaṃsa*, and discussed in depth in the journal of Prinsep (*Journal of the Asiatic Society of Bengal*, vol. 6, p. 714). One can henceforth form an idea of the discrepancies that exist among the various Indian authorities on this important historical point, by comparing the passage of our text with the list of the Mongol *Sagang Sechen*, examined by Klaproth (*Foe koue ki*, p. 230), and the Brahmanical tables of Wilford (*Asiatic Researches*, vol. 5, p. 286).

her to king Bindusāra to make her his wife: "O king, here is a fortunate, perfect girl." Finally she was placed by king Bindusāra in his inner apartments. The wives of the king then had this reflection: "Here is a pleasant, charming woman who is the delight of the country; if the king comes to have intercourse with her, he will never look at us again." They began to teach her the trade of barber; and the daughter of the brahman proceeded to trim the beard and hair of the king, so much so that she became very skilled at it. Now, each time that she commenced to carry out her duties for the king, the latter lay down. One day the king, who was pleased with her, offered to grant her the favor she desired, and asked her: "Which favor do you wish?" "Lord," the young woman replied, "may the king consent to unite with me." "You are of the caste of barbers," Bindusāra told her, "and I, I am from the race of the kṣatriyas who has received royal anointing; how is it possible that you have intercourse with me?" "I am not of the caste of barbers," she replied. "I am the daughter of a brahman who has given me to the king in order that he make me his wife." "Who then has taught you the trade of barber?" said the king. "It is the women of the inner apartments." "In the future, I do not want you to do this work anymore," said Bindusāra. In the end, she was recognized by the king as the first of his wives.[225]

The king then had intercourse with the maiden; he enjoyed himself with her, with her he indulged himself in pleasure and sensual delight. The queen became pregnant and gave birth after eight or nine months; she gave birth to a son. When the festival of birth had been celebrated magnificently, one wondered: "What will be the name of this child?" The queen then said: "At the birth of this child, I did not feel any grief (*aśokā*)"; consequently the name Aśoka (without grief) was given to the child. Later, she gave birth to a second child; since he was born without the queen feeling suffering, he was given the name of Vigatāśoka (one from whom grief is far away).[226]

Aśoka's limbs were rough to the touch; he was not pleasing to king Bindusāra. One day, the king, desiring to put his sons to the test, called for the mendicant Pingalavatsājīva and said to him: "Let us, O master, put these children to the test, in order to know which of them will be capable of being king when I am no more." The mendicant Piṅgalavatsājīva responded: "Take your sons, O king, to the garden where the golden maṇḍapa is, and there let us put them to the test." The king took his sons with him and went to the garden where the golden maṇḍapa was. Meanwhile, the queen said to the young Aśoka: "The king, who wants to put his children to the test, has left for the garden where the golden

225. A part of this piece has already been cited above, section 2, p. 177, on the occasion of the prejudices of the royal caste. I believed that I could reproduce it here without great inconvenience, because it is indispensable for understanding the rest of the legend.

226. We learn from another passage of the legend of Aśoka that this child was also called Vītāśoka, a name which has the same meaning as that of Vigatāśoka.

maṇḍapa is; you must go there as well." "I do not please the king," replied Aśoka. "He does not even want to see me; what good would there be for me to go there?" "Go nevertheless," replied his mother. Aśoka then said to her: "Send some food ahead." Aśoka thus left Pāṭaliputra. Rādhagupta, the son of the prime minister, then said to him: "Aśoka, where are you going?" "The king," responded Aśoka, "will today put his sons to the test in the garden of the golden maṇḍapa." There was an old elephant there that had been ridden by the king.[227] Aśoka used this old animal to go to the garden of the golden maṇḍapa, he got down among the children and sat on the ground. Food was then offered to the children; the queen had sent cooked rice with curds in an earthen bowl for Aśoka.

Then, king Bindusāra addressed the mendicant Pingalavatsājīva in this way: "Put the children to the test, O master, in order to see which one will be able to rule when I am no more." Pingalavatsājīva began to watch them and to reflect: "It is Aśoka who will be king; and yet he is not pleasing to the king. If I am going to say: 'It is Aśoka who will be king,' I am not certain to stay alive." Thus he spoke in this way: "O king, I will make my prediction without distinguishing the person." "Do so," the king said to him. Then, the mendicant replied: "The one who has a beautiful mount, Lord, will be king." And each of the children conceived this thought: "I have a beautiful mount, it is I who will be king." Aśoka, for his part, had the following reflection: "I came on the back of an elephant; I have a beautiful mount, it is I who will be king."

Bindusāra then said: "Continue with the test, O master." Pingalavatsājīva expressed himself in this way: "O king, the one who has the best seat will be king." And each of the children conceived this thought: "I have the best seat." Aśoka, for his part, had the following reflection: "The earth is my seat, it is I who will be king." After having used the children's bowl, food, and drink as the object of his predication in this way, the mendicant withdrew.

The queen then said to her son Aśoka: "Who is the one for whom it has been predicted that he would be king?" Aśoka answered: "The prediction has been made without distinguishing the person, in this way: the one who has the best mount, seat, bowl, drink, food, this one will be king. If I am not mistaken, it is I who will be king. My mount was the back of an elephant; my seat, the earth; my bowl, an earthen pot; my food, cooked rice seasoned with curds; my drink, water. This is why the mendicant Pingalavatsājīva has said: 'It is Aśoka who will be king.' If I see well, it is I who will be king, since my mount was the back of an elephant and my seat the earth." [The mendicant] began to seek the favor of

227. The word that I translate as "old" is *mahallaka* in the text; it is doubtful that this term is Sanskrit; at least the *mahallaka* of the Wilson dictionary, which means "eunuch," seems to be of Arabic origin. What compels me to translate the word *mahallaka* as "old" is that I have found it in the *Lotus of the Good Law* used as a synonym of *vṛdda*, and forming part of some enumerations of qualities related to old people.

the mother, so that one day she said to him: "O master, which of my sons will be king at the death of Bindusāra?" "It will be Aśoka." "It may be that the king would question you insistently; thus go away; take refuge in the country beyond the frontier. When you hear that Aśoka is king, then you will be able to return." Consequently, the mendicant took refuge in the country beyond the frontier.

Then, king Bindusāra wished to lay siege to the city called Takṣaśilā.[228] He sent his son Aśoka there, telling him: "Go, my son, lay siege to the city of Takṣaśilā." He gave him an army composed of four corps of troops, but he refused him chariots and arms. When the young Aśoka set out from Pāṭaliputra, his people addressed this warning to him: "Son of the king, we have neither soldiers nor arms; with what and how will we fight?" Then, Aśoka exclaimed: "If there is some virtue in me that has to ripen in order for me to be given the throne, may soldiers and arms appear!" The son of the king had hardly spoken when the earth opened slightly and the devatās brought him soldiers and arms.

Then, the son of the king departed for Takṣaśilā with his army composed of four corps of troops. The citizens who inhabited the city had cleared the route over a distance of two and a half yojanas and, carrying bowls full [of offerings], went out to meet him; and having come into his presence, they said to him: "We are not the enemies of the son of the king, or of king Bindusāra; it is evil ministers who oppress us." Thus, Aśoka entered Takṣaśilā amid great pomp. Moreover, he entered in the same manner in the kingdom of the Svaśas.[229] Two naked giants came to seek refuge from him.[230] They received from him means of subsistence and began to walk before him, dividing the mountains in their wake; and the

228. I do not need to recall that the ancient existence of this city is demonstrated by the testimony of the historians of Alexander. This is also not the place to summarize the numerous discussions that this celebrated name has created; it will suffice for me to indicate the newest of the results that they have produced, namely the identity of the *Tachashiluo* of the traveler Faxian with the *Takṣaśilā* of the Indians, a result at which Mr. Lassen and Mr. Wilson have arrived independently from one another, through a careful study of the text of Faxian (Lassen, *Zeitschrift für die Kunde des Morgenlandes*, 1:224. Wilson, *Journal of the Royal Asiatic Society*, vol. 5, p. 118. *Ariana antiqua*, p. 196).

229. I do not know this name of a people, and I suspect that there is some fault here in our manuscripts. It is probable that we have to read *Khaśa* instead of *Svaśa*, the signs स्व *sva* and ख *kha* are very easily confused, as one knows. But the presence of Khaśas not far from Takṣaśilā gives rise to a difficulty that Lassen has already indicated on the occasion of a stanza of the *Mahābhārata*, where Wilson read, according to his manuscripts, *Khaśa*, and where Lassen has recognized in that of Paris another name of a people, that of Bāśati (*Commentatio geographica atque historica de Pentapotamia indica*, p. 87). Lassen does not find that the existence of Khaśas in the Punjab is justified by the texts. Should our legend not modify this opinion in part, and could we not believe that Khaśas existed in the north of this country? These peoples, who are so often the subject in the history of Kashmir, have probably been nomads; and the rare indications that one possesses thus far on their ancient existence permits bringing them closer to the north of India (*Mānavadharmaśāstra*, chap. 10, st. 44). My excellent friend Mr. Troyer has collected a great amount of interesting information on this ethnic group in his translation of the history of Kashmir (*Rājataraṅginī*, 2:321ff.).

230. The text uses the expression *mahānagna*; these *nagnas*, or naked men, appear in the legend in the role of warriors who perform almost supernatural exploits. This meaning appears to me preferable to that of "bard," which the word *nagna* has according to Wilson.

devatās pronounced these words: Aśoka will be a sovereign cakravartin, master of the four quarters of the earth; no one must obstruct him. In the end, the earth, to the limits of the ocean, submitted to his orders.

One day Susīma, one of the sons of the king, returned from the garden in Pāṭaliputra. Khallātaka, the prime minister of king Bindusāra, departed from Pāṭaliputra. Susīma, the son of the king, threw his gauntlet on his head with the intention of playing. The minister had this reflection: "Today, he makes his gauntlet fall; but when he will be king, it will be the law that he will cause to fall. I will take my measures so that he will not become king." He thus detached five hundred counselors [from the prince], telling them: "Aśoka is destined to become a cakravartin, master of the four quarters of the earth; we will have to place him on the throne."

However, the inhabitants of Takṣaśilā revolted, and Susīma, the son of the king, was dispatched against them by his father; but he could not subjugate the city. King Bindusāra then fell ill, and he said: "Bring me my son Susīma, I want to place him on the throne; establish Aśoka in Takṣaśilā." But the ministers rubbed Aśoka, the son of the king, with saffron. After having boiled lacquer in an iron bowl and having rubbed bowls of the same metal with the sap produced by this decoction, they dyed them with it.[231] Then, they said to Bindusāra: "Aśoka, the son of the king, has fallen ill." But when Bindusāra was reduced to such a state that almost no life remained in him, the ministers, having adorned Aśoka with all kinds of ornaments, brought him to the king, telling him: "In the meantime, place this one on the throne; when Susīma returns, then we will reinstate him in turn." But the king became angry; and then Aśoka pronounced these words: "If the throne comes to me by right, may the devatās place the royal fillet on me"; and immediately the diadem was placed on him by the devatās. At the sight of this miracle, king Bindusāra coughed up hot blood and died.

When Aśoka was established on the throne, the yakṣas proclaimed the news at the height of one yojana above the earth; the nāgas proclaimed it at the depth of one yojana below. This news made Rādhagupta come out of his retreat and he heard it repeated in the environs: "Bindusāra has had his day, and Aśoka has just been placed on the throne." On hearing of this event, [Susīma], full of anger, set out [for Pāṭaliputra], and left the place where he was with all possible speed. But king Aśoka set at the first gate of the city of Pāṭaliputra a naked giant; at the second gate, a second giant; at the third, Rādhagupta; and himself stood at the eastern gate. Rādhagupta erected in front of the eastern gate an elephant made of

231. I confess that I do not understand the purpose of this preparation well. Here is the text itself: *lākṣaṃ ca lohapātre kvāthayitvā, kvathitena rasena lohapātrāṇi mrakṣayitvā chorayanti.* It may be that the red dye given by the ministers to iron bowls has the aim of causing belief that the young prince had lost a more or less great quantity of blood, which had been received in these bowls.

wood; and after having dug a pit the size of the body of Aśoka[232] and having filled it with charcoal of khadira,[233] he covered it with grass on which he spread dust. He then told Susīma: "If you can slay Aśoka, you will be king." Then, Susīma made for the eastern gate, saying: "I will do combat with Aśoka." But he fell into the pit full of burning charcoal, and he perished miserably there. When Susīma had been put to death in this way, his giant called Bhadrāyudha, accompanied by a retinue of several thousand men, entered into the religious life under the law of Bhagavat and became an arhat.

When Aśoka had been placed on the throne, his ministers showed signs of disobedience. This is why he said to them: "Have the flowering trees and the fruit trees cut down, and keep the thorn trees." His ministers said to him: "What is the king thinking about? One must instead cut down the thorn trees, and keep the flowering trees and the fruit trees." Three times, they resisted the order that the king gave them. So Aśoka, furious, drawing his sword, made the heads of his five hundred ministers roll.

Another time, Aśoka, surrounded by the women of the inner apartments, went to the garden in the east of the city in springtime, when the trees are covered with flowers and fruits. While he was walking there, he saw an aśoka tree in full flower. He immediately bowed to it, making this remark: "Here is a tree that bears the same name as me." But king Aśoka had limbs rough to the touch; the young women took no pleasure in caressing him. The king fell asleep; then, the women of the inner apartments out of spite broke off the flowers and branches of the aśoka tree. When he woke up, the king saw the tree in that state and demanded: "Who broke it in this way?" One answered him: "It is the women of the inner apartments." On learning the fact, the king, overcome with anger, had the five hundred women encircled with wood[234] and had them burned. Seeing the acts of cruelty he indulged in, the people said to themselves: "The king is furious, he is Caṇḍāśoka, Aśoka the furious." Then, the prime minister Rādhagupta made the following remonstrations: "O king, it is not fitting that you yourself carry out such actions, which are unworthy of you. There must be established men charged with delivering the death blow to those condemned by the king, who will carry out the sentence conveyed by the king." Thus, Aśoka gave this order to his people: "Look for a man who executes criminals."

Not far from there, at the foot of a mountain, there was a cottage inhabited by a weaver. This weaver had a son to whom the name of Girika (the mountain dweller) was given. This child, quick-tempered, cruel, abused his father and his

232. Was it not *Susīma* that we should read? Besides, nothing is more confused than the text in the greater part of this legend.

233. *Mimosa catechu.*

234. I read *kāṣṭakaiḥ* instead of *kiṭikaiḥ*, of which I can make nothing.

mother and beat small boys and small girls. He put to death ants, flies, mice, birds, and fish with the aid of skewers and snares. He was a furious child, thus he was given the name Caṇḍagirika, Girika the furious. One day, he was seen, busy with this mischief, by the people of the king, who said to him: "Can you discharge the office of torturer for king Aśoka?" The child responded: "I would discharge the duty of torturer for all of Jambudvīpa." This response was made known to the king, who said: "Let him be brought." The people of the king went thus to say to the child: "Come, the king calls for you." Caṇḍagirika responded: "Go ahead, I go to see my father and my mother." Then, he went to say to his parents: "O my father and my mother, grant me your permission; I will exercise the office of torturer for king Aśoka." But his parents sought to dissuade him from it; so he deprived them of their life. Meanwhile, the people of the king asked him: "Why did you delay so much in coming?" He revealed to them what had happened in detail. Then, they conducted him to the king, to whom he said: "Have a house made for me." The king had a house built for him, a very beautiful house but which only had a pleasant entrance, and to which the name Pleasant Prison was given. The young Girika then said: "Grant me a favor, O king, may the one who enters this house never be able to leave it"; to which the king responded: "Let it be so."[235]

Then, Caṇḍagirika went to the hermitage of Kukkuṭārāma.[236] The monk Bālapaṇḍita read a sūtra there. "There are beings who are reborn in the hells," he said. "The guardians of the hells, having seized them and having laid them on their back on the ground made of red-hot iron, heated, and making a single flame, open their mouth with an iron skewer and insert balls of red-hot iron, heated, making a single flame. These balls burn the lips of these unfortunate beings; and after having consumed their tongue, their throat, the canal of their gullet, their heart, the parts near their heart, their entrails, their ropes of the entrails, escape from below. These, O monks, are the pains of hell.

"There are beings who are reborn in the hells. The guardians of the hells, having seized them and having laid them on their back on the ground made of red-hot iron, heated, and making a single flame, open their mouth with an iron skewer and throw in molten copper that burns the lips of these unfortunate beings, and which, after having consumed their tongue, their palate, their throat, the canal of their gullet, their entrails, their ropes of the entrails, escapes from below. These are, O monks, the pains of hell.

"There are beings who are reborn in the hells. The guardians of the hells, hav-

235. This part of our legend is the subject of a special chapter of the travels of Faxian; it is, however, told there with some slight variations of little importance (*Foe koue ki*, p. 293ff.).

236. It is the famous hermitage called Kukkuṭa, or of the cock; it was located on the mountain called Kukkuṭapāda, "the foot of the cock," which, according to Faxian, is not very far from Gayā (*Foe koue ki*, p. 302).

ing seized them and having laid them facedown on the ground made of red-hot iron, heated, and making a single flame, run them through with a chain of red-hot iron, heated and all in flames; then, they rub them, grind them, plane them down with a hoe of red-hot iron, heated, and all in flames. They thus remove from their body an eighth, a sixth, or a quarter, plane them either lengthwise, or in a circle, or from the top, or from the bottom, or softly, or very softly. These are, O monks, the pains of hell.

"There are beings who are reborn in the hells. The guardians of the hells, having seized them and having laid them facedown on the ground made of red-hot iron, heated, and making a single flame, run them through with a chain of red-hot iron, heated and all in flames; then, they rub them, grind them, plane them on the ground of red-hot iron, heated, and making a single flame.[237] They thus remove from their body a sixth, an eighth, or a quarter, plane them either lengthwise, or in a circle, or from the top, or from the bottom, or softly, or very softly. These are, O monks, the pains of hell.

"There are beings, O monks, who are reborn in the hells. The guardians of the hells, having seized them and having laid them facedown on the ground made of red-hot iron, heated, and making a single flame, inflict on them the punishment that consists of being enchained in five places. These unfortunate beings walk with their hands on two iron bars; they walk with their two feet on a bar of the same metal; they walk with an iron bar through the heart. Because the hells, O monks, are filled with sufferings, and these are the five punishments that are inflicted there." "Put these tortures into practice," he said to Caṇḍagirika; and he started to inflict on criminals these various types of punishment and others similar.

There was then in the city of Śrāvastī a merchant, who, accompanied by his wife, crossed the great ocean. There, on the sea, this woman, who was pregnant, brought into the world a boy, who was given the name of Samudra (the ocean). Finally, after twelve years, the merchant returned from the great sea; but he was kidnapped by five hundred brigands and slain. Then, Samudra, the son of the merchant, entered into the religious life under the law of the Bhagavat. While traveling through the country to collect alms, he reached Pāṭaliputra. Having dressed at daybreak, he took his bowl and his mantle, and entered the city to collect alms. There, he entered, without knowing it, the beautiful dwelling [of the torturer]. Seeing this house of which only the entrance was beautiful, but which inside was frightening and similar to the abodes of hell, he wanted to leave; but he was seized by Caṇḍagirika, who had seen him, and who said to him: "You must die here." [The monk recognized well that] he had to submit in the end.

237. I follow my manuscripts here; but it is probable that this paragraph is only the repetition of the preceding, and that it is necessary to say: "with a hoe, etc."

Then, filled with pain, he started to sob. The torturer then said to him: "Why do you weep so, like a child?" The monk responded: "I certainly do not weep for the loss of my body; I weep only for the interruption of the duties of salvation, which thus will take place for me."

"After having obtained the state of a human so difficult to encounter, and the religious life that is the source of happiness;

"After having had Śākyasiṃha as master, I will, in my misfortune, abandon all that."

The torturer then said to him: "The king granted me as a boon [the right to put to death all those who enter here]; so be steadfast; there is no salvation for you." But the monk started to beg him, with pitiful words, to grant him one month; the torturer conceded seven nights to him. Yet, his heart troubled by the dread of death, the monk felt his spirit preoccupied by this thought: In seven nights I will exist no more.

The seventh day, king Aśoka surprised a woman of the inner apartments who watched and conversed with a young man with whom she was in love. At the mere sight of this, enflamed by anger, he sent the woman and the young man to his torturer, who crushed them in a bronze mortar with pestles, in such a manner that nothing remained of their bodies but their bones. Moved by this spectacle, the monk exclaimed:

"Ah! How right was the great recluse, this master filled with compassion, to say: 'Form is like a ball of foam; it has neither solidity nor consistency.'

"Where has this charm of the face gone? Where is this beauty of the body? Woe to this world, where the insane take delight!

"My sojourn in the house of the torturer has provided me with help, which I will use today to cross the ocean of existence."

Having applied himself to the teaching of the Buddha during this entire night, and having broken all his bonds, he acquired the supreme rank of arhat. When day had come, Caṇḍagirika said to him: "Monk, the night is finished; the sun has just appeared; here is the moment of your punishment." "Yes," the monk responded to him. "The night, which put an end for me to such a long existence, is finished; the sun that marks for me the moment of supreme favor is risen; thus do as you will." "I do not understand you," replied Caṇḍagirika. "Explain your words." Then, the monk responded to him [with these stanzas]:

"The fearsome night of error is dissipated in my soul, this night made thick by five veils and haunted by pains like brigands.

"The sun of science is risen; my heart is happy in the sky, whose luster allows me to perceive the three worlds as they really are.

"For me the moment of supreme favor is the imitation of the conduct of the master; this body has lived a long time; thus do as you will."

In this moment, the pitiless torturer, with a hard heart, who took no account of another life, seized the monk and, filled with fury, threw him into an iron cauldron filled with water mixed with blood, grease, urine, and human excrement. Then, he lit a large fire under the cauldron. But though it consumed a considerable mass of wood, the monk did not experience any pain. The torturer wanted to rekindle the fire, but the fire did not burn. While he sought the cause, he saw the monk seated crossed-legged on a lotus, and he immediately hastened to go inform the king of this miracle. When the king had come with a retinue of several thousand people, the monk, seeing that the moment to convert him had arrived, began to display his supernatural power. From the middle of the iron cauldron, where he bathed in water, he soared into the air like a swan, in sight of the crowd that watched him; and there he began to produce various miraculous apparitions; it is this that this stanza expresses:

"From half of his body came water, from the other half sprang fire; producing in turn rain and flames, he was resplendent in the sky like a mountain from whose summit springs would pour forth among flaming plants."

At the sight of the monk suspended in the air, the king, whose face showed astonishment, said to him, looking at him, hands joined and with an extreme earnestness:

"Your form, friend, is that of a man; but your power is superhuman. Lord, I have no idea of your nature; which name to give you, you whose essence is perfect?

"Tell me thus in this moment who you are, so that I can know your majesty, and knowing it, according to my strength and like a disciple, I honor the grandeur of your qualities and your merits."

In this moment, the monk recognized that the king should be favored with the teaching, that he was destined to spread the law of the Bhagavat, and that in this way he should bring about the good of a great number of beings; and then he told him, expounding his qualities to him:

"I am, O king, a son of the Buddha, of this being filled with mercy, who is free from the bonds of all defilements, and who is the most eloquent of men; I observe the law, and have no attachment to any type of existence.

"Tamed by the hero among men who has tamed himself, calmed by this sage who has himself reached the height of quietude, I have been freed from the bonds of existence by one who is delivered from the great terrors of the world.

"And you, O great king, your coming has been predicted by the Bhagavat, when he said: 'One hundred years after I will have entered into complete nirvāṇa, there will be in the city of Pāṭaliputra a king named Aśoka, sovereign king of the four parts of the earth, a just king, who will distribute my relics, and who will establish eighty-four thousand edicts of the law.'[238] Yet, O king, you had

238. The text uses the compound *dharmarājikā*, which appears to me susceptible to only these two meanings: "monument of the law" or "edict of the law." According to the first interpretation, it would be here a

this residence similar to hell built, where thousands of creatures are put to death. It is necessary that, [by destroying it], you give the people proof of safety, and that you satisfy the desire of the Bhagavat." Then, he pronounced this stanza:

"Thus, O king of men, give safety to the beings who implore your compassion; satisfy the desire of the master, and multiply the edicts that recommend the law."

Then, the king, who felt benevolence toward the Bhagavat, joining his hands in a sign of respect, spoke in this way to placate the monk: "Forgive me, O son of the sage, who possesses the ten strengths, forgive me this evil deed. Today before you, I blame myself for it, and I seek refuge in the Buddha the ṛṣi, in the first of the assemblies, in the law proclaimed by the āryas.

"And I make this determination: Today imbued with respect for the Buddha, and filled with the benevolence that I feel for him, I will embellish the earth by covering it with caityas of the chief of jinas, which will shine like the wing of the swan, like the conch and like the moon."

Meanwhile, the monk left the house of the torturer, with the help of his supernatural power. The king also proceeded to withdraw; but Caṇḍagirika said to him with joined hands: "O king, you have granted me this boon, that a man once entered here can never leave." "What!" replied Aśoka. "You would also like to put me to death?" "Yes," responded the torturer. "And which one of us," said the king, "entered here first?" "I did," said Caṇḍagirika. "Someone come!" exclaimed the king; and immediately Caṇḍagirika was seized by the torturers, who threw

matter of the stūpas, whose establishment the tradition attributes to king Aśoka; and this interpretation would be confirmed by the expression *dharmadharā*, "container of the law," which appears in the following stanza. Then, *rājikā*, coming from *rāj* (to shine), would allude to the radiance that the coating of stucco which covered them gave to the stūpas. According to the second explanation, *rājikā* would mean "order, edict, royal command," and with *dharma*, "royal edict related to the law"; this term would be another name of the celebrated *dharmalipi* engraved on columns, or of these moral inscriptions so successfully deciphered by Prinsep. There is on one of these monuments, the lāth of Delhi, a word that is still obscure, at least for me, which could well be an analog of the *rājikā* of our text; it is the term that is sometimes written *lajakā*, and sometimes *rajakā* (*Journal of the Asiatic Society of Bengal*, vol. 6, p. 578, lines 2 and 4, and p. 585, note 1). Prinsep has translated this term as "devotees" or "disciples," by deriving it from the Sanskrit *rañj;* and he has noted that if the first vowel had been long, he would have rendered it as "assembly of princes or kings." Prinsep must be right concerning the orthography; and he could have even observed that at line 12 of the same inscription this word is written *lājakā*, doubtless for *rājakā*, in this sentence: *hevaṃ mama lājakā katā*, "it is in this way that my royal order is accomplished." I say "royal order" by conjecture, perhaps it is "duty of king" that must be said. But first, since *rājakā* appears to be a derivative of *rājan*, it is necessary that the idea of king appears there; then, the content of the inscription, where this word crops up several times, seems to announce a commandment. One would almost expect to see this word defined on this monument, because the text says *kiṃti lājakā*, "What is this royal commandment?" Unfortunately what follows is not a definition, but rather a succession of injunctions of a quite moral character, which is of no help for the precise determination of the meaning of *rājakā*. In sum, I prefer to translate the *rājikā* of the text of the legend as "royal edict"; and this interpretation can be reconciled with the first, if one accepts that the king ordered that there be raised next to or on the occasion of each stūpa a column bearing a royal edict related to the fundamental principles of the Buddhist law. See the additions at the end of the volume.

him into the hall of tortures and made him perish in fire. The prison called the Pleasant was demolished, and safety was returned to the people.

Then, the king, wishing to distribute the relics of the Bhagavat, took his place at the head of an army formed of four corps of troops; and having opened the monument called the Stūpa of the Bowl, which had been built by Ajātaśatru, he took possession of the relics.[239] Then, he distributed these relics at the place from which they had been extracted; and above each of the portions that he made he raised a stūpa. He did the same for the second stūpa, and so on until the seventh, from which he removed the relics to distribute them in [new] stūpas. He then betook himself to Rāmagrāma; there the nāgas caused him to descend to their palace and said to him: "We will worship this stūpa at this very place." This is why the king allowed them [to keep it without it being opened]; and the nāgas transported the king from their palace. There is a stanza that says at this occasion:

"The eighth stūpa is at Rāmagrāma; at this time, the faithful nāgas kept it. May the king, [they said], not withdraw the relics from that which contains them. Filled with faith, the monarch reflected; and conforming to what was asked of him, he withdrew."[240]

The king had eighty-four thousand boxes of gold, silver, crystal, and lapis lazuli made; then he had the relics enclosed in them. He then gave to the yakṣas and placed between their hands eighty-four thousand urns with as many strips,[241] distributing them on the entire earth to the shores of the ocean, in the inferior, principal, and medium-sized cities, where [the fortune of the inhabitants] rose

239. The stūpa discussed at this point is that which king Ajātaśatru had built in Rājagṛha, above the portion of relics he had taken possession of at the time of the division of the bones of Śākyamuni Buddha (Csoma, *Asiatic Researches*, vol. 20, p. 316). But the expression used here by the text obliges me to note a difference between the elements of our legend and those of the Tibetan account translated by Csoma. According to this latter, the Stūpa of the Bowl (*Droṇa stūpa*) was raised not by Ajātaśatru, but by the brahman who, reconciling the rival claims of those who wished to seize the relics, had divided them. This account must be the true one, for it agrees with the legend of Buddhists of the South.

240. The text is singularly confused; so even if you know that a stanza must be found here, which is announced by the formula *vakṣyati hi*, "indeed, one will say," the legend would not be very understandable. It seems, in the use of the words *vistareṇa yāvat*, "in detail until," that we have only one extract of it here. I had nonetheless believed it necessary to translate this passage, which is probably truncated here, very literally. The general meaning of what remains from it here accords well with the account of the visit that Aśoka made to the king of the *nāgas*, or dragons, guardians of the eighth stūpa, an account preserved for us by the Chinese traveler Faxian (*Foe koue ki*, p. 227ff.). The kingdom of *Lanmo* of the Chinese Buddhist is indeed our Rāmagrāma, as Klaproth had conjectured, without knowing the present legend. In the translation of the account of Faxian there is only one expression that I do not understand, and of which there is no trace in our texts; it is this: "When the king Ayu [Aśoka] went forth from the world." It seems that these words mean: "when he became a monk." But though it is true that Aśoka was converted to Buddhism, it is not true that he embraced the religious life.

241. The strips in question here were intended to fix the lid to the body of the bowl; it is not rare that one still finds remains of them in stūpas.

to one koṭi [of suvarṇas]. And for each of these cities he had an edict of the law established.

In this time one counted in the city of Takṣaśilā thirty-six koṭis [of suvarṇas]. The citizens said to the king: "Grant us thirty-six boxes." The king reflected that he could not do so, for the relics were to be distributed. Here is the means he employed: "It is necessary to subtract," he said, "thirty-five koṭis." And he added: "The cities that exceed this number, like those that do not reach it, will have nothing."[242]

In the meantime, the king went to the hermitage of Kukkuṭārāma, and addressed himself to the sthavira Yaśas in this way: "Here is my desire: I would like to be able to establish on the same day and at the same hour eighty-four thousand edicts of the law." "May it be so," responded the sthavira. "I will take care, during this time, to hide the disc of the sun with my hand." Indeed, the sthavira Yaśas carried out what he had promised; and on the same day, at the same hour, eighty-four thousand edicts of the law were established. This is what this stanza expresses:

"Having removed the relics of the ṛṣi from the seven ancient constructions, the descendant of the Mauryas had eighty-four thousand stūpas, resplendent like the clouds of autumn, raised in the world on the same day."

Since king Aśoka had established eighty-four thousand edicts of the law, he became a just king, a king of the law; thus, the name of Dharmāśoka, Aśoka of the Law, was given to him. This is what this stanza says:

"The respectable Maurya, the fortunate one, had all these stūpas erected for the benefit of creatures; previously he was named Caṇḍāśoka on the earth; this good deed earned him the name of Dharmāśoka."[243]

It still had not been a very long time since the king was favorably disposed toward the law of the Buddha, and already, each time that he encountered sons of Śākya, either in a group or alone, he touched their feet with his head and worshipped them. He had Yaśas as minister, who was filled with faith in the Bhagavat; Yaśas said to the king: "Lord, you must not prostrate in this way before mendicants of all castes. Indeed, the śrāmaṇeras of Śākya are coming from the four castes to enter into the religious life." The king did not respond to him at

242. Here again the passage is not perfectly intelligible, apart from the exaggeration of the number rendering it hardly probable. In supposing that the term *koṭi* applies to the fortune of the inhabitants, we see from the preceding paragraph that the principle of distribution followed by Aśoka was to give an urn of relics to each city that possessed ten million coins. At this count, Takṣaśilā had to receive thirty-six urns; but to extricate himself from this exaggerated demand, the king declares that the number of ten million is required, and that it is necessary to reach it, but not surpass it, in order to have the right to an urn. See the additions at the end of the volume.

243. The account is interrupted here in our manuscripts by the title *Pāṃśupradānāvadāna*, or "The Legend of the Alms of a Handful of Earth." But the narration continues regularly, and it is clear that this division is only a matter of form.

all; but some time after that, he addressed all his gathered counselors in this way: "I want to know the value of the head of various animals; thus, you bring me such a head, and you such another." Then, he said to his minister Yaśas: "You, bring me a human head." When all the heads were brought, the king said to them: "Go and sell all these heads for any price." All the heads were sold, except the human head, which no one wanted. Thus, the king said to his minister: "If you cannot have money for it, give it to whomever wants it for nothing"; but Yaśas did not find a buyer. Then, the minister, ashamed for not having been able to rid himself of this head, went to see the king and told him what had happened. "The heads of cows, of asses, of rams, of gazelles, of birds," he said to him, "have been purchased by one or another for money; but this human head is an object without value that no one wanted even for nothing." So the king said to his minister: "Then why did no one want this human head?" "Because it is a contemptible object," the minister responded. "Is it this head alone," replied the king, "that is contemptible, or is it all human heads?" "All human heads," said Yaśas. "What!" said Aśoka. "Is my head also a contemptible object?" But the minister, held back by fear, did not dare speak the truth. "Speak according to your conscience," the king said to him. "Well, yes!" the minister replied. The king, having in this manner made his minister confess what he thought, expressed himself in these terms, by addressing to him these stanzas:

"Yes, it is because of a feeling of pride and of elation, inspired by beauty and power, that you wish to turn me away from prostrating myself at the feet of monks.

"And if my head, this miserable object that no one wants for nothing, encountering an occasion to purify itself, acquires some merit, what is there that is contrary to good order?

"You are looking at the caste of the monks of Śākya, and you do not see the virtues hidden in them; this is why, inflated with the pride of birth, in your error you neglect yourself and others.

"One inquires about caste when it is a question of an invitation or a marriage, but not when it is a question of the law, for it is virtues that accomplish the law, and virtues are not troubled by caste.

"If vice touches a man of high birth, this man is blamed in the world; how then would virtues that honor the man of base extraction not be an object of respect?

"It is in consideration of the mind that men's bodies are either scorned or honored. The souls of Śākya's ascetics must thus be venerated, for they are purified by Śākya.

"If a man regenerated by the second birth is deprived of virtue, one says: 'He is a sinner, and he is scorned.' One does not do the same for the man born in a poor family; if he has virtues, one must honor him by prostrating oneself before him."

And the king added: "Have you not heard this word of the compassionate hero of the Śākyas: 'The sages know how to find value in things that have none,' this word of the truthful master, which a slave would be able to comprehend? And if I wish to carry out these commandments, it is not a proof of friendship on your part to divert me from it.

"When my body, abandoned like fragments of sugarcane, sleeps on the ground, it will be incapable of taking pains to greet, to stand up, and to join the hands in a sign of respect.

"Which virtuous action would I be able to perform with this body? Thus, it is not suitable that I attach any price to a body whose end is the cemetery. It is worth no more than a burned-down house, no more than a treasure of precious stones lost in the waters.

"Those who, in this body made to perish, are incapable of distinguishing what has value, those not recognizing the essential, are ignorant of what has worth and what does not; these insane people fall into a swoon at the moment when they enter the mouth of the monster of death.[244]

"When one has removed from a bowl the best of what it contained, curds, melted butter, fresh butter, milk, sour milk, and when nothing is left but foam, if this pot comes to be broken, there is little reason for complaint. It is the same for the body: if the good deeds that give worth to it are taken from it, one need not lament when it comes to perish.

"But when in this world, death violently breaks the bowl of the body of these proud men who turn away from good deeds, then the fire of grief consumes their heart, as when one breaks a pot of curds, of which the best is thus entirely lost.

"Thus do not oppose, Lord, my bowing before the person [of monks]; for he who, without examination, says to himself: 'I am the most noble,' is enveloped in the gloom of error.

"But he who examines the body by the torchlight of the discourses of the sage possessed of the ten strengths, he is a sage who does not see the difference between the body of a prince and that of a slave.

"The skin, the flesh, the bones, the head, the liver, and the other organs are the same in all men; only ornaments and jewels make the body of one superior to another.

"But what is essential in this world is that which can be found in a vile body, and which sages deserve merit for saluting and honoring."

King Aśoka, having thus recognized that the body had less value than eggshells filled with balls of sand made with the tears of a snake, and being persuaded that the advantages resulting from the respect shown [to the monks] surpassed

244. The text says "the makara of death." The makara is this fabulous fish of which the dolphin has perhaps suggested the idea to the Indians.

a multitude of great earths existing with their Sumeru during numerous kalpas, the king Aśoka, so I say, wished to adorn himself in order to honor the stūpas of the Bhagavat. Then, surrounded by the multitude of his ministers, he went to Kukkuṭārāma, and there, holding the place of honor, he said, with hands joined in a sign of respect: "Is there a second person who has been, from the sage who saw everything, the object of a prediction similar to that which he has made for me, when I offered to him [in another existence] a handful of earth?"[245] Then, Yaśas, the elder of the assembly, responded to him in this way: "Yes, great king, there is one. When the Bhagavat, at the point of entering into complete nirvāṇa, after having converted the nāga Apalāla[246] and the cāṇḍālī Gopālī, the wife of the potter,[247] was on his way to Mathurā, he addressed the respectable Ānanda in this way: "In this city of Mathurā, O Ānanda, a hundred years after I have entered into complete nirvāṇa, there will be a merchant of perfumes named Gupta. This merchant will have a son named Upagupta,[248] who will be the first of the

245. This is an allusion to the virtuous action that Aśoka performed in a previous existence, one day when Śākya passed near him. Aśoka was then a small boy named Jaya, who played on the great road, in the dust, with another child of his age named Vijaya. At the sight of the perfections of the Buddha, he was touched with benevolence; and with the intention to give flour to the monk, he threw a handful of earth into his bowl (*Divyāvadāna*, fol. 228b of my manuscript). The legend in which this fact is recounted has the title of *Pāṃśupradāna*, "The Alms of a Handful of Earth"; it is the preamble to that of Aśoka; and this is natural according to Buddhist ideas, since this legend recounts one of the ancient existences of Aśoka, where he acquires the merits that would later elevate him to the throne and make him the most glorious protector of Buddhism. It is important to bring this note together with the beginning of the chapter where Faxian briefly recounts the story of Aśoka. The translation of Mr. A. Rémusat, corrected by Klaproth, is not sufficiently clear; it makes Aśoka while still a child a contemporary of Śākyamuni, which is an error that a note of Klaproth augments further (*Foe koue ki*, pp. 293 and 295). All becomes clear if one accepts, as is indispensable, that Faxian wished to say something analogous to this: "At the time when he who later becameAśoka was a small child contemporary of Śākyamuni."

246. The nāga Apalāla was a dragon who resided in the spring of the river that Faxian named Supofasudu, that is to say, in Sanskrit Śubhavastu, and in the ancient geography Svastus, the Swat of our maps, as Lassen has shown (*Zur Geschichte der griechischen und indoskythischen Könige in Baktrien, Kabul und Indien*, p. 135). The legend of this nāga, which the Chinese call very exactly Apoluoluo, is recounted in great detail by Mr. A. Rémusat (*Foe koue ki*, p. 53).

247. I have not found in our anthologies of legends those of the cāṇḍālī Gopālī.

248. It was a general usage in India, at the time of Buddhism, to give a son the name of his father, while distinguishing it through the addition of the prefix *upa* (under), as here: Gupta the father, and Upagupta the son; Nanda and Upananda, Tiṣya and Upatiṣya. The addition of this prefix gave the compound the meaning of "he who is under Nanda," and by extension "little Nanda." Research could be done on proper names that would not be without interest for the history of Indian literature. Thus, Buddhist names are in general borrowed from those of the lunar constellations, like Puṣya, Tiṣya, Rādha, Anurādha, and others; but one does not find any that recall the names familiar to modern mythology, like Kṛṣṇa, Gopāla, Mādhava, Rādhā, Devī, Pārvatī, Gaurī, and similar others. One can say with complete assurance that there is, between Buddhist proper names and those of the Purāṇas, the same difference as between the latter and those of the Vedas, to which the Buddhist denominations offer one striking analogy. This subject would furnish the material for an interesting monograph. Here I only note, in passing, that the name Tiṣya, which is so common in our legends of the North, is the original Sanskrit of the Pāli name Tissa, which is no less familiar to the Sinhalese Buddhists.

interpreters of the law, and a true buddha, without the exterior signs.[249] It is he, a hundred years after I have entered complete nirvāṇa, who will fulfill the role of a buddha. *Under his teaching a great many monks will see face to face the state of arhat through the destruction of all corruptions of evil. These monks will fill a cave eighteen cubits deep by twelve wide with sticks four inches long.[250] The first of my listeners, O Ānanda, among those capable of interpreting the law, will be the monk Upagupta.* Do you see there, O Ānanda, this band of woods which is so blue?" "Yes, Lord." "It is, O Ānanda, the mountain called Urumuṇḍa.[251] There, when a hundred years have passed after the entry of the Tathāgata into complete nirvāṇa, there will be a dwelling place in the woods called Naṭabhaṭikā.[252] Among all the places for one to sit or lie down, and which favor the calm [of contemplation], the first to my eyes is this hermitage of Naṭabhaṭikā."

Then, the sthavira pronounced this stanza: "The chief of the world has predicted that the glorious Upagupta, first of the interpreters of the law, would fulfill the duties of a buddha."

"Is this perfect being," replied the king, "thus already born, or is he still to be born?" The sthavira answered: "He is born, this magnanimous sage, who has triumphed over corruption; he lives on Mount Urumuṇḍa, surrounded by a multitude of arhats, out of compassion for the world." And he added:

"This perfect sage who takes pleasure in the games of he who knows all, sets forth the pure law to the multitude of his disciples, conducting gods, chiefs of asuras, uragas, and humans by the thousands to the city of deliverance."

Now, at that time, Upagupta, surrounded by eighteen thousand arhats, re-

249. One does not see clearly in the text if one must read *alakṣaṇako buddhaḥ* or *lakṣaṇako*. Attentive reading of the legend of Upagupta allows me to believe that the true reading is *alakṣaṇaka*. The text means that Upagupta will be a buddha without the *lakṣaṇāni*, or the thirty-two signs of physical beauty.

250. The passage inserted between two asterisks is borrowed from the legend of Upagupta, which is of very great help for understanding that of Aśoka (*Divyāvadāna*, fol. 173b). But at this very place the text is so altered that without the clarifications which the legend contains elsewhere, it would be almost impossible to understand anything of it. Here is the summary of the clarifications in question. When Upagupta had acquired the profound science that made him the first of the interpreters of the law, he began to preach constantly to the masses, and converted up to eighteen thousand persons who, through the force of application, reached the rank of arhat. "Now, there was in the mountain of Urumuṇḍa a cave eighteen cubits deep and twelve wide. The sthavira Upagupta said to those of his listeners who had fulfilled their duties: 'He who, by following my teaching, comes to see face to face the state of arhat through the annihilation of all corruptions of evil will have to throw a stick of four inches into this cave; and it happened that in a single day ten thousand arhats each threw a stick into the cave'" (*Divyāvadāna*, fol. 181a). It is to this fact that the sentence with which the present note deals is related; but it was difficult to have an idea of the meaning, in the manner in which our two manuscripts give this passage. Besides that, they omit the word *guhām* (cave), they read *śaṇakābhiḥ* instead of *śalākābhiḥ* and *pūjayiṣyanti* instead of *pūrayiṣyanti*.

251. This mountain is sometimes called Urumuṇḍa and sometimes Rurumuṇḍa; the first spelling is the more usual.

252. This hermitage takes its name from that of two brothers, Naṭa and Bhaṭa, who had it built (*Divyāvadāna*, fol. 173b).

sided in the hermitage called Naṭabhaṭikā. The king, having been informed of it, summoned the multitude of his ministers and said to them: "Equip a corps of elephants, of chariots, and of horsemen; I wish to go promptly to the mountain of Urumuṇḍa. I wish to see with my eyes the sage called Upagupta, free of all defilements." But the ministers responded: "Lord, a messenger must be sent there; the sage who inhabits this place will certainly come himself to the king." "It is not for him," replied the king, "to come before me but rather for me to betake myself to meet him." And he added: "It is, I think, made of diamond, the body of Upagupta that resembles the master, this body that equals, if it does not surpass, rock [in hardness]; such a man would reject the order one would address to him." So the king did not send a messenger to the sthavira Upagupta, and he said: "I myself will go to see the sthavira."

In the meantime, Upagupta had the following reflection: "If the king comes here, it will result in harm to a great multitude of people and to the country." This is why he said to himself: "It is I who will go to meet the king." Consequently, Aśoka, thinking that the sthavira Upagupta will come by water, had boats placed in the space that divides Mathurā from Pāṭaliputra. So, Upagupta, to show his benevolence to king Aśoka, having embarked with his retinue of eighteen thousand arhats, arrived in the city of Pāṭaliputra. At this moment, the people of the king came to announce the news to him. "Lord, you have good fortune! Upagupta, this master of his thoughts, this pilot of the teaching, approaches on foot to show his favor to you, followed by sages who have reached the shore of the ocean of existence." At these words, Aśoka, enraptured with joy, untied from his neck a necklace of pearls worth a hundred thousand [suvarṇas], and gave it to the one who had brought him this happy news; then, having summoned the one who rang the bell, he told him: "Ring the bell in Pāṭaliputra to announce the coming of the sthavira Upagupta, and shout:

'He who renounces a poverty that has neither price nor value, who desires in this world a flourishing and happy felicity, may he come to see Upagupta, this compassionate sage, who is [for all beings] the cause of deliverance and heaven.

'May those who have not seen the first of men, the master filled with mercy, the being existing by himself, come to see the sthavira Upagupta, this noble torch of the three worlds, so similar to the master.'"

When the king had the news spread at the sound of the bell in Pāṭaliputra, and had the city adorned, he went out from it to the distance of two and a half yojanas and approached the sthavira Upagupta, accompanied by the sound of all kinds of instruments, through perfumes and garlands of flowers, and followed by all his ministers and all the inhabitants. The king saw from afar the sthavira Upagupta among his eighteen thousand arhats, who surrounded him like the two ends of the crescent of the moon; and no sooner had he caught sight of him, he descended from his elephant and went on foot toward the bank of the river;

there, putting one of his feet on the shore, he placed the other on the edge of the boat, and taking the sthavira in his arms, he carried him to land. When he had deposited him on the ground, he fell to his full height at the feet of the sthavira, like a tree whose root had been cut, and he kissed them. Then, rising again and placing his two knees on the ground, he joined his hands in a sign of respect, and looking at the sthavira, he spoke to him in this way:

"When, after having triumphed over the multitude of my enemies, I saw united under my sole power the earth with its mountains, to the shores of the ocean that surrounds it, I have not felt as much pleasure as seeing the sthavira.

"The sight of you doubled the favorable dispositions that I have for this excellent law; though he is absent, the purifying sight of you makes the incomparable being who owed everything to himself appear to my eyes today.

"Now that the compassionate chief of the jinas is entered into repose, fulfill for the three worlds the office of a buddha; like the sun, make the light of science shine on the destroyed universe whose illusions of the world cloud the vision.

"You who are similar to the master, you the only eye of the universe and the first of the interpreters [of the law], be my asylum, Lord, and give me your orders; I will rush immediately, accomplished sage, to obey your voice."

Then, the sthavira Upagupta, caressing the head of the king with his right hand, spoke to him in this way: "Fulfill with attention the duties of royal rank; the three precious objects are something difficult to obtain; honor them constantly, Lord.

"O great king, the Bhagavat, the venerable Tathāgata, perfectly and completely buddha, has entrusted to me as well as to you the repository of the law; let us make all our efforts to preserve that which the guide of beings has transmitted to us when he was among his disciples."

The king replied: "Sthavira, I comply with the orders that the Bhagavat gave me. I have embellished the surface of the earth with beautiful stūpas, similar to the summits of mountains, decorated with parasols and raised standards, and ornamented with various precious stones; and I have multiplied the urns that contain his relics. Women, children, houses, myself, likewise, the possession of land and of my treasures, there is nothing I have not renounced under the teaching of the king of the law." "Good, good," replied the sthavira Upagupta. "You have done well, great king, in executing the orders of the Buddha. He who uses his body for the profit of what is truly essential, and who uses material objects to sustain his life, will not lament when his time comes, and he will go to the abode desired by the gods."

The king, having then introduced the sthavira Upagupta with great pomp in his royal abode, took him in his arms and had him sit on the seat intended for him.

The body of the sthavira Upagupta was smooth and perfectly soft, as soft as a tuft of cotton. The king, having noticed that, said to him, with hands joined in a sign of respect: "Noble creature, your limbs are soft like cotton, soft like silk from Benares; but I, unfortunate being, my limbs are rough, and my body is harsh to the touch." The sthavira responded: "It is that I made a precious gift, an incomparable present to the being without peer; I did not make the gift to the Tathāgata of a single handful of sand, as you did long ago." "O sthavira," replied the king, "it is because I was a child that, long ago, having encountered a personage without equal, I gave him a handful of sand, an action whose fruit I gather today." Then, the sthavira, wishing to restore joy to the heart of Aśoka, responded to him in these terms: "Great king, see the excellence of the soil in which you have sown this dust; it is to it that you owe the radiance of the throne and supreme power." At these words, the king, opening astonished eyes, called his ministers and said to them: "I have obtained the empire of a balacakravartin solely for having given a handful of earth; thus what efforts must you not make, lords, to honor the Bhagavat?" Then, falling at the feet of the sthavira Upagupta, he exclaimed: "Here, O sthavira, is my desire: I wish to honor all the places where the blessed Buddha stayed; I wish to mark them with a sign for the sake of posterity." And he pronounced the following stanza:

"All the places where the blessed Buddha resided, I wish to go to honor them and mark them with a sign for the sake of posterity."

"Good, good, O great king," replied the sthavira. "You have a beautiful thought. Today, I will show you the places where the blessed Buddha stayed; I will honor them with joined hands, I will go to visit them, and I will mark them with a sign, have no doubt."[253]

Then, the king, having equipped an army composed of four corps of troops, took perfumes, flowers, and garlands, and departed accompanied by the sthavira Upagupta. This latter commenced by leading the king to the garden of Lumbinī; then, extending his right hand, he said to him: "It is in this place, O great king, that the Bhagavat was born"; and he added:

"Here is the first monument consecrated in honor of the Buddha whose view is excellent. It is here that, one instant after his birth, the recluse took seven steps on the ground."[254]

Having cast his gaze over the four points of the horizon, he pronounced

253. These last words must be placed, without doubt, in the mouth of the king; however, our manuscripts do not indicate it in this way.

254. The wood of Lumbinī is celebrated in all the legends related to the life of Śākya; see especially the chapter of the *Lalitavistara* devoted to the account of the birth of the young Siddhārtha (*Lalitavistara*, fol. 45ff. of my manuscript). This garden is located near Kapilavastu. Faxian spoke about it in his travels (*Foe koue ki*, p. 199, and the note of Klaproth, p. 219). The Chinese traveler also reports the story of the seven steps that the miraculous child took on the ground (*Foe koue ki*, *ibid.* Klaproth, *ibid.*, p. 220).

these words: 'Here is my last existence; it is the last time that I inhabit a human womb.'"[255]

At this moment, Aśoka fell to his full height at the feet of the monk; then, rising again, he joined his hands in a sign of respect and said, weeping: "They are happy, and they have accomplished virtuous actions, those who saw the great recluse at the moment when he came into the world, and who heard his pleasant voice." Then, the sthavira, wishing to increase the joy of Aśoka, spoke to him in this way: "Great king, would you like to see the divinity who was present at the birth of the most eloquent of men, and who heard him speak, when he came into the world in this wood and took three steps?" "Yes, sthavira, I would like to see her." Immediately, the sthavira, pointing his hand toward the tree whose branch queen Mahāmāyā had held, spoke in this way: "May the divinity who resides here in this aśoka tree, this daughter of gods who saw the perfect Buddha, show herself here in person in order to increase the feelings of benevolence [for the law][256] in the heart of king Aśoka." And at that instant the divinity appeared in her own form next to the sthavira Upagupta, and holding her hands joined, she said to him: "Sthavira, what is your command?" Then, the sthavira, turning toward Aśoka: "Here, O great king, is the divinity who saw the Bhagavat at the time of his birth." Immediately joining his hands in a sign of respect, the king addressed the divinity in this way: "You thus saw him at the time of his birth, this sage whose body was marked with the signs of beauty and whose great eyes resembled the lotus! You thus heard the first words of the hero among men, the pleasant words that he pronounced in this wood!" "Yes," responded the divinity. "I saw him at the moment when he was just born, the first of men whose body was brilliant like gold; I saw him at the moment when he made seven steps, and I heard the words of the master." "Thus, tell me, O divinity," replied the king, "what was the radiance of the Bhagavat at the instant he came into the world?" "I cannot express it in words," the divinity told him, "but judge it with a single word:

255. As for the words pronounced by the young prince at the moment of his birth, see the legend of Śākya translated from the Chinese by Klaproth (*Foe koue ki*, pp. 220 and 223). The various versions of these words reported by the numerous authorities cited by this scholar all come down more or less exactly in meaning to the passage of the *Lalitavistara* related to this event, which I have cited elsewhere some time ago (*Journal des Savants*, 1837, pp. 353 and 354. *Lalitavistara*, p. 49b of my manuscript). This must not be surprising, since the tradition of the various peoples who have adopted Buddhism rests after all on Indian authorities. But what is more useful to note is that the words placed in the mouth of the young Śākya by the legend of the North are the same as those reported by the legends of the South. I do not have the Pāli text of it, but I judge it according to the translation, likely quite accurate, that Mr. Turnour has given of a considerable fragment of the commentary composed by Buddhaghosa on the *Buddhavaṃsa* (*Journal Asiatic Society of Bengal*, vol. 7, p. 801).

256. I continue to translate *prasāda* as "benevolence"; but it would be quite possible to replace it here with *grace*, and one understands easily that the Tibetans have taken it in such passages as synonymous with *faith*.

"Brilliant with a miraculous light, resplendent like gold, pleasant to the eyes, the earth in this system of the three worlds where Indra reigns trembled, as did the mountains, to the shores of the ocean, like a vessel carried on the great sea."

The king, after having given a hundred thousand [suvarṇas] to the people of the country, had a stūpa erected in this place and withdrew.

The sthavira Upagupta, having then led the king to Kapilavastu, said to him, extending his right hand: "It is in this place, O great king, that the bodhisattva was presented to king Śuddhodana [his father]. At the sight of this body, which was adorned with the thirty-two signs characteristic of a great man, from which he could not detach his eyes, Śuddhodana fell to his full height at the feet of the bodhisattva. Here, O great king, is the divinity of the family named Śākyavardha (she who makes the Śākyas prosper); it is to her that the bodhisattva was presented just after his birth in order for him to worship the god. But it was the divinities who all threw themselves down at the feet of the bodhisattva. So, king Śuddhodana exclaimed: 'This child is a god for the divinities themselves; that is why he was given the name of Devātideva (god superior to the gods).'"[257]

"It is here, O great king, that the bodhisattva was presented to the clairvoyant brahmans who predict the future. It is here that the ṛṣi Asita declared that the child would one day be a buddha in the world. Here, O great king, the child was entrusted to Mahāprajāpatī, his nurse. There, he was taught to write; here to ride an elephant and a horse,[258] to drive a chariot, to handle the bow, the arrow, the mace, the goad, to practice, in short, the other exercises appropriate to his birth. Here is the hall where the bodhisattva trained himself. It is in this place that, surrounded by a hundred thousand divinities, the bodhisattva indulged in pleasure with his sixty thousand women. It is here that, disgusted with the world at the sight of an old man, a sick man, and a dead man, the bodhisattva [left his abode] to retire to the forest.[259] It is here that he sat in the shadow of a jambu and that, disengaging himself from the conditions of sin and misery, he reached, by reflection and judgment, the first degree of *dhyāna* (contemplation), which is the result of clear view, which gives satisfaction and happiness, and which resembles the state free from all imperfection. It is then that a little after noon, at the time when one takes one's meal, the shadow of the other trees was seen to

257. This legend is again the brief summary of the corresponding chapter of the *Lalitavistara* (*Lalitavistara*, chap. 8, fol. 67ff. of my manuscript). It is necessary to see also the account of the birth of Śākya, translated from the Chinese by Klaproth (*Foe koue ki*, p. 221).

258. The text uses characteristic and very Indian expressions, "to ride on the neck of an elephant and on the back of a horse."

259. This part of the legend of Śākya has been known for a long time and celebrated with good reason, because it expresses the ideas of compassion and of charity that are considered the principal motives of the mission to which Śākya devoted himself. One finds it amply developed in the *Foe koue ki*, p. 204ff.

be cast [in the ordinary way], to go toward, to bend toward the East,[260] whereas the shadow of the jambu tree did not abandon the body of the bodhisattva. At this sight, king Śuddhodana fell to his full height a second time at the feet of the bodhisattva. It is through this door that, escorted by a hundred thousand divinities, the bodhisattva set out from Kapilavastu in the middle of the night. Here, the bodhisattva handed over his horse and his jewels into the hands of Candaka [his servant] and dismissed him. This is what this stanza said:

'Candaka, having received his jewels and his horse, was dismissed by him; the hero entered alone and without a servant into the forest where he was to mortify himself.'

"It is here that the bodhisattva, exchanging with a hunter his clothes of Benares silk for robes of yellow color, embraced the life of a mendicant. Here, he was received in the hermitage of the Bhārgavides. In this place, king Bimbisāra invited the bodhisattva to share the throne with him. It is there that he met Ārāḍa[261] and Udraka, as this stanza expresses:

'In this hermitage lived the ṛṣis Udraka and Ārāḍa; the bodhisattva, this Indra among men, this protector, became familiar with the practice of their doctrine.'

"Here the bodhisattva submitted himself to harsh penance for six years. This is what this stanza says: 'The great recluse, after giving himself over to harsh pen-

260. The text here uses an expression that I saw only in this style: *prācīnaprāgbhāra*. According to Wilson, *prāgbhāra* means only "summit of a mountain." By comparing the compound of our text with this meaning, one could assume that the adjective *prāgbhāra* means "that of which the weight is on top."

261. This brahman has already been mentioned above, section 2, p. 181, note 150. I believe I recognize the name of the first of these anchorites, Ārāḍa, in the Chinese transcription *Alan*, as it is given by Klaproth according to a legend of the life of Śākyamuni (*Foe koue ki*, p. 281). I even conjecture that Klaproth, or the text that he follows, makes a mistake by making *Jialan* into another brahman different from the first (*ibid.*). Indeed, if one compares the Sanskrit name of the brahman in question, Ārāḍa Kālāma, with the Chinese double name Alan Jialan, one will naturally be led to believe that the four Chinese monosyllables are the little altered transcription of the two Sanskrit trisyllables. A passage from the legend of Śākyamuni, as written by Buddhaghosa and translated from the Pāli by Mr. Turnour, seems to say that Ārāḍa was living in Magadha, not far from Rājagṛha (*Journal of the Asiatic Society of Bengal*, vol. 7, p. 810). But the *Lalitavistara* expressly affirms that the brahman Ārāḍa was living in the great city of Vaiśālī (*Lalitavistara*, fol. 125b of my manuscript). This fact is confirmed by a passage of the Pāli *Parinibbāṇa Sutta*, of which Mr. Turnour has given an excellent analysis. It is indeed beyond Vaiśālī, after the last visit of Śākya to this city, that a discussion between a Malla and a disciple of Ālāra Kālāma (as he is called by the Sinhalese) on the relative merits of Śākya and Ālāra took place (*Journal of the Asiatic Society of Bengal*, vol. 7, p. 1004). It seems natural to conclude from this latter circumstance that the residence of Ārāḍa was not far from Vaiśālī. As for Rudraka, son of Rāma, it is really in Rājagṛha that Śākyamuni met him, as I have said above (section 2, p. 181, note 150); the *Lalitavistara* expressly affirms this fact (*Lalitavistara*, fol. 128b of my manuscript). I do not know which of these two authorities is to be preferred: the *Lalitavistara*, which named this latter brahman Rudraka Rāmaputra, or the present legend, which names him Udraka. What is certain is that this latter orthography is confirmed by the Pāli commentary of Buddhaghosa, which mentions this same brahman with the name of Uddakaramo (*Journal of the Asiatic Society of Bengal*, vol. 7, p. 810). It must probably be read *Uddaka Rāma*. As for the facts summarized in this passage, after the time when Śākya sat under a *jambu* tree, see the oft-cited legend of the life of Śākya (*Foe koue ki*, p. 231ff. and p. 281ff.).

ance for six years, recognized that it was not the true path and abandoned this practice.'

"It is in this place that Nandā and Nandabalā, the daughters of the villager, presented the bodhisattva with an offering of honey and milk, which [miraculously] multiplied into ten offerings, and from which he fed himself.[262] The following stanza is cited on this occasion:

'Having eaten in this place the offering of milk and honey that Nandā had presented to him, the great hero, the most eloquent of men, went to sit in the shadow of the Bodhi tree.'

"It is here that Kālika, king of the nāgas, came to meet the bodhisattva, who was seated next to the Bodhi tree, and started to sing his praises. Consequently, it is said: 'The most eloquent of men was praised by Kālika, king of the snakes, when, desirous of immortality,[263] he entered into the path that leads there, on the throne of bodhi.'"[264]

At this moment, the king, prostrating at the feet of the sthavira, spoke to him in this way, hands joined in respect: "If I could see this king of the nāgas who gazed at the Tathāgata, when, having the vigor of the king of furious elephants, he walked on this path!" Immediately the king of the nāgas, Kālika, appearing next to the sthavira Upagupta, said to him, hands joined in respect: "Sthavira, what is your command?" Then, the sthavira said to the king: "Here, O great king, is Kālika, king of the nāgas, who sang the Bhagavat's praises when, seated next to the Bodhi tree, he advanced on the path of salvation." Immediately, the king, hands joined in respect, spoke in this way to Kālika, king of the nāgas: "You thus saw him, the one whose complexion equaled the radiance of melted gold, you saw him, my incomparable master, whose face resembles an autumn moon. Set

262. See this part of the legend of Śākya recounted in detail in the *Foe koue ki*, pp. 283 and 284. Cf. *Asiatic Researches*, vol. 20, p. 165.

263. Here again there is an incorrect form, *amṛtārthinaḥ* for *amṛtārthī*. See in the *Foe koue ki*, p. 285, the legend of this blind dragon.

264. This is the way I translate the compound *bodhimaṇḍa*, an expression quite proper to Buddhist Sanskrit. Interpreted literally and according to the rules of the classical style, it should mean "the essence of bodhi or of intelligence"; and it is in this way that I have understood it for a long time, and in particular when I was reading the developed sūtras, like the *Lotus of the Good Law*, where nothing illuminates the special meaning of this term for the reader; but I have since acquired the conviction that it designates, notably in the old legends, the throne or miraculous seat that is supposed to have risen from earth in the shadow of the Bodhi tree when Śākya had fulfilled the duties that gave him the right to the title of *buddha*. One finds on this subject, in the *Foe koue ki*, a note from Klaproth that leaves no doubt as to the quite special application of this term (*Foe koue ki*, p. 286, note, col. 1). It is only necessary to add that the "platform of the Bodhi tree," as the Chinese call it, is the *bodhimaṇḍa* of our legends, of which I was ignorant before having seen this term several times, either in the avadānas or in the *Lalitavistara*, not forgetting that this name applies by extension even to the city of Gayā, where the Bodhi tree was, in whose shadow the platform or the throne in question appeared. This is what Csoma indicates in his analysis of the life of Śākya (*Asiatic Researches*, vol. 20, pp. 292 and 423). This throne was also called *vajrāsana*, "the diamond seat" (*ibid.*, pp. 75 and 292); but this name is less common than the other.

forth to me one part of the qualities of the sage with ten strengths; tell me what then was the splendor of the Sugata." "I cannot express it with words," said the dragon to him, "but judge it with a single word":

"Touched by the sole of his feet, the earth with its mountains trembled in six different ways; illuminated up by the light of the Sugata, which rose like the moon above the world of men, it seemed beautiful and more resplendent than the rays of the sun." After this conversation, the king had a caitya erected at this place and withdrew.

Then, the sthavira Upagupta, having led the king next to the Bodhi tree, told him, extending his hand: "It is here, O great king, that the bodhisattva, endowed with great charity, after having defeated all the forces of Māra, reached the state of perfectly accomplished buddha.[265] This is expressed by the following stanza:

'It is there, next to the Bodhi tree, that the hero of recluses dispersed in a few instants the army of the humiliated Namuci; it is there that this incomparable being obtained the noble, the supreme, and immortal state of buddha.'"

Consequently, the king gave a hundred thousand [suvarṇas] for the Bodhi tree and had a caitya erected in this place; after that, he withdrew.

Then, the sthavira Upagupta said to king Aśoka: "It is here that the four great kings of heaven offered four bowls made of stone to the Bhagavat and that he chose one of them.[266] In this place, he received the alms of a meal from the hand of the two merchants Trapuṣa and Bhallika.[267] Here the Bhagavat, at the point

265. This is always a topic in the legends of Śākya's stay near the Bodhi tree under which he obtained the dignity of buddha; this tree was in Gayā. The details of Śākya's stay in this country are amply set forth and developed in the notes related to chapter 31 of the *Foe koue ki* (see p. 275ff., pp. 285 and 290). Faxian saw stūpas erected at almost all the places that our legend designates. I must add here that when speaking above about the origin of the name *bodhi* given to the Indian fig tree, I have forgotten to speak in favor of my opinion, that each buddha had, according to popular mythology, his particular Bodhi, which was not always a *ficus religiosa*. Thus, the Bodhi tree of the first buddha of the present epoch was a śirīṣa, that is to say, an *acacia sirisa* (*Asiatic Researches*, vol. 16, p. 453. *Foe koue ki*, p. 193. *Journal of the Asiatic Society of Bengal*, vol. 7, p. 793. *Mahāvanso*, p. 90, ed. in -4°). That of the second was an udumbara, that is to say, a *ficus glomerata* (*Asiatic Researches*, vol. 16, p. 454. *Foe koue ki*, p. 195. *Journal of the Asiatic Society of Bengal*, vol. 7, pp. 794 and 795. *Mahāvanso*, p. 92). That of the third was a nyagrodha, that is to say, a *ficus Indica* (*Foe koue ki*, p. 189. *Journal of the Asiatic Society of Bengal*, vol. 7, p. 796). This proves that the name *bodhi* is a generic term designating the tree under which a buddha must obtain the consecration of his sublime mission, and is not the proper and popular name of this species of fig tree. This is what I had wished to establish above, section 2, p. 120, note 15, and which already indicates the sole analogy of the words *buddha* and *bodhi*.

266. See on this legend a note of Klaproth in the *Foe koue ki*, p. 291. Śākya preferred the most simple bowl among all those offered by the gods. This legend, which belongs to that which follows, is recounted in the *Lalitavistara*, fols. 197b and 198a of my manuscript.

267. This legend is also reported in the previously cited note of Klaproth, according to Sinhalese sources and in part according to the Chinese Xuanzang (*Foe koue ki*, p. 291). But in the passage that Klaproth has borrowed from Upham (*The Sacred and Historical Books of Ceylon*, 3:110ff.), the words are singularly distorted. These two merchants are the very same ones who are mentioned in the inscription of the famous bell of Rangoon, and to whom I have made allusion above, p. 343, note 219. The legend in question here is the object of a chapter (the twenty-fourth) of the *Lalitavistara*, fol. 196b of my manuscript.

of betaking himself to Benares, was praised by a certain Upagaṇa."[268] Finally, the sthavira, having led the king to the place called Ṛṣipatana, told him, extending his right hand: "Here, O great king, the Bhagavat turned the legal wheel of the law which in three turns appears in twelve different ways." And he pronounced this stanza:

"In this place, the Lord, in order to put an end to the revolution of the world, has turned the beautiful and excellent wheel, which is the law itself."

"It is here that he made one thousand ascetics with plaited hair adopt the life of the mendicant; here that he taught the law to king Bimbisāra, and here that the truths were seen by this prince as well as by eighty thousand divinities, and by several thousand brahmans and householders of Magadha. It is here that the Bhagavat taught the law to Śakra, the Indra of the devas, and that the truths were seen by this god as well as by eighty thousand devatās. There, he has performed a great miracle. Here, the Bhagavat, after having spent the time of the varṣa among the Trayastriṃśa devas, in order to teach the law to his mother to whom he owed his birth, descended again [from heaven] escorted by a multitude of gods."

Finally, the sthavira Upagupta, having led the king to the city of Kuśinagarī, said to him, extending his right hand: "It is in this place, O great king, that the Bhagavat, after having fulfilled all the duties of a buddha, completely entered into the domain of nirvāṇa, where nothing is left of the accumulation of the elements of existence." And he added this stanza:

"After having submitted to the discipline of the imperishable law the world with devas, humans, asuras, yakṣas and nāgas, the great ṛṣi, this sage endowed with intelligence and with an immense compassion, entered into repose, tranquil hereafter because he had no more beings to convert."

At these words, the king fainted and fell on the ground; water was thrown [on his face] and he rose again. Then, when he had regained some of his senses, he gave a hundred thousand [suvarṇas] for the [place of the] nirvāṇa and had a caitya built in this place. Having then thrown himself on the sthavira's knees, he said to him: "Here, O sthavira, is my desire: I wish to honor the relics of those of the listeners of the Bhagavat who have been designated [by him] as being the foremost." "Good, good, O great king," replied the sthavira. "That is a good thought." Then, the sthavira, leading the king to Jetavana, said to him, extending his right hand: "Here, O great king, is the stūpa of the sthavira Śāriputra; you now can honor it." "What were the merits of Śāriputra?" asked the king. "He was," said the sthavira, "like a second master; he was the general of the army of the law, while the Buddha turned its wheel; it is he who was designated as the first of those who possess wisdom when the Bhagavat said: 'Apart from the

268. This fact is also recounted in the *Lalitavistara*, chap. 26, fol. 209b of my manuscript. It took place between the throne of bodhimaṇḍa and the city of Gayā.

Tathāgata, however, the wisdom in the entire universe does not equal a sixteenth of the wisdom of Śāriputra.'" And Upagupta pronounced this stanza:

"The incomparable wheel of the good law that the Jina turned, the sage Śāriputra also turned, following his example. What man other than the Buddha could know and set forth in this world, omitting nothing, the treasure and the multitude of qualities of the son of Śāradvatī?"

Then, the king satisfied, after having given a hundred thousand [suvarṇas] for the stūpa of the son of Śāradvatī, the sthavira, exclaimed, hands joined in a sign of respect: "I honor with a deep devotion the son of Śāradvatī, who is free from the bonds of existence, whose glory illumines the world, this hero, the first of those possessed of wisdom."

The sthavira Upagupta, then showing the stūpa of the sthavira Mahāmaudgalyāyana, expressed himself in this way: "Here is, O great king, the stūpa of the great Maudgalyāyana; you can honor it." "What," said the king, "were the merits of this sage?" "He was designated by the Bhagavat," replied the sthavira, "as the foremost of those possessed of supernatural power, because with the big toe of his right foot, he shook Vaijayanta, the palace of Śakra, the Indra of the devas; it is he who converted Nanda and Upananda, the two kings of the nāgas."[269] And he pronounced this stanza:

"It is necessary to honor, with all one's power, Kolita,[270] the foremost of the brahmans, who, with the big toe of his right foot, has shaken the palace of Indra. Who could, in this world, surpass the ocean of the qualities of this sage with perfect intelligence, who tamed the sovereigns of the snakes, these fearsome beings so difficult to subdue."

The king, having given a hundred thousand [suvarṇas] for the stūpa of Mahāmaudgalyāyana, exclaimed, hands joined in a sign of respect: "I honor, bowing my head, the celebrated Maudgalyāyana, the foremost of the sages endowed with supernatural power, who is free from birth, old age, grief, and suffering."

The sthavira Upagupta then showed the king the stūpa of the sthavira Mahākāśyapa, saying to him: "Honor it." "What," replied the king, "were the merits of this sage?" "This magnanimous sage, O great king, was designated by the Bhagavat as the foremost of those with few desires, who are satisfied, who have triumphed over those who speak of qualities; the Bhagavat invited him to share his seat; covered with a robe of white color, compassionate for the poor

269. The Chinese also say that Maudgalyāyana is the disciple of Śākya who acquired the greatest supernatural power (A. Rémusat, *Foe koue ki*, p. 32).

270. Csoma informs us, in his analysis of the Dul-va, that Kolita, which was another name of Maudgalyāyana, means "lap-born" (*Asiatic Researches*, vol. 20, p. 49). Klaproth has committed a slight inaccuracy in transcribing this last name as *Kālitha*; but he has rightly recognized the meaning according to the Tibetans, the Mongols, and the Manchus (*Foe koue ki*, p. 68, note a). His error comes in part from the Vocabulaire Pentaglotte, which records this name as *Kālitaḥ* (sec. 21, no. 3).

and unhappy, he preserved the repository of the law." And he pronounced this stanza:

"This noble treasure of virtue, this monk compassionate for the poor and the destitute, who never rested, who wore the costume of the sage who knows all, this intelligent master who preserved the repository of the law, is there a man who could enumerate his qualities completely? It is to him that the benevolent Jina ceded half of the best of seats."

Then, king Aśoka, having given a hundred thousand [suvarṇas] for the stūpa of Mahākāśyapa the sthavira, spoke in this way, hands joined in a sign of respect: "I honor the sthavira Kāśyapa, who retired into mountain caves, who did not like combat or hatred, this sage filled with peace of mind, in whom the virtue of contentment was at its peak."

The sthavira Upagupta then showed the king the stūpa of Vakkula[271] the sthavira and said to him: "Here is, O great king, the stūpa of Vakkula; honor it." "What," replied the king, "were the merits of this sage?" "This magnanimous monk," responded the sthavira, "was designated by the Bhagavat as the foremost of those who know few obstacles." But the sthavira did not add for this sage a stanza formed of two pādas. The king then said: "Give here one kākaṇi."[272] "Why," the ministers asked him, "after having fixed an equal sum for the other stūpas, do you give here one kākaṇi?" "Here," responded the king, "is my thought: although this sage has completely dispelled the darkness that obscured the house of his heart with the light of the teaching, because of his few desires, he did not do good for creatures as the others did; for he never encountered obstacles." At these words, the ministers were struck with astonishment, and falling at the feet of the king, they exclaimed: "Ah, the moderation of desires of this magnanimous sage was useless, since he did not encounter difficulties."

The sthavira Upagupta, then showing the stūpa of the sthavira Ānanda, said to the king: "Here, O king, is the stūpa of the sthavira Ānanda; honor it." "What," said Aśoka, "were the merits of this monk?" "This monk," replied the sthavira, "was the servant of the Bhagavat; it is he who was the foremost of those who heard much and who understood the word [of the master]." And he added this stanza:

271. The text spells the name of this monk Vatkula; but I do not hesitate to correct this orthography and to replace it with Vakkula, the name of one of the listeners of Śākyamuni, mentioned in the *Lotus of the Good Law* (fol. 114a of the text, p. 126 of the trans.) and in the Vocabulaire Pentaglotte (sec. 21, no. 17). This name would perhaps be more regularly written in one of these two ways, *Vakula* or *Vākkula*. I have not dared to identify him with *Vakkalin* (for *Valkalin*), the brahman spoken of above, in the legend of Pūrṇa, p. 272.

272. I have retained this word without translating it because the meaning given to it by Wilson in his lexicon is not relevant here. It is evident that, in our text, it is a matter of money and certainly money of little value. Since *kāka* is one of the words synonymous with *raktikā*, that is to say, of the grain of the *arbrus precatorius* which shows a weight of a value of 2 3/16 English troy grains, it is permissible to believe that *kākaṇi* is either this same weight or a given measure of kākas or raktikās, which seems more probable.

"Careful in keeping the bowl of the recluse, filled with memory, with steadfastness, and with intelligence, Ānanda, this ocean of knowledge, this bowl of virtues, this sage whose sweet words were clear and who, always intelligent, was skillful at penetrating the thought of the perfect Buddha, Ānanda at last, vanquisher in all battles and praised by the Jina, is constantly honored by men and by gods."

The king gave ten million [survaṇas] for his stūpa. "Why," said the ministers, "does the king thus honor this stūpa more than the others?" "Here, responded the king, is my thought:

"This sage, whose name expresses the absence of sadness, deserves to be particularly honored, because he sustained the pure body of the most eloquent of masters, the body of the one who was the law itself.

"If the torch of the law that dispels the deep darkness of suffering shines today among men, it is thanks to the power of this son of the Sugata; this is why he deserves to be particularly honored.

"Just as in order to have the water of the ocean, no one seeks it in the footprint of a cow; in the same way, it is after recognizing his nature and his condition that the sovereign master consecrated this sthavira as the repository of the sūtras."

The king, after having rendered these honors to the stūpas of the sthaviras, threw himself at the sthavira Upagupta's feet and said to him, his heart filled with joy: "I have given purpose to the human condition one obtains through the sacrifice of a hundred offerings;[273] I have extracted the essence of the passing and vain advantages of royal power; I have assured for myself the other world, and I have adorned this one with hundreds of caityas, more brilliant than the cloud with shades of white; have I not thus today accomplished the law, so difficult to perform, of the incomparable being?" Finally, the king, having bowed before Upagupta, withdrew.

When king Aśoka had thus given a hundred thousand [survarṇas] to each of these places, the place of birth, the Bodhi tree, the place where the Buddha turned the wheel of the law, where he entered into nirvāṇa, he principally favored the Bodhi tree, thinking that it was there that the Bhagavat had obtained the state of a perfectly accomplished buddha. He thus sent to this tree all that he had of the most precious jewels. The foremost of the wives of king Aśoka was named Tiṣyarakṣitā. The queen, [seeing the piety of the king], had the following reflection: "The king takes pleasure with me and yet he sends all that he had of the most precious jewels to the Bodhi tree!" Then, she had a woman from the mātaṅga caste come and said to her: "Couldn't you destroy this Bodhi tree for me, which is a kind of rival for me?" "I can do so," replied the woman, "but I need

273. It would perhaps be more in accordance with Buddhist ideas to say "which one does not obtain . . ." Our manuscripts are quite incorrect at this point.

kārṣāpaṇas." The mātaṅgī attacked the tree with her mantras and tied a thread to it; and the tree soon began to wither. The people of the king came to announce to him that the Bodhi tree was withering, and they pronounced this stanza:

"This tree in whose shadow the Tathāgata succeeded in knowing the entire world as it is, and in obtaining omniscience, this Bodhi tree, O king of men, begins to waste away."

At this news, the king lost consciousness and fell to the ground, but water was splashed on his face and he returned to himself. When he had regained a little of his senses, he exclaimed while weeping: "Seeing the trunk of the king of trees, I believed I saw Svayaṃbhū himself; but once the tree of the Lord is destroyed, my very life will also be extinguished."[274]

Meanwhile, Tiṣyarakṣitā, seeing the king troubled by grief, said to him: "Lord, if the Bodhi tree came to die, I will fill the king with happiness." "It is not a woman," said the king, "it is the Bodhi tree [that can make me happy], this tree under which the Bhagavat reached the supreme state of a perfectly accomplished buddha." Tiṣyarakṣitā thus said to the mātaṅgī: "Can you restore the Bodhi tree to its original state?" "I can," responded the woman, "if it still has some life." She thus untied the thread [that tied it], dug the earth all around the trunk, and watered it with one thousand vases of milk in one day. After some days the tree came back to its original state. The people of the king hastened to announce the news to him: "Lord, happiness to you; here is the tree back to its original state." Enraptured with joy, Aśoka, gazing at the Bodhi tree, exclaimed: "What Bimbisāra and the other chiefs of kings shining with radiance did not do, I will do. I will pay the greatest homage to the Bodhi tree by washing it with water imbued with fragrant substances, and to the assembly of arhats by fulfilling for it the duties of hospitality during the five months of the varṣa."[275] Then, the king,

274. This attempt by the queen against the Bodhi tree is related in brief by Faxian (*Foe koue ki*, p. 294); with other details in the *Mahāvaṃsa*, chap. 20, p. 122. A common tradition forms the core of these various accounts.

275. The text says *pañcavārṣika*; now, since the *varṣa*, or the rainy season, which it was the custom of the monks to spend among the laity, lasts for four or five months, I suppose that it is to this custom that the aforementioned word of the text alludes. But it could be that this term referred to what Mr. Abel Rémusat calls, according to Faxian, "the great quinquennial assembly" (*Foe koue ki*, p. 26). Since I do not have sufficient precise details on the nature and object of this assembly, I have believed that, in order to translate *pañcavārṣika*, I must adopt the meaning that recalls a known usage. However, I must not forget to remark that this great quinquennial assembly of Faxian is very likely the one instituted by the Buddhist king Piyadassi, in the third of the edicts of Girnar, and whose object was to recommend again the principal rules of Buddhist morality: the obedience one owes to one's father and to one's mother, liberality toward brahmans and śramaṇas, and other equally humane principles (Prinsep, in *Journal of the Asiatic Society of Bengal*, vol. 7, pp. 228, 242, 250, and 439). In this edict of Girnar as in the lāths of Delhi, of Allahabad, and of other provinces of the North, brahmans are again mentioned before śramaṇas; but in the fourth edict, as it is reproduced at Dhauli in Cuttack, śramaṇas rank before brahmans, as in the Sanskrit texts of the North. In my view, it is a circumstance most worthy of remark and which proves the anteriority of Brahmanism to Buddhism in the most obvious manner. It is necessary to add this fact to those I have put forward above (section 2, p. 168ff.) in favor of the thesis I have tried to prove.

having had one thousand vases made of gold, of lapis lazuli, and of crystal filled with perfumed water, a considerable quantity of food and drinks gathered, and a mass of perfumes, garlands, and flowers collected, took a bath, covered himself in new robes, not yet worn and ornamented with long fringe, submitted to the fast one practices in consideration of eight conditions; then, having taken a bowl of incense, he mounted the platform of his palace and exclaimed, turning toward the four points of the horizon: "May the śrāvakas of the blessed Buddha agree to come here out of benevolence for me!" And he pronounced these stanzas:

"May the disciples of the Sugata who have walked on the right path, whose senses were calm, may these sages, vanquishers of desires and sin, worthy of respect and honored by gods and humans, arrive in this place out of compassion for me.

"Friends of quietude, masters of themselves, free of all attachment, may these sons beloved by the Sugata, by the king of the law, these sages who have become āryas, who asuras, suras, and humans venerate, come here out of compassion for me.

"May the sages filled with steadfastness who inhabit the pleasant city of Kāśmīrapura, may the āryas who reside in the gloomy forest of Mahāvana,[276] in the chariot of Revataka,[277] come here on my behalf.

"May the sons of the Jina who live near the lake Anavatapta, in the mountains, near the rivers and in the valleys, may these sages, friends of contemplation, filled with perseverance, come here with the energy of compassion.

"May the sons of the most eloquent of men, who reside in the excellent divine palace of Śerīṣaka,[278] may these monks free from grief and whose nature is filled with mercy, come here out of compassion for me.

At the time of Piyadassi, that is to say, two centuries after Śākya, the political superiority of the brahmans was still sufficiently incontestable that a Buddhist king, in one of his edicts, was obliged to name them before the Buddhist monks themselves. But in the books written, or at least revised later, at the time of the predominance of Buddhism, the compilers took the same liberty toward their opponents that, according to the remark of Prinsep, the writer of the edicts of Cuttack had already given to himself, and from that time śramaṇas invariably came before brahmans.

276. It is the monastery of Mahāvana, so called from the wood in which it was located in the country of Udyāna (*Foe koue ki*, p. 54).

277. I have not seen the indication of this locality elsewhere. The name *Revata*, from which that of *Revataka* stems, is, however, not foreign to the Buddhist tradition. The *Lalitavistara* so named the brahman, chief of one of the hermitages that Śākyamuni visited at the beginning of his life as a mendicant (*Lalitavistara*, fol. 125b of my manuscript). The tradition of Southern Buddhism mentions a Revata even more celebrated, who directed the third council and who was contemporary with Dharmāśoka (Turnour, in *Journal of the Asiatic Society of Bengal*, vol. 7, p. 791). The latter plays a very important role in the *Mahāvaṃsa* (*Mahāvanso*, p. 16ff., ed. in -4°). Nothing indicates to us which of these two Revatas could have given his name to what the text of our legend calls "the chariot of Revataka." This expression *chariot* itself appears quite mythological; it recalls the word *vimāna*, which designates the divine chariots among the brahmans or the kinds of moving palaces given to the gods, and of which clouds probably furnished the first idea.

278. I find nothing in our legends related to this probably fabulous palace. The Buddhists of the South speak of a place called Sirīsamālaka, in the legend of the first buddha of the present epoch (*Mahāvanso*, pp. 90

"May the monks filled with energy who reside in the mountain of Gandhamādana[279] come out of benevolence for me, summoned by my invitation."

As soon as the king had pronounced these words, three hundred thousand monks found themselves gathered in his presence. But among these hundreds of thousands of arhats, of disciples, and ordinary men filled with virtues, there was no one who presented himself to occupy the seat of honor. "Thus, how is it," said the king, "that the seat of the elder is not occupied?" Then, the aged Yaśas, possessed of the six supernatural knowledges, responded to him in these terms: "Great king, here is the seat of the elder." "Is there, O sthavira," replied the king, "a monk older than you?" "Yes," said the sthavira. "There is one who has been designated by the most eloquent of sages as the chief of those who made the lion's roar heard: it is Piṇḍola, descendant of Bharadvāja; and this seat, the foremost of all, is his." Immediately, the king, on whose body all the hair bristled like the filaments of the kadamba flower, addressed this question to him: "Is there still in the world a monk who saw the Buddha?" "Yes," responded the sthavira. "There is one who has seen the Buddha; it is Piṇḍola, descendant of Bharadvāja; and he still lives." "Could I not see him?" said Aśoka. "You will see him, O great king; this is the moment of his coming." Enraptured with joy, the king exclaimed: "What advantage it would be for me, what superior and incomparable advantage if I could see face to face this noble creature who belongs by his name to the race of Bharadvāja!" Then, the king, joining his hands in a sign of respect, stood with eyes fixed on the sky. Immediately, the sthavira Piṇḍola, descendant of Bharadvāja, surrounded by several thousand arhats, who deployed themselves on his right and on his left like the ends of the crescent of the moon, dropped from the skies, like the rājahaṃsa, and came to sit in the place of honor. At the sight of Piṇḍola the Bharadvājide, these numerous thousands of monks came forward to meet him. The king saw Piṇḍola, whose head was white, whose forehead was covered by long eyebrows that hid the pupil of his eyes, and whose aspect was that of a pratyekabuddha; and hardly had he seen him than, falling to the ground to his full height at the feet of Piṇḍola like a tree cut at the root, he kissed the feet of the monk; then, having risen and having put his two knees on the ground, he joined his hands in a sign of respect, and looking at the monk, he said, shedding tears:

"When, after having triumphed over the multitude of my enemies, I saw gath-

---

and 93, ed. in -4°). It was the enclosure that surrounded the sirīsa tree (*śirīṣa* in Sanskrit) under which this Buddha reached his state of perfection (*ibid.*, p. 90). I would not dare to assert that it is this place that our legend recalls with the name Śerīṣaka. This word, which would be more correctly written *śairīṣaka*, may, however, mean "the place of the śirīṣa."

279. It is known that Mount Gandhamādana is a fabulous place; it was spoken of above, section 2, p. 200, note 187. However, the continuation of the dialogue of Piṇḍola and Aśoka seems to place this mountain to the north of the lake Anavatapta. Could one with this name not exist in the country of Gandhāra?

ered under my sole power the earth with its mountains to the shores of the ocean that surround it, I did not feel as much pleasure as seeing the sthavira.

"The sight of you, which in your compassion you accord me, makes the Tathāgata appear to my eyes today; the sight of you doubles my benevolent disposition.

"You thus saw him, O sthavira, the sovereign of the three worlds, my preceptor, the blessed Buddha?" Then, the sthavira Piṇḍola, descendant of Bharadvāja, raising his eyebrows with his two hands, responded, looking at Aśoka: "Yes, I saw him more than once, the great and incomparable ṛṣi, whose splendor resembled the radiance of burning gold; I saw him adorned with the thirty-two signs of beauty, with his face like an autumn moon, with his superior voice like that of Brahmā; I saw him living in solitude." "In which place, O recluse, and how did you see the Bhagavat?" The sthavira responded: "When the Bhagavat, O great king, after having routed the army of Māra, went, for the first time, to pass the time of the rainy season at Rājagṛha with five hundred arhats, I was in this city at that time. It is there that I perfectly saw this being worthy of respect." And he pronounced this stanza:

"When, surrounded by monks free like him from passions, the great recluse, the Tathāgata, went to Rājagṛha to pass there the time of the varṣa;

"I was at that moment in this city, and I found myself in the presence of the perfect Buddha; then, I saw the recluse as you yourself see me today.

"And, moreover, O great king, when the Bhagavat, wishing to defeat the tīrthyas at Śrāvastī, performed a great miracle, making this crown of buddhas who ascended to the Akaniṣṭha heaven appear, I was then in this city, and there I saw this sport of the Buddha." Then, he pronounced this stanza:

"When the tīrthyas, who walked on the evil path, were brought down by the Bhagavat, who used his supernatural power, I then saw, O king, the noble sport of the hero with ten strengths that filled creatures with joy.[280]

"And, moreover, O great king, when after having passed the time of the varṣa among the Trayastriṃśa devas, to teach the law to his mother to whom he owed his birth, the Bhagavat descended again in the city of Sāṃkāśya, followed by the multitude of gods, I was there at that moment in this city; I attended the brilliant feast of gods and humans, and I also saw the glorious metamorphosis of Utpalavarṇā, who transformed herself into a cakravartin king."[281] And he pronounced this stanza:

280. This is an allusion to the facts recounted in the legend, the main part of which I have translated above, section 2, p. 205.

281. See above what was said about the travel and the miraculous descent of Śākyamuni in the city of Sāṃkāśya (section 2, p. 194, note 180). As for the miraculous transformation of the mendicant Utpalā, Faxian made a short allusion to it in his passage through Sāṃkāśya (*Foe koue ki*, p. 124). There is, in addition, in our text a new trace of Pāli or Prakrit: it is the word *saṃpadā* for the Sanskrit *saṃpad* (prosperity).

"When after having passed the varṣa in the world of the gods, the most eloquent of men descended again [to earth], I was in this place, and then I saw the recluse, the foremost of beings.

"And, moreover, O great king, when invited by Sumāgadhā, the daughter of Anāthapiṇḍika, the Bhagavat went miraculously to Puṇḍravardhana,[282] escorted by five hundred arhats; then, seizing the summit of a mountain by virtue of my supernatural power, I soared into the skies and went to Puṇḍravardhana. And, at this moment the Bhagavat gave me this order: 'You will not enter into complete nirvāṇa as long as the law has not disappeared.'" Then, he pronounced this stanza:

"When, by the strength of his supernatural power, the guide, the preceptor, at the invitation of Sumāgadhā, went [to her], then, seizing the summit of a mountain through my superhuman strength, I transported myself rapidly to Puṇḍravardhana.

"Then, the sage, friend of mercy, who was born in the family of the Śākyas, gave me the following order: 'You will not enter into complete nirvāṇa as long as the law has not disappeared.'

"And, moreover, O great king, when, long ago, at the moment when the Bhagavat had entered Rājagṛha to beg for his meal, you threw a handful of earth into his bowl, saying to him with the childishness of your age: 'I will give him flour,' and Rādhagupta[283] approved of you; when on this occasion, the Bhagavat made the following prediction about you: 'A hundred years after I have entered into complete nirvāṇa, this child will be the king named Aśoka in the city of Pāṭaliputra; he will be a cakravartin, sovereign of the four parts of the earth; he will be a just king, a sovereign king, who will distribute my relics and who will establish eighty-four thousand royal edicts of the law'; at the time of all these events, I was in this city." And he added this stanza:

"When you had thrown a handful of earth into the bowl of the Buddha, wishing to show benevolence to him with the childishness of your age, I was there at this moment."

The king then replied: "Sthavira, where are you staying now?" "To the north of the first of ponds, on the mountain Gandhamādana," responded the sthavira. "I live, O prince, with other monks who follow the same rule as me." "What,"

282. See the additions at the end of the volume.

283. The presence of the name of Rādhagupta could cause a difficulty here, from which the continuation of the legend gives us the means to escape. We have seen above that the young child who played with Jaya, that is to say, Aśoka, in the one of his existences when he was contemporary with Śākya, was named Vijaya (above, p. 360, note 245). How thus can Piṇḍola say, as he does in our text, that Rādhgupta gave his assent to the generosity of little Jaya? It is that, according to the continuation of the legend that we will soon see, Rādhagupta, the minister of Aśoka, had been Vijaya himself, and that Piṇḍola calls these two personages by the name they bear at the very time that he speaks to them.

said the king, "is the number of those who surround the sthavira?" "My retinue, O king of men, is of sixty thousand arhats; it is with these sages free from desires and vanquishers of sin that I spend my life. But, O great king, why would I allow doubt to penetrate the mind of the assembly of monks? As soon as the assembly has taken its meal, I will satisfy it with a pleasant instruction." "Let it be as the sthavira orders," replied the king. "As for me, in memory of the Buddha, I will give a bath to the Bodhi tree, and immediately afterward I will offer excellent food to the assembly of monks." Then, the king, having called Sarvamitra the herald, said to him: "I will give a hundred thousand [suvarṇas] to the assembly of āryas, and I will give a bath to the Bodhi tree with the water of a thousand vases. Proclaim in my name [that the monks will be received by me during] the five months of the varṣa."

At that time, Kunāla[284] had already lost his two eyes, and he stood to the right of his father. He held out two fingers without pronouncing a word; his intention was to announce that he wished to give double. But at the moment when Kunāla increased the sum in this way with a sign of his hand, the multitude of people began to laugh. The king, laughing in his turn, said to Rādhagupta: "Oh! who has thus so doubled the sum?" "There are many beings," responded Rādhagupta, "who have need of the merit of good deeds; it is one of those who has doubled it." "Well!" said the king. "I will give three hundred thousand [suvarṇas] to the assembly of āryas, and I will give a bath to the Bodhi tree with the water of a thousand vases. Let it be proclaimed in my name [that the monks will be received by me during] the five months of the varṣa." At this moment, Kunāla raised four fingers; but the king said in anger to Rādhagupta: "Who thus, Rādhagupta, is the one who fights with me so? Who is he, this ignoramus of the world?" At the sight of the irritated king, Rādhagupta, throwing himself at his feet, said to him: "Lord, who would have the power to fight with the king of men? It is the virtuous Kunāla who plays with his father." Immediately, the king, turning to the right, saw Kunāla and exclaimed: "Sthavira, I give, first to the Bodhi tree and then to the assembly of āryas, my monarchy, my wives, the multitude of my advisers, Kunāla and my very person, except for my treasure; I will bathe the great Bodhi tree with milk and water perfumed with sandalwood, with saffron, with camphor, contained in five thousand vases of gold, of silver, of crystal, of lapis lazuli, filled with various kinds of perfumes; I will offer thousands of flowers to it. Let it be proclaimed in my name [that the monks will be received by me during] the five months of the varṣa." And he pronounced this stanza:

284. Kunāla is this son of Aśoka whose eyes the queen Tiṣyarakṣitā had put out because he had resisted her advances. He was so named because of the beauty of his eyes, which resembled those of a bird called *kuṇāla*. His name is written with an *n* or an *ṇ*.

"My flourishing monarchy, my wives, the whole multitude of my advisers, I give all that, except for my treasure, to the assembly, which is like a vase of virtues; I give myself and Kunāla, who is filled with qualities."

Then, the king, having departed in the presence of the assembly, at the head of which was the sthavira Piṇḍola, descendant of Bharadvāja, had a platform built on the four sides of the Bodhi tree; then, mounting this platform himself, he bathed the Bodhi tree with the water of four thousand vases. And hardly had the tree been so watered than it became again as it was in the past. There is a text that says:

"Hardly had the king of men given this excellent bath to the Bodhi tree than the tree came to be covered with a delicate and green foliage; at the sight of the green leaves that adorned it and its soft buds, the king felt utmost joy, as did the multitude of his ministers who surrounded him."

When the king had given a bath to the Bodhi tree, he proceeded to usher the assembly of monks [into his palace]. At this moment, the sthavira Yaśas addressed him with these words: "Great king, the numerous assembly of āryas gathered here is worthy of the greatest respect; it is necessary to usher it in in such a way that no wrong is done to it." This is why the king himself ushered the monks in with his own hand until the last.[285]

There were two śrāmaṇeras there who gave themselves over to a mutual exchange of good offices.[286] If one gave flour to his companion, the other gave him the same; and they exchanged food and sweets in this way. The king, seeing them, began to laugh: "Here," he said to himself, "are śrāmaṇeras who play a children's game." Meanwhile, when the king had ushered in the entire assembly of monks, he went to sit at the place of honor. At this moment, he received this warning from the sthavira: "Has the king not committed some oversight due to lack of attention?" "None," responded the king. "Yet there are these two śrāmaṇeras who amuse themselves with a children's game, like little boys who play in the dust. These śrāmaṇeras amuse themselves with flour, food, and sweets." "Enough," replied the sthavira. "These are two arhats who each gives up his share with equal detachment." At these words, Aśoka, his heart filled with joy,

285. I translate the word *navakānta* in this way by conjecture; it seems to me that it must be the opposite of *vṛddhānta*, which is one line below in our legend and which appears rather frequently elsewhere, always with the meaning of: "the place of the elder, the first place." The *vṛddhānta* means in effect, I believe, "the limit of the old man," the term that the old man reaches and by extension "the place of honor." The term *navakānta* must mean "the limit of the new," the last place.

286. Here again is a not very clear expression: *saṃrañjanīyaṃ dharmaṃ samādāya vartataḥ*. This passage could also mean "they happened to have received the law that inspires affection." But the prefix *sam* of the adjective *saṃrañjanīya* seems to me to express an idea of reciprocity that determines the meaning. The root *rañj*, like *mud*, is used in our legends of the North as in the Pāli of the South with the special meaning of "to please, to be gracious" in a conversation; and when two personages meet, one uses terms derived from these roots, like *rañjanī* and *saṃmodanī*, to express the way in which they open their conversation.

conceived this thought: "When I have approached these two śrāmaṇeras, I will give the assembly of monks enough material for it to dress." The two śrāmaṇeras, having divined the intention of the king, said to each other: "We must cooperate in increasing his merits." Immediately, one appeared holding a tortoise shell and the other brought colors. At this sight, the king said to them: "Śrāmaṇeras, what are you going to do?" "We have divined," they responded, "that the king desired to give the assembly of monks enough material for it to dress, and we come to dye this material." "I have just conceived the thought," the king said to himself, "and I have not pronounced a single word. They thus know the thought of the others, these magnanimous sages?" Immediately falling at their feet to his full height, he said to them, with hands joined in a sign of respect:

"The descendant of the Mauryas, with his servants, his people, and the inhabitants of his cities, has reached the height of happiness, has happily celebrated all the sacrifices, since virtuous beings show him enough benevolence to make him such a present today."[287]

The king then said to them: "I wish, after having approached you, to give the assembly of monks enough material for each to have three robes." Consequently, when the five months of the varṣa had elapsed, king Aśoka presented each monk with three robes; and when he had given four hundred thousand mantles to the assembly, he bought back from the [monks] the land, his wives, the multitude of his ministers, himself, and Kunāla [his son].[288] His faith in the teaching of the Bhagavat had only increased; and he established eighty-four thousand royal edicts of the law.

The day when the king promulgated his edicts, the queen Padmavatī gave birth to a beautiful, pleasant to see, graceful son; the eyes of this child shone with most sparkling radiance. One went to announce the news to the king: "Happiness to the king; a son is born to him." Enraptured with joy, Aśoka exclaimed: "An extreme joy, a limitless joy fills my heart; the splendor of the Mauryan race is at its height; it is because I govern according to the law that a son was born to me; may he also make the law blossom!" This is why the name Dharmavivardhana[289] was given to him. The child was then brought to the king, who, seeing him, was overjoyed and exclaimed:

"How pure are the beautiful eyes of this child, these eyes resemble a blue

287. The text is here altered in our two manuscripts; the last verse lacks a syllable that I restore by conjecture.

288. It is most interesting to find in the Chinese travelers the historical trace of this event, which is here indicated only in a very abridged manner. According to Faxian, there still existed in his time, near Pāṭaliputra, a column erected by Aśoka that bore this inscription: "The king Ayu (Aśoka) had given Yanfuti (Jambudvīpa) to the monks of the four sides; he bought it back from them with money, and did so three times" (*Foe koue ki*, pp. 255 and 261). This is the reason why in our legend it is said that Aśoka gives everything to the assembly of monks save his treasure. He wished to save the means to repeat these acts of generosity in this way.

289. See the additions at the end of the volume.

lotus in full bloom! His face, adorned with beauty, shines like the disc of the full moon."

Then, the king said to his ministers: "Do you see, lords, whose eyes the eyes of this child resemble?" "We do not know a man," replied the ministers, "who has such eyes; but, there is, in the Himavat, this king [of mountains], a bird named kunāla, whose eyes resemble the eyes of your son." This is what this stanza expresses:

"On the summit of one of the mountain peaks, king of snow, rich in shrubs, in flowers, and in waters, lives a bird named kunāla; the eyes of your son resemble those of this bird."

"Bring a kunāla," exclaimed the king. Thus, the yakṣas heard the orders he gave at a distance of one yojana in the sky, and the nāgas heard them at a distance of one yojana beneath the earth. So, the yakṣas brought a kunāla to him at that very instant. The king, after having examined the eyes of the bird for a long time, could not discover any difference between its eyes and those of his son. This is why he said to his ministers: "The prince has eyes like those of a kunāla; thus, give him the name Kunāla." This is what this stanza expresses:

"Struck by the charm of his eyes, the king of the earth exclaimed: 'My son must be called Kunāla.' This is how the name of this prince who had the virtues of an ārya was celebrated on earth."

When the prince was grown, he was given a young girl named Kāñcanamālā as his wife. One day, the king went with his son to the hermitage of Kukkuṭa. At this moment, Yaśas, the sthavira of the assembly, who possessed the five supernatural knowledges, saw that Kunāla would not be long without losing his eyes, and he made it known to the king. "Why?" [replied Aśoka]. "It is that Kunāla does not fulfill his duties." "Kunāla," the king said to him, "take good care to do what the sthavira of the assembly commands you to do." Immediately throwing himself at the feet of the sthavira, Kunāla said to him: "Lord, what do you command me?" "Convince yourself well, O Kunāla, that the eye is something perishable." And he added this stanza:

"Reflect constantly, O prince, that the eye is by its nature perishable, that it is the source of a thousand sorrows; becoming too attached to it, many ordinary men commit actions that make their misfortune."

Kunāla began to reflect on this maxim and he had it ceaselessly in mind. He liked only solitude and repose. Seated at the back of the palace, in a solitary place, he imagined the eye and the other senses as perishable. One day Tiṣyarakṣitā, the foremost of the wives of Aśoka, passed through this place and saw Kunāla, who was alone. Seduced by the beauty of his eyes, she clasped him in her arms and said to him:

"At the sight of your ravishing gaze, of your beautiful body, of your charming eyes, all my body burns like dried straw that the forest fire consumes."

At these words, Kunāla, covering his ears with his two hands, responded to her: "Do not pronounce such culpable words in front of a son, for you are like a mother to me; renounce licentious passion; this love would be the path to hell for you." But Tiṣyarakṣitā, seeing that she could not seduce him, said to him in anger: "Since you push me away here, at the moment when, enraptured with love, I come to offer myself to you, in a short time, insane one, you will cease to live." "O my mother," responded Kunāla, "it is better to die persisting in duty and remaining pure; I have nothing to do with a life that would be an object of blame for good people, a life that, in closing the path to heaven to me, would become the cause of my death and would be scorned and condemned by the sages." From this moment, Tiṣyarakṣitā dreamed only of finding the occasion to harm Kunāla.

It happened that the city of Takṣaśilā, which was located in the North and which obeyed king Aśoka, began to revolt. At this news, the king wished to go there himself, but his ministers said to him: "O king, send the prince there; he will bring the city back to duty." Consequently, the king, having called Kunāla, spoke to him in this way: "My dear son, go to Takṣaśilā and subdue this city." "Yes, Lord, I will go," responded Kunāla. [This is what this stanza expresses:]

"The king, having learned thereby the desire of the one he called his son and knowing in his heart what he could expect from his affection, himself renounced the journey and destined Kunāla for it."

Aśoka, having the city and the road ornamented and having the old, the sick, and the destitute moved to a distance, mounted a chariot with his son and left Pāṭaliputra. At the moment of leaving his son to retrace his steps, he threw his arms around his neck, and contemplating his eyes, he said to him while bursting into tears: "The eyes are fortunate and the eyesight happy for mortals who will constantly see the prince's lotus face." But a brahman astrologer predicted that in a short time Kunāla would lose his sight. Therefore, king Aśoka, unable to tire of contemplating the eyes of his son, exclaimed when he looked at them:

"The eyes of the prince are perfect," and the king felt an extreme attachment for him. "Today, I contemplate these eyes whose radiance is so pure, which spread happiness; these eyes destined to perish.

"This city, happy as heaven itself, is overjoyed because it sees the prince; but when he has lost his eyes, all the hearts of the city will plunge into grief."

The young prince soon arrived in the vicinity of Takṣaśilā. At the news of his approach, the inhabitants, having ornamented the city and the main road to a distance of two and a half yojanas, went out to meet him with bowls [full of offerings]. This is what this stanza expresses:

"At this news, the inhabitants of Takṣaśilā went out in respect to meet the son of the king, carrying bowls filled with jewels in their hands."

When they had arrived in his presence, they said, with hands joined in a sign of respect: "We are not revolting against the prince and king Aśoka; there are evil ministers who have come to heap outrage on us." Thus, Kunāla entered the city of Takṣaśilā with great pomp.

Meanwhile, king Aśoka was affected by a terrible malady. His excrement came out of his mouth; an impure humor escaped from all his pores and nothing could cure him. He then said: "Let Kunāla come, I wish to put him on the throne."

[Here, the legend recounts how Tiṣyarakṣitā cured the king and seized his mind. I do not believe it useful to reproduce here this passage, which I have translated above, section 2, p. 178, and I beg the reader to be kind enough to refer to it if he wants to know the continuation of the story.]

When the king was cured, full of joy, he asked Tiṣyarakṣitā which favor she desired: "What gift will I make to you?" he said to her. "May the king," she responded, "grant me the monarchy for seven days." "And I, what will become of me?" "After seven days," said the queen, "the king will again take royal power." Thus, Aśoka ceded the monarchy to Tiṣyarakṣitā for seven days. The first thing the queen thought of was to satisfy her hatred against Kunāla. She wrote a false letter [in the name of the king] that ordered the inhabitants of Takṣaśilā to tear out the eyes of Kunāla. And she added this stanza:

"For Aśoka, this strong and violent king, has ordered the inhabitants of Takṣaśilā to tear out the eyes of this enemy; he is the shame of the Mauryan race."

When king Aśoka gave an order that must be carried out promptly, he sealed it with an ivory seal. Tiṣyarakṣitā said to herself: "I will seal this letter with the ivory seal when the king is asleep"; and she went near Aśoka. But at that moment the king awakened, quite afraid. "What is it?" the queen said to him. "I just had a sad dream," the king responded. "I saw two vultures who wanted to tear out Kunāla's eyes." "Happiness to the prince!" exclaimed the queen. A second time, the king again awakened, quite afraid. "O queen," he said, "I just had a sad dream." "And what dream?" the queen asked him. "I saw Kunāla," said the king, "who had entered the city with long hair, nails, and beard." "Happiness to the prince!" exclaimed the queen. Finally, the king having fallen asleep again, Tiṣyarakṣitā sealed her letter with the ivory seal and had it sent to the city of Takṣaśilā.

Meanwhile the king saw his teeth fall out in a dream. As soon as it was day, he called the soothsayers and said to them: "What does the dream I just had foretell?" "O king," answered the soothsayers, "he who has such dreams, he who during his sleep sees his teeth fall out and be destroyed, will see his son deprived of his eyes and will learn of his death." At these words, king Aśoka rose with all possible speed from his seat and, pointing his joined hands to the four sides of the horizon in a sign of respect, began to beseech the divinity, and he pronounced this stanza:

"May the divinity who is benevolent to the preceptor, to the law and to the assembly, the foremost of troops, may the ṛṣis who are foremost in the world, protect our son Kunāla."

During this time, the letter of the queen reached Takṣaśilā. At the sight of this missive, the inhabitants of Takṣaśilā, those of the city and of the country who were happy with the numerous virtues of Kunāla, did not have the courage to make known to him the inhuman order it contained; but after having reflected for a long time, they said to themselves: "The king is violent; he is naturally hot-tempered; if he does not forgive his son, all the more reason for him not to spare us." And they pronounced this stanza:

"He who could conceive hatred against a prince so calm, whose mores are those of a recluse, and who desires only the welfare of all beings, how will he be for others?"

Finally, they decided to inform him of this news, and handed the letter to him. Kunāla, having read it, exclaimed: "The order is worthy of confidence. Do what you are commanded." Cāṇḍālas were thus made to come and the order was given to them to tear out the eyes of Kunāla, but the torturers, joining their hands in a sign of respect, exclaimed: "We do not have the courage for it. And why?

"Only an insane man capable of wiping out the radiance of the moon could tear out the eyes of your face, which resembles the star of the night."

The prince gave them the crown that covered his head and said to them: "Do your duty for the price of this gift"; [but they refused, saying:] "This action must necessarily lead to misfortune." Then, a man with a deformed aspect and covered with eighteen marks of a repulsive color appeared, who offered to tear out the eyes of the prince. He was thus led to Kunāla. At this moment, the words of the sthaviras came to the young man's mind; the prince, recalling them, pronounced this stanza:

"It is because they predicted this misfortune that these sages who know the truth have said: 'Behold, this entire world is perishable; no one remains in a permanent situation.'

"Yes, they were virtuous friends to me who sought my advantage and wished for my happiness, these magnanimous sages, free from passion, who have taught me the law.

"When I consider the fragility of all things and reflect on the counsel of my masters, I no longer tremble, friend, at the idea of this torture; for I know that my eyes are something perishable.

"Let them be torn out or preserve them for me, according to what the king commands; I have taken in with my eyes the best that they could give me, since I have seen that objects are perishable."

Then, addressing himself to this man: "Go on," he said, "tear out one eye first and place it in my hand." The torturer proceeded to perform his duty; and at this moment, thousands of men uttered lamentable cries: "Ah! misfortune!

"Here is this moon of pure splendor that falls from the sky; a beautiful lotus is torn from the clump of white water lilies."

While this multitude of people made these lamentations heard, the eye of Kunāla was torn from him and he received it in his hand. Taking it, the prince said:

"Why thus do you not see shapes as you did a little while ago, crude globe of flesh? How mistaken and how blameworthy, the insane who become attached to you, saying: 'It is me.'

"Those who, always attentive, know to recognize in you an organ that resembles a ball which one cannot grasp, which is pure but dependent, those will be sheltered from misfortune."

While the prince reflected in this way on the instability of all beings, he acquired the reward of the state of śrotāpatti in the sight of the multitude of people. Then, Kunāla, who saw the truths, said to the torturer: "Now the second eye; tear it out." Indeed, the man tore it out and put it in the hand of the prince. At this moment, Kunāla, who had just lost the eyes of flesh but in whom those of science had been purified, pronounced this stanza:

"The eye of flesh, although difficult to seize, has just be taken from me; but I have acquired the perfect and irreproachable eyes of wisdom.

"If I am abandoned by the king, I become the son of the magnanimous king of the law, whose child I am called.

"If I am deposed from the supreme grandeur that brings so much grief and suffering in its wake, I have acquired the sovereignty of the law that destroys suffering and grief."

Some time later, Kunāla knew that his torture was not the work of his father Aśoka but that it was the effect of the intrigues of Tiṣyarakṣitā. At this news, he exclaimed:

"May queen Tiṣyarakṣitā, who has here put to use this means to ensure me such a great advantage, keep her happiness, life, and power for a long time."

However, Kāñcanamālā learned that the eyes of Kunāla had been torn out. Immediately, using her right as spouse, she rushed through the multitude to go to meet Kunāla and saw him deprived of his two eyes and his body completely covered with blood. At this sight, she fainted and fell to the ground. Someone hastened to throw water on her and to revive her. When she began to regain her senses, she exclaimed while shedding tears:

"These ravishing and beloved eyes, which looking at me made my happiness, now that they are thrown to the ground and deprived of the faculty of sight, I feel life abandoning my body."

Then, Kunāla, wishing to soothe his wife, replied in this way: "Cease your tears; you must not give yourself over to grief. Each collects the recompense of the actions he has done in this world"; and he pronounced this stanza:

"Recognizing that this world is the fruit of deeds and that creatures are condemned to misfortune; knowing that men are made to see their dear ones taken from them, you must not, dear friend, shed tears."

Then, Kunāla departed from Takṣaśilā with his wife. Since the time he had been conceived in the womb of his mother, the prince always had a very delicate body. He thus could not engage in any profession, and he only knew how to sing and play the vīṇā. He went begging for his food and shared what he gathered with his wife. Kāñcanamālā, returning on the route by which she had been brought from Pāṭaliputra, followed it accompanied by the prince; and once arrived in the city, she proceeded to enter the residence of Aśoka. But they were stopped by the guard at the door. Meanwhile, they were ushered into the place where the chariots of the king were kept. At the break of day, Kunāla began to play his vīṇā and to sing of how his eyes had been torn out and how the view of the truths had appeared to him. And he pronounced this stanza:

"The sage who sees the eye and the other senses with the pure torch of science is free from the law of transmigration.

"If your mind, indulged in sin, is tormented by the sufferings of existence and if you desire happiness in this world, hasten to renounce forever the objects of the senses."

King Aśoka heard the songs of the prince, and he said with a feeling of joy:

"It is to me that are addressed the songs of Kunāla and the sounds of this vīṇā that I have not heard for so long. The prince has returned to my residence, but he does not want to see anyone."

Immediately calling one of the guards, the king said to him: "Do you not find some resemblance between this song and that of Kunāla? It seemed that this performance betrayed some trouble. This voice has strongly moved my soul; I am like the elephant who, having lost its young, would come to hear its voice. Thus go and bring me Kunāla." The guard immediately went to the place where the chariots were kept; and there he found Kunāla, deprived of his eyes and whose body was burned by the ardor of the sun and by the wind; but not having recognized him, he returned to king Aśoka and said to him: "O king, it is not Kunāla; it is a blind mendicant with his wife in the place where the chariots of the king are kept." At these words, the king, quite troubled, had this reflection: "Here is the effect of the disastrous dreams I have had; certainly, it is Kunāla whose eyes have been torn out." And he pronounced this stanza:

"According to the omens I saw long ago in a dream, no, there is no more doubt, the eyes of Kunāla have been torn out."

Bursting into tears, he exclaimed: "Quickly bring this mendicant into my presence; for my heart cannot find calm while thinking about the misfortune that could have struck my son." The guard, having returned to the hall of the chariots, said to Kunāla: "Of whom are you the son and what is your name?"

"Aśoka," replied Kunāla, "this king who increases the glory of the Mauryas, whose authority the entire earth obeys with submission, this king is my father, and my name is Kunāla. But today, I am the son of the Buddha, this descendant of the solar race who established the law." Immediately Kunāla was conducted with his wife into the presence of king Aśoka. On seeing Kunāla, who was deprived of his eyes, whose body, burned by the ardor of the sun and by the wind, was covered with a shabby robe drained of color by water during his travels,[290] the king to whom the crime was unknown, gazed at his son several times without being able to recognize him, and seeing only a human form before his eyes, he said: "Are you Kunāla?" "Yes," responded the prince. "I am Kunāla." At these words, the king fainted and fell on the ground. This is what this stanza expresses:

"Seeing the face of Kunāla, whose eyes had been torn out, king Aśoka, ripped by suffering, fell to the ground, consumed by the fire of grief at the sight of his son's misfortune."

Water was thrown on the king, he was helped back up, placed again on his seat. When he had regained a little of his senses, he clasped his son in his arms. This is what this stanza says:

"The king, after some moments, returning to himself, threw his arms around his son's neck; and caressing the face of Kunāla several times, many moans were heard, his voice broken with sobs:

"In the past, at the sight of these eyes like those of the kunāla, I called my son Kunāla; today these eyes are extinguished, how could I continue to give him this name?"

Then, he said to him: "Tell me, tell me, my dear son, how this face with beautiful eyes has been deprived of its light and has come to be like the sky where the setting of the moon had taken away its splendor."

"He has a merciless heart, O my son, the spiteful one who, driven by his hatred against a good man, stranger to all feelings of hatred, has destroyed the eyes of the best of men, of the very image of the recluse, cruel act that is a source of sorrows for me.

"Speak quickly to me, O you whose face is so beautiful. Consumed by the grief that the loss of your eyes causes in me, my body perishes like a forest devoured by the thunderbolt thrown by the nāgas."

290. At this point our two manuscripts are quite altered; I translate this otherwise not very important detail by conjecture.

Then, Kunāla, having thrown himself at his father's feet, spoke to him in this way:

"O king, you need not lament so over an event that has passed; have you not heard quoted the words of the recluse who has said that the jinas themselves, or the pratyekabuddhas, cannot escape the inevitable influence of deeds?

"They collect, like all ordinary men, the fruit of bad deeds committed here below; it is in this world that one finds the reward for what one has done: how could I call the treatment that I have experienced the deed of another?

"I committed some fault [long ago], O great king, and it is under the influence of this fault that I have returned [to this world], I whose eyes have been the cause of my unhappiness.[291]

"Sword, thunderbolt, fire, poison, birds, nothing injures the ether, whose nature is inalterable; it is on the body in which souls are enveloped, O king, that cruel sufferings that somehow take it as a target fall."

But Aśoka, whose heart was ripped by grief, replied in this way: "Who thus has deprived my son of his eyes? Who thus has resolved to renounce [for the price of this crime] life, this good so dear? Anger descends into my heart devoured by the fire of grief; tell me quickly, O my son, on whom must I make punishment fall." In the end, the king learned that this crime was the work of Tiṣyarakṣitā. Immediately, having the queen called, he said to her:

"How, cruel one, are you not swallowed into the earth? I will make your head fall under the sword or under the axe. I renounce you, woman covered by crimes, unjust woman, just as the sage renounces fortune."

Then, looking at her with a face blazing with the fire of anger, he added:

"Why would I not break her limbs after having torn out her eyes with my sharp nails? Why would I not place her alive on the execution post? Why would I not cut off her nose?

"Why would I not cut out her tongue with a razor or would I not make her die by poison?" Such were the tortures with which the king of men threatened her.

The magnanimous Kunāla, full of compassion, having heard these words, said to his father: "It would not be honorable for you to put Tiṣyarakṣitā to death; act in conformity with honor and do not kill this woman.

"There is indeed no reward superior to that of benevolence; patience, Lord, has been celebrated by the Sugata." Then, throwing himself again at his feet, the prince made his father hear these truthful words:

"O king, I experience no suffering and despite this cruel treatment, I do not

291. A verse is missing to this stanza; the words put into square brackets are added to complete the meaning.

feel the fire of anger; my heart has only benevolence for my mother, who gave the order to tear out my eyes.

"In the name of the truth of these words, may my eyes become again as they were before." Hardly had he pronounced these words than his eyes reappeared with their original radiance.

However, king Aśoka, incensed at Tiṣyarakṣitā, had her thrown into a place of torture where she died by fire; and he had the inhabitants of Takṣaśilā massacred.

The monks who conceived some doubts questioned in this way the respectable sthavira Upagupta, who settles all doubts: "What action had Kunāla thus committed so that his eyes had been torn out?" The sthavira responded: "Listen, respectable personages. Long ago, in times past, there was in Benares a certain hunter who went to the Himavat and killed wild animals there. One day when he went to the mountain, at the end of a cave, he came upon five hundred gazelles that had gathered there, and he caught them all in a net. He then had this reflection: 'If I kill them, I will be encumbered with all this meat.' This is why he put out the eyes of the five hundred gazelles. These animals deprived of sight were unable to escape. It is in this way that he put out the eyes of several hundred gazelles.

"What do you think about that, O monks? This hunter was Kunāla himself. Because at that time, he put out the eyes of several hundred gazelles, he has undergone the sufferings of hell during several hundred thousand years as the price for this action. Then, to complete the expiation of the remainder of his fault, he has had the eyes torn out during five hundred existences in the form of a human." "But what action had he done to merit rebirth in a high family, to have a pleasant outward appearance, and to know the truths?" "Listen, respectable personages:

"Long ago, in times past, when the lifespan of humans was forty-four thousand years, there appeared in the world a perfect buddha called Krakuchanda. When he had completely fulfilled the duties of a buddha, he entered into the domain of nirvāṇa, where nothing remains of the elements of existence. A king named Aśoka had built for him a stūpa made of four kinds of precious stones. But, after the death of Aśoka, his throne was occupied by a monarch who had no faith. The precious stones were stolen by thieves who left only earth and wood. The people who had gathered in this place, seeing the stūpa destroyed, burst into tears. Now, the son of a chief of artisans was at that time [among the people]. This young man asked: 'Why are you crying?' 'The stūpa of Krakuchanda the buddha was made of four kinds of precious stones,' the multitude replied to him. 'Now it is destroyed.' The young man [raised it again]. There was, moreover, in this place a statue of the perfect buddha Krakuchanda that was of natural size; it had been destroyed. The young man restored it also and pronounced this prayer: 'May I make myself agreeable to a master like Krakuchanda! May I not be disagreeable to him!'

"What do you think about that, respectable personages? This son of the chief of the artisans was Kunāla himself. It is he who at that time had the stūpa of Krakuchanda raised again, and it is in recompense for this action that he was born into an illustrious family. Because he restored the statue of the buddha, as recompense for this good deed he was reborn with an agreeable outward appearance. Because he pronounced the prayer reported above, he had the privilege of pleasing a master similar to Śākyamuni, the perfect buddha, he was not displeasing to him, and he knew the truths."[292]

When king Aśoka conceived faith in the law of the Bhagavat, he had eighty-four thousand royal edicts of the law established; he fed three hundred thousand monks during the months of the varṣa; namely, a hundred thousand arhats, and two hundred thousand disciples and ordinary men filled with virtue. The multitude of inhabitants, who covered the earth to the limits of the ocean, had feelings of benevolence for the law of the Bhagavat. The brother of Aśoka, who was named Vītāśoka, was favorable to the tīrthyas. They had convinced him of this opinion: there is no deliverance for the śramaṇas, sons of Śākya; for they seek pleasure and dread pain. One day, king Aśoka said to his brother: "Vītāśoka, you must not show benevolence to that which has no foundation; it is to the Buddha, to the law, and to the assembly that you owe your confidence; your benevolence will then have a real object."

Another day, king Aśoka went out to hunt antelope. Vītāśoka saw then in the forest a ṛṣi surrounded by the five fires, who submitted himself to harsh mortifications. The prince approached him, and having saluted his feet, he asked him this question: "O Blessed One, how long have you lived in this forest?" "Twelve years," responded the anchorite. "And with what do you feed yourself?" "With fruits and roots." "And what are your robes?" "Rags and leaves of darbha." "And your bed?" "A carpet of grass." "Is there some suffering which bothers you [in your penitence]?" "Yes," replied the ṛṣi. "These antelopes mate during the rutting period. Now when I see their frolic, I am consumed with desire." "If this anchorite," exclaimed Vītāśoka, "cannot tame passion with this harsh penance, what will it be for the śramaṇas, sons of Śākya, who seek carpets and broad seats? How could they triumph over passion?" And he pronounced this stanza:

"If the ṛṣis inhabiting this deserted forest who feed themselves only on air, water, and roots, cannot, through such harsh austerities practiced during so long a time, succeed in mastering their desires,

"How could the Śākyas gain mastery of their senses, they who eat so great a

292. This part of the legend has a special title in our manuscripts, *Kunālāvadāna*, "Legend of Kunāla."

quantity of meat with rice well seasoned with curds and butter? If this were possible, mount Vindhya would be able to cross the ocean.

"Yes, king Aśoka is completely the dupe of the śramaṇas, sons of Śākya to whom he shows respect."

Aśoka heard these words; and as his mind was fecund with expedients, he said to his ministers: "Vītāśoka has benevolence only for the tīrthyas; it is necessary that, by cleverness, I make him conceive similar sentiments for the law of the Bhagavat." "What does the king command?" responded the ministers. "When I have entered the bath," said the king, "after having taken off my crown and fillet, symbols of royalty, you will have to, by whatever means, put the crown and royal fillet on Vītāśoka and make him sit on the throne." "It will be done," responded the ministers. The king, having taken off his crown and fillet, symbols of royalty, entered the bath. Then, the ministers said to Vītāśoka: "When king Aśoka is dead, it is you who will be king; thus while waiting, don these royal ornaments. We will put the crown and the royal fillet on you and have you sit on the throne; we will see if these ornaments fit you well or poorly." Consequently, the ministers adorned Vītāśoka with the marks of royal rank and put him on the throne; then, they immediately informed the king. Seeing Vītāśoka adorned with the crown and fillet, symbols of royalty, and seated on the throne, he exclaimed: "I am still living, yet you, you already play the king. Someone come!" At that very instant executioners appeared covered with blue robes, having long hair, and carrying a bell in their hands; and prostrating themselves at the feet of the king, they said to him: "What does the king command?" "I turn Vītāśoka over to you," he responded. Then, addressing the prince, the executioners said to him: "We, executioners armed with the sword, we seize your person." But the ministers threw themselves at the feet of Aśoka, imploring him. "Pardon, O king, Vītāśoka is your brother." "I pardon him," responded Aśoka, "but only for seven days. He is my brother and in consideration of my affection for him, I grant him the monarchy during these seven days."

Immediately hundreds of instruments were heard to resound; the prince was saluted with cries of "Long live the king!" Thousands of people joined their hands as a sign of respect before him, and hundreds of women surrounded him. But the executioners did not leave the door of the palace. At the end of the first day, they presented themselves to Vītāśoka and said to him: "One day has passed, Vītāśoka; you have only six more days left." They did the same the second day and the following days; finally on the seventh, Vītāśoka, adorned with royal ornaments, was conducted into the presence of Aśoka, who said to him: "Vītāśoka, how did you find the songs, dances, and concert of instruments?" "I did not see anything or hear anything," responded Vītāśoka; and he pronounced this stanza:

"I have not listened to the songs, I have not looked at the dances of the women: how could one who has enjoyed none of these pleasures give you his opinion?"

"Vītāśoka," replied the king, "I have granted you the monarchy for seven days; hundreds of instruments have resounded for you; you were saluted with cries of 'Long live the king!' The multitude has honored you by holding their hands joined as a sign of respect to you; you have been served by hundreds of women; how then can you say: 'I have seen nothing and heard nothing'"?

"No," responded Vītāśoka. "I have not seen the dances or heard the sound of the songs; I have not smelled the fragrances or tasted the flavors; I have not perceived the contact of the gold, the jewels, the necklaces, or the bodies that I touched; the multitude of women could not charm an unfortunate one condemned to death.

"Women, dances, songs, palace, beds, seats, youth, beauty, fortune, all that and even the earth with its various jewels have been without charm and empty for me while I saw the executioners in their blue robes sitting tranquilly on their seats at my door.

"Hearing the sound of the blue-robed executioner's bell, I felt, O chief of kings, the fearsome terrors of death.

"Surrounded by the goads of dread, I have not heard the ravishing voices, I have not seen the dances, and I have not desired food.

"Struck by the fever of death, I have no longer known sleep; I have spent the entire night thinking about death."

"What!" replied Aśoka. "If the dread of a death that would deprive you of only one life could prevent you from enjoying the happiness of being king, with which eyes do you believe that monks, frightened at the thought of the death that must end hundreds of existences, envisage all the places where one can be reborn and the sorrows related to them? In hell, the distress to which the body consigned to fire is condemned; among animals, the terrors that the dread of seeing themselves devour one another inspires in them; among pretas, the torments of hunger and thirst; among humans, the disquiet of an existence of projects and efforts; among gods, the dread of falling and of losing their felicity: here are the five causes of misery by which the three worlds are enchained. Tormented by the sufferings of mind and body, they see true torturers in the attributes that compose existence; in the sense organs, desolate villages; in objects, brigands; finally, they see the totality of the three worlds devoured by the fire of instability. And how then could passion be born in them?" Then, he pronounced these stanzas:

"What! The dread of death that would deprive you of but one life prevents you from enjoying the pleasant objects made to flatter the heart, because the terror does not cease troubling you!

"Thus, what pleasure can the heart of the monk find in food and other objects of the senses, they who contemplate the future terrors of death, repeated over several hundred existences?

"How could clothes, beds, seats, bowls, inspire attachment in hearts who think only about deliverance, who see enemies and assassins in these objects, for whom the body is similar to a burning abode, and who regard beings as perishable.

"And how would deliverance not belong to those who desire only it and who turn away from existence, to those whose heart is no more attached to the various causes of pleasure than water to the leaf of the lotus?"

So favorably disposed toward the law of the Bhagavat thanks to the ruse of the king, Vītāśoka said to him, holding his hands joined in a sign of respect: "Lord, I seek refuge in the blessed Tathāgata perfectly and completely buddha; I seek refuge in the law and in the assembly." And he pronounced this stanza:

"I take refuge in him whose eyes are as pure as a newly blooming lotus and who is honored by gods, sages, and humans; I take refuge in the pure law of the Buddha and in the assembly."

Then, Aśoka threw his arms around his brother's neck: "No," he said to him. "I have not abandoned you; but it is a means I have employed to inspire in you feelings of benevolence in favor of the law of the Bhagavat." From that moment, Vītāśoka began to honor the caityas of the Bhagavat by offering them perfumes, garlands of flowers, and by making a multitude of instruments resound; and he heard the law and he showed respect to the assembly. One day, he went to the hermitage of Kukkuṭārāma; there was the sthavira called Yaśas, who was an arhat endowed with the six supernatural knowledges. Vītāśoka came to sit before him to listen to the law. The sthavira began to observe him, and he immediately recognized that the causes [of his conversion] were accumulated in him, that he had reached his last existence, and that he would reach the state of arhat in this very body. This is why he began to praise the life of the mendicant, in order to persuade him to embrace it. As soon as Vītāśoka heard him, he conceived this desire: "May I become a mendicant under the law of the Bhagavat!" Then, standing, he spoke in this way to the sthavira, holding his hands joined in a sign of respect: "May I embrace the religious life under the discipline of the well-renowned law! May I obtain investiture and become a monk! May I practice before you the duties of the religious life!" "Friend," the sthavira responded to him, "make your desire known to king Aśoka." Vītāśoka, having thus gone to the place where the king was, said to him, his hands joined in a sign of respect: "O king, grant me your permission; I desire to embrace the religious life under the discipline of the well-renowned law by leaving the house with perfect faith." And he pronounced this stanza:

"I was lost like the elephant who no longer knows the goad; but thanks to the powerful bridle of your intelligence, I was saved from my straying by the instructions of the Buddha.

"Therefore, O sovereign master of kings, you must grant me a favor; permit me to bear the happy signs of the perfect law, of the foremost of the lights of the world."

Hearing these words, Aśoka, tears in his eyes, threw himself on his brother's neck and said to him: "Vītāśoka, renounce this resolution: in the life of a mendicant, one has relations with and one lives with people of inferior castes; for a robe one has only rags of material picked up in the dust where slaves have discarded them; as food, only what one obtains by begging among others; as bed and as seat, only grass spread at the foot of a tree. When one is sick, one has only leaves to lie on; it is difficult to procure medicines; as food, one has only what others reject.[293] And you, you are delicate; you are incapable of bearing the sufferings of hunger, thirst, heat, and cold; renounce your intention, I beseech you." "No, Lord," replied Vītāśoka. "It would be to think like a man who thirsts for objects; but he who desires to embrace the religious life does not suffer from the fatigue that they cause us; he does not see the enemy stealing power from him; he is not reduced to indigence.[294] At the sight of the world that undergoes suffering, which is the prey of death, which exhausts itself in impotent effort, I have dreaded being born in it again and I have formed the idea of entering into the path of happiness and security." At these words, king Aśoka started to shed tears while moaning. But Vītāśoka, wishing to console him, pronounced this stanza:

"Having once climbed into the agitated litter of the world, men are condemned to fall from it; why does this emotion possess you? Are we not all made to separate one day?"

"Good!" said Aśoka. "Begin your mendicant apprenticeship here." In an enclosure planted with trees, in the midst of the palace, a carpet of grass was spread for the prince, food was given to him. He began to go begging in the inner apartments, but he did not receive very good food.[295] The king said to the women of the inner apartments: "Give him food like that which begging monks collect." As a consequence, the prince collected spoiled and rotten wheat, and he proceeded to eat it. But Aśoka, having seen him, prevented him: "Live the life of a mendicant, since I allow you to; but when you have collected alms, show them to me."

Some time later, Vītāśoka went to the hermitage of Kukkuṭārāma. However, this thought came to his mind: "If I live the life of a mendicant here, I will be among the multitude." This is why he withdrew to the countries of Videha[296] and

293. The text says: *dhūtibhojanam*; should it not rather read *pūtibhojanam*, "spoiled food"?

294. This passage is very altered; I take the most likely meaning.

295. It is necessary, for the clarity of the story, to suppress this negation; I would thus propose to read: *āhāram alabhata* instead of *āhāraṃ na labhate*, and I would translate in this way: "and he received very good food."

296. Videha is, as is known, the old Mithila or the modern Tirhut.

began to beg there. Finally, after a good many efforts at application, he obtained the rank of arhat. When the respectable Vītāśoka had reached this high rank, he felt the happiness and the pleasure of deliverance, and he had this reflection: "I am indeed an arhat." The first thing he did was to go to the door of king Aśoka. "Go," he said to the guard, "and announce to king Aśoka that Vītāśoka is at his door and that he desires to see the king." The guard, going immediately to the king, said to him: "O king, happiness to you. Vītāśoka is at your door and desires to see the king." "Go quickly," responded the king, "and have him enter." Immediately, Vītāśoka was ushered into the palace. No sooner had Aśoka seen his brother than, rising from his throne, he fell to his full height at the feet of the monk, like a tree cut at the root; then, looking at the respectable Vītāśoka, he said to him while shedding tears:

"Although he sees me, he does not feel this emotion that men always feel when they meet; he is doubtless satisfied with the savory food of science that the energy of distinction has procured for him."

Rādhagupta was the prime minister of king Aśoka. He saw the patched robe of the respectable Vītāśoka and his earthen bowl, and in this bowl, alms of rice that Lūha had given to him; and at this sight, having prostrated at the feet of the king, he said to him, holding his hands joined in a sign of respect: "O king, since this monk has so few desires and is satisfied, he must certainly have reached his aim."

"What can cause pleasure in one who has only some alms for food, only rags picked up in the dust for robes, and only the surrounding trees for his abode?

"One with a vast heart to whom nothing is attached, for whom the healthy body is exempt from sickness, and who has his existence at his disposal, he sees for himself a perpetual festival in the world of humans."

The king, having heard these stanzas, exclaimed with joy in his heart:

"By seeing this scion of our race who has renounced the family of the Mauryas in the city of Magadha and all his precious goods, exempt from pride, haughtiness, and turmoil, it seems to me that my ardent capital city rises again, purified by glory.

"Thus, set forth for us nobly the law of the sage with ten strengths." Then, the king, taking his brother in his arms, had him sit on the seat intended for him; then, he offered him cooked food with his own hand; finally, when he saw that he had finished his meal, washed his hands, and put his bowl aside, he sat before the respectable Vītāśoka to listen to the law. Then, the respectable monk, wishing to instruct Aśoka with a discussion related to the law, said to him: "Fulfill with attention the duties of royal power; the three precious objects are something difficult to obtain; Lord, honor them constantly." And when he had delighted him in this way with a discourse related to the law, he withdrew. But Aśoka, hands joined, surrounded by his five hundred ministers and accompanied by a procession of several thousand inhabitants of the city and of the countryside who encircled him with respect, proceeded to follow the respectable Vītāśoka. This is what this stanza expresses:

"The brother is followed by the king his elder, who accompanies him with respect; this is a visible result of the adoption of the religious life, quite worthy of celebration."

Then, the respectable Vītāśoka, wishing to give an idea of his merit, soared into the skies by means of his supernatural power, in the sight of the multitude. And king Aśoka, joining his hands in a sign of respect, and encircled by several hundred thousands of inhabitants, kept his eyes fixed on the sky; and looking at the respectable Vītāśoka, he pronounced these stanzas:

"Free from all attachment of your family, you soar like a bird, leaving us enchained in the bonds of passion that man has for pleasure.

"If this sage full of calm and master of his heart appears with this power, it is the fruit of contemplation, a fruit that does not show itself to men blinded by desire.

"This supreme supernatural power covers us with shame, we whom the pride of prosperity inflates; this intelligence bows our head, we who exalt the idea of our own knowledge.

"This sage, whose goal is in sight, frightens us, we who in our blindness believe we have received our reward; in the end, a cloud of tears darkens our face; we are not really free."

Meanwhile, the respectable Vītāśoka went to the countryside beyond the borders, and he placed his bed and seat there. There, he suffered from a grave malady. King Aśoka, having been informed of it, sent him medicines and servants. When the monk was suffering from this malady, his head was covered with leprosy; but as soon as the sickness had disappeared, his hair grew back and he sent back the medicines and the servants. He began to eat mainly food to which milk was added and consequently went to a park in whose vicinity he lived as a mendicant.

Around the same time, it happened that, in the city of Puṇḍravardhana, a man devoted to Brahmanical mendicants knocked over a statue of the Buddha at the feet of a mendicant, who broke it. A faithful Buddhist informed the king, who immediately ordered that this man be brought to him. The yakṣas heard this order at the distance of one yojana in the sky, and the nāgas at the distance of one yojana beneath the earth in such a way that the culprit was brought before the king at the very same instant. At this sight, Aśoka, overcome with fury, exclaimed: "Put to death all those who live in Puṇḍravardhana." In conformity with this order, eighteen thousand inhabitants were put to death in a single day.

Some time after, in Pāṭaliputra, another man devoted to the brahmans again knocked over a statue of the Buddha at the feet of a mendicant, who smashed it to pieces. The king learned the fact and in fury went to the house of the mendicant, of the devotee, as well as to the houses of their parents and their friends and had all consumed by fire; then, he had this order proclaimed: "He who brings me the head of a Brahmanical mendicant will receive one dīnāra[297] from me."

Meanwhile, the respectable Vītāśoka had retired to the hut of an ābhīra for the night. Since he was still suffering from his malady, his robes were in rags, his hair, his beard, and his nails were of a disproportionate length. The wife of the shepherd had this reflection: "This man who has come to our hut to pass the night is doubtless a brahman mendicant." She thus said to her husband: "Son of my master, here is an opportunity to earn one dīnāra; let us kill this mendicant and let us take his head to king Aśoka." Immediately drawing his sword from the sheath, the ābhīra went toward Vītāśoka. This respectable monk possessed the science of what had happened to him in the past. He saw that he was at the point of collecting the fruit of actions he had formerly accomplished himself. So, quite sure of this fact, he remained tranquil. The ābhīra thus chopped his head off with his sword and took it to king Aśoka, saying to him: "Give me one dīnāra." At the sight of this head, the king believed he recognized it; however, this thin hair did not accord with the likeness he was seeking. The doctors and servants were summoned, and said upon seeing it: "Lord, it is the head of Vītāśoka." At these words, the king fell to the floor in a faint. Water was thrown to revive him and then, his ministers said to him: "Your orders, O king, have attracted misfortune on the very head of a sage exempt from passion; grant security to everyone in the world by revoking them." Thus the king restored repose to the people by forbidding that anyone be put to death from then on.

Meanwhile, the monks who had conceived doubts questioned the respectable Upagupta, who settles all the doubts, in this way: "Which action had the respectable Vītāśoka thus committed to deserve, as result of his behavior, to perish by the sword?" "Learn, respectable personages," responded the sthavira, "the

297. The use of this word *dināra*, whose western origin and relatively recent introduction into India Prinsep has definitively demonstrated ("Note on the facsimile," etc., in *Journal of the Asiatic Society of Bengal*, vol. 6, p. 45), is a more convincing proof than everything I could put forward concerning the modern date of the legend of Aśoka. This word is very rarely used in the Sanskrit books of the North, and I have never encountered it in those sūtras I regard as ancient, at least in their content. Until now, I can only cite two examples. The first is borrowed from the legend of Hiraṇyapāṇi, which belongs to the *Avadānaśataka*. The hero of this story had been named Hiraṇyapāṇi, "he who has gold in his hand," because at the moment of his birth, *lakṣaṇāhataṃ dīnāradvayam*, which must mean "two dīnāras marked with signs," were found in his hands (*Avadānaśataka*, fol. 195). The second example I can put forward of the use of this word is in a semihistorical passage of the *Divyāvadāna*, which we will see below. Puṣpāmitra, this king of Magadha that the legend calls the last of the Mauryas, promises one hundred dīnāras for each head of a Buddhist monk in the city of Śākala (*Divyāvadāna*, fol. 211b). In the ancient sūtras, the term that most often appears is *suvarṇa*.

actions he had done in his past existences. Long ago, O monks, in a time since long past, there lived a hunter who supported himself by killing antelopes. In the forest, there was a well near which the hunter set his nets and traps, and it is there that he killed antelope. When there is no buddha in this world, pratyekabuddhas are born here. Now a certain pratyekabuddha, having withdrawn to this well to make his meal, departed from it and went to sit cross-legged near a tree. Warned of his presence by the scent he had left there, the antelopes did not come to the well. The hunter, having gone there, recognized that the game had not appeared as usual; and step by step, he reached the place where the pratyekabuddha was sitting. Seeing him, this idea came to his mind: 'Here is the one who has made my hunt fail'; and drawing his sword from the sheath, he put the pratyekabuddha to death.

"How do you understand that, respectable personages? This hunter was Vītāśoka himself. Since he formerly had killed antelopes, he has had to suffer a great malady as the effect of this action. Because he had killed the pratyekabuddha with his sword, as the effect of this action he has experienced the sufferings of hell during several thousand years, and he was born again among humans during five hundred years, seeing always his life cut off by the sword; finally, it is in order to expiate the remainder of this action that today, although he reached the rank of arhat, he has perished by the sword." "But which action did he commit to be reborn in an illustrious family and to obtain the rank of arhat?" The sthavira responded: "There was under Kāśyapa, the perfectly accomplished buddha, a certain Pradānaruci, who entered into the religious life. Thanks to him, generous donors used their liberality to feed the assembly of monks by giving them pleasant drinks of wheat flour or by inviting them to their house. Thanks to him, parasols were erected above the stūpas; they were honored by offering them flags, standards, perfumes, garlands, flowers, and by performing concerts. It is as a reward for this action that he was born in a high family. Finally, after having fulfilled the duties of the religious life during ten thousand years, he has expressed a virtuous wish, and it is owing to this wish that he has reached the rank of arhat."[298]

When king Aśoka, by offering half an āmalaka,[299] had shown his faith in the law of the Bhagavat,[300] he spoke to the monks in this way: "Who, under the

298. This part of the legend bears the title *Vītāśokāvadāna*, or the "Legend of Vītāśoka," in our two manuscripts.

299. It is the fruit of the *phyllanthus emblica*, or the myrobolan.

300. At the beginning of this piece, which concludes the legend of Aśoka, there is a confusion that would not be easy to disentangle if one did not know with what negligence the compilers of legends sew together the various episodes of the accounts that the tradition transmits to them. It is not after having offered half of an āmalaka to the assembly of monks that king Aśoka inquired of the monks about the name of the one who had ever given the most abundant alms. On the contrary, the continuation of the account proves that Aśoka gave this half fruit only when he had exhausted his treasures, and the heir apparent had taken measures to

law of the Bhagavat, has given abundant alms?" "It is Anāthapiṇḍika the householder," responded the monks. "What amount of alms did he give?" "A hundred koṭis." This response made the king reflect: "Here," he said to himself, "is a householder who has given a hundred koṭis for the law of the Bhagavat!" Then, he said loudly: "I too, I wish to give a hundred koṭis." He had [as one knows] established eighty-four thousand royal edicts of the law; he gave a hundred thousand [suvarṇas] to each place where they were erected, and he did as much to the place where Śākyamuni was born, where he had become a buddha, where he turned the wheel of the law, and where he had entered into complete nirvāṇa. He received the monks during the five months of the varṣa and on this occasion, he gave four hundred thousand [suvarṇas]; he fed three hundred thousand monks, namely a hundred thousand arhats and two hundred thousand disciples and ordinary men filled with virtues. He gave to the assembly of āryas the great earth, his wives, the multitudes of his ministers, Kunāla, and lastly himself, keeping, however, his treasure for himself, and he bought back all these goods for four hundred thousand [suvarṇas]. Finally, he had given in this way ninety-six thousand koṭis for the law of the Bhagavat when he fell into languor. Then, he said to himself: "Soon, I will be no more," and this idea cast him into discouragement.

Rādhagupta was the minister of the king; he was the one with whom, [in one of his previous existences,] he had given a handful of earth [to Śākya]. Seeing the king fallen into discouragement, he prostrated himself before him, and said to him, with hands joined in a sign of respect:

"Why, Lord, is this face which, similar to the star that devours the day, cannot be looked at by the multitude of your powerful enemies, and from which hundreds of women with lotus-eyes cannot turn away, flooded with tears"?

"Rādhagupta," responded the king, "I do not weep at the loss of my treasures or at that of my monarchy or at the misfortune of being separated from the world; I weep at being far from the āryas.

"No, I will see no more the assembly possessed of all virtues, revered by humans and gods; I will no longer be able to honor it by offering it excellent food and drink; and this thought makes my tears flow.

"And then, Rādhagupta, my intention was to give a hundred koṭis for the law of the Bhagavat, and I have not put my project into action." Having spoken in this way, he said to himself: "I will still gather four koṭis to make up my alms"; and from that moment, he began to send gold and silver to the hermitage of Kukuṭārāma.

---

prevent him from abandoning to the monks the totality of what remained to him. The first sentence of this paragraph can thus pass for a kind of title of the legend, which must be more or less understood in this way: "How Aśoka, by the offering of half an āmalaka, shows his faith for the law of the Bhagavat." What follows this sentence is the summary of the first part of the legend of Kunāla; that of Vītāśoka begins with a similar summary.

At that time, it was Saṃpadī, the son of Kunāla, who was the *yuvarāja,* or heir apparent. The ministers said to him: "Prince, king Aśoka does not have much longer to live, and he sends all his treasures to Kukkuṭārāma; now, there are other sovereigns who have great wealth; we thus must prevent the king from ruining himself." Consequently, the young prince forbade the treasurer [from giving money to the king]. There was the custom of presenting him food in golden bowls; Aśoka, having taken his meal, proceeded to send these bowls to Kukkuṭārāma. Then, it was forbidden to present him bowls of this metal, and from that moment, his food was brought to him in silver bowls; but the king in the same way sent them to Kukkuṭārāma. The silver bowls were suppressed in turn and replaced by iron bowls; but the king continued to send them like the others to the hermitage. Finally, it was necessary to present his food in clay bowls. Then, Aśoka, taking in his hand half of an āmalaka fruit, summoned his ministers with the inhabitants and, filled with sadness, said to them: "Who, then, is now the king of this country?" The ministers, immediately rising from their seats and making their way toward Aśoka, their hands joined in a sign of respect, said to him: "It is you, Lord, who is king of this country." But Aśoka, his eyes darkened by a cloud of tears, said to his ministers: "Why are you saying with kindness what is not true? I am deposed from the monarchy; I only have half of this fruit at my disposal as sovereign.

"Shame on a miserable power that resembles the movement of the waters of a swollen river, since despite the sovereignty I exert over men, fearsome misery has also affected me!

"But who could flatter himself by belying these words of the Bhagavat: 'All felicities end in ill fortune'? Indeed, it is not deceitful language, that of the Bhagavat who never lies.[301]

"After having commanded the earth gathered under his single power, after having suppressed all combat and all disorder, destroyed the multitude of his enemies swollen with pride, and consoled the poor and the unfortunate, the deposed king Aśoka lives now in misery without radiance. Like the flower or the leaf that fades when it is cut or pulled out, king Aśoka withers."

Then, king Aśoka called a man who was close to him: "Friend," he said to him, "although I am deposed from my power, please consent, on behalf of my old merits, to carry out my last order. Take this half āmalaka that belongs to me;

301. Here, I omit a stanza that is absolutely unintelligible and hardly legible in our two manuscripts; half is even missing in the copy of the *Divyāvadāna* I possess. This stanza certainly contains one of these moral maxims on the vanity of human power, which the legends of the North ordinarily express in a rather flat and rather vulgar style. The end of the stanza, if I am not mistaken, concerns a comparison to a river that flows back, stopped by rocks removed from a great mountain. I desire that the reader not regret its absence more than I. I hope at least that he will forgive this lacuna in consideration of the torture I have imposed on myself in translating manuscripts that are so incorrect.

go to the hermitage of Kukkuṭārāma and give it to the assembly. Then, saluting the feet of the assembly in my name, speak to them in this way: 'This is what the wealth of the sovereign monarch of Jambudvīpa amounts to now; here is his final alms; you must eat this fruit in order for the offering to be distributed to all the assembly to whom it is directed.'" And he pronounced these stanzas:

"Here today is my last alms; my monarchy and my power are gone; deprived of health, of doctors, of medicines, I have no other support than the assembly of āryas.

"Thus, eat this fruit in order for my last alms to be distributed to the entire assembly to whom it is my intention to offer it."

"It will be done," responded the man to the king; and taking this half fruit, he went to the hermitage of Kukkuṭārāma. There, having gone forward to the place of honor, he offered this half fruit to the assembly, hands joined in respect, and pronounced these stanzas:

"He who commands the earth gathered under his single power, who in the past illuminated the world like the sun when it has reached the middle of its course, this king, feeling today his prosperity interrupted, sees himself betrayed by his deeds; and like the sun at the end of the day, he is deprived of his power.

"Bowing his head with respect before the assembly, he gives it this half āmalaka, a visible sign of the instability of fortune."

Then, the elder of the assembly addressed the monks in this way: "Today, venerable personages, you are permitted to experience suffering; and why? Because the Bhagavat has said: 'The misfortune of another is an appropriate occasion to grieve.' And who is the man who, being good-hearted, would not grieve today?

"Aśoka, hero of the Mauryas, this monarch, model of generosity, after having been the sole sovereign of Jambudvīpa, possesses but half an āmalaka.

"Today, deprived of his power by his subjects, he gives this half fruit, thus showing his thought to ordinary men, inflated with pride by the intoxication of enjoyments and felicities."

Then, this half fruit was crushed and reduced to one mass, which was circulated in the assembly.

Meanwhile, king Aśoka said to Rādhagupta: "Tell me, dear Rādhagupta, who is now the sovereign of the country." Then, Rādhagupta, throwing himself at Aśoka's feet, said to him, hands joined in a sign of respect: "Lord, it is you who are the sovereign of the country." At these words, Aśoka, lifting himself up a little and casting his eyes over the four parts of the horizon, exclaimed while pointing his hands, joined with respect, toward the assembly: "Today, I give to the assembly of the listeners of the Bhagavat the totality of the great land to the shores of the ocean, except, however, my treasure." And he pronounced these stanzas:

"This earth that the ocean envelops like a beautiful cloth of sapphire, whose face is somehow adorned with mines of various jewels, this earth that supports creatures and Mount Mandara, I give to the assembly; may I collect the fruit of this action!

"For the price of this good deed, I do not desire possession of the palace of Indra or that of the world of Brahmā; all the more reason I do not desire the happiness of the monarchy, which disappears more quickly than water flows.

"What I wish for the price of the perfect faith with which I make this donation is to exercise this self-control so worthy of respect, honored by the āryas, a benefit free from change."

After having this donation written, he handed it [to his minister] and had it sealed with his seal. As soon as the king had given the earth to the assembly, he was subjected to the law of time. The ministers, having transported his corpse in a litter adorned with blue and yellow fabric, rendered to him the last duties and occupied themselves with giving him a successor. But Rādhagupta said to them: "Aśoka, the great king, has given the great earth to the assembly." "Why did he make this donation?" replied the ministers. "It was his desire," responded Rādhagupta. "The king said that he wished to give a hundred koṭis for the law of the Bhagavat. His liberality came to the sum of ninety-six koṭis, but the heir apparent prevented him from continuing. So the king gave the great earth to the assembly." As a consequence, the ministers paid four koṭis to the assembly, bought back from it the property of the earth, and put Saṃpadī on the throne. Saṃpadī was succeeded by Vṛhaspati, his son; Vṛhaspati by Vṛṣasena; Vṛṣasena by Puṣyadharman; Puṣyadharman by Puṣpamitra. One day, this latter summoned his ministers and said to them: "What means would I have to perpetuate the memory of my name for a long time?" The ministers responded to him: "Lord, there was in your family a king named Aśoka who established eighty-four thousand edicts of the law; his glory will live as long as the law of the Bhagavat will remain. Thus, you can, by his example, establish eighty-four thousand edicts of the law." "King Aśoka was great and fortunate," replied the king. "I desire to find another means to achieve celebrity."

The king had as household priest a brahman who was an ordinary man and who did not have faith in the Buddha. This brahman said to the king: "Lord, there are two means to make your name endure." Puṣpamitra, having then equipped an army composed of four corps of troops, left for Kukkuṭārāma with the project of destroying the law of the Bhagavat. Arriving at the door of the hermitage, he heard the roar of the lion.[302] Terrified, the king returned to

302. This expression must be taken figuratively: in the ancient sūtras as in the modern ones, the "roar of the lion" designates the preaching of the law considered as victorious and putting its opponents to flight. This figure is probably one application of the name Śākyasiṃha that is given to Śākyamuni; indeed, once the sage is called "the lion of Śākyas," it is natural that his word is named "the roar of the lion." The lion plays also another role in Buddhism; and the columns surmounted by a recumbent lion that one finds standing or knocked down in the north of India are a manifest allusion to the name "lion of Śākyas."

Pāṭaliputra. A second time, a third time, he was repulsed in this way. Finally, he convened the assembly of monks and said to them: "I wish to annihilate the law of the Bhagavat; which do you prefer that I destroy, the stūpa or the hermitage where the assembly resides?" The monks preferred to abandon the hermitage to the king. Puṣpamitra thus knocked it down from top to bottom and massacred the monks who inhabited it. From there, he went to Śākala,[303] where he made this declaration: "One who will bring me the head of a śramaṇa will receive from me a hundred dināras." Now a monk offered his head in order to save the edicts of the law and the life of the arhats.[304] The king, having learned of it, had the arhats of the country massacred. But he encountered opposition and did not carry out his destructive enterprise any further.

Leaving thus this country, he went to Koṣṭhaka.[305] The yakṣa Daṃṣṭrānivāsin then had the following reflection: "The law of the Bhagavat will perish, and I who observe its precepts, I am unable to commit evil against anyone." Kṛmisena asked for the daughter of this divinity; but the father did not wish to give her to this yakṣa, and he responded to him: "You are a sinner." However, Daṃṣṭrānivāsin consented to give her to Kṛmisena, who asked for her, on the condition that he would protect the law of the Bhagavat. King Puṣpamitra was constantly followed by a great yakṣa[306] who was commissioned to defend and protect him, and it was the power of this yakṣa that rendered the king invincible. The yakṣa Daṃṣṭrānivāsin, having seized this guard who did not abandon the king, went for a pilgrimage in the mountains. However, Puṣpamitra made his way for the great southern ocean. Then, the yakṣa Kṛmisena, having rolled down a great mountain, imprisoned Puṣpamitra as well as his soldiers and his chariots. From that moment, the king was given the name Munihata (he who has put recluses to death). At the death of king Puṣpamitra, the family of Mauryas was extinct.

Before indicating to the reader the main points of this legend that merit his attention at this moment, I believe it necessary to join to it another fragment extracted from the *Avadānaśataka*. I borrow it from a legend entitled the *Council*. One will soon see why this text needs to be compared with the preceding.

303. See on this name a note at the end of this volume, Appendix no. 6.

304. The text is here quite altered; I interpret this sentence according to the entire account.

305. I do not find anything in our legends that permits me to determine the location of this place. But if one relates it to the name of the yakṣa who, according to the text, seemed to make his residence there, a name that means "one who lives near the tooth," and if one remembers that one of the teeth of the Buddha, the one considered to have been carried later to Ceylon, was kept in Kalinga or modern Orissa, perhaps it will be permissible to conjecture that Koṣṭhaka is one of the old names of the modern city of Cuttack (Csoma, "Life of Shakya," in *Asiatic Researches*, vol. 20, p. 317. Turnour, *Journal of the Asiatic Society of Bengal*, vol. 6, p. 860ff.; vol. 7, p. 1014).

306. After the words *yakṣo mahān*, one reads in our two manuscripts *pramāṇe yūyaṃ*, with which I can do nothing; do we have to read *mahāpramāṇo 'bhavat*?

Two hundred years after the blessed Buddha had entered into complete nirvāṇa, a king named Aśoka reigned in the city of Pāṭaliputra. His kingdom was wealthy, flourishing, prosperous, fertile, populous, rich in men; one saw neither dispute nor quarrel; attacks, invasions, and robberies by thieves were unknown there; the earth was covered with rice, sugarcane, and cattle. This just monarch, king of the law, governed the kingdom according to the law. One day while he enjoyed himself with the queen, indulging in pleasure and sensual delight with her, she became pregnant. After eight or nine months she delivered and brought into the world a beautiful son, pleasing to see, graceful, having eyes like those of the kunāla bird. As soon as he was born, his birth festival was celebrated and they were occupied with giving him a name. "Which name will this child have?" said the parents between themselves. Since at the time of his birth his eyes resembled those of the kunāla bird, his name will be Kunāla. The young child was entrusted to the care of eight nurses: two to suckle him, two to make him drink milk, two to clean him, and two to play with him. One day when he was adorned with all his ornaments, the king, holding him in his arms, began to look at him several times; and delighted by the perfection of his beauty, he exclaimed: "No, I do not have a son who equals his beauty!"

Now at that time there lived in the province of Gandhāra a man called Puṣpabherotsa. It happened that a son whose beauty surpassed that of humans but did not equal that of the gods was born to a certain householder. At his birth, a pond appeared built of precious stones and filled with a divine perfumed water as well as a great garden full of flowers and fruits, which traveled. Wherever the child took a step, the pond and the garden appeared there. This is why the name Sundara (the beautiful) was given to him. With time, Sundara grew up.

Some time later, Puṣpabherotsa went with merchants for a certain matter to the city of Pāṭaliputra. Taking with him a gift intended for the king, he had himself ushered into his presence; then, having prostrated at his feet, he offered his gift and stood before him. The king had the merchants see his son Kunāla. "Merchants," he said to them, "did you ever see in the countries you have visited a child endowed with beauty so perfect?" The merchants, joining their hands in a sign of respect, prostrated at the feet of the king; and after having obtained assurance that they could speak without dread, they gave this response to him: "There is in our country, O king, a young man named Sundara whose beauty surpasses that of humans but does not equal that of the gods. At his birth, a pond appeared built of precious stones and filled with a divine perfumed water as well as a great garden full of flowers and fruits, which travel. Wherever this young man takes a step, the pond and the garden appear there."

On hearing these words, the king was struck by an extreme astonishment; and filled with curiosity, he sent a messenger to Sundara to give him the following notice: "King Aśoka desires to come to see the young Sundara; perform what you have to do or prepare." But the great multitude of people, frightened, had this reflection: "If the king is coming here with a great procession of troops, great disasters will result." This is why Sundara, having had a good chariot hitched up and having provided himself with a necklace made with one thousand pearls as a present for the king, was sent to king Aśoka. Arriving at the end of his travel, he reached the city of Pāṭaliputra; and taking the necklace made of one thousand pearls, he went to king Aśoka. As soon as he saw the beauty, the radiance, the splendor, and the perfection of young Sundara as well as the divine pond and garden, he was seized by an extreme astonishment.

Then, the king, in order to arouse the astonishment of the sthavira Upagupta, went to Kukkuṭārāma, taking the young Sundara with him. In this garden resided eighteen thousand arhats with Upagupta at their head and a double number of disciples and ordinary men filled with virtues. The king, having saluted the feet of the sthavira, sat before him to listen to the law, and Upagupta set it forth to him. Then, the young Sundara, whose dispositions had arrived at perfect maturity, after having heard the law, felt the desire to enter into the religious life. After having informed king Aśoka of it, he entered into the religious life in the presence of the sthavira Upagupta. After long efforts, after sustained studies and application, he recognized what the wheel of transmigration which bears five marks is, which is at once moving and fixed; and having triumphed over all the routes by which one enters into the world, by destroying them, by overturning them, by dissipating them, by annihilating them, he succeeded, through the destruction of all corruptions of evil, in seeing face to face the state of arhat. Once becoming an arhat [etc., as above, p. 320 at the end, until:] he became one of those whom all the devas accompanied by Indra and Upendra worship, honor, and salute.

Then, king Aśoka, feeling doubts arise in his mind, addressed the following question to the sthavira: "Which actions has Sundara thus done to have such beauty? Which actions has he done in order that [at his birth] a pond appeared filled with a divine perfumed water as well as a great garden full of flowers and fruits, which travel?" The sthavira Upagupta responded: "This Sundara, O great king, has long ago, in other existences, performed and accumulated actions that have reached their completion [etc., as above, p. 277, until the end of the paragraph].

"Long ago, O great king, when the Bhagavat had entered into complete nirvāṇa, the respectable Mahākāśyapa, who, with a retinue of five hundred monks traveled the provinces of Magadha, desired to gather an assembly of the law. It happened that a poor plowman saw this great assembly of monks that the death of the master plunged into suffering, who were fatigued by traveling through the country, and whose bodies were covered with dust. At this sight, he felt touched by compassion, and he invited the five hundred monks with Kaśyapa to come to take a religious bath. There, when he had presented them with hot water perfumed with various kinds of fragrances, the monks bathed and cleaned their mantles. Then, having offered them food prepared with care, he received the formulas of refuge as well as the precepts of teaching, and he pronounced the following prayer: 'May I, entering into the religious life under the law of Śākyamuni himself, obtain the state of arhat!'

"How do you understand that, O great king? The one who in this time and in this epoch was a poor plowman is the monk Sundara. Because he offered a sacred bath to the monks, he has obtained this beauty that distinguishes him, and with him has appeared this pond built of precious stones and filled with a divine perfumed water as well as a great garden full of flowers and fruits, which travel. Because he received then the formulas of refuge as well as the precepts of teaching, he has seen face to face in this present existence the state of arhat. This is so, O great king, for completely black actions is reserved also a completely black reward" [etc., as above, p. 278, until the end of the paragraph].

From the comparison of this fragment with the more extensive legend with which I have preceded it, it evidently results that it is the same king who is spoken about in the one and the other; the Aśoka from the fragment entitled the *Council* as well as the Aśoka of the legends called the *Alms of a Handful of Earth,* the *Story of Aśoka,* and the *Story of Kunāla* is the king, father of this young man celebrated for his beauty and for his misfortunes. In the one as in the other text, Aśoka is contemporary with Upagupta, the eminent monk who made the law of the Buddha blossom under this same monarch. That is, I believe, a point that cannot be in doubt.

Now in the first of our two fragments, the time of Aśoka is placed at the hundredth year since the death of Śākyamuni Buddha. This date is repeated more than once, ordinarily in the form of a prediction, the only form with whose aid the compilers could include a legend later than the death of Śākya among the number of books emanated from his teaching and given as the very expression of his word. But as if the redactors of the avadānas had had doubts about the credulity of the faithful, an indication of an apparently more historical nature presents itself to somehow give this date all desirable certitude: it is the meeting of king Aśoka with a hundred-year-old monk who said that he had seen Śākyamuni. This monk undoubtedly made too many miracles, to the point that his longevity is the least incredible of all. The monk, his memories, and his meeting with Aśoka, all that is probably only a pure invention of the compilers of the legends; but these various details agree no less with the predictions that place Aśoka a hundred years after Śākyamuni. Invented by the redactors of the legends, or found by them in traditional recollections, the intervention of Piṇḍola, the hundred-year-old monk and the contemporary at once of Śākyamuni and Aśoka, certainly has as its object to give the date ascribed to this latter the appearance of a historical event.

Now, in the fragment borrowed from the legend entitled the *Council,* this king Aśoka is said to have lived two hundred years after Śākyamuni. How to reconcile these two contradictory pieces of information, if not in one of these two manners: either by recognizing that two Aśokas existed, confused as only one by the tradition; or by acknowledging that there is a double tradition among the Buddhists of the North or, if one prefers, two historical opinions on the one and only Aśoka? When we compare the traditions of Southern Buddhism with those of the Nepalese, we will see how the first supposition is more likely than the other. Indeed, one knows that the Buddhists of Ceylon recognize two Aśokas: one who lived around the year 100 since the death of Śākya; the other who was the sovereign of central India, two hundred eighteen years after this same event, and to whom is attributed the erection of numerous stūpas and columns of which many remains are still found in various provinces of India.[307] At this time, it suffices for the special object of this memorandum, which is the critical examination of the written authorities of Northern Buddhism, to state that the collection of avadānas contains treatises that certainly do not belong to the preaching of Śākyamuni. And what is even more important to remark is that these treatises are mingled with works contemporary with Śākyamuni, at least in the content, with nothing to warn the reader of the major difference distinguishing one from the other. We will also have to take this particularity into account again when we study the collection of the South, where this confusion, against which the critic must early be on guard, has certainly not taken place.

It is time to summarize in a few words the results of the discussion to which the collection called the avadānas, or legends, has given rise. I believe to have established in the course of this discussion.

1. That it is the avadānas, or legends, which, in the Sanskrit collection of Nepal, represent the second of the three divisions of the Buddhist scriptures, called the *vinaya,* or discipline.

2. The rules of discipline are no more dogmatically set forth in the avadānas than are those of moral doctrine in the sūtras, which I have demonstrated with ample extracts from the avadānas.

3. In studying the avadānas, one finds details that are old and contemporary with Śākya on the ordination of monks, on the names they bear, on the various orders of which the assembly of the listeners of the Buddha is composed, on their way of living in the retinue of the master as well as in the monasteries; on the hierarchy and on the ranks assigned to monks according to merit; on various in-

307. Turnour, *Journal of the Asiatic Society of Bengal,* vol. 6, p. 714ff.

stitutions, such as those of the retreat called the *varṣa*, or the rainy season, and of confession; on the distinction and enumeration of faults; on various obligations imposed on the ascetics related to robes and food, details that I have supported with extracts from various avadānas and that I have followed with observations on the general character of the Buddhist discipline, on worship and on the objects to which it is addressed, on the statues of the Buddha, and on the stūpas.

4. Finally, among the avadānas, it is still necessary to distinguish those that recall events contemporary with Śākyamuni from those that recount facts or mention personages obviously posterior to the epoch of the founder of Buddhism.

SECTION 4

Abhidharma, or Metaphysics

If the collection of Nepal that Mr. Hodgson was able to gather includes few books having the special title *vinaya*, it offers us many contained in the section of *abhidharma*, or metaphysics. The third of the *piṭakas*, or anthologies, is indeed fully represented by the three editions of the *Prajñāpāramitā*: the first in a hundred thousand articles contained in four great sections; the second in twenty-five thousand articles, and the third in eight thousand. These voluminous collections are now in the Bibliothèque royale; in addition, I possess a copy of the redaction in eight thousand articles, which I owe to the friendship of Mr. Hodgson. As one sees, assistance is not lacking for the study of the metaphysics of Buddhism.

To these works, it is necessary to add other books whose aim is in part analogous to that of the *Prajñāpāramitā*. These are several *vaipulya*, or developed sūtras, such as the *Samādhirāja*, a treatise on various types of contemplation; the *Daśabhūmīśvara*, an exposition of the ten degrees of perfection through which a buddha passes; the *Saddharmalaṅkāvatāra*, or the teaching of the good law given in Laṅkā, which will be discussed later; and also most probably the *Saddharmapuṇḍarīka*, or the *Lotus of the Good Law*, the dogmatic part of which has the object of establishing that there are not three distinct paths of salvation for the three classes of beings, named *śrāvakas*, or listeners, *pratyekabuddhas*, or individual buddhas, and *bodhisattvas*, or future buddhas, but that there is but one vehicle, and that if Śākya speaks of three vehicles, it is solely to adjust his teaching to the more or less powerful faculties of those who listen to him.[1] It is true that in the greater part of the works I have just mentioned, the speculative part is not dominant, and it is mixed with subjects of another order and, in general, practical. However, as far as the redaction and style are concerned, there is an incontestable analogy between the vaipulya sūtras and the books of the *Prajñāpāramitā*. This analogy, which I have announced above in discussing the two categories of sūtras, one formed of simple sūtras and the other of developed sūtras, concerns the preamble that opens the books of *Prajñā*, the number of personages who attend the assembly of Śākyamuni, and finally the rank of these personages, who almost always are fabulous bodhisattvas, miraculously coming from all points of the horizon. In short, the context of the various redactions of the *Prajñā* is exactly that of any of the developed sūtras one wishes to choose; and to complete this resemblance, the various redactions of the *Prajñā* bear the title *mahāyāna sūtras*, or sūtras serving as a great vehicle; they are true sūtras, but of the type I call developed.

It would seem, seeing the length of these works, that although it must be a rather lengthy undertaking to read them in full, it must not be very difficult to form an idea of their content through more or less developed abstracts. One would, however, be mistaken in so thinking; and personal experience, acquired through several attempts, gives me the right to admit that the second undertaking is no less difficult than the first is tedious. This comes from the very form of these books and from the manner in which the subject is presented there. This subject, which is essentially speculative, is set forth with the most ample developments in the *Prajñā*, but nowhere explained; the psychological and metaphysical terms that Buddhist philosophy uses are enumerated there in a certain order. Each of these terms forms a *dharma*, that is to say, a law, a condition, or a thesis; for nothing is more extensive than the meaning of this word *dharma*. Each of these theses is posed in three forms there: the first affirmative, the second negative, the third neither affirmative nor negative. But the books do not teach us what each of these terms signifies. This silence is doubtless because they are assumed to be known in the school, a circumstance from which I infer that the great collections in which they are found were compiled at a time when Buddhism was definitively constituted. In addition, there exist commentaries in which the fundamental term of each thesis must be etymologically and philosophically analyzed, and Mr. Hodgson mentions a commentary on the *Prajñāpāramitā in Eight-Thousand Articles*[2] in one of his lists, but we do not have it in Paris and it is perhaps not easy to

1. This is also what was established by Mr. Schmidt according to his Mongol and Tibetan authorities (*Mémoires de l'Académie des sciences de Saint-Pétersbourg*, 4:125).

2. "Notices of the Languages, Literature and Religion of the Bauddhas of Nepal and Bhot," in *Asiatic Researches*, vol. 16, p. 428.

find, even in Nepal. I shall return below to some of these theses, and I shall place the reader in the position to judge for himself the difficulty one experiences in forming an idea of the metaphysics of Buddhism, according to books in which enumeration almost exclusively takes the place of explanation. These difficulties are such that they have stopped Csoma de Kőrös himself, whose knowledge and rare patience no one would suspect. After having reproduced, without any commentary, some of the most important series of these philosophical terms, this learned man confesses that he is unable to say more about the doctrine of the *Prajñāpāramitā*.[3] The reading of a commentary and the comparative study of some other Buddhist texts would doubtless have furnished him with the means to enter into the greatest detail on this difficult subject.

Fortunately for us, several points of the philosophy of Śākya have already been the object of important works in Asia and in Europe. The most extensive portion of the first dissertation of Mr. Hodgson is dedicated to the metaphysical systems and schools of Nepal, and the scholarly research that Mr. Schmidt began long ago and which he pursues with ardor on Mongol and Tibetan books have made known to us the loftiest points of the metaphysics of Buddhism. It is beyond my plan to reproduce here everything that these authors have taught us about the doctrine attributed to Śākya; their memoranda, some recorded in the *Asiatic Researches* of Calcutta and of London; the others in the *Mémoires de l'Académie des sciences de Saint-Pétersbourg*, are easily accessible to all European readers, and I must not forget that my sole intention is to give an introduction to the history of Buddhism here, and not a dogmatic exposition of Buddhism that extends to all its developments. I nonetheless have one reason to make less frequent use of the dissertations of Mr. Schmidt than those of Mr. Hodgson: it is that the first are written according to books that are not at my disposal, books whose Indian origin is certainly not doubtful to my eyes, but from which I had to prevent myself from drawing, except in cases of absolute necessity, because my special aim is to study Buddhism according to works written either in Sanskrit or in an Indian language. The memoranda of Mr. Hodgson, on the contrary, are composed of documents that owe their origin to the two sources to which I have particularly had recourse for the writing of my work, namely the tradition of Nepal and the books preserved in this country. I thus propose to quickly summarize, while joining to it observations of my own, the main features of the picture that Mr. Hodgson has drawn of the metaphysics of Buddhism, in order to then pass on to the special examination of some points I will study according to the texts themselves. This is more or less the course I followed when I analyzed the sūtras.

At the present time, one counts four great philosophical schools in Nepal, those of the Svābhāvikas, the Aiśvarikas, the Kārmikas, and the Yātnikas. The

3. "Analysis of the Sher-chin," in *Asiatic Researches*, vol. 20, p. 399.

school of the Svābhāvikas is that of the philosophers of nature;[4] but the word *nature* only renders what the Buddhists understand by *svabhāva* in an incomplete manner; they see in it at once nature that exists by itself, absolute nature, the cause of the world, and the intrinsic nature of each being, that which constitutes what it is.[5] The Svābhāvikas, which Mr. Hodgson regards as the oldest Buddhist philosophical school known at present in Nepal,[6] deny the existence of a spiritual principle. They only recognize nature taken absolutely, to which they attribute energies, among which not only is activity included, but also intelligence. Nature is eternal, as are its energies, and it has two modes, that of *pravṛtti*, or existence, and that of *nirvṛtti*, or cessation, repose. The powers of nature in their own form are in the state of *nirvṛtti*;[7] they take an animate and material form in the state of *pravṛtti*, a state that nature enters spontaneously, and not by the will or action of some being different from it. The creation and the destruction of the universe are the effect of the eternal succession of the two states of nature, and not that of the will of a creator God, who does not exist. To the state of *pravṛtti*, or activity, belong the material forms of nature: they are transitory, like the other phenomena among which they appear. Animate forms, on the contrary, of which man is the most elevated, are judged capable of reaching the state of *nirvṛtti* by their own efforts, that is to say, they can free themselves from the necessity to reappear among the transitory phenomena of *pravṛtti*.[8] Arrived at this point, the Svābhāvikas split, with some asserting that the souls that have attained *nirvṛtti* retain the feeling of their personality and are aware of the repose they eternally enjoy,[9] the others believing that the man freed from *pravṛtti* and arrived in the state of *nirvṛtti* falls into absolute emptiness, that is to say, is annihilated forever.[10] This emptiness is what the Buddhists call *śūnyatā*, "vacuity," a state which, according to the most rigid Svābhāvikas, is a good although it is nothing; because apart from that, man is condemned to pass eternally through all forms of nature, a condition to which nothingness itself is preferable.

I believe I must refer the reader to the luminous elaborations with which Mr. Hodgson has followed this presentation, which I have reduced to its most essential terms. Nor do I stop to indicate an ancient division of the Svābhāvika school that does not bring this doctrine any other change than to put into re-

4. "Notices of the Languages, Literature and Religion of the Bauddhas of Nepal and Bhot," in *Asiatic Researches*, vol. 16, p. 423.

5. See the additions at the end of the volume.

6. "Notices of the Languages, Literature and Religion of the Bauddhas of Nepal and Bhot," in *Asiatic Researches*, vol. 16, p. 439.

7. *Ibid.*, p. 435.

8. See on this part of the doctrine of the Svābhāvikas the judicious observations of Benfey ("Indien," p. 197, extract from the *Encyclopédie* of Ersch and Gruber).

9. *Asiatic Researches*, vol. 16, p. 436.

10. *Ibid.*, p. 437.

lief, under the name *prajñā*, "wisdom," the sum of all the active and intelligent energies of nature and to absorb man into the state of *nirvṛtti*.[11] I hasten to set forth the particular principles of the school most directly opposed to that of the naturalists, I wish to say the school of the Aiśvarikas, or theists, who assert a God, an intelligent essence who, under the name *ādibuddha*, is for some the sole divinity and for others the first term of a duality whose second term is the material principle that is coexistent and coeternal with him.[12] But here I let Mr. Hodgson himself speak for fear of altering his thought: "Although the theists recognize an immaterial essence and a God, they deny his providence and his dominion over the world; and although they regard deliverance as the state of being absorbed into the divine essence, and they vaguely appeal to God as the giver of the good things of *pravṛtti*, they regard the union of virtue and happiness, as long as one remains in this state of *pravṛtti*, as utterly independent from God. They believe that man can only reach it through his own efforts with the aid of austerities and meditation; and they think that this effort can render him worthy of being honored as a Buddha on earth and raise him to heaven after his death to participate in the attributes and happiness of the supreme Ādibuddha."[13] One sees that the idea of God, even in this school that Mr. Hodgson regards as more modern and less numerous than that of the naturalists,[14] has not put down very deep roots. It seems evident to me that it is superimposed onto a system that was previous to it and that was not aware of it; for, omitting this Ādibuddha, the ontological system of Buddhism as the naturalists conceive it remains almost in its entirety. It seems that the conception of an *ādibuddha* has been accepted by the theist school only to furnish a more peremptory and more popular response to a question to which one found that the naturalists responded obscurely and imperfectly. When they were asked: "Where do beings come from?" they responded: "*Svabhāvāt*, from their own nature." "And where do they go after this life?" "Into other forms produced by the irresistible influence of this same nature." "And where must they go to escape from this inevitable necessity of rebirth?" "Into emptiness." To these questions, the theists made these following responses, which, save for the names, are truly Brahmanical solutions: beings come from Ādibuddha, or from God, who has created them more or less directly; and to avoid the fatality of transmigration, they must return to the bosom of God.[15]

11. Hodgson, "European Speculations on Buddhism," in *Journal of the Asiatic Society of Bengal*, vol. 3, p. 502.

12. "Notices of the Languages, Literature and Religion of the Bauddhas of Nepal and Bhot," in *Asiatic Researches*, vol. 16, p. 438.

13. *Asiatic Researches*, vol. 16, p. 438.

14. "European Speculations on Buddhism," in *Journal of the Asiatic Society of Bengal*, vol. 3, p. 503. We should be able to say *naturists* instead of *naturalists*.

15. *Asiatic Researches*, vol. 16, p. 440.

Let us now summarize what Mr. Hodgson informs us about the two other schools, which he regards as more modern than the preceding,[16] and which come closer to the school of the theists than to that of the naturalists,[17] that of the *Kārmikas*, or the followers of action, and that of the *Yātnikas*, or the followers of effort. By *action* Mr. Hodgson understands moral action accompanied by consciousness (*conscious moral agency*), and by *effort*, intellectual action accompanied by consciousness (*conscious intellectual agency*). The birth of these schools results from the need to combat the exaggerated quietism of the previous sects, which removed personality, providence, and activity from the first cause, and which deprived man of liberty absolutely.[18] For while accepting the general principles set by their opponents, the founders of these two schools sought to establish that man can obtain happiness either by the culture of the moral sense (these are the Kārmikas), or by the good direction of his intelligence (these are the Yātnikas).[19] But Mr. Hodgson has judiciously noted: one does not have to believe that these schools conceived the idea of divine providence or that of free will. The general principles that were the basis of the other sects, which the Kārmikas and Yātnikas, like their adversaries, adopted, were fundamentally opposed to these two ideas.[20]

Only the study of commentaries written according to the views of these two schools could indicate to us the extent to which the works belonging to the Nepalese collection we have in Paris support or contradict their theories. For in general these are the same texts that serve as foundation for all the doctrines; only the explication of these texts marks their naturalist, theist, moral, or intellectual tendency. This point has been brought to light by the quotations that Mr. Hodgson extracted from various Buddhist works of Nepal and that he gathered to serve as proofs for his various expositions of Buddhism that have appeared in India and England.[21] One can appreciate thereby what part the commentators must have had in the formation and development of the sects; and at the same time, one sees that it is necessary to accept that the redaction of the texts that

16. *Ibid.*, p. 439. "Quotations from Original Sanscrit Authorities in Proof and Illustration of Mr. Hodgson's Sketch of Buddhism," in *Journal of the Asiatic Society of Bengal*, vol. 5, p. 90.

17. "Notices of the Languages, Literature and Religion of the Bauddhas of Nepal and Bhot," in *Asiatic Researches*, vol. 16, p. 439.

18. *Asiatic Researches*, p. 439, and *Journal of the Asiatic Society of Bengal*, vol. 5, p. 82, note and p. 90.

19. "Notices of the Languages, Literature and Religion of the Bauddhas of Nepal and Bhot," in *Asiatic Researches*, vol. 16, p. 439. "Quotations from Original Sanscrit Authorities in Proof and Illustration of Mr. Hodgson's Sketch of Buddhism," in *Journal of the Asiatic Society of Bengal*, vol. 5, p. 90.

20. "Quotations from Original Sanscrit Authorities in Proof and Illustration of Mr. Hodgson's Sketch of Buddhism," in *Journal of the Asiatic Society of Bengal*, vol. 5, p. 90.

21. "Quotations from Original Sanscrit Authorities in Proof and Illustration of Mr. Hodgson's Sketch of Buddhism," in *Journal of the Asiatic Society of Bengal*, vol. 5, p. 71ff., and *Journal of the Royal Asiatic Society*, vol. 5, p. 72. Cf. "European Speculations on Buddhism," in *Journal of the Asiatic Society of Bengal*, vol. 3, p. 502, note.

give them authority is very much anterior to the birth of the various schools, which each interprets in its own interest. Here again, we are brought back to this observation of Mr. Hodgson, that Buddhism is a vast system to whose formation the time and efforts of more than one philosopher contributed. To distinguish the epochs and the doctrines is doubtless a quite delicate enterprise, but it must be the aim of the critic. Now in order to distinguish, it is necessary to limit the field of research, to examine some chosen texts, and to apply to these texts alone the consequences one draws from them. It is only when all the books have been subjected to such an examination that it will be possible to have an idea of their similarities and their differences. This is why I no longer emphasize the schools of the Kārmikas and the Yātnikas, to which the *Prajñāpāramitā* has doubtless provided elements, without being their fundamental book, or the theist school, to whose opinions the *Prajñāpāramitā* is equally foreign. But I alert those readers who would now desire to form an exact idea of what I regard as relatively modern developments of Buddhism that the first two schools are appraised in the often cited memoranda of Mr. Hodgson, and that it is in the dissertations of Mr. Schmidt, so rich in extracts of Mongol texts, that it is necessary to search for how the primitive system of the metaphysics of Śākya rose to the notion of an absolute and supreme divinity, which, in my view, was lacking at the origin.

The summary of the four great philosophical schools we have just read can be taken as the expression of the Nepalese tradition verified by the texts to which Mr. Hodgson had access. But we will see that this summary is not complete, and that the indications drawn by Csoma from the Tibetan sources reveal to us the existence of other sects about which the Nepalese Buddhists consulted by Mr. Hodgson maintain a profound silence. This is not all; one of the manuscripts discovered in Nepal furnishes us with information in complete conformity with the Tibetan indications. Another circumstance adds new interest to the information I will describe. It is that they assign to the Buddhist schools the very names given them in the commentaries of the brahmans who have occasion to mention the Buddhists. Mr. Hodgson, in gathering the most appropriate passages for establishing the exactitude of the presentation he had given previously of the metaphysics of Buddhism, remarked that in the books of Nepal he had not found texts that justified the classification of the philosophical schools of the Bauddhas as the brahmans present it.[22] The information that will follow, however little developed as it is, will at least have the advantage of filling the blank indicated by Mr. Hodgson to a certain point.

At the word *lta* ("doctrine, system") of his Tibetan dictionary, Csoma indicates to us that among the Buddhists there are four theories or four systems of

22. "Quotations from Original Sanscrit Authorities in Proof and Illustration of Mr. Hodgson's Sketch of Buddhism," in *Journal of the Asiatic Society of Bengal*, vol. 5, p. 82.

philosophy, named in Sanskrit Vaibhāṣika, Sautrāntika, Yogācāra, and Madhyamika.[23] Here I let Csoma de Kőrös speak for himself, while completing the indications of his dictionary with those he gives elsewhere on the first of these four systems.[24] "The first school, that of the Vaibhāṣikas, is composed of four principal classes with their subdivisions. These four classes had four of the principal disciples of Śākya as founders, namely Rāhula, Kāśyapa, Upāli, and Kātyāyana. Rāhula was the son of Śākya; his disciples divided into four sections; they read the *Sūtra of Emancipation* (doubtless the *Prātimokṣa Sūtra*) in Sanskrit and asserted the existence of all things. At about the time of the third council, the school linked to Rāhula, known under the generic name of Sarvāstivādāḥ, or Those Who Assert the Existence of All Things, divided into seven subdivisions: 1. Mūlasarvāstivādāḥ, 2. Kāśyapīyāḥ, 3. Mahīśāsakāḥ, 4. Dharmaguptāḥ,[25] 5. Bahuśrutīyāḥ, 6. Tāmraśāṭīyāḥ, 7. Vibhājyavādinaḥ. Kāśyapa was a brahman; his disciples divided into six classes and were called the Great Community. They read the *Sūtra of Emancipation* in a corrupt dialect. At the time of the third council, five divisions of this school were counted, which had the title Mahāsāṃghikāḥ, "Those of the Great Assembly"; these were: 1. Pūrvaśailāḥ, 2. Aparaśailāḥ, 3. Haimavatāḥ, 4. Lokottaravādinaḥ, 5. Prajñāpativādinaḥ. Upāli was a śudra; his disciples divided into three classes; they read the *Sūtra of Emancipation* in the paiśācika dialect. . . . They were called The Class Honored by Many People. Indeed, this school had this title at the time of the third council; its members were named Saṃmatāḥ and were divided into: 1. Kaurṇkullakāḥ (?), 2. Āvantikāḥ, 3. Vātsīputrīyāḥ. Kātyāyana was a śūdra; his disciples divided into three classes; they read the *Sūtra of Emancipation* in the vulgar dialect. . . . They were called the Class that has Fixed Dwellings. These were the Sthävirāḥ of the third council, namely: 1. The Mahāvihāravāsinaḥ, 2. the Jetavanīyāḥ, 3. the Abhayagirivāsinaḥ.

"In general, the Vaibhāṣikas stop at the inferior degrees of speculation; they

23. *Tibetan Dictionary*, p. 276, col. 2. "Notices of the Different Systems of Buddhism," in *Journal of the Asiatic Society of Bengal*, vol. 7, p. 143.

24. *Asiatic Researches*, vol. 20, p. 298.

25. Klaproth has inserted in the *Foe koue ki* a note touching on the division of the Buddhist scriptures accepted by the Chinese, which could contain some allusions to the sects enumerated by Csoma. This note is obscure, and perhaps the texts according to which it was written would need to be examined again. The first of the divisions mentioned by Klaproth has for its title: *Tanmojuduo*; he translates it as "Destruction of Obscurity" and sees in it the Sanskrit *tamoghna*; the title *Dharmagupta*, in its Pāli form, *Dhammagutta*, would give a closer form of the Chinese transcription. The second division is that of *Sapoduo*; it is attributed to Upāsi, a bad reading of *Upāli*. Would it not be too bold to see here the school of *Sammata* which had Upāli as chief? The third division is that of *Jiashe wei*; it is probably an altered transcription of the term *Kāśyapīya*. The fourth is that of *Mishase*; is it not again a very strong alteration of the word *Mahīśāsaka*? The fifth and last division of the list of Klaproth is that of *Pocuo fuluo*; I believe to be able to recognize in it the *Vātsīputrīyas*, as I will say below (*Foe koue ki*, pp. 325 and 326). On the four sects, see Lassen, *Zeitschrift für die Kunde des Morgenlandes*, 4:492ff. See the additions at the end of the volume.

take everything that the scriptures contain in the most vulgar sense; they believe in everything and discuss nothing.

"The second school, that of the Sautrāntikas, is composed of followers of the sūtras; it divides into two sects, one which tries to prove all things through the authority of the scriptures, the other which uses argumentation for that.

"The third school, that of the Yogācāras, counts nine subdivisions; the principal works of this system, which flourished around the seventh century of our era, are attributed to the monk Ārya Saṃgha.

"The fourth school, that of the Madhyamikas, properly speaking constitutes the philosophical system of Buddhism. It owes its origin to Nāgārjuna, who appeared around four hundred years after the death of Śākya.[26] His main disciples were Āryadeva and Buddhapālita. They are probably the founders of the two classes into which the Madhyamikas are subdivided."[27]

If the Tibetans know these names and can give the true Sanskrit form, it is because these names existed in Indian Buddhism; and the testimony of the Tibetan interpreters, regardless of all other proof, would already suffice to establish the authenticity of this separation of Buddhism into four schools bearing the titles I have just enumerated. But fortunately we have a more direct proof of their existence. I find it in a work already mentioned, in the commentary on the *Abhidharmakośa*, this inexhaustible mine of precious information on the speculative part of Buddhism. At the very beginning of his work, the commentator, explaining a word of little importance, believes that the author used this word to express the following thought:

"Such is the feeling of those who follow the Abhidharma, but it is not that for us Sautrāntikas. The tradition indeed teaches us the existence of authors of treatises on the Abhidharma, as, for example, the ārya Kātyāyanīputra, author of the *Jñānaprasthāna*; the sthavira Vasumitra, author of the *Prakaraṇapāda*; the sthavira Devaśarman, author of the *Vijñānakāya*; the ārya Śāriputra, author of the *Dharmaskandha*; the ārya Maudgalyāyana, author of the *Prajñapatiśāstra;* Pūrṇa, author of the *Dhātukāya*; Mahākauṣṭhila, author of the *Saṃgītiparyāya.* What is the meaning of the word *Sautrāntikas*? One refers in this way to those who take the sūtras and not the books as authority. But if they do not take the books as authority, how then do they accept the triple division of the books into *sūtrapiṭaka*, *vinayapiṭaka*, and *abhidharmapiṭaka*? One speaks indeed of the *abhidharmapiṭaka* in the sūtras, at the point at which it is a matter of a monk knowing the three piṭakas. And this is not surprising, for there are some sūtras, like the *Arthaviniścaya* and others having the name *abhidharma*, in which

26. "Notices on the Different Systems of Buddhism," in *Journal of the Asiatic Society of Bengal*, vol. 7, p. 143ff.

27. *Tibetan Dictionary*, p. 216. A commentary on these names would be one of the most instructive books.

the definition of the Abhidharma is given. In response to this objection, the author says: 'The Abhidharma has been set forth by the Bhagavat amid other matters.'"[28]

This text, one sees, leaves no doubt on the meaning of the title *Sautrāntika*; this title designates those who follow a doctrine, in which one accepts the authority of the sūtras above all. As to the double sect of the Sautrāntikas of whose existence Csoma informs us, I do not find it expressly indicated by the commentary on the *Abhidharmakośa*. However, one must probably see an allusion to some division of the Sautrāntikas in this passage, where it is said of a certain author: "He is not of the school of the sūtras nor of that of the similitudes, *na dārṣṭāntikaḥ*."[29] When one puts forward a similitude, an example, one must use reason to apply it to the thesis one wishes to demonstrate.

The title *Vaibhāṣika* is no less familiar to our author, and he defines it in this way: "Those who are dismissive or who follow the alternative" or also "who know the alternative."[30] By *alternative*, one must doubtless understand the use of the dilemma, a process that this school possibly made particular use of to change the position of its opponents. This is the school that the author of the commentary on the Abhidharma mentions most often. He attributes to it the belief in the existence of ether or space, which all Buddhist schools do not equally recognize. "The Vaibhāṣikas," he says, "base themselves on this text that emanates from the teaching of the Bhagavat. 'On what does the earth rest, O Gautama?' asks Kāśyapa. 'The earth, O brahman, rests on the circle of water.' 'And the circle of water, Gautama, on what does it rest?' 'It rests on the wind.' 'And the wind, Gautama, on what does it rest?' 'It rests on the ether.' 'And the ether, Gautama, on what does it rest?' 'You go too far, O great brahman, you go too far. The ether, O brahman, has nothing on which it rests, it has no support.'"[31]

The commentary of the *Abhidharma* also mentions the Yogācāras in this passage: "While gathering together the receptacles (*āśraya*), the received things (*āśrita*), and the supports (*ālambana*), which are each formed of six terms, there are eighteen terms, which are called *dhātus*, or containers. The collection of the six receptacles are the organs of sight, of hearing, of smell, of taste, of touch, and *manas* (or organ of the heart), which is the last. The collection of the six received things is the knowledge produced by sight and by the other senses up to *manas* inclusively. The collection of the six supports are form and the other sensible attributes up to *dharma* (the law or being) inclusively. But, in the opinion of the

28. *Abhidharmakośavyākhyā*, fols. 9b and 10a of the MS of the Société Asiatique.

29. *Abhidharmakośavyākhyā*, fols. 32a and 36b of the MS of the Société Asiatique.

30. *Abhidharmakośavyākhyā*, fol. 10a of the MS of the Société Asiatique.

31. *Abhidharmakośavyākhyā*, fol. 13a of the MS of the Société Asiatique. All readers to whom the philosophical processes of ancient Brahmanism are familiar will note the striking analogy of this exposition with that of some Upaniṣads.

Yogācāras, there is a *manodhātu*, distinct from the six knowledges,"[32] and doubtless perceived by the *manas*, or heart.

Finally, our author indicates the existence of the Madhyamikas,[33] a circumstance of interest for us, in that the school of the Madhyamikas is one of the four great sects enumerated by him about which we possess the most certain notions and details having a true historical character. Csoma informs us that it owes its origin to a celebrated philosopher, Nāgārjuna, who lived four hundred years after Śākyamuni, and that it is based entirely on the *Prajñāpāramitā*, of which it gives (still according to Csoma) an interpretation equally distant (*madhyama*) from the two extreme opinions accepted before, namely that the soul survives eternally or that it is entirely annihilated, doubtless after death.[34] The *Dharmakośavyākhyā* is not, as I will soon say, a book easy to make use of in order for me to be able to extract the opinions of the Madhyamikas from it, which are, moreover, rarely mentioned there. These opinions belong to what I call the middle age of Buddhism; and the books that contain them have so little authority, if not for the sect of the Madhyamikas itself, that they do not form part of the collection of works deemed canonical in Tibet and are only found in the Stangyur (*bstan 'gyur*), that is to say, in the collection of glosses and literary works.[35] As for the existence of Nāgārjuna, I will return to that in my Historical Sketch of Indian Buddhism; what is important to examine at the moment are the names of these four schools, the Sautrāntikas, the Vaibhāṣikas, the Madhyamikas, and the Yogācāras.

Now, these four schools are exactly those of which the brahmans speak when refuting the Buddhists; they are those that the famous Vedantist Śaṃkarācarya mentions. They are, as Colebrooke has remarked, anterior to the writing of the Brahmanical *Brahmasūtras*.[36] They also are anterior to the sixth or seventh century of our era, since the Yogācāra recognizes as its founder the philosopher Ārya Saṃgha, whom Csoma places around this epoch. Their authenticity, which is established by the quotations I have just borrowed from the commentator on the *Abhidharmakośa*, is further confirmed, if it were necessary to do so, by the testimony of the brahmans themselves. Without doubt, there is still a great deal, I should say almost everything, to learn about these schools; but it is not possible to complete the picture of a doctrine so vast and so complicated as Buddhism on

32. *Abhidharmakośavyākhyā*, fol. 32b of the MS of the Société Asiatique, fol. 28b of my manuscript.

33. *Abhidharmakośavyākhyā*, fol. 477a of my manuscript.

34. "Analysis of the Sher-chin," in *Asiatic Researches*, vol. 20, p. 400. I do not flatter myself that I understand what Csoma wished to say at this point.

35. Csoma, *Asiatic Researches*, vol. 20, p. 400.

36. Colebrooke, *Miscellaneous Essays*, 1:202, note. I quite keenly regret not being able to consult the commentary by Śaṃkara on the *Brahmasūtras*. It had been of the utmost interest for me to seek to determine if the axioms of Buddhist philosophy mentioned by the commentary are found in the books of Nepal that I have before me and that serve as the basis of my research.

the first attempt. Let us first draw the frame and hope that dedication like that of Messrs. Hodgson and Csoma will give the scholars of Europe the means to fill it in later. While waiting, I regard as a most interesting result of my studies to be able to note that one of the longest compositions of the scholarly literature of Nepal gives us, as far as the exposition of philosophical schools is concerned, information that accords so well with that which Colebrooke borrowed, already some years ago, from ancient Brahmanical commentators, and with those that Csoma de Kőrös has found among the Tibetan authors. It is not less worthy of attention to see this information at least omitted, if not forgotten, by the Nepalese tradition. Finally, it is remarkable that to the silence of the Nepalese concerning the four great sects I have just enumerated according to the *Abhidharmakośa* and according to the Sanskrit commentators extracted by Colebrooke, there answers the silence that the *Abhidharma* itself maintains on the four Nepalese sects of the Svābhāvikas, Aiśvarikas, Yātnikas, and Kārmikas.

In the section of this memorandum dedicated to works bearing the names of authors and above all in the Historical Sketch of Buddhism, I shall discuss what consequences appear to me to result from this silence. It suffices for me at the moment to summarize in a few words the results of the double presentation I have just made: 1. according to Mr. Hodgson, who informs us of the existence of two great sects, that of the naturalists and that of the theists, of which one is anterior to the other, and of two secondary schools, that of the moralists and that of the spiritualists, more intimately connected with that of the theists; 2. according to the *Abhidharmakośa*, which indicates to us four sects, that of the Sautrāntikas, Vaibhāṣikas, Yogācāras, and Madhyamikas. I confess that his presentation summarizes, in a very general form, all that we know up to the present about the most important divisions of the metaphysics of the Bauddhas. It naturally is separated into two portions: one that draws its authority from the still existing tradition in Nepal, it is that whose elements Mr. Hodgson has furnished us; the other that rests on the testimony of the *Abhidharmakośa*, it is that which I have extracted from this same book. These two portions most probably represent the whole of the different phases through which Buddhism has passed. To determine up to which point the four sects enumerated by Mr. Hodgson are included in those mentioned by the *Abhidharmakośa*, or to show that there are quite different sects who later shared the heritage of primitive beliefs, is a task for which we need new assistance. Let me remark, however, that the four Nepalese sects of Mr. Hodgson do not exist, according to Csoma, in the Tibetan books, or to speak with more precision, they do not rest on written authorities admitted into the voluminous collection of the Kah-gyur.[37] It is, it seems to me,

37. "Notices of Different Systems of Buddhism," in *Journal of the Asiatic Society of Bengal*, vol. 7, p. 146.

a presumption in favor of the latter hypothesis, that which regards the four sects of the Svābhāvikas, Aiśvarikas, Kārmikas, and Yātnikas as more modern, at least in the name, than those of the *Abhidharmakośa* and of the Tibetan authors.

Be that as it may and until the assistance of which I was just speaking is assembled, we probably possess in the present collection of Nepal, as Mr. Hodgson has collected it, the works on which the vast edifice of these developments is raised and of whose extent the previous observations have given a presentiment. I have already found several interesting confirmations of the elements gathered by Csoma touching on the four sects I have mentioned so many times. This is not the place, however, to show everything that the presentation of the ancient sects that Csoma has borrowed from the Tibetan authors contains which is of interest for the primitive history of Buddhism; this presentation, which I have reproduced above, will be examined elsewhere with the attention it merits. I only note here, because it is information that casts daylight on one of the most voluminous works of the Nepalese collection, that the school directed by Kāśyapa was called the Great Assembly. Now, I find among the books discovered in Nepal by Mr. Hodgson a treatise that manifestly belongs to this school; it is the *Mahāvastu*, or *Great History*, a voluminous anthology of legends related to the religious life of Śākya. Indeed, a considerable portion of this volume bears this title: *āryamahāsāṃghikānāṃ lokottaravādinām pāṭhena*, which means: "according to the lesson of the *Lokottaravādins* (those who claim to be superior to the world) being a part of the venerables of the Great Assembly." It is not doubtful that the Mahāsāṃghikas, or venerables of the Great Assembly, are none other than the monks who recognized Kāśyapa as chief; and it is no more so that the Lokottaravādins form the fourth of the subdivisions of this school. And what is quite worthy of attention is that this volume is written in a Sanskrit mixed with Pāli and Prakrit forms, which is often obscure. I do not wish to say that this is the corrupt dialect which Tibetans claim that Kāśyapa used, even less that the *Mahāvastu* was written as we have it from the first times of Buddhism. But while supposing that the style of this anthology has been revised, I regard this book no less to be one of the most ancient compilations that the collection of Nepal has preserved for us; and the indication alone contained in this title, the "Lesson of the Mahāsāṃghikas," brought together with the Tibetan tradition related to the name of the disciples of Kāśyapa, in my eyes ensures to it a great value and an incontestable antiquity.

This opinion seems again confirmed by the testimony of Faxian regarding the *Mohe sengzhi*, monks who were established in Jetavana in Kośala. Faxian informs us that the opinions of these monks were those to which the greatest number of the Buddha's disciples were connected while he was in the world, and he mentions specifically one *apitan* or *abhidharma* which belonged to them in particular.[38] Perhaps this simply means that the Mohe sengzhi was the most numerous subdivision of the disciples of Śākya; and it must be so, since they are called the monks of the Great Assembly. I indeed do not doubt that the Mohe sengzhi of Faxian are the Mahāsāṃghikas of the *Mahāvastu*; and I regard the connection of these two titles, supported as it is by the existence of the *Mahāvastu*, as more well founded than what the Brahmanical name Mahāsāṃkhya has suggested to Mr. Wilson.[39]

I would have wished to find the titles of the other schools in the same manner, and notably that of Kātyāyana, a personage who, we will see elsewhere, has a considerable importance for the history of Southern Buddhism; but until now, I have encountered only one name in the Sanskrit books of Nepal relating to one of these titles; I will indicate it below in its place.

Independent of these scattered indications that are important to collect in the interest of history, we possess the great collections of the *Prajñāpāramitā*, to which one of the four sects cited by the *Abhidharmakośa*, that of the Madhyamikas, is certainly posterior. Now, it would be a result of great interest to find in the *Prajñāpāramitā*, at least in part, the picture of Buddhist ontology as set forth by Mr. Hodgson. But the features of this picture are dispersed in such enormous collections, they are marked by such a weak hand, and lost under a mass of words so empty in appearance that I do not hesitate to say that they have gained a great deal by passing through the clear and pragmatic mind of the English scholar. Thus, if the details into which I will enter do not correspond completely to those that Mr. Hodgson has reported according to the Nepalese tradition, one must not conclude from that that his picture is not accurate or that my details have been badly chosen. As I occupy myself by design only with particular and consequently very special points, it is difficult for me to encounter generalities that result from the assembly of a considerable number of these particular points and above all of the successive work of the centuries, assisted by the mutual action of the schools on one another. But this part of my work will not be useless if I succeed in marking the true place of the *Prajñāpāramitā* in the whole of the literary monuments of Northern Buddhism, as I have done for the sūtras.

I said at the beginning of this memorandum, in my general description of the Nepalese collection, that, according to the Buddhist commentators, the section of the Abhidharma had not been set forth directly by Śākyamuni, but that it was formed after his death from a certain number of philosophical passages

38. A. Rémusat, *Foe koue ki*, p. 318. Would the *Mahāvastu* be the work Mr. A. Rémusat speaks about in this way in his *Recherches sur les langues tartares*: "In the same epoch (1332), a decree of the emperor ordered that a Buddhist book in one thousand sections on the longevity of the Buddha be written in golden letters and in Uighur characters, like another work of theology entitled the *Great History*" (*Recherches*, etc., p. 212). Is the book on the longevity of the Buddha the *Suvarṇaprabhāsa*?

39. *Journal of the Royal Asiatic Society*, vol. 5, p. 134.

dispersed throughout his teaching. Assembled like the other parts of the scriptures after the death of Śākya, the Abhidharma differs from them in that it does not truly offer us any work that, whatever the Tibetans say,[40] can in its entirety be considered the word of the last buddha, whereas the sūtras, by their form, by their length, and above all by the opinions of the Buddhists themselves, are much closer to the preaching of the Master. One understands easily the interest of information of this kind. In the first place, it is useful to know if Śākya indeed mixed with his preaching, whose most apparent character is that of a pure morality, the exposition or at least the suggestion of more general principles by which he must have resolved the great problems of the existence of God, of nature, of mind, and of matter. As far as I am concerned, I am convinced that he never separated metaphysics from morality and that he always connected these two parts of antique philosophy in the same teaching. But it is not a matter here of a demonstration *a priori*: at this moment it is a question of criticism; and it is through the testimony of the texts that it is necessary to ascertain if Śākyamuni was a philosopher and how he was one. If, as seems obvious to me, the founder of Buddhism resolved the questions I have just indicated in his own way, by that alone he is placed at a more exalted rank than this multitude of ascetics, perhaps as holy, but less celebrated than he, who content themselves with meditating in solitude on the truths accepted or disputed by the various philosophical schools of the brahmans. He takes his place immediately next to Kapila, to Patañjali, to Gotama, founders of flourishing philosophical schools, and he is different from them only because his philosophy became a religion. But where to find these first essays and these fundamental propositions of the metaphysics of Śākya, if not in the books considered to have preserved the repository of his word, that is to say, in the sūtras? Thus, it is necessary to return to the sūtras; it is in these books that one must study the beginnings of metaphysics in the same way as we have studied the beginnings of morality and discipline there.

In the second place, if the books of which the Abhidharma is composed are collections of principles, axioms, theses, whatever one wishes to call them, borrowed from treatises that are not exclusively philosophical, the place of the Abhidharma is marked immediately after these treatises. But if, on the other hand, the books of the Abhidharma form a whole almost as considerable as the treatises from which they are extracted, these books must have been amply developed, whether the development did nothing but reproduce the primitive core in more vast proportions, or if it was allied with new subjects. It cannot be supposed that this almost complete identity of volume between the *Prajñāpāramitā*

40. Csoma, "Analysis of the Sher-chin," in *Asiatic Researches*, vol. 20, p. 339. The doctrine contained in the *Prajñā* is attributed in its entirety to Śākya. According to the Tibetan authors, he set forth this doctrine sixteen years after becoming a buddha, that is to say, in his fifty-first year.

and the class of sūtras is the result of development alone, for Śākya's metaphysics, while taking a scientific form, necessarily had to be completed. I nevertheless have no fear in asserting that development (and our language has no word to express the extent of this development) played by far the greatest part in the identity I have just indicated. I am convinced that all readers who have the courage to browse through one or two volumes of the *Prajñāpāramitā in One Hundred Thousand Articles* and to compare the results of his reading with some portions of the sūtras or legends I regard as the most ancient will recognize that, except for consequences it draws from previously enunciated principles, the redaction of the *Prajñā* often adds nothing but words to that of the sūtras.

These observations, which appear to me indispensable preliminaries for the analysis of these books, take us back, as one sees, to the study of the sūtras and the avadānas envisaged from the point of view of metaphysics. I will thus extract from these treatises a passage appropriate to establish that the oft-mentioned commentator on the *Abhidharmakośa* was right to make the origin of the Abhidharma date back to these books and consequently to the *Prajñāpāramitā*, which in the Nepalese collection represents this part of the Buddhist scriptures.

The piece I will cite is borrowed from the *Avadānaśataka*: it is a conversation between Śākya and a brahman; its object is the detachment one reaches through the consideration that sensation is transitory. Here, as one will see, metaphysics and moral doctrine are intimately joined and almost inseparable. This piece gives us, in addition, the method of Śākya and puts into action this process of his dialectic that he applies to all theses, affirmation, negation, and neutrality.

The blessed Buddha[41] was with the assembly of his listeners in the city of Rājagṛha, in the Bamboo Wood, in the place called Karaṇḍakanivāpa.[42] Now at that time, in the village of Nālanda lived a brahman called Tiṣya who married Śāri, daughter of the brahman Māṭhara. When the child of Śāri entered into the womb of his mother, this woman, who debated with her brother Dīrghanakha, convinced this latter of a mistake in reasoning. This is why Dīrghanakha [vanquished], having withdrawn to the Dakṣiṇapatha, started to read a great number of books. During this time, the son of Śāri [named Śāriputra] came into the world. At sixteen years of age, he had read the grammar of Indra and vanquished all those who disputed with him. After some time, he then adopted the religious life under the teaching of the Bhagavat. However, this rumor reached the ears of Dīrghanakha the mendicant: "All the tīrthakaras have been vanquished by

41. Same preamble as for the legend translated above, section 2, p. 130.

42. One finds mention of this place in Faxian and in Xuanzang (*Foe koue ki*, pp. 272 and 273). Csoma informs us that a *vihāra*, or monastery, was built there, which was given to Śākyamuni by Bimbisāra, king of Magadha (*Asiatic Researches*, vol. 20, p. 294).

your nephew; he is, at this moment, the disciple of the śramaṇa Gautama." On learning this news, Dīrghanakha conceived a not very favorable idea about his nephew; and after having cursorily examined [as he had done himself] all the sciences, he pictured Śāriputra as a disciple who had remained with his master for only a limited time. This is why he went to Rājagṛha.

At that time, the Bhagavat, who just woke up, taught the four assemblies a pleasant law, sweet as the honey of the bee and filled with flavor. Śāriputra was standing behind the Bhagavat, holding a flywhisk in his hand, with which he fanned his master. Then, Dīrghanakha the mendicant saw the Bhagavat who taught the law, seated in the center of a circle that spread out on each side like the crescent of the moon, and Śāriputra, who, flywhisk in hand, fanned his master, and at this sight he addressed the Bhagavat in this way: "O Gautama, all that does not appeal to me." The Bhagavat answered: "The opinion, O Agnivaiśyāyana,[43] which makes you say: 'All that does not appeal to me,' does it itself not appeal to you?" *"O Gautama," continued the mendicant, "the opinion that makes me say: 'All that does not appeal to me,' does itself not appeal to me."*[44] "Consequently, O Agnivaiśyāyana, if it is thus that you know, if it is thus that you see, do you abandon, do you give up, do you reject your opinion without accepting, without admitting, without producing another?" "Yes, Gautama," answered the mendicant. "Knowing thus and seeing thus, I abandon, I give up, and I reject my opinion without accepting, without admitting, without producing another." "O Agnivaiśyāyana," replied the Bhagavat, "you are like the multitude of men; *since you say what the multitude of men say owing to such an opinion, you do not differ from them. But he who is a śramaṇa, O Agnivaiśyāyana, or a brahman, whoever he is, if he abandons an opinion without adopting another,* it is said in the world that he is the most subtle being among the most subtle beings. Now, there are, O Agnivaiśyāyana, three opinions; and what are they? Here, O Agnivaiśyāyana, some say, by virtue of one opinion: 'All that appeals to me.' On another side, here too, O Agnivaiśyāyana, others say by virtue of a different opinion: 'All this does not appeal to me.' On the other hand, here too, O Agnivaiśyāyana, there are some who say by virtue of another opinion: 'This appeals to me and that does not appeal to me.' Now here, the opinion that makes one say: 'All that appeals to me' ends in attachment and does not end in the absence of attachment, ends in aversion and does not end in the absence of aversion, ends in error and does not end in the absence of error, ends in union and does not end in separation, ends in corruption and does not end in purity, ends

43. This is a patronymic epithet of Dīrghanakha; it means "the descendant of Agnivaiśya." This latter name is that of an old Brahmanical family.

44. The passage contained between two asterisks is missing in the manuscript, which is here extremely incorrect; I have restored it according to the rest of the text. This observation applies equally to some other passages of this sūtra, where the reader will find the same sign.

in augmentation and does not end in diminution, ends in pleasure, in acquisition, in greed.

"The second opinion, which makes one say: 'All that does not appeal to me,' ends in the absence of attachment and does not end in attachment, ends in the absence of aversion and does not end in aversion, ends in the absence of error and does not end in error, ends in separation and does not end in union, ends in purity and does not end in corruption, ends in diminution and does not end in augmentation, ends in the absence of pleasure, in the absence of acquisition, in the absence of greed.

"Here, finally, the third opinion, which says: 'This appeals to me and that does not appeal to me'; as far as the proposition *That appeals to me* is concerned, it ends in attachment and does not end in the absence of attachment [etc., as above, until:] it ends in pleasure, in acquisition, in greed; and as far as the proposition *That does not appeal to me* is concerned, it ends in the absence of attachment and does not end in attachment [etc., as above, until:] it ends in the absence of pleasure, in the absence of acquisition, in the absence of greed. Among these three opinions, a respectable listener who has studied a great deal learns in a distinct and perfect manner what follows: 'If I have the first opinion and say: "All that appeals to me," I will be in discord with two other opinions, that which says: "All that does not appeal to me," and that which says: "This appeals to me and that does not appeal to me." From discord, dispute will arise, from dispute, hate.' Thus, recognizing clearly that this opinion brings with it discord, dispute, and hate, he renounces it and does not adopt another. It is in this way that one can abandon, give up, and reject an opinion without accepting, without admitting, without producing another.

*"Here again, a respectable listener who has studied a great deal learns in a distinct and perfect manner what follows: 'If I hold the second opinion and I say: "All that does not appeal to me," I will be in discord with two other opinions, that which says: "All that appeals to me" and that which says: "This appeals to me and that does not appeal to me." From discord, dispute will arise, from dispute, hate.' Thus, recognizing clearly that this opinion brings with it discord, dispute, and hate, he renounces it and does not adopt another. It is in this way that one can abandon, give up, and reject an opinion without accepting, without admitting, without producing another. *"Here again, a respectable listener who has studied a great deal learns in a distinct and perfect manner what follows: 'If I hold the third opinion and I say: "This appeals to me and that does not appeal to me," I will be in discord with two other opinions, that which says: "All that appeals to me," and that which says: "All that does not appeal to me." From discord, dispute will arise, from dispute, hate.' Thus, recognizing clearly that this opinion brings with it discord, dispute, and hate, he renounces it and does not adopt

another. It is in this way that one can abandon, give up, and reject an opinion without accepting, without admitting, without producing another.

"This material and coarse body, O Agnivaiśyāyana, is formed of the collection of the five great elements. A respectable listener must dwell on the consideration that the body is perpetually subject to birth and death. He must dwell on the consideration of the absence of attachment, on that of annihilation, on that of abandonment. When a respectable listener dwells on the consideration that the body is perpetually subject to birth and death, then what he experiences in his body: love, attachment, affection, complaisance, satisfaction, passion for this body itself, all that, vanquished by his mind, does not survive.

"There are, O Agnivaiśyāyana, three kinds of sensations; and what are these three kinds? These are pleasant sensation, unpleasant sensation, and the sensation that is not pleasant or unpleasant. At the moment when a respectable listener who has learned a great deal perceives a pleasant sensation, the two other sensations, namely unpleasant sensation and neutral sensation, do not exist for him; the respectable listener perceives in that moment only pleasant sensation; but this sensation itself is transitory and subject to annihilation. At the moment when a respectable listener perceives an unpleasant sensation, the two other sensations, namely pleasant sensation and neutral sensation, do not exist for him; the respectable listener perceives at that time only unpleasant sensation, but this sensation itself is transitory and subject to annihilation. At the moment when a respectable listener perceives a neutral sensation, the two other sensations, namely pleasant sensation and unpleasant sensation, do not exist for him; the respectable listener perceives at that time only neutral sensation; but this sensation itself is transitory and subject to annihilation.

"Then, he has this reflection: 'What is the cause, what is the origin, what is the birth, what is the production of these sensations?' It is contact that is the cause, the origin, the birth, the production of these sensations. When the production of such-and-such contact takes place, such-and-such sensations are produced; when the cessation of such-and-such contact takes place, such-and-such sensations also cease, are calmed, are cooled, and disappear. Whatever sensation he perceives, be it pleasant, unpleasant, or neutral, he knows the origin, the annihilation, the diminution, the appearance, and the production in their reality. Knowing in that way the origin, the annihilation, etc., of these sensations in their reality, when these sensations come to be produced, he dwells on the consideration that they are passing, on the consideration of annihilation, on that of the absence of attachment, on that of cessation, on that of abandonment. Experiencing a sensation that lasts as long as his body lasts, he knows this truth as it is: 'I perceive a sensation that lasts as long as my body lasts.' Experiencing a sensation that lasts as long as his life, he knows this truth as it is: 'I perceive a sensation that lasts as long as my life lasts.' And, after the dissolution of his body, as also when his life reaches only half of its duration, all the sensations perceived by him in this very world cease without anything remaining of them, they disappear, are destroyed, are annihilated without anything remaining of them. He thus has the following reflection: 'Even when I perceive a pleasant sensation, the dissolution of my body will take place: it is there that is the end of pleasure.[45] Even when I perceive an unpleasant sensation or a neutral sensation, the dissolution of my body will take place: it is there that is the end of suffering.' Even when he perceives a pleasant sensation, he perceives it detached and not attached. Even when he perceives an unpleasant or neutral sensation, he perceives it detached and not attached. And from what is he detached? It is from attachment, from aversion, from error; it is from birth, from old age, from sickness, from death, from grief, from lamentations, from suffering, from disquietude, from despair, from miseries. That, O Agnivaiśyāyana, is what I say."

Now at that moment, the respectable Śāriputra, who had only received investiture half a month before, stood behind the Bhagavat, having a flywhisk in his hand with which he fanned his master. This reflection then came to his mind: "The Bhagavat celebrates the abandonment of those conditions in this way: he celebrates their detachment, their cessation, their renunciation. Why would I not dwell on the consideration of abandonment, on the consideration of detachment, on that of cessation, on that of renunciation?" Consequently, the respectable Śāriputra, having dwelled on the consideration that conditions were transitory, that they were subject to perish; having dwelled on the consideration of detachment, of cessation, of renunciation, rid his mind of all its imperfections while admitting none of them. On his side, the mendicant Dīrghanakha felt born in him the pure and unblemished vision of conditions. When he had seen, attained, known the law; when he had probed its depth, when he had passed beyond doubt and uncertainty, no longer seeking the assistance of others, envisaging with intrepidity the laws of the doctrine in which one instructs oneself by oneself, Dīrghanakha, having risen from his seat and having thrown his upper robe back on his shoulder, pointed his hands, joined in a sign of respect, in the direction of the Bhagavat and spoke to him in this way: "Lord, may I embrace the religious life under the discipline of the well-renowned law! May I obtain investiture and the rank of monk! May I accomplish the duties of the religious life in the presence of the Bhagavat!" Consequently, Dīrghanakha the mendicant embraced the religious life under the discipline of the well-renowned law; he obtained investiture and the rank of monk. When he had entered into it, this respectable personage, alone, retired to a deserted place, attentive, assiduous, the

45. The text says "of suffering," but this thesis comes in a short while in its own place, and it cannot be repeated twice.

mind collected, soon succeeded to see by himself, to see face to face the supreme and unequaled goal of the religious life, which is that for which young men of good family, shaving their hair and their beard and dressing in robes of yellow color, leave their house with a perfect faith to embrace the life of a mendicant. And when he had received investiture, he felt in himself this conviction: "Birth is annihilated for me; I have accomplished the duties of the religious life; I have done what I had to do; I will not see another existence after this one." Arrived thus at omniscience, this respectable personage became an arhat and his mind was perfectly free.[46]

The principal aim of the piece I have just translated is to establish the necessity of detachment, a subject that reappears at almost any moment in the sūtras and the legends. It is to this thesis, at once metaphysical and moral, that these beautiful words refer, which, according to a passage of a legend cited above, make themselves heard in the sky when the luminous rays produced by Śākya's smile penetrate it: "That is transitory, that is misery, that is empty, that is lacking in substance."[47] The last two theses are obviously metaphysical; they are the abridged expression of these two propositions that occupy so great a place in the *Prajñāpāramitā*, that all phenomena are empty and that no one phenomenon has its own substance, which is expressed by the two words *śūnya* and *anātmaka*. One must also connect to this order of ideas this axiom, which I already mentioned above: "All concepts or all compounds are perishable."

It is now necessary to bring a fragment borrowed from the *Prajñāpāramitā* to the text I have just cited. But first, it is necessary to describe quickly the voluminous collections that bear this title. These collections are distinguished from one another by the number of stanzas or articles of which they are composed. The foremost and the most considerable is that called *Śatasāhasrikā*, that is to say, that which contains one hundred thousand articles. It is divided into four large books to which one joins another *Prajñāpāramitā in Twenty-five Thousand Articles*, and the whole forms five *skandhas*, or divisions, that the Nepalese name *pañcaraṣa* or *rakṣa*.[48] It is probable that the second spelling is the best, and that *raṣa* is a provincial alteration of the Sanskrit *rakṣa* (protection). These divisions as a whole receive the generic name *rakṣabhagavatī*, which is an epithet related to the true title of this great compilation, *Prajñāpāramitā*. It appears to me quite probable that *rakṣabhagavatī* represents for the Nepalese the two words *āryā bhagavatī* that open the full title of the work thus conceived: *Āryābhagavatī*

46. *Avadānaśataka*, fol. 245b ff.

47. It is like a kind of philosophical act of faith. *Brāhmaṇadārikā*, in *Divyāvadāna*, fol. 33a. *Aśokavarṇa*, *ibid.*, fol. 68a. *Jyotiṣka*, *ibid.*, fol. 133a. *Paṃśupradāna*, *ibid.*, fol. 182b. *Avadānaśataka*, fol. 3a.

48. Hodgson, "Notices of the Languages, Literature and Religion of the Bauddhas of Nepal and Bhot," in *Asiatic Researches*, vol. 16, p. 423.

Prajñāpāramitā, "The Venerable Blessed Perfection of Wisdom."[49] Thus, in naming the collection *rakṣabhagavatī*, the Nepalese are only designating it with epithets connected to it through respect or superstition; they are almost like a Christian who, instead of calling the Old Testament the *Holy Bible*, would content himself with saying the *Holy*. This is how I explain a difficulty I dwelled on for a long time at the beginning of my Buddhist studies; it is on the one hand the frequent use that Mr. Hodgson made of this title *Rakṣabhagavatī* in all his memoranda, and on the other hand the impossibility in which I found myself of discovering it in a single one of the manuscripts of the compilation so named. This comes from Mr. Hodgson having always designated this collection with the title in use today among the Nepalese, whereas the manuscripts copied from ancient originals exclusively reproduce the true title of the collection.

This title is thus *Prajñāpāramitā*, and it must mean "the perfection of wisdom"; but however clear the meaning of this expression seems to be, its formation is nevertheless not regular, and I do not know that the word *pāramitā* is ever used in Brahmanical works with the meaning of "perfection." This word is indeed the feminine of the adjective *pāramita*, meaning: "one who has gone to the other shore, transcendent"; but it is not and cannot be a substantive. But the Buddhists use it as a substantive, not only those of the North but also those of the South, since they count several pāramitās, that of alms, of charity, and of several other virtues whose names I have already given. Perhaps, the term *pāramitā* is related to some implied terms, like that of *buddhi*, "intelligence," for example, such that one should translate the names of the various perfections in this way: "[the intelligence] that has reached the other shore of wisdom, of alms, of charity," and so for the others.[50] I nevertheless give this explanation only as a conjecture I could not support with the testimony of any definitive text, because

49. "Analysis of the Kah-gyur," in *Journal of the Asiatic Society of Bengal*, vol. 1, p. 375.

50. The Tibetans, like the Mongols, make of the term *pāramitā* a participle meaning "which has reached the other shore" (Csoma, *Asiatic Researches*, vol. 20, p. 393, Schmidt, *Mémoires de l'Académie des sciences de Saint-Pétersbourg*, 2:14). But, in their translations, they remove the difficulty that the gender of the term *pāramitā* creates. I believe I will please the reader by transcribing here two other explanations of this difficult word, which I owe to Mr. Theodor Goldstücker, with whom I had spoken on this subject. "The first explanation which I propose consists of taking *pāramitā* as an abstract substantive in *tā*, derived from *prajñāpārami*, a *tatpuruṣa* compound, of which the last part would be then composed, with the *vṛddhi* of the first syllable by the affix *i* or *in*, which is used, according to Pāṇini, only in the derivation of patronymics. In this case, *Pārami* would mean a descendant of *Parama*, and if this last word could be taken for a denomination of the Buddha, the meaning of the abstract compound would be: *Prajñā*, or supreme science, who is a daughter of the Buddha. However, this explanation appears to me a bit artificial and I would rather ask if there would not be a good reason to consider *prajñā* and *pāramitā* as two distinct words: the science which has arrived beyond all doubts; because I believe that there is no difficulty in using *pāra* in this absolute manner when the ambiguity becomes impossible." This last explanation, as one sees, is not very far from the one I propose; but I imply *buddhi* instead of *prajñā*; as far as the first is concerned, I think with Mr. Goldstücker that one could not defend it. I do not believe any less that *pāramitā* is regarded by Buddhist authors as a substantive, and I find myself confirmed in this hypothesis by the word *pāramī*, which in Pāli is synonymous with *pāramitā*.

I do not have any commentary on the *Prajñā* at my disposal. I will only say that the expression *pāramitā,* once introduced into the language with the ellipsis I suppose, could have remained and by extension taken the value of a substantive because of its exterior resemblance to an abstract noun, such as those formed by means of the syllable *tā,* a well-known formative of nouns of quality.

The four sections of the *Prajñāpāramitā in One Hundred Thousand Articles* and the abridged edition of the same work in twenty-five thousand are not the only philosophical treatises to which this title *prajñā* applies. Two other redactions are also mentioned, one in eighteen thousand articles, the other in ten thousand, the first of which is considered the abridgment of the redaction in a hundred thousand, the second as the extract of the redaction in twenty-five thousand articles.[51] Finally, the collection ends with a shorter redaction in eight thousands stanzas, this same one that I mentioned at the beginning, and for which the Nepalese appear to especially reserve the title *Prajñāpāramitā.*[52] I say a shorter redaction in order not to decide anything about the question of whether, as the Tibetans wish it, it is only an abridgment of the more ample collections, or if, on the contrary, this edition, as the Nepalese claim, is the primitive work of which the others would be only developments.[53] It is also necessary not to forget the *Vajracchedikā*, which is an even more condensed extract of all the doctrine contained in the *Prajñāpāramitā*; it is the book that Mr. Schmidt has translated, as I have said at the beginning of this volume, from the Tibetan and included in the *Mémoires de l'Académie des sciences de Saint-Pétersbourg.*

The piece we are going to read is borrowed from the *Prajñāpāramitā in Eight Thousand Articles*, that is to say, from the redaction the Nepalese regard as the most ancient. I have extracted it from the first chapter, because it seems to indicate to me, more clearly than any other, the general tendency of this collection. I have compared this passage with the corresponding part of the *Prajñāpāramitā in One Hundred Thousand Articles*, and I can affirm that the doctrine is identical in these two collections. What I say of the first chapter applies equally to the whole of the two works. I have translated, for my personal use, almost all of the *Prajñā* in eight thousand articles, and I have compared a considerable portion of it with the longest redaction in one hundred thousand stanzas. Now, I have found in the two collections the same subjects, treated exactly in the same way, often in the same terms. There is hardly a difference between the most considerable redaction and the most brief redaction except in the development and in

51. Csoma, "Analysis of the Sher-chin," in *Asiatic Researches*, vol. 20, p. 394. *Journal of the Asiatic Society of Bengal*, vol. 1, p. 376.

52. Hodgson, "Notices of the Languages, Literature and Religion of the Bauddhas of Nepal and Bhot," in *Asiatic Researches*, vol. 16, p. 427.

53. Hodgson, "Notices of the Languages, Literature and Religion of the Bauddhas of Nepal and Bhot," in *Asiatic Researches*, vol. 16, p. 424.

the tedious repetition of formulas, which, in the redaction in eight thousand articles, are sometimes abridged.

In this assembly, the Bhagavat addressed the respectable Subhūti the sthavira in this way: "Deploy your vigor, O Subhūti, when commencing with the perfection of wisdom for bodhisattva mahāsattvas[54] in order that bodhisattvas penetrate it entirely." Then, this reflection came to the mind of the respectable Śāriputra: "Is it that the respectable sthavira Subhūti will teach the perfection of wisdom to bodhisattvas by deploying the strength of the energy of his own and personal wisdom and by the benediction of this very strength, or will he do it by the power of the Buddha?" Then, the respectable Subhūti, knowing with his thought, thanks to the power of the Buddha, the thought and the reflection that rose in the mind of the respectable Śāradvatīputra, spoke to him in these terms: "All that the listeners of the Bhagavat say, O Śāriputra,[55] all that they show, all that they teach, all that they develop, all that they explain, all that they elucidate, all that must be recognized as the effect of the virile strength of the Tathāgata. Why is that? It is that when they learn the exposition of the law taught by the Tathāgata, they see it face to face, they possess it with its character of law; and when they have seen it face to face with this character and possess it, all that they say, all that they show, all that they teach, all that they develop, all that they explain, all that they elucidate, all that accords with the character of law that the teaching of the law by the Tathāgata possesses. In this way, O Śāriputra, it is explained how it happens that these young men of good family while teaching that which has the character of law are not in contradiction with that which has this character."

Then, Subhūti, thanks to the power of the Buddha, spoke to the Bhagavat in this way: "When the Bhagavat has said: 'Deploy your vigor, O Subhūti, when commencing with the perfection of wisdom for bodhisattvas in order that bodhisattvas penetrate it entirely,' he used the term *bodhisattva mahāsattva.* But what, O Bhagavat, is this name of the being called *bodhisattva mahāsattva*? I do not see, O Bhagavat, the being who is named *bodhisattva*; nor do I see the being who is designated with the name *perfection of wisdom.* Thus seeing, O Bhagavat, neither bodhisattva nor being of bodhisattva, not comprehending, not grasping that; neither seeing, understanding, nor grasping the perfection of wisdom, what is the bodhisattva whom I must instruct, and what is the perfection of wisdom in which I must instruct him? Yet, O Bhagavat, if while speaking, setting forth, and teaching as I just have, the thought of the bodhisattva does not dissolve, does

54. The epithet *mahāsattva*, which means "great being or great creature," is always added to the title of *bodhisattva* in the collections of the *Prajñā* and in the developed sūtras; I believe I am excused from repeating it in this translation.

55. It is the most ordinary name of this celebrated disciple of Śākya; that of Śāradvatīputra is a synonym of it.

not melt, does not subside, does not experience weakness; if it does not recede, if his mind does not recede in defeat, if it is not frightened, if it is not afraid, if it does not experience terror; that is the very bodhisattva who must be instructed in the perfection of wisdom; that is what must be recognized as the perfection of wisdom of the bodhisattva; finally that is the very teaching of the perfection of wisdom. When the bodhisattva is so established, this teaching, this instruction then takes place.

"Still one more thing, O Bhagavat. The bodhisattva who courses in the perfection of wisdom, who comprehends it, must study in such a way that while studying, he does not pride himself in possessing the thought of bodhi or the intelligence of a buddha. Why is that? It is that even then this thought is a nonthought; the nature of the thought is that of light." [?]

Then, Śāriputra spoke to Subhūti in this way: "But Subhūti, is there a thought that is a nonthought?" That said, Subhūti spoke to Śāriputra in these terms: "But, Śāriputra, in the state of nonthought, is there found, does there exist, reality or nonreality?" Śāriputra responded: "Neither reality nor absence of reality, O Subhūti." "If so, O Śāriputra, in the state of nonthought, there neither exists nor is there found reality or absence of reality, do you not see the answer that is suitable to the objection that the respectable Śāriputra has made when he has said: 'Is there a thought that is a nonthought?'" This said, Śāriputra spoke to Subhūti in this way: "But what, O Subhūti, is the state of nonthought?" "The state of nonthought," continued Subhūti, "is immutable, O Śāriputra, it is indisputable."

Then, Śāriputra expressed his assent to Subhūti: "Good, good, Subhūti; it is good that you have been designated by the Bhagavat as the chief of the monks who lives in the absence of all corruption. This is why the bodhisattva must be recognized as being unable to turn away from the supreme state of a perfectly accomplished buddha. The bodhisattva must be recognized as not being deprived of the perfection of wisdom. One who desires to instruct himself in order to arrive at the rank of listener must listen, learn, retain, recite, comprehend, promulgate the perfection of wisdom itself. He has to instruct himself in this perfection of wisdom; he has to apply his efforts to it. One who desires to instruct himself in order to arrive at the rank of pratyekabuddha must listen, learn, retain, recite, comprehend, promulgate the perfection of wisdom itself; he has to instruct himself in this perfection of wisdom; he has to apply his efforts to it. One who desires to instruct himself in order to reach the rank of bodhisattva must listen [etc., as above, until:] promulgate the perfection of wisdom itself. It is necessary that one who is endowed with the skillful use of means apply his efforts to it in order to arrive at the comprehension of all the conditions of bodhisattvas. Why is that? Because it is in the perfection of wisdom itself that all the conditions which the bodhisattva must study, to which he must apply his efforts, are taught at length. One who desires to instruct himself in order to reach the supreme state of a perfectly accomplished buddha must listen [etc., as above, until:] promulgate the perfection of wisdom itself. It is necessary that one who is endowed with the skillful use of means apply his efforts to it to arrive at the comprehension of all the conditions of a buddha. Why is that? Because it is in the perfection of wisdom itself that all the conditions of a buddha, which a bodhisattva must study, to which he must apply his efforts, are taught at length."

Then, Subhūti spoke to the Bhagavat in this way: "For me, Bhagavat, I do not know, I do not comprehend, I do not grasp this very name *bodhisattva.* Nor do I know, do I comprehend, do I grasp the perfection of wisdom. Now in this ignorance in which I find myself about the name *bodhisattva* and about the perfection of wisdom, who is the bodhisattva I must instruct, and what is the perfection of wisdom I must teach him, which I must impart to him? It would be, O Bhagavat, an evil action on my part, if, not knowing, not comprehending, not grasping the thing itself, I contented myself to explain it with only the name that it bears, that of *bodhisattva.* There is more, O Bhagavat. This name itself is neither stable, nor not stable; it is neither unstable, nor not unstable. Why is that? Because this name has no existence. It is in this way that it is neither stable, nor not stable, neither unstable, nor not unstable. If, while this profound perfection of wisdom is spoken of, set forth, taught to the bodhisattva, his thought does not dissolve, does not melt, does not subside, does not experience weakness, does not recede; if his mind does not recede in defeat, if it is not frightened, if it is not afraid, if it does not experience terror, this bodhisattva, who owes his favorable dispositions to the practice of reflection, must be recognized as not separated from the perfection of wisdom. Established on the field of a bodhisattva, incapable of turning away from his aim, he is well established in the manner of not really being so.

"Still another thing, O Bhagavat. The bodhisattva who courses in the perfection of wisdom, who meditates on it, must not dwell on form, any more than on sensation, on idea, on concepts, on knowledge. Why is that? It is that if he dwells on form, he courses in the notion that form exists; he does not course in the perfection of wisdom. And likewise if he dwells on sensation, idea, concepts, knowledge, he courses in the notion that all of that exists; he does not course in the perfection of wisdom. Why is that? It is that he who courses in the notion does not grasp the perfection of wisdom, does not apply his efforts to it, does not accomplish it entirely. Not accomplishing the perfection of wisdom entirely, he will not reach omniscience, because he grasps what is not grasped. Why is that? It is that in the perfection of wisdom, form is not grasped, and it is the same for sensation, for idea, for concepts, for knowledge, for all things that are not grasped in the perfection of wisdom. Now, this state of form that is not being grasped, it is not form; and it is the same for sensation, for idea, for concepts, for knowledge. The perfection of wisdom itself is not grasped; for it is in this way that the bodhisattva must course in the perfection of wisdom. It is that which is called the meditation which does not grasp any condition; an immense meditation placed before [all the others], incommensurably certain and which is appropriate neither for listeners nor for congregating pratyekabuddhas.

"Omniscience itself is not grasped; for it does not have characters by which one can grasp it. If it was graspable by some character, the mendicant carrying a rosary would not have faith in it; for the mendicant carrying a rosary who has dispositions favorable for omniscience is, according to the degree of his faith, instructed in a partial science. Once he is instructed, he does not grasp form, any more than sensation, idea, concepts, knowledge; and he does not take delight with pleasure and happiness in seeing science there. He does not recognize science as that of interior form; he does not recognize it as that of exterior form; he does not recognize it as that of exterior and interior form; he does not recognize it as that of all things other than form. In the same way, he does not recognize science as that of sensation, of idea, of concepts, of interior knowledge any more than as of these exterior conditions, as that of these interior and exterior conditions, as that of all other things than these conditions. In the preceding enumeration, the term *mendicant carrying a rosary* is qualified as *favorably disposed*. Now it is when, always in proportion to his faith, he has taken as authority that which has the character of law that he is said to be favorably disposed for omniscience. By such a man, no one condition is grasped; if he happens to grasp one, this condition, whatever it is, is not apparent. And he does not glory in having arrived at nirvāṇa.

"Here, O Bhagavat, is what it is necessary to recognize for the perfection of wisdom of the bodhisattva. This perfection consists in that he does not grasp form and, in the same way, that he does not grasp sensation, idea, concepts, knowledge. Yet he has not reached thereby, in the course [of the existence where he finds himself] complete nirvāṇa, because he has not acquired the ten strengths of a tathāgata, the four intrepidities of a tathāgata, the eighteen distinct conditions of a buddha. So, O Bhagavat, this is what must be recognized as the perfection of wisdom of the bodhisattva mahāsattva.

"Still one more thing, O Bhagavat. The bodhisattva who courses in the perfection of wisdom, who meditates on it, must think, must reflect in this way: 'What is this perfection of wisdom and to whom does it belong? What? Would the perfection of wisdom be a condition that does not exist, that is not to be found?' If thinking and reflecting in this way, the mind of the bodhisattva does not dissolve, does not melt, [etc., as above, until:] if it does not experience terror, this bodhisattva must be recognized as being not deprived of the perfection of wisdom."

Then, Śāriputra spoke to Subhūti in this way: "Why, Subhūti, must the bodhisattva be recognized as not being deprived of the perfection of wisdom, when form is deprived of the intrinsic nature of form, and it is the same for sensation, for idea, for concepts, for knowledge, all of which are deprived of intrinsic nature; when omniscience itself is deprived of the intrinsic nature of omniscience?"

That said, Subhūti spoke to Śāriputra in this way: "That is it, Śāriputra, that is exactly it. Yes, form is deprived of the intrinsic nature of form; and it is the same for sensation, for idea, for concepts, for knowledge, which all are deprived of intrinsic nature. In the same way, O Śāriputra, the perfection of wisdom itself is deprived of intrinsic nature and it is so for omniscience. The perfection of wisdom is deprived of the attributes of the perfection of wisdom. The attribute itself is deprived of the intrinsic nature of attribute. The subject itself is deprived of the intrinsic nature of subject. The intrinsic nature itself is deprived of the attributes of intrinsic nature."

That said, Śāriputra spoke to Subhūti in this way: "O Subhūti, will the bodhisattva who studies in this way reach omniscience?" "Yes, Śāriputra," responded Subhūti. "That is exactly it; the bodhisattva who studies this will reach omniscience. Why is that? It is, O Śāriputra, that all conditions are not produced, are uncreated. The bodhisattva, O Śāriputra, who courses in this conviction approaches omniscience. To the degree that he approaches omniscience, in that proportion, for the maturity of creatures, he approaches the perfection of body and mind, the perfection of the attributes, the perfection of the field of the Buddha and [the state of] the Buddha himself. It is in this way, O Śāriputra, that the bodhisattva, coursing in the perfection of wisdom, approaches omniscience."

Still one more thing. Subhūti spoke in this way, commencing with the bodhisattva: "The bodhisattva courses in the sign if he courses in form, if he courses in the sign of form, if he courses saying: 'Form is the sign,' if he courses in the production of form, if he courses in the cessation of form, if he courses in the destruction of form, if he courses saying: 'Form is empty,' if he courses saying: 'I course,' if he courses saying: 'I am a bodhisattva'; finally, in the very fact of conceiving this idea: 'I am a bodhisattva,' he courses. And in the same way that he courses in the sign, if he courses in sensation, in idea, in concepts, in knowledge, if he courses in the sign of knowledge, if he courses saying: 'Knowledge is the sign,' if he courses in the production of knowledge, if he courses in the cessation of knowledge, if he courses in the destruction of knowledge, if he courses saying: 'Knowledge is empty,' if he courses saying: 'I course,' if he courses saying: 'I am a bodhisattva,' finally in the very fact of conceiving this idea, he courses. If he makes this reflection: 'He who courses in this way certainly courses in the perfection of wisdom, he meditates on it, he courses in the sign.' Now this bodhisattva must be recognized as not possessing skill of means."

Then, Śāriputra spoke to Subhūti in this way: "But how, O Subhūti, does the bodhisattva course when he courses in the perfection of wisdom?" That said, Subhūti spoke to Śāriputra in this way: "If the bodhisattva, O Śāriputra, courses neither in form, nor in the sign of form, nor saying: 'Form is the sign'; if he courses neither in the production of form, nor in the cessation of form, nor in the destruction of form, nor saying: 'Form is empty,' nor saying: 'I course,' nor saying: 'I am a bodhisattva'; if finally he does not course in the very conception of this idea: 'I am a bodhisattva'; in the same way, if he does not course in sensation, in idea, in concepts, in knowledge; if he does not course in the sign of knowledge, if he does not course saying: 'Knowledge is the sign'; if he does not course in the production of knowledge, in the cessation of knowledge, in the destruction of knowledge; if he does not course saying: 'Knowledge is empty,' while saying: 'I course,' while saying: 'I am a bodhisattva'; if he does not make this reflection: 'He who so courses, certainly courses in the perfection of wisdom, he meditates on it,' if, I say, he so courses, he courses in the perfection of wisdom; for coursing in this way, he does not carry this judgment: 'I course,' or this one: 'I do not course,' or this one: 'I course and I do not course,' or this one: 'I do not course and I am not coursing'; he does not carry this judgment: 'I will course,' or this one: 'I will not course,' or this one: 'I will course and I will not course,' or this one: 'I will not course and I will not not course.' Why is that? It is that all these conditions, whatever they are, are not perceived, not accepted by him. That is what is called the meditation of the bodhisattva who does not accept any condition; an immense meditation, placed before [all the others], incommensurably certain and which is appropriate neither for śrāvakas nor for congregating pratyekabuddhas. The bodhisattva who practices this meditation rapidly reaches the supreme state of a perfectly accomplished buddha."

Then, Subhūti the sthavira spoke in this way, thanks to the power of the Buddha: "He has heard, O Bhagavat, from the mouth of the ancient tathāgatas, venerable, perfectly and completely buddhas, the prediction which announces that the bodhisattva who devotes himself to this meditation will obtain the supreme state of a perfectly accomplished buddha. He does not perceive this very meditation, he is not proud of it. 'I devote myself to the meditation,' 'I will obtain the meditation,' 'I obtain the meditation,' 'I have obtained the meditation' are reflections which do not exist for him, not in the least, in any manner, in no way, absolutely not."

That said, Śāriputra spoke to Subhūti in this way: "Can, O Subhūti, the meditation to which the bodhisattva devotes himself be shown, the bodhisattva who has heard the prediction from the mouth of the tathāgatas, venerable, perfectly and completely buddhas, that announces to him that he will obtain the supreme state of a perfectly accomplished buddha?" Subhūti responded: "No, Śāriputra. Why is that? It is that this young man of good family does not know this very meditation, that he has no idea of it." Śāriputra replied: "Do you not say, Subhūti, that he does not know it, that he has no idea of it?" "Yes, Śāriputra, I say it," responded Subhūti. "He does not know it, he has no idea of it. Why is that? It is because this meditation does not exist that he does not know it, that he has no idea of it."

Then, the Bhagavat showed his assent to Subhūti by saying: "Good, good, Subhūti; it is just that, Subhūti, that is exactly it. It is good that, thanks to the power of the Buddha, you deploy your energy and you teach thanks to the benediction of the Tathāgata. This is what the bodhisattva must study in this way. Why is that? It is that the bodhisattva who studies in this way studies the perfection of wisdom."

Then, Śāriputra spoke to the Bhagavat in this way: "The bodhisattva who studies in this way, O Bhagavat, does he study the perfection of wisdom?" That said, the Bhagavat spoke to Śāriputra in this way: "The bodhisattva who studies in this way studies the perfection of wisdom." That said, Śāriputra spoke to the Bhagavat in this way: "The bodhisattva who studies in this way, which condition does he study?" That said, the Bhagavat spoke to Śāriputra in this way: "The bodhisattva, O Śāriputra, who studies in this way does not study any condition. Why is that? It is that conditions, O Śāriputra, do not exist as ordinary and ignorant men who are not instructed believe while becoming attached to them." Śāriputra said: "How thus do they exist, O Bhagavat?" "They exist, O Śāriputra," replied the Bhagavat, "in such a manner that they do not really exist. And since they do not exist, because of that they are called *avidyā*, that is to say, what does not exist or ignorance. It is to that that ordinary and ignorant men who are not instructed become attached. They imagine as existing all conditions of which none exists. When they have imagined them in this way, then, chained to two limits, they do not know, they do not see conditions. This is why they imagine all conditions as existing, when none exists. When they have imagined them in this way, they become attached to two limits. Once attached in this way, and having conceived the idea of the chain of cause and effect, they imagine past conditions, future conditions, and present conditions. After they have imagined them in this way, they become attached to name and form. It is in this way that they imagine all conditions, when none exists. Imagining all conditions as existing, when none exists, they do not know, they do not see the true path. Not knowing, not seeing the true path, they do not depart from the collection of the three worlds; they do not know the true aim; so they go among the number of those who are called ignorant; they do not believe in the true law. This is why, Śāriputra, bodhisattvas do not become attached to any condition."

That said, Śāriputra spoke to the Bhagavat in this way: "Does the bodhisattva who so learns, O Bhagavat, learn omniscience?" The Bhagavat said, "The bodhisattva, O Śāriputra, who learns in this way learns omniscience itself. The bodhisattva, O Śāriputra, who learns in this way learns all conditions. The bodhisattva, O Śāriputra, who learns in this way learns omniscience, approaches omniscience, must reach omniscience."

Then, Subhūti spoke to the Bhagavat in this way: "If anyone, O Bhagavat, asks the following question: 'Will a man produced from a magical illusion learn omniscience, will he approach omniscience, will he reach omniscience?' how, O Bhagavat, must this question be answered?" That said, the Bhagavat spoke to Subhūti in this way: "About that, I ask you, O Subhūti, to explain the matter as you can." "Good, Bhagavat," responded Subhūti, who began to listen, and the Bhagavat spoke in this way: "How does it seems to you, O Subhūti? Is illusion one thing and form another thing? Is illusion one thing and sensation another; idea, another; concepts, another; knowledge, another?" Subhūti responded: "No, Bhagavat, no, illusion is not one thing, and form another thing. Form itself is illusion, and illusion itself is form. No, Bhagavat, illusion is not one thing and sensation another, idea another. Sensation, idea, and concepts themselves, O Bhagavat, are illusion; illusion itself is sensation, idea, and concepts. No, Bhagavat, illusion is not one thing, and knowledge another thing. Knowledge itself, O Bhagavat, is illusion; illusion itself, O Bhagavat, is knowledge." The Bhagavat said: "O Subhūti, are there in the five attributes, which are causes of conception,[56] the idea, knowledge, acceptation, the notion of that which is called *bodhisattva*?"

That said, Subhūti spoke to the Bhagavat in this way: "Yes, without doubt, Bhagavat; yes, without doubt, Sugata. It is for that, O Bhagavat, that the bodhisattva who learns the perfection of wisdom must learn the supreme state of a perfectly accomplished buddha as if he was a man produced by a magical illu-

56. These five attributes are what are called *skandhas*, or aggregates, namely: form, sensation, idea, concepts, and knowledge, to which I will return below. I will show in my analysis of the metaphysical terms of Buddhism that the five *skandhas* embrace the various accidents of the fact of knowledge, conceived in the manner of the Buddhists, from that which provides the occasion, that is form, to the fact of knowledge itself. I agree for the present that the term *attribute* is quite imperfect, and I will say below how that of *means, support* seems to correspond better to one of the ideas that the Buddhists make of the word *skandha*. Nevertheless, considered in a general way, the five *skandhas* are intellectual attributes of the subject, which are supplemented with the five senses and the six material elements, as is proved by a major passage of the *Pūrṇāvadāna* (above, section 3, p. 277). The *skandhas* constitute what I will call the domain of knowledge or mind in man, and it is for that that I consider them intellectual attributes. But the difficulty is not entirely there; the word *skandha* is employed by our text in combination with that of *upādāna*, in this manner *upādānaskandha*, and then, we have to determine: 1. the relation of these two terms to each other, 2. the signification of that placed first, that is to say, *upādāna*. As for the first question, I find two solutions to it in the commentary on the *Abhidharmakośa*: "One calls *upādānaskandhas*, the *skandhas* or attributes produced by *upādāna* (seizing or conception). It is a compound of those types in which the middle term is suppressed in this manner: *upādāna* [*sambhūtāḥ*] *skandhāḥ*, that is to say, the attributes produced by conception. It is like calling a fire produced by grass, *grass fire*; a fire produced by straw, *straw fire*" (*Abhidharmakośavyākhyā*, fol. 18b). Here now is the second solution, that which is preferred by the commentator: "*Upādānaskandhāḥ* designates the attributes that are the origin or the cause of seizing or of conception, just as when one says: *a flower and fruit tree*. The tree that is the origin or the cause of the flowers and of the fruits is called *flower and fruit tree*" (*ibid.*, fol. 18b). It in no way follows from that, according to me, that *skandha* means "cause"; on the contrary, the idea of cause is implied between the two ideas expressed by the two terms *skandha* and *upādāna*; it is as if one said: the *skandhas*, or attributes, that are used or that end in *upādāna*. This latter term will be explained below.

sion. Why is that? It is that it is necessary to take what is called *the five attributes*, causes of conception, to be the man produced by a magical illusion. And why is that? Because the Bhagavat has said that form is like an illusion. Now, form is the collection of the five senses, and that of the five attributes. It is that the Bhagavat has said that sensation, idea, and concepts are similar to an illusion. It is that the Bhagavat has said that knowledge is similar to an illusion. But knowledge is the gathering of the five senses and that of the five attributes. O Bhagavat, will bodhisattvas newly entered into their vehicle, listening to this demonstration, not be frightened, not be afraid, not conceive terror?" The Bhagavat responded: "If bodhisattvas, O Subhūti, newly entered into their vehicle fall into the hands of a sinful friend, they will be frightened, they will be afraid, they will experience terror. But if bodhisattvas, O Subhūti, newly entered into their vehicle fall into the hands of a virtuous friend, they will not be frightened, they will not be afraid, they will not experience terror."

That said, Subhūti spoke to the Bhagavat in this way: "Who are those, O Bhagavat, who must be recognized as virtuous friends for the bodhisattva?" The Bhagavat responded: "They are those who instruct him and train him in the perfections, and those who make him see the deeds of Māra, telling him: 'In this way must the faults of Māra be recognized, these are the faults of Māra; in this way the deeds of Māra must be recognized, these are his deeds; once you have recognized them, you must avoid them.' These are, O Subhūti, those who must be recognized as virtuous friends for a bodhisattva dressed in the great armor, who has entered into the great vehicle, who has mounted the great vehicle."

That said, Subhūti spoke to the Bhagavat in this way: "When the Bhagavat has said: 'These are those who must be recognized as virtuous friends for a bodhisattva dressed in the great armor, who has entered into the great vehicle, who has mounted the great vehicle, and when he has pronounced the name *bodhisattva*, who then, O Bhagavat, is the being named *bodhisattva*?"

That said, the Bhagavat spoke to Subhūti in this way: "It is not a being, O Subhūti, the one who calls himself *bodhisattva.* Why is that? It is that the bodhisattva, O Subhūti, learns to detach himself from all conditions. Arrived at detachment from all conditions that result from his recognizing them, the bodhisattva reaches the supreme state of a perfectly accomplished buddha. Arrived then at the perfection that results for him in the state of *bodhi*, he is called by this name *bodhisattva.*" Subhūti replied: "But the Bhagavat has said: 'The *bodhisattva mahāsattva*'; Now, why is this being so called?" The Bhagavat answered: "It is said: He will obtain the first rank in the great mass of creatures, in the great body of creatures; this is why he is called *bodhisattva mahāsattva.*"

Then, Śāriputra spoke to the Bhagavat in this way: "I will have the courage, O Bhagavat, to say for which reason this being is called *bodhisattva mahāsattva.*" The Bhagavat responded: "Have the courage, O Śāriputra, to say what you believe now." The respectable Śāriputra replied: "He will teach the law in order to destroy these great doctrines and still others, namely the doctrine of self, of creatures, of life, of individuality, of birth, of destruction, of interruption, of eternity, of body; it is for this reason that this being is called *bodhisattva mahāsattva.*"

Then, Subhūti spoke to the Bhagavat in this way: "I will also have the courage, O Bhagavat, to say for which reason this being is called *bodhisattva mahāsattva.*" The Bhagavat responded: "Have the courage, O Subhūti, to say what you believe now." Subhūti replied: "The thought of bodhi which is that of omniscience, which is a thought free from imperfections, dissimilar, dissimilar and similar, which is not appropriate for any śrāvaka or to any pratyekabuddha, is a thought to which he is not attached or enchained. Why is that? It is that the thought of omniscience is free from imperfections, is absolutely detached. Now it is because he is not attached or enchained to the thought of omniscience which is free from imperfections and absolutely detached that he is counted in the number of those called *bodhisattva mahāsattvas.*"

Then, Śāriputra spoke to Subhūti in this way: "For which reason, O Subhūti, is he not attached or enchained to this thought?" Subhūti responded: "It is because it is a nonthought, O Śāriputra, that he is not attached or enchained." Śāriputra replied: "But, Subhūti, is there a thought which is a nonthought?" Subhūti replied: "But, Śāriputra, in the state of nonthought, is there found, does there exist reality or nonreality?" Śāriputra responded: "Neither reality nor absence of reality, O Subhūti." Subhūti replied: "If thus, O Śāriputra, in the state of nonthought, there does not exist and there is not found reality or nonreality, how, Śāriputra, could you have said: 'Is there a thought which is a nonthought?'" Śāriputra responded: "It is good, O Subhūti, it is good that after having been designated by the Bhagavat as the chief of those who live in the absence of all corruption, you teach in this way."

Then, Pūrṇa, son of Maitrāyaṇī, spoke to the Bhagavat in this way: "The one called *bodhisattva mahāsattva*, O Bhagavat, is a being dressed in the great armor, is a being entered into the great vehicle, mounted the great vehicle. It is for that that he is called *mahāsattva* (great being)."

Then, Subhūti spoke to the Bhagavat in this way: "He is called, O Bhagavat, dressed in the great armor, covered with the great armor. But at which point, O Bhagavat, is the bodhisattva dressed in the great armor?" The Bhagavat responded: "It is, O Subhūti, when this reflection comes to the mind of the bodhisattva: 'I must lead into complete nirvāṇa creatures whose number is immense, I must lead them there; yet there exist no creatures who must be led into it, or creatures who lead into it'; and yet nonetheless he leads all these creatures into complete nirvāṇa. But there do not exist creatures who arrive in complete nirvāṇa or creatures who lead others. Why is that? Because, O Subhūti, the particular character that constitutes beings is the character of an illusion. It is, O

Subhūti, as if a skilled magician or the disciple of a magician made appear in the crossroads of four large roads an immense multitude of people and that, after having made it appear, he made it disappear. What do you think about that, O Subhūti? Is there someone that another has killed, has made to die, has annihilated, has made disappear?" Subhūti responded: "Certainly not, Bhagavat." "That is exactly it, O Subhūti," replied the Bhagavat. "The bodhisattva mahāsattva leads into complete nirvāṇa an immense, incalculable, infinite number of creatures; and there exist no creatures who are led into it or creatures who lead into it. If the bodhisattva mahāsattva, in listening to this exposition of the law, is not frightened and does not experience fear, he must be recognized, O Subhūti, all the more as dressed in the great armor."

Then, Subhūti spoke to the Bhagavat in this way: "If I understand well the meaning of what the Bhagavat has said, the bodhisattva must be recognized as not being dressed in the great armor." The Bhagavat replied: "It is that, Subhūti, it is exactly that. The bodhisattva must be recognized as not dressed in the great armor. And why is that? It is that omniscience is not a thing that is made, that is modified, that is composed. In the same way, the creatures in whose interests he is dressed in the great armor are not made, not modified, and not composed."

That said, Subhūti spoke to the Bhagavat in this way: "It is that, Bhagavat, it is exactly that. Why is that? It is, O Bhagavat, that form is not tied or untied and it is the same for sensation, for idea, for concepts, for knowledge, which are not tied or untied."

Then, Pūrṇa, son of Maitrāyaṇī, spoke to Subhūti in this way: "Do you not say, Subhūti: 'Form is not tied or untied and in the same way, sensation, idea, concepts, knowledge are not tied or untied?' Do you not say, O Subhūti: 'The very essence of form is not tied or untied; and in the same way, the essence of sensation, of idea, of concepts, of knowledge is not tied or untied?' What thus, O Subhūti, is the form that you call a form which is not tied or untied? In the same way, what thus is the sensation, the idea, the concepts, the knowledge, all the things that you call neither tied nor untied? What thus, O Subhūti, is the essence of form that you call an essence of form which is not tied or untied? In the same way, what is the essence of sensation, of idea, of concepts, of knowledge that you call neither tied nor untied?"

That said, Subhūti spoke to Pūrṇa, son of Maitrāyaṇī, in this way: "The form, O Pūrṇa, of a man who is only the product of magic is a form which is neither tied nor untied. In the same way, the sensation, the idea, the concepts, the knowledge of a man produced by magic are all things which are neither tied nor untied. The essence of the form, O Pūrṇa, of a man who is only the product of magic is neither tied nor untied. In the same way, the essence of the sensation, of the idea, of the concepts, of the knowledge of this man are all things which are neither tied nor untied. Why is that? It is because these things have no real existence that they are neither tied nor untied; it is because they are isolated that they are neither tied nor untied; it is because they are produced that they are neither tied nor untied. It is in this manner that the bodhisattva who is dressed in the great armor, who has entered the great chariot, who has mounted the great chariot is not really dressed in the great armor." That said, Pūrṇa, son of Maitrayani, kept silent.

Then, Subhūti spoke to the Bhagavat in this way: "How, O Bhagavat, has the bodhisattva dressed in the great armor entered the great chariot, mounted the great chariot? What is this great chariot, and how must he be recognized as having entered it? Where will this great chariot depart, and by what means is it mounted? Where will it stop? Who will depart on this great chariot?" That said, the Bhagavat spoke to Subhūti in this way: "The expression *great chariot*, O Subhūti, is a word that means 'immensity.' One says an immense thing because this thing has no measure. As far as what you say, Subhūti: 'How must he be recognized as mounted on this great chariot? Where will this chariot depart? By what means is it mounted? Where will this great chariot stop? Who will depart on this great chariot?' I answer: Entered by means of the perfections, it will depart from the enclosure of the three worlds; entered by means of what is not visible, it will stop in omniscience; it is the bodhisattva who will depart on it. But fundamentally, Subhūti, it will depart from nowhere; it is not entered by any cause, it will not stop anywhere. Quite to the contrary, it will stop in omniscience in a manner that is not really stopping; and nobody has departed, will depart, or departs on this great chariot. Why is that? It is that one who would depart and that by which he would depart are two beings that do not exist, that are not seen, one more than the other. Since no being exists in this way, who is the one who would depart, and with the aid of what would he depart?"

That said, Subhūti spoke to the Bhagavat in this way: "It is said: What is called the great chariot, O Bhagavat, triumphing over the world formed by the gathering of devas, men, and asuras, will depart [from the three worlds]. This chariot is great by its resemblance to space. Just as in space there is room for immense creatures without number and without measure, so there is in this chariot room for immense beings without number and without measure. The great chariot of the bodhisattvas is like this. One does not see its arrival, one no more sees its departure any more than one knows where it stops. It is in this way, O Bhagavat, that one does not see the front part of this great chariot, nor does one see the back part, or the middle. It is equal to the three epochs of duration, O Bhagavat; this is why it is called a great chariot."

Then, the Bhagavat showed his assent to Subhūti in this way: "Good, good, Subhūti; it is that, Subhūti, it is exactly that. Such is this great chariot of the bodhisattvas. The bodhisattvas who have learned that have acquired, acquire, will acquire the perfection of wisdom."

Then, Pūrṇa, son of Maitrāyaṇī, spoke to the Bhagavat in this way: "Subhūti, the sthavira who, thanks to the benediction he has received, has studied in order to obtain the perfection of wisdom, thinks that the great chariot must be shown." Then, Subhūti spoke to the Bhagavat in this way: "I do not believe, O Bhagavat, to have spoken of the great chariot contrary to the perfection of wisdom." The Bhagavat responded: "No, certainly, Subhūti; you define the great chariot correctly, in accord with the perfection of wisdom."

That said, Subhūti spoke to the Bhagavat in this way: "It is by the favor of the Buddha, O Bhagavat. There is more: the bodhisattva does not conceive of the beginning, no more than the end or the middle. Why is that? It is that he does not conceive. Just as form has no limit, the bodhisattva must be recognized as something unlimited. In the same way, since sensation, idea, concepts, knowledge have no limit, the bodhisattva must be recognized as something unlimited. He does not conceive this: 'The bodhisattva is form,' for even that is not, does not exist. In the same way, neither does he conceive this: 'The bodhisattva is sensation, idea, concepts, knowledge,' because that itself is not, does not exist. It is in this way, O Bhagavat, that not encountering in any way, not at all, absolutely no condition[57] of bodhisattva, I do not recognize a being to whom this name *bodhisattva* applies. I do not recognize, I do not see perfection of wisdom. I do not recognize, I do not see omniscience anymore. Not encountering, O Bhagavat, not recognizing in any way, not at all, absolutely none of these conditions, in which condition will I train and will I instruct? With the aid of which condition and in which condition will I do so?

"The name *buddha*, O Bhagavat, is only a word. The name *bodhisattva*, O Bhagavat, is only a word. The name *perfection of wisdom*, O Bhagavat, is only a word; and this name is unlimited, as when one says: 'the self'; for the self, O Bhagavat, is something unlimited, because it has no end. In the same way, what is the unseizable, unlimited form of the conditions of which none has intrinsic nature? What is sensation, idea, concepts? What is the unseizable, unlimited knowledge? Again in the same way, the absence of an intrinsic nature for all conditions, this is the state of nonlimitation. But the state of nonlimitation of all conditions, this is not what the conditions themselves are called. How thus will I train, how will I instruct in the unlimited perfection of wisdom by means of the state of nonlimitation? Yet, O Bhagavat, it is nowhere else than in nonlimitation that all conditions are encountered, either that of the buddha or that of the bodhisattva, conditions which course toward the state of buddha.

57. I have already noted that the word I translate as "condition" is *dharma*: I chose *condition* by design because this word gives an abstract notion like the Sanskrit *dharma* itself. But I hardly need to say that the words *being*, *reality*, and even *individual* can quite often be substituted for that of *condition* in the course of this singular exposition.

"If while one speaks, one teaches, one explains, and one elucidates the subject in this way, the thought of the bodhisattva does not dissolve, [etc., as above, until:] does not experience terror, here is what one has to recognize. Such a bodhisattva courses in the perfection of wisdom, he understands it; he reflects on the perfection of wisdom, he meditates on it. Why is that? It is that at the time when the bodhisattva reflects on these conditions, according to the perfection of wisdom, at this very time, he does not conceive of form, he does not grasp form, he does not recognize the production of form, he does not recognize the cessation of form. In the same way, he does not conceive of sensation, idea, concepts, knowledge; he does not grasp these things; he does not recognize their production; he does not recognize their cessation. Why is that? It is that the nonproduction of form is not form; the nondestruction of form is not form; the nonproduction and the form do not make two things, it is not a difference. The nondestruction and the form do not make two things, it is not a difference. On the other hand, when one pronounces the name *form*, one does not count two things. In the same way, the nonproduction of sensation, of idea, of concepts, of knowledge, it is not sensation, idea, concepts, knowledge; the nondestruction of knowledge is not knowledge; the nonproduction and knowledge do not make two things, it is not a difference; the nondestruction and knowledge do not make two things, it is not a difference. On the other hand, when one pronounces the name *knowledge*, one does not count two things. It is in this way that the bodhisattva, O Bhagavat, who reflects in all these manners on all conditions according to the perfection of wisdom, does not conceive, in this very moment, form; he does not grasp it, he does not recognize the production of form, he does not recognize the cessation of it; [etc., as above, until:] On the other hand, when one pronounces the name *knowledge*, one does not count two things."

More than one reader will perhaps find that I could have dispensed with extracting such a long passage, and that instead of giving this bizarre fragment, I could have presented the summary at the start and in almost these terms: The books of the *Prajñāpāramitā* are dedicated to the exposition of a doctrine whose aim is to establish that the object to be known, or the perfection of wisdom, has no more real an existence than the subject who must know it, or the bodhisattva, or the subject who knows it, or the Buddha. Such is indeed the common tendency of all the redactions of the *Prajñā*; whatever difference there is in the developments and circumlocutions in which the fundamental thought envelops itself, all end in the equal negation of subject and object. But I pray the reader to note that here it is less a matter of setting forth the metaphysics of the *Prajñā* in all its details than of determining, as much as this is possible, the place that this collection occupies in the whole of the books of Nepal. Now, there is no one who, after reading a portion of the aforesaid passage, is not able to immediately appreciate the distance that separates the metaphysics of the sūtras from that of the *Prajñā*. It is clear that in this latter work the doctrine has reached all its developments, to the point of not retreating before the absurdity of its conclusions; whereas in the sūtras, metaphysics, inserted ordinarily into morality, is still in its first attempts. Thus, I quite doubt that in any sūtra (I speak about those I believe to be the oldest), it was possible to encounter a proposition like this one: "The name *buddha* is just a word," and like this one: "The Buddha himself, O respectable Subhūti, is like an illusion, the conditions of the Buddha themselves are like an illusion, like a dream."[58] Speculation, doubtless through a sequence of reasoning, can reach the negation of the subject, considered in its most elevated form; but it is difficult to believe that Śākyamuni would have become the chief of a gathering of ascetics destined later to form a body of monks, if he had started with axioms such as those I have just recalled.

It is no less true that the germ of the most audacious negations of the *Prajñā* is already contained in the sūtras, and that the Buddha, for example, or the most enlightened man, as he appears amid the phenomena produced by the chain of causes and effects, has really no more existence than these phenomena themselves. Now, the theory of causes and effects is as familiar to the ancient sūtras as it is to these great developed sūtras named the *perfection of wisdom*. It is not explained in one any more than in the other; but it is set forth and recalled at each instant in all of them. This is the truly ancient philosophical part of Buddhism, which could be called psychology and ontology, in the same way that the theory of the four sublime truths represents morality more particularly; and the Reverend W. H. Mill has been quite fortunately assisted by the recollection of his classical erudition when, examining the famous philosophical formula by which the knowledge of all causes is attributed to the Buddha, he recalls the famous verse *Qui potuit rerum cognoscere causas*, and names Śākya the Epicurus of this great Oriental system.[59] It is not to say, however, that these three parts of speculation are clearly distinguished in this double theory, that of causes and effects and that of the four truths. Quite to the contrary, the relations that unite all parts of philosophy among themselves (and this is natural) struck the Buddhist ascetics much more than the differences that separate them, and their analysis did not clearly mark the domain of each of them. This very circumstance is what renders their exposition very difficult to comprehend, where facts of all kinds are intermingled and where in particular the distinction between mind and matter is almost completely lacking, that is to say, in order to express myself in a manner more in accordance with Buddhist ideas, where the distinction is lacking between the

58. *Vinayasūtra*, fol. 136b, according to the *Prajñāpāramitā*.
59. *Journal of the Asiatic Society of Bengal*, vol. 4, pp. 214 and 215.

phenomena which fall under the senses, and those which escape them and which intelligence conceives. Indeed, and this is a point that is important not to forget, for the greatest number of Buddhists, who believe only in the testimony of direct observation, all phenomena, whether material or immaterial, are essentially homogeneous; they are not fundamentally different from one another. Material, they are called *external*; intellectual, they are named *internal*; it is a simple difference of location, and Mr. Hodgson could have said, that according to the greatest number of Buddhists, notably the naturalists, mind is only a modification of matter and that the order of the universe, which is one, is the physical order.[60]

Whatever these difficulties may be, I nevertheless will try to summarize here what my studies have taught me about the important theory of causes and effects. While perusing this part of my work, the reader will be kind enough to recall that I do not have any commentary at my disposal and that, to clarify this delicate matter, I do not possess other assistance except for the comparison of passages borrowed from various treatises that are all equally obscure because, ordinarily, they are only the repetition of one another.

The persons who have had the patience to read the aforesaid fragment of the *Prajñāpāramitā* have seen that beings and their qualities do not exist with the reality that ordinary men attribute to them. Present beings owe their existence to the ignorance which does not know what they are, or rather which does not know that they do not have real existence. According to this doctrine, the starting point of all existences is *avidyā*, which, as I will indicate below, signifies at once nonbeing and nonknowledge. How, now, does the object which is and the subject who knows emerge from this nonbeing and this nonknowledge? This is what the theory of causes, or *nidāna*, the theory that receives the generic title *pratītyasamutpāda*, "the production of the successive causes of existence," or the production of what is successively cause and effect,[61] is aiming to show. It is thus important to set forth the terms or degrees, twelve in number, by which phenomenal being indeed comes out of nonbeing; but instead of following the sequence of the *Prajñā*, which descends from nonbeing, that is to say, from ignorance, I prefer to proceed in the reverse sense and to start from the current state of being in order to go back to its past. Moreover, I again have here a Buddhist authority of great weight, that of the *Lalitavistara*, which shows Śākyamuni rising through meditation to the knowledge of this truth that all comes from nonbeing, and starting from the current state of being to recover his origin. I will quote this piece, in which it appears to me rather easy to grasp the course of the philosophical thought that dominates there. It is borrowed from the chapter

60. "European Speculations on Buddhism," in *Journal of the Asiatic Society of Bengal*, vol. 3, p. 500.

61. See, at the end of this volume, a note related to this expression, Appendix no. 7.

where Śākya, named in the text the *bodhisattva*, passes successively through the different degrees of contemplation.

Then, he recalled the whole of his numerous previous dwellings and those of other creatures in this way: one existence, two, three, five, ten, twenty, forty, fifty, one hundred, one thousand, one hundred thousand, several hundred thousand, several koṭis, one hundred koṭis, one thousand koṭis, ten thousand koṭis, several hundred thousand koṭis, several hundred thousand myriads of koṭis, one kalpa of destruction, one kalpa of reproduction, one kalpa of destruction and of reproduction, several kalpas of destruction and of reproduction, such is the number of existences that he recalled.[62] "I was in this place, I had such a name, I was from such lineage, I was from such a family, from such a caste; my life lasted for so much time; I remained for so much time in the world; I experienced such happiness and such unhappiness; after having departed from this existence, I was born again in such a place; after having departed from this existence, I was born again in such a place; lastly, having departed from this last place, I was born here." It is in this manner that he recalled the whole of his old dwellings and those of all creatures, each with its character and its description.[63]

Then, the bodhisattva, with his thought collected, perfect, completely pure, luminous, exempt from stains, cleared of all imperfection, resting in the facility of his action and arrived at immobility,[64] the bodhisattva, I say, in the last watch of the night, at the time when dawn is breaking, at the moment when sleep is deepest and when it is so difficult to awake, collected his intelligence and brought it back in himself through the direct contemplation of science, with the aid of the view of the knowledge that destroys all imperfection. Then, this thought appeared in his mind: "The existence of the world, which is born, grows old, dies, falls, and is born again, is certainly an evil." But he could not recognize the means to depart from this world, which is only a great accumulation of sufferings. "Alas!" he said to himself, "there is no end to this great accumulation of sufferings, which is only composed of decrepitude, maladies, death, and other miseries of which it is entirely formed."

This reflection brought the following thought to his mind: "What is the thing which, existing, gives rise to decrepitude and death, and what is the cause of de-

62. For the explanation of these terms, "*kalpa*, or age of reproduction and of destruction," which designate the different periods of the birth and annihilation of the visible world, see Turnour, *Journal of the Asiatic Society of Bengal*, vol. 7, p. 699.

63. This passage is found almost word for word in the Pāli books of the Buddhists of the South; it has been translated by Turnour (*Journal of the Asiatic Society of Bengal*, vol. 7, p. 690).

64. My manuscript is not very correct at this point, and it could be that I did not perfectly grasp the special signification of the fifth of the epithets that characterize the thought of the bodhisattva; nevertheless I have omitted nothing.

crepitude and death?" This reflection came to his mind: "Birth (*jāti*) existing, decrepitude and death exist; for birth is the cause of decrepitude and death."

Then, this other reflection came to the mind of the bodhisattva: "What is the thing which, existing, gives rise to birth, and what is the cause of birth?" This reflection then came to his mind: "Existence or being (*bhava*) being, birth exists; for existence is the cause of birth."

Then, this other reflection came to the mind of the bodhisattva: "What is the thing which, existing, gives rise to existence, and what is the cause of existence?" This reflection then came to his mind: "Conception (*upādāna*) existing, existence is; for conception is the cause of existence."

Then, this other reflection came to the mind of the bodhisattva: "What is the thing which, existing, gives rise to conception, and what is the cause of conception?" This reflection then came to his mind: "Desire (*tṛṣṇā*) existing, conception exists; for desire is the cause of conception."

Then, this other reflection came to the mind of the bodhisattva: "What is the thing which, existing, gives rise to desire, and what is the cause of desire?" This reflection then came to his mind: "Sensation (*vedanā*) existing, desire exists; for sensation is the cause of desire."

Then, this other reflection came to the mind of the bodhisattva: "What is the thing which, existing, gives rise to sensation, and what is the cause of sensation?" This reflection then came to his mind: "Contact (*sparśa*) existing, sensation exists; for contact is the cause of sensation."

Then, this other reflection came to the mind of the bodhisattva: "What is the thing which, existing, gives rise to contact, and what is the cause of contact?" This reflection then came to his mind: "The six seats [of sensible qualities] (*ṣaḍāyatana*) existing, contact exists; for six seats [of sensible qualities] are the cause of contact."

Then, this reflection came to the mind of the bodhisattva: "What is the thing which, existing, gives rise to the six seats [of sensible qualities], and what is the cause of the six seats?" This reflection then came to his mind: "Name and form (*nāmarūpa*) existing, the six seats [of sensible qualities] exist; for name and form are the cause of the six seats."

Then, this other reflection came to the mind of the bodhisattva: "What is the thing which, existing, gives rise to name and form, and what is the cause of name and form?" This reflection then came to his mind: "Knowledge (*vijñāna*) existing, name and form exist; for knowledge is the cause of name and form."

Then, this other reflection came to the mind of the bodhisattva: "What is the thing which, existing, gives rise to knowledge, and what is the cause of knowledge?" This reflection then came to his mind: "When concepts (*saṃskāra*) exist, knowledge exists; for concepts are the cause of knowledge."

Then, this other reflection came to the mind of the bodhisattva: "What is the thing which, existing, gives rise to concepts, and what is the cause of concepts?" This reflection then came to his mind: "Ignorance (*avidyā*) existing, concepts exist; for ignorance is the cause of concepts."

Then, the bodhisattva, O monks, made these reflections: "Concepts have ignorance for their cause; knowledge has concepts for its cause; name and form have knowledge for their cause; the six seats have name and form for their cause; contact has the six seats for its cause; sensation has contact for its cause; desire has sensation for its cause; conception has desire for its cause; existence has conception for its cause; birth has existence for its cause; decrepitude and death, with pains, lamentations, suffering, grief, despair, have birth for their cause. It is in this way that the production of this world, which is only a great mass of suffering, takes place. Production! Production!" [exclaimed the bodhisattva]; and since he had envisaged face to face, in a fundamental way and on several occasions, these conditions of which he had not heard spoken before, he felt produced in him knowledge with view, science, the plenitude [of knowledge], reflection, wisdom; light appeared to him. What is the thing which, not existing, makes decrepitude and death not to exist? Or again, what is the thing by the annihilation of which the annihilation of decrepitude and of death takes place? This reflection then came to his mind: "Birth not existing, decrepitude and death do not exist; from the annihilation of birth results the annihilation of decrepitude and death."

Then, this other reflection came to the mind of the bodhisattva: "What is the thing which, not existing, makes birth not exist? Or again, what is the thing by the destruction of which the destruction of birth takes place?" This reflection then came to his mind: "Existence not being, birth does not exist; from the annihilation of existence results the annihilation of birth."

Then, this other reflection came to the mind of the bodhisattva: "What is the thing which, not existing, [and so forth for each of the aforesaid conditions, until:] makes concepts not exist; or again; what is the thing by the annihilation of which the annihilation of concepts takes place?" This reflection then came to his mind: "Ignorance not existing, concepts do not exist; from the annihilation of ignorance results the annihilation of concepts. From the annihilation of concepts results the annihilation of knowledge; [and so forth, until:] from the annihilation of birth results the annihilation of decrepitude, death, pains, lamentations, suffering, grief, and despair. It is in this way that the annihilation of this world, which is only a great mass of suffering, takes place."

It is in this way, O monks, that the bodhisattva who had envisaged face to face, in a fundamental way and on several occasions, these conditions of which he had not heard before, felt produced in himself knowledge with vision, science, the plenitude [of knowledge], reflection, wisdom; light appeared to him.

It is I, O monks, who at that time recognized with certitude: "That is suffering, that is the production of corruption, that is the annihilation of corruption; this is the degree that leads to the annihilation of corruption": such are the truths I recognized with certitude. "This is the corruption of desire; that, the corruption of existence; this, that of ignorance; that, that of false doctrines. It is here that corruptions are completely annihilated; it is here that imperfections disappear without leaving a trace, without leaving a reflection. Here is ignorance; here the production of ignorance; here the annihilation of ignorance; there the degree that leads to the annihilation of ignorance": such are the truths I recognized with certitude; "It is here that ignorance disappears without leaving a trace, without leaving a reflection"; and so forth for the other conditions. "Here are concepts; here the production of concepts; here the annihilation of concepts; there the degree that leads to the annihilation of concepts": such are the truths I recognized with certitude. "Here is knowledge; here the production of knowledge; here the annihilation of knowledge; there the degree that leads to the annihilation of knowledge": such are the truths I recognized with certitude. "Here are name and form; here the production of name and form; here the annihilation of name and form; there the degree that leads to the annihilation of name and form": such are the truths I recognized with certitude. "Here are the six seats [of sensible qualities]; here the production of the six seats; here the annihilation of the six seats; there the degree that leads to the annihilation of the six seats [of sensible qualities]": such are the truths I recognized with certitude. "Here is contact; here the production of contact; here the annihilation of contact; there the degree that leads to the annihilation of contact": such are the truths I recognized with certitude. "Here is sensation; here the production of sensation; here the annihilation of sensation; there the degree that leads to the annihilation of sensation": such are the truths I recognized with certitude. "Here is desire; here the production of desire; here the annihilation of desire; there the degree that leads to the annihilation of desire": such are the truths I recognized with certitude. "Here is conception; here the birth of conception; here the annihilation of conception; there the degree that leads to the annihilation of conception": such are the truths I recognized with certitude. "Here is existence; here the production of existence; here the annihilation of existence; there the degree that leads to the annihilation of existence": such are the truths I recognized with certitude. "Here is birth; here the production of birth; here the annihilation of birth; there the degree that leads to the annihilation of birth": such are the truths I recognized with certitude. "Here is decrepitude; here the production of decrepitude; here the annihilation of decrepitude; there the degree that leads to the annihilation of decrepitude": such are the truths I recognized with certitude. "Here is death; here the production of death; here the annihilation of death; here the degree that leads to the annihilation of death": such are the truths I recognized with certitude. "Here are pains, lamentations, suffering, grief, despair. It is in this way that the production of this world, which is only a great mass of suffering, takes place [and so forth, until:] and so its annihilation takes place": such are the truths I recognized with certitude. "Here is suffering; here the production of suffering; here the annihilation of suffering; there the degree that leads to the annihilation of suffering": such are the truths I recognized with certitude.[65]

Let us now return to the series of these terms, in the order in which the *Lalitavistara* presents them to us, that is to say, starting from the current state.

That which we find first and which is last in the order of production is *jarāmaraṇa*, "decrepitude and death." This term cannot be an object of any difficulty; it only marks clearly the point of departure of all Buddhist theory; it is indeed from the direct observation of the great fact of the destruction by death of all that has life that they begin to explain the generation of all things. Decrepitude and death take place, according to the Buddhist authors, in conformity with the mode and the time assigned to each being.[66] The brahman philosophers who, while refuting the Buddhists, mention this theory of the successive chain of causes and effects, define decrepitude and death in the same way, after which, according to the law of transmigration, the departure for another world takes place.[67] The first part of this compound, *jāra,* or decrepitude, old age, is, according to the Chinese Buddhists[68] and the Brahmanical authorities to which I allude, the maturity of what are called the five *skandhas*, or attributes, which are gathered by birth and of which I will speak below. Decrepitude and death are the product of birth; for all that is born must die, according to a maxim attributed to Śākya. "It is short, O monks, the life of humans; its end is inevitable; one must practice virtue, for death is the condition of that which is born."[69] Decrepitude and death are thus the effect of birth, which is their cause, and to which we will now turn.[70]

The second term going backward is *jāti*, "birth," which is the cause of the pre-

65. *Lalitavistara*, fol. 178ff. of my manuscript.

66. Hodgson, "Quotations from Original Sanscrit Authorities in Proof and Illustration of Mr. Hodgson's Sketch of Buddhism," in *Journal of the Asiatic Society of Bengal*, vol. 7, p. 78ff.

67. Colebrooke, *Miscellaneous Essays*, 1:397.

68. Klaproth, in the *Foe koue ki*, p. 288, note.

69. *Abhidharmakośavyākhyā*, fols. 327a and b.

70. I believe I must add here a note that Mr. Theodor Goldstücker has kindly given me on this term, and I will do as much for those that follow it. Since it is almost the first time that I have had the advantage of being able to consult, before printing, a competent judge on the matters with which I occupy myself, the reader will permit me to quote a separate opinion, although it is not quite in conformity with mine. "I propose to translate *jarāmaraṇa* by *wearing away* and *destruction*, for I believe that *jarā* expresses all the conditions that elapse between birth and death, not only those of the last period of life, but the decay which is the consequence of each passing instant. I interpret *maraṇa* as *destruction*, because I suppose that this term must apply to all that exists, as much to animate beings as inanimate, beings equally subjected to wearing away and destruction." Mr. Goldstücker is perfectly right here, and it is with the same idea of generality that I have translated *jarā* as "decrepitude." But since it seems obvious to me that Śākya started from man in building his theory of causes and effects, I do not see any inconvenience in keeping the word *old age*. The Tibetans translate this term as *rga shi*, "old and dead."

viously explained term. There are six paths or routes in which birth takes place, and four manners in which it occurs. The six paths, frequently spoken of in the texts, are the conditions of deva, human, asura, preta, animal, and inhabitant of the hells. The four manners in which birth occurs are defined, conforming to Brahmanical ideas, as humidity, egg, womb, metamorphosis.[71] One understands thereby why the term *jāti* is defined sometimes as "birth," as the brahmans refuting the Buddhists do, sometimes by species as other brahmans[72] and one of the great modern schools of Buddhism[73] understand it. Indeed, since to be born it is necessary to enter into the six paths of existence, to be born is to take on one of the varieties of species that distinguish animate natures from one another; hence it follows that for each given nature, birth merges with species. I nonetheless believe that it is preferable to render *jāti* as "birth" because of the proximity of these two conditions, birth and death, which mark the two terms of the visible life of the individual. In addition, if one does not see *birth* in *jāti*, it will be necessary to seek it in *bhava*, as one of the Buddhist schools does, a term that comes immediately after *jāti*. But if, as everything leads one to believe, these conditions, as they ascend, express more and more general notions, *bhava* must designate existence rather than birth. I have said concerning the previous article that at the moment of birth the five *skandhas*, or attributes, gather, and here would be the place to define these five attributes; but this research would divert us from the object which occupies us at present. The five *skandhas* are, moreover, subordinated to the condition of the birth or species of which they are a part, and as such they can be suitably examined only after the relation of birth to the conditions that precede it has been clearly determined. But the condition of which birth is the effect is *bhava*, or existence, to which I now turn.[74]

Existence is the third condition going backward. According to one of the Buddhist schools, *bhava* is the present physical existence, which one commentator of this school defines in this way: physical birth.[75] I just gave the reasons I had

71. Klaproth, *Foe koue ki*, p. 288, note.

72. Colebrooke, *Miscellaneous Essays*, 1:396.

73. Hodgson, "Quotations from Original Sanscrit Authorities in Proof and Illustration of Mr. Hodgson's Sketch of Buddhism," in *Journal of the Asiatic Society of Bengal*, vol. 5, p. 78ff.

74. Here is the note of Mr. Goldstücker on *jāti*: "The term *jāti* expresses *real existence*; in Mīmāṃsā and Vedānta, *jāti* always means 'species'; in Mīmāṃsā, it even seems to be synonymous with the term *ānantya*, although I do not disregard the nuance that always differentiates two apparently synonymous words. But I do not find incompatibility between the species of the Mīmāṃsakas and the birth or real existence of the Bauddhas. Because for the philosophy that is able to arrive at an absolute and real being, there can be an infinite generality; whereas for that which arrives at nothingness, this generality itself, from whatever point of view one regards it, is something finished, consequently endowed with a perishable existence. And I believe that for the Buddhists, it is the same thing to say *general* or *individual*, general existence being for them the same as real existence." The Tibetans translate *jāti* as *skye ba*, "birth."

75. Hodgson, "Quotations from Original Sanscrit Authorities in Proof and Illustration of Mr. Hodgson's Sketch of Buddhism," in *Journal of the Asiatic Society of Bengal*, vol. 5, p. 78.

to reserve the word *birth* for *jāti*, and consequently that of *existence* for *bhava*. Indeed, this term means "being or state"; now, this notion is more general than that of birth, birth being only the mode of external appearance of the being. The Buddhists, moreover, and after them the brahmans who refute them,[76] give an explanation for *bhava*, or existence, taken from the very heart of Indian ideas, and which adds more precision to this general idea. According to the Indian commentators, the Buddhists would define *bhava* as "the condition of *dharma* (merit) or of *adharma* (demerit)," and I hesitate all the less to take as authentic the explanation of the brahmans, which is this same one contained, although very obscurely, in a passage of a Chinese Buddhist that Klaproth perhaps has not completely understood, since he did not compare it with the opinion of the brahmans.[77] *Bhava* is thus the state of being worthy of reward or punishment, *moral existence*, as made by previous actions, according to the theory of transmigration. It is not merely material existence or spiritual existence, it is also and above all moral being that this term designates; and this point is even more necessary to establish: it is one of those by which the Buddhist theory of causes and effects is linked to the theory, at once Brahmanical and Buddhist, of transmigration. One sees now the manner in which it is necessary to widen the notion of *existence*; and this word can be given as an example of the difficulties encountered in translating such comprehensive expressions into our modern languages. Thus, once existence is well determined, it is necessary to go backward to its cause, that is, *upādāna*, or conception.[78]

This cause is the fourth condition, always going backward. It is called *upādāna*, "grasping, seizing, attachment, conception." I do not know why Csoma de Kőrös has always written this term *apādāna*, translating it as "privation, ablation."[79] The Tibetan interpreters render it not only as *len pa*, as does the Vocabulaire Pentaglotte, but as *nyer bar len pa*, an expression that I have found in the previously quoted piece from the *Prajñāpāramitā*, in the context of the five attributes of conception.[80] These five attributes are the *skandhas*, about which I have promised to speak soon when I have finished the exposition of causes and effects: *grasping* or *conception* is the same *upādāna* in question here. The expression with which the Tibetan interpreters render this difficult term is lacking in the dictionaries of Csoma and Mr. Schmidt; it is found only in that of Mr. Schröter, which is, whatever one can say about it, very rich in precious information. There, the term that represents *upādāna skandha*, namely *nyer len gyi phung po*, is inserted in one

76. Colebrooke, *Miscellaneous Essays*, 1:396.

77. *Foe koue ki*, p. 288, note.

78. According to Mr. Goldstücker, *bhava* is *virtual existence*, existence in potential, which is comparable to the δύνἄμις of Aristotle as *jāti* is to ἐνεργεία.

79. "Analysis of the Kah-gyur," in *Journal of the Asiatic Society of Bengal*, vol. 1, p. 377; and "Analysis of the Sher-chin," in *Asiatic Researches*, vol. 20, pp. 398 and 399. Cf. Vocabulaire Pentaglotte, sec. 22, no. 9.

80. Above, p. 441, note.

phrase that the editor of Schröter has translated in this way: "the trouble or the pain arising from transmigration."[81] I believe that the word *transmigration* is not accurate, but it certainly leads us quite close to the meaning that very respectable Buddhist authorities attribute to the original term. Thus, a text quoted by Mr. Hodgson defines *upādāna* in this way: "the physical existence of the embryo," which a commentator determines in this way: "conception of the body."[82] The brahmans, adversaries of the Buddhists, define this term as follows: "the effort or the exertion of the body or the voice";[83] but I do not know on what this definition, which offers only a vague memory of the meaning of *upādāna* (grasping, accepting), is based.

Whatever the case may be, the Chinese Buddhist drawn on by Klaproth contents himself with representing this word with "grasping," and makes it an accident of the existence of a man twenty years old, who rushes with ardor to seize the object of his passion.[84] I cannot believe that it is a case here of a grown man, and I suspect that the Chinese Buddhist cited the ardor of the young man toward the object of his desire as an example "of grasping, of attachment." I thus prefer the meaning of "conception," and I think that it is a case here of the evolution of the being who passes through conception to arrive at existence. This notion is better connected with the following conditions, just as it results rather well from the condition from which it issues. But, since conception is an act in which the conceived being is to a certain point passive, it appears to me that it is necessary, to judge the full force of the word *upādāna* well, to accord to the being passing through this phase which precedes existence a certain degree of activity, which is expressed by the original term *seizing*, an activity which makes him take for himself, which makes him grasp the five attributes of form, sensation, idea, concepts, and knowledge, which, united to the five senses and to the coarse elements of which the body is formed, mark his appearance in one of the six paths of existence.

What confirms this idea for me is that the word *upādāna* has, besides the special acceptation that we study, a very moral sense, that of attachment, adherence, a sense which figures in these five terms: *kām-upādāna*, "attachment to pleasure"; *diṭṭh-upādāna*, "attachment to false doctrines"; *śīlappat-upādāna*, "contrary or negative attachment with regard to morality"; *atthavād-upādāna*, "attachment to controversy."[85] I do not hide the fact that these terms are borrowed from the

81. *Bhotanta Dictionary*, p. 117, col. 1.

82. Hodgson, "Quotations from Original Sanscrit Authorities in Proof and Illustration of Mr. Hodgson's Sketch of Buddhism," in *Journal of the Asiatic Society of Bengal*, vol. 5, p. 78.

83. Colebrooke, *Miscellanous Essays*, 1:396. This meaning seems too limited.

84. *Foe koue ki*, p. 288, note.

85. Judson, *Burman Dictionary*, p. 45. I am not sure about the meaning of the third term; in order for my translation to be certain, it would be necessary that the original word be *śīlappacupādāna*, for the Sanskrit *śīla-prati-upādāna*.

Pāli, that is to say, from the Buddhism of the South, and that one might contest the appropriateness of the application I am making here to the Sanskrit texts of the North. But I entreat the reader to accept for a moment what will be amply proved later, namely that as regards philosophical terms and in what touches on the value of these terms, the Pāli is as useful to the interpretation of the Sanskrit texts of Nepal as the Sanskrit to that of the Pāli books of Ceylon.[86] I add here, to conclude, a passage that shows in some detail the mode in which the act is brought about, which I believe to be conception or grasping of existence.

"Man, O monks, is formed of six elements (*dhātu*). This results from this axiom, that the gathering of the six elements is the cause of the descent of the seed into the mother's womb. For these elements are the containers (*dhā-tu*) of birth, because they engender it, nourish it, and make it grow. Now, the element that engenders here is that of knowledge (or consciousness, *vijñāna*), because it is the

86. Before concluding, I place here the explanation of Mr. Goldstücker: "*Upādāna* or *upādāna-skandhas* are the cause of virtual or embryonic existence but embryonic, I believe, in a broader sense and not restricted to the embryonic state of man. I first translate *upādāna* as 'material cause.' This term has been for me one of the most difficult; nevertheless, I believe that the passages I will cite will remove some of its obscurity. It is said in the *Vedāntasāra* (ed. Franck, p. 5, 1.23; and p. 6, 1.1 and 2) that Caitanya (Brahma) is, by his two strengths *nimitta* and *upādāna*, and one adds: like the spider, in relation to its web is *nimitta* by its nature and *upādāna* by its body. Windischmann, on Śaṃkara, interprets (p. 19, on *śloka* 12 of the sixth page) *upādāna* as *causa materialis*, while advancing other examples. In all of Mīmāṃsā, this word has the same meaning, and I content myself with citing a passage that gives a complete and very satisfying definition of it (*mādhavīya Jaiminīnyāyamālāvistara*, fol. 58b of your manuscript): *ananuṣṭhitasya anuṣṭhānam upādānam*, that is to say: *Upādāna* is attachment to that which is without attachment, to that which is primitive. But what can serve as a point of attachment without having one, without having cause, must be, if I can express myself in this way, palpable, consequently material; it is thus visible cause. And for added clarity (which does not happen often in the ślokas of Mādhava and in the commentary he has himself given to it) the author adds: *tacca karmaviṣ ayaḥ puruṣa vyāpāraḥ*. And this is found, this is said about an object, and this becomes the work of man. This is said in contrast to *vidhāna*, which is *apravṛttapravartanam* and *puruṣaviṣayaḥ śabdavyāpāraḥ*. He ends with: *iti mahān bhedaḥ*. Other passages are in perfect conformance with this explanation, which removes all doubt about the meaning of *upādāna*. The etymology of this word also seems to me to provide it, by expressing the object that one can seize, *ādā* (and which consequently is material), but which is the *upa* of the senses, that is to say, the base, the cause, that is to say, also the perceptible, material cause. If I retain this explanation, the word *skandha* also loses its darkness; for I would be tempted to take it in its primitive sense from which the other senses of *aggregate*, *accumulation* derive. I translate *skandha* as 'shoulder' and *upādānaskandha* is a *tatpuruṣa* like those described by Pāṇini (2, 1, 36) where the term *upādāna* is the dative of the declined word. From the meaning 'shoulder for the material causes,' one derives: 'that on which material causes rest, that by which they become knowable'; in this manner, I conform perfectly to the commentator you cite p. 441, note; and the explanation of *upādānaskandhas* as *rūpa*, etc., according to whether one grasps them with the body or with the mind, becomes quite clear. I will even ask if this word *skandha*, in its acceptation of *aggregate* or *cause* (as the commentator says p. 441), must not necessarily be part of a compound. It is only in this condition that this meaning appears justifiable to me. As for me, I do not recall having encountered it alone with this acceptation; and that of the verb *skandh* (to accumulate) is, as indicated by its conjugation and the *dhātupāṭha* of Westergaard, very probably a denominative formation made when the reason for the application had been forgotten. I thus believe that the *upādānskandhas* are the *bases of the visible causes*, which would correspond to the *invisible* elements of the brahmans, just as real existence implies visible elements. So, for the Buddhists, *bhava* has *invisible elements* for the cause or the base of the visible causes." Being little familiar with the doctrine of the Mīmāṃsā, I do not possess the necessary elements to discuss this opinion; however ingenious it appears to me, it is still not sufficiently demonstrated in my eyes to commit myself to modifying my interpretation at this point.

origin of the grasping of a new body. The elements that nourish are the coarse elements, earth, water, fire, wind, because by gathering, they constitute the body. The element that makes growth is that of space (*ākāśa*), because it is that which gives it the place it needs. This is why these elements have the name *dhātu*; they are *dhātus*, containers, because they contain principle taking a new body."[87]

We have to come now to the cause from which *upādāna* issues, a word that for lack of a more precise expression, I translate as "conception."

This cause, which is the fifth, is *tṛṣṇā*, "thirst or desire." The meaning of this term is not in doubt. The commentator cited by Mr. Hodgson expresses himself in this way with regard to that: "Then desire or mundane love is born in the archetypal body";[88] and the brahmans who refute the Buddhists define this desire in this manner: "Thirst is the desire to renew agreeable sensations and to avoid what is disagreeable."[89] Here again, the Chinese Buddhist has, at least according to Klaproth, attributed to a human youth this condition that occurs at a certainly more primitive period of his existence.[90] If indeed, I have well determined the previous word, if *upādāna* is physical conception that constitutes the existence of the individual and prepares it for birth, *tṛṣṇā* is a condition of the individual prior to conception, or of the archetypal being, according to Mr. Hodgson; that recalls rather well the *liṅgaśarīra*, or the body composed of pure attributes accepted by the Sāṃkhya school, and which the previously cited commentator seems to define.

Let me thus note that from desire, we enter into a series of conditions that are envisaged independently from all material subjects, and which form the envelope of an ideal subject. It is not easy for our European minds (I speak after all only for myself) to imagine qualities without substance and attributes without subject; even less easy to understand how these qualities can form an ideal individual, who will later be a real individual. But nothing is more familiar to Indians than the realization and, in some way, the personification of absolute entities, detached from the being we are accustomed to seeing joined to these entities; and all their systems of creation are only more or less direct passages, more or less rapid, from the abstract quality to the concrete subject. Applying these remarks that would be susceptible to longer development to the term with which we are concerned, I will say that in the term *tṛṣṇā*, "thirst or desire," we do not have to see a material being who desires, but only an abstract desire, a pure desire, which

87. *Abhidharmakośavyākhyā*, fols. 48a and b, MS of the Société Asiatique. The commentator teaches us in another place (fol. 55b) that this passage is borrowed from the sūtra entitled *Garbhāvakrānti* (Descent of the Fetus).

88. "Quotations from Original Sanscrit Authorities in Proof and Illustration of Mr. Hodgson's Sketch of Buddhism," in *Journal of the Asiatic Society of Bengal*, vol. 5, p. 79.

89. Colebrooke, *Miscellaneous Essays*, 1:396.

90. *Foe koue ki*, p. 287, note.

ends the evolution of the immaterial and primitive forms of the individual and which produces conception, which commences the series of its material and present forms. Desire, although the cause of conception, is thus not, according to me, the attraction the two sexes feel for each other; for in that case the subject would be changed; since the one or those who desire are not the one who is conceived. Now, in all this series of twelve causes and effects, the subject remains always the same; at least, nothing allows me to suppose that the last four conditions belong to one being, and that the eight others (of which seven still remain to be studied) designate another being. Desire,[91] whose true character I believe to have thus determined, has for its cause the condition I will examine, sensation.

This cause, which is the sixth, is *vedanā*, or sensation, and in a more general manner sensibility. Doubt is no more possible about this article than the preceding. The text cited by Mr. Hodgson explains it in this way: "Sensation is definite perception," and the commentator adds: "Perception or definite knowledge as, for example, that is white, this is black, that is good and this is bad."[92] Colebrooke defines this word in the same way: "The sensation of pain and of pleasure."[93] We see from the gloss of the previously cited commentator that here it is not only a case of internal sensation, a sensation that we have to consider as giving a perception, that is to say, as a sensation accompanied by knowledge, but that *vedanā* also contains moral notion or judgment; that would not be easy to understand if one did not recall that these types of judgments are the work of *manas*, or the heart, the true internal sense that the Buddhists as well as the brahmans made an organ, as much as the eye, the hand, and the other instruments of sensation. Let us add that here it is again necessary to envisage sensation in itself, independently of the material subject, as I have just said about desire, the effect of sensation. For we are still in the abstract qualities of the ideal being who, in all likelihood, is the primitive type of the real being who only begins at conception. This is so true that sensation will appear among the five *skandhas*, or attributes, that birth aggregates; from which it follows that there are two sensations or sensibilities, one of the ideal being before his birth, the other of the real being after he is born. Assuming this to be the case, we can pass on to the cause of sensation,[94] that is to say, contact.

91. Here is how Mr. Goldstücker understands this term: "I believe that *tṛṣṇā* expresses *appetitus*, the desire to be active or the internal fermentation that the invisible elements experience in order to proceed to their creation of *bhava*, or of the *visible elements*. Then, one can say that the impetus, as the essence of these invisible elements, is their cause, is what precedes them virtually. As *bhava* is the δύναμις of *jāti*, in the same way one can suppose that *tṛṣṇā* is the δύναμις of the *upādāna skandhas*."

92. "Quotations from Original Sanscrit Authorities in Proof and Illustration of Mr. Hodgson's Sketch of Buddhism," in *Journal of the Asiatic Society of Bengal*, vol. 5, p. 79.

93. Colebrooke, *Miscellaneous Essays*, 1:396.

94. Mr. Goldstücker defines this term in this way: "*Vedanā* is *irritability*, which, taken in the literal sense, applies only to animate and organic beings, but which appears here in an analogous meaning although broader."

This cause is the seventh; it is called *sparśa*, "touch, contact." According to the commentary cited by Mr. Hodgson, contact occurs "when the thinking principle endowed with a body in the form of an archetype comes to exercise itself over the properties of things."[95] Colebrooke gives an almost identical definition according to Brahmanical authorities: "It is the feeling of hot and cold experienced by the embryo or the being endowed with a body."[96] I do not need to dwell on this cause, whose relation with sensation, which is its effect, is so easy to grasp. It is only necessary to note that this theory relates to the evolution of the archetypal body, a fact that direct observation shows us only in the already formed material body.[97] The cause of contact is the gathering of the *ṣaḍāyatana,* which is placed immediately above.

These *ṣaḍāyatana* are thus the eighth cause going backward; they are the six places or seats of sensible qualities and of the senses. The text cited by Mr. Hodgson defines them in this way: "The six seats or external objects of the senses," and according to a commentator: "The six properties, which can be felt and known, of natural, moral and physical objects."[98] The explanation borrowed by Colebrooke from the Brahmanical commentators is less clear: "The seats of the six organs or the places of the senses, which are formed of feeling, of the elements such as earth, etc., of name and of form, or of the body, in relation to which they are the organs."[99] The commentator on the *Abhidharma* gives for the word *āyatana* (place) an explanation which grammatically speaking is wrong, but which is important to report here to make one understand what the Buddhists mean by this term: "It is what extends (*tan-oti*) production or birth (*āy-us*) of the mind and thoughts."[100] The senses, indeed, by placing the mind into relation with the external world, extend and develop knowledge, or even extend it itself somehow in each sensation it perceives. The *ṣaḍāyatana* are thus the six seats of sensible qualities, or otherwise, the six senses, namely, seeing, hearing, smell, taste, touch, and the internal sense, or *manas.*[101]

But this name *āyatana* does not apply solely to the eye and to the other senses, including the internal organ, senses that are collectively called *adhyātmika āyatana*, "internal seats"; it is given also, according to the previously cited commentator, to form and to the other sensible attributes, including *dharma*, the law,

95. "Quotations from Original Sanscrit Authorities in Proof and Illustration of Mr. Hodgson's Sketch of Buddhism," in *Journal of the Asiatic Society of Bengal*, vol. 5, p. 78.

96. Colebrooke, *Miscellaneous Essays*, 1:396.

97. According to Mr. Goldstücker, who is consistent in his system of explanations, "the term *sparśa* designates sensibility extended equally to the whole of nature, to all beings indistinctly."

98. "Quotations from Original Sanscrit Authorities in Proof and Illustration of Mr. Hodgson's Sketch of Buddhism," in *Journal of the Asiatic Society of Bengal*, vol. 5, p. 78, note.

99. Colebrooke, *Miscellaneous Essays*, 1:396.

100. *Abhidharmakośavyākhyā*, fol. 32b of my manuscript.

101. The Tibetans translate *ṣaḍāyatana* with *skye mched*, "the senses."

merit, or being, attributes collectively called *bāhya āyatana*, "external seats."[102] Hence it results that the word *āyatana* designates the five organs of the senses, including the internal organ, and the five sensible qualities, including the law that only the internal organ can grasp. As for the manner in which the senses place the mind in communication with external objects, there are two opposing opinions among the Buddhists. Some believe that the mind grasps only an image, a representation of the object; the others believe in the direct perception of the object. These latter take the following passage of a sūtra cited by a commentator as authority: "Seeing forms with the aid of the eye, it does not grasp a secondary representation; and because it is the eye that sees, the person (*pudgala*) sees through the eye."[103] The six seats of sensible qualities or senses[104] have for their cause name and form, which immediately precede them in the evolution.

Name and form, *nāmarūpa*, are the ninth cause; it is a compound expression like *jarāmaraṇa*, "decrepitude and death." The text cited by Mr. Hodgson defines this condition as: "individual notions," to which the commentator adds: "It is an organized and definite body, but which still is only an archetype, and which is the seat of individual consciousness,"[105] which will be discussed later. The Brahmanical authorities quoted by Colebrooke express themselves in this way: "From the gathering of feeling or consciousness with the paternal semen and the uterine blood derives the rudiment of the body, its flesh and its blood, its name, *nāman*, and its form, *rūpa*."[106] It is not in doubt that here it is a question of the name and form of an ideal subject or archetype, as the texts quoted by Mr. Hodgson say; and I will make the same observation here as concerning sensation: it is that form will appear later among the five attributes gathered by birth; hence the result is that form is double, one that belongs to the ideal body, the other received by the material body. *Nāmarūpa* thus represents that which is most external in individuality; but, I repeat, this individuality is that of the ideal being, a type of real being who shows himself externally only at the instant of conception.[107] Name and form, or the external sign of individuality, have knowledge for their cause.

102. *Abhidharmakośavyākhyā*, fol. 48b of the MS of the Société Asiatique.

103. *Abhidharmakośavyākhyā*, fol. 67b of the MS of the Société Asiatique.

104. Here is the note of Mr. Goldstücker on the *āyatanas*: "According to the commentator, the six seats express not only the six organs of man but also form and the other sensible attributes. This application proves to me even more that *sparśa*, *vedanā*, and all the previous notions are the attributes *of all beings*; for if they were only the attributes of man or of animate beings, it would be difficult to understand why the *six seats* would also include form, etc., attributes which can now, with the aid of a metaphor, be taken for the organs by which inorganic nature is susceptible to sensibility or irritability."

105. "Quotations from Original Sanscrit Authorities in Proof and Illustration of Mr. Hodgson's Sketch of Buddhism," in *Journal of the Asiatic Society of Bengal*, vol. 5, p. 78.

106. Colebrooke, *Miscellaneous Essays*, 1:396.

107. Here is how Mr. Goldstücker understands *nāmarūpa*: "I believe that *nāmarūpa* must be rendered by 'substantiality' or, if we conform to Buddhist conceptions, by 'reality.' But the word *reality* has the disadvantage

Knowledge, *vijñāna*, or feeling, for this term is quite comprehensive, is the tenth cause. The texts cited by Mr. Hodgson define it in this way: "general notions," to which the commentator adds: "When *saṃskāra*, or desire which is the cause of *vijñāna*, becomes excessive, individual consciousness begins to appear."[108] According to the Brahmanical authorities cited by Colebrooke, "*Vijñāna* is feeling or the beginning of consciousness."[109] This term means, strictly speaking, "distinct knowledge," and its meaning is not always easy to determine, even in the monuments of Brahmanical literature. Here I believe that the word *knowledge* is the most convenient expression; but we have to bring together the notion of feeling and that of knowledge, which are given separately by the authorities just cited. It seems to me that that of pure knowledge would be too restricted, although it is the meaning adopted by Csoma, who translates this word as "cognition."[110] The Tibetan interpreters who are, in their usual way, materially exact, render the prefix *vi* very well with *rnam par*, "totally, completely," and the substantive *jñāna* with *shes pa*, "knowledge"; but this version does not tell us anything new about the meaning of *vijñāna*. Here again, the lexicon of Schröter comes to our rescue by translating this term as "soul, life, reasonable soul."[111] It is perhaps to say a little too much, for here it is a case of an abstract quality rather than a concrete being; nevertheless we must admit that this interpretation, which is absent from the dictionaries of Csoma and Schmidt, leads us quite directly to the idea of consciousness that is also expressed by the term of *vijñāna*.[112] I add that *vijñāna*, or

---

of not expressing clearly enough the inseparable union (duplicated in the compound) of essence and form. The meaning of *nāman* is 'essence' in all of Mīmāṃsā. It is opposed to *guṇa*, to accident that perishes, and employed, for example, to designate indefinable sacrifices that provide final emancipation, heaven, and to the consumption of which other sacrifices will be as *guṇas*. For me, *nāmarūpa* expresses this substantiality in which essence is married to form and which is, so to speak, the final limit of the corporeal world. From that everything derives: and indeed the following notions rise or try to rise above the corporeal world; for the cause of substantiality, which is already the idea itself, but the idea still attached by a part of itself to the corporeal world, by *rūpa*, by form, the cause of substantiality, I say, can only be something ideal." I have not been able to justify this interpretation with the texts thus far.

108. "Quotations from Original Sanscrit Authorities in Proof and Illustration of Mr. Hodgson's Sketch of Buddhism," in *Journal of the Asiatic Society of Bengal*, vol. 5, p. 78.

109. Colebrooke, *Miscellaneous Essays*, 1:396.

110. "Analysis of the Sher-chin," in *Asiatic Researches*, vol. 20, p. 398; and *Tibetan Dictionary*, p. 255, col. 1.

111. *Bhotanta Dictionary*, p. 342, col. 2.

112. Here are the observations of Mr. Goldstücker on this article: "If I believe that until now the entire development of the Buddhist theory progresses in a perfect and almost irrefutable order, in spite of its enormous lacunae and intellectual leaps that the mind is obliged to make to follow it, I am equally convinced that it is in the three last notions, from the tenth, that commence abysses that are impossible to fill. The term *vijñāna* is, it seems to me, exactly our *learning*, that is to say, the quantity of knowledge that a man has acquired. It is in this way that this term is employed constantly all through Vedānta, where it is also opposed to *jñāna*, 'real learning.' So, *vijñāna* is the learning of what is *vi*, multiple, diverse, without unity, consequently, according to Vedānta, false. On the contrary, *jñāna* is the learning par excellence, the learning of what is, of Brahma, it is true learning. And I will go so far as to say that since *ṣaḍāyatana* expresses the six organs of man and the *organs* of inorganic nature, in short, all organs in general, *vijñāna* expresses *learning* and everything that is at the basis of learning, all this unreal world, filled with apparitions, with varieties. *Vijñāna* thus has this duplicity, however intellectual,

knowledge, is of two kinds, one (and it is this that it is the topic here) which is an attribute of the ideal being, the other which is the fifth attribute of the material being. Let us pass now to the cause of knowledge that is called *saṃskāra*.

This cause, which is the eleventh, is always indicated in the texts of Nepal only with a noun in the plural, *saṃskāras*. I do not believe that this circumstance is entirely insignificant. Nevertheless, it does not seem to have struck the authors, who thus far have spoken about the doctrine of the evolution of the being. The text cited by Mr. Hodgson defines the term *saṃskāra* as "illusory impression"; to which the commentator adds: "The belief of the sensible principle, not endowed with a body, in the reality of that which is only a mirage, is accompanied by a desire for this mirage, and by the conviction of its merit and its reality: this desire is called *saṃskāra*."[113] According to the Brahmanical authorities cited by Colebrooke, "*Saṃskāra* is passion, which consists of desire, aversion, fear, joy."[114] The notion of desire and that of passion appear to me a little too restricted; I believe them to be quite implicitly contained in the term *saṃskāra*, but its etymological value reveals to us a nuance that the completely moral interpretation just cited masks entirely. Originally, *saṃskāra* means "accomplishment, achievement" in the literal sense, then "conception, apprehension" figuratively. The *saṃskāras* are thus things *quæ fingit animus*, what the mind creates, makes, imagines (*saṃskaroti*); in short, these are the products of the faculty that it has to conceive, to imagine; and if the word *saṃskāra* were employed in the singular, I would not hesitate to translate it as "imagination."[115] The plural form has led me to decide

---

by which it becomes the cause of substantiality, or to say it better, the notion to which that of substantiality is subordinate. Consequently, I will translate *vijñāna* as 'variety,' known or to be known."

113. "Quotations from Original Sanscrit Authorities in Proof and Illustration of Mr. Hodgson's Sketch of Buddhism," in *Journal of the Asiatic Society of Bengal*, vol. 5, p. 78.

114. Colebrooke, *Miscellaneous Essays*, 1:394 and 396.

115. Among many passages by which I could justify the meaning I attribute to the term *saṃskāra*, I will content myself with citing only one, which I borrow from a very respected book, the *Lalitavistara*, the Tibetan version of which is in the hands of the scholarly public. This passage will give me a new occasion to support with a direct example the general opinion I have expressed above on the value of these versions. After having announced that a day will come when unfaithful monks will refuse to believe in the miraculous birth of the bodhisattva, Śākyamuni adds: *paśya ānanda kiyantaṃ te mohapuruṣā bahvapuṇyābhisaṃskāram abhisaṃskariṣyanti, ye buddhadharmān pratikṣepsyanti, lābhasatkāraślokābhibhūtā, uccāralagnāḥ, lābhasatkārābhibhūtā itarajātīyāḥ*; which must mean: "See, O Ānanda, how numerous are the reprehensible imaginations in which the insane men who will reject the laws of the Buddha will indulge; these men, slaves of gain, of honors, and of fame, plunged into the mire, vanquished by gain and love for respect, and naturally coarse" (*Lalitavistara*, fol. 51b). The Tibetan version has furnished Mr. Foucaux with the following translation: "These confused men will mock stanzas of perfection acquired and worthy of respect; given over to impurity, trampling underfoot what is venerable, see them, these men of base condition, rejecting the doctrine of Sangs gyas and abandoning themselves openly and without reserve to the innumerable imaginations that vice brings forth" (Foucaux, *Spécimen du Gya tcher rol pa*, p. 24 and of Tibetan text, pp. 32 and 33). I do not know how the Tibetan interpreters could have translated the epithet so clear in the Sanskrit text, *lābhasatkāraślokābhibhūtāḥ*, "defeated by gain, by respect, and by fame," so obscurely "will mock stanzas of perfection acquired and worthy of respect." The Ti-

on the meaning of "conception"; I have replaced it with that of *concepts*, which is doubtless slightly technical but which avoids the confusion that could have been caused in French between conceptions (*saṃskāra*) and conception (*upādāna*).

The word *concept*, taken in the very broad meaning of "product of the imagination," seems to me also justified by the following passage of a Sinhalese commentator. The book from which I borrow it is the *Jinālaṃkāra*, or the poetic description of the perfections of the Jina, or Buddha, written in Pāli and accompanied by a commentary composed in the same language. The text asks: "Who is the one called Buddha?" *Buddho ko ti*? and the commentator develops this question in this way: *Buddho ti ko satto vā saṃkhāro vā*, "What real being or what conception is the one called Buddha?"[116] In this text, if I am not mistaken, *saṃkhāra* (for the Sanskrit *saṃskāra*) is opposed to *satta* (for *sattva*); and since *sattva* means "creature, real being," it is not doubtful that *saṃskāra* means "conception." But, it is important not to forget, these conceptions or concepts must be taken in a very broad sense; it is necessary to see in them, with the commentator cited by Mr. Hodgson, conceptions of intelligence, like that of the existence of the external world, then conceptions of the heart, if I can express myself in this way, like love and hate and the other passionate movements that the view of this illusory world arouse.[117] Here again the observation already made about form, sensation, and consciousness applies; it is that *saṃskāras*, or concepts, are of two forms: those which were just now the topic, the others will appear again

betan interpreter has certainly overly restricted the meaning of the word *śloka*, which not only means "stanza" but also "renown, glory," whether the glory results from stanzas or songs of poets, or whether that *śloka* derives from an ancient and now unknown transformation of the root *śru* (to hear). Whatever it is, the meaning of "stanza" is not convenient here, and the interpretation I propose cannot cause difficulties. Would it not even be possible, by looking at it closely, to translate the Tibetan passage very literally in this way: "O Ānanda, sic homines stupidi, quæstu et veneratione et laudibus victi, sordibus immersi, honorum splendore victi, ignobiles genere, hi Buddhæ legem despicientes, quam multas impias imaginationes mente concipiunt, vide." If this version, as I suppose, came directly from the Tibetan text, it would have the advantage of rendering word for word the Sanskrit original, whose meaning, however, does not appear doubtful to me.

116. *Jinālaṃkāra*, fol. 12b of my manuscript.

117. Here is the note of Mr. Goldstücker concerning this major term. "You have already brought out the importance of the plural of *saṃskāra*, and I am convinced that this number is decisive for the interpretation of this notion. But I permit myself to hold to the established sense in Mīmāṃsā, which, far from opposing your explanation, on the contrary renders it perfectly, with the sole difference of a small nuance that on its side restores the good harmony between your interpretation and the ordinary usage of this word. The word *saṃskāra* expresses in this philosophy the notion of *means* in opposition to that of the aim it helps to accomplish. The aim remains, the means is leaving, disappears. *Saṃskāra* is thus the term or the notion of inferiority, because it is used only in view of the superiority of the aim. Buddhism can very well say, I suppose, that all this here below is inferior, is pure means; and this condemnation to *means-ness*, which only means, to inferiority, to degradation, or rather this inferiority itself then becomes the cause of *variety*. So many different objects, so many objects having the nature of means. Speaking according to the view of Buddhism, I can say that *means-ness* (the sum of all that is means because of the plural) is the δύναμις of the variety. The term *imagination*, I believe, would apply only to man, while the term indicated finds its place as much in intellectual creation as in the corporeal world."

in a short time among the five attributes aggregated by birth. The first result in the belief in the existence of what is not; and this is why it is said that they have their causes in *avidyā*, "ignorance or nonbeing."

To these observations, I will add that the term *saṃskāra* is often translated in a very satisfying manner as "composite"; I will only give as an example a passage I have cited above[118] and to which this meaning is more convenient than that of "concept or imagination." These two interpretations are not as far from each other as one would believe at first glance: they differ only according to the point of view one takes. Does one view the *saṃskāras* in an abstract manner? They are imaginations, conceptions, creations of the mind resulting from an erroneous belief in the existence of what is not. Does one consider them, on the contrary, in a concrete manner or in reality? The *saṃskāras* are the beings, these various creations, who are true composites, not only because one imagines them to be formed of parts (*saṃskṛta*, *confecta*) but because no relative being is absolutely simple.

Avidyā, or ignorance, is the twelfth and last cause going backward. It is, as the text often cited by Mr. Hodgson says, "false knowledge," to which its commentator adds: "The existence of the world which is in perpetual movement derives uniquely from the imagination or the belief one has in the reality of things; and this false opinion is the first act of the sensible principle not yet individualized or endowed with a body."[119] It is also in this manner that the Brahmanical authorities understand it according to Colebrooke: "*Avidyā*, ignorance or error, is the misunderstanding that consists in considering durable what is only passing."[120] There cannot remain the slightest doubt about the value of this term; nevertheless, it is important to remark that it has a double meaning, one that is objective, drawn from the very etymology of the word *avidyā*, that is to say, *avidyamānam*, "what is not found, what does not exist, nonbeing"; the other subjective, drawn from the ordinary use of the word *avidyā*, that is to say, *a-vidyā*, "nonscience, ignorance." Nonbeing and nonknowledge are thus identical; and so the existence of the object or the world, and to a certain point, of the essentially relative subject that lives in the world, is denied in its origin.[121]

118. Section 2, p. 126. The Tibetans understand the term in the same way, for Csoma translates the word *'du byed*, the Tibetan synonym of *saṃskāra*, as "any real or fancied thing" (Vocabulaire Pentaglotte, sec. 22, no. 2). See the additions at the end of the volume.

119. Hodgson, "Quotations from Original Sanscrit Authorities in Proof and Illustration of Mr. Hodgson's Sketch of Buddhism," in *Journal of the Asiatic Society of Bengal*, vol. 5, p. 78.

120. Colebrooke, *Miscellaneous Essays*, 1:396.

121. Here is the note of Mr. Goldstücker on *avidyā*: "The term *avidyā* is, in my view, different from *ajñāna*, often employed in Vedānta; for I do not doubt that this would have been employed if the Buddhist doctrine had not wanted to bring out another notion, or at least a nuance of an existing notion. The word *ignorance* or *nonscience* gives rise to the difficulty about which I have already made some observations, namely that it is applicable only to man. I rather believe that the significance you have indicated according to the etymol-

One sees that one should not have to press this principle too much to draw from it the absolute emptiness that the brahmans, adversaries of the Buddhists,[122] say is the dogma of the Madhyamika school, a school which is, we have seen, that of the famous monk Nāgārjuna. But to take the previously cited definition of *avidyā* literally, it always remains a sensitive principle, as the commentator of Mr. Hodgson says, a mind or a soul, in a word, the subject or the person, who can be ignorant or aware of the truth related to things, and who, if he is ignorant of it, falls under the influence of causes and effects, and revolves in the eternally moving circle of transmigration until he can free himself from it. The books of *Prajñā* sometimes speak of this principle, which I believe to be their *citta* (mind) or their *pudgala* (person, soul). But it is certain that the theory of causes and effects presupposes its existence; for there must be an intelligent subject, since there is the possibility of error or ignorance with regard to the object. The existence of a thinking subject is, moreover, directly established by the following fragment of a sūtra, which I cite according to the commentator on the *Abhidharmakośa*.

"I will teach you, O monks, what existence (*bhava*) is, what is the act of receiving existence and that of rejecting it, what is the one who takes on existence. Listen to that and fix it well and completely in your mind: I will speak. What is existence? There are the five attributes, causes of conception. What is the act of receiving existence? It is desire, which is reborn ceaselessly, which is accompanied by love and enjoyment, which is satisfied here and there. What is the act of rejecting existence? It is the complete abandonment, the absolute rejection, the expulsion, the destruction, the detachment, the suppression, the cessation, the disappearance of this desire, which is reborn ceaselessly, which is accompanied by love and enjoyment, which is satisfied here and there. What is the one who takes on existence? It is the person (*pudgala*), it should be said; [but Śākya says:] It is this respectable personage whom you see, who has such a name, who is from such a family and from such a lineage, who takes such food, who experiences such pleasure and such pain, who is so old, who has lived so long, who is so respectable; there is the one who takes on existence. Now, by these words, *who takes on existence*, Śākya means to designate the person, the *pudgala*. Existence is not the one who takes on existence."[123]

I will also cite other authorities that are no less explicit. It is an axiom accepted

---

ogy *avidyamāna* is that which would be best related to the notion of *saṃskāras* as I have explained it. For *avidyamāna* would only be the same thing as *ajñānamāna* and would have the general use needed here. However, I would not identify *avidyā* with nothingness; for the subsequent passages of your memorandum prove that man must destroy all these notions and above all their root, *avidyā*, in order to reach nothingness. I am thus led to believe that *avidyā* is illusion, the exterior that lacks a core, the same notion as *māyā* with nonetheless this difference, that *māyā* is the reflection of the absolute and existing truth, whereas *avidyā* is the reflection of nothingness." See the additions at the end of the volume.

122. Colebrooke, *Miscellaneous Essays*, 1:331.

123. *Abhidharmakośavyākhyā*, fol. 474a.

by the Buddhists that no condition is the soul or the self, or that all conditions are nonself: *sarvadharmā anātmānaḥ*, and the commentators on the *Abhidharma* explain this axiom in this way: "Conditions have no intrinsic nature of soul or of self, the self is not in them";[124] then it adds: "the person is not a *dharma*, a condition, *sa pudgalo na dharmaḥ*. Now, the person is the one who in the proposition: 'In a past time, I took on a form' says I or self. This I or self (*aham*) is the person, the *pudgala*. The self (*ātman*) is not the attributes (*skandha*), or the seats of the sensible qualities (*āyatana*), or the elements (*dhātu*)."[125] That is to say, in other words, the self is not the body of the individual, which is composed of the intellectual attributes, the senses, and the elements.[126] Now, this theory is based on texts that I consider respectable, notably on a passage of the *Avadānaśataka* which is important to cite here: I borrow it from the legend of a certain Guptika, who became a monk at the time of Śākya.

The young men of his age who accompanied him were led to enter into the religious life by his example. Having gone to the place where the respectable Guptika was, they spoke to him in this way: "Respectable Guptika, what is it in the world that has the condition of being perishable, and what is it in the world that does not have the condition of being perishable?" "Respectable personages," replied Guptika, "form has the condition of being perishable; and nirvāṇa, which consists in the cessation of form, does not have the condition of being perishable. Sensation, idea, concepts, and knowledge have, O respectable personages, the condition of being perishable, and nirvāṇa, which consists in the cessation of these various accidents, does not have the condition of being perishable. What do you think, respectable personages, is form, permanent or passing?" "It is passing, O respectable Guptika." "And that which is passing, is it an evil or is it not an evil?" "It is an evil, respectable Guptika." "But, respectable personages, what is passing, what is an evil, what is subject to change, is it its nature to inspire the following sentiments in a respectable listener who is very educated: 'This belongs to me, this is me, this is my very soul'?" "Not at all, respectable Guptika." "What do you think, respectable listeners, are sensation, idea, concepts, and knowledge, permanent or passing?" "They are passing, respectable Guptika." "And that which is passing, is it an evil or is it not an evil?" "It is an evil, respectable Guptika." "But, respectable personages, what is passing, what is an evil, what is subject to change, is it its nature to inspire the following sentiments in a respect-

124. *Abhidharmakośavyākhyā*, fol. 474a. It is the idea expressed by the *anātmaka*, in Tibetan *bdag med pa*, of the Vocabulaire Pentaglotte (sec. 29, no. 4).

125. *Abhidharmakośavyākhyā*, fol. 474a of my manuscript.

126. See above, section 3, p. 277, end of the second paragraph, and p. 441, note.

able listener who is very educated: 'This belongs to me, this is me, this is my very soul'?" "Not at all, respectable Guptika."

"This is why, respectable personages, any form, whether it is past, future, or present, whether it is internal or external, whether it is coarse or subtle, whether it is bad or good, whether it is distant or close, all form, I say, must be envisaged as it really is, with the aid of perfect wisdom, which must make us say: 'This does not belong to me; this is not me; this is not my very soul.' All sensation, all idea, all concept, all knowledge whatsoever, whether it is past, future, or present, whether it is internal or external, whether it is coarse or subtle, whether it is bad or good, whether it is distant or close, all sensation, I say, must be envisaged as it really is with the aid of perfect wisdom, which must make us say: 'This does not belong to me; this is not me; this is not my very soul.' The respectable listener having learned much, O respectable personages, who envisages the subject in this way, is disgusted even by form; he is disgusted also by perception, by idea, by concepts, and by knowledge; and once he is disgusted by all that, he is detached; and once he is detached, he is free. Then, he has the liberated view of the science that makes him say: 'Existence is annihilated for me; I have fulfilled the duties of the religious life; I have done what I had to do; I will not see a new existence after this one.'"[127]

If I am not mistaken in applying the theory of causes and effects to these texts, one should probably see in them the origin of one of the fundamental opinions of the school of the Yogācāras, who, according to Brahmanical commentators, believed that all is empty, except for the thinking principle, whose existence and eternity they accepted.[128] But at the same time that the enumeration of causes and effects presumes the subject, does it also presume the object? I do not think so, since the subject is mistaken in regard to the object through, according to this latter, an existence it does not really have. It occupies itself only with these two terms, the world and man: the world, which exists only from the vain existence that man attributes to it in his error; man, who exists as we see him only as a result of his ignorance of the world. It is most probable that this doctrine is that of the Sautrāntikas, who claim to follow the authority of the sūtras of Śākyamuni exclusively.[129] The doctrine of the twelve causes thus presupposes, as I have said, one of two terms, that which is man; and I believe that the ancient sūtras also accepted it. The *Prajñāpāramitā*, to the contrary, and notably the Madhyamikas, who take this book as authoritative, go much farther, and one cannot deny that their deductions destroy the subject and the object equally. This, if I am not mis-

127. *Avadānaśataka*, fol. 238a.
128. Colebrooke, *Miscellaneous Essays*, 1:391.
129. Colebrooke, *Miscellaneous Essays*, 1:391.

taken, is a point that further research will only confirm. But even reduced to the terms of the theory of the twelve causes, the primitive ontology of the Buddhists has a rather great analogy with that of the Brahmanical school of the Sāṃkhya. The Buddhists recognize in man an intelligent principle, a life, a soul, which transmigrates through the world; it is the *puruṣa*, or the spirit of the Sāṃkhyas. Apart from this principle, the Svābhāvikas accept the existence of *prajñā*, or intelligent nature; would it not be, as Mr. Hodgson has already conjectured, the material principle of the Sāṃkhyas?[130] Before having life descend among coarse forms, they imagine it taking on various abstract qualities, which create for it a kind of ideal body, a type of material and visible body; it is the *liṅgaśarīra*, or the body of attributes, that is to say, the subtle body of the Sāṃkhyas. Here, if I judge well, are many new links by which the philosophy of the Buddhists is related to that of the brahmans; but it is nevertheless necessary to confess that the Sāṃkhya doctrine, and notably the section of this doctrine which denies the existence of God, is not recognized as rigorously orthodox by anyone in India.

In the course of this analysis, I have recalled more than once the five *skandhas*, or attributes, which gather when the fact of birth occurs. These skandhas are true sensible and intellectual attributes, more intellectual than sensible; and this is not surprising when one reflects on the idealist tendency of Buddhism, a tendency that emerges at every instant from the evolution of causes producing animate beings. It is to the state of the thinking and sensible principle, once it is born, that is to say, to its actual state, that these five attributes are related, which are: *rūpa*, form; *vedanā*, sensation; *saṃjñā*, idea; *saṃskāra*, concepts; and *vijñāna*, knowledge. Of these five attributes, four have already appeared in the enumeration of the twelve causes I have made a short while ago; I return to them here only to say that these five attributes are not abstract qualities, as above, but real attributes of the living subject.

The only one that did not yet appear is that of *saṃjñā*, or idea; Csoma de Kőrös sees in it awareness; but the Brahmanical commentators, refuting the Buddhists, appear to me to better understand the value of this term when they translate it as "the knowledge or the opinion that results from names, words, signs, and characters."[131] The word *idea* seems to me to render this nuance exactly.

But how is it that these five attributes of the living subject are called *skandhas*, "branches or aggregates"? The various peoples who have adopted Buddhism, at least as much as their works are known to me, give us little light in this regard; and to cite only two examples, the Tibetans, with their translation of "heap, accumulation" and the Chinese, with that of "pile," teach us absolutely nothing more than the Sanskrit *skandha*. Schröter, it is true, translates the Tibetan

130. "European Speculations on Buddhism," in *Journal of the Asiatic Society of Bengal*, vol. 3, p. 428.

131. Colebrooke, *Miscellaneous Essays*, 1:394. It is also the meaning of the Tibetan *'du shes*, "idea."

term *phung po lnga* (which is the Sanskrit *pañcaskandha*) as "the five bodies, that is to say, the five composite corporeal attributes," but this version is not sufficiently clear. As much must be said for that of the Burmese, who render the Pāli *khandha* in this way: "Body, living animal, composed of five parts, namely: materiality, *rūpakkhandha*; sensation, *vedanakkhandha*; perception (for me, idea), *saññānakkhandha*; will (for me, concepts), *saṃkhārakkhandha*; and intelligence (for me, knowledge), *viññānakkhanddha*."[132] This interpretation is clearer, but it exceeds the aim: *skandha* cannot mean "living body"; rather, one would have to say *part,* the body produced from birth being formed of five *skandhas*, or parts. But in the commentary on the *Abhidharma*, I find a passage that in a very satisfying manner gives account of the use of this term, whose meaning is so difficult to understand according to the etymological value alone. After having set forth that *skandha*, "mass," is a synonym of *rāśi*, "heap, pile," Yaśomitra adds: "Sensation, whatever its nature is, past, future, present, internal, external, considerable, subtle, distant, immediate, being gathered in a single mass, takes the name of *vedanāskandha*, the aggregate of sensation; and it is so for the other aggregates, up to and including that of knowledge."[133] One sees thereby that in a French translation, for example, there is no disadvantage in omitting the word *aggregate*, for the abstract expression *sensation* summarizes by its very generality the various accidents of sensation indicated in the previously cited commentary; these are all sensations and all their types. It is with this character of generality that the word *skandha* is employed in the following passage of a sūtra cited by the author of the commentary on the *Abhidharmakośa*: "These conditions of the buddhas, like the conditions called *āveṇikas* and others, because of their excessive subtlety and depth, there is only ignorance with regard to them for others than the Buddha. It is said in this way: 'Do you know, O Śāriputra, the mass of morality or all morality, *śīlaskandha*, of the Tathāgata, all his meditation, all his science, all his freedom, all his science of freedom?'"[134]

To translate this difficult term exactly, one would have to employ the word *aggregate*; but this term is no clearer than *skandha*, and it would need perpetual commentary to be well understood. I doubt, moreover, whether to say "the aggregates that serve conception" gives a true idea of the role this term plays in the compound expression *upādānaskandha*. I have thus preferred the word *attribute* because, as I have already said on the occasion of a fragment of the *Prajñāpāramitā*, the *skandhas*, which are form, sensation, idea, concepts, and knowledge, are true intellectual attributes that constitute the domain of intelligence in man, since they embrace the different phases of the fact of knowing,

132. Judson, *Burman Dictionary*, p. 88.

133. *Abhidharmakośavyākhyā*, fol. 31b of my manuscript.

134. *Abhidharmakośavyākhyā*, fol. 4b of the MS of the Société Asiatique.

from the point of departure, which is somehow the occasion for it, that is to say, form, to the last term, which is knowledge itself. A perfectly exact translation of the word *skandha*, at least in the compound *upādānaskandha*, would render this term by "means, aid," in this way: "the means that serve conception," more or less as Mr. Goldstücker understands it in a note I just transcribed. But this interpretation, by showing only the special application of *skandha* in the compound *upādānaskandha*, would lack generality and would leave in the dark the collective meaning that this word takes on when it is joined to one or the other of the five intellectual attributes, like *vedanāskandha*, "the mass of sensations," to refer to all sensations, all types of sensation.

While beginning the analysis of the works preserved in Nepal that are specially related to the *abhidharma*, or metaphysics, I said that the voluminous redactions of the *Prajñāpāramitā* were not the only treatises from which one could draw knowledge of the speculative part of Buddhism. I mentioned, among others, several sūtras that offer a striking analogy with the books of *Prajñā*, not only in form, but to a certain point in content. I leave aside the *Saddharmapuṇḍarīka*, which only touches on a special point, that of the unity of the three means of transport, and I only wish to dwell on a book enjoying equal authority and whose speculative tendency is incontestable. This book, which appears also to be highly valued among all the peoples who received Buddhism to the north of India, is already known under the title *Laṅkāvatāra*, that is to say, the teaching given in Laṅkā or Ceylon. What confirms this last explanation for me is that the title of the work, as repeated at the end of each chapter, is *Saddharmalaṅkāvatāra*, the "Revelation of the Good Law in Laṅkā."[135] This work, composed of one hundred and six leaves, or two hundred twelve very large and very full pages, is said to be a Mahāyāna sūtra. It is written in prose and verse, and the poetic part offers rather numerous traces of this mixed style of Prakrit forms whose existence I have noted in the *Lotus of the Good Law*. A stanza that does not belong to the primitive redaction of the work clearly marks the quite philosophical aim of this treatise: "The sūtra in which the king of the law taught that conditions (dharmas) are deprived of soul is transcribed here with care." Śākya is depicted as being in Laṅkāpurī, on the summit of Malayagiri mountain. Recalling that the ancient tathāgatas set forth the law in this place, he feels disposed to imitate them; and Rāvaṇa, king of Ceylon, who perceives his intention, experiences the desire to hear him. Rāvaṇa goes to Śākya and addresses some stanzas to him, praying that he teach his doctrine to the inhabitants of Ceylon, as the previous buddhas did. Śākya yields to the wish

135. Mr. W. von Humboldt, who knew the work of which I speak here only by the truncated title *Laṅkāvatāra*, nevertheless recognized and set forth its true meaning, save for a nuance of little importance: "Die Schrift von dem auf Langkā (Ceylon) offenbar Gewordnen" (*Über die Kawi-Sprache*, 1:268). The derivatives of the root *trī* preceded by *ava* and employed in the causal form lend themselves very easily to the meaning of "to communicate, to transmit," literally "to make the teaching descend."

of Rāvaṇa and out of compassion for him, he manifests himself in his full glory, surrounded by a great number of devas and the assembly of his listeners.

The dialogue then takes place and continues afterward between Śākya and Mahāmati, one of the bodhisattvas of the assembly; and it turns on the nature of laws or beings, and on a great number of points peculiar to Buddhist doctrine, such as production, annihilation, intelligence, the sublime truths, the emptiness of various types of causes. Śākya sometimes recalls in a summary form the opinions of the *tīrthakaras*,[136] the name by which he designates Brahmanical ascetics, as I have said above. One sees supernatural beings taking part in the dialogue, like Kṛṣṇapakṣika, king of the nāgas, who, in the form of a brahman, comes to ask Śākya if, according to him, another world exits. I add that the *Saddharmalaṅkāvatāra* possesses, like the *Saddharmapuṇḍarīka*, a chapter with magical formulas, called *dhāraṇīs*, a circumstance that to a certain point links this book to the category of the tantras.[137]

One sees that there is nothing historical in this work, and one would wrongly hope to use it to support this opinion of the Sinhalese that Śākyamuni came to Ceylon, as, they say, the previous buddhas did, to preach the law.[138] This encounter of Śākya with Rāvaṇa is no less fabulous than the existence of the king of Ceylon, whom the Brahmanical tradition made contemporary with Rāma, that is to say, with a hero who, if he ever existed, certainly preceded Śākyamuni Buddha by several centuries. The *Laṅkāvatāra* appears to me as a book composed in the school, and in an epoch, in which Buddhism had attained its full development. I will cite as proof the following piece, where are set forth various opinions that various sects of Buddhists and brahmans had formed about this common aim of their efforts and their teaching, nirvāṇa.

Then, the bodhisattva mahāsattva Mahāmati spoke again to the Bhagavat in these terms: "One says, O Bhagavat, nirvāṇa, nirvāṇa. What is the thing designated by this name *nirvāṇa*, about which all the tīrthakaras argue?" The Bhagavat said: "Thus, listen, Mahāmati, and engrave my words in your mind well and completely; I will tell you what nirvāṇa is, in conformity with the various ideas that

136. One could believe that the *tīrthakaras* of whom this work speaks in more than one place are the deified sages of the Jainas; but although this denomination could be borrowed from this sect, which must doubtless have taken place only in a rather modern epoch, I believe that in our Buddhist texts the word *tīrthakara* is simply synonymous with *tīrthika* and with *tīrthya*, terms by which all the ascetics who are not Buddhist and in particular all Brahmanical mendicants are designated.

137. *Saddharmalaṅkāvatāra*, fols. 78a and b.

138. After this analysis of the *Laṅkāvatāra*, I do not need to signal that I renounce the point of view from which Mr. Lassen and I had believed, a long time ago, we had to consider this work (*Essai sur le Pāli*, p. 43). One will permit us to no longer accept the opinion of a judge to whose sentiments I never have difficulty in submitting myself; here indeed, his opinion, like the one I abandon, does not rest on the direct examination of the work in question (A. Rémusat, *Nouveau Journal Asiatique*, vol. 7, p. 295).

the tīrthakaras have." "Good, Bhagavat," responded the bodhisattva Mahāmati, and he began to listen. The Bhagavat spoke to him in this way:

"There are tīrthakaras, Mahāmati, who define nirvāṇa in this way, saying that by the suppression of intellectual attributes, of the elements, and of the senses, by indifference with regard to objects, by consideration of the perpetual contradiction of duties, thoughts, and what results from them cease to occur in abundance; then, the cessation of any exercise of thought, produced by an annihilation of its cause, like that of a lamp, of a sprout, of the wind, and resulting from forgetting past, future, and present things, there is nirvāṇa; it is from there that the idea they have of nirvāṇa comes. But these men, O Mahāmati, who see only annihilation, do not reach nirvāṇa.

"Others define it in this way: It is the deliverance which is the action of passing into another place as quickly as the wind, an action that results from the cessation of all exercise of thought with regard to objects. Other tīrthakaras define it in this way: It is the deliverance resulting from the destruction of the view of these two things, the mind that knows and the object that must be known. Others imagine deliverance as resulting from the cessation of all exercise of the faculty of thinking, cessation that comes from the view of that which is temporary and that which is eternal. Others define it in this way: starting from this conviction that the multitude of thoughts related to the attributes carries with it the production of suffering, incapable of knowing the measure of the view in their own mind, terrified by fear of the attributes, they imagine finding nirvāṇa in a character that is the desire for happiness resulting from the view of the attributes. Others, knowing entirely the particular as well as the general characters that belong to all conditions, either internal or external, imagine nirvāṇa as the imperishable substance of past, future, and present beings. Others also imagine nirvāṇa as the imperishable existence of the soul, of being, of life, of the nutritive principle, of the person, and of all conditions.

"Other tīrthakaras, Mahāmati, whose minds have only a false penetration, imagine that nirvāṇa results from the distinction they make between mind and nature and from the unique action of the successive modification of qualities. Others imagine nirvāṇa as resulting from the complete annihilation of virtue and vice; others, of the science that completely annihilates suffering; others, of the consideration that the world is the work of a creator God. Others, asserting that the creation of the universe is the product of the mutual action [of the elements] and not of a cause, do not see, in their error, that a cause is still accepted there; it is according to this point of view that they imagine nirvāṇa.

"Other tīrthakaras, Mahāmati, imagine nirvāṇa as resulting from perfect intelligence of the truth and the path. Others, engaging in the examination of qualities and the subject that supports them, draw their ideas about nirvāṇa from these diverse points of view: that qualities and the subject are one, that they are different, that they are at the same time one and the other, and that they are neither one nor the other. Others, starting from this view that the intrinsic nature of each being comes from its nature (*svabhāva*) passing to the state of activity (*pravṛtti*), as for example the variety of colors for the peacock, precious stones of various types for mines, the property of being prickly for thorns, imagine nirvāṇa according to this idea. Others, Mahāmati, imagine nirvāṇa as resulting from the knowledge of the twenty-five principles; and others, from the acquisition of the science that has six qualities and protects humans. Others, starting from this view that time is that which acts, imagine nirvāṇa according to the knowledge of the following principle: The existence of the world is dependent on time. Others, Mahāmati, imagine nirvāṇa by existence; others by the knowledge of existence and of nonexistence; others by this idea that there is no difference between existence and nirvāṇa.

"To the contrary, others, O Mahāmati, imagine it as follows: making heard the roar of the lion uttered by him who has omniscience (the Buddha), that is to say, recognizing everything to be the conception of their own mind,[139] not accepting the existence or the nonexistence of external objects; considering [nirvāṇa] as a place essentially deprived of four sides; not falling to the two extreme terms of reflection applied to that which is visible to their mind, because they do not see the object to accept, or the subject which accepts; not believing that any proofs, whatever they are, can cause a principle to be grasped; rejecting the existence of a principle because the illusory character of all principles leads them to accept none; each possessing individually the sublime law; recognizing the double nonexistence of a spiritual element;[140] having made the two corruptions of evil cease; having dispelled the two types of darkness; detached from the mind, the heart, and the knowledge that the heart gives, due to deep meditation on the image reflected by the illusory appearance that is in the role of the Tathāgata, the highest of all;[141] these men imagine nirvāṇa according to these ideas. Such opinions and others like them that the logicians of the evil schools of the tīrthyas support are, because of their falsity, rejected by the sage. [All indeed], Mahāmati, imagine nirvāṇa according to an idea that dwells on two terms. These are, Mahāmati,

139. This passage appears to me to be explained by another text of the same work, fol. 23b: "The three worlds are a pure conception of mind; they are deprived of self, of substance."

140. Or perhaps, "recognizing that there are two things which have no self": *nairātmyadvayāvabodhāt*, doubtless the soul and the body. When there is no commentary, one is never sure of being able to rigorously determine the meaning of these abstract formulas.

141. Here is true philosophical gibberish, many words for few ideas. It seems to me that this wants to say that the role, that is to say, the condition of the Tathāgata, which is the most elevated of all these to which an animate being can reach, does not really exist; that it is an illusory appearance; that the image reflected by this appearance deprived of reality, doubtless, that is to say, the individual Buddha, must be for the monk, etc. the object of a deep meditation. I could have separated all that into shorter propositions; but I have believed it necessary to give an idea of this style with a very literal version.

among others, the ideas that all the other tīrthakaras have of nirvāṇa. But with such opinions, one cannot be said to be in action (*pravṛtti*) or inaction (*nirvṛtti*). Each tīrthakara, O Mahāmati, has his nirvāṇa; examined according to the ideas of their own books, such opinions are inconsistent; they do not stand up as they present them. Nirvāṇa does not result for anyone from the movement, the arrival, or the departure of the heart. After having instructed yourself in this truth, as have the other bodhisattvas, you must reject all the nirvāṇas of the tīrthakaras as false doctrines."[142]

According to the manner in which this piece ends, it would seem that all the opinions he set forth about nirvāṇa are equally rejected by the author. I believe, however, that the last is the one he accepts; and this opinion, which, moreover, is expressed in obscure terms, amounts to the absolute negation of the subject and the object. I am well founded in believing that this way of envisaging nirvāṇa is one of the dominant opinions in the Buddhism of the North; that it is very probably that of the various redactions of the *Prajñā*, perhaps that of the Madhyamikas, and certainly that of the Yogācāras, toward whose opinions the *Laṅkāvatāra* seems to me to incline.[143] I find again in this work other details on nirvāṇa that amount almost to those expressed by the last of the opinions reported in the previous piece. After having described nirvāṇa as corresponding to the absolute emptiness in these singularly obscure terms: "the domain of the essence of vacuity of all intrinsic nature that belongs to nirvāṇa," the Bhagavat adds: "One more thing, Mahāmati, the nirvāṇa that is the domain of a science seen by each of the āryas individually is shielded from the various ideas one can have about it, namely that it is eternal, that it is interrupted, that it is and that it is not. How is it that it is not eternal? It is that it does not give rise to the idea that it has attributes, either particular, or in common [with something else]: because of that it is not eternal. How is it that it is not interrupted? It is that all the past, present, and future āryas, each understands it individually; because of that it is not interrupted. Moreover, Mahāmati, the great complete nirvāṇa is not destruction or death. If the great complete nirvāṇa, O Mahāmati, were death, after it the chain of rebirths would resume. If, moreover, it were destruction, it would fall under the definition of a composite being. This is why the great complete nirvāṇa is not destruction or death. Yogins understand it as death not followed by passage to another world.[144] Yet another thing, Mahāmati: nirvāṇa is called by this name because it is neither removed nor acquired, neither interrupted nor

142. *Saddharmalaṅkāvatāra*, fol. 54b ff.

143. *Saddharmalaṅkāvatāra*, fols. 3b, 13a, 23b.

144. That is to say, the true and last death in the eyes of an Indian, since for him what we call *death* is the end of a given existence, which must be followed by several other existences and so on indefinitely according to the law of transmigration.

eternal, neither identical nor different. Yet another thing, Mahāmati: nirvāṇa for the śrāvakas and pratyekabuddhas is not an idea resulting from the view of particular or common characters [that would belong to nirvāṇa], or of the abstinence of all active life, or of the consideration of the slight reality of objects."[145]

This passage can provide an idea of the method constantly followed by the writer of this treatise, a method which, we have seen, is also that of the Madhyamikas. From that argumentation which recognizes no authority other than that of logic and which uses it sophistically to deny everything that can be asserted about anything, the yes and the no, there results a Pyrrhonism of which there is no example in any of the Brahmanical schools. I repeat, and it is with this reflection that I wish to end this rapid analysis of the most considerable treatises related to the metaphysics of Buddhism. I cannot believe that such a book, any more than the different redactions of the *Prajñā*, gives us the doctrine spread by the recluse of the Śākya race several centuries before our era. There is no trace of these radically negative theories in the first sūtras, or to put it more exactly, these theories are there only in seed, and this seed is not more developed there than in the Brahmanical schools, where, while contesting the reality of the external world, one accepts its passing existence, as well as the permanent existence of a supreme spirit of which the universe is but a kind of visible manifestation.

Whatever the danger of precisely formulating opinions that are so difficult to grasp through texts still so completely unknown as those of Nepal, I imagine that Śākyamuni, in entering into the religious life, began from the elements that the atheistic doctrines of Sāṃkhya provided him, which for ontology were the absence of a god, the multiplicity and the eternity of human souls, and for physics was the existence of an eternal nature endowed with qualities, transforming itself and possessing the elements of the forms that the human soul assumes in the course of its voyage through the world. Śākyamuni took from this doctrine the idea that there is no God, as well as the theory of the multiplicity of human souls, of transmigration, and of nirvāṇa or deliverance, which belonged in general to all the Brahmanical schools. Only, it is not easy to see today what he understood by nirvāṇa, for he defines it nowhere. But because he never speaks of God, nirvāṇa for him cannot be absorption of the individual soul into a universal god, as the orthodox brahmans believed; and since he hardly speaks of matter, his nirvāṇa is also not the dissolution of the human soul into the physical elements. The word *emptiness,* which already appears in the monuments that all prove to be the most ancient, induces me to think that Śākya saw the supreme good in the complete annihilation of the thinking principle. He imagined it, as an oft-repeated comparison implies, to be like the exhaustion of the light of a lamp going out.

One has seen through the exposition of the twelve causes of existence that I

145. *Saddharmalaṅkāvatāra*, fols. 29a and b.

have made above what difficulty one experiences to discover his true opinion, not on the past of the human soul, but on its very origin. The soul of man, according to him, necessarily transmigrates through an infinite number of forms; that of the greatest saint, that of a buddha who will enter into complete nirvāṇa, has had an immense past of misery and happiness, of virtues and crimes. But whence comes this multitude of individual souls that the brahmans said come from the bosom of Brahma, and that the Sāṃkhyas believed distinct and eternal? Śākya does not say, as least as far as I could recognize; and I suppose that he accepted with the Sāṃkhyas that they existed for all eternity. For, one must not forget, Śākya could not separate himself completely from the world in which he lived; and Brahmanical society, in which he took birth, must have left the deep imprint of its teachings on his mind. One recognizes its trace notably in the quite orthodox theory of transmigration. If his doctrine thus appears incomplete to us, if for us it leaves in the dark a good many problems with whose solution it does not seem to have occupied itself, it is that these problems were not a question for him, it is that he did not contest the explanation given for them up to that point. Envisaged from this point of view, his doctrine places itself in opposition to Brahmanism as a morality without God and as an atheism without nature. What he denies is the eternal God of the brahmans and the eternal nature of the Sāṃkhyas; what he accepts is the multiplicity and individuality of human souls of the Sāṃkhyas, and the transmigration of the brahmans. What he wishes to attain is the deliverance or freedom of mind, as everyone wished for in India. But he does not free the mind as the Sāṃkhyas did by detaching it from nature forever, nor as the brahmans did by plunging it again into the eternal and absolute Brahma; he annihilates the conditions of its relative existence by hurling it into emptiness, that is to say, to all appearances, by annihilating it.

After that, it is not surprising that this doctrine produced the Pyrrhonism of the *Prajñā* and the nihilism of the other schools, like that of Nāgārjuna. But neither this Pyrrhonism nor this nihilism are written explicitly in the sūtras emanating from the preaching of Śākya, as they are in the *Prajñāpāramitā* and the other works that rely on this collection. That is enough to justify the opinion I have advanced in commencing this analysis, namely that there is an interval of several centuries between the sūtras regarded as the sources of the metaphysics of Buddhism and the *Prajñā* or the books that depend on them, the difference that separates a doctrine at its very beginnings from a philosophy that has reached its final development.

SECTION 5

Tantras

The part of the Nepalese collection to which this section is dedicated is distinguished in such a definite manner from all those I have examined thus far that the Tibetans themselves place it apart from the most general classification they make of their religious books, calling *mdo* or *sūtra* everything that is not *rgyud* or *tantra.*[1] The tantras are indeed treatises with a very special character, where the cult of bizarre or terrible gods and goddesses is combined with a monotheistic system and other developments of Northern Buddhism, that is to say, with the theory of a supreme buddha and superhuman buddhas and bodhisattvas. In the tantras, all these personages are the object of a cult for which these books minutely delineate rules; several of these treatises are merely collections of instructions directing devotees in the art of drawing and arranging circles and other magical figures (*maṇḍala*) intended to receive the images of these deities. Offerings and sacrifices addressed to them in order that they be favorable to oneself, such as prayers and hymns sung in their honor, also occupy a considerable place in these books. Lastly, they all contain magical formulas, or *dhāraṇīs*, veritable spells supposed to have been composed by these very divinities, which usually bear their name and which have the virtue of saving from the greatest perils one who is fortunate enough to possess and repeat them.

This part of the Nepalese collection is not the first that Mr. Hodgson discovered, and his Buddhists revealed its existence to him only when he had already

1. Csoma, "Analysis of the Sher-chin," in *Asiatic Researches*, vol. 20, p. 412.

obtained from them many other works of a different character. If, as the title *tantra* indicates, and as this analysis will prove, the impure and coarse cult of the personifications of the female principle, as accepted among the Śivaists, found a place in these books, one can understand that an honest Buddhist hesitated to reveal to a foreigner proofs of so monstrous an alliance. But another reason must have also long shielded this part of Buddhist literature from the researches of Mr. Hodgson: it is the idea that the Nepalese and the Tibetans seem to possess about the value and the importance of the tantras. Nowhere, indeed, is Buddhism reduced to more human proportions and to conditions of a practice more easy, in general, than in these books. It is no longer a matter, as in the ancient sūtras, of preparing oneself through the exercise of all virtues, in order to one day fulfill the duties of a buddha. It suffices to trace a figure, to divide it into a certain number of compartments, to draw here the image of Amitābha, the buddha of a world as fabulous as he is, there that of Avalokiteśvara, the famous bodhisattva, the tutelary saint of Tibet; somewhere else those of some female divinities with singular names and terrible forms; and the devotee assures himself the protection of these divinities, who arm him with the magical formula or spell that each possesses. For coarse and ignorant minds, such books certainly have more value than the moral legends of the early days of Buddhism. They promise temporal and immediate advantages; in the end, they satisfy this need for superstitions, this love of pious practices by which the religious sentiment expresses itself in Asia, and to which the simplicity of primitive Buddhism responded but imperfectly.

It is, moreover, easy to judge the character of this part of Buddhist literature through the translation of two treatises made by Mr. Wilson from a manuscript sent by Mr. Hodgson to the Asiatic Society of Bengal.[2] One sees there the most complicated mythology and the conceptions of the most scholarly schools of Buddhism mingled with the names of divinities, several of whom belong in particular to the special cult of Śiva. This is the general character of these two treatises. To these fundamental characters, which probably form the most important part of the tantras, the first of these two treatises adds some that are peculiar to Nepal, and which prove that this small book was written in the valley since Buddhism was established there.[3] It is thus a Buddhist work composed in Sanskrit outside India; but this fact is not in itself of very great importance if, as Mr. Wilson establishes, one has reasons to believe that the ensemble of mythological personages who figure in this treatise were already part of Buddhism when it still flourished in Northern India.[4] Moreover, the treatise in honor of the Nepalese divinities, where there is this trace of a hand foreign to India, is not

2. Wilson, "Notice of Three Tracts Received from Nepal," in *Asiatic Researches*, vol. 16, p. 450ff.

3. *Asiatic Researches*, p. 470.

4. *Asiatic Researches*, p. 469.

regarded as an inspired book, and there is no reason to apply to it the severe rules of criticism to which it is necessary to submit books accepted into the canon of sacred scriptures.

Mr. Hodgson has furnished Mr. Wilson with a mythological commentary on these two works, which is full of details essential to know; and in his turn, Mr. Wilson has followed them with remarks whose importance is appreciable above all from the point of view at which I believe one must place oneself in order to examine the Buddhist books. The first of these remarks is that the Sanskrit vocabulary of Hemacandra and above all the *Trikaṇḍaśeṣa* mention, besides the names of Śākyamuni, those of a great number of buddhas and other divine personages who play the principal role in the tantras of the Buddhists of Nepal. The author of the *Trikaṇḍaśeṣa*, who must have written around the tenth or at the latest around the eleventh century of our era,[5] could not have spoken about these divinities, unknown to the brahmans, if they had not already existed in Buddhism, which had still not been proscribed in all parts of India in that period. The second remark is that so far nothing proves that these various developments of Buddhist mythology are known in Ceylon, in the kingdom of Ava, and in Siam,[6] that is to say, in the countries where what I propose to call the school of Southern Buddhism reigns. It is an important fact, whose verification is of the highest degree of interest for the ancient history of this religion. But this is not the place to make a complete study of it and develop its consequences. This subject will naturally find its place when I compare the Buddhist collection of the North to that of the South. While waiting, it suffices for me to say that the tantras are as unknown in Ceylon as the numerous divinities to whose adoration they are dedicated.

The tantras thus belong to the most complicated form of Northern Buddhism. At any rate, one finds in them the trace of the most diverse conceptions, which could elaborate themselves only in succession. So, alongside the human buddha Śākyamuni appears the system of celestial buddhas and bodhisattvas, which is quite difficult to regard as the primitive form of Buddhism, and the notion of an *ādibuddha*, or supreme buddha, corresponding to the Brahma of brahmanism, a notion which, according to Csoma, would be primitively foreign to India and would not have been introduced there before the tenth century of our era.[7] To the five dhyāni buddhas, the tantras add even a sixth named Vajrasattva, who corresponds to the sixth sense or to the internal sense, *manas* (the heart), and to the sixth sensible object, *dharma* (merit or moral law), that is seized by the manas, in the same way as the other five buddhas correspond, as has been said above,

5. *Sanscrit Dictionary*, preface, p. xxvij.
6. Wilson, "Notice of Three Tracts Received from Nepal," in *Asiatic Researches*, vol. 16, pp. 468 and 469.
7. Csoma, "Analysis of the Sher-chin," in *Asiatic Researches*, vol. 20, pp. 488 and 564.

to the five senses and the five sensible qualities.[8] All these notions, joined to the adoration of the female energies of the buddhas and bodhisattvas and to that of other divinities known for the most part from the Śivaists, are associated in these books in the closest manner to the cult whose object is Śākyamuni, as well as to the speculative doctrines that his teaching seeks to popularize. The founder of Buddhism is even expressly depicted in them as the institutor of the ritual and magical prayers of the tantras. The mixture of these two orders of ideas, which in their expression and their object are almost the opposite of one another, is so intimate in the tantras that if one did not possess other specimens of Nepalese Buddhism, one would form an idea of this belief far distant from that given by the texts of which I have spoken thus far.

I well understand that the character of inspired books is also attributed to the tantras since, like the canonical works, these treatises are taken to be the very word of the last human buddha. But these books themselves furnish a very strong objection against this claim, which is drawn from the character of the divinities whose cult they recommend and whose practices they enjoin. Nothing proves, indeed, that these divinities figured in the primitive teaching of Śākya; proof to the contrary follows from their being entirely unknown to the sūtras and the Buddhist legends of Nepal I have examined above. There, neither the female energies of the Buddha and Śiva, nor the obscene worship one renders to them, nor the formulas by which one assures their protection appear.

To this observation, which I believe to be decisive, I will add another, which, although concerning a point of a lesser value, no less merits consideration. I wish to discuss the extreme difference one notices between the style of the tantras and that of the primitive sūtras. Apart from this style being sometimes obscure and incorrect to the point of barbarism, it employs with a quite special meaning terms that in the ancient sūtras appear only with their ordinary and classical sense. I will mention in particular the word *vajra* (diamond, thunder), which plays a great role in the language of the tantras and which figures, among others, at the beginning of the name Vajrasattva, this sixth superhuman buddha who is the invention of the tantrists. This same word appears also in the name *vajrācārya*, or the Buddhist priest of the Nepalese. The true character of this priest has been clearly traced by Mr. Hodgson,[9] and the research of this scholar

8. Hodgson, "Quotations from Original Sanscrit Authorities in Proof and Illustration of Mr. Hodgson's Sketch of Buddhism," in *Journal of the Asiatic Society of Bengal*, vol. 5, p. 79, note. "Notices of Three Tracts Received from Nepal," in *Asiatic Researches*, vol. 16, p. 458 and note 1. It is for this that Csoma, in his analysis of the Tibetan collection of the tantras, usually accompanies the name Vajrasattva, literally "precious being," with this definition, "supreme intelligence" ("Analysis of the Sher-chin," in *Asiatic Researches*, vol. 20, pp. 491, 496, 503, and 549).

9. "Quotations from Original Sanscrit Authorities in Proof and Illustration of Mr. Hodgson's Sketch of Buddhism," in *Journal of the Asiatic Society of Bengal*, vol. 5, pp. 34 and 35. See above, section 3, p. 328, note 184.

has indicated that the vajrācāryas were of a rather modern date. This testimony comes to support the observation I make at the moment on the use of the word *vajra*. I suppose that the name *vajrācārya*, "the diamond preceptor," or "the precious preceptor," which according to Mr. Hodgson is not found in any canonical book, belongs to the same epoch and to the same source as that of Vajrasattva, "one who has the essence of the diamond," or "precious being." Here, doubtless, *vajra* must have a figurative meaning, that of "precious, supreme,"[10] like *ratna*, "jewel," which appearing in the sacramental expression *triratna*, that is to say, the three jewels (Buddha, the law, and the assembly), has lost its specific meaning to take on the general meaning of "precious, eminent." I cannot refrain from believing that the so frequent use that the ancient texts make of *ratna*, with the special meaning of "precious," has given birth to that of *vajra*, which is no less familiar to the authors of the tantras. Moreover, whatever influence the use of the word *ratna*, taken in this special sense, exerted on the adoption of the word *vajra*, used in an analogous sense, it remains no less certain that this latter characterizes the style of the tantras in a particular manner. I can thus say of these works what I have said of the more developed sūtras: like them, they belong to a second age of beliefs and Buddhist literature; it is not that I claim thereby that they were written at the same time as the longest sūtras and the great collections of the *Prajñāpāramitā*, but that they mingle the simple notions of primitive Buddhism with religious practices and divine names also mentioned in the large sūtras.

It is not my intention to long dwell on this part of the Nepalese collection, which I am inclined to regard as the most modern of all, and whose importance for the history of human superstitions does not compensate for its mediocrity and vapidity. It is certainly not without interest to see Buddhism, which in its first organization had so little of what makes a religion, end in the most puerile practices and the most exaggerated superstitions. But this deplorable spectacle has quite quickly wearied the curiosity and humiliated the intelligence. The idea of a supreme god undoubtedly occupies a considerable place there; and I well believe that morality also must have had its own place in the developments that took place in this part of Buddhist literature. They all must not be as poor as the ones I know, since Csoma de Kőrös mentions in several places of his analysis a number of tantras that in his view are very beautiful.[11] I am surprised nonetheless

10. "Notice of Three Tracts Received from Nepal," in *Asiatic Researches*, vol. 16, p. 475ff. See also for the value of application of this word, Schmidt, *Geschichte der Ost-Mongolen*, p. 310.

11. "Analysis of the Sher-chin," in *Asiatic Researches*, vol. 20, pp. 492, 496, 499, 502, 513, and 545. At one point, he expresses himself in this way: "This tantra and the preceding are well worthy of being read and studied because they will give an idea of what the ancients thought of the human soul and of God" (*ibid.*, p. 497). But would it not have been necessary to establish beforehand that these tantras are indeed ancient productions? And was it not useful to remark that nothing they teach is found in either the Vinaya or the Sūtras, which on the contrary are filled almost entirely with the story of Śākyamuni or of his first disciples, whose relative precedence cannot be contested by anyone?

that this scholar, who has given a full analysis of the legends of the Vinaya, where the story of the preaching of Śākyamuni is sometimes recounted in so captivating a manner, and who has done so without allowing the slightest sentiment of interest in these fascinating stories to come through, has only found words of admiration and enthusiasm for books that appear to me the miserable product of ignorance and the most coarse credulity. But the tantras, in replacing the simple worship of Śākya with the adoration of a multitude of fantastic divinities, evidently transformed Buddhism and consequently gave birth to a special literary development that could also have its beautiful side. I only regret either not having seen them, or perhaps having lacked the courage necessary for the search.

I must nevertheless provide an analysis of some of these books, and I commence by design with that which appears the most celebrated of all, at least according to the report of Csoma de Kőrös, that is to say, the *Suvarṇaprabhāsa.*[12] The importance that the Buddhists of the North attach to this work is proved, moreover, by this fact alone: that it is included among the nine dharmas or sacred books of Nepal. It is found, like all works reputed to be canonical, translated into Tibetan in the collection of the Kah-gyur; but I have noticed that the Tibetan version was in general more developed than the Sanskrit text whose manuscript belongs to the Société Asiatique. I conclude from this that there are two redactions of this work that are similar in content but that differ from each other in the length of development. This conclusion, moreover, is supported by more than one fact. Csoma, in his analysis of the Tibetan collection of the tantras, notes the existence of two *Suvarṇaprabhāsas*, which equally treat the same subject and contain the same matters, but which differ in their origin, the first being translated from Chinese, the second from Sanskrit.[13] On the other side, in recalling a passage extracted by Mr. Schmidt from the Mongol *Suvarṇaprabhāsa*, I have advanced that I did not know its Sanskrit text;[14] this passage indeed is not found in the Indian *Suvarṇaprabhāsa* owned by the Société Asiatique. As much must be said of another fragment extracted by Mr. Schmidt from the second chapter of his Mongol *Suvarṇaprabhāsa*,[15] with, however, this difference: that the same subject forms the core of the Mr. Schmidt's fragment and of the second chapter of our *Suvarṇaprabhāsa*. One must thus consider it certain that there are two redactions of this work: the one that is not long, which the Société Asiatique owes to the liberality of Mr. Hodgson; the other, which is longer, of which one Mongol translation is known and from which Mr. Schmidt has made two important borrowings. It is for scholars who know both Tibetan and Mongol to

12. "Analysis of the Sher-chin," in *Asiatic Researches*, vol. 20, pp. 515 and 516. See the additions at the end of the volume.

13. *Asiatic Researches*, vol. 20, pp. 514 and 515. *Journal of the Asiatic Society of Bengal*, vol. 1, p. 388.

14. Above, section 2, p. 152, note 75.

15. *Geschichte der Ost-Mongolen*, p. 307ff.

determine the relation of the versions of the Kah-gyur and the *Altan gerel*. As for the Sanskrit *Suvarṇaprabhāsa* that the Société Asiatique owns, I have believed it necessary to distinguish it clearly from the Mongol version in order to make clear that what I have to say about this work applies exclusively to the hardly considerable volume we possess in Paris.

The title *Suvarṇaprabhāsa*[16] that this volume bears means "Golden Radiance," and the work is regarded as a sūtra that would have been preached by Śākya on the mountain of Gṛdhrakūṭa in Magadha.[17] Ānanda asks the Bhagavat if he is going to teach him the law; and he responds that he wishes to set forth the king of sūtras, the *Suvarṇaprabhāsa*, of which he makes pompous praise in mediocre verses, which fill the first chapter. The second opens with the question that a bodhisattva named Ruciraketu asks himself about the reasons for the short duration of the existence of Śākya, which must be only eighty years. He finds that the Bhagavat has given as the motive for such a short existence the aversion one experiences in depriving any being of life, and the disposition one feels to give food to those who need it, even at the cost of one's own body. At the moment when he conceives this thought, there appears to him a vast edifice made of lapis lazuli and filled with the most precious furnishings and objects. In the east, he sees the tathāgata Akṣobhya, in the south Ratnaketu, in the west Amitābha, and in the north Dundubhīśvara. At the sight of these marvelous apparitions, Ruciraketu is not able to contain his astonishment; the question he had asked himself regarding the duration of Śākyamuni's life returns to his mind, and then the tathāgatas who have appeared before his eyes address him in these terms: "Do not say, O son of good family, that the life of Śākyamuni is short in length; for we do not see in the universe anyone capable of knowing the term of the tathāgata Śākyamuni's life, so composed is it of an incommensurable number of millions of ages and years." At that instant, gods of different orders gathered in immense number in the palace of Ruciraketu; and then the tathāgatas who had appeared to him begin to set forth the duration of life of Śākyamuni the tathāgata in measured stanzas in the presence of the assembly gathered before them.

Meanwhile, in the assembly of Mount Gṛdhrakūṭa there was a brahman

16. The word *prabhāsa*, according to Wilson, does not mean "splendor," and it is doubtful that this word is classical with this meaning; however, it is formed regularly from *bhāsa*, which has this meaning.

17. The mountain of Gṛdhrakūṭa is the celebrated Vulture Peak of which Faxian speaks in more than one place in his account (*Foe koue ki*, pp. 253 and 269). Klaproth has perfectly determined the position of this mountain, whose name is preserved, to all appearances, in that of Gidhaur (*Foe koue ki*, pp. 260 and 270), which is applied at present to the fort situated at its most elevated part (*The History, Antiquities, Topography, and Statistics of Eastern India*, 2:51ff.). This denomination, moreover, is ancient in India, for one finds it already in the traditions collected in the *Mahābhārata*. The personified earth revealed there to Kāśyapa that several descendents of the kṣatriya race, and notably Vṛhadratha, who had escaped the vengeance of Paraśurāma, son of Jamadagni, had taken refuge at Gṛdhrakūṭa (*Mahābhārata, Śāntiparvan*, chap. 49, st. 1796, 3:428, Calcutta edition).

named Vyākaraṇa Kauṇḍinya, who, having heard about the complete nirvāṇa of Śākyamuni, asked him, in the name of his immense mercy, to grant him a favor. The Bhagavat kept silent; but a young man from the tribe of the Lichavis, named Sarvasattvapriyadarśana, who was present, said to the brahman: "Thus why, O great brahman, do you ask a favor of the Bhagavat? Indeed I can grant you one myself." To which Kauṇḍinya responded: "I desire to possess a fragment of the relics of the Tathāgata, even if it is no larger than a mustard seed, to make it the object of a religious cult." But the young Lichavi replies to him in verse that he will see a relic of the Tathāgata, even if it is no larger than a mustard seed, when hair grows on the back of a tortoise. The brahman comprehends the sufficiently clear meaning of these words, and responds to them with other approbatory stanzas, in which he says that indeed the Bhagavat was not born like other men, and that one would search in vain after his death for a relic the size of a mustard seed, since his body has neither bones nor blood, and that his true body, his true bones are the law, *dharmakāya*, *dharmadhātu*. This profound exposition disposes the minds of a great number of devas to comprehend what the supreme intelligence of a perfectly accomplished buddha is, and inspires in them stanzas in which they say that a buddha does not enter into complete nirvāṇa, that his law does not perish, and that his body is an eternal body. The chapter ends with the expression of the joy that Ruciraketu experiences.

At the beginning of the third chapter, one learns that this latter saw in a dream a golden drum resplendent like the disc of the sun, and in all points of space buddhas infinite in number who taught the law to immense assemblies. Then, he saw a brahman who beat the drum, and the drum produced the sound of poetic stanzas on the law. When he awoke, the bodhisattva Ruciraketu recalled these stanzas. He then sets out from Rājagṛha; and accompanied by a countless multitude, he went before the Bhagavat on the mountain of Gṛdhrakūṭa, and recited to him the stanzas that he had heard in the dream. These stanzas, which fill the fourth chapter, are related to the importance of the teaching of the law, and in particular to the merit of the *Suvarṇaprabhāsa*. Ruciraketu announces at the same time his desire to save creatures by setting forth this sūtra; and he makes a long confession of his faults in order to make himself worthy of the mission to which he aspires.

In the fifth chapter, the Bhagavat speaks, telling the story of a king named Suvarṇabhujendra, who addressed praise to all the past, present, and future buddhas and who requested as his reward to one day become worthy to set forth the *Suvarṇaprabhāsa*. At the beginning of the sixth chapter, the Bhagavat announces that the laws of emptiness have been set forth in a very considerable number of sūtras, but in order to facilitate their understanding, he has summarized them in the *Suvarṇaprabhāsa*.

He then explains in some stanzas the action of the senses, the origin and destruction of the body, the emptiness of all conditions and of all beings, the misery of the world and the necessity to free oneself from it. At the beginning of the seventh chapter, the four great kings of the four points of space celebrate in prose the merits of the *Suvarṇaprabhāsa*; they promise at the same time to protect the creatures of Jambudvīpa, in particular monks who possess this excellent sūtra. The Bhagavat approves of the speech of the four great kings. They return to the same subject while developing it further, always in prose. The Bhagavat in turn enumerates the advantages and honors promised to one who possesses this sūtra. I greatly abridge this presentation, which occupies a considerable place in the work, and which is followed by stanzas the four great kings pronounce in honor of Śākya.

In the eighth chapter, the great goddess Sarasvatī promises her protection and a magical formula to one who sets forth this sūtra. She joins to it the description of some superstitious practices that must accompany the recitation of this formula. The Bhagavat approves of her good disposition. The brahman Kauṇḍinya then sings the praises of the goddess in prose and verse. At the beginning of the ninth chapter, Mahādevī appears, who in the presence of the Bhagavat gives the same assurances of protection to the possessor of this sūtra. The goddess at the same time traces the rules of the cult whose object she must be for one who wishes to acquire wealth. The tenth chapter, which has only a few lines, is composed of invocations (*namas*) to various buddhas and bodhisattvas. In the eleventh, Dṛḍhā, goddess of earth, promises to make fertile and flourishing the place where the sūtra of the *Suvarṇaprabhāsa* is, or a monk who possesses it. In the twelfth chapter, Saṃjaya, chief of the armies of yakṣas, makes similar promises for the interpreter of the sūtra.

The authors of this long and tiresome dialogue change in the thirteenth chapter. The son of a king named Rājabalendraketu is pleased to possess a royal book having *Devendrasamaya* as its title. On this occasion, the *lokapālas*, or guardians of the world, gather around Brahmā and ask him how it is that a mortal king can become monarch of the gods. Brahmā responds that it is when, after having reigned with justice on earth, he is reborn among the devas. Brahmā then sets forth the duties of a good king and the vices of an unjust monarch. At the beginning of the fourteenth chapter, there is the story of king Susaṃbhava, who lived when the tathāgata Śikhin was in the world. In a dream he saw a monk setting forth the *Suvarṇaprabhāsa*, and upon waking, he rendered eminent honors to him and heard this precious sūtra from his mouth. Śākyamuni, who recounts this story, applies it to himself and tells his listeners that it is he who, in times past, was king Susaṃbhava and that Akṣobhya, one of the celestial buddhas, was the monk who set forth the sūtra to the king. The fifteenth chapter is dedicated to the development that Śākya makes in verse of this idea that by setting forth the *Suvarṇaprabhāsa*, one worships all the past, present, and future buddhas. One learns that in the future the bodhisattva Ruciraketu will be a tathāgata named Suvarṇaratnākarachatraketu.

This chapter also contains similar predictions for a great number of other personages and particularly for the ten thousand sons of the devas who belong to the assembly. The Bhagavat, whom one of the divinities present, named the bodhisattva Samuccayā, asks how these gods could deserve such happiness, responds that it is the merit they have accumulated by listening to the law, and recounts in the sixteenth chapter that under the ancient buddha Ratnaśikhin, there was a king named Sureśvara who was eminent for his justice. He had a skilled physician named Jātiṃdhara to whom was born a son named Jalavāhana, who was filled with all the physical and moral perfections. Terrible sicknesses swept down on the kingdom and struck an immense number of inhabitants. Touched by compassion, the son of the physician said to himself: "Here is a great multitude of sick people, and my father is quite old and cannot save them all. Suppose I was to ask my father to impart his knowledge of medicine to me?" He carried out his project and made his request in verse. His father imparted to him various principles of medicine founded on the distinction of the six seasons into which the twelve months of the year are divided. Nearly all of these principles amount to the need to vary the food and medicines of humans according to the seasons. Jalavāhana, sufficiently instructed, succeeds in curing all the sick people of the kingdom.

In the seventeenth chapter, one learns that Jalavāhana had two sons by his wife, one named Jalāmbara and the other Jalagarbha. One day, Jalavāhana was in a forest and saw a multitude of wild animals and birds all running toward a pond located in the middle of the woods. He asked himself what the cause could be and decided to find out. After a long walk, he reached the banks of the pond and saw a great quantity of fish without water. This spectacle moved him with pity and immediately divinities appeared before his eyes and told him: "Good, good, son of good family, you are named Jalavāhana (one who brings water); give water to these fish; act in conformity with the meaning of your name." The physician sets out to look for water but did not find it anywhere. Finally, he devises a way to strip a great tree of its branches and uses them to shade the pond and the fish. After much investigation, he discovers that long ago, the pond had been supplied by a great river, whose waters had been diverted by a malevolent being to make the fish perish. Recognizing that it is impossible for him to restore the river to its old course, he returns to the city and the king, tells him what he has seen, and asks him for twenty elephants; the king grants them to him. Then, going to the river, he fills the water-skins he has brought with water, loads them on his elephants, and immediately goes to the pond, where he empties them. He sees that the fish move as a group to the side where he appears, and he immediately guesses that hunger must be the cause of this movement. He thus sends his son

Jalāmbara to search his grandfather's home for all the prepared food there was. When his son has returned, he breaks all this food into small pieces and throws it into the pond.

He then remembers having learned that one who at the moment of death hears the name of the buddha Ratnaśikhin pronounced will be reborn one day in the world as a buddha. Consequently, he has the idea to cause the fish he has just saved to hear this precious name. But at that time, there were in Jambudvīpa two prevailing opinions: one that gave credence to the Mahāyāna, the other that rejected it. Jalavāhana, who followed the first, enters the waters up to his knees and pronounces the formula of adoration in honor of the buddha Ratnaśikhin. He then teaches the theory of the causes of existence, almost in the same terms as the *Lalitavistara*; then, he returns to his house with his two sons. The next day, all the fish were dead and had taken a new existence among the Trayastriṃśa devas. There, remembering their past life and recognizing to whom they are indebted for their present happiness, they resolve to show their respect to their benefactor, and during the night they go to his house, where they offer him precious necklaces amid a rain of flowers and the sound of divine drums. When day had come, king Sūreśvaraprabha asked the treasurer, his minister, the cause of the miracles that had taken place during the night; the minister also learned that the son of the physician had become the possessor of a great number of precious necklaces. The king wished to see this fortunate man and asked him to tell him the cause of all that had happened. Jalavāhana responded that the fish might be dead; the king desired to verify the fact, and the physician sent his son Jalāmbara to the pond to find out what had happened to the fish. He found them dead and saw in the pond a mass of divine māndārava flowers. Then, Jalavāhana presented himself to the king and affirmed to him that the fish had changed their abode, and that having become devas, they had produced the miracles that astonished him.

This story concluded, Śākyamuni applies it to various personages who are his contemporaries. King Sūreśvaraprabha was Daṇḍapāṇi the Śākya. Jātiṃdhara was king Śuddhodana, the father of Śākyamuni; and Jalavāhana, Śākyamuni himself. Jalāmbugarbha, the wife of Jalavāhana, is the young Gopā, of the race of Śākyas; his son Jalāmbara is Rāhulabhadra, son of Śākyamuni; Jalagarbha is Ānanda. Finally the ten thousand devas are the ten thousand fish of the pond; and the divinity of the tree that Jalavāhana strips of its branches is the bodhisattva goddess Samuccayā herself, whom the Bhagavat addresseses.

In the nineteenth chapter, Śākyamuni, continuing to speak to the same goddess, tells her that a bodhisattva must always be ready to abandon his own body in the interest of others. On this occasion, he recounts to her that one day he showed the assembly of monks the relics of an ancient personage who had performed this difficult sacrifice. It is the young prince Mahāsattva, who offered his body as food to a tigress who had just given birth. Śākya applies this story to himself, saying that long ago he was this prince, and finding the other personages of this legend in some of his contemporaries; the king Mahāratha is Śuddhodana, the queen is Māyādevī, and so on with some others, among whom Mañjuśrī and Maitreya are mentioned.

This story concluded, the innumerable bodhisattvas of the assembly make their way toward the tathāgata Suvarṇaratnākarachatrakūṭa and sing his praises. This piece is in verse, as is the praise of Śākyamuni then made by Ruciraketu. Finally, the work ends with stanzas in honor of the same buddha, pronounced by the goddess bodhisattva Samuccayā, in which she repeats in several forms that all beings and all conditions are empty.

Such is the content of this book, mediocre and indeed vapid, like the things of which it speaks, despite the great esteem it enjoys among the Buddhists of the North. Certainly, if one compares it to some of the tantras we have in Paris, it will appear superior to them on several points. The magical formulas and the superstitious practices occupy much less of a place than in other tantras almost as esteemed. The worship of Śākya and the observation of moral virtues that his teaching aimed to spread are still recommended; Śākya is the main personage and he is still not replaced, as takes place almost completely in the other books of the same genre, either by imaginary buddhas, or by other personages strange or terrible, of a less peaceful and less pure character. But despite these advantages, how little value this book has for us compared with the legends where the real life of Śākyamuni is recounted, and with the so profound parables of the *Lotus of the Good Law*! It bears all the characteristics of a treatise that does not belong to the preaching of Śākya, and which must have been composed at leisure in some monastery, at the time when Buddhism was completely developed. It is written in prose and in verse, like all the compositions of the second age of Buddhism, and the poetic parts bear traces of this mixture of Prakrit forms that I have indicated in the developed sūtras.

Then, and this touches on the very content, this book is so filled with praises of itself made by the Buddha or his listeners, and with the account of the advantages promised to one who studies and reads it, that one searches for it in vain beneath this mass of praise, and one arrives at the last page, almost without knowing what the *Suvarṇaprabhāsa* is. This feature is, to my mind, quite decisive. Nothing, indeed, better shows to what mediocre proportions Buddhism was reduced by the tantras than this tiresome repetition of the advantages and merits assured to the owner of a book which, in itself and apart from these developments, would be almost reduced to a few pages. It is the flavor and the style of the worst of the Brahmanical Purāṇas, those exclusively dedicated to defending the interests of a sect. The less mediocre piece of the work is the story of Mahāsattva, who feeds his body to a starving tigress; still, this legend has no more merit than all those with which the collections of the *Divyāvadāna*, the *Avadānaśataka*, and the *Mahāvastu* abound. The reader can judge for himself from the translation given by Mr. I. J. Schmidt, according to the text of the *Altan gerel*, the Mongol version of the *Suvarṇaprabhāsa*.[18] The philosophical part, belonging to the most negative school of Buddhism, is very brief and poorly treated there.

Finally, one wonders what the reasons can be for the attraction that the Buddhists of the North have for this book. Will one claim that this comes from its being a sūtra, that is to say, a book attributed to Śākyamuni himself? But this circumstance is not, either for the Nepalis or for us, sufficient reason to prefer it to other sūtras also attributed to the founder of Buddhism. It is clear that the title *sūtra* given to a book does not prove that this book must be ranked in the category of primitive treatises. I have already shown in analyzing several sūtras that there were different epochs in this part of the sacred literature, easy to distinguish, if not to date. The existence of the title *sūtra* given to a tantra proves only that the sūtras are regarded as the very word of Śākya in the eyes of the Buddhists of Nepal, and brings us back to this result, mentioned several times in the course of this research: that it is to the sūtras that one must always return if one wishes to recover either the most ancient form of his teaching, or the most popular form in which it subsists in our day to the north of India.

I have also browsed through several other tantras; but I feel, I confess, some scruples about making the reader share the boredom this study has caused me. I will mention, among others, the *Saṃvarodaya Tantra*, or the Raising of the Mystery or of Saṃvara, if this last word is really a proper name. According to Csoma, Saṃvara is the name of one of the divinities who belong especially to the followers of the tantras and the practices they set forth. The treatise of which I speak is written less in honor of Saṃvara than to the glory of Heruka, another god of the same type, perhaps the same under another name. I shall not pause to report the prayers, magical formulas, and ceremonies recommended by this book; in some, the substances one uses are hair collected in cemeteries and the hair of a camel, donkey, and dog. The coarsest superstition predominates in this work, where nothing would remind one of Buddhism if one did not see the name of the Buddha appear at rare intervals. The reward promised to these ridiculous practices is much less the state of a buddha than a kind of perfection (*siddhi*), which consists in the possession of a supernatural power that ordinarily serves purely human interests. This book contains a chapter on the signs that announce death; another on the four *yugas*, or ages of the world; another on the four islands or continents;

18. *Grammatik der Mongolischen Sprache*, p. 163ff. I have compared this translation with the Sanskrit text of our *Suvarṇaprabhāsa*, and I have found it, save on a small number of points, so accurate that one would believe that it was carried out from the Sanskrit and not from the Mongol. Apart from this circumstance proving the care that Mr. Schmidt brings to all his works, I conclude that, save for the differences of developments indicated a short while ago, it is one and the same core that forms the base of the two redactions of the *Suvarṇaprabhāsa*, that of the Mongols and that of the Nepalese.

one on the preparation of the fire for sacrifice and on the *homa*, or fire offering; some subjects take us far from Buddhism and bring us nearer to Brahmanism.

In a chapter especially dedicated to mantras, the cult of the Śivaite divinities is expressly recommended, and the first mantra is conceived in this way: "Oṃ! Adoration to the servant of Mahākāla who inhabits the cemeteries." The liṅga figures among the objects of this superstitious adoration. One is given the means to rid oneself of an enemy by drawing his image in a certain manner and with specific formulas. At the end of the work, there is a chapter filled with obscene practices written in a Sanskrit so incorrect and probably so particular that I do not flatter myself to have completely understood it; I have, however, seen enough of them to recognize that the Buddhist tantras are not worse than the Śivaite tantras in that regard. The passage to which I allude is dedicated to the description of the worship one must render to a *yoginī*, that is to say, to a woman charged to represent the female divinity one adores. The work, composed of thirty-three chapters, has the form of a sūtra; the dialogue takes place between the Bhagavat and the bodhisattva Vajrapāṇi, the son of the superhuman buddha Akṣobhya. It is written in verses of anuṣṭubh meter in a very incorrect Sanskrit and rarely mingled with Pāli forms (for example, *bhonti* for *bhavanti*); but the incorrectness of the text comes most often from the fault of the copyist, who perhaps did not always know how to read the original manuscript, which must have been written in the ancient ranjā script.

In the *Mahākāla Tantra*, of which there exists a translation in the Tibetan collection of the Kah-gyur,[19] one finds the ridiculous practices whose existence I have noted in the preceding tantra. Mahākāla is, as we know, one of the most familiar names of Śiva; here again, the union of Śivaism and Buddhism is manifest, expressed in its coarsest symbols. One finds in this treatise an explanation of the mystical value of the letters that compose the name Mahākāla; one is taught the means to discover hidden treasures, to attain the monarchy, to obtain the woman one wishes to marry; one is given the recipe for several concoctions, one of which has the marvelous property to make the person who rubs his eyes with it invisible. I leave it to the reader to guess the substances of which this unguent is composed; the spleen of a cat appears in the first line. One chapter contains various details given in the form of predictions related to some cities and some kings of India; but the text is so confused and the manuscript so incorrect that I could draw nothing from it. I find also in another place this rather curious reference, that the bodhisattva Avalokiteśvara resides in the land of Uttarakuru.[20] Perhaps one must see here an allusion to the northern origin of Avalokiteśvara and of the legends related to this personage, true tutelary saint of Tibet. This tan-

19. Csoma, "Analysis of the Sher-chin," in *Asiatic Researches*, vol. 20, p. 495.
20. *Mahākāla Tantra*, fol. 79b.

tra, written in a pitiable style, has the form of a sūtra and of a dialogue between Śākya and a goddess whose name I could not discover; it is in prose with some accidental traces of versification.

I will not dwell further on this part of Buddhist literature; it would, however, make it imperfectly known not to indicate the use it can have for the literary history of Buddhism, in particular in modern times. Thus, it is important to note, among the tantras, the *Kālacakra*, or the Wheel of Time, whose detailed analysis we owe to Csoma, but which we unfortunately do not have in Paris. The subjects treated in this book are cosmography, astronomy, chronology, to which is joined the description of some gods. One finds in it the indication of various epochs and chronological calculations; it speaks of Mecca as well as about the origin, the progress, and decline of Mohammedanism. The work is regarded as having emanated from the supreme Ādibuddha, or from this first buddha, an abstract being who corresponds, as I have said, to the Brahma of the orthodox: "It is," says Csoma, "the first original work relative to the tantrika system to have been written in the North, in a probably fabulous city named Shambala, near the Sihoun (the Sītā). From there, it was introduced into India in the tenth century and into Tibet in the eleventh."[21] One sees that this tantra is very modern; but it contains traditions that may not have left traces in more ancient books.

The same kind of merit recommends the *Ārya Mañjuśrīmūlatantra*, a treatise that, attributed like all the others to Śākyamuni, contains the indication of some historical events and the names of important personages in the form of predictions. It is in this way that Śākya predicts the future coming of Nāgārjuna, four hundred years after him. He announces also that of Pāṇini, of Candragupta, and of Ārya Saṃgha; this latter is the celebrated philosopher, chief of the Yogācāra school that Csoma places in the sixth or seventh century of our era.[22] These indices confirm what I have said at the outset about the place the tantras must occupy in the whole of Buddhist literature, of which they obviously form the most modern part. They already suffice, however, to make one appreciate how advantageous it would be to carry out a regular perusal of these books in order to extract the historical documents found scattered there.

I have said above that one found in the tantras, mantras and *dhāraṇīs*, or magical formulas, which in the eyes of the devotees constitute one of the most important parts of these books. I was not able to discover the difference between a mantra and a dhāraṇī, if it is not that the mantra has always appeared to me to be shorter than the dhāraṇī, which is sometimes very developed. This is what I conclude from the mantras contained in the famous leaves of Ablaikit, definitively translated by Csoma de Kőrös; they are in general shorter, more similar to

21. "Analysis of the Sher-chin," in *Asiatic Researches*, vol. 20, pp. 488 and 564.
22. "Analysis of the Sher-chin," p. 513.

a formula of adoration than the dhāraṇīs, of which I will speak in a short while.[23] One must add to this difference that the term *mantra* is a noun equally familiar to Brahmanical literature and Buddhist literature, while that of *dhāraṇī* seems exclusively peculiar to the second. This word, which Wilson gives in his dictionary as belonging to the Buddhists, means "one which contains or possesses a great efficacy." Ordinarily, the dhāraṇīs form an intelligible sentence, ending in bizarre monosyllables that generally have no meaning. Other times, they are composed of terms, some significant, others obscure, which are almost always put in the locative: one finds some specimens in the *Lotus of the Good Law*;[24] some occupy several lines there.

In comparing the simple sūtras to the developed sūtras, I have already said that the latter were influenced by ideas familiar to the tantras, at least in that they accepted dhāraṇīs, or magical formulas, made to assure incalculable advantages for those who read the books in which they are found. This alliance of dhāraṇīs with the Mahāyāna sūtras merits notice in more than one respect. In the first place, it does not exist in the primitive sūtras, where I have recognized only a single trace of it. This unique trace is, as I have said above,[25] in the legend of Śārdūlakarṇa, where Śākyamuni reveals the mantra in six letters to Ānanda, this celebrated formula of which Avalokiteśvara is regarded as the inventor, which Mr. Hodgson has found carved in ranjā and Tibetan characters on a temple situated between Nepal and Tibet, and which has led to so many different interpretations.[26] But I have set forth my reasons to believe that this legend was not one of the most ancient. In the second place, the presence of dhāraṇīs in the Mahāyāna sūtras can be explained in two ways: either the dhāraṇīs are contemporary with the redaction of the text, or they have been introduced afterward. It is quite difficult to decide between these two hypotheses; I only note that the most important Mahāyāna sūtras each have their dhāraṇī, and that collections of them have even been made. A compilation of this kind exists in the Société Asiatique, where one is able to gain an idea of the composition and meaning of these formulas. Each one bears a title that indicates at once its origin and its goal. Thus the volume opens with the dhāraṇīs of several celebrated works, like the *Prajñāpāramitā in One Hundred Thousand Stanzas*, the *Gaṇḍavyūha*, the *Samādhirāja*, the *Saddharmalaṅkāvatāra*, the *Saddharmapuṇḍarīka*, the *Tathāgataguhyaka*, the *Lalitavistara*, the *Suvarṇaprabhāsa*, and the *Prajñāpāramitā in Eight Thousand Stanzas*. The existence of such a collection does not, I confess, decide the ques-

23. "Translation of a Tibetan Fragment," in *Journal of the Asiatic Society of Bengal*, vol. 1, p. 273ff. Csoma has provided the lithographed text of it.

24. *Le lotus de la bonne loi*, chap. 21, fol. 208a ff. of the text; and p. 238ff. of the translation.

25. Section 2, pp. 155 and 156.

26. "Remarks on an Inscription in the Ranjá and Tibetan (Utchhén) Characters, Taken from a Temple in the Confines of the Valley of Nepál," in *Journal of the Asiatic Society of Bengal*, vol. 4, p. 196ff.

tion I just asked, for this collection can be modern and well later than the interpolations that would have introduced the dhāraṇīs into the works just mentioned. I prefer, however, the first solution to the second, and I think that the dhāraṇīs have not been added afterward into the books where they have a place. Furthermore, the use of these formulas must have been general at the time these books were written; otherwise, the need would not have been felt to accept them there. This is also a point to which I will return later.

One encounters among these formulas works of a slightly different character, for example, sūtras named *mahāyāna*, but in which there still appear often quite long dhāraṇīs, and above all *stotras*, or praises, notably the stotra of the seven human buddhas, the same one that Mr. Wilson has translated;[27] that of Āryatārā, called Sragdharā, a goddess who is the spouse of the superhuman buddha Amoghasiddha; that of Vasudharā, one of the nine great goddesses; that of Avalokiteśvara, a *Sūryaśataka*, or hundred stanzas in honor of the sun. One even finds there, in the form of a dialogue between Vasiṣṭha and Daśaratha, a fragment of the *Skandhapurāṇa*, this inexhaustible collection that furnishes so great a number of legends to the popular literature of modern India. Some of these treatises bear names of authors, such as Sarvajña, Ārya Maitrīnātha, Śrīvajradatta. But among these three names, the first is that of every buddha and in particular Śākyamuni, and the second, that of Maitreya; and it is probable that these names have been placed at the end of these treatises by some devotee who wished them to be accepted as the work of these holy personages. A singular association that results, in my opinion, from an obvious anachronism shows us Śākyamuni in the palace of Avalokiteśvara, in Potaraka, in this same city that is the ancient capital of Tibet, the Potala of our day. Now, this city is regarded, according to the tradition, to have been founded by Avalokiteśvara, a personage whose existence is related intimately to the first establishments of Buddhism in the Himalaya. This is a trace of a fact, purely local and peculiar to Tibet, which cannot be contemporary with the times when Śākyamuni must have lived; I will return to it later on the occasion of Avalokiteśvara. I also notice another trace of the same kind; it is the name of a divinity, if not exclusively peculiar to, at least very celebrated, in Kashmir, a country whose name is, moreover, mentioned in the text. "Adoration to the Blessed Mahākāla who has the names of Nandikeśvara, of Adhimuktika and who inhabits the cemeteries of Kaśmīra."[28]

The dhāraṇīs, or rather the books that contain the so-called formulas, appear not to be composed exclusively of these formulas; at least, I find in the commentary of the *Vinayasūtra* a citation extracted from a book of this kind, which has the title: *Vajramaṇḍā dhāraṇī*. It is perhaps the same work as the *Vajrahṛdaya*

27. *Recueil de Dhāraṇīs*, MS of the Société Asiatique, fol. 69a ff. *Asiatic Researches*, vol. 16, p. 453.
28. *Recueil de Dhāraṇīs*, fol. 29b.

of the Tibetan collection.[29] This piece is exclusively speculative, and it offers us new proof of the intimate alliance that the system of the tantras contracted with the most elevated Buddhist philosophy. I cite it because it is a passage where nihilism, resulting as I have shown from the doctrine of the *Prajñāpāramitā*, is pushed to its final limits.

"It is because one uses a stick, because one takes a flammable piece of wood, because the man moves his hand, it is, I say, from all these causes that smoke is born and that then fire appears. But this smoke and this fire must not be exclusively attributed to the stick, or to the flammable piece of wood, or to the movement of the man's hand; it is in the same manner, O Mañjuśrī, that, for the soul of the man bewildered by the belief in what does not really exist, the fire of love, of hate, of error are born. And this fire is not produced [exclusively] inside, or outside, or independently of the inside and the outside.

"Now, O Mañjuśrī, why does what is called *error* bear this name? It is, O Mañjuśrī, that error (*moha*) is what is completely sent forth [produced outside, *mukta*] by all conditions: this is why error is called *moha*.[30] All conditions, O Mañjuśrī, are the door of the hells; this is an axiom of the dhāraṇī." Mañjuśrī replied: "How is this axiom of the dhāraṇī understood, O Bhagavat?" "The hells, O Mañjuśrī, are created by ignorant men who are mistaken due to their belief in what does not really exist; they are the product of their imagination." Mañjuśrī replied: "On what, O Bhagavat, do the hells rest?" The Bhagavat responded: "They rest on space, O Mañjuśrī. What do you think about that, O Mañjuśrī? Do the hells exist only in the imagination [of those who invent them]; or rather do they exist by their own nature?" Mañjuśrī replied: "It is by an act of their imagination, O Bhagavat, that ignorant men believe in the hells, in animal wombs, in the world of Yama. It is by giving a false reality to what does not exist that they experience the sensation of suffering, that they feel the suffering of these three states inflicted on them as punishment; and the vision I have of the hells, O Bhagavat, I have also of the suffering of the hells.

"It is, O Bhagavat, as if a sleeping man came, in the middle of a dream, to believe he had fallen into hell; that he believed he had been thrown into this cauldron of iron, burning, filled with men, of which so much is spoken; that he experienced there a feeling of suffering, cruel, piercing, sharp; that he experienced there a complete faintness of heart; that he was frightened; that he felt dread. That he then exclaims, as if he were awake: 'Ah! what suffering! Ah! what

29. Csoma, "Analysis of the Sher-chin," in *Asiatic Researches*, vol. 20, p. 499.

30. This is quite bad grammar to support theories that are no better; the brahmans often have some that are as pitiable.

suffering!' That he cries, that he laments. That at this moment, his friends, his relatives, his acquaintances ask him: 'Where does the suffering you experience come from?' But that he responds to his friends and his relatives: 'I experience the suffering of hell,' that he loses his temper at them, that he abuses them, 'I undergo the suffering of hell, and you, you ask me in turn: "Where does the suffering you experience come from?"' That then his friends, his relatives, his acquaintances speak to this man in this way: 'Do not be afraid, do not be afraid, O man, for you are asleep, you did not leave your house.' That then reason returns to him: 'Yes, I fell asleep, what I imagined to feel has no reality,' and that so he regained his composure.

"In the same way, O Bhagavat, that this sleeping man, having a dream, would believe, through a false imagination, to have fallen into hell, just so, O Bhagavat, all ignorant men, chained by the belief in what does not really exist, imagine that the person called *woman* exists; they feel enjoyment with her. The vulgar man has this reflection: 'I am a man, and here is a woman; this woman is mine.' It is thus, that chained to the false imaginations of desire and passion, they imagine the condition of woman as existing; [the text repeats the previous sentence until: this woman is mine]. The mind of the man thus obsessed by desire and by passion, his thought turns to the illusions of enjoyment. As a consequence, he reaps disputes, dissension, and quarrels; his organs are disturbed and hate is born in him. With this false imagination that these ideas give him, the man, believing he is dead, believes that he experiences suffering in the hells during several thousand kalpas. In the same way, O Bhagavat, that the friends, the relatives, the acquaintances of the [sleeping] man tell him: 'Do not be afraid, do not be afraid, O man, you are asleep, you did not leave your house,' just so, O Bhagavat, the blessed buddhas teach the law in this way to creatures troubled by the four types of false imagination. 'Here [they tell them] there is no man, or woman, or creatures, or life, or mind, or person; all these conditions have no reality; all these conditions are nonexistent; all are the product of the imagination; all are like an illusion, like a dream, like something artificial, like the image of the moon reflected in water.' Here is the exposition that they set forth. Creatures, after having heard this teaching of the law by the Tathāgata, see all conditions free from passion; they see them free from error, not having their own nature, having nothing that envelops them. With their thought resting on space, these creatures, as if their time were finished, enter in a complete manner into the domain of nirvāṇa, where no trace is left of the aggregation of the elements that constitute existence."[31]

31. *Vinayasūtra*, fol. 13b ff. This piece is certainly known by the Chinese Buddhists, for Des Hauterayes, in his *Recherches sur la religion de Fo*, gives a rather long abstract that presents the most striking analogy with our text; he attributes these opinions to the followers of the Inner Doctrine (*Journal Asiatique*, vol. 8, p. 87).

To set forth in a few words the result of the analyses developed in this section, I will say that the tantras are composed of the mixture of the most diverse elements. They contain, first of all, Buddhism, and I would almost dare to say all Buddhisms, each represented by their most respected symbols: namely, primitive Buddhism by the name Śākyamuni; that of the celestial buddhas by the names Amitābha, the other dhyāni buddhas, and the equally celestial bodhisattvas, like Avalokiteśvara and the others; lastly, that of the theists by the name *ādibuddha*. With these theological elements, one finds associated metaphysical speculations of the most abstract order, like the nihilism of the *Prajñā*. Finally, these purely Buddhist elements are combined with the most shameful part of popular Brahmanism; namely with the cult of female divinities worshipped by the sects that were the last to emerge from the antique stock of Śivaism. Indeed, not content with paying idolatrous homage to the *śaktis*, or female energies, whom they imagine to be the spouses of the six divine buddhas and of the supreme Ādibuddha, the followers of the tantras have adopted en masse all the śaktis that the Śivaite tantras possessed, from that of Brahmā to that of Śiva, the most frequently invoked, as much for her frightening and sanguinary character as for the multiplicity of names she bears, thus offering to these miserable superstitions inexhaustible subjects for adoration. If one had to express in numbers the proportions in which these so diverse conceptions occur, one could say that the practices and formulas especially related to female divinities ordinarily occupy twice as much space as all the purely Buddhist elements together; and that among these same elements, that which appears most seldom is the name Śākyamuni, who is mentioned only as Master, as he is in all the sūtras. Thus, if the tantras had not taken themselves to be sūtras, that is to say, books emanated from the preaching of Śākyamuni, his name could well have not appeared in them, replaced as it had been by those of superhuman buddhas whose existence and marvelous qualities much better satisfy modern superstition. This is enough, I think, to prove that these books are the result of a rather recent syncretism, and that they can on no account be regarded as contemporary with Śākya.

But this result, which, thus presented in a general manner, seems to me shielded from all serious objection, needs to be examined more closely in order to be definitively admissible, for it touches on the difficult question of the alliance of Buddhism with Śivaism, a question that cannot be so settled in such an expedited fashion. The two scholars who have studied this subject with the most profound knowledge of Oriental documents, Messrs. Schmidt and W. von Humboldt, have wondered why Buddhism became allied with Śivaism rather than with Viṣṇuism.[32] Without seeking the reason for the preference of the

32. Schmidt, *Mémoires de l'Académie des sciences de Saint-Pétersbourg*, 1:119. W. von Humboldt, *Über die Kawi-Sprache*, 1:281.

Buddhists for Śiva, Mr. Schmidt observed that the Śivaite divinities, regarded by the Buddhists as protectors and guardians of their belief,[33] are, in their eyes, strictly speaking Buddhist intelligences (*eigne Buddhaische Intelligenzen*) who have taken such forms for certain particular aims, and that it is on this account only that they receive worship. On his side, Mr. von Humboldt, contesting the greatest part of the proofs drawn from the hypogeal temples of western India, in favor of an ancient alliance between the cult of Śākyamuni and that of Śiva,[34] hardly accepts testimony other than that of the present state of Buddhism in Nepal. Resting in particular on the opinion of Wilson, who establishes by very specious reasoning that the Śivaism of the Nepalese Buddhists is that of the Indian sect of the Pāśupatas, or followers of Śiva called Paśupati,[35] he notices, following Colebrooke, that the Pāśupatas, while substituting for the Brahmanical Vedas a *śāstra*, or sacred collection, that has become their fundamental book, come close on this important point to the Buddhists who, as one knows, reject the authority of the Vedas.[36] He then seeks a secret analogy with Buddhism in the tendency that the Śivaite sects manifest for the exaggerated practice of meditation; but as if this last proof, which one could assert for most of the other Indian sects, did not satisfy him, he supposes that the Buddhists and the Śivaites could find themselves closer less in the core of doctrine than in external circumstances; in other words, that Śivaism flourished more than Viṣṇuism in the provinces and in the epoch when Buddhism makes an alliance with it.

This discussion, like everything we owe to the pen of Mr. von Humboldt, is filled with instructive observations; the very solution he seems to settle on, since he sets it forth last, is still the most likely of all. Thus, it is less to the result than to the slightly vague manner in which it was obtained that I would dare make some objections. I find that if ever it was necessary to distinguish monuments and epochs clearly, it is on a question as complex as that of the relation of Buddhism to Śivaism; one will see that it is there above all that it is indispensable to know quite precisely of which one speaks.

What does one mean by the alliance of Buddhism and Śivaism? Does one wish to speak of one of these intimate fusions of two or of several sects, as the

33. Schmidt, *Geschichte der Ost-Mongolen*, pp. 342 and 355.

34. It is the learned Erskine who, in his oft-cited memoranda, had extended to the temple of Elephanta the opinion that Buddhism was formerly associated with Śivaism there (*Transactions of the Literary Society of Bombay*, vol. 1, p. 231 ff.). Mr. von Schlegel has made well-founded objections against this opinion (*Indische Bibliothek*, 2:447), which are adopted by Mr. von Humboldt (*Über die Kawi-Sprache*, 1:281). But Mr. von Humboldt perhaps carries the doubt a little too far when he advances that, save for Buddha Gayā, the figurative temples and monuments of India do not demonstratively prove the existence of an alliance between Buddhism and Śivaism (*ibid.*, p. 283). However, the caves of Ellora are real Buddhist temples, and very attentive travelers say that statues of Śiva are found there.

35. *Asiatic Researches*, vol. 16, p. 472.

36. *Über die Kawi-Sprache*, 1:285 and 286.

religious history of India offers us so many examples?[37] Does one have in view to assimilate this union of Buddhist beliefs and the practices of the coarsest Śivaism with the easy syncretism of several Viṣṇuvites, who, taking from any hand, make from the most heterogeneous elements an amalgam that they decorate with the name *religion*? I do not believe that one can think anything like this when it is the question of Buddhism and Śivaism. Let us read, for example, the tantrika treatise that Mr. Wilson has extracted and commented on in the *Asiatic Researches of Bengal*, and one will recognize that it consists of a series of formulas and ceremonies peculiar to the Śivaites that a Nepalese Buddhist put into practice for an entirely temporal aim. What Mr. Wilson has proved touching on this treatise can equally be said of all those I have browsed through in manuscript. They are either true Śivaite tantras in which the ceremonies peculiar to the worshippers of Śiva are described and recommended in the name of the last buddha, or they are works called *mahāyāna sūtras* because of their form and their tendencies, works in which divinities, most often Śivaite, appear to promise their sovereign protection to the Buddhist faithful. Here, in very general terms, is what one finds in the Sanskrit tantras of Nepal, that is to say, in those Buddhist books where the name Śākya is found mingled with that of Śiva and with the names of terrible and bizarre gods who walk behind him.

But however general this description is, it already puts us in possession of two quite important points for the continuation of our research. First, it proceeds, as one sees, from the elements accepted by Mr. von Humboldt, to whose eyes the alliance of Buddhism with Śivaism shows itself quite clearly only in the present state of the religion in Nepal; at the same time, as it embraces the *Suvarṇaprabhāsa* and the other great treatises of the same kind, it brings us to another observation of Mr. Schmidt that Mr. von Humboldt seems to have lost sight of and upon which we will soon pause.

Let us thus see which consequences result from our description. The first is that there is no complete fusion of Śivaism and Buddhism, but only a practice of various ceremonies and an adoration of various Śivaite divinities by Buddhists who seem hardly disquieted by the discordance that exists between their old faith and their new superstitions. This is so true that the most abstract philosophy remains complete among the magical formulas, the diagrams, and the gesticulations of the tantras. These are thus Buddhists who, while keeping their beliefs and their philosophy, consent to practice certain Śivaite rites that promise them happiness in this world, and take their origin back to Śākyamuni in order to further authorize them; or if one wishes, these are Śivaites who, to give credence to their innovations among a Buddhist people, resign themselves to believe that Śākyamuni, the apostle of the people, was the institutor of their rites. The first

37. Wilson, "Notices of Three Tracts Received from Nepal," in *Asiatic Researches*, vol. 16, pp. 450 and 451.

supposition appears to me the more likely; and one will see in the Historical Sketch of Buddhism that it accords better with the results of the research of Mr. Wilson on the introduction of tantras in Nepal, which he places between the seventh and the twelfth centuries of our era. This union of the fundamental beliefs of Buddhism with the practices of a barbarous Śivaism exists at the moment in Nepal, and it is in this sense that I regard the tantras that recommend it as modern. Furthermore, the qualification of modern is relative to my eyes; I intend to say by that that the religious state to which it applies is later than another state whose existence it is possible for us to note.

The observation I have just made leads us directly to the second consequence resulting from my general description of the books arranged under the category of tantras. This consequence is that several of these books, instead of showing us Buddhists practicing what is most ridiculous or most monstrous in the ceremonies addressed to Śivaite divinities, present these divinities promising spells, formulas, and the support of their redoubtable power to one who reads this or that book, who honors this or that relic, and who presents offerings to this or that buddha. This, as far as the alliance of Buddhism with Śivaism is concerned, is what appears clearest in the *Suvarṇaprabhāsa*, such as we have it in Paris. Suppress the content of this book that is composed of a discussion on the duration of the life of Śākya and a legend where long ago he is supposed to have given up his body to feed a tigress, and you will find there only praises of the *Suvarṇaprabhāsa* sung by divinities of all kinds, some Brahmanical in general, others Śivaite in particular. I say as much about the chapters accepted into the Mahāyāna sūtras where magical formulas called *mantras* or *dhāraṇīs* appear; these are Śivaite divinities, ordinarily female divinities, who commit themselves to communicate them to the worshipper of the Buddha, while assuring him the support of the terrible power that superstition attributes to them.

It is, one sees, a new relation of Buddhism with Śivaism; and if one wishes there to be the alliance of two cults, one will have to acknowledge that the treaty was not concluded on the same bases as the previous one. Whereas in the practical tantras, the Buddhist makes himself Śivaite, as much as this is possible for him, in books like the *Suvarṇaprabhāsa*, he remains Buddhist, asking the Śivaite divinities, for the price of his persevering faith in the Buddha, only their protection and the spells they possess. And, moreover, while the tantras strictly speaking have hardly preserved the name of Śākya except to make him the institutor of the rites they recommend, the Śivaite part of the Mahāyāna sūtras preserves for Śākyamuni his antique and incontestable superiority over the redoubtable dispensers of spells and magical formulas.

Here, the observation of Mr. Schmidt touching on the relation of Śivaite divinities to the Buddha appears in all its accuracy, an observation that Mr. Hodgson had already made on his part and that Mr. Wilson had accepted without discussion.[38] Mr. Schmidt has seen quite well that, according to the opinion of the Buddhists, these divinities are only beings of undoubtedly immense power if compared to humans, but in reality it is quite inferior to that of the Buddha, who entrusts them to guard his religion. But he goes perhaps a bit too far when, contesting the true Śivaite character of these divinities, he sees in them Buddhist intelligences incarnated in terrible images. Here still, it is necessary to distinguish with care. Without objection, the Buddhists who practice the tantras honor certain divinities that belong properly to them.[39] These can be the hypostases of which Mr. Schmidt speaks, although I must confess that I have not found a trace of this notion in the texts I have perused. But the fact remains that there are still a considerable number of gods and goddesses, like Mahākāla, Yamāntaka, Bhairava, Durgā, Mahākālī, and so many others who truly are Śivaite divinities, real borrowings made by Buddhism from the popular religion of the Indians. If the followers of Śākya imagine that these great forms are animated by Buddhist intelligences, according to Mr. Schmidt's own words, this belief, quite suspect to my eyes, must be modern; for nothing allows me to believe that the least trace of it exists in the Mahāyāna sūtras themselves.[40] I thus persist to see in all these forms of the Indian Śiva, venerated in the Buddhist tantras and whose protection the Mahāyāna sūtras accept, real Śivaite gods previous to Buddhism and adopted by it; both of these two characters seem to me to be obviously recognizable.

From all this, I conclude that the Sanskrit texts of Nepal present us with the relations of Buddhism with Śivaism in a double aspect, depending on whether the Śivaite divinities are the object of a more or less direct adoration, in other words, depending on whether they are worshipped through the practice of special ceremonies or whether one contents oneself with requesting spells and magical formulas from them. But since this double aspect corresponds to different books, first the Mahāyāna sūtras, in which these gods are only guardians and protectors of the Buddhist faith, and then the tantras, in which they walk as peers with the Buddha himself, I again conclude that these two categories of works do not belong equally to the same form of Buddhism, consequently they are not of the same epoch, and I do not hesitate to believe, as I said in the beginning, that those in which the union of Śivaism with Buddhism is less intimate must be taken as most ancient.

38. *Asiatic Researches*, vol. 16, p. 465, n. 26.

39. See especially the four divinities accepted by the Svābhāvika system invoked in the list of the gods of Nepal (*Asiatic Researches*, vol. 16, p. 465, n. 25). Wilson also accepts the existence of tantrika divinities who are the original product of the various schools of Buddhism (*ibid.*, p. 468).

40. Here again I will repeat that it would be indispensable to distinguish the systems. So, the divinities of the tantras are regarded, according to the Svābhāvika system, as being born spontaneously, while among the Āiśvarikas their genealogy, as given by the brahmans, appears to be adopted without discussion (*Asiatic Researches*, vol. 16, p. 465, notes 26 and 30), or related to the supreme Ādibuddha (*ibid.*, p. 468).

Finally, if continuing our research, we ask ourselves to what point this alliance of Buddhism with Śivaism is general, or to what point it appears in the texts of all epochs, then we will find that the names of Śivaite divinities are as foreign to the moral and metaphysical sūtras and avadānas as they are familiar to the Mahāyāna sūtras. I have already sufficiently explained myself on this point in speaking about the characteristics that distinguish the simple sūtras from the developed sūtras, and in this very section, while dealing with the dhāraṇīs. It thus suffices for me to recall this result here in order to show what the comparative study of Buddhist texts touching on the alliance of Buddhism with Śivaism teaches us. We can be certain that this alliance, unknown to primitive Buddhism, because it is contrary to its spirit, begins to show itself only in the developed sūtras, that it is still only there in its first beginnings, and that it is only consummated in the tantras by means of obvious borrowings that the Buddhists make from the language and practices of the Śivaites.

The Sanskrit texts of Nepal are the only source of the remarks and conclusions that precede, and the reader will perhaps find that I have been quite late in consulting the ordinarily decisive authority of the monuments. But he will not reproach me, I hope, for imitating here the prudent reserve of Mr. von Humboldt, for whom the alliance of Buddhism and Śivaism does not appear so clearly written on the monuments as it is in the testimonies of the religious state of Nepal. Why, instead of these descriptions where mythological interpretation occupies so much space, do we not possess accurate drawings of the hypogeal temples of western India, where the distinctive characters of the divinities they contain are reproduced with scrupulous exactitude? Unfortunately, with very few exceptions, the memoranda to which these interesting temples have given rise are only more or less ingenious tissues of hypotheses without foundation. The descriptions are made in an approximate manner, and it is not rare to see statues, whose determination would be the most important, receiving successively all the attributions and taking in turn the names Buddha, Jina, Indra, Śiva, and others. It is right to say that these descriptions have been made for the most part in an epoch when the study of Brahmanical and Buddhist mythologies was still not widespread, and by persons who had only modest claims to this kind of knowledge. But this concession, which I make without regret, although certain memoranda merited all the severities of the critic, does not improve the position of European erudition; I believe that it must beware of adding the confusion of the hypotheses to the inadequacy of the descriptions; its task would already not be so easy, even if it possessed the full collection of all the edifices and all the Buddhist caves of India depicted with a scrupulous and scholarly exactitude.

Nevertheless, in this matter there are a small number of points I desire to indicate to the reader, less as fixed opinions than as presentiments that can one day be confirmed by the more attentive study of the statues and scenes that decorate the Buddhist temples of India. The first point is that if one brings these figurative monuments closer to the written monuments, they are not strictly speaking related to the tantras; in other words, the tantras are not the commentary on the scenes represented in the Buddhist caves. This fact, which can be affirmed with near certitude, confirms the opinion I have developed touching on the modern date of the tantras. It seems evident to me that those of the hypogeal temples of India that must be attributed to Buddhism with complete assurance are earlier by a good many centuries than the mixture of Buddhist beliefs with the ridiculous or obscene practices of the Śivaites. On the other hand, I suspect that the Śivaite divinities do not play a very different role in these temples from the one they fulfill in the Mahāyāna sūtras. They are guardians, protectors who are placed at the door or at the first approaches to the temples in order to dispel the enemies of the Buddha, whose statue occupies the most honorable place. If the images of Śiva and the scenes where he is represented sometimes take a considerable place, it is that they were sculpted by Śivaist Indians, or perhaps even added later and after the construction of the temple. This is a point I touch on only with reserve, because it is one on which the present descriptions give us the least light.

Whatever it may be, we are naturally brought back to the opinion of Mr. von Humboldt, who conjectures that the predominance of Śivaism in the west of India, in the period when the Buddhist caves were carved out, sufficiently explains the presence of statues of Śiva near those of the Buddha. Quite simple as it is, and to my mind, for the very reason that it is very simple, this explanation seems to me to be the best. I do not believe under any circumstances in a secret alliance of Buddhism with Śivaism, founded on the analogy of philosophical principles. The sole point on which these two doctrines meet is the power that they attribute to the personal efforts of man, since, like the Buddha, the Śivaite yogin owes nothing but to himself and that it is exclusively by the practice of a quite individual asceticism that he rises above the world. But the similarity between Buddhism and Śivaism amounts to that alone; one would search in vain elsewhere for proofs of agreement between these two doctrines, and one must descend to the tantras to see them associated in a manner monstrous and unknown to all Buddhist schools, except to that of the North.

I believe that it would be neither profitable nor very easy to push this discussion further. I shall have a double occasion to return to it, first when I summarize what we know of the religious collection of Nepal, then when I sketch the history of Indian Buddhism.

SECTION 6

Works Bearing the Names of Authors

The works to which this section is dedicated would certainly be one of the most interesting parts of the Nepalese collection if they were dated and if they were more numerous. Dated, they would give us an accurate history of noninspired Buddhist literature; numerous, they would offer us a more considerable mass of useful information for knowledge of the doctrine and its developments. But no one will be surprised that works bearing the names of authors do not appear in greater number in a collection intended first and foremost to gather the books regarded as inspired, that is to say, as emanated from the very preaching of the last buddha. However, although rare and in general of little importance, the Sanskrit works composed by Buddhist monks who are their acknowledged authors are not, as one will see, without value or without interest.

A religion whose productions reputed to be sacred were so numerous must have necessarily aroused a vast literary movement; and indeed, what I am permitted to glimpse, from the works in my hands, gives me the right to affirm that this movement was as varied as it was long. These works, although belonging in all likelihood to the last ages of Buddhism, take up and develop the ancient traditions and opinions in new forms. Legends, philosophy, religious practices, they deal with everything and fix the frame of the sacred literature for us in a definitive manner. For if their authors were able to add foreign developments to the primitive core, they must not have innovated to the point of inventing entire classes and categories of works; and in order for monks to write avadānas that they signed, it was necessary that there first existed in the canon of sacred scriptures avadānas received as the work of Śākya.

The part of the sacred literature that seems to have most inspired the authors is that of the legends. I find, among others, in the collection of Nepal, a volume entitled *Avadānakalpalatā*, whose real title, as I read it in the manuscript itself, is *Bodhisattva avadānakalpalatā*. The author is Kṣemendra; it is at least the name that seems to me to correspond best to the different spellings of our manuscript *Śyomendra*, *Kṣyemandra*, *Kṣyemendra*, and *Kṣemindra*, according to the list of Mr. Hodgson.[1] It is a collection of legends related to the ancient existences of the buddhas and of their principal disciples; these legends bear, as one knows, the name *jātakas*, or births. I have counted in it twenty-six of these histories written in Sanskrit and in verses of the anuṣṭubh meter; the author has borrowed their subject from more ancient accounts, and I have recovered the source of some of his jātakas in several sūtras or avadānas of the great collection of legends often cited, the *Divyāvadāna*. The exposition of Kṣemendra is one of extreme exactitude, and it comes as close to the primitive text as the poetic form of the anuṣṭubh meter permits, which is, moreover, the most supple of all and the least removed from prose.

It is also an ancient legend that forms the core of the *Saptakumārikāvadāna*, or the Story of Seven Maidens, a composition of mixed prose and verse contained in twenty-two leaves, or forty-four pages. This small book is given as the work of the ācārya Bhadanta Gopadatta: it is the story of seven daughters of a fabulous king named Kṛkin, who is said to live at the time of the ancient buddha Kāśyapa. These maidens obtain from their father permission to enter into the religious life under Kāśyapa, and then triumph over the opposition of Māra. This mediocre core is developed in verses burdened with epithets that indicate nothing and that revolve around these commonplaces set forth, ordinarily with much more talent, in the mahākāvyas of Brahmanical literature.

One observes slightly more merit in the *Buddhacarita*, which bears the very title *mahākāvya*, or great poem, a title as familiar to the Buddhists as to the brahmans. The *Buddhacarita* is a poetic exposition of the life of the buddha Śākyamuni; this poem, not of considerable length (eighty-seven leaves), is attributed to the monk Aśvaghoṣa. It is written in verses of the anuṣṭubh and indravajra meters; its style is, if not very poetic, at least correct and perfectly intelligible. The *Buddhacarita* is only a substantial abridgement of the *Lalitavistara*; and this circumstance merits being taken into consideration all the more, since one does not observe in Aśvaghoṣa's poem any of the grammatical particularities that belong to the Pāli and Prakrit dialects. Thus we have here a work manifestly later

1. "Notices of the Languages, Literature and Religion of the Bauddhas of Nepal and Bhot," in *Asiatic Researches*, vol. 16, p. 431.

than the *Lalitavistara*, written in a language more grammatically correct than the *Lalita* itself. The name Aśvaghoṣa (one who has the voice of a horse) is, as we will see later, celebrated in the history of migrations of Buddhism. But nothing indicates to us that our author is the one about whom I will have occasion to speak in my summary of the history of this belief abroad. This name could certainly have been borne by more than one Buddhist monk, and something other than the identity of the name would be necessary to conclude that the Aśvaghoṣa of the North is the Buddhist monk that the Chinese named *Ma-ming*. It is more probable that our author is the same monk as the author of the *Vajraśuci*, which I have discussed above.[2]

The work of the authors extended to still other parts of Buddhist literature. The tantras themselves, or to put it more exactly, the works written in honor of the divinities whom the tantras honor, have been commented on and explained. Thus the Société Asiatique has a small volume named *Sragdharāstotra*, the "Praise of Sragdharā," that is to say, of one who wears a garland; a volume that is nothing other than a literal commentary on a poem of the same title, which very much resembles these small compositions brought forth by the devotion of the Śivaists and dedicated to the celebration of Śiva, Kālī, and the other divinities of this special pantheon. The goddess named Sragdharā seems to me to be the same as Āryatārā; at least I find this latter name in the margin of the manuscript. In this quite mediocre work, Amitābha and Avalokiteśvara, these two favorite personages of the Buddhists of the North, appear next to the goddess Āryatārā. It is true that I do not know the name of the author of this stotra; it must, however, be a noninspired writer; for apart from the fact that Śākya could not have preached or composed such a work, he would certainly not have commented on it himself, had he been its author.

But among the authors of works related to the practices of the tantras, there is none more celebrated than Nāgārjuna, a monk I have already had more than one occasion to mention. I find in the collection of Mr. Hodgson a book by this celebrated writer entitled *Pañcakrama* and to which is related a commentary having the title *Pañcakramaṭippanī*: it is a treatise written according to the principles of yoga tantra,[3] and which is exclusively dedicated to the exposition of the principal practices of the tantrika school. One learns there to draw magical figures named maṇḍalas, where the images of buddhas, bodhisattvas, and other fabulous personages appear, like Amitābha, Akṣobhya, Vairocana, Kṣitagarbha, Khagarbha, Vajrapāṇi, Lokeśa, Mañjughoṣa, Samantabhadra, Sarvanivaraṇaviṣkambhin, personages who, as I have said, are totally unknown to the sūtras and ancient legends, and who appear only in the developed sūtras and the tantras. The author

2. Section 2, pp. 230–31.
3. *Pañcakrama*, fol. 15b.

notes the importance of maxims like this one: "My own nature is that of the diamond of the science of emptiness" or "of the precious science of emptiness,"[4] and it is this very maxim that one must pronounce when one has drawn the diagram called *of the truth*. Each of these diagrams, that of the sun, for example, and of the other divinities, has its corresponding philosophical formula; this formula is always borrowed from the theories of the most absolute nihilism.

All the ideas, one sees, are commingled in this work, which, regardless of the author's name that it bears, belongs by its very content to the epoch when all the elements of Buddhism were completely developed. What dominates there, however, is the doctrine of the tantras, with its absurd formulas and its unintelligible monosyllables. It is difficult to express the type of discouragement one experiences upon reading such a composition. It is a sad thing to see serious men propose the most bizarre syllables and words as means of salvation and moral perfection. And what morality, other than that of indifference and a quietism so exaggerated that the distinction between the just and the unjust, good and evil, no longer exists for one who has attained it! This book, indeed, leads the ascetic by degrees to excesses that, I am deeply convinced, are completely foreign to primitive Buddhism. I shall cite only one example, borrowed from the final chapter, which deals with indifference, the practice to which all efforts of the ascetic must aim. "For the ascetic, an enemy or himself, his wife or his daughter, his mother or a prostitute . . . all this is the same thing!"[5] The pen refuses to transcribe doctrines as miserable in form as they are odious and degrading in content. Moreover, everything in this work should not be unequivocally attributed to Nāgārjuna, for I find the name Śākyamitra at the end of a chapter.[6] Perhaps this latter name is also only a title of Nāgārjuna. The light that such a treatise is able to cast on the other monuments of Buddhist literature is, one understands, very weak. The only information I find in it is a quotation from the *Lalitavistara*, with its title *mahāyāna sūtra*.[7] As for the commentary, which is very short and which does not extend to the totality of the work, it has the paṇḍita Parahitarakṣita as its author.

The collection of Nepal offers us still other traces of the part that Nāgārjuna played in the development of the philosophical literature of the Buddhists. Thus, we have in one of the volumes of this collection definitive proof that he composed works of metaphysics, and that these works even acquired enough authority to become the object of the efforts of commentators. I wish to speak about a volume belonging today to the Bibliothèque royale and bearing the title *Vinaya-*

4. *Pañcakrama*, fol. 4a.
5. *Pañcakrama*, fol. 33b.
6. *Pañcakrama*, fol. 26a.
7. *Pañcakrama*, fol. 23b.

patra on the first leaf and that of *Vinayasūtra* in the list of the books discovered and collected by Mr. Hodgson.[8] But neither of these titles is found in the work itself; the only one I encountered at the end of the chapters is *Madhyamakavṛtti*, or the "Explanation of the Madhyamaka, or Madhyamika Doctrine," a work composed by the ācārya Candrakīrti. Some lines of introduction indicate to us that the *Madhyamakavṛtti* is a commentary that deals with the *kārikās*, or memorial axioms, of which Nāgārjuna is the author. It is most probably to these kārikās that the name *Vinayasūtra* or *Vinayapatra*, which has remained on our volume, despite the testimony of the manuscript itself, is applied. This treatise confirms the opinion of the Tibetans regarding the school called Madhyamika, a school whose origin they attribute to the ārya Śrī Nāgārjuna; for the commentator of the kārikās, after having announced that these axioms are by Nāgārjuna, adds that they belong to the Madhyamika school. It is even likely that we have here the original work, or at least one of the principal treatises of Nāgārjuna; for Csoma indicates to us that according to the Tibetans, Candrakīrti, of whom, however, he says nothing more, wrote a commentary on the principal book of Nāgārjuna.[9] Now, as our manuscript contains axioms of Nāgārjuna explained by Candrakīrti in a work that has the form of a running commentary, we have every reason to believe that this is the treatise, or if one wishes, a treatise analogous to the one indicated by the Tibetan tradition.

The axioms of Nāgārjuna are generally cited only briefly by the commentator; nevertheless, and although the manuscript is quite incorrect, it is easy to see what the opinions of the primitive author and his commentator are; it is at bottom the same doctrine as that of the *Prajñāpāramitā*, pushed even further, if that is possible. Thus, among the *Prajñā* texts, the commentator cites those which assert most clearly that absolutely nothing exits; it is he who, for example, cites this axiom reported above: "The Buddha himself is like an illusion."[10] One can define the doctrine of Nāgārjuna as a scholastic nihilism. This philosopher does not let stand any of the theses posed in the various Buddhist schools, on the world, beings, laws, and the soul; he shatters positive, negative, and indifferent assertions, placing them in doubt; nothing is spared, God and the Buddha, mind and man, nature and the world. It is probably to this Pyrrhonism that his school owes the name Madhyamika (intermediate); it indeed places itself between the affirmative and the negative; when speaking about things, it established that it is no more possible to affirm than to deny their eternity. One is at pains to comprehend how this book can claim to be one of the authorities of the doctrine of

8. "Notices of the Languages, Literature and Religion of the Bauddhas of Nepal and Bhot," in *Asiatic Researches*, vol. 16, p. 431.

9. "Notices of Different Systems of Buddhism," in *Journal of the Asiatic Society of Bengal*, vol. 7, p. 144.

10. *Vinayasūtra*, fol. 136b.

Śākyamuni. It seems that a brahman wishing to reduce this doctrine to nothing could not do better than to adopt the negative arguments of Nāgārjuna and his commentator.

Moreover, a treatise of this type always has a particular kind of merit for us, regardless of the more or less considerable value of the content; this merit is that it cites monks or commentators who otherwise would be completely unknown to us. While awaiting other works that show us their names, accompanied by whatever circumstances suitable to fix their dates more or less rigorously, I believe it useful to mention them here: they are the ācārya Buddhapālita,[11] Āryadeva,[12] and the ācārya Bhāvaviveka.[13] The first two are known among the Tibetans as the principle disciples of Nāgārjuna, which places them four hundred years after the Buddha, like their master.[14] These three authors, only because Candrakīrti cites them in his commentary, are previous to the epoch in which he wrote.

The gloss of Candrakīrti abounds in citations of canonical works like the *Prajñāpāramitā* and other sūtras; but these works are those I attribute to the second age of the sacred literature: these are Mahāyāna sūtras. It is not my plan to reproduce these citations here; I believe it useful, however, to give two of them as specimens of the doctrine that the commentator intends to support above all. I only warn the reader that the manuscript I use is extremely incorrect, and that I have been obliged to omit a word that is found, it is true, in an enumeration of similar terms and probably has little importance.

"Here is what is said in the book entitled *Ratnacūḍāparipṛcchā.* Examining thought (or the mind, *citta*), he seeks to recognize its edge.[15] Where does the origin of thought come from, he says to himself. Here is the idea he has: When there is an [exterior] support, thought appears. But what? Is the support one thing, and thought another thing? No, that which is the support, that is thought itself. If on the contrary, something else was the support, something else was thought, then there would be double thought: thus that which is the support is thought itself. But how can man see thought with his thought? Thought does not see thought. It is, for example, like a blade of a given sword that cannot cut this same blade; it is like the end of a given finger that cannot touch this same finger: in the same way, a given thought cannot see this same thought. It is in this way that, engaged in this meditation in a profound manner, he really sees thought's quality

11. *Ibid.*, fols. 4a, 6b, and 10a.

12. *Ibid.*, fol. 4b.

13. *Ibid.*, fol. 10a.

14. Csoma, "Notices of Different Systems of Buddhism," in *Journal of the Asiatic Society of Bengal*, vol. 7, p. 144.

15. This expression is explained by the continuation of the text; it is a figure borrowed from the shape of a sword whose blade, as our author says, cannot cut itself. He employs this figure to show that thought cannot see itself.

of not having a place to rest, of not being interrupted or permanent, of not being absolute, of not being without cause, of not being stopped by an occasional cause.[16] . . . He sees there, I say, the edge of thought, its character, its condition; he sees the quality it possesses, to have no place to rest, to be passing, invisible, contained in itself. It is in this way that he sees the true reality, and he does not suppress it; he really knows, he really sees the special character of thought. It is there, O son of good family, looking at thought with thought, and not an act of the presence of the memory."[17]

I have cited this passage because it contains two of the most characteristic features of Buddhist psychology. The first is that thought or the mind (for the faculty is not distinguished here from the subject) appears only with sensation and does not survive it; the other, that the mind cannot grasp itself, and by looking at it, it only derives the conviction of its impotence to see itself as other than passing and as successive: two theses of which the second is but a consequence of the first, and which are radically contrary to the opinions of the brahmans, for whom the perpetuity of the thinking subject is an article of faith.

The second piece, which is even shorter, is borrowed from a sūtra entitled *Ratnakūṭa Sūtra*. I cite it because it gives an idea of the dialectic of the developed sūtras.

"Thought or the mind (*citta*), O Kāśyapa, is taken as the object to seek; what is not grasped [by the senses] is not perceived; what is not perceived is neither past, nor future, nor present; what is neither past, nor future, nor present has no particular nature; what has no particular nature has no origin; what has no origin has no destruction."[18]

This argumentation rests entirely on the thesis that the mind does not perceive itself through direct and external observation, the only one accepted by the Buddhists. Hence, the route is neither long nor difficult to conclude that the mind does not exist. Moreover, the method and the philosophical point of view of Buddhism allow themselves to be easily recognized in this piece as well as in the previous one. That which seems to have struck the Buddhists above all, that which entirely dominates their manner of philosophizing, is the fact, accepted by them, that experience only gives particular knowledge, that it furnishes only multiplicity, a dispersed multiplicity, if I can express myself in this way, and facts detached from one another, subjectively and objectively. The consideration of this principle has been decisive, from what appears to me, for their entire philosophy, and it has exerted a profound influence on the notions they have about things.

16. Here I omit some unreadable syllables.
17. *Vinayasūtra*, fol. 18a.
18. *Vinayasūtra*, fol. 11b.

The examination of the *Vinayasūtra*, or rather of the *Madhyamikavṛtti*, a commentary on the *Vinayasūtra*, despite the interest it offers for the study of the most developed metaphysics of Buddhism, due to its extreme specialty, still allows one to understand only imperfectly the full benefit one can draw from reading the commentators devoted to the explanation of either canonical books or of works composed by modern authors. It is necessary, to form an idea of it, to browse through a most voluminous compilation I have mentioned several times in the course of these memoranda, and which contains more details on Buddhist philosophy than it would be possible for me to set forth here without greatly exceeding the limits of this present work. I wish to speak of the enormous volume entitled *Dharmakośavyākhyā* owned by the Société Asiatique. This book is, as its title indicates, the commentary on an older work whose title is *Abhidharmakośa*, the "Treasure of the Superior Law or of Metaphysics," and the author, Vasubandhu. This work, which is composed of four hundred eighty-four leaves, or nine hundred sixty-eight pages in folio, must have enjoyed considerable authority among Buddhist monks; for it is regarded as the summary of a great number of glosses on metaphysics, and its author, Vasubandhu, receives in it the illustrious title "wise like a second Buddha." The writer of the commentary is called Yaśomitra, and the commentary itself has the title *Sphuṭārthā*, "That Whose Sense Is Clear."

The most general observations among those that the examination of this voluminous treatise has suggested to me encompass three principal points. The first concerns the writing and the system of the commentator; the second, the indications he gives of other works, regardless of the subject he treats; the third conveys the subject itself. As far as the writing and the system of the commentator are concerned, it must be recognized that he belongs to the good school of Indian glossarists. Yaśomitra certainly possessed all the resources of the Sanskrit language, and he made excellent use of them for the explanation of the primitive text. His gloss is at once grammatical and philosophical. For grammar, he follows the school of Pāṇini; and as for the philosophical system, he develops the opinions set forth or only suggested in those canonical books called sūtras. From that comes the quality of Sautrāntika, or philosopher of the school of the sūtras, which he assumes in a great number of passages. From this point of view, the indications contained in this commentary are as numerous as they are varied, and one finds on almost every page more or less lengthy fragments of these treatises, several of which are found in the volumes we have in Paris. The examination of such a book to my eyes shields the authenticity of the sūtras from all contestation; and it renders the sacred literature of the Buddhists a service of the same kind as the philosophical commentaries of the brahmans render the Vedas, which they cite at every moment.

Yaśomitra accepts the division of Buddhist scriptures into three great classes, the gathering of which is called *tripiṭaka*,[19] "the three baskets." I have spoken above about this division, and I have also indicated the existence of the tradition related to the eighty-four thousand texts of the law, according to a passage borrowed from the very work I examine at this moment. He sets forth in a manner as detailed as it is interesting the different sources of the Abhidharma, and shows that the work of extracting from the preaching of Śākyamuni all the passages related to metaphysics, in order to form a body specially distinguished by the title *abhidharma*, goes back very far and is almost contemporary with Śākyamuni, since several of his foremost disciples are considered to have gathered the principles of high philosophy in a scientific form.[20] I cited above, in the section related to metaphysics, this piece, which I regard as very important for the literary history of the first times of Buddhism. Although the treatises whose titles it provides are, for the present, completely unknown, I believed it was good to refer to them in the chapter just mentioned, because if they ever reach Europe, their place will be marked in the series of works from which one must draw knowledge of the metaphysics of Buddhism. Now, it is permissible not to renounce the hope of recovering them one day, when one considers how unexpected was Mr. Hodgson's discovery, made before our eyes, of this important mass of works of which no one before him suspected the existence, and when one reflects on the richness of some of the libraries of Tibet, where, according to Csoma de Kőrös, such considerable collections of Sanskrit and Tibetan books are kept. But what is important to note at the moment is the great development that the study of metaphysics had taken at the time of Śākyamuni himself; for among the authors of the treatises mentioned by the commentary with which we are occupied, there are five, namely Kātyāyanīputra, Śāriputra, Maudgalyāyana, Pūrṇa, Mahākauṣṭhilya, who appear among the foremost disciples of the Buddha in the sūtras and avadānas. The works of these authors form a group of texts accepted as an authority for those Buddhists who occupy themselves exclusively with the Abhidharma. But this authority is not so imperative that it is not permissible to go back further, that is to say, to seek the principles of philosophy in the sūtras themselves. Our commentator is of this latter sentiment, and this is what explains, as I have just indicated, the title *Sautrāntika*, or philosopher of the school of the sūtras, which he assumes each time there is a question of an important or controversial point of doctrine. These ancient monks decorated with the title *ārya*, "respectables," or *sthavira*, "elders," are in some way the apostles and first fathers of the Buddhist church; but they cede their authority to that of the inspired books, which the tradition dates back to the teaching of the Master himself.

19. Above, section 1, p. 84.

20. *Abhidharmakośavyākhyā*, fol. 8a.

It would be impossible for me to note, in this rapid examination, all the citations of sūtras and other treatises that enrich the commentary of Yaśomitra. These citations, sometimes rather developed, other times very brief, would only prove to us the vast reading and orthodoxy of our author. I shall content myself with adding to the extracts that I have just made from them, two passages that cast daylight on some parts of the Buddhist collection in general. In one of these passages, the commentator speaks of sūtras known by the title *Arthavargīya*, and which belong to the *Kṣudraka*.[21] It is quite probable that these sūtras, judging by their title, deal with temporal objects, objects arranged under the generic name *artha* by all the schools of India. This conjecture is almost turned into certitude by this fact, that the collection named *Kṣudraka*, which is translated in the Tibetan collection of the Kah-gyur, and which forms there a special section entitled *Vinayakṣudrakavastu*, "Small Details on Religious Discipline," treats, among other subjects, the customs and practices of the peoples of central India.[22] It would be most interesting for us to possess a treatise of this kind, if, however, the content corresponds exactly to the description given by Csoma. But the title alone that it bears furnishes us with elements whose full importance I would not be able to make felt until I compare the collection of the Pāli books of Ceylon to that of the Sanskrit books of the North. Let it suffice for me at the moment to say that the Sinhalese also possess the *Kṣudraka*, which they know under the Pāli title *Khuddaka*.

The second passage I desire to bring to the reader's attention is related to dreams that appeared, it says, to a certain king Kṛkin, dreams that Śākyamuni explains as presages of the future destinies of his religion. The commentator, before recounting these dreams, announces that their presentation is found in the Vinaya. I discovered them by chance exactly as Yaśomitra reports in the manuscript of the *Sumāgadhāvadāna*, that is to say, in the history of the beautiful woman of Magadha. This legend, which I have translated according to the Sanskrit text owing to the interesting details it provides about the first disciples of Śākyamuni, is found also in the Tibetan collection, from which I have extracted it and compared it word for word with the Sanskrit original.[23] But the Tibetan version, instead of placing this legend in the section of the Vinaya, or discipline, ranks it in the category of Sūtras. If our commentator is not mistaken in writing *vinaya* instead of *sūtra*, it will be noted, at least for this legend, that the compilers of the Kah-gyur did not follow the Nepalese classification very exactly. Moreover, that of the Kah-gyur itself is not absolutely rigorous; for one finds in the class of discipline legends that are more specially connected to morality

21. *Abhidharmakośavyākhyā*, fol. 28a.

22. Csoma, "Analysis of the Dul-va," in *Asiatic Researches*, vol. 20, pp. 85 and 86.

23. *Bka 'gyur*, sec. *Mdo*, vol. *ha* (29), p. 430. Perhaps I will publish this work on another occasion.

or philosophy, and which as such should have instead been placed among the Sūtras. What I nonetheless can conclude from this comparison is that I was not wrong to say, in analyzing the category of the Sūtras and that of the Vinaya, that the limits were not very rigorously marked; and this fact, added to those I have put forward in my description of the collection of Nepal, proves that the legends the Tibetans place in the Vinaya took their place in the category of the Sūtras among the Nepalese.

In addition to the ancient names of authors to whom I alluded above, the commentary of the *Abhidharmakośa* mentions others, some also ancient, others probably more modern. I notice, among others, the sthavira Aśvajit, who ordinarily appears in the enumerations of the listeners of Śākya that generally open the sūtras of Nepal;[24] I presume that this sage is contemporary with Śākya. I notice also the sthavira Dharmatrāta[25] and the sthavira Buddhadeva.[26] One finds more frequently the names of the *ācāryas*, or masters, Guṇamati and his disciple Vasumitra,[27] who commented on the *Abhidharmakośa* that he himself explains, those of the ācārya Saṃghabhadra,[28] bhadanta Śrīlābha,[29] probably the same as the ārya Śrīlābha,[30] bhadanta Rāma,[31] Rāma,[32] bhadanta Dharmatrāta,[33] the ārya Dharmagupta,[34] who is perhaps just the previous one, the ācārya Manoratha,[35] bhadanta Goṣaka.[36] Finding in his author's text the name bhadanta, which generally means "Buddhist" but designates in particular a respectable master,[37] in order to determine who this Bhadanta is, he devotes himself to a discussion I believe it useful to translate in order to make known, by a short example, our author's manner of commenting.

"*Bhadanta*," says the text, "is a certain sthavira of the school of the sūtras or it is his own name. But Bhagavadviśeṣa has claimed that this title designated the sthavira Dharmatrāta. To that we will respond in turn: the sthavira Dharmatrāta upholds the existence of past things and of future things; he is neither of the school of the sūtras nor of that of the similitudes. And, however, the text will say

24. *Abhidharmakośavyākhyā*, fol. 107b.
25. *Ibid.*, fol. 32a.
26. *Ibid.*, fol. 475b of my manuscript.
27. *Ibid.*, fols. 5a, 93b, 119a, 147b, 153a, 193b, 338b.
28. *Ibid.*, fol. 22a, 30b, 99b, 154a, 163b, 164b, 190a, 318b, 345a, 351a, 352b, 391b, 448b, 462a.
29. *Ibid.*, fols. 44b and 88b.
30. *Ibid.*
31. *Ibid.*, fols. 327b, 328a, 409b.
32. *Ibid.*, fols. 209b, 210a, 213b, 216a, 218b, 221a, 222b.
33. *Ibid.*, fol. 219b.
34. *Ibid.*, fol. 375b.
35. *Ibid.*, fol. 209a.
36. *Ibid.*, fol. 119a.
37. It is, to say in passing, from this title, which is among the Nepalese almost unique to Buddhist Sanskrit, that the Pāli title *bhanta*, which one ordinarily addresses to monks, is derived.

later: The respectable Dharmatrāta believes in the diversity of existences, since he has said: 'For the being who transmigrates in the three paths of time, there is diversity of existence and not diversity of substance.' Now the personage who is called by the title *bhadanta* is presented by the school of the Vibhāṣā as connected to the opinions of the Sautrāntikas, as one sees in various passages such as the following: 'The respectable one has said,' etc. I add that the respectable Dharmatrāta is mentioned by name in passages like this one: 'The respectable Dharmatrāta has said.' All of that proves that here, by *bhadanta*, the text wishes to designate a personage of the school of the sūtras other than Dharmatrāta; it so designates some sthavira or some monk [whose name is not given]."[38]

Among the monks mentioned in the preceding discussion, there is one whose name suggests to me a remark whose application can become of some interest; it is Vasumitra, the celebrated commentator on the *Abhidharmakośa*. The Mongols, according to Mr. Schmidt, know a Vischumitra contemporary with Kaniṣka, the king of Kashmir, whom they place three hundred years after the Buddha's entry into nirvāṇa; and they make him the chief of the third and final council, which, according to the tradition of the North, occupied itself with the redaction of the sacred scriptures and which admitted dhāraṇīs and magical formulas into the religious canon.[39] Klaproth, who hardly forgives such peccadilloes when he discovers them in others, replaces the *Vischumitra* of Mr. Schmidt with *Viṣṇumitra*, without alerting us whether *Viṣṇumitra* is the true reading of the Mongol texts.[40] The spelling preferred by Klaproth has the advantage of providing a regular name, while that of *Vischumitra* is manifestly corrupt. But the Mongol transcriptions are so negligently executed that *Vischumitra* could be a misspelling of Vasumitra. If this supposition came to be verified, the epoch of the monk Vasumitra would be related to that of the greatest events in the history of Buddhism; it is a point to which I intend to return in my Historical Sketch.

I find, in addition, two or three titles of works whose authors are not indicated, like the *Pañcaskandhaka*[41] and the *Nirgranthaśāstra*.[42] The first is certainly a Buddhist book, but the second is most probably a work foreign to the belief of the Buddha, for in the legend of the *Sumāgadhāvadāna* I find the title *nirgrantha* employed with the meaning it has in Sanskrit, to designate a brahman mendicant. It is not the only work opposed to Buddhism that our author mentions: thus, he makes allusion in one place to the *Śatarudrīya*, which he says is the work of Vyāsa.[43] This *Śatarudrīya* is probably the hymn of the hundred rudras, a

38. *Abhidharmakośavyākhyā*, fol. 32a; and MS of the Société Asiatique, fol. 36b.
39. Schmidt, *Geschichte der Ost-Mongolen*, pp. 17 and 315.
40. *Foe koue ki*, p. 248.
41. *Abhidharmakośavyākhyā*, fol. 224a.
42. *Ibid.*, fol. 192a.
43. *Ibid.*, fol. 172a.

Vedic piece that appears among the Upaniṣads and that belongs to the collection translated from the Persian by Anquetil du Perron.[44] Our commentator speaks about several Indian sects that seem to have existed in his time, like the Pāṇḍaras, the Pāśupatas, the Kāpālikas.[45] He frequently refutes the Vaiśeṣikas, a name that doubtless indicates the atomist philosophers of the Sāṃkhya school, who recognize Kaṇāda as their founder.

He accepts that there exists among the Buddhists a rather great variety of opinions on several points, and he sometimes notes various theses on which all schools agree, as for example, when he says that *hemanta*, "winter" (November, December), is the first of the seasons for all Buddhists.[46] Those that he mentions most often, either to refute or only to note divergences of sentiment, are the Buddhists of Kashmir, those of Ceylon, and the Vātsīputrīyas. The Kāśmīras are named in more than one place;[47] the author calls them *foreigners*;[48] and in a passage in which he refutes philosophers that he says are modern, he depicts them as recently coming from Kashmir;[49] it is true that the expression he uses: *pāścātyāḥ paścādbhavāḥ*, can still better signify "westerners." Whatever meaning we choose, it is permissible to conclude from this term that the work we examine was composed in India: the latter version would make one suppose that our author wrote in a province situated to the east of Kashmir. I also believe I recognize the Buddhists of Ceylon in the Tāmraparṇīyas, or inhabitants of Tāmraparṇa, the Taprobane of the ancients, mentioned in a passage where our commentator expresses himself in this way: "The Tāmraparṇīyas make the substance of the heart (*hṛdaya*) the asylum of knowledge and the intellect, *manas*."[50] Elsewhere, he uses this remarkable expression: "The text says *in all the other books*, which means the books of the Tāmraparṇīyas and others"[51]; from which I conclude that the collections (*nikāyas*) of Ceylon were known to the Buddhists of the North, and that they had enough importance in their eyes to be mentioned first when it was a question of collectively designating Buddhist works other than those whose authority was accepted in India.

As for the Vātsīputrīyas, who appear often in this work and who ordinarily are refuted, it is a name as interesting for the history of Buddhism as those I have mentioned previously. I do not doubt that they are the monks forming the third subdivision of the school that originally recognized Upāli as its founder.[52] They

44. *Oupnek'hat*, 2:171ff.
45. *Abhidharmakośavyākhyā*, fols. 217a and b.
46. *Ibid.*, fol. 241b.
47. *Ibid.*, fols. 61b, 121a, 469a of my manuscript.
48. *Ibid.*, fol. 95a of my manuscript.
49. *Ibid.*, fol. 115a of my manuscript, *pāścātyaḥ kaśmīra maṇḍalāt paścādbhavāḥ*.
50. *Abhidharmakośavyākhyā*, fol. 28b of my manuscript; fol. 32b of the MS of the Société Asiatique.
51. *Ibid.*, fol. 474a of my manuscript.
52. Csoma, "Notices on the Life of Shakya," in *Asiatic Researches*, vol. 20, p. 298.

are unquestionably the same as the sectarians called *Pocuo fuluo* by the Chinese, and about whom Klaproth has inserted a note in the *Foe koue ki* that unfortunately is not very clear.[53] This name, according to the Chinese, means "calf" and has become that of a family; this is perfectly correct, and the patronymic Vātsīputrīya indeed really has its origin in the word *vatsa* (calf). Klaproth makes of this title a category of books that support the existence of the self, contrary to the opinion of the greatest number of Buddhist schools. Moreover, the commentator of the *Abhidharmakośa* speaks about the Vātsīputrīya as perfectly known personages of his time.[54] There is even one passage where he seems to assimilate them in part into the Madhyamikas, that is to say, into the philosophers who follow the Madhyamika system, which owes its origin to Nāgārjuna. In the passage to which I allude, after having spoken of an opinion attributed to some Vātsīputrīyas, he adds: "That means those who have the ideas of the Madhyamikas."[55] There are thus Vātsīputrīyas who follow the school of the Madhyamikas.

Moreover, we do not need this passage to be convinced that our author knew Nāgārjuna, for it is obviously he that he designates with the name sthavira Nāgasena, whose opinion he harshly criticizes at one point.[56] We will see, in speaking of the Sinhalese collection, that Nāgasena is celebrated among the Buddhists of the South; and Benfey has already conjectured rightly, without having the work that occupies us before his eyes, that the Nāgasena, who according to the Sinhalese Buddhists converted the king of Sagala, is the same as the Nāgārjuna of the Buddhists of the North.[57] There is in addition a decisive reason to believe that Yaśomitra could not have been unaware of the existence of Nāgārjuna; it is that in more than one place, he speaks of the Madhyamika system, which, according to the commentator of the *Vinayasūtra*, owes its origin to Nāgārjuna. We will conclude also from all this that our author is more modern than this great philosopher, that is to say, that he came after all the events that had an influence on the destinies of Northern Buddhism. His work, it is true, bears rather few traces of these events, among which he mentions, to my

53. *Foe koue ki*, p. 326.

54. *Abhidharmakośavyākhyā*, fols. 56b, 311b, 470b, 471a, 476b, 477a of my manuscript.

55. *Ibid.*, fol. 477a of my manuscript.

56. *Ibid.*, fol. 475b of my manuscript.

57. "Indien," p. 85, extract of the *Encyclopédie* of Ersch and Gruber. It is probably our Nāgārjuna whose name the Chinese or their interpreters transcribe as *Naqieheshuna*. This sage would have appeared eight hundred years after the nirvāṇa of Śākyamuni, and one of his disciples would have composed the book entitled *Bailun*, or the *Hundred Discourses* (A. Rémusat, *Foe koue ki*, p. 159). Elsewhere, this sage is called *bodhisattva* (*Ibid.*, pp. 162 and 177). This name *Naqieheshuna* certainly offers a rather great similarity to that of Nāgārjuna, and the hundred discourses seems to recall the collection *Śatasāhasrikā*. What is also worthy of remark is the date of eight hundred years after Śākya that the Chinese assign to the coming of this sage. I conclude, as I will try to show in my Historical Sketch, that the Chinese Buddhists who have adopted this date wished to reconcile what they knew of the real epoch of *Naqieheshuna* with the date that they previously accepted for the epoch of Śākyamuni.

knowledge, only the third of the councils where the Buddhist scriptures were submitted to a new revision.[58]

These indications are still not sufficient to allow us to fix the age and the homeland of Yaśomitra with precision; but it is necessary to also acknowledge that the purely philosophical subject to which his work is dedicated is not one of those where historical facts generally come to take place. This subject itself is not easy to follow because of the form of the commentary, which takes each word of the text separately and develops it or drowns it in a gloss that ordinarily is very long. It is only very rarely possible to distinguish the text from these commentaries, among which it is lost. The work of Vasubandhu that Yaśomitra proposes to explain is itself a composition written about previous sūtras. This composition is probably only a commentary; at least, this is what we would be permitted to conclude from the words of Yaśomitra, the latter commentator, who expresses himself in this way: "Many sūtras are omitted because the exposition of the text is lost; here the master has not commented."[59] The *master* is without doubt none other than Vasubandhu, the author of the *Abhidharmakośa*; and this passage, if it must be understood as I propose, gives light to the nature and the form of Vasubandu's treatise, quite difficult to find in other parts of Yaśomitra's gloss.

Be that as it may, this work is a compilation of philosophical texts and interpretations. The author deals with the general characters of beings, conditions, and laws, for the word *dharma* means all these things; of sensible qualities, the senses, the elements, sensation, and knowledge; of the succession of effects and causes; affection, hate, error, and other moral modifications of the subject; of the birth of man, destiny, the fruit of deeds, the passage of man through the different paths of existence; of the different degrees of virtue and intelligence man can attain in this world; of the action of the organs of sense on the fact of knowledge, and of the conditions that arrest or favor this action; of man and woman considered from the physical perspective; of the passions, and the necessity of taming them; of pleasure and pain, of the necessity of freeing oneself from them to reach nirvāṇa, that is to say, the perfection of absolute repose; of the conditions of human existence and the functions of the organs; of *pravṛtti* (action) and *nivṛtti* (repose); of the different degrees of humanity as far as instruction is concerned, and the relative perfection of the senses of man; of supernatural faculties; of the passage of superior intelligences through the different degrees of existence; of the devas and the numerous categories into which they are divided; of the

58. *Abhidharmakośavyākhyā*, fol. 197a of my manuscript. The text designates this council with the very name that the Buddhists of the South give to these kinds of assemblies: *tṛtīyaṃ dharmasaṃgītim anupraviśya*; but nothing indicates to us the date of this council, and one does not know if the author wishes to designate that which the Sinhalese Buddhists place 218 years after Śākya, or that of the Buddhists of the North, four hundred years since the death of the Master.

59. *Abhidharmakośavyākhyā*, fol. 157a of my manuscript.

hells and the worlds. These subjects, none of which is examined in a coherent, much less a dogmatic manner, are intermingled with one another, and the same matter appears at several points in the work. The doctrine belongs manifestly to the most ancient school of Buddhism, that is to say, to the atheist school. I find on the question of the existence of God a very striking passage, which leaves no doubt on the tendency of this work or at least on the ideas of the latter commentator. I believe that this passage deserves to be translated as a specimen of the method that Yaśomitra follows when his duties as commentator leave him enough leisure to speak in his own name.

"Beings are neither created by God (*īśvara*) nor by mind (*puruṣa*), nor by matter (*pradhāna*). If, indeed, God was the only cause, this god being Mahādeva, Vāsudeva, or any other principle like mind or matter, then by the sole fact of the existence of this cause, it would be necessary that the world was created in its totality at once; for one cannot accept the cause without its effect existing. But one sees beings coming successively into the world, some from a womb, others from a bud; from that one must conclude that there is a succession of causes, and that God is not the only cause. But, one objects, this variety of causes is the effect of the will of God, who has said: 'May this being be born now, in such a way that another is then born'; it is in this way that the succession of beings is explained and that proves that God is its cause. To that, one responds that to accept several acts of the will of God is to accept several causes, and that destroys the first thesis, that there is only one cause. There is more: this plurality of causes can be produced only at once, since God, the source of the distinct acts of will that have produced this variety of causes, is one and indivisible. Here again appears the objection just made, namely, that it would be necessary to accept that the world has been created at once. But the sons of Śākya hold this maxim, that the revolution of the world has no beginning."[60]

This passage is remarkable in several respects, and the most rapid examination suffices to recognize how the theory it expresses is far from the pantheistic naturalism of the principal Brahmanical schools; but the consequences that one is able to draw for the history of Buddhism itself must occupy us above all. It is evident that the work from which this passage is borrowed belongs to the most ancient of the philosophical systems of the Buddhists, to that which reproduces in the most faithful manner the first attempts made to regularize through speculation the purely metaphysical elements of this belief; and as for the commentary on this work, I believe it to be earlier than the four great sects into which the philosophers of Nepal are divided today. I draw this conclusion from the fact that Yaśomitra does not mention them once by name. The absence of the title *Aiśvarika* (Deist) seems conclusive to me, above all after the passage we just read

60. *Abhidharmakośavyākhyā*, fol. 171a of my manuscript.

touching on the question of the existence of God. Will one say that if the author does not make any allusion to the Ādibuddha of the Aiśvarikas, it is possible to explain his silence by conceding that, exclusively occupied with the system he had adopted, he does not have occasion to deal with a theory that is not his? This explanation would be insufficient in my opinion, and I am convinced that the system of an ādibuddha could not have existed at the time of Yaśomitra without his speaking of it in his commentary. If, thus, wishing to combat the belief in the existence of God, he has only mentioned the Mahādeva of the Śivaists, the Vāsudeva of the Viṣṇuvites, the mind or matter of the Sāṃkhya school, it is that he has not found in Buddhism itself the belief in the existence of God, which was, however, in the interest of his system to refute where he found it. These considerations lead me to think that the work of Vasumitra, with the commentary of Yaśomitra that accompanies it, are both earlier than the epoch when belief in a supreme God was established in Buddhism, a belief that Csoma does not date further back than the end of the tenth century of our era. On the other side, since our author mentions the school of the Yogācāras whose founder, Ārya Saṃgha, lived, according to the Tibetans, from the sixth to the seventh century of our era, our commentator is necessarily later than this latter personage, and we must place his gloss between the sixth and the tenth centuries of our era, around the end of the Middle Ages of Buddhist literature.

SECTION 7

History of the Collection of Nepal

The history of the sacred collection of Nepal is not recorded in any of the books of which this collection is composed; and this is no reason for surprise, if one examines only those books regarded as inspired, that is to say, as emanated from the preaching of Śākyamuni. Indeed, it must be one or the other: either these books are in reality contemporary with Śākya, and then the historical information we would hope to find there can concern only these two points, the date itself of the books, if it is given, and the indication of some events contemporary with the redaction; or these books were composed long after Śākya and attributed by popular faith to the founder of Buddhism, and then it is easy to understand that all the indications that could betray their modern origin were carefully excluded. But since the collection of Nepal contains works other than inspired books, since one finds, for example, treatises composed by authors whose names are celebrated, it is permissible to regret that one of these writers did not compose a history of Buddhist books, a history for which the tradition and the knowledge of these books themselves supplied a Buddhist with material that perhaps will be impossible for us to ever gather.

Is it thus true to say with Mr. Wilson that history is even more foreign, if that is possible, to the books of the Buddhists than to those of the brahmans?[1] This is not the place to discuss in detail a question whose examination will naturally find its place in the Historical Sketch of Buddhism; I must confine myself here

1. "Abstract of the Contents of the Dul-va," in *Journal of the Asiatic Society of Bengal*, vol. 1, p. 6.

to what touches especially on the sacred collection of Nepal, as Mr. Hodgson has made it known to us. Yet while accepting that this collection cannot pride itself in possessing a work as really historical as the *Mahāvaṃsa* of the Sinhalese Buddhists, or the *Rājataraṃginī* of the Kashmiri Brahmans, it is no less true to say that the Buddhist books of the North contain even more history, or in a more general manner, are able to better serve the history of Buddhism than those of the brahmans do for that of Brahmanism. Is it not already an advantage for these books to be so decidedly later than they are to the definitive establishment of Indian society and to the development of the sacred literature of the brahmans? Have we not seen above, in analyzing the sūtras, how these works contain allusions to the state of Brahmanical society, to the sacred literature, and finally to the men amid whom they were preached or written? It is this that in general distinguishes the religious compositions of the Buddhists from those of the brahmans. Never descending from heaven and remaining constantly in the vague regions of mythology where the reader grasps only vain forms that are no longer possible for him to fix in time or space, the sacred books of the Buddhists ordinarily present us with a series of entirely human events, a kṣatriya who makes himself an ascetic, who does battle with brahmans, who teaches and converts kings whose names these books have preserved for us.[2] The only Brahmanical monuments that can compete with the books of the Buddhists in this regard are the most authentic portions of the old epics, dramas, and some collections of stories.[3]

In order for the various indications that present themselves in the books of Nepal with the striking character of reality to become true history, it suffices that some of the personages mentioned in the Buddhist books are well known from elsewhere, and that the epoch when they lived is determined by means independent from these books themselves. Where, indeed, must we search for the points to which the redactors of the Buddhist works would have linked the events whose memory they have preserved for us, if not in the general history of India? But if this history did not yet exist at their time, can we reproach them for knowing it less well than those who should have composed it? Thus, far from accusing the Buddhists of being greater strangers to all notions of true history than the brahmans themselves, it must be said that if there is no factual history in their books, there was none in those of their adversaries; for if there had existed in India a slightly developed corpus, at the time when Buddhism appeared, the realistic spirit of this doctrine, its materialism and even its ordinariness, which

2. Lassen, *Zeitschrift für die Kunde des Morgenlandes*, 4:503 and 504.

3. I allude here to the collection entitled *Kathāsaritsāgara*, whose publication is due to the care of Mr. H. Brockhaus. Several of the tales contained in this collection offer striking analogies with some of our legends. I indicate, among others, that of Udāyana, whose capital was Kauśambhī. The Buddhist tradition makes him contemporary with Śākyamuni. I will return to this interesting synchronism in the Historical Sketch.

here are qualities, its position as a reform of a previous order of things, all these circumstances in short, would have compelled the redactors of the sacred texts to give all desirable precision to the facts whose memory they believed it useful to preserve.

I thus persuade myself that by noting with care the names of the kings who attended the teaching of Śākya, and those of the brahmans who resisted him or who made themselves his disciples, by recalling the place where he was born and where he lived, and by determining with a remarkable precision the theater of his preaching, the redactors of the sacred books obeyed a historical instinct that one would seek in vain in the compositions of the brahmans, where gods take such a place that man and his history disappear completely. Finally, there is a decisive fact, entirely to the advantage of Buddhist literature: it is that the history of India begins to become clear only in the epoch of Śākyamuni. Starting with this sage, central India is covered with truly historical monuments and inscriptions; one sees precious synchronisms being established between this country and the history of Occidental peoples; in the end, the Buddhist books are enriched with details and indications of a truly factual character, which are still the most interesting of those we possess on the state of India beginning from about the sixth century before our era. I add that, although based on the personal study of the Buddhist books, the appreciation I express for it here is not peculiar to me; Benfey dates the history of India from the epoch of Śākya; and Lassen, in his research on the antiquities of this country, also takes this epoch as the certain point of departure for all works related to the history of India in the times before and after the last buddha.[4]

The preceding remarks not only have the object of placing the Buddhist books in their true light; they are also intended to explain why it is not necessary to search in them for the history of the collection to which they belong. One will find in them, as I have proved by the analysis of the sūtras, the picture of Indian society at the time when Śākyamuni lived, and apart from these general notions, the precise indication of the personages whom he attracted through his preaching. These are precious elements that I will strive to make use of in my Historical Sketch of Indian Buddhism. But they do not indicate anything about the date of the books where we encounter them, since these books could have been written quite long after the events they report. The sole assistance we possess in order to study the history of the sacred books of Nepal is the information that the tradition has passed on to us and that with which the detailed examination of these books themselves furnishes us. It is from this double source that the facts are

4. Benfey, *Göttingische gelehrte Anzeigen*, May 1841, p. 746ff. and especially pp. 748 and 749. Lassen, *Indische Alterthumskunde*, 1:471. One is unable to study the excellent remarks of this latter scholar too much. I will return to them in my Historical Sketch of Indian Buddhism.

drawn for this abbreviated picture I will present in this section, the last, which is dedicated to the study of the Buddhist collection of the North.

By tradition, I understand here not only the ensemble of opinions and facts that Mr. Hodgson has collected in Nepal, in his conversations with educated Buddhists, or in the study he has made of their books, but the opinions and facts recognized by the Buddhists of the North in general, and in particular by the Tibetans. I have already said how I believed myself to be authorized to invoke the testimony of the Tibetans every time it is a question of Northern Buddhism, although the works taken as authoritative among this people are only translations of Sanskrit texts and these translations are not previous to the seventh century of our era. I content myself with adding here that this date of the seventh century is the last limit at which, in modern times, the history of the sacred collection of the Northern Buddhists stops. This limit is not absolutely rigorous, since all the translations that took their place in the Tibetan library of the Kah-gyur were carried out, according to Csoma de Kőrös, between the seventh and the ninth centuries of our era, and the work of interpretation continued still later. But however fluctuating it is, it assures to the most important part of the Nepalese collection several more centuries of existence than one would perhaps be tempted to accord it when only considering the date of 1822, the year Mr. Hodgson discovered it in the valley of Nepal. Who knows if one of these critics who, in order to judge the history of a people, believes himself to be excused from knowing its language and its literature, would not have concluded, after long meditations, in convincing himself that the Buddhist collection of Nepal has been fabricated quietly at the beginning of the nineteenth century, with a view to consummate the fraud that had been so successful for the brahmans, when some time previously, they had created a literature for themselves in order to deceive the English whom they saw approaching and above all, to lead astray the European governments, who have the naïvete to pay some scholars to teach languages that have never been spoken and literatures that no one has composed?

At the end of the section of the Vinaya, or discipline, which opens the collection of the Kah-gyur, one finds details of great interest concerning the facts, so important for the question that occupies us, of the writing of the books that are the repository of Śākya's teaching. These details, obviously preserved by the tradition, inform us that there were, at three different epochs, three successive redactions of the Buddhist scriptures, redactions made by monks gathered in council, and invested, it seems, by public assent, with the authority necessary for this major work. The first redaction took place immediately after the death of Śākyamuni, not far from Rājagṛha, through the efforts of five hundred monks who had Kāśyapa as their chief.[5] The task of gathering the word of the Master

5. Csoma, "Analysis of the Dul-va," in *Asiatic Researches*, vol. 20, pp. 41, 91, and 297.

was divided among three of his principal disciples, whose names always figure in the legends. It was Kāśyapa who wrote the Abhidharma, or metaphysics, Ānanda compiled the Sūtras, and Upāli, the Vinaya.[6] The second redaction of the sacred books took place one hundred and ten years after the death of Śākya, at the time of Aśoka, who reigned at Pāṭaliputra. Discord was introduced among the monks of Vaiśālī, and seven hundred arhats felt it necessary to gather in order to write down the canonical scriptures anew.[7] Finally, a little more than four hundred years after Śākya, at the time of Kaniṣka, who is said to have been the king in the north of India, the Buddhists were separated into eighteen sects who grouped themselves into four great principal divisions, the names of which Csoma has preserved for us. These discords gave rise to a new compilation of the scriptures, which was the third and last of those of which the Tibetans speak.[8]

However brief these details may be, whatever difficulties they may even create, if one compares them to those preserved for us by the Sinhalese on analogous events, they are already, taken in themselves, fecund with precious consequences for the history of the Buddhist collection of the North. One must conclude first that of the three redactions whose memory the tradition has preserved for us, we possess only the last; or to express myself with an indispensable reserve, in view of the silence of the Buddhist writers, one is able to say that the books that we actually have before our eyes are either ancient works belonging to the previous redactions but revised under the influence of the last one, or works quite new and coming exclusively from the work of the third assembly. It is permissible to doubt, as Lassen has judiciously remarked, that the canon of scriptures had been fixed in full as early as the first council in such a way as to include, since this epoch, the totality of what is comprised there today.[9] I believe that the truth will be in the simultaneous adoption of these two hypotheses, namely that we possess at once ancient books emanating from either the first or the second redaction, but modified through the revision of monks contemporary with Kaniṣka, and books quite entirely new, introduced by the sovereign authority of this last council, or even of some influential sage, like Nāgārjuna.

Two considerations offer a very high degree of likelihood to this manner of envisaging the question. The first is that the authority of the last council, however great one presumes it to have been, could not go as far as destroying the previous books in order to substitute entirely different ones. Indeed, it is necessary not to lose sight of the circumstances that made the last two redactions of the canonical books necessary. These are the existence and the claims of sects that in the course

6. *Id., ibid.*, pp. 42, 91, and 297.
7. *Id., ibid.*, pp. 92 and 297.
8. *Id., ibid.*, pp. 41 and 298.
9. Lassen, *Zeitschrift für die Kunde des Morgenlandes*, 3:157. The continuation of this research will prove the exactitude of this opinion.

of time, and thanks to the principle of freedom that Buddhism contained, must have developed early on within the school founded by Śākya. Now, these ancient sects doubtless only differed from one another in the manner of interpreting the sacred texts that each of them equally invoked to support its theories. From the origin, and it is permissible to say, in all the ages of Buddhism, there must have occurred the circumstances that we still see in our day in Nepal,[10] and that Faxian encountered in India at the beginning of the fifth century of our era. The same texts served as authority for the most divergent opinions, and a difference of sect was but a difference of interpretation. Thus, as Mr. Hodgson remarks, the very texts of the school of the naturalists, differently explained, became the basis of theist opinions.[11] It was not, therefore, a matter of writing new books for the councils who gathered for the purpose of making the dire divisions cease, but to cause to prevail the interpretation of ancient books that the council, which was ordinarily only the most numerous sect, recognized as orthodox. That some parts, subject to controversy, were struck from the ancient scriptures; that other parts or even entire works were introduced into them by this systematic labor, this is what is easy to conceive, and which will be not impossible to demonstrate through the facts. But however extended one supposes such labor to be, this must have been no more than a work of revision, a reshaping of the previous texts, whose form and content, preserved by tradition and by religious respect, could not have been completely changed. In summary, if it is permissible to suppose that the last council introduced new books into the canon of scriptures recognized by the previous councils, it is no less necessary to accept that it allowed a more or less significant number of these scriptures to remain, while modifying them according to the dominant ideas of its time. This supposition is too natural not to be accepted, even in the silence of the texts.

The second consideration is furnished to me by the examination I have made above of the collection of the North, and it comes entirely to the support of the first. Through the study of the principal works of this collection, I have acquired a conviction that I have endeavored to pass on to the mind of the reader: it is that in identical forms, and often even in entirely similar language, are hidden works that are very different from one another, through developments given to earlier opinions and the presence of completely new opinions. I could even advance without exaggeration that under the name of ***buddhadharma***, "the law of the Buddha," the collection of Nepal had preserved several Buddhisms for us, three Buddhisms, if I can express myself in this way: that of the simple sūtras, where only the human buddha, Śākyamuni, appears; that of the developed and

10. Hodgson, "Quotations from Original Sanscrit Authorities," in *Journal of the Asiatic Society of Bengal*, vol. 5, p. 72, note.

11. "European Speculations on Buddhism," in *Journal of the Asiatic Society of Bengal*, vol. 3, p. 502, note.

Mahāyāna sūtras, where, next to the human buddha, are found other fabulous buddhas and bodhisattvas; finally that of the tantras, where above these two elements the cult of the female divinities of Śivaism came to take its place. I should probably count a fourth, that of Ādibuddha, with the developments that the Nepalese have given to it and which are recorded in the *Svayaṃbhū Purāṇa.*

It is not my intention to connect these three great forms of Northern Buddhism to the three councils of which the Tibetan tradition speaks. I even confess that I would not be able to justify this connection by proofs of great weight. What I only wish to say is that the core of the different parts that compose the canon of Buddhist scriptures attests to a series of changes that coincide, if not with each of the councils in particular, at least with the fact of the existence of the councils; for if there had been councils, the doctrine was modified, and the doctrine indeed shows itself to be modified in the three fundamental sections of the Buddhist scriptures, the sūtras, the Mahāyāna sūtras, and the tantras.

But what is the nature of these modifications? I have said and I do not need to insist further on the results of the comparison I have established between the simple sūtras and the developed sūtras. These modifications are those whose character is not unrecognizable. They allow us to see a doctrine, simple at first, which then grows and becomes complicated. They permit us to grasp differences of redaction that announce differences of epochs. These epochs are undated, without doubt; but they mark perfectly defined divisions in the development of Buddhist literature that succeed each other according to an order drawn by necessary laws that the course of human ideas obeys. Thus, we have books which by their content (and through that I understand the facts they report and the ideas they support) must be taken as ancient books, as books contemporary, as far as their content is concerned, with the preaching of Śākya. We have others where speculation takes the place of reality, and where hardly anything remains from the previous books except the frame and some proper names. We have, finally, those where elements most foreign to the institution of Buddhism, where practices most contrary to its spirit, alter the simplicity of the doctrine preserved in the first, extended and already modified in the second. Nothing more is necessary, I think, to justify the supposition I have just made touching on the actual existence of books belonging to the one or the other of the first two redactions, but more or less reshaped by the last. I do not need to add that the other hypothesis, namely that the last council authorized new books, remains no less likely. The number and the importance of these books doubtless depended on the more or less high degree of fervor that animated the monks at the time of this council. But in that it is the last, we must boldly conclude that it is its work which survived that of the two preceding assemblies and whose result we have in very great part before our eyes. The opposite supposition would be, to me, far too unlikely.

Neither the tradition nor the study of the Nepalese collection permits us to attain a more rigorous precision; with the help of these alone, we are unable to definitively affirm that this part of the collection emanates more particularly than another from such-and-such council. I must not, however, neglect to bring together with the previous observations that which the Mongol tradition informs us concerning the successive redactions through which the religious books have passed. According to *Sagang sechen*, with whose chronology I am not occupied at the moment, the monks who were the first to put the teaching of Śākya into writing collected those of his discourses related to the first principle of the doctrine, that is to say, the four truths, which was so often the topic elsewhere. The second redactors focused on the discourses related to the middle doctrine, that is to say, to the nothingness of everything that exists, and the chiefs of the council joined to the words of the Master a great number of subjects suitable to edify the mind. Finally, the third redactors, who had gathered to put an end to the schism instigated by a false monk, collected the words related to the last principles of the doctrine and put the finishing touches on them. This third collection includes all the dhāraṇīs.[12] The reflections with which the Mongol authors accompany this classification of the three redactions remove, to my mind, a part of its historical character; it is not possible to believe that the first collection is directed exclusively to the most feeble intelligence, the second to average intelligence, and the third to superior minds. These distinctions were invented afterward to give the philosophical reason for a fact that history is quite sufficient to explain. But leaving the explanation of the goal of the three councils to the Mongol writers, who are here undoubtedly only the copyists of the Tibetans, I content myself in indicating these three facts preserved without doubt by the tradition: 1. that the first council occupied itself with discourses related to the four truths; now this is exactly the subject which the sūtras I consider the most ancient deal with most often; 2. that the chiefs of the second council connected to the discourses of Śākya various subjects suitable to edify the mind; now, I have conjectured that more than one new book could have slipped quietly into the repository of ancient traditions; 3. finally, that the dhāraṇīs belong to the last redaction; now this returns to the same opinion I tried to establish when I analyzed some tantras and that I indicated as the most modern part of the Nepalese collection.

Let us, however, carry these connections a little further and see what we are permitted to conclude. I take as an example the sūtras for which I have distinguished two classes, the simple sūtras and the more developed sūtras, also called *mahāyāna*. I presume that because of their simplicity, one must regard the sūtras of the first class, where only Śākya is spoken about, as the work of the first council.

12. Schmidt, *Geschichte der Ost-Mongolen*, pp. 17 and 315.

It will be necessary to immediately express a reservation concerning the second council; indeed, the sūtras and the legends where Śākya alone is on the stage offer such striking and such numerous similarities to those where Aśoka, the king said to be contemporary with the second council, appears, that it is impossible to separate them. The legends related to Śākya could thus have been collected by the first council; but they must also have been reshaped by the second, and still later when those related to king Aśoka were redacted. What is more, they must also have been reshaped by the third, for I have already indicated, in the course of my remarks on the sūtras, the existence of some particularities that announce a hand more modern than the core elements of the books where they are found. I will recall at the moment only the indication of numerous sects that the tradition makes contemporary with the last council, a circumstance that places the sūtras where one notices it at a point much later than one would if they did not contain this index of posteriority.[13] But it might be only an interpolation there, and the difference between these treatises and those called *mahāyāna* remains complete. This difference is such that it permits one to affirm with full assurance that the same assembly could not have redacted these two classes of works at the same time. Otherwise, the conceptions that dominate in the Mahāyāna would have slipped more often into the simple sūtras, where the traces of their presence are, on the contrary, extremely rare.

Assuming this to be the case, if the primitive sūtras are the work of the first council, successively reshaped by the two following councils, and if the examination of their content excludes the idea that they could have been redacted at the same time as the Mahāyāna, there remain for us only the second and the third councils, to which we have to attribute the compilation of the most developed sūtras. It is hardly probable that they emanate from the second; the date of this council is too close to that of Śākya for his doctrine to have had the time to be subjected to so considerable a transformation as that to which the Mahāyāna sūtras testify. It is thus from the third council that they emanate; and indeed the high esteem they still enjoy today in the North, where they are considered, as I have said elsewhere, to contain the very word of the Buddha, is, to a certain point, an argument in favor of this sentiment. I add that it is in these sūtras that these long pieces of poetry where the Sanskrit is so faulty are found, a circumstance that coincides in a quite remarkable manner with the tradition that places the meeting and the labor of the third council in Kashmir and under a king of foreign origin. These are, one sees, simple comparisons where the reasoning has as much a place as the facts. I daresay, however, that the continuation of this research should fully confirm them.

One cannot say anything more precise touching on the tantras. There are,

13. Csoma, "Notices on the Life of Shakya," in *Asiatic Researches*, vol. 20, p. 298.

however, grounds for believing that these books were redacted neither by the first nor by the second council. Were they redacted by the third? Or, after already being spread through India as a consequence of the mixture of Buddhism with Sivaism, were they accepted by the third council, which was unable to reject them from the canon of sacred scriptures? These are two suppositions whose value we do not have many means to decide, although it is possible, as I will show later, to bring arguments of some weight in favor of the second. What I can already say is that here Nāgārjuna seems to have exercised a considerable influence, and that the tradition, in accordance with the testimony of one of the books analyzed above, the *Pañcakrama*, presents him as having taken an active part in the propagation of the tantras.

If we now attempt to connect to this general survey, which is concerned only with the books considered to be inspired, what we learn from the analysis of the books whose authors are known, we will find ourselves in a position to complete the history of the Nepalese collection and to follow it, at least in its principal phases, almost up to our day. The tradition, I have said, informs us that three councils successively had a hand in the Buddhist scriptures; and it places these three councils in the period of time comprised between the outer limits of these two epochs, the first year and the four hundredth year after the death of Śākyamuni. This period of time embraces what I call the ancient times of Northern Buddhism. The end of these times is marked naturally by the last council. Starting from this event, Buddhism does not cease to live in the provinces of India where it took birth; far from it, it is evident to me that it continues to develop there and that it expands rapidly again; but the modifications it undergoes do not receive, at least to my knowledge, the sanction of a council, and I regard them as the effects of individual works and efforts. Buddhism, in short, enters a new era that I call the Middle Ages, as opposed to the ancient times of which the tradition preserved for us a more or less precise memory. During this second age, which is that of the commentators, Northern Buddhism had very diverse destinies. First, it persisted, filled with radiance and vigor, in places where it was established for centuries; there it gave birth to systems as numerous as they are varied; but successively attacked throughout India by Brahmanism, it ends in disappearing entirely from this country. For me, its complete expulsion dates to the end of the Middle Ages of which I just spoke, and the beginning of modern times. I do not conceal from myself, I confess, how vague this limit is, since, on the one hand, Brahmanical persecution lasted many centuries (from about the fifth to the fourteenth of our era) before triumphing entirely over Buddhism, and that, on the other hand, the proscribed cult only step by step left the different provinces where it had plunged such deep roots. This limit, however, becomes more precise, if one combines the elements relating to the proscription of Buddhism with those related to its establishment among the peoples who inherited it, notably to the north of India. It is clear, indeed, that as Buddhism moved away from its cradle, it lost a portion of the life that it drew from its long abode in the country where it had flourished for so many centuries, and, obliged to use, in order to propagate among new peoples, diverse idioms sometimes little amenable to the expression of its own conceptions, little by little it hid its original forms under borrowed cloth. The transformation was not made everywhere at once, but it began rather early and continued until epochs markedly closer to our time. It is this that I call the modern age of Northern Buddhism; when the Historical Sketch I intend to draw of Indian Buddhism reaches this age, my research must stop.

Such are the principal phases that I believe to be able, with some confidence, to indicate in the history of the Nepalese collection; for me they result from the combination of traditional elements with those provided by the study of the texts. But all is still not achieved; we have obtained up to now only some dates, or rather some epochs whose mutual relation we are able to indicate well, but that we still cannot connect to anything. We lack, in short, the fundamental point from which we must proceed to place them in the annals of India and of the world. This initial point is furnished to us by the Buddhists of the North: it is the death of Śākyamuni, the last buddha; here is the major fact that sets the foundation for the entire historical development of Buddhism, notably for this chronology of the councils of which I have spoken above; but the tradition and the texts leave us almost in ignorance on the real date of this fact, on whose positive determination depends that of all those which follow it. Instead of a fixed point, the tradition gives us only a collection of dates that differ from one another by several centuries, of which none has obtained the assent of the Buddhists of all schools. It is thus necessary, before placing the series of events related to the sacred collection definitively in history, to have made a choice among the numerous dates assigned to the death of Śākya by the Buddhists of all countries. We are, we see, naturally led to the examination of this difficult question, on whose solution depends the definitive determination of the historical information assembled up to now.

We are unable to approach that, however, without having looked at another region where Buddhism also flourishes and where it is preserved until today in books written in a language of Indian origin, and which, like those of the North, claim to be inspired; I wish to speak of Ceylon and the collection of Pāli books that are taken as authoritative by the Buddhists of this island, as well as those of Burma, Pegu, and Siam. The study of this collection is a preparation indispensable to the discussion of the date of Śākya, and to the historical presentation of Indian Buddhism that must follow from it. Indeed, either the collection of Ceylon is the same as that of Nepal, and then its value increases all the more, since the identity is more complete: there is only one single source for the study of Buddhism; one can, with complete confidence, follow it in one or the other of these two currents, that of the North and that of the South, and it remains only to examine the circumstances that separated this single trunk into two branches now so far from each other. Or rather the collection of Ceylon differs from that of Nepal, not only in language but also in content; and then these differences open a new course to our research and offer us precious subjects of study. What are the number and the scope of these differences, and at the same time, what are the points of resemblance that exist between these two collections? Are these differences so considerable as to constitute two schools, one of the North, the other of the South? And does the nature of these resemblances authorize us to think that where they are found, there is primitive Buddhism? Have the councils exercised some influence on the separation of this belief into two schools, and is the date as well as the number of these councils fixed in the same manner in the North and the South? Such, in a few words, are the principal questions that the study of the Sinhalese collection compared to that of Nepal contains, supposing that these two collections are recognized as different from each other; one sees that we are unable to pass to the historical exposition of Indian Buddhism without having examined this Sinhalese collection in itself and in its relations with that of the North.

I thus intend to analyze it, as much as this will be possible for me, as I have done for that of Nepal; and this analysis finished, I will bring together the results with those that the examination of the Buddhist books written in Sanskrit and preserved in the North has furnished me. Then, I am confident, many facts that I have presented as only probable will be recognized as certain; many circumstances on which the tradition of the North is silent or itself explains obscurely will be placed in their true colors; in short, the history of the collection of Nepal will be illuminated with a new light, and it will henceforth be possible, not only to determine the relations among the various parts of which it is composed, but to mark its place in the ensemble of the written monuments of Buddhism.

Appendixes

No. 1. On the Word *Nirvāṇa*
(Second Memorandum, Section 2, Page 121)

This, I believe, is the place to determine, following examples taken from texts, the meaning of the word *nirvāṇa*; one will better understand thereby how it is possible that the Buddhists make such diverse applications of it. Let us recall at the outset that in his memorandum on the heterodox sects of India, Colebrooke has given its etymological meaning: "This word," he says, "used as an adjective, means *extinct*, as for example a fire that is consumed or a luminary that ceases to shine; moreover it means *dead* as when one applies it to a saint who has departed this world for the other. This word derives from *vā*, to blow like the wind, and from the preposition *nir*, which here has a negative meaning; *nirvāṇa* thus means: calm and not moved by the wind. The notion that is associated with this word employed [substantively] in a philosophical sense is that of complete apathy." And further on: "It is not an annihilation, but an unceasing apathy that Jainas and Buddhists intend to designate by nirvāṇa, that is to say the extinction of their saints."[1] I do not know on which authority Colebrooke relies in order to so limit the meaning of *nirvāṇa* among the Buddhists; I certainly believe that this must be the sentiment of some schools, but it does not prove to me that it is for them all, and in particular the most ancient. This question, moreover, even presuming that its solution is possible, could be examined only when we have compared the opinions of the Buddhists of the North with those that prevail in the South.

1. *Miscellaneous Essays*, 1:401 and 402.

I thus return to the meaning of the word *nirvāṇa*, and I note at the outset that the proper acceptation of this term is that of "extinction." In a passage of the *Divyāvadāna* I find the root from which this word derives employed verbally with this special meaning. There, it is a matter of a lamp that is offered to the Buddha by a woman, and that Ānanda, his faithful servant, cannot extinguish. Here is the sentence itself: "'If I extinguish (*nirvāpayeyam*) this lamp,' he said to himself; and trying to extinguish it with his hand, he could not succeed."[2] This circumstance, to mention in passing, is related to Maudgalyāyana by the redactor of one of the legends that Mr. Schmidt has translated from the Tibetan;[3] and I find there a new confirmation of what I have said in my first memorandum[4] touching on the inferiority of the Tibetan language with regard to Sanskrit. Here, indeed, the interpreter, holding to the particular meaning of *nirvāpay*, renders it rightly by "extinguish," in Tibetan *bsab pa*; but we have already seen, and we will say again, that *nirvāṇa* in the philosophical sense is uniformly rendered in Tibetan by "the exemption of suffering," in such a way that the beautiful analogy that exists between *nirvāpay* taken literally and *nirvāṇa* employed figuratively cannot even be suspected in the Tibetan version.

The meaning of "extinction" is so intimately particular to this term *nirvāṇa*, that the nirvāṇa which a buddha is said to attain when death finally frees him from the bonds of the world is compared to a fire that dies out. I find a proof of it in this interesting passage of the *Avadānaśataka*: *yāvad vipaśyī samyaksaṃbuddhaḥ sakalabuddhakāryaṃ kṛtvā indhanakṣayād ivāgnir nirupadhiśeṣe nirvāṇadhātau parinirvṛtaḥ*,[5] a passage whose Tibetan version can be read in the Kah-gyur,[6] which means: "until finally Vipaśyin, the completely perfect Buddha, after having fulfilled all of the duties of a buddha, was, like a fire whose fuel is consumed, entirely annihilated in the element of nirvāṇa, where nothing remains of that which constitutes existence." This sentence contains all the expressions related to nirvāṇa; it is thus important to examine it closely. First, I observe that the idea of extinction dominates there, and that a buddha who enters into the definitive nirvāṇa (*parinirvṛta*) is compared to a fire that dies out through lack of fuel. Second, the term *nirvāṇa* is accompanied by the word *dhātu*, an element whose value it is important to fix. I regard *dhātu* as one of these denominations of categories that abound in the style of the Buddhists, and which stem from the classificatory system of their doctrine. The element of nirvāṇa is certainly nothing more than the element called *nirvāṇa*, or in other words, nirvāṇa.

The expression *nirupadhiśeṣa* is not nearly as easy. One finds it also writ-

2. *Divyāvadāna*, fol. 42.

3. *Der Weise und der Thor*, p. 262 of the text, and p. 328 of the translation.

4. Above, First Memorandum, p. 63ff.

5. *Avadānaśataka*, fol. 150b.

6. *Mdo*, vol. *ha* (29), fol. 254a.

ten *anupadhiśeṣa*,[7] which comes to absolutely the same thing. The Buddhists of the South give a good deal more divergent spellings of this word. Thus the commentary of the *Mahāvaṃsa* of which Mr. Turnour has had a copy made in Ceylon, which he has obligingly given me to use, cites among the epithets of a Buddha *anupādisesanibbāṇasampāpakam*,[8] "one who makes nirvāṇa completely obtained." The word *anupādisesa*, written in the same way by Clough,[9] is reproduced with a short *a, anupadisesa*, in another passage of the same commentary of the *Mahāvaṃsa*. In all the research I have done in the Buddhist books written in Sanskrit at my disposal, I have nowhere found a complete commentary on this term. The gloss of the *Pañcakrama*, a small treatise I have discussed above,[10] and which is certainly not from the early times of Buddhism, is the only book where I have found some trace of explanation, in the following passage: *sopadhiśeṣam pañcaskandhamātraśūnyam, anupadhiśeṣaṃ sarvaśūnyaṃ nirvāṇam.*[11] If the relations I presume between these terms really exist, it will be necessary to translate them in this way: "The *sopadhiśeṣa*, or that in which some *upadhi* remains, is empty only of the five *skandhas*; the *anupadhiśeṣa*, or that in which no *upadhi* remains, is empty of everything, it is nirvāṇa."

Now, what does *upadhi* mean? Wilson gives these meanings to this term: 1. fraud, 2. wheel of a chariot, 3. terror; but none of these meanings seems to fit here. I note, however, that the meaning of "wheel" brings us closer to the explanation adopted by Clough, who, reading *anupādisesa*, analyzes this term in this way: "*na* (not) *upadi* (producing) *sesa* (transmigration)," that is to say, "that which put an end to transmigration, that which leads to nirvāṇa."[12] I regard this explanation as entirely untenable; it teaches us only one thing, that the result of nirvāṇa is to put an end to transmigration. In citing it here, I solely have the intention to show that if *upadhi* had the meaning of "wheel" in our Buddhist expression, one would find in it the elements of the translation given by Clough, "that in which the wheel does not remain," in order to say, "the revolving of the world." But besides the fact that the commentary of the *Pañcakrama* does not say anything about this interpretation, it further is not supported by the authority of the Tibetan translators. In the passage just cited, as well as in several places of the *Lotus of the Good Law*, the Sanskrit formula *nirupadhiśeṣe nirvāṇadhātau parinirvṛtaḥ* is translated into Tibetan in this way: *phung po'i lhag ma med pa'i mya ngan las 'das pa'i dbyings su mya ngan las 'das so.* It is this expression that we must examine to find the true opinion of the Tibetans.

7. *Pañcakramaṭippanī*, fol. 16b.
8. *Mahāvaṃsaṭīkā*, fol. 2b init.
9. *Singhala Dictionary*, 2:30.
10. Second Memorandum, section. 6, p. 507.
11. *Pañcakramaṭippanī*, fol. 16b, l. 4.
12. *Singhala Dictionary*, 2:30, col. 2.

Our Tibetan dictionaries furnish us, for the explanation of this sentence, with the following interpretations: "He is completely delivered from suffering in the element of the exemption of suffering where nothing remains of the aggregates." The compound expression *phung po'i lhag ma med pa'i*, which has the form of a genitive preceding the substantive that governs it, certainly corresponds to the Sanskrit compound *anupadhiśeṣe*; and in this expression *upadhi* is rendered by *phung po*, and *śeṣa* by *lhag ma.* I understand the word *phung po* as the Tibetan dictionaries translate it: "accumulation, heap, aggregation of material elements"; and what confirms me in that view is that this word *phung po* is the common translation of the Buddhist term *skandha*, "aggregate" and "intellectual attribute." Schröter gives us this expression with this meaning. The very phrase that occupies us is also in Schröter, under a verbal form, with the meaning of "going to heaven." This interpretation is doubtless too limited, and it has a theist tendency that is certainly not ancient. It proves, however, that one must seek in *phung po* the notion of the *skandhas*, or the five intellectual attributes constitutive of human existence. Finally, Csoma de Kőrös understands the Tibetan expression that occupies us exactly in this way, since he translates it thus: "Entirely delivered from pain with respect to the five aggregates of the body."[13]

All these comparisons lead me to believe that the term *upadhi* designates the collective gathering of the five *skandhas*, a gathering that is one of the main elements of human individuality, and I propose to give this term a meaning analogous to that of "support, sustain," that is to say, that on which the intellectual attributes of individuality rest, or to translate it as "supposition," that is to say, that which one supposes to be; such that *upadhi* designates individuality, taken somehow subjectively and objectively. It will result from all this that the expression *anupadhiśeṣaṃ nirvāṇaṃ* could be translated in this manner: "annihilation, where nothing remains of individuality." It is this that the gloss of the *Pañcakrama* calls the void of everything, complete vacuity. But it is not as easy for me to understand the manner in which this gloss explains *sopadhiśeṣam*, seeing in it the void of the five *skandhas* only. It is clear that this gloss distinguishes two voids: one where the *upadhi*, or the individuality supported or presumed, still remains, if I can express myself in this way; the other absolute, or the total void, in which the Tibetan interpreters teach us to see the annihilation of individuality itself. It might be, however, that the *Pañcakrama* understands by *upadhi* the person itself, or what is elsewhere called the *pudgala*, in a way that the void where *upadhi* still subsists represents the human person or the pure mind released from all its attributes. We are stopped here, one sees, by the absence of a special commentary on these difficult terms; however, since the *Pañcakrama* is a book certainly more modern than the terms it uses, and since it probably makes a special application

13. *Asiatic Researches*, vol. 20, p. 312.

of them, its opinion, whatever it is, can be left aside without inconvenience in a discussion related to these manifestly ancient terms.

One sees them figure, in addition, in all the schools and all the ages of Buddhism. I find a very complete example in the Sanskrit text of the *Vajracchedikā*, known to be a succinct summary of the *Prajñāpāramitā*. Here is this example: *sarve 'nupadhiśeṣe nirvāṇadhātau parinirvāpayitavyāḥ*, and in the Tibetan version: *de dag thams cad phung po lhag ma med pa'i mya ngan las 'das pa'i dbyings su yongs su mya ngan las bzla'o.* Mr. Schmidt, in his German version of the Tibetan *Vajracchedika*, renders this passage in this way: "I must, while delivering them completely and without remainder of suffering, transport them to the region exempt from suffering."[14] I do not flatter myself to possess sufficiently great practice in the Tibetan language to definitely deny that this translation faithfully reproduces the text. It seems to me, however, that the expression *phung po lhag ma med pa'i*, which means, according to Mr. Schmidt, "completely and without remainder," refers by its ending *'i* to the term *mya ngan las 'das pa'i*, literally "of the state of the exemption of suffering," words that represent the Sanskrit *nirvāṇa.* Let us add that the likelihood is due to this feeling: for if the Tibetan versions are as accurate as one must believe, it is permissible to think that the Buddhist translator of the *Vajracchedikā* would not have wished to disturb the connection of these two Sanskrit terms *anupadhiśeṣe nirvāṇadhātau*, which are both in the locative; while if the first of these terms was related to *sarve* (all the beings of the world to be saved), the interpreter would have taken care not to give it any case ending in his version.

I must remark, however, that Mr. Schmidt has not consistently translated the expression *anupadhiśeṣa* in this manner, and that in another passage he seems to come closer in part to the meaning I believe to be the true one.[15] Thus, he says elsewhere: "The beings without the remainder of any accumulation." This expression is not sufficiently clear; and one does not see what must be understood by *Anhäufung* if it is not the *skandhaṣ* But this translation still has the inconvenience of making *anupadhiśeṣa* relate to *sattvāḥ*, whereas it must determine *nirvāṇadhātau.*

Since I had occasion to speak of the word *dhātu* (element), may I be permitted to add here a new example of the use of this term, where I suspect Mr. Schmidt has given it too much value. It is a question of a passage of the *Vajracchedikā* where the Bhagavat establishes that whatever the number of the beings saved by a bodhisattva, there is not one being who is really saved. Here is

14. "Über das Mahayana und Pradschna-Paramita der Bauddhen," in *Mémoires de l'Académie des sciences de Saint-Pétersbourg*, 4:130 and 187.

15. "Über das Mahayana und Pradschna-Paramita der Bauddhen," in *Mémoires de l'Académie des sciences de Saint-Pétersbourg*, 4:202.

the Sanskrit text: *yāvantaḥ . . . sattvāḥ sattvadhātau sattvasaṃgraheṇa saṃgṛhītā aṇḍajā vā jarāyujā vā saṃsvedajā vā aupapādakā vā*; and I translate it literally in this way: "All the beings there are included in the domain of beings, in the collection of beings, whether their birth is from an egg, or a womb, or from humidity, or from a supernatural manner." Mr. Schmidt interprets the Tibetan version of this passage[16] in the following manner: "*Was alles zu lebenden Wesen sich aus der Ansammlung (Materie) angesammelt hat*," which comes almost to this: "All that, coming from accumulation or from matter, has accumulated in the manner of beings, or to become living beings." I will note at the outset that the Tibetan version of this passage, *sems can ji tsam sems can du bsdus bas bsdus pa*, lends itself well to the meaning I find in the Sanskrit text, since, literally meaning "all the beings that are gathered by the collection of beings," one can see there in clearer terms, "all the beings there are included in the collection of beings." Then, and to confine myself to the Sanskrit, which has the merit here of being the original, it is clear that *sattvadhātau* cannot signify the element of beings or matter, as Mr. Schmidt proposed, but that it is one of these expressions familiar to Sanskrit Buddhism, where *dhātu* does not have very great value and where one has at most to translate it as "domain of beings," in order to say "among beings." This tiresome repetition of the word *being* to express an idea as clear as that of the text is again a feature peculiar to this Sanskrit. In general, the more simple the idea, the more the Buddhists emphasize it and develop it with an ample apparatus of words, which eventually contribute in no small way to obscure it.

16. *Ibid.*, 4:187.

No. 2. On the Expression *Sahalokadhātu*

(Second Memorandum, Section 2, Page 93)

The expression the text uses here is *Sahalokadhātu*: it is a term familiar to Buddhists of all schools to designate the universe inhabited by humans. The last word *dhātu*, which means "element," is not very explanatory, and it does not add anything to the signification of the word *loka*. It is this that the following passage from a commentary on the *Jinālaṃkāra*, a Pāli poem in honor of the Jina (or the Buddha) proves: *tīsūpi lokadhātusu jeṭṭhaseṭṭhattam patto*, "having obtained excellence and superiority in the three worlds themselves."[1] It thus must be admitted that *Sahalokadhātu* does not say more than *Sahaloka*.

Several explanations have already been proposed for this difficult term. When it appeared for the first time in the History of Kashmir, Mr. Wilson, translating it at the beginning of the second verse of stanza 172, *asmin sahalokadhātau*, gave this explanation of it, which is, to say the least, obscure: "in this essence of the world."[2] Later, speaking of the fabulous universe of Śukhavatī, this fortunate land that the Buddhists of the North imagine to be situated in the west,[3] he distinguished *lokadhātu* as the special title of a division of the universe; and finding the expression *Sahalokadhātu* in the small treatises sent to Calcutta by Mr. Hodgson, he rendered it in this way: "in the lokadhātu called *Saha*." To this translation, Mr. Wilson added that the division called Saha apparently des-

1. *Jinālaṃkāra*, fol. 5b of my manuscript.

2. *Asiatic Researches*, vol. 15, p. 111.

3. "Notice of Three Tracts Received from Nepal," in *Asiatic Researches*, vol. 16, p. 471.

ignated a part of the Himalaya and included Kashmir; and while continuing to declare that the meaning "essence of the world" he had given previously was acceptable, he nevertheless withdrew it, because this meaning was not technical in this context.[4] Finally, giving an account in the *Asiatic Journal of Bengal* of the first works of Csoma de Kőrös on the Kah-gyur, he defines the Sahalokadhātu in a more general manner: "the region or the world of Śākya, that is to say, the world of mortals that is governed by Brahmā."[5]

My learned friend, Mr. Troyer, while publishing the text and translation of the History of Kashmir by Kalhana, had before his eyes the Calcutta edition and India Company manuscript no. 310, which also have *Sahalokadhātu*;[6] but he doubtless ceded to the authority of Mr. A. Rémusat, who read *Savalokadhātu*,[7] and of Mr. Schmidt, who had also found *sava*[8] in the Mongol authors. He thus accepted *śavalokadhātau* in his text;[9] and starting from the meaning of *śava* (cadaver), he translated the whole expression in this way: "at the bottom of this perishable world." However, the reading *Sahalokadhātau* was preserved by Mr. Turnour in his research on Buddhist chronology, and he translated it as "in all the world."[10] Lassen, while quite accurately critiquing the aforementioned memorandum of Turnour, noted how obscure the expression *Sahalokadhātu* was; and while asking if it could not be related to the three Turuṣka kings whose simultaneous presence it indicated in Kashmir, he acknowledged that this supposition would not make all the difficulties of the passage where it is found disappear.[11]

In this state of things, it is important to return to the texts themselves and to consult the peoples foreign to India who have been forced to translate this entirely Buddhist expression. First, the texts give us the word *saha* in two forms: at the outset, as I have just transcribed it and in combination with the word *lokadhātu*, in this manner, *Sahalokadhātu*; then ending with a long vowel and separated from the following *lokadhātu*, with which it declines: *sahā lokadhātuḥ*, *sahāyāṃ lokadhātau*, etc. In this latter form, it is a true adjective whose substantive is *lokadhātu*. From the joining of these two words, there results an expression similar to all those that designate the fabulous universes with which the Buddhists populate space, for example *Sukhavatī lokadhātuḥ*. I

4. *Asiatic Researches*, vol. 16, pp. 473 and 475.
5. *Journal of the Asiatic Society of Bengal*, vol. 1, p. 384.
6. *Histoire du Kachemire*, 1:371.
7. "Essai sur la cosmographie et la cosmogonie des bouddhistes," in *Journal des Savans*, 1831, p. 670.
8. *Geschichte der Ost-Mongolen*, p. 301.
9. *Histoire du Kachemire*, vol. 1, st. 172.
10. *Journal of the Asiatic Society of Bengal*, vol. 5, p. 530.
11. *Zeitschrift fur die Kunde des Morgenlandes*, 1:239.

find an example characteristic of that which occupies us in this sentence of the *Saddharmalaṅkāvatāra*: *evam eva mahāmate aham api sahāyāṃ lokadhātau tribhir nāmāsaṃkhyeya śatasahasrair bālānāṃ śravaṇāvabhāsam āgacchāmi*: "It is in this way, O Mahāmati, that in the Saha universe, I myself am known to the ignorant by three hundred thousand asaṃkhyeyas of names."[12]

But what can *saha*, which appears here in the role of an adjective, signify? This word must certainly belong to the root *sah* in one of its meanings that are only nuances of one another, "to hold up, to support, to tolerate, to resist"; and it is without question the adjective *saha*, "suffering, patient." This explanation leads us directly to the translation of the Chinese Buddhists, among whom *Sahalokadhātu* designates "the abode or the world of patience," because, Des Hautesrayes says, "all the beings who live in it are subjected to the ordeals of transmigration and to all the vicissitudes that are the consequence."[13] One sees that Mr. A. Rémusat knew the true meaning of the term, although he had adopted a faulty spelling; but one must at the same time abandon the explanations that this bad spelling has suggested to Mr. Schmidt.[14]

It is important to compare this expression with the title given to Brahmā in the Buddhist books of the North as well as in those of the South. One finds him called *sahāṃpati*, and in Pāli *sahaṃpati*.[15] This title is even compounded with that of Brahmā in the following passage of the *Thūpavaṃsa*, the history of the stūpas: *sahaṃpati mahābrahmuṇā āyācita dhammadesano*, "he who the great Brahmā Sahaṃpati has implored to teach the law."[16] I see here the joining of two words *pati* (master, lord), and *saham* (Pāli for *sahām*), genitive plural of a name derived directly from the root *sah*, and I translate it as "the lord of those who endure, of patient beings." Brahmā is indeed the sovereign of the Sahalokadhātu, that is to say, of the world of patience. It is this that the Tibetans probably understand by the expression *mi mjed kyi bdag po*, which to their eyes represents *sahāṃpati*. The first part, *mi mjed*, is translated in our Tibetan dictionaries as "who is not subject, who is not subjected" (Csoma), and by "not subjected, independent" (Schmidt). This vague expression lacks the necessary precision, and the words "who is not subjected" must be understood in the sense of "who suffers, who endures without ceding." In closing, I must mention here, if only not to omit it, the explanation of the term *sahāṃpati* given by Mr. W. von Humboldt

12. *Saddharmalaṅkāvatāra*, fol. 57b.

13. Des Hautesrayes, "Recherches sur la religion de Fo," in *Journal Asiatique*, vol. 8, p. 43; and A. Rémusat, "Essai sur la cosmographie et la cosmogonie des bouddhistes," in *Journal des Savans*, 1831, p. 670. *Foe koue ki*, p. 116.

14. *Geschichte der Ost-Mongolen*, p. 301, note 8. *Mémoires de l'Académie des sciences de Saint-Pétersbourg*, 2:23.

15. Clough, *Singhala Dictionary*, 2:722, col. 1.

16. *Thūpavaṃsa*, fol. 9a of my manuscript.

without proving it and as if it was sufficiently self-evident. This scholar believes that *sahāṃpati* is identical to *jagatpati*, "the sovereign of the universe."[17] It is true that he had borrowed the original term from the bad transcriptions of Upham, who writes it *sagampati*, and whose work was not as discredited as it has become since the publication of the *Mahāvaṃsa.*

17. *Über die Kawi-Sprache*, 1:297.

No. 3. On the Words *Purāṇa* and *Kārṣāpaṇa*

(Second Memorandum, Section 2, page 175)

It is not easy to arrive at a rigorous evaluation of the sum expressed in our text, because the values of the bases according to which it is possible for us to calculate it are not known with all desirable precision. Indeed, on the one hand, these values have varied in periods that are not historically determined; on the other hand, the Indian authors themselves give evaluations for these bases that are very different from one another, and whose divergence can be explained only by accepting that they stem from the same sign having been variously employed in various provinces.

It is, however, possible to obtain an approximate result with the aid of elements of comparison that the memorandum of Colebrooke on weights and measures of India furnishes us. It is important in the first place to notice that the *puraṇa* mentioned in the text is a currency of weight, that is to say, a currency belonging to a purely Indian system, and consequently prior to the influence that the monetary system of the Greeks of Bactria exerted in India. Now, in the system to which the purāṇa belongs, which is a weight of silver, the unit is the *raktikā*, that is to say, the weight of a red grain of gunja, or *abrus precatorius.* W. Jones weighed a very great number of these grains and ascertained that their average weight equaled 1 3/16 English troy grains. But Colebrooke affirms that the raktikā (vulgarly *retti*) in practice has a value by convention considered to be double the weight of the grain of the abrus and which, however, does not quite reach 2 1/4 grains; it is nearly, Colebrooke says, 2 3/16 English troy grains.[1] In thus accepting that the raktikā equals 2³⁄₁₆ troy grains, the silver māṣaka, which is equal to two raktikās, will be worth 4⁶⁄₁₆ troy grains; and since it takes 16 of these māṣakas to make one purāṇa, this latter weight will be exactly equal to 70 troy grains; from which we will have 35,000 troy grains for 500 of these purāṇas. Finally, since the English troy grain is worth 0.065 French milligrams according to the reduction tables of the directory of the Bureau des longitudes, 500 purāṇas will be worth 2,275 milligrams, or 455 francs.

One understands that one would arrive at a much higher result if it was a question of a weight of gold; but the use of the word *purāṇa* absolutely forbids this supposition, since the purāṇa is expressly given as a weight of silver. This consideration exempts me from investigating what 500 purāṇas would be worth in the several following suppositions, namely: that the māṣa sometimes equals 5 raktikās or 10¹⁵⁄₁₆ English troy grains, and in round numbers 11 troy grains, that is to say, 715 milligrams; sometimes four raktikās or 8¾ troy grains, that is to say, 569 milligrams; sometimes 16 raktikās or 35 troy grains, that is to say, 2 grams 275 milligrams. Colebrooke has not said clearly whether we had to understand these māṣas to be weights of gold or silver; but since he has expressly specified the *māṣaka* (diminutive for *māṣa*) as a silver currency, there is a very great likelihood in believing that the māṣas properly speaking are weights of gold. This consequence can also be deduced from the comparison of two articles in Wilson's dictionary, that for *māṣa* and that for *māṣaka*.

Whatever it may be, the terms *māṣa* and *māṣaka* belong, like that of *raktikā*, to this system of weights provided by nature and very likely quite ancient, which characterizes the epochs of a still not very advanced civilization; for the *māṣa* is a bean of the species called *phaseolus radiatus*.

The text of our legend speaks of yet another currency, the kārṣāpaṇa, which is, according to Colebrooke,[2] equal to 80 raktikās of copper, that is to say, to 175 English troy grains, or according to Wilson (at the word *kārṣāpaṇa*), to 176 grains. Although the kārṣāpaṇa can be a weight of gold or silver as well as of copper, the entirety of the text seems to me to prove that we must understand a kārṣāpaṇa of copper, for the courtesan certainly wishes to say that she does not even ask for the smallest sum from Upagupta. Now, since the kārṣāpaṇa, at the rate of 175 English troy grains, would equal 11 grams 375 milligrams of copper (that is to say, a coin of 5 French centimes with a fraction of 1.375 milligrams, which does not come to 1 centime), to say: "I do not want even a kārṣāpaṇa" is to say almost the equivalent of this: "I do not ask for even one centime from you."

1. "On Indian Weights and Measures," in *Asiatic Researches*, 5:92, ed. in -8°.
2. *Asiatic Researches*, vol. 5, p. 93.

No. 4. On the Names of Gods among the Buddhists
(Second Memorandum, Section 2, Page 220, Note 228)

Georgi has given, according to the Tibetan sources gathered by Father Orazio della Penna, a list of superposed heavens according to the ideas of the Tibetans, which I believe are useful to compare with those of our sūtra.[1] This comparison can be interesting in more than one respect. In the first place, since the Tibetan names of the heavens and the divinities who inhabit them are only translations of names originally in Sanskrit, and since Georgi has not given these latter names, which were unknown to him, it is necessary to compare the Tibetan list with that of our sūtra, in order to furnish some more elements to this comparison of two Buddhist literatures, that of Tibet and that of Nepal, which can be so profitable to each other. Then, from a more elevated point of view, it is indispensable to know which additions the Buddhists made to the popular pantheon of the brahmans that they adopted, or at least that they did not proscribe; it is, indeed, only in accordance with the nature of these additions that one will be able to judge the peculiar character of their mythology.

The enumeration of Georgi, which follows the same sequence as that of our sūtra, starts by ascending from the levels closest to the earth; but it only commences at the heaven of Tuṣita, and it thus omits the three first orders which our sūtra names. But Georgi returns to this subject in other passages of his compilation, and it is possible, by gathering all these passages, to present a complete

1. *Alphabetum Tibetanum*, p. 182ff.

picture of the number and formation of the levels of which the world above is composed according to the ideas of the Buddhists.

One knows that it is on the slopes of Mount Meru, that is to say, of this fabulous mountain which, according to the exact definition of Mr. A. Rémusat, is at once the highest part of the terrestrial world and the central point of the visible sky,[2] that the Buddhists place the inferior levels of heavens that gradually ascend above the earth. The four continents of which the earth we inhabit is composed are arranged around this mountain, which rises above their surface as far as it descends below.[3] The upper part of Meru is divided into several levels, of which the first, in ascending order, is inhabited by spirits whose prince the Tibetans call *gnod byin lag na gzhong thog.*[4] I do not know the Sanskrit word corresponding to this name, which is obviously a compound. Georgi has not given its translation; but it can be interpreted with the aid of the dictionary of Csoma, according to which *gnod sbyin* means "a mischievous fancied spirit," and *lag na gzhong thog* (or rather *thogs*) designates an imaginary being who holds a basin in its hand. To these notions, Mr. Schmidt adds that *gnod sbyin* is synonymous with the Sanskrit *yakṣa*,[5] which I believe to be quite accurate, because the yakṣas, in Indian mythology, are spirits whose abode is the atmosphere; but Mr. Schmidt does not indicate anything more about the epithet added to the name of these yakṣas, "who have a vase in their hand." All that we know about them is due to Georgi, who represents them occupied in fetching with their vases water that the waves of the sea splash onto Mount Meru. Thus far, I have found nothing in the texts of Nepal related to this category of beings superior to man. Furthermore, it is not entirely an invention of the Tibetans; since the Buddhists of the South know something analogous, it is actually based on truly Indian and antique elements, for nothing is more common than to see yakṣas figure in legends. They are spirits of the air, endowed with a great power, who, like all the other inhabitants of the Buddhist pantheon, are subject to the supreme power of the Buddha, and even to that of monks or some privileged personages, like the kings who are protectors of Buddhism. The name the Tibetans give them recalls in part that of *kumbhāṇḍa*, which designates beings placed by the Sinhalese immediately above the earth, along the slopes of Meru;[6] I must speak elsewhere of these purely Indian spirits.

The second level is inhabited by beings who hold a rosary in their hand; the prince who governs them is called, according to Georgi, *pran thog*,[7] a faulty reading that is easily rectified with the aid of the notion that Georgi gives us of these

2. *Journal des Savans*, 1831, p. 609.

3. Georgi, *Alphabetum Tibetanum*, p. 480.

4. *Ibid.*, and p. 237.

5. *Tibetisch-deutsches Wörterbuch*, p. 308, col. 2.

6. *Mahāvansi*, 3:51.

7. *Alphabetum Tibetanum*, p. 481.

spirits. If, indeed, one reads *phreng thogs*, this name will mean: "one who holds a garland." This term would translate quite exactly the Sanskrit *sragdhara*; but thus far I have found only one divinity of this name in the books of Nepal; it is the goddess of the tantras, of whom I have spoken above in the section dedicated to these books,[8] and who, I believe, is not relevant here. I must not, however, forget to say that, according to Schröter, the Tibetans have a word, *phreng ldan*, by which they designate *garuḍa*, the Indian bird dedicated to Kṛṣṇa;[9] *phreng ldan*, which means "having a garland," is not very far from *phreng thogs*, an expression that has the same meaning. If these two words were synonyms, we could suppose that the beings who inhabit the second level are the garuḍas, which the Buddhists make a class of divine birds. We will see, in studying the classification of the Buddhists of the South, that they place the garuḍa at the third level above the earth.[10]

The third level is the abode of beings called, according to Georgi, "drinkers and stupid ones," and who in Tibetan have the name *rtag myos*.[11] These two monosyllables are literally translated as "continuously inebriated," and this interpretation accords well with the notion that Georgi gives us of these gods; but here again the texts of Nepal, at least those I can consult, are absolutely silent, and I do not find the Sanskrit name of these divinities in our legends. Perhaps these continuously inebriated spirits are the nāgas, or the dull and stupid dragons that the Buddhists of the South place, it is true, at the fourth degree.

The fourth level is inhabited by beings that Georgi calls the *lha ma yin*,[12] that is to say, "those who are not gods," in other terms, who are *asuras*; for the Tibetan expression is the exact translation of this latter Sanskrit name. Here again, we lack the testimony of the Nepalese texts as to the precise determination of the abode of the asuras; but their name is nonetheless authentic, and their existence is proved by these texts. It is, with the yakṣas, one of these ancient borrowings made by Buddhism from the popular religion of India. The asuras, like the spirits of the three lower levels, do not figure in the classification of the gods, the inhabitants of the celestial levels superposed above the earth; but that must not surprise us, for they are not gods. The asuras, on the contrary, are the enemies of the *devas*, or of these luminous divinities of whom Buddhists of all schools received ideas quite in conformity with Brahmanical conceptions.[13] This is why the sūtra to which the present note is related, speaking of rays of light that rise in the sky and go to illuminate the residences of the devas, takes its point of departure from

8. Second Memorandum, section 5, p. 495.
9. *Bhotanta Dictionary*, p. 199, col. 1.
10. *Mahāvansi*, 3:51.
11. *Alphabetum Tibetanum*, p. 481, no. 10.
12. *Alphabetum Tibetanum*, p. 481, no. 11.
13. A. Rémusat, *Foe koue ki*, pp. 138 and 139.

the *caturmahārājika*, that is to say, from the divinities who inhabit the lowest of the six superposed heavens that constitute the first of the three regions, that of the *kāmāvacara*, or beings who indulge in concupiscence.[14]

The classification that I have just set forth according to Georgi is found, without the fourth level of the asuras, in Pallas, whose interesting collection in general merits great confidence for all that regards the Buddhism of Central Asia. This proves that it is very familiar to the Mongols; it seems indispensable to me to set it forth in a few words. On the inferior degree of levels that Meru encompasses reside the spirits with a vase; these are the yakṣas of the Tibetans. Above them come those that Pallas calls *free* (*freye*); they apparently correspond to the Georgi's spirits wearing a garland; for they have above them those who are called *always inebriated*, who are placed at the third degree by Pallas as well as by Georgi; but I am unaware of the reason for the name *free* that Pallas gives them. The Chinese, as one will see later, have an order of spirits they call *delivered*, and to whom the *free* of Pallas correspond. Finally, above these three classes of spirits come the *macharansa chane*, that is to say, the mahārāja kings who command all these secondary spirits, and whose palaces survey the four cardinal points of which they are the protectors.[15] One sees that Pallas does not speak of the asuras, whom some Tibetans make the inhabitants of the fourth heaven; doubtless, he confuses them with the always inebriated spirits of the third division of Meru. Mr. Schmidt, to whom one owes the most elaborated memoranda on the celestial levels of the Mongol Buddhists, places the asuras in the depths of the subterranean regions.[16]

The Chinese also seem to know these various orders of spirits; at least, I find in the oft-cited memorandum of Mr. Abel Rémusat on Buddhist cosmography some details that have an obvious relation to the subject that occupies us. It concerns the mountains arranged in a circle around Meru, and that are represented rising by degrees from the range that surrounds the earth to that which reaches half of the height of the central mountain. These mountains thus form veritable levels that are inhabited by beings superior to humans. I do not believe it necessary to insist on the number of these ranges, who for some are seven and for others ten; and I do not pause further to note the striking analogy that this description offers with the cosmological system of the brahmans. I only observe that

14. See Second Memorandum, section 2, p. 122, note 23. I use the word *region* (*dhātu*) intentionally, to avoid the confusion entailed by the use of the word *world* (*loka*), a confusion that Mr. Schmidt has perfectly disentangled (*Mémoires de l'Académie des sciences de Saint-Pétersbourg*, 2:55, note 7).

15. *Sammlungen historischer Nachrichten über die mongolischen Völkerschaften*, 2:46. Pallas, with his ordinary exactitude, has referred to the presentation of Georgi, of whom he notes in general terms the divergence from his own.

16. *Mémoires de l'Académie des sciences de Saint-Pétersbourg*, 2:34.

the yakṣas live on one of these ranges, on another the immortals who are called *delivered*, and lastly the asuras on the one closest to Meru.[17] The system of the Chinese, which consists in placing atmospheric spirits on ranges concentric to Meru and rising at unequal heights along its slope, is perhaps preferable to that of Georgi, who represents these spirits in tiers on the slopes of this mountain; at least, it accords better with the Brahmanical theory of the great ranges that surround Meru.

Be that as it may, above these orders of spirits that inhabit the atmosphere, one places in the fourth station of Meru the four great kings. Georgi informs us that there are two opinions in Tibet on this point.[18] Indeed, according to whether one attributes to the asuras the third or the fourth degree, the four great kings ascend to the fourth or descend to the third level of Meru. I do not waver in coming to the first opinion, that of Pallas and Mr. A. Rémusat; it seems to me to rest on accurate and more carefully studied documents than those so often confused by Georgi;[19] it is that which I have followed when I had occasion to speak of the four great kings.[20] The list of our sūtra starts with this order of divinities, who are called *caturmāharājika*. The Tibetans, according to Georgi, designate them with the name *rgyel chen bzhi*,[21] which must be read *rgyal*, etc., which means exactly "the four great kings." The Vocabulaire Pentaglotte gives their name in this manner: *gyal* (*rgyal*) *chen bzhi rigs*, "the tribe of the four great kings";[22] it is the literal translation of the Sanskrit title adopted by this Vocabulaire: *catur mahārāja kāyika*. The Tibetans call them also *'jigs rten skyongs ba bzhi*, "the four protectors of the universe,"[23] which is only a translation of the Brahmanical name *lokapāla*.

These kings are frequently mentioned in the books of Nepal, and I have explained their names in the notes to a sūtra I have translated above.[24] I only add here that the compound and derived term employed by our sūtra means "the gods that form the retinue of the four great kings." It is exactly in this manner

17. *Journal des Savans*, 1831, p. 606. In this part of the memorandum of Mr. Rémusat, there are several names of mountains whose Sanskrit form is easy to find, under the rather feeble alteration of the Chinese transcriptions. Thus *Yougantuo* is the Yugaṃdhara (*Mahāvansi*, 3:67); *Nimintuoluo*, Nemīndra; *Jidu modi*, Ketumatī. This name does not mean "vexilli perspicacitas," as Mr. A. Rémusat says, but "the region that has banners"; it seems that the Chinese have made a play on words on the suffix *matī*, which they have taken for *mati*, a word meaning "intelligence." The name *Jiaduolo* recalls Kedāra, and *Cakra* is this range that the Buddhists call Cakravāla and which they make the belt of the earth; it is very often a topic in the Buddhist books of Ceylon.

18. *Alphabetum Tibetanum*, pp. 481 and 482.

19. *Journal des Savants*, 1833, p. 609. *Foe koue ki*, pp. 139 and 140.

20. See Second Memorandum, section 2, p. 192, notes 174–77.

21. *Alphabetum Tibetanum*, p. 482, no. 12.

22. Vocabulaire Pentaglotte, sec 49, no. 1.

23. Csoma, *Tibetan Dictionary*, p. 243, col. 2. Schmidt, *Tibetisch-deutsches Wörterbuch*, p. 176.

24. See Second Memorandum, section 2, p. 192, notes 174–77.

that the Pāli texts designate this class of divine beings; for, since they follow this name with the word *deva*,[25] they do not permit us to doubt either the meaning or the role of the word *caturmahārājika*. I have just said that the Vocabulaire Pentaglotte gives a synonym of this term in the reading *catur mahārāja kāyikāḥ*, "those who form the retinue of the four great kings";[26] there it is a collective expression whose analog we will soon see. The four great kings, considered independently of their court, are called *caturmahārāja*; this latter denomination is the one the Tibetans have translated. The idea itself of the four great kings who are the guardians of the four cardinal points, their names, and even the way in which each of them is placed are purely Indian conceptions that the Buddhists modified very little. But what is peculiar to them is the belief that these gods occupy the inferior degree of a ladder composed of six ranks which, comprised under the generic name *kāmāvacara*, "gods of desire," constitutes the region of the desires or of love, which the Buddhists of all schools call *kāmadhātu*,[27] because the beings who populate it are all equally subject, although in different forms, to the effects of concupiscence.[28]

Above the four great kings, Georgi places the *gsum bcu rtsa gsum*, or "the thirty-three gods";[29] they are the *trayastriṃśa* of our sūtra and of the Vocabulaire Pentaglotte.[30] The Tibetans, if we must believe Georgi, have established a relation between the name of these gods and their system of the earth, of which I have not found any trace in our Sanskrit texts. They suppose that the thirty-three gods are so named because they govern the universe, which is composed of thirty-three parts, namely: five levels, eight seas, seven golden mountains, twelve continents and islands, and an iron wall. This explanation appears to me invented afterward, and I am firmly convinced that the trayastriṃśa of the Buddhists are exactly the thirty-three gods of Brahmanism, one of the most ancient classifications of the atmospheric and elemental divinities known in India.

One knows that it is Indra who, for the Buddhists as for the brahmans, is the king of the thirty-three gods, or more exactly, of the thirty-two, since it is the presence of Indra that forms the number thirty-three.[31] Georgi gives Indra the name *kia-cjin*, which, in Tibetan, is written *brgya byin*; this title appears to correspond to that of Śatamanyu or Śatakratu, as Indra is commonly known among

25. *Pārājika*, fol. *kha* recto. *Mahavamsi*, 3:135.

26. Vocabulaire Pentaglotte, sec.. 49, no. 1.

27. Vocabulaire Pentaglotte, sec. 48, no. 1.

28. *Journal des Savans*, 1831, p. 610. Des Hauterayes, "Recherches sur la religion de Fo," in *Journal Asiatique*, vol. 7, p. 315.

29. *Alphabetum Tibetanum*, p. 482, no. 13.

30. Vocabulaire Pentaglotte, sec.. 49, no. 2. The Tibetan name is a little altered in the book.

31. A. Rémusat, *Foe koue ki*, pp. 64 and 65, 128 and 129, and, moreover, the cross-references to other books indicated in these two substantial notes. See *Journal des Savans*, 1831, p. 610; Schmidt, *Mémoires de l'Académie des sciences de Saint-Pétersbourg*, 2:30ff.

the brahmans. Moreover, the Buddhists have exactly the same idea as the orthodox Indians of the Heaven of the Thirty-Three Gods and of the felicity one enjoys there. They place it at the summit of Meru, and say it is inhabited by personages whose virtue or glory has elevated there; but what appears peculiar here to the Buddhists is the idea so often repeated in the sūtras, that even humans and animals may, after their death, be reborn there for the price of their virtue.[32] Regarding this characteristic Mr. Schmidt permits himself to advance the view that the thirty-three gods are not the sole inhabitants of this land of delights.[33] I cannot confirm or contest this assertion, for the books in my hands do not say anything in this regard. I prefer, however, to believe that among the Buddhists as among the brahmans, the number thirty-three is taken literally and employed in a restrictive sense. The Buddhists have even preserved with a perfect exactitude the four categories of which these thirty-three divinities are composed. The eight *vasus* are the eight gods dispensing all goods, which accords with one of the interpretations of the word *vasu* and that recalls the antique formula *dātāro vasūnām*, δωτῆρες ἐάων. The eleven *rudras* are the eleven redoubtable divinities, which is very accurate. The twelve *ādityas* are twelve manifestations of the sun, and the two *aśvins* are two divinities who are always young: they are not invoked differently in the Vedas or the Zend Avesta.

Immediately above the thirty-three gods, that is to say, at the third level of the region of desires, come the Yāma, whom Georgi calls *thob bral ba.*[34] One must read, as in the Vocabulaire Pentaglotte,[35] *'thabs* instead of *thob*, and translate: "those who are shielded from quarrels," which would return to the meaning given to this name among the Mongols, who, according to Mr. Schmidt, translate it as "exempt from combat."[36] This explanation is, in addition, not very far from that of the Chinese, who, according to Mr. A. Rémusat, give the name *yāma* the meaning of "good time."[37] According to Mr. Schmidt, the gods of this heaven have received this name because they are outside the domain of the good and evil terrestrial spirits who are in a perpetual battle among themselves, and because the asuras of the abyss can do nothing against them.[38] If this interpretation is really authentic, it is peculiar to the Buddhists, just like the place they give these gods in their classification of the celestial levels. But one cannot say as much of the name *yāma* itself, which is quite Brahmanical, and which designates, as one knows, a class of gods whose role is not perfectly defined in mythology, although

32. *Foe koue ki*, p. 144.
33. *Mémoires de l'Académie des sciences de Saint-Pétersbourg*, 2:30.
34. *Alphabetum Tibetanum*, p. 483, no. 13.
35. Vocabulaire Pentaglotte, sec. 49, no. 3.
36. *Mémoires de l'Académie des sciences de Saint-Pétersbourg*, 2:30 and 4:216.
37. *Foe koue ki*, p. 144.
38. *Mémoires de l'Académie des sciences de Saint-Pétersbourg*, 2:30.

it is frequently mentioned in the Purāṇas.[39] The interpretation the Chinese give of the name *yāma* comes much closer than that of the Mongols to one of the significations of the primitive Sanskrit from which this name is derived. According to them, the Yāma are so named because they measure their days and their nights on the blooming and closing of lotus flowers.[40] This explanation recalls in part one of the most common meanings of the Sanskrit *yāma*, which means "a watch of three hours." From this point of view, the Yāma would be the divinities who are protectors of the divisions of the Indian day.

The fourth level of the region of desires is inhabited by the *tuṣita,* whom the Tibetans call *dga' ldan*;[41] it is exactly the translation of the Sanskrit *tuṣita*, "those who are satisfied." Georgi renders this name rather well in applying it to the heaven that these gods inhabit, *magnæ lætitiæ locus.* This meaning is known from Buddhists of all nations, Mongols and Chinese;[42] but the Chinese, according to Mr. A. Rémusat, see in it the meaning of "sufficient knowledge," which does not appear to me justified by the etymology.[43] I am likewise unaware of the reason Mr. Rémusat preferred this interpretation to that of *lætus* (joyful) that he had given to *tuṣita* in his handwritten copy of the Vocabulaire Pentaglotte, a work on which he had undertaken considerable labor that death has unfortunately interrupted.[44] The name of the Tuṣita gods is also a borrowing made by the Buddhists from Brahmanical mythology; but the Buddhists, besides the place they have given to them in their classification of the celestial levels, have made the abode they inhabit the privileged residence where there comes to be reborn, in order to descend one day among men, he who has no more than one existence to spend on earth and who is predestined to become a perfectly accomplished buddha. This is a notion about which I had occasion to speak more than once and which one finds reproduced in the sūtras at any instant.

The fifth level of the same region is the abode of the gods that Georgi calls *'phrul dga'*,[45] which he explains in this way: *gaudium ingens ex prodigiis.* It is the name that Mr. Schmidt writes, according to the erroneous transcription of the Mongols, *nirmāṇavati*, but which he translates accurately in this manner: "the region of those who find their pleasure in their own transformations or productions."[46] The word *production* appears to me less accurate than that of *transformation*; for the original term *nirmāṇarati*, as indeed our sūtra writes

39. Wilson, *Viṣṇu Purāṇa*, p. 54, note 10.

40. *Journal des Savans*, 1831, p. 610.

41. *Alphabetum Tibetanum*, pp. 182 and 483.

42. Schmidt, *Mémoires de l'Académie des sciences de Saint-Pétersbourg*, 2:30. Rémusat, *Journal des Savans*, 1831, p. 610.

43. *Foe koue ki*, p. 145.

44. Vocabulaire Pentaglotte, sec. 49, no. 4.

45. *Alphabetum Tibetanum*, p. 182 and p. 483, no. 15.

46. *Mémoires de l'Académie des sciences de Saint-Pétersbourg*, 2:29 and 4:216.

it, means: "those who find their sensual delight in their miraculous transformations." It is in this manner that Mr. A. Rémusat understands it in his unpublished work on the Vocabulaire Pentaglotte, where he translates it: *spiritus gaudens in permutationibus.*[47] The translations that the same author has preferred later, that of "heaven of conversion" or "happiness of conversion," have the disadvantage of being obscure: one does not know if one must understand *conversion* in a religious sense, which would be inaccurate; for *nirmāṇa* and the terms belonging to the same family as this word never have other meanings, in the Buddhist style, than that of "transformation resulting from magic." The name and the role of these divinities belong exclusively to the Buddhists, and I do not find anything among the brahmans that corresponds to that.[48] One would not deny, however, that the idea of attributing to the gods the faculty to take whatever form they wish by their own free will is ancient in India, since it already appears in the Vedas. It is, I believe, to this notion of supernatural power of the gods that one must attribute the idea the Buddhists had to invent a special heaven for divinities who can assume all kinds of forms. Mr. Rémusat thought that this heaven was so named because the desires born from the five principles of sensations were converted to purely intellectual pleasures there.[49]

The sixth level of the region of desires is inhabited by the gods that Georgi calls *gzhan 'phrul nbang bye*, whose name he translates in this way: *prodigiorum virtute dominantes.*[50] Our author corrects himself in another place[51] and reads, as in the Vocabulaire Pentaglotte, *dbang* instead of *nbang*, which is not given in any of our lexicons. The meaning that results from these four monosyllables is not perfectly clear; but it is elucidated by the unpublished translation of the Vocabulaire Pentaglotte of Mr. A. Rémusat, who interprets it in this way: *spiritus permutans aliena*,[52] and by that of Mr. Schmidt, who defines the heaven in question in this way: "the region of one who acts according to his will on the transformations of others," that is to say, adds the learned interpreter, "the region of one whom all forms are under his order, who acts on all the forms."[53] I must, however, skip over the other developments into which Mr. Schmidt enters on the occasion of this heaven, which he makes the abode of Māra, the god of love and passion; not that these developments are not filled with elevated views on the role of Māra in Buddhist doctrine, but they would lead me too far,

47. Vocabulaire Pentaglotte, sec. 49, no. 5.

48. Indeed, the Nirmāṇarati who, according to the *Viṣṇu Purāṇa*, form one of the classes of the gods of the eleventh Manvantara, appear to me not to have any analogy with the Nirmāṇarati of the Buddhists. (See *Viṣṇu Purāṇa*, p. 268.)

49. *Journal des Savans*, 1831, p. 610.

50. *Alphabetum Tibetanum*, p. 182.

51. *Ibid.*, p. 483, no. 16.

52. Vocabulaire Pentaglotte sec. 49, no. 6.

53. *Mémoires de l'Académie des sciences de Saint-Pétersbourg*, 2:24 and 4:216.

and save for some details, I do not find justification for them in our Sanskrit texts. I only add that the interpretations I have just mentioned are verified by that which one can give in addition of the slightly obscure term in our sūtra, *paranirmatavaśavartin*, "those who use by their own will forms that others have assumed." I do not need to note that these divinities, like the previous ones, are peculiar to the Buddhist system.

With this sixth level the first of the three regions, that of desires and concupiscence, ends. I say the first, because I follow the classification of our sūtra, which proceeds by ascending from the earth; it is obvious that this region should be called the third if one descended from the highest sphere, as Mr. Schmidt has done in the memoranda to which I cannot do better than refer the reader. Continuing to ascend, we enter the second region, that of forms, inhabited by more perfect beings; they are divided into several classes that we will enumerate in their order.

Immediately above the divinities to whom one attributes the power of transforming other creatures miraculously and by their own free will come, according to our sūtra, the *brahmakāyika*, that is to say, "those who form the retinue of Brahmā." It is the name of the gods of whom Brahmā is the chief, and the Buddhists of the South do not name this class of divinities differently. In the Vocabulaire Pentaglotte this order corresponds to the *Brahma paripatyā*, a faulty spelling that I do not hesitate to replace with *brahmapariṣadyāḥ*, supported by the easy confusion of the letters प *pa* and ष *ṣa*. The Tibetan version of the Vocabulaire Pentaglotte translates this name by *tshangs 'khor*, "troop of Brahmā," or *turma spirituum Fan*, as Mr. A. Rémusat understands it according to the Chinese.[54] The Nepalese also know this class of divinities, although they transcribe the name in a faulty manner, *brahmapraṣādyā*.[55] I will return to these differences of denomination below.

Georgi, who does not give the Tibetan name of this class of gods, at least in the place where it would be natural to look for it, replaces it with a collective term that embraces four classes of divinities and that is expressed by the Tibetan words *tshangs pha'i gnas bzhi* (or rather *pa'i*);[56] Georgi translates this expression as *sedes quadruplici contemplationis generi vacantium*, but this translation is obviously erroneous,[57] and the four Tibetan words can only mean "the four habitations of Brahmā." While admitting that the analogy of the Tibetan list and that of our sūtra continues here with the same regularity as with the previous heavens,

54. Vocabulaire Pentaglotte, sec. 50, no. 1.

55. *Transactions of the Royal Asiatic Society*, vol. 2, p. 233.

56. *Alphabetum Tibetanum*, p. 182.

57. It seems that it has been borrowed from the title borne by this section in the Vocabulaire Pentaglotte: the *Three Contemplative Gods*.

one would be led to think that the four habitations of Brahmā comprise the three terms of our sūtra where the name Brahmā figures, plus the Parīttābha who come after; but that would be an error, for we will soon recognize that the Parīttābha open a new category of gods. One thus must admit that the four habitations of Brahmā of the Tibetans correspond to the three spheres of our sūtra, namely the *brahmakāyika*, "those who form the retinue of Brahmā"; the *brahmapurohita*, "the priests or ministers of Brahmā," in Tibetan *tshangs pa mdun na 'don*;[58] and the *mahābrahmā*, in Tibetan *tshangs pa chen po.*[59]

It would now remain to determine which of these two enumerations is preferable: that of the Tibetans, who accept four heavens of Brahmā, or that of our sūtra, which recognizes only three of them. But whatever efforts I have made to find decisive reasons in favor of one or the other, it was impossible for me to succeed. I have found the one and the other supported by equally respectable authorities. Thus, the classification of Georgi is warranted by the opinion of the Nepalese, who, according to Mr. Hodgson,[60] count four heavens where Brahmā rules, and who name them in this way: *brahmakāyika*, *brahmapurohita*, *brahmapariṣadya*, and *mahābrahmāṇa*. Now, if one compares this classification with that of our sūtra, it seems that it results from the division in Nepal into the two distinct orders of the Brahmakāyika and the Brahmapariṣadya, which our sūtra and the Vocabulaire Pentaglotte appear to gather in only one category. On the other side, the classification that recognizes only three heavens of Brahmā is first adopted by the sūtra that gives rise to the present note; then by the Vocabulaire Pentaglotte that alters their names but, after all, recognizes only three orders;[61] by the Sinhalese Buddhists;[62] finally, by the Mongols according to Pallas and Mr. Schmidt.[63] Thus, a Sanskrit sūtra from Nepal speaks of three residences of Brahmā; the Mongols, who ordinarily follow the Tibetan tradition so religiously, recognize only three residences; and the Tibetans count four of them. It is one of these differences that Mr. A. Rémusat indicated while treating the very matter which occupies us,[64] and that will be possible to reconcile only when one

58. Vocabulaire Pentaglotte, sec. 50, no. 2.

59. *Ibid.*, no. 3.

60. *Transactions of the Royal Asiatic Society*, vol. 2, p. 233.

61. Vocabulaire Pentaglotte, sec. 50.

62. *Mahāvansi*, 3:136. There is, however, a confusion in the presentation of Upham; the Mahābrahmā are missing and are replaced by the Brahmakāyika. I believe it to be a substitution rather than an omission.

63. *Sammlungen historischer Nachrichten über die mongolischen Völkerschaften*, 2:48. *Mémoires de l'Académie des sciences de Saint-Pétersbourg*, 1:101. It is the suppression of the Brahmakāyika that, among the Mongols, reduces to three the number of heavens of Brahmā; but this class is not, to speak truthfully, suppressed, if one accepts as I do that it is merged with that of the Brahmapariṣadya. We will see in studying the classification of the Buddhists of the South that this latter order is the only one they accept and that in this way the Brahmakāyika and the Brahmapariṣadya make only one.

64. *Journal des Savans*, 1831, p. 610.

possesses the complete translation of the Indian, Tibetan, Chinese, and Mongol authorities, on which these various classifications rest; as for the present, I consider that of our sūtra as more supported than the other.

After all, these divergences affect only the number of the superposed heavens; as for the ideas that the names borne by these heavens express, they are exactly the same in each classification. On one side, we have four orders of gods set each above the other in this way: 1. those who form the retinue of Brahmā; 2. the ministers of Brahmā; 3. those who compose the assembly of Brahmā; 4. the great Brahmās. On the other side, we have three orders: 1. those who form the retinue of Brahmā; 2. the ministers of Brahmā; 3. the great Brahmās. It is very easy to understand that those of the retinue and those of the assembly could have been merged into a single category; on the other side, one also easily conceives that the unique class of gods called by some "those who form the retinue of Brahmā," and by the others "those who compose his assembly," could divide in two if some reason, unknown to us, required that the classification complete itself by means of one more level. For my part, I thus attach rather little importance to these differences, although I have believed it necessary to indicate them. What appears to me more worthy of remark is the systematic character of this classification, where it seems that one wished to enlarge the domain of Brahmā in forming two or three orders of the gods who approach him. We have then to note that our texts, in accord with the Nepalese tradition, call the third or the fourth of these heavens the Mahābrahmā (*mahābrahmāṇaḥ*). There are thus several superior Brahmās who populate the third or fourth heaven, and these Brahmās are doubtless beings whose holiness has elevated them to this high rank. This does not preclude that in the books of Nepal, the existence of a unique Brahmā is recalled at any instant, and that this Brahmā is known under the title *brahmāsahāṃpati*, "Brahmā, the sovereign of beings who suffer." It is probable that Brahmāsahāṃpati is the most elevated and the chief of these great Brahmās who inhabit the heaven we have just studied.

Be that as it may with these explanations, which I will not emphasize further for want of possessing a rather large number of texts that confirm them definitively, it appears to me that the difficulties we experience in finding our way in this chaos of Brahmās come exclusively from the fact that the ideas subjected to our examination belong to different epochs. I am convinced, although I cannot give all desirable proofs for this opinion, that the notion of a unique Brahmā borrowed by the Buddhists from Brahmanism is the most ancient of all those that this series of three or four heavens subordinate to Brahmā offers us. This notion shows itself as purely and as clearly as possible in Brahmāsahāṃpati, sovereign of the world inhabited by humans. The creation of two or three heavens populated by beings who serve this Brahmā is a sort of homage rendered to the grandeur of this god, who primitively belonged to Indian religion before the coming of Śākya. But at the same time, it is the work of a later classification that could only have been carried out when Buddhists felt the need to incorporate into their own system the notions they had received from their predecessors. In the end, I will say as much about this multiplication of Brahmās, who appear in the heaven of the Mahabrahmās, while asserting that it is necessary, as I propose, to take this plural literally. If the name *mahābrahmāṇaḥ*, which one must only see as a plural, is so called here in imitation of the other heavens inhabited by more or less numerous troops of divinities of the same name, then there would be only one Mahabrahmā, and this notion would be even more Indian. Finally, to complete what we know of these three orders of gods, I will add that they form the first degree of the spheres of *dhyāna*, or contemplation, as they are called, and that, according to the Vocabulaire Pentaglotte, they belong to the first contemplation. It is a division to which we will return when we will be in a position to embrace it as a whole.

Immediately above the Mahabrahmās, the gods of the second contemplation take their place, which, according to the Vocabulaire Pentaglotte,[65] is composed of three levels, like the previous contemplation. The common character of these gods, as Mr. A. Rémusat[66] has well noticed, is the radiance or light at different degrees. The first of the levels in ascending order, that is to say, that which is occupied by the last category of gods of this new sphere, is inhabited by the *parīttābha*, who are called in Tibetan *'od bsal.*[67] Georgi translates this term as *magni luminis atque splendoris*; but this interpretation is certainly inaccurate, for comparing it with other Buddhist authorities proves that this title must signify: "those who have weak light," or who are deprived of light. In our Sanskrit texts of Nepal, *parītta* (participle of *pari-dā*) ordinarily has the meaning of "limited." Moreover, the Vocabulaire Pentaglotte translates this name as *'od chung*, which has the meaning that I find in *parīttābha*. The Chinese, according to Mr. A. Rémusat, understand the name of these gods in the same way; they say that in the first degree of the second sphere dwell gods whose radiance is weak;[68] and in his unpublished translation of the Vocabulaire Pentaglotte, this author translates the Chinese version of the barbarous spelling *parīrtābha* (for *parīttābhāḥ*) in this manner, *spiritus fulgens parvus.*[69] It is, I believe, a point that cannot be the object of any doubt.

Above these gods, whose radiance is weak, one finds beings of a superior character, called by our sūtra the *apramāṇābha*, that is to say, "those whose radiance

65. Vocabulaire Pentaglotte, sec. 51.

66. *Journal des Savans*, 1831, p. 668. *Foe koue ki*, p. 145.

67. *Alphabetum Tibetanum*, p. 182 and p. 484, no. 21.

68. *Foe koue ki*, p. 145.

69. Vocabulaire Pentaglotte, sec.. 51, no. 1. Mr. Schmidt understands it in the same way (*Mémoires de l'Académie des sciences de Saint-Pétersbourg*, 4:217).

is immeasurable." The Tibetans call them *tshad med 'od*, which Georgi translated accurately as *luce infinita micantium.*[70] Mr. A. Rémusat was also not mistaken when he translated the corresponding article of the Vocabulaire Pentaglotte as *fulgens sine fine.*[71]

Finally, still above, at the third and last level of this sphere, come the *ābhāsvara*, or "those who are all radiance." Thus far, I could not discover the Tibetan name of this category of gods in Georgi; it is certainly not in its place in any of the lists he gives of the celestial levels; that is what one can be convinced of through the examination of these two lists[72] and by the observations of which the following sphere will be the object. But the Vocabulaire Pentaglotte gives it in this form: *'od gsal*, "those who have a shining radiance."[73] Here, Mr. A. Rémusat has been less fortunate than with the other articles; he believed that the name *ābhāsvara* designated gods for whom light took the place of the voice,[74] in the supposition that the word *ābhāsvara* should be divided in this way: *ābhā-svara*, "who have light for voice." We have translated this word, breaking it down in this way, *ā-bhāsvara*; and the Chinese appear to understand it in the same way according to Mr. Rémusat himself, since in his unfinished work on the Vocabulaire Pentaglotte, he translates this article as *spiritus fulgens clarus.*[75] It is also the opinion of Mr. Schmidt.

We enter now into the region of the third *dhyāna*, or third contemplation, which, according to the division of the Vocabulaire Pentaglotte, is composed of three degrees, like the previous one.[76] These gods, as Mr. A. Rémusat has well put it, have virtue and purity for their common attribute.[77] One calls the gods of the inferior level *parīttaśubha*, "those whose purity is limited"; and in Tibetan *dge chung*, that which Georgi renders accurately as *exiguarum virtutum.*[78] One sees that this category of gods is designated according to the same system as the levels of the previous contemplation.

Above come the *apramāṇaśubha*, "those whose virtue is immeasurable." The Tibetans call them *tshad med dge*, which Georgi renders accurately as *virtutum infinitarum regio.*[79] It is also the idea that the Chinese have of them, according to

70. *Alphabetum Tibetanum*, p. 182 and p. 484, no. 22.

71. Vocabulaire Pentaglotte, sec. 51, no. 2. *Foe koue ki*, p. 145. Schmidt, *Mémoires de l'Académie des sciences de Saint-Pétersbourg*, 4:217.

72. *Alphabetum Tibetanum*, pp. 182 and 484.

73. Vocabulaire Pentaglotte, sec. 51, no. 3.

74. *Foe koue ki*, p. 145.

75. Vocabulaire Pentaglotte, sec. 51, no. 3.

76. *Ibid.*, sec. 52.

77. *Journal des Savans*, 1831, p. 668. *Foe koue ki*, p. 145.

78. *Alphabetum Tibetanum*, pp. 182 and 484. We have to read *chung* and not *tshung* in the two cited places; the Vocabulaire Pentaglotte does not make this mistake (sec. 52, no. 1).

79. *Alphabetum Tibetanum*, p. 182 and p. 484, no. 24.

Mr. A. Rémusat.[80] The remark indicated concerning the previous article applies also to this one; it corresponds to the second level of the second contemplation, as the previous one corresponded to the first. I observe further with Mr. Schmidt that this class of gods is missing from the Nepalese list, but that it is known to the Mongols.[81]

The third and the highest of the levels of this sphere is inhabited by the *śubhakṛtsna*, "those who are complete purity." The two lists of Georgi do not give this expression at the place where it should be; but I have acquired the conviction, after a careful search, that the translation of the word *śubhakṛtsna* must be sought in no. 17 of his second list,[82] where following an inexplicable confusion he has placed it, against all the authorities known to me. If, indeed, in place of *ged rgyes*, one reads *dge rgyas*, as in the Vocabulaire Pentaglotte,[83] one will translate this compound as "extended purity," that is to say, "those who have absolute purity," exactly as the Chinese and the Mongols understand *śubhakṛtsna*.[84]

Above this level where the sphere of the third dhyāna ends, we enter the fourth, that is to say, the superior contemplation, which, according to our sūtra, is composed of eight degrees, and according to the Vocabulaire Pentaglotte of nine, for a reason I will mention in a short while. The inferior degree of this sphere is occupied by the *anabhraka*, or "those who are without clouds." One would vainly search in the list of Georgi for the Tibetan denomination of these gods, if one did not make use of a little of this liberty I have allowed myself on the preceding article. Indeed, immediately after *dge rgyas*, which I believe to be *śubhakṛtsna*, I find *pri med*,[85] a term that in a faulty form hides the compound *sprin med*, that is to say, "who is without clouds." This is again a correction confirmed by the Vocabulaire Pentaglotte.[86] The Chinese and the Mongols understand the name of these divinities in the same way;[87] and Mr. A. Rémusat adds that they are so called because they no longer need the support of the clouds necessary to the gods placed below them.

After the Anabhraka come the *puṇyaprasava*, whose name is susceptible to several interpretations that are only nuances of one another. One can translate it in three ways: 1. "those whose origin is purity," that is to say, "those who are born from purity"; 2. "those who produce purity"; 3. "those whose productions or descendants are pure." The two last interpretations are almost included within

80. *Journal des Savans*, 1831, p. 668. *Foe koue ki*, p. 145.

81. *Mémoires de l'Académie des sciences de Saint-Pétersbourg*, 1:102 ; and 4:217.

82. *Alphabetum Tibetanum*, p. 484, no. 17.

83. Vocabulaire Pentaglotte, sec. 52, no. 3.

84. *Foe koue ki*, p. 145. *Mémoires de l'Académie des sciences de Saint-Pétersbourg*, 4:217.

85. *Alphabetum Tibetanum*, p. 484, no. 18.

86. Vocabulaire Pentaglotte, sec. 53, no. 1.

87. *Foe koue ki*, p. 145. Vocabulaire Pentaglotte, sec. 53, no. 1. Schmidt, *Mémoires de l'Académie des sciences de Saint-Pétersbourg*, 4:217.

each other, and I do not hesitate to prefer the first, as more true to the spirit of the classical language. The list of Georgi does not put the Tibetan translation of this title in its place; but in continuing the corrections to which this list appears to me to be susceptible, I find the class of the gods that we seek in the expression *so rnam rgyes*,[88] which I read *bsod nams skyes*, like the Vocabulaire Pentaglotte,[89] and which I translate in this way: "those born from purity." Here again, I present this correction with all the more confidence, since the article with which it is concerned comes in the list of Georgi immediately after the title I have proved corresponds to the previous article, *anabhraka*. Mr. A. Rémusat translates this word according to the Chinese as "happy life,"[90] which is a bit vague. His unpublished work on the Vocabulaire Pentaglotte has *spiritus nascens ex divitiis*,[91] an expression where *divitiis* is certainly wrong, but with a kind of inaccuracy that is found in *bsod nams*, Tibetan words that mean at once, "fortune," "happiness," and "moral merit" or "purity." The Sanskrit term *puṇya* fortunately does not have such a great number of meanings.

The third level of the sphere of the fourth contemplation is inhabited by the *vṛhatphala*, "those who have great rewards." In following the new order I propose for the list of Georgi, one finds *'bres bu che ba*,[92] which I correct in this way, in agreement with the Vocabulaire Pentaglotte, *'bras bu*, etc., which I translate "great rewards," that is to say, "those who have great rewards." The Chinese, according to Mr. A. Rémusat,[93] do not understand this title, which cannot cause any difficulty, differently. I only caution persons who would be tempted to accord to the Vocabulaire Pentaglotte a confidence that this volume does not appear to me to completely merit, that the name of the Vṛhatphala is there altered in such a way that it cannot be recognized. It is necessary besides to notice the difference that the Nepalese classification offers here, as Mr. Hodgson has received it from his Buddhist, from those of our sūtra, the Vocabulaire Pentaglotte, and the Mongol books: it is that after the heaven of the Vṛhatphala, the Nepalese place the *arangisattva*, or nonpassionate beings, of whom our other lists do not speak.[94] It seems that this new name is only a synonym of the already known other classes, perhaps of the Avṛha, to which we will proceed and who are probably called gods free from efforts only because they are free from passion and all attachment. I will note below the existence of another category of gods peculiar

88. *Alphabetum Tibetanum*, p. 484, no. 19.

89. Vocabulaire Pentaglotte, sec. 53, no. 2.

90. *Foe koue ki*, p. 146.

91. Vocabulaire Pentaglotte, sec. 53, no. 2. Compare with Schmidt, *Mémoires de l'Académie des sciences de Saint-Pétersbourg*, 4:217.

92. *Alphabetum Tibetanum*, p. 484, no. 20.

93. *Foe koue ki*, p. 146. Vocabulaire Pentaglotte, sec. 53, no. 3.

94. *Transactions of the Royal Asiatic Society*, 2:234.

to the Nepalese, whose invention would also explain itself well in this manner. I must remark, however, that the Buddhists of Ceylon have here an order of gods that Upham calls *assanjasatthaya*,[95] of which the Pāli title, if one reads it *asangasatta*, has the same meaning as the *arangisattva* of the Nepalese.

At the fourth degree come the *avṛha*, whose name is not perfectly clear; it can signify "those who do not grow," or "those who are not making efforts." The Chinese version of the Vocabulaire Pentaglotte, as Mr. A. Rémusat understands it, gives this latter interpretation the precision that it lacks; this scholar renders it, in fact, as *spiritus sine cogitationibus*,[96] or "the heaven where there is no reflection." I do not have difficulty accepting this meaning, which I fix with still a little more clarity, in saying: "those who are not making efforts (to think)." As for the Tibetan translation of this title, one finds it, after having exhausted the transpositions I have indicated previously, in this form, *mi che ba*,[97] a compound that appears to me susceptible to a sole signification, "one who is not tall." But this signification does not come close enough to the primitive *avṛha* in order for me not to suspect some error; and I would propose to read *mi mched pa*, which according to the dictionary of Csoma could be translated by "those who do not lie down," with the same degree of vagueness as the Sanskrit *avṛha*. It is also the version adopted by Mr. Schmidt according to his Mongol authorities, who appear to closely follow the Tibetans here.[98]

Above the Avṛha come the *atapa*, "those who do not experience suffering." Georgi calls them in Tibetan *mi dung ba*;[99] but he does not translate this name any more than the previous ones. I do not waver in restoring here the reading that I think the true one, and to read *mi gdung ba*, "those who are free from distress," exactly like the Vocabulaire Pentaglotte. The Chinese understand *atapa* well, and Mr. A. Rémusat translates their version in these two different manners, *spiritus sine mærore* and "heaven without fatigue."[100] Mr. Schmidt translates this name likewise as "gods free from distress."

There come after that, at the sixth degree, the *sudṛśa*, "those who see well"; they are the *shin tu mtho ba* of Georgi,[101] a reading that I correct in this way, *shin tu mthong ba*, to translate "those who see perfectly." The Vocabulaire Pentaglotte shifts this interpretation, putting it under the following article, and vice versa; it could be that on this point it was less accurate than Georgi. The explanation

95. *Mahāvansi*, 3:136.

96. Vocabulaire Pentaglotte, sec. 53, no. 4. *Foe koue ki*, p. 146.

97. *Alphabetum Tibetanum*, p. 182; and p. 485, no. 25; and *Mitchhe* in the Vocabulaire Pentaglotte, sec. 53, no. 5.

98. *Mémoires de l'Académie des sciences de Saint-Pétersbourg*, 1:103; and 4:217.

99. *Alphabetum Tibetanum*, p. 182; and p. 485, no. 26.

100. Vocabulaire Pentaglotte, sec. 53, no. 5. *Foe koue ki*, p. 146.

101. *Alphabetum Tibetanum*, p. 182; and p. 485, no. 27.

I propose is also that of the Chinese, at least according to Mr. A. Rémusat, who translates their version in this way: *spiritus bonus vivus*, or "the heaven of the gods who admirably see all the worlds."[102] Here too, the Vocabulaire Pentaglotte altered the Sanskrit term very greatly.

At the seventh degree of the same sphere are established the *sudarśana*, whose name must signify "those whose appearance is beautiful." The Tibetans, according to Georgi, give them the name *gya nom snang ba*,[103] which can mean "those who have a beautiful appearance." The Chinese, according to Mr. A. Rémusat, understand it in this way; because in his unpublished translation of the Vocabulaire Pentaglotte, he translates their version in this way, *bonus apparens*;[104] but in his notes on the *Foe koue ki*, he renders the name *sudarśana* as "heaven of the gods for whom all is present and manifest."[105] The first interpretation appears to me far preferable; the second would only reproduce the idea expressed by the name of the gods of the preceding heaven.

Above these gods, and before the Akaniṣṭha who will follow, the Nepalese list of Mr. Hodgson places a category quite unknown to the other Buddhist authorities, that of the *sumukha*.[106] This title *sumakha* means "gods with a beautiful face,"[107] and it recalls so well the *sudarśana* who precede it that I am tempted to regard it as a simple synonym of the name *sudarśana*. It is possible that this term has slipped into the list in its capacity as a commentary on the preceding name, without which it could have been confused with that of the Sudṛśa. I have already made an analogous observation with regard to the Arangisattva; but I confess that this remark has for me more value here than with regard to the category of gods I recall above. I only add that by means of the addition of these two categories, the Nepalese Buddhists count ten heavens of the fourth contemplation instead of eight that the Chinese and the Mongols recognize in accord with our sūtra.

Finally, there comes at the eighth degree the *akaniṣṭha*, that is to say, "the highest ones," on whose name I had occasion to explain myself above.[108] I have shown that this name means literally "those who are not the smallest." The Tibetans call them *'og min*, "those who are not inferior," an exact translation of the Sanskrit *akaniṣṭha*. Georgi renders this expression as *altissimus*:[109] the good

102. Vocabulaire Pentaglotte, sec. 53, no. 6.

103. *Alphabetum Tibetanum*, p. 182; and p. 485, no. 28.

104. Vocabulaire Pentaglotte, sec. 53, no. 7. The original Sanskrit term is here also almost distorted by the editor of this work.

105. *Foe koue ki*, p. 146.

106. *Transactions of the Royal Asiatic Society*, vol. 2, p. 234.

107. Mr. Schmidt translates this name as: *höchste Vortrefflichkeit*, "the highest excellence." I do not know on what this interpretation is based, which Mr. Schmidt modifies elsewhere by adding to it the idea of *light* (*Mémoires de l'Académie des sciences de Saint-Pétersbourg*, 1:102; and 4:217).

108. Above, section 2, p. 205, note 199.

109. *Alphabetum Tibetanum*, p. 182.

father who hardly has any verve, except to insult Beausobre, forgot to interpret the greatest number of previous words; he remembered here that he had to translate it or say that he could not. The Chinese understand the title of these gods in the same way; thus, in his unpublished work on the Vocabulaire Pentaglotte, Mr. A. Rémusat renders it as *princeps supremus*;[110] but they add, at least if we must believe the Vocabulaire Pentaglotte, a higher heaven that crowns the sphere of the fourth contemplation. This work writes it in a barbarous manner: *mahāśvarivasanamra*, a spelling that Mr. A. Rémusat has well restored by reading *maheśvaravasanam*,[111] that is to say, "the residence of Maheśvara."

I believe I am able to advance the idea that this addition of a ninth heaven to the eight given by our sūtra is not justified by any of the ancient Sanskrit books at my disposal. It could be at the very most justified by the tantras; for the idea of this heaven of the great Īśvara is manifestly a borrowing from Śivaism. One can boldly conclude that the Vocabulaire Pentaglotte has been compiled by monks to whom the mixture of Śivaism with Buddhism was familiar. Perhaps this addition was favored by the necessity to have twenty-four heavens, from the lowest, or that of the four great kings, to the highest. Indeed, without the abode of the great Īśvara, the Vocabulaire Pentaglotte, like our sūtra, has only twenty-three gods; while, if instead of the three levels that these two authorities assign to the heaven of Brahmās, one counts four of them, as the Nepalese and the Tibetans do, the total number of twenty-four heavens is obtained, without it being necessary to count nine heavens of the third contemplation instead of eight. In any case, the addition of a heaven, special abode of Maheśvara, is all the more remarkable, since the Buddhists who have collected the materials that figure in the Vocabulaire Pentaglotte could place Maheśvara in the heaven of the Akaniṣṭha, as the Nepalese have done with regard to their Ādibuddha.[112] It proves that these Buddhists did not know this Ādibuddha, of which the sūtras of the North, as I have said more than once, do not speak more than the Mongol books.[113]

Let us now summarize what results from this presentation for the knowledge of Buddhist mythology. It is evident that from the four great kings to the great Brahmās, Brahmanical ideas dominate, and gain in number and in importance

110. Vocabulaire Pentaglotte, sec. 53, no. 8.

111. *Foe koue ki*, p. 146.

112. Hodgson, *Transactions of the Royal Asiatic Society*, vol. 2, p. 233. The Nepalese write the name of this heaven *agniṣṭha*. This spelling is even more wrong in that it offers a meaning.

113. Schmidt, *Mémoires de l'Académie des sciences de Saint-Pétersbourg*, 1:97. Mr. Schmidt asserts that the supreme Ādibuddha is completely unknown to the Tibetans, and that not the least trace of him is found in their books; however, the Tibetans who have translated the tantras where he is a subject, in particular the *Kālacakra Tantra*, must know him. The assertion of Mr. Schmidt is certainly too general, unless he does not count the tantras among the number of canonical books. I am quite close to sharing this sentiment; but I believe it no less necessary to distinguish and to say which category of books one speaks about.

over the ideas peculiar to the Buddhists.[114] That which belongs to these latter is, besides the invention of two orders of divinities unknown to the brahmans, the classification resting on this hypothesis: that to the degree that the heavens are distant from the earth, they increase in power and in purity. Above the Great Brahmās up to the Akaniṣṭha, all is Buddhist, invention and disposition. These fourteen heavens, which with the four of Brahmā constitute the world of forms divided in four spheres of contemplation, allow us to see well, as Mr. A. Rémusat had said, that one has striven to gradually increase perfection by piling up ideas of purity, light, and grandeur.[115]

Can one say that all this is contemporary with Śākya? It is this that I would not dare to affirm; it is still certain that these conceptions are ancient in Buddhism, for they belong to the two great schools that started to separate from the common trunk three centuries before our era. One will doubtless later recognize that it is necessary to distinguish between the container and the manner of which it is filled; the container is the belief in four degrees of contemplation that Śākya and his foremost disciples are said to have passed beyond. These degrees of contemplation are purely philosophical and all the more perfect since they are of a higher rank. The inhabitants of the three or four heavens of Brahmā, like those of the fourteen superior levels, are connected to these four degrees of dhyāna, probably because each of these dhyānas is the kind of speculation in which these various gods indulge, and which merited their residence in one of the corresponding spheres.[116] I say probably, for I must recognize that I have not found any definite assertion in this regard in the Sanskrit texts I have consulted.

In order to complete the exposition of the system of superior worlds, as the Buddhists conceive it, it would be necessary to speak of the third region, that is to say, of the highest of all, which under the collective name of "region without form, or what has no form," comprises four heavens, which the Vocabulaire Pengaglotte names.[117] I could refer to the special memorandum of Mr. Schmidt in which this learned author gives a philosophical theory of this immaterial region, where the infinity in space and in intelligence is crowned by a heaven where there are no ideas and no absence of ideas.[118] But not having found in our Sanskrit texts of Nepal confirmation of this theory, of which the principal idea is that the Buddha is united in these heavens with *prajñāpāramitā* or with a perfect nirvāṇa,

114. Mr. Hodgson had already made this remark (*Transactions of the Royal Asiatic Society*, vol. 2, p. 248, note 7).

115. *Foe koue ki*, p. 146. *Journal des Savans*, 1831, p. 669.

116. A. Rémusat, "Essai sur la cosmographie et la cosmogonie des bouddhistes," in *Journal des Savans*, 1831, p. 668.

117. Vocabulaire Pentaglotte, sec. 54.

118. *Mémoires de l'Académie des sciences de Saint-Pétersbourg*, 1:101 and 102. See also the same collection, 4:217.

apart from all relation with matter, I would be obliged, in order to discuss it, to enter into clarifications that would considerably augment this already quite long note. I shall have, moreover, a favorable occasion to return to this subject in the second volume of the present work, in examining a most interesting passage of the Pāli texts; I will show then what idea the Buddhists have on the creation of all these worlds, which is for them the necessary result of the conduct of the moral beings who inhabit them, and not the work of a creator God that Buddhism has never known.

No. 5. On the Sandalwood Called *Gośīrṣa*

(Second Memorandum, Section 3, Page 254)

The name of this sandalwood means "head of a cow"; it appears that this species is the most esteemed of all, for one finds it often mentioned in the legends. The Tibetans transcribe it rather exactly in this manner, *gor shi sha*, and rightly consider it a proper noun that they preserve in their versions.[1] I am convinced that it is this same name that the Mongols express with the word *gurschoscha*, a species of sandalwood which, according to the legend related to the discovery of the miraculous image of Avalokiteśvara, grows only on the northern part of the Malaya mountains.[2] Nothing indicates to us if the Mongols know the true meaning of their *gurschoscha*; but it appears evident to me that they knew, although modifying it slightly, that of the primitive Sanskrit term *gośīrṣa*. I do not hesitate to recognize the sandalwood *cow's head* in the species that the Mongols call *elephant's head*.[3] This change of meaning comes from the Mongols having borrowed this denomination from the Tibetans, in whose language the name of the ox, *glang po*, takes on, with the addition of *chen* (large), the meaning of "elephant," that is to say, a large ox. The Mongols, who owe to the Tibetans what they know of the natural products of India, can well have made this error that, after all, does not have great importance.

1. Schmidt, *Der Weise und der Thor*, p. 282, text; and p. 353, German translation.
2. *Id. Geschichte der Ost-Mongolen*, p. 332.
3. Schmidt, *Geschichte der Ost-Mongolen*, pp. 15, 313, and 314.

The name *gośīrṣa* is, moreover, classical in India; one finds it in the *Vocabulary of Amara*, and Wilson explains it in this way: "a species of sandalwood the color of copper and with a strong smell."[4] It is no less familiar to the Buddhists of the South, and Clough gives it in his *Pāli Vocabulary* under its mild form *gosīsa.*[5] Abul-Fazel cites another kind of sandalwood whose name has eluded the authors of *Kurdish Studies*;[6] it is that of *mekasiry*,[7] which is certainly the same as the مقاصری, or sandalwood of Macassar, a name that these authors report according to Sprengel.

The Tibetan legend of the statue of Avalokiteśvara speaks also of another kind of sandalwood whose Mongol name means "snake's heart," for which I do not have the means to restore the Sanskrit name; it appears, according to the legend, that it is a divine sandalwood that grows only in the highest region of the heaven of the Buddhists, among the Akaniṣṭha gods.[8] It is, however, not useless to remark that the two words *snake's heart*, in Sanskrit *sarpa hṛdaya*, could, if they were shifted, *hṛdaya sarpa*, take the meaning of "which has snakes in the heart." Now, one knows that among some Indian poets, and notably in Jayadeva, the author of the *Gītagovinda*, the sandalwood trees of the Malaya mountains are frequently marked as the den of snakes that withdraw into the cavities of their trunks. If it were thus established that the sandalwood of which the Tibetan legend speaks had been called in Sanskrit *hṛdaya sarpa*, one would see in this denomination of a sandalwood that is in other respects fabulous only a figurative expression to designate all kinds of sandalwood in general, according to a character common to all varieties of this tree.

It would remain to seek the reason for this name given to the first kind of sandalwood, *cow's head.* Does it come from the brown color of this wood? I would not know how to assert this, for grayish cows are in general more common in India than tawny ones. Dr. Roulin, whom I have consulted on this subject, thinks that the name *cow's head* could result from the analogy that exists between the slightly musky smell of certain sandalwoods and that which the body of animals of the oxen type gives off in general. This smell, among the species where it is most pronounced, exists above all in the tuft of hair that covers the forehead. According to this hypothesis, the name *candanagośīrṣa* would amount to saying "sandalwood that has the smell of the head of an ox." Before concluding, I have to remark that the name of the sandalwood I have just examined is the only one, to my knowledge, that appears in the Buddhist legends. I do not recall

4. *Sanscrit Dictionary*, p. 302, col. 1, 1832 ed.
5. *Pāli Grammar and Vocabulary*, p. 28, st. 18b.
6. Pott and Rödiger, "Kurdische Studien," in *Zeitschrift für die Kunde des Morgenlandes*, vol. 5, p. 80.
7. Gladwin, *Ayeen Akbery*, 1:92, in -4°.
8. Schmidt, *Geschichte der Ost-Mongolen*, pp. 330 and 332.

having come across the name of the sandalwood produced in the Malaya mountains more than once, namely *malayacandana.* It is in the legend of the prince who gives his body to a starving tigress to devour, a legend that is a part of the *Suvarṇaprabhāsa*, whose antiquity is very doubtful in my opinion.[9]

9. *Survarṇaprabhāsa*, fol. 110a of the MS of the Société Asiatique. Compare Schmidt, *Grammatik der Mongolischen Sprache*, p. 161.

No. 6. On the Name Śākala
(Second Memorandum, Section 3, page 404)

This name recalls that of the formerly celebrated city of Śākala or Sakala, which is already mentioned in the *Mahābhārata*,[1] and which the Greeks knew under the name Σάγγαλα according to Arrian,[2] under that of Σάγαλα according to Ptolemy, and finally under that of Συθυδημία, a name that, according to the same Ptolemy, is synonymous with Σάγαλα and is related, as Bayer said long ago, to the name of the Bactrian king Euthydemus.[3] Whatever difficulties still exist concerning the precise position of this city because of the imperfect knowledge we have about the present Punjab, where all the critics agree to seek it, nothing is less fabulous than its existence. It would be quite difficult to add something new to the thorough discussions of which it has been the object on the part of Lassen[4] and of Wilson.[5] Let us only recall that Lassen, while renouncing, on the authority of Droysen, the idea that the Śākala of the *Mahābhārata* is the Sangala of Arrian, recognizes that Śākala is the capital of the Bahīkas, and that it is consequently in the Punjab; and, moreover, that he does not move away from this region, in making Śākala the capital of the Madras. I regard as less demonstrated the link he tries to establish between this name and the Śākaladvīpa of the *Mahābhārata*.

1. Lassen, *Commentatio geographica atque historica de Pentapotamia indica*, p. 64.
2. *De Expeditione Alexandri*, bk. 5, chaps. 21 and 22.
3. Lassen, *loc. cit.* pp. 20 and 36. Cf. Benfey, "Indien," p. 85 of the extract.
4. Lassen, *Zeitschrift für die Kunde des Morgenlandes*, vol. 1, p. 353, and vol. 3, p. 157ff., and p. 212.
5. *Ariana antiqua*, p. 196ff.

Alexander Burnes identifies the Sāgala of Arrian with Lahore;[6] and Benfey, without going that far, does not believe the two cities to be very far from each other.[7] Finally, Masson[8] finds the ruins of Sāgala or Sangala on the site of Harrīpa, sixty miles southwest of Lahore. It is this opinion, whose perfect evidence Lassen rightly contests,[9] that Mr. Wilson seems to side with.[10]

The name Śākala is mentioned in the Buddhist legends of the North, without it being possible to discover the true position of the city that bears it. At the end of the legend of Aśoka, it is said that Puṣpamitra, the fifth successor of this prince, went to Śākala to destroy the religion of Śākya, promising a hundred dināras for each śramaṇa's head brought to him.[11] The name Śākala is also known from the Buddhists of Ceylon, in the form *Sāgala*; and Mr. Turnour has provided interesting extracts of a Pāli book, the *Milindapañha*, where Milinda, king of Sāgala, is depicted discussing the main points of the Buddhist religion with the wise Nāgasena.[12] I will return, in speaking of Nāgasena, to this work of which I possess a Sinhalese version, which to my eyes does not have all the importance that Mr. Turnour accords it. I content myself at the moment, as far as the word that occupies us is concerned, in making the following observations.

The difference between these two spellings, *Sāgala* and *Sangala*, cannot cause any difficulty. That of *Sangala* is a provincialism found in the Sinhalese transcriptions of a great number of Sanskrit words; thus, the king Nāgasena is ordinarily called Nangasena; Nagara is written *Nangara* and the Sāgala of the Pāli text of the *Milinda* is read *Sangala* in the Sinhalese gloss of this book. The addition of this nasal before a guttural ordinarily has the effect of necessitating the substitution of the sign of the short vowel for that of the long one, in the manner that the sign changes but the quantity remains the same. In this respect, I compare it to doubling a consonant in Pāli words, a doubling that needs to be preceded by a short vowel. Although peculiar to the Pāli of Ceylon, I persuade myself that the insertion of this nasal has also taken place in India in ancient epochs. One finds traces of it in dialects of Prakrit origin and, in order not to depart from our subject, the two Greek spellings *Sāgala* and *Sangala* are not explained otherwise; obviously, the first reproduced the scholarly form and the second the popular form. I do not need to caution that this connection pertains only to the name, and that it presumes nothing about the contested identity of the Sāgala

6. *Travels in Bokhara*, 3:182.

7. *Göttingische gelehrte Anzeigen*, May 1841, p. 759.

8. "Suggestions on the Sites of Sangala and the Altars of Alexander," in *Journal of the Asiatic Society of Bengal*, vol. 6, p. 58.

9. *Zeitschrift für die Kunde des Morgenlandes*, vol. 3, p. 154ff.

10. *Ariana antiqua*, pp. 197 and 198.

11. *Divyāvadāna*, fol. 211 b. Above, Second Memorandum, section 3, p. 464.

12. *Journal of the Asiatic Society of Bengal*, vol. 5, p. 530ff.

of Arrian and the cities of Śākala, Sāgala, and Sangala of the Indians. I add that if my analysis is accurate, then all the etymologies of this word one would like to seek that take the nasal into account, as Mr. Masson has tried to do, accomplish nothing.[13] It is not that I regard the reading *Sāgala* to be a perfectly accurate spelling; on the contrary, I do not hesitate to see in it the alteration of *Śākala*, owing to the substitution of the soft for the strong, which takes place in several dialects of North India. The true reading is certainly that of the *Mahābhārata* and the Buddhist legends. One can neither be in doubt on the nature of the initial sibilant; this must be *Śākala*, as Lassen writes it according to Pāṇini and a manuscript of the *Rāmāyaṇa*.[14] This spelling is the only one that lends itself well to a regular etymological explanation; I propose, in fact, to see in it "the habitation of the Śakas," by virtue of an analogous derivation to that which Lassen has given of the ethnic term Siṃhala, "the abode of lions." The presence of the Śakas or Saces in this part of India, prior to the invasion of Alexander, however novel it may appear, is still not impossible. One knows, moreover, that the denomination Śaka in antiquity was that for the generality of equestrian and nomadic peoples, in opposition to peoples established in cities. This interpretation of the name Śākala would even explain, if it could be more explicitly demonstrated, the reproach and blame with which the *Mahābhārata* stigmatizes the dissolute mores of its inhabitants.

13. *Journal of the Asiatic Society of Bengal*, vol. 6, p. 60.
14. *Zeitschrift für die Kunde des Morgenlandes*, vol. 3, p. 212.

No. 7. On the Expression *Pratītyasamutpāda*

(Second Memorandum, Section 4, Page 449)

Here is an explanation of the sacramental term *pratītyasamutpāda*, which the commentator of the *Abhidharmakośa* attributes to the philosopher Śrīlābha. In this compound, *prati* has the meaning of "succession, repetition"; *itya* means "made to go," to go away; it is the suffix *ya*[1] that here gives the word *itya* the meaning of "*made to* go away, disappear"; in a word, *itya* means "unstable." The preposition *sam* means "together, in connection"; and *pad* preceded by *ut* means "apparition." From that, it results that the compound *pratītyasamutpāda* can be translated in this way: "production related to conditions made to disappear successively"; for, the commentator adds, no condition is ever born alone.[2]

I will return to this important term in my examination of the Sinhalese collection. I only note here that, although formed of completely Sanskrit elements, the word *pratītya* does not exist, at least to my knowledge, in the classical language of the brahmans; I only find *pratyaya*[3] there, which means "cause, origin." Such must be, I do not doubt, the meaning of the Buddhist *pratītya*, and if the commentator Śrīlābha prefers to this meaning that of "unstable," it is 1. that he holds more strictly to the etymology according to which *pratītya* is a participial adjective, 2. that he envisages only the philosophical meaning according to which

1. This suffix is called *kyap* in Pāṇini (*Pāṇini*, vol. 3, bk. 1, 109).
2. *Abhidharmakośavyākhyā*, fol. 213b.
3. Derived from the same root as *pratītya*.

conditions, which are successively causes and effects, have a character of instability. But without going as far as the Sinhalese, who translate *pratītya* as "cause," and while remaining with the authorities of the North, we find the meaning of "cause" given by the Tibetan interpreters, who, remarkably enough, surrender this word to their system of material literalness. Thus, the Tibetan version of the *Saddharmapuṇḍarīka*[4] translates *pratītyasamutpāda* by *rten cing 'brel bar 'gyur ba*, "linked production, related to causes," an expression for whose interpretation Schröter[5] provides the formula *rten cing 'byal bar 'byung ba*, "two things united together, as cause and effect," and the phrase *rten cing 'brel bar 'byung ba yan lag bcu gnyis ni*, "twelve roots united with cause and effect," or perhaps that are united between themselves in that they are mutually the effect and cause of each other; that is precisely the coming together of the twelve nidānas. Now, if one analyzes the Tibetan version, one finds first *rten cing*, which Schröter translates as "cause"; it is the word that corresponds to the Sanskrit *pratītya*. Then comes *'brel bar*, a word that appears in an adverbial form and means "in a related manner." This adverb certainly modifies the word that follows *'byung ba*, "production," and it represents the prefix *sam* in the expression *samutpāda*. I thus literally render this compound "related production," which gives me for the entire expression: "production related to causes." From this Tibetan expression, which plays so great a role in the primitive system of Buddhist philosophy, the only part that I find in the dictionaries of Csoma and of Schmidt is *rten 'brel*, "fundamental connection, reciprocal agreement." And as far as the first monosyllable is concerned, which in the version of the *Lotus of the Good Law* is followed by *cing*, formative of the gerund, one sees that it translates, as I indicated at the outset, not the etymological meaning but, by extension, *pratyaya*.

Furthermore, the translation given by the *Lotus* and Schröter of the compound *pratītyasamutpāda* is classical; for I find it in the collection of legends recently published by Mr. Schmidt.[6] It is the topic, in the third chapter of this work, of a sūtra entitled: *Rten cing 'brel bar 'byung ba bcu gnyis kyi mdo*, which is translated by Mr. Schmidt: *Der aus den zwölf gegenseitigen Bedingungen Entstandene*. The present note sufficiently explains why I would translate this title in the following manner: "The Sūtra of the Twelve Productions Related to Causes." I believe I recall having seen a similar title in a collection of the Vinaya of the Sinhalese in Pāli; but the searches I have made thus far to find it have been unsuccessful; I hope to be able to return to it in the second volume of the present work.

4. Sanskrit text, chap. 1, fol. 11a.
5. *Bhotanta Dictionary*, p. 338, col. 2.
6. *Der Weise and der Thor*, text, p. 26; trans., p. 30.

No. 8. Additions and Corrections

Page 109, end of the third paragraph.—[It is indispensable to add what follows to the clarifications I have given on the application of the title *upadeśa* to the books called *tantras*.] It is only natural, moreover, to see the tantras called *upadeśa*; for this latter word, apart from its general meaning of "advice, instruction," also has the very special meaning of "initiation," that is to say, of "communication of a mantra or a formula by which the master initiates the disciple."[1] This word is familiar to all the Brahmanical schools, and nothing is more common in India than to hear it said: "The *upadeśa*, or the formula of initiation of such-and-such sect, is such-and-such mantra." It is exactly in this latter sense that the Buddhist tantras employ the word *upadeśa*, and this is all the more natural since these tantras are only Śivaist books originally, that is to say, books whose core is Indian and independent of Buddhism, as I try to prove in section 5 of my Second Memorandum.

Page 118, line 15 and note 10 of the page 119.—The four principles of supernatural power, or more exactly, the four foundations of this power, are enumerated in a more complete manner in the Vocabulaire Pentaglotte[2] than in our text, where two of the names they bear are only indicated in brief. I have said in note 10, to which this addition is related, that without commentary, one could not flatter

1. Wilson, *Sanscrit Dictionary*, p. 154, 1832 ed.
2. Vocabulaire Pentaglotte, sec. 27.

oneself to understand these obscure formulas perfectly; however, the comparison of the version given by the Tibetans with the original terms permits me to attempt the explanation. The fundamental term is *ṛddhipada*, which the Tibetans represent by *rdzu 'phrul gyi rkang pa*, "the foundation of miraculous transformations." The first of these foundations is, for the Vocabulaire Pentaglotte, as for our text, *chanda samādhi prahāṇa saṃskāra samanvāgata*, a compound the examination of the Tibetan version of which allows me to place all the terms in the following relation: "endowed with the conception of renunciation of the meditation of desire." From which it follows that the first foundation of supernatural power consists in the faculty of conceiving the abandonment of all ideas of desire, or is the effect of this faculty. The second foundation, whose name is only given in brief in the text of our sūtra, is developed in this way in the Vocabulaire Pentaglotte: *citta samādhi prahāṇa saṃskāra samanvāgata*, and one can translate it literally in the same system: "endowed with the conception of renunciation of the meditation of thought." It follows from that that the second foundation of supernatural power consists in the faculty of conceiving the abandonment of all ideas of thought. The third foundation is *vīrya samādhi prahāṇa saṃskāra samanvāgata.* After what I just said concerning the two previous terms, I can put forward, without insisting further on the latter, that the third foundation of supernatural power consists in the faculty of conceiving the abandonment of all ideas of energy. The fourth foundation is called *mīmāṃsā samādhi prahāṇa saṃskāra samanvāgata*; it consists in the faculty of conceiving the abandonment of all ideas of investigation. It results from all this that the Buddhists attribute supernatural faculties to one who has succeeded in imagining that he has renounced all ideas of desire, thought, effort, investigation, or meditation, that is to say, one who, somehow, has detached himself from all interior operation. Since that is hardly possible in the ordinary state of humanity, one understands that those who one believed capable of this prodigious detachment could have been taken, by people who believed in the possibility of such a power, to be endowed with a power superior to that of man.

Page 119, note 11.—See also, touching on the title *tathāgata*, the discussion in which Mr. W. von Humboldt was engaged, who has distinguished, as the Sinhalese do, two meanings in *tathāgata*, according to whether this word is divided in this way, *tathā gata*; or in this way, *tathā āgata.*[3]

Page 120, note 14, on the word *sugata.*—According to the explanations that Mr. W. von Humboldt gives of this term, it seems that he finds in it the meaning of "one who has progressed well, who has arrived at the end, at perfection."[4]

3. *Über die Kawi-Sprache*, 1:270 and 271.
4. *Ibid.*, p. 270.

I do not deny that this meaning cannot be preferred to that of "well come," which I have asserted. Among the observations of which the title of *sugata*, like that of *tathāgata*, is the object on the part of Mr. von Humboldt, I cannot prevent myself from noticing the astonishment he experiences that the titles *sugata* and *tathāgata*, which imply an idea of progressing, of departure, or of arrival, can be applied to the primitive Ādibuddha, the independent and invisible being. According to my point of view, this erroneous application is easily explained. The titles of *sugata* and *tathāgata* properly belong to the human buddha Śākyamuni; but when the divine buddha Ādibuddha was invented, it was the least that could be done to accord him the superior qualities that a simple mortal had possessed. One thus decorated him with all the titles that Śākyamuni had borne, whatever their practical or material meaning could have been; one had in one's possession the resource of mystical interpretations, and one could always say that it was only as a mortal buddha that the supreme Ādibuddha received these various titles.

Page 126, line 22.—The expression that I have translated as "the four supports of memory" is *catuḥ smṛtyupasthāna*; these *smṛtyupasthāna* are enumerated in the Vocabulaire Pentaglotte with the following names: *kāyasmṛtyupasthānam*, *vedanāsmṛtyupasthānam*, *cittasmṛtyupasthānam*, *dharmasmṛtyupasthānam*.[5] It seems from this that the objects or the means of the four *smṛtyupasthāna* are the body, sensation, thought, and the law. The Tibetans translate this term so literally that it is rather difficult to recognize their opinion with regard to its true meaning. It is with the monosyllables *dran pa nyer bdag*, doubtless "the action of placing his memory," that they render *smṛtyupasthāna*. One can, however, conclude from this that the original term *upasthāna* must be translated as "application," in this manner: "the application of memory to the body, or with the help of the body, etc." The Chinese version, at least as Mr. A. Rémusat interprets it, permits us to go a little further, since it translates the words corresponding to *smṛtyupasthāna* with *cogitare respiciendo corpus*, etc. It is not a case here of memory; and in fact, the word *smṛti* (like the Pāli *sati*) has in the Buddhist style the special meaning of "thought, reflection." It is probably in this manner that one must understand it here; and *smṛtyupasthāna*, which literally interpreted means "the placement of reflection," perhaps must be translated as "the application of thought." I prefer this latter explanation to that of "supports of memory," which I had adopted not having examined the enumeration of the Vocabulaire Pentaglotte closely enough.

Page 152, line 20.—When I sought to establish that the system of the dhyāni buddhas should be independent of the existence of Ādibuddha, I could have

5. Vocabulaire Pentaglotte, sec. 25.

taken the sentiment of Mr. W. von Humboldt as my authority, who recalls that Hemacandra already mentions in the eleventh century a great number of divinities, today worshipped by the Nepalese, and who concludes from that that these divinities were honored in India before Buddhism had been transported to Nepal.[6] The truth is that Mr. von Humboldt does not express himself in a manner as affirmative as I do; and I must note it, in order that one not believe that I wish him to partake in my error, if I commit one. But I am confident that if he had had in his hands the material I have at my disposal, his conclusions would not have differed from those I set forth in my text.

Page 192, note 178. The monk whose decent aspect struck Śāriputra, at a time when he was still not converted to Buddhism, is called Upasena by the *Mahāvastu.*[7] Faxian, who has preserved the tradition of this meeting for us, calls this monk *Epi.*[8] On the other side, Xuanzang, according to Klaproth, calls him *Ashiposhi*, that is to say, as Klaproth has well seen, Aśvajit, the name of a monk who is in fact celebrated among the first disciples of Śākya.[9] Should it be concluded from this connection that the names Upasena and Aśvajit designate the same personage? This is possible, for these two names are both military titles.

Page 206, fifth paragraph, on the proper noun Pāñcika.—I have forgotten to make note, on the occasion of the proper noun Pāñcika (which is given as that of the general of the yakṣas in the legend of the miracles), that it is perhaps the same as *Banzhi*, taken by Faxian, at least according to Klaproth, for a celestial musician who played the lyre in honor of Śākyamuni, not far from Nālanda.[10] But I must caution that Mr. A. Rémusat translated this passage differently and that he made *banzhi* a tune or an instrument.[11] Now, we know that the Sanskrit numeral *pañcan* applies to the fifth of the Indian musical modes, which is called *pañcama*, or the fifth;[12] in addition, the Indians sometimes call music "the sound of the five instruments." It is probably between these latter two meanings that one must choose to explain the *Banzhi* of the Chinese traveler.

Page 209, second paragraph, at the word *jina.* The name *jina* is one of the synonyms of *buddha*, or rather it is one of the numerous epithets given to a buddha.

6. *Über die Kawi-Sprache*, 1:298.
7. *Mahāvastu*, fol. 265a of my manuscript.
8. *Foe koue ki*, p. 262.
9. *Foe koue ki*, p. 267, note 11.
10. *Foe koue ki*, pp. 263 and 264.
11. *Foe koue ki*, p. 263.
12. *Sanscrit Dictionary*, p. 493, 1832 ed.

It means "conqueror," in a moral and religious sense. It is known to be common to the Buddhists and the Jainas.[13]

Page 218, note 226. When I conjectured that the sūtra called *Dahara* in our manuscripts should probably be entitled *Dahra Sūtra*, "the Sūtra of the Blaze," my intention was to recall, in favor of this conjecture, that according to the Sinhalese Buddhists, there exists a treatise entitled *Aggikkhanda upama*, that is to say, the "Sūtra Like a Blaze," preached by a monk Yonaka, or from the country of Yona (in Sanskrit Yavana), a name which is that of the Greek empire of Bactria.[14] The existence of a sūtra called "like a mass of fire" gives some likelihood to the substitution I propose to make *dahra* (blaze) from *dahara* (small). Prinsep seemed to believe that the name of the Pāli sūtra *Aggikkhandha* was mentioned in the fourth edict of Piyadassi at Girnar.[15] But I think that it is an error; and the compound *agikhaṃdhānī* of this inscription must be translated in the literal sense "masses of fire," in order to say "fires of joy," which are part of the exhibitions with which the king wished to celebrate the establishment of the law he protected.

Page 274, note 42.—The expression *atyaikapiṇḍapāta*, which I have translated as "quickly collected alms," most probably designates instead "alms or meals that are extraordinary or are at the wrong time," of which Faxian speaks and on which Mr. A. Rémusat has one note in the *Foe koue ki*.[16] This supposition is strongly confirmed by the meaning of the word *atyaya*, from which the adjective *atyayika* derives: *atyaya*, in fact, means "the action of going beyond, to pass over"; and speaking of a rule, "to transgress." The meal, of which the passage to which the present note is related speaks, is taken, in reality, outside the time fixed by the rule of discipline. The excuse given for this transgression, as one sees from the examples of the text, derives from such-and-such case of absolute necessity.

Page 287, note 94.—It is probable that it is the time of the varṣa that the Chinese traveler Faxian designates as "to make a stay, or to sit in summer,"[17] which he names in another place "the summer repose."[18]

Page 291, note 101.—I notice that I have forgotten to present the theory of the four sublime truths in their original form, according to the texts of the North, although I committed myself to it in the same note to which the present addi-

13. *Sanscrit Dictionary*, p. 250.
14. Turnour, *Mahāvanso*, chap. 12, p. 73, ed. in -4°.
15. *Journal of the Asiatic Society of Bengal*, vol. 6, pp. 237, 243, and 266.
16. *Foe koue ki*, p. 107, note 18.
17. *Foe koue ki*, p. 1; and p. 4, note 8.
18. *Ibid.*, p. 362; and p. 366, note 11.

tion refers. Here is the presentation according to a passage of the *Mahāvastu*. As this latter work is a book that is not canonical, since it belongs to the school of the Mahāsaṃghikas, I have compared this passage with a corresponding text of the *Lalitavistara*; and having recognized that there was identity of doctrine between the two books, I have not hesitated to use the fragment of the *Mahāvastu* I give here.

"There are, further, O monks, four sublime truths. What are they? Suffering, the production of suffering, the annihilation of suffering, the path that leads to the annihilation of suffering; each of these terms is a sublime truth. Now, O monks, what is the suffering that is a sublime truth? Here it is: birth, old age, sickness, death, the encounter with what one does not love, the separation from what one loves, the incapacity to obtain what one desires and what one seeks, form, sensation, idea, concepts, knowledge, in short, the five attributes of conception, all this is suffering. This, O monks, is what suffering is, which is a sublime truth. What is the production of suffering that is a sublime truth? It is ceaselessly recurring desire, accompanied by pleasure and passion, which seeks to satisfy itself here and there. This, O monks, is what the production of suffering is, which is a sublime truth. What is the annihilation of suffering, which is a sublime truth? It is the complete destruction of this ceaselessly recurring desire accompanied by pleasure and passion, which seeks to satisfy itself here and there; it is the detachment of this desire, it is the annihilation of it, the giving up, the destruction; it is the complete renunciation of this desire. This, O monks, is what the sublime truth of the annihilation of suffering is. What is the sublime truth of the way that leads to the annihilation of suffering? It is the sublime way formed of eight parts, namely: right view, will, effort, action, life, language, thought, right meditation. This, O monks, is what the sublime truth of the way that leads to the annihilation of suffering is."[19]

One can also consult Csoma de Kőrös relating to the four *āryasatyāni*, or sublime truths, that were just enumerated.[20]

Page 334, note 190.—The observation that serves as the object of this note is certainly changed by the following passage of Faxian: "those who will have received the three *guiyi* and the five precepts."[21] In fact, the three *guiyi*, or the three supports, correspond to the expression *śaraṇagamana* or *triśaraṇa*, "the three refuges"; and this expression itself is the abridged summary of the three formulas *buddhaṃ śaraṇaṃ gacchāmi*, *dharmaṃ śaraṇaṃ gacchāmi*, *saṃghaṃ śaraṇaṃ*

19. *Mahāvastu*, fol. 357a of my manuscript; fol. 371b in the MS of the Société Asiatique. See also *Lalitavistara*, fol. 216a ff.

20. *Asiatic Researches*, vol. 20, p. 294.

21. *Foe koue ki*, p. 352.

gacchāmi, as I have shown above.[22] As for the five precepts, these are five fundamental commandments, the basis of Buddhist morality, as a note of Mr. Landresse on the *Foe koue ki*[23] indicates, exactly as I have conjectured in the note, the object of the present remarks. It is what our texts call *śikṣāpada*.

Page 337, note 200.—To the clarifications I have given on the term *caitya*, I could have added the information we owe to Mr. Hodgson touching on the use made of it in Nepal. According to Amṛtānanda, *caitya* is the name of a temple dedicated to the supreme Ādibuddha or to the five dhyāni buddhas; and all temples erected to Śākyamuni or to another human buddha are called *vihāra*.[24] It is to the theist system of the religious consulted by Mr. Hodgson that we owe this most modern definition. But this scholar gives us a more accurate idea of a caitya when, speaking in his own name, he says that the most essential part of a caitya is a solid hemisphere, and that the greatest number of the caityas of Nepal have this hemisphere surmounted by a pyramid or a cone invariably divided in thirteen tiers.[25] Below he adds: *caitya* signifies, properly speaking, a temple of the Buddha; and *vihāra*, the habitation of the disciples of the Buddha who have embraced the monastic life. In the square space left in the middle of the vihāra is placed a caitya. At the base of the hemisphere of all caityas of Nepal are placed images of the buddhas of contemplation.[26] One sees that Mr. Hodgson had particularly in view to compare the caitya to the vihāra, that is to say, the abode of the dead master to that of the living master. This was not entirely the object of the note to which this addition refers. I will only add to the observations that it contains that I have never seen the name *caitya* given to monuments erected above the relics of a personage other than a buddha; for a disciple, for example, the name *stūpa* is employed.

Page 354, note 238. Since having written the note related to the word *rājikā*, I have found in the *Journal* of Prinsep a passage of the *Mahāvaṃsa* that had escaped my memory at the time when I looked for the meaning of the term *rājikā*. Here is the literal translation according to the edition of Mr. Turnour: "After he had listened to the eighty-four thousand articles of the law, the king of the earth said: 'I will honor each of them with the consecration of a vihāra.' Consequently, having given ninety-six silver koṭis to eighty-four thousand cities of the earth, he made the kings in each of these places build vihāras; then, he himself began to

22. Second Memorandum, section 2, p. 123, note 25.
23. *Foe koue ki*, p. 358 compared to p. 104.
24. *Transactions of the Royal Asiatic Society*, vol. 2, p. 241.
25. *Id., ibid.*, p. 248.
26. *Id., ibid.*, p. 250.

erect the Aśoka ārāma."[27] The text says, *tatta tattheva rājuhi vihāre ārabhāpayi*; and by *rājuhi*, Mr. Turnour understands well the local kings who reigned in each of these cities. Now, does this text connected to the term *rājikā* not seem to confirm the meaning I have proposed in the latter place, in the note to which the present observation refers, namely that of "duty of the king, work of the king," which can be applied to an edict emanating from sovereign power as well to the erection of a religious monument that is the work of a king? One sees, besides, with this text that the number of eighty-four thousand stūpas was an allusion to that of the eighty-four thousand articles of the law. I must therefore not omit to indicate an expression that seems to return us to another interpretation. I find it in a translation that Mr. Turnour has given of a passage of the Pāli *Buddhavaṃsa*; it is an instance of the law that is established as solidly "as a caitya decorated with the embellishments of the law."[28] Does this expression not seem to be a commentary on that of our texts, *dharmarājikā*? But not having the Pāli original, whose translation I give according to Mr. Turnour, I do not dare to push this connection further.

Page 357, note 242.—I fear I still have not explained myself clearly enough on this perplexing passage. In putting forward, in agreement with the text, that the king had taken for the basis of his distribution the number of ten million golden coins, considered the expression of the wealth of the inhabitants in each of the cities in which he wanted to erect a stūpa, I had said that this number should be reached and not exceeded. This must be understood in this sense, that the cities where the fortune of the inhabitants did not rise to ten million coins had no right to an urn of relics, and that those where the public fortune exceeded ten million had, however, the right to only one of these urns. This is why Aśoka responds to the inhabitants of Takṣaśilā that from their thirty-six koṭis, it was necessary to subtract thirty-five of them, in other words, that he recognized only one of them.

Regarding the miracle through which Yaśas the sthavira satisfied the desire of the king, who wished to erect his eighty-four thousand edifices on the same day, I will remark that it is an absurdity of which the Sinhalese Buddhists do not make themselves culpable, since they say that this great operation cost three years' work to those Aśoka charged with it.[29]

Page 378, line 5.—I have forgotten to note, at the occasion of the name Puṇḍravardhana, that it must be the same as that of Puṇḍra, which designates,

27. *Mahāvanso*, p. 26, ed. in -4°.
28. "Examination of the Pāli Buddhistical Annals," in *Journal of the Asiatic Society of Bengal*, vol. 7, p. 795.
29. *Mahāvanso*, p. 34, ed. in -4°.

according to Wilson,[30] the greatest part of Bengal and a portion of Bihar. The inhabitants, named *puṇḍras* in Manu,[31] are taken for fallen kṣatriyas; and Lassen[32] judiciously notes the analogy of origin that exists between this name, which designates a kind of red sugarcane, and that of Gauḍa, another denomination of a part of Bengal, which designates the molasses extracted from the sugarcane. The same scholar has shown by the comparison of two passages of the *Viṣṇu Purāṇa*[33] and one verse of the *Trikaṇḍaśeṣa*[34] that this geographical denomination is employed with a more or less considerable extension in these different texts. I add, as far as the name Puṇḍravardhana is concerned, which means "what makes the Puṇḍras prosper," that the word *vardhana* recalls that of *vardhamāna* or *bardhwān*, "the country that prospers." These names are obvious allusions to the great fertility of these provinces. This part of Bengal is named Pauṇḍraka in a Sanskrit inscription of the year 1136 of our era.[35]

Page 381, fourth paragraph, at the word Dharmavivardhana.—It is necessary to place under this word the following note, which I had omitted at the printing of this part of my volume: This prince is the one called *Fayi* by Faxian, and whose name is translated as "advantage" or "increase of the law." Mr. Rémusat had quite ingeniously conjectured that the Chinese *Fayi* should be in Sanskrit Dharmavardhana,[36] a name found in Brahmanical lists; our text fully confirms his conjecture. I add that we have in the existence of this name Dharmavivardhana, given to a prince whom legend named Kunāla, a new example of this fact, that the rājas, or more especially the Buddhist kings, generally carried two names, one that they took at their birth, the other that was religious or political. So, Kunāla is the name that the legend celebrated, and Dharmavivardhana is the official title; for it was under this latter that he was still known at the time of Faxian, in the fifth century of our era, and that he was considered to have governed Gandhāra. This fact has no reason at all to surprise us here, since king Aśoka, father of Kunāla, appears in the inscriptions with the name Piyadassi.

Page 414, line 2.—The second of the two significations of the word *svabhāva*, which I set forth in my text, is perfectly indicated in a passage of the *Pañcakramaṭippanī* that I believe it useful to cite. The yogin must, according to the text of this work, pronounce the following axiom: *svabhāvaśuddhāḥ sarvadharmāḥ*

30. *Sanscrit Dictionary*, p. 540, col. 1, 1832 ed.
31. *Mānavadharmaśāstra*, bk. 10, st. 44.
32. *Indische Alterthumskunde*, 1:140 and 141.
33. *Viṣṇu Purāṇa*, p. 117, note; and p. 190, note.
34. *Trikaṇḍaśeṣa*, chap. 2, st. 7.
35. *Journal of the Asiatic Society of Bengal*, vol. 7, p. 50.
36. *Foe koue ki*, p. 67.

svabhāvaśuddho 'ham iti, "All conditions and all beings are produced from their own nature; I am myself produced from my own nature."[37] I believe that this signification of *svabhāva* is the most ancient; if, as Mr. Hodgson thinks, the Buddhists understand abstract nature by this term, this metaphysical notion can be added afterward to this word, whose natural interpretation is that which results from the axiom I have just cited. It is not useless to note the meaning that the participle *śuddha* takes, "achieved, accomplished"; this meaning is common in Buddhist Sanskrit.

Page 418, note 25.—To the indications furnished by Klaproth contained in the note on page 418, it is necessary to add those given by Mr. A. Rémusat in a passage related to another text of the *Foe koue ki*. According to a Chinese notice on the Western countries, at the time of the Tang Dynasty, there were five Buddhist sects in the province of Udyāna. The first was that of *Fami*, "silence of the law." I suppose that it is the fourth of the subdivisions of the school of Rāhula, the one Csoma calls Dharmagupta. The second was that of *Huadi*, "conversion of the earth"; these are the Mahīśāśakas of Csoma. The third was that of *Yinguang* or Kāśyapa, "the light that is drunk"; these are the Kāśyapīyas of Csoma who belong, like the two latter sects, to the school of Rāhula. The fourth was that of *Shuoyiqieyou*. Mr. Rémusat has not translated this title; consequently, I lack the means to find the Sanskrit synonym. The fifth was that of *Dazhong*, "the multitude"; these are very likely the Mahāsaṃghikas, or the school of Kāśyapa, the celebrated disciple of Śākya.[38]

Page 466, note 118.—It is necessary to also add to these testimonies that of Mr. Turnour, who is going still further, at least apparently, since at the occasion of the last words pronounced by Śākya, he translates the word *saṃkhāra* (for *saṃskāra*) as "perishable thing" in this passage: "perishable things are transitory."[39] It is the same word I have translated as "compound" in the translation of the sūtra where the last moments of Śākyamuni are announced.[40]

Page 466, note 121.—Following this note, I should have indicated the observations that are going to follow with a reference to the Appendix; but this reference was forgotten, and I only have the resources of the additions to repair this oversight. These observations have been suggested by the manner in which Mr. Schmidt, according to his Mongol authorities, envisages the theory of the

37. *Pañcakramaṭippanī*, fol. 1, line 3.
38. A. Rémusat, *Foe koue ki*, p. 53.
39. *Journal of the Asiatic Society of Bengal*, vol. 6, p. 1051.
40. Second Memorandum, section 2, p. 126.

nidānas, or the successive causes of existence. As this theory is found framed in a piece where all the theses that figure in the *Prajñāpāramitā* are enumerated, I believe it indispensable to reproduce the greatest part of this piece, while accompanying it with short observations intended for the most part to restore the Indian form of these terms, a form to which it is necessary to always return in the final analysis, since this alone is primitive and original. On the other side, since the piece of Mr. Schmidt is a translation of a Mongol text, which is probably a translation of a Tibetan text, which is certainly a translation of a Sanskrit text, I believed I was liable for not giving anything more original to the reader if I again translated the last result of these successive translations into French. One will find here the text itself of Mr. Schmidt, divided in short paragraphs and accompanied by the necessary observations.

"Es gibt sechs Grundursachen (Stoffe, Elemente), und fünf ausgebildete Kategorien; diese letzteren sind: die Farbe (die Gestalt, das Aussehen), das Vermuthen, das Denken, das Thun (Handeln, Wirken) und das Wissen (Erkennen)."

These six elements are the *dhātus*, or material elements, which will be the topic below; and what the Mongols or their learned interpreter call the five *ausgebildete Kategorien* are the five *skandhas*, that is to say, the five aggregates or intellectual attributes: *rūpa*, form; *vedanā*, sensation; *samjñā*, idea; *saṃskārāḥ*, concepts; and *vijñāna*, knowledge. I do not believe that the German word *Vermuthen* can be an accurate translation of *vedanā*, a term than can express only one of these three things: 1. sensation restricted to pure sense impression; 2. perception resulting from this sensation; 3. knowledge resulting from this perception; three significations, the first of which seems to me to accord best with the rest of the enumeration. I do not believe furthermore that *saṃskāra* is "action"; this translation is far too vague: unless one understands by this term the action of the imagination or of this faculty that the mind has, *formas effingendi*.

"Die zwölf Sinnvermögen (Werkzeuge) nebst den Sinnen sind: die Augen, die Ohren, die Nase, die Zunge, der Körper, der Wille (das Verlangen) und demnächst die Äusserungen dieser Werkzeuge oder Vermögen: das Aussehen (die Farbe, Gestalt), die Stimme (der Laut, Ton), der Geruch, der Geschmack das Gefühl und die Feststellung (irgend eines Gegenstandes und dessen Begriffes). Es gibt ein Wissen (Erkennen) mittelst der Augen, eines mittelst der Ohren, eines mittelst des Nase, eines mittelst der Zunge, eines mittelst des Körpers und eines mittelst des Willens (Verlangens). Es gibt ferner ein Auffassen (Aneignen) mittelst der Augen, eines mittelst der Ohren, eines mittelst des Nase, eines mittelst der Zunge, eines mittelst des Körpers und eines mittelst des Willens. Auch gibt es ein Empfinden durch das Auffassen der Ohren, eines durch das Auffassen der Nase, eines durch das Auffassen der Zunge, eines durch das Auffassen des Körpers und eines durch das Auffassen des Willens."

This passage is perfectly clear, and the restitution of the original terms does not teach us much more than the German version of the Mongol text. The reason for this is easy to understand: these terms are among those that direct observation gives; the ideas peculiar to Buddhism occupy only a rather limited space there. The twelve organs or instruments that the Mongol text enumerates are in one part the six sense organs, in Sanskrit *ṣaḍāyatanāni*, the eyes, ears, nose, tongue, body, or rather the skin that envelops the body and that is the seat of touch, and finally the inner organ, in Sanskrit *manas*, a multiple organ, as much moral as intellectual, of which the Mongols reproduce only one facet by translating it as "will, desire." To these organs, which are true instruments, it is necessary to add the function assigned to each of them, viewing, hearing, smelling, tasting, touching, and feeling. The manner in which the Mongols represent this last term is doubtless not very clear; it is not that I believe it less based on knowledge of the Buddhist theory, although it expresses only one part of it. The function of *manas*, or the heart, as an organ, is to grasp the *dharma*, which is the moral law or duty; to grasp it as a given organ perceives an impression, which is a sensation determined at once by the object that gives it and by the organ that receives it. The object that sends the *manas* the sensation it is intended to receive is any individual being, capable of merit or demerit, in a word, of morality. The proper name of this sensation is *dharma*, the law, duty, merit, as one will wish to call it, while taking into account an imperfection of analysis that the antiquity of this theory sufficiently explains. At the same time that the *manas* receives, if I can express myself in this way, the sensation of morality, it also receives that of individuality; in other terms, it perceives the being or the individual subject of the dharma; for a being is necessary to have merit or demerit. It is this second kind of sensation that the Mongol definition represents. This manner of envisaging *manas*, if, however, I understand it well, is consistent with the psychological system of the Buddhists; for not accepting a source of knowledge other than our senses, and convinced that the senses give only notions of qualities isolated from one another, it was necessary for them to have an organ that grasped the individual, the unique subject of these multiple qualities, and who somehow experienced the impression of duty; or of good and bad.

What comes after that, in the text translated by Mr. Schmidt, is a summary of the various manners in which the senses give us impressions. There is, says this text, a knowing that comes from the eyes, and so from the other senses, up to and including the inner organ, which the Mongols continue to translate as the will; in this case, man is passive, knowledge somehow offering itself to him without his seeking it. There is, the text again says, an action of grasping or of appropriating knowledge from the eye, and so with the other senses; in this second case, man is active. Finally, there is a feeling, a sensation, or an *experiencing*, if I can express myself in this way, which results from this action of grasping or of appropriating the knowledge from the eye and from each of the other senses; in this last case, man is passive and active together.

"Die sechs Grundstoffe (Elemente) sind ihrem Begriffe nach: die Erde, das Wasser, das Feuer, die Luft, der materielle Himmel, das Wissen (Erkennen)."

This enumeration of the six elements is remarkable on more than one account. First, it summarizes all that the Buddhists know of nature, and it is, as far as its bases are concerned, the same as that of the brahmans. With this enumeration, the Buddhists can dispense with speaking of matter, an abstract notion of which I do not believe they have occupied themselves. Beyond the four elements generally accepted in India, earth, water, fire, air, it counts with the brahmans a fifth, which is ether, an element whose existence is contested by some Buddhist schools. I do not know how the Mongols can translate the original term that designates this element as "the material sky," unless this translation is an overly strict interpretation of the Tibetan *nam mkha'.* What is definite is that the Sanskrit word *ākāśa* means "ether" or "space" among the Buddhists, and more often "space" than "ether."

As for the sixth element, which is, according to the enumeration of the Mongols, that of knowing or knowledge, it is called *vijñāna* in Sanskrit, a word that in fact has the signification given to it by Mr. Schmidt. It is here a pure invention of the Buddhists, and, I believe to be able to put forward, a rather modern invention. To my knowledge, no trace of this element exists in the ancient sūtras, where the enumeration one finds most often is restricted to these four terms: earth, water, fire, air, elements that are classified in the successive order of their immateriality. The *Prajñāpāramitā* adds an even less material element, space, and above this, *vijñāna*, or intelligence and mind; since knowledge is a relative term, if *vijñāna* should be translated with the precision given it by the Mongols, one would ask where are the beings among whom this fact of knowledge passes. The addition of mind or of intelligence to the material elements is no less an extremely remarkable fact; and as it appears only in the books that I believe to date from later than the ancient sūtras, I have every reason to regard it as a recent invention. It seems to me that at the beginning of their research, the Buddhists viewed the mind only in its individual form, and in each of the beings that they believed were endowed with it. I do not find any trace of an absolute or elementary mind, as this *vijñāna* or this intelligence of the *Prajñā* must be; and if this intelligence appears in the theory that forms the core of this collection, it is that it was introduced by the need that was felt to regularize and to complete a doctrine which, without that, had appeared incomplete. Indeed, when one wished to explain man, one did not know where to discover the source of the intelligent principle that animates him, while one believed oneself authorized to search in each of the material elements for the origin of the different parts of which the body is composed. The addition that was made of intelligence to the fundamental elements seems to have been to obviate this difficulty. This addition, moreover, is, to all appearances, only an imitation of the *cit* of the Vedāntists, and it is likely on it that the Svābhāvikas later depended to make intelligence one of the attributes of material nature.

"Die zwölf dazu gehörigen und damit verbundenen Bedingungen sind ihrem Begriffe nach: die Thorheit (Verfinsterung), das Thun (Wirken), das Wissen (Erkennen), die Farbe (Gestalt oder Gestaltung), die sechs Regionen (der Wesen), das Empfinden, das Vermuthen (Ahnen), die Begierde (Lust), das Nehmen (Geniessen, Aneignen), der *Sansāra* (Kreislauf der Geburten), das Geborenwerden und endlich das Altern und Sterben."

That which the Mongols name the twelve conditions here are the twelve *nidānas* that are linked to each other as effect to cause. I occupied myself with this in the section on metaphysics with enough details not to return to it here. I only recall the precautions I took to grasp the true character of each of these terms of this enumeration. It is possible that I did not completely succeed; but the manner in which the Mongols view them does not appear to me to better reach the goal. There are obvious errors in their translation. One will judge by the comparison with the original terms following each of their interpretations. The first or the highest, *avidyā*, "ignorance," can, if absolutely necessary, be translated as "darkening" or "obscurity"; but "action" or "acting" is a very incomplete interpretation of *saṃskāra*. One finds again in *vijñāna* the *learning* or *knowing* of the Mongol interpreters; but they certainly go too far when they represent *nāmarūpa*, "name and form," with "color and figure"; they omit in addition the idea of name, this necessary element of individuality. I can accept even less the manner in which they view the *ṣaḍāyatanas*, the six seats of the senses, where they find the six regions of beings. Not only do they not say what these six regions are, but it is easy to recognize where the error of the Mongols comes from: it is that they have taken the word *āyatana*, "place, site," literally. I pass rapidly over the four following terms: *sparśa*, contact; *vedanā*, sensation; *tṛṣṇā*, desire; *upādāna*, conception, of which their version gives sufficient analogues, if they were accompanied with a commentary. But I cannot omit to indicate the overly general manner in which they translate *bhava*, "existence," which they believe to be a synonym of *saṃsāra*, the circle or circular movement of births. The error is certainly not very grave, since it is by birth that man enters into the circle or into the revolution of the world, in other terms, that he is submitted to the law of transmigration. Birth, however, is only one of the acts of the passage through the world, and it is not possible to identify one of the degrees of the revolution with the entire revolution. The fact is that it is the twelve *nidānas*, or these twelve terms successively connected to one another, as cause to effect, that make man enter inevitably into the circle of the transmigration.

I end here what I had to say on the manner in which the Mongols envisage the difficult theory of the twelve causes of existence; it is hardly necessary to add that if, surrounded by all the aids they had at their disposal, they were not able to render it more clearly, it is enough to justify all those who occupy themselves with the same subject and will not be more successful.[41]

Page 484.—Before passing on to the analysis of the *Suvarṇaprabhāsa*, it was necessary to indicate the subdivisions of the class of books called tantras, of which Csoma indicates the existence. According to this author, one recognizes in Tibet four classes of tantras, namely: 1. *kriyā tantra*, the tantras of action; 2. *ācāra tantra*, the tantras of practices; 3. *yoga tantra*, the tantras of mystical union; 4. *anuttarayoga tantra*, the tantras of superior yoga.[42] These divisions are sufficient to show the considerable developments in the literature of the tantras, I will not say solely in Tibet, but in India and very likely in Kashmir; for the Sanskrit titles of these divisions seem to me to establish that the works that they embrace were originally composed in Sanskrit. The great distinction of *kriyā* (action) and *yoga* (meditation) is, one knows, familiar to Brahmanism.

Since I speak here of the tantras accepted in Tibet, I must make mention of the existence of a monastery of Tantrist monks, whom Georgi described in this way in his prudish language: "Formis anaglypticis carnalium conjugationum duabus atque triginta contaminatum."[43] This monastery is called, according to him, *Ra mo che'i.* Would these images be the figurative representations of the rites of the tantras? It would be one of the hardly common traces in India, at least to my knowledge, of the influence of the tantras on figurative monuments.

41. *Mémoires de l'Académie des sciences de Saint-Pétersbourg*, 4:215.

42. *Tibetan Dictionary*, p. 245, col. 1.

43. *Alphabetum Tibetanum*, p. 223.

General Index of Proper Names and Place-Names, of Buddhist Expressions, and of Works in Sanskrit, Pāli, Sinhalese, etc.

A

Ābbhokāsikaṅga (meaning of the Pāli word), 306

Ābhāsvara, gods of the third level of the first sphere, 560

Abhayagirivāsinaḥ (philosophical school), 418

Abhidharmakośavyākhyā, philosophical compilation, 84, 93—Its importance, 419

Abhidharma Piṭaka, treatise of metaphysics and one of the three Buddhist collections, 89—Not from Śākyamuni, 90—Its length, 419

Abhijñā (five), 294

Ābhyavakāśikaḥ (meaning of the word), 306

Abotuona, Chinese transcription of *avadāna*. See this word.

Action (meaning of the word), among the Karmikas, 416

Adbhutadharma, treatise of supernatural events, 107

Adhimuktika, name of a divinity, 495

Ādibuddha, 151, 154—His other names, 235—Recognized only by the theist school, 241, 415, 529, 565

Ādinātha, one of the names of the Ādibuddha, 235

Āgama (great), religious treatise, 62—The four Āgama, 95, 311

Aggikkhanda, name of a Pāli sūtra, 583

Aggregates (five) of conception, 133. See Skandha.

Agnidatta, name of a king, 224

Aiśvarikas (sect of), 413, 520

Ajātaśatru, Ajatasattu, name of a king, 174, 217, 345, 356

Ajita, name of a bodhisattva, 101, 139

Ajita Keśakambala, name of a tirthya, 188

Akaniṣṭha (heaven of the gods), 205, 377, 564

Ākāśa (ether), according to the Buddhist system, 459

Akṣobhya, name of a buddha, 152, 485, 507

Ālambana (meaning of the word), 420

Alanruo (meaning of the Chinese expression), 306

Altan Gerel, Mongol title of *Suvarṇaprabhāsa*, 60, 485

Alternative (meaning of the word), 420

Āmalaka, name of a fruit, 399

Amitābha, name of a divine buddha, 138, 139, 485, 507—The fourth buddha, 152, 154—His residence, 235
Amitāyus, same as Amitābha, 140
Amoghasiddha, name of a buddha, 152, 495
Amṛtānanda, name of a Nepalese commentator, 585
Anabhraka, gods of the first level of the fourth sphere, 562
Anāgāmin (state of), 292ff.
Anan, Chinese transcription of Ānanda. See this word.
Ānanda, disciple of Śākyamuni and compiler of the sūtras, 92, 527—Makes miracles, 216—Cousin of Śākyamuni, 222—His continence, 222—His stūpa, 372—Is the same as Jalagarbha, 489
Anāthapiṇḍika or piṇḍada, name of a householder, 72, 130, 218, 258, 400
Anātmaka (meaning of the word), 431
Anavatapta, name of a lake, 194, 322, 375
Anekadharmakathā, varied exposition of the law, 101
Aniyatā dhammā, Pāli treatise on religious discipline, 300
Anupadhiśeṣa (meaning of the word), 537
Anupapādakas (sectarians), 151
Apalāla, name of a nāga, 360
Apitan, Chinese transcription of *abhidharma*, 148, 423
Apramāṇābha, gods of the second level of the first sphere, 559
Apramāṇaśubha, gods of the second level of the third sphere, 560
Apriya, name of a yakṣa, 264
Ārāḍa, name of a ṛṣi, 367
Arangisattva, gods of the fourth sphere according to the Nepalese, 562
Āraṇyakaḥ (meaning of the word), 306
Arhat, holy personage of the Buddhist hierarchy, 122, 294, 320
Artha (meaning of the word), 514
Arthavargīya, canonical works, 514
Arthaviniścaya, treatise of metaphysics, 90, 419
Ārya (meaning of the word), 291, 513—Eight classes of Āryas, 291–292
Āryabhagavatī. See Rākṣabhagavatī.
Āryadeva, disciple of Nāgārjuna, 419, 510
Āryatārā, name of a goddess, 495
Asangasatta and Assanjasatthaya. See Arangisattva.
Asita, name of a ṛṣi, 170
Aśoka, name of a king, 164, 177, 240, 345—His legend, 346ff.—Another legend, 405ff.—His epoch, 407
Āśraya (meaning of the word), 420
Āśrita (meaning of the word), 420
Assembly (great), 418
Asura, their place in the Buddhist pantheon, 549
Aśvajit, name of a sthavira, 515
Aśvaghoṣa, name of a Buddhist writer, 230, 506—Fought against the pre-eminence of the brahmans, 231
Atapa, gods of the fifth level of the fourth sphere, 563
Attributes. See the Five Attributes.
Atyayika piṇḍapāta (meaning of the expression), 583
Avadāna (compilation called), 344
Avadānakalpalatā, collection of legends, 506
Avadānas (treatises called), 108—Chinese transcription of the word *avadāna*, 109—Their analogy with the sūtras, 117—Deal with discipline, 245—Two categories of avadānas, 344—Which of the three divisions of the scriptures they represent, summary of what they contain, 408
Avadānaśataka, collection of legends, 60, 150, 217, 232, 344, 490
Avalokiteśvara, name of a bodhisattva, 139, 148—Renowned as the son of Amitābha Buddha, 154—Author of two sūtras, 234—His pre-eminence among all beings, 235—Qualities of his body, 236—Explanation of his name, 239—Included among the ārya, 291—His residence, 492—Stanzas in his praise, 495—Tibetan legend of the statue of Avalokiteśvara, 569
Āvantikāḥ, philosophical school, 418
Avaraśailāḥ, philosophical school, 418
Avidyā (meaning of the word), 440, 449, 466
Avṛha, gods of the fourth level of the fourth sphere, 563
Āyatana (meaning of the word), 461, 592
Ayiduo, Chinese transcription of Ajita. See this word.

B

Bahuśrutīyāḥ (philosophical school), 418
Bāhya āyatana (meaning of the word), 462
Bālapaṇḍita, name of a monk, 351
Balendraketu (Rāja), name of a king, 487
Banruo boluomi, Chinese transcription of *prajñāpāramitā*, 148
Bhadanta (meaning of the word), 515
Bhadanta Dharmatrāta, Buddhist writer, 515
Bhadanta Gopadatta (ācārya), Buddhist writer, 506
Bhadanta Gośaka, Buddhist writer, 515
Bhadanta Rāma, Buddhist writer, 515
Bhadanta Śrīlābha, Buddhist writer, 515, 577
Bhadrakalpa (meaning of the expression), 322
Bhadrakanyā, name of a woman, 276
Bhadraṃkara, name of a city, 209
Bhadramukha, name of a nāga, 313
Bhadrāyudha, name of a giant, 350
Bhagavat, one of the names of Śākyamuni, 118 passim.
Bhallika, name of a man, 369
Bhava, name of a man, 247ff.
Bhavanandin, name of a man, 247ff.
Bhavatrāta, name of a man, 247ff.
Bhāvaviveka, Buddhist writer, 510
Bhavila, name of a man, 247ff.
Bhikṣu (meaning of the word), 279, 297
Bhikṣuṇī, mendicant nun, 281
Bhikṣusaṃgha (meaning of the expression), 285
Bimbisāra, name of a king, 174, 190, 331—List of his successors, 345
Bindusāra, name of a king, 177, 346
Blag ba med pa (meaning of the Tibetan expression), 306
Bodhi, name of a tree, 120, 368, 373
Bodhi (meaning of the word), 295, 443
Bodhisattva (meaning of the word), 123, 145, 411, 434—How one reaches the state of bodhisattva, 436ff.
Boluodi tisheni, Chinese religious treatise, 301
Boluoyi, Chinese religious treatise, 299
Botuo. See Abotuona.
Boyiti, Chinese transcription of *pācittiyā*, 301
Brahmā, his role in the Buddhist pantheon, 163
Brahmādatta, name of a king, 170
Brahmakāyika, gods from the retinue of Brahmā, 557
Brahmanical deities mentioned in the sūtras, 163—Twenty-three orders of divinities mentioned in the sūtras, 219–220—Accepted by Buddhism, 547–567
Brahmans (caste of), Relations with Buddhism, 171—Grievances against Buddhism, 187—Vices and passions of the Brahmans, 225—Observances of the Brahmans, 319—Persecution of Buddhists, 532
Brahmapariṣadyāḥ, category of gods from the retinue of Brahmā, 556
Brahmapurohita, gods, priests, or ministers of Brahmā's court, 557
Brahmāsahāṃpati (meaning of the word), 558. See Sahāṃpati.
Brahmāyus, the name of a Brahman, 170
Buddha, possesses four principles of supernatural power, 118—His role in the sūtras, 145—Unique in each century, 146. See Śākyamuni.
Buddha, dharma, saṃgha (meaning of the formula), 285
Buddha Gayā. See Gayā.
Buddhacaritakāvya, a Nepalese work, 230, 506
Buddhadeva, name of a sthavira, 515
Buddhadharma (meaning of the word), 528
Buddhaghosa, name of a commentator, 294
Buddhajñāna (meaning of the word), 29n.
Buddhapālita, name of a disciple of Nāgārjuna, 419, 510
Buddharakṣita, name of a man, 310
Buddhas (five), 152—Have a magical figure, 208
Buddhavacana (meaning of the expression), 85, 91
Buddhist (books), Language in which they were written, 66—Epoch in which they were translated into Tibetan, 75—Where they were written, 75—Buddhist books of Nepal, 83ff.—Classification of the Buddhist books, 85, 95—Classification of the Buddhist books in twelve sections, 98ff.—Presumed epoch of the redaction of the Buddhist books, 526
Buddhism, later than Brahmanism, 161, 172—Its relations with Brahmanism, 186—Odious to the brahmans and well received by the inferior castes, 228—Considered as a moral system and as a religion, 327—

Buddhism (*continued*)
Alliance with Śivaism, 498ff.—Divided into eighteen sects, 527—Different ages of Buddhism, 532ff.
Buddhist Councils, 302, 516, 528—Philosophical schools dated from the third Buddhist council, 446
Buddhist monks, in Brahmanical dramas, 161—Clothes, utensils, appearance of monks, 201, 272—How novices became monks, 246—Rules monks must follow, 279—Various orders of religious, 281—Admission of women in the religious orders, 281—Monasteries of monks, 287—Hierarchy of monks, 289—Their life in monasteries, 310ff.—Must practice hospitality, 327—Mendicant monks, their way of living, 395—Kashmiri monks, those from Tāmraparṇa, 517
Buddhopāsaka (the meaning of the word), 283

C

Cailaka, type of Buddhist, 102
Caityas (buildings named), 337, 585—Caitya stick, 266, 267
Campā, name of a city, 177
Campū, Sanskrit books, 65, 140
Candaka, name of a man, 367
Candragupta, name of a Buddhist writer, 493
Candrakīrti (ācaryā), Buddhist writer, 509
Candraprabha, name of a sūtra, 186
Cāpāla Caitya, name of a temple, 118, 125
Castes (four), their relations with Buddhism, 168, 174
Caturmahārāja and Caturmahārājakāyika, gods of the highest of the sixth heavens, 550
Cela. See Cailaka.
Ceylon (legend related to the island), 236, 241
Chain of causes, successive, 577
Chariot (meaning of the word "great"), 443. See Vehicle.
Chos gos gsum pa (meaning of the Tibetan expression), 304
Confession, instituted by Śākyamuni, 298
Cunda, name of a man, 196, 202

D

Dahara Sūtra, religious treatise, 218, 583
Dakṣiṇapatha, name of a place, 426
Dakṣhiṇāvarta, name of a country, 275
Damṣṭrā, name of a yakṣa, 404
Dānādhikāra, religious treatise, 149
Dānapāramitā, one of the six perfections, 137
Dānaśūra, name of a bodhisattva, 235, 238
Daṇḍapāṇi, name of a man, 179
Dārukarṇin, name of a man, 249
Daśabhūmīśvara, one of the nine dharmas, 111, 411
Dasalatha. See Daśaratha.
Daśaratha, name of a king, 495
Devasarman, Buddhist writer, 419
Devātideva, another name of Śākyamuni, 366
Devendrasamaya, royal book, 487
dge bsnyen, Tibetan translation of *upāsaka*. See Upāsaka.
dgon pa pa (meaning of the Tibetan expression), 306
Dhammaguttikā (sectarians). See Dharmaguptaḥ.
Dhāraṇīs, charms and formulas, 97—Not counted among the sacred books, 11—Are tantras, 155, 473, 493ff.—See Magical formulas.
Dharma (various meanings of the word), 90, 235
Dharmabhaginī (meaning of the expression), 281
Dharmaguptaḥ, philosophical school, 418
Dharmākara, name of a monk, 138
Dharmakośavyākhyā, philosophical treatise, 421, 512
Dharmaratna, collective name of the sūtras, 110
Dharmaruci (legend of), 187
Dharmas (nine), 65—Titles of the dharmas, 111
Dharmaskandha, a philosophical treatise, 84, 419
Dharmatrāta, name of a sthavira, 515
Dharmavivardhana, name of a prince, 381—same as Kunāla, 587
Dhātu (meaning of the word), 458, 536, 539, 589
Dhātukāya, philosophical treatise, 419
Dhyāna (meaning of the word), 559
Dhyāni buddhas and bodhisattvas (system of), 150, 235, 481, 581
Dīghanikāya, Pāli religious treatise, 294
Dīrghanakha, name of a brahman, 426
Disciples of Śākyamuni who recorded his doctrine, 93, 526

Divyāvadāna, collection of Buddhist legends, 60, 232, 298, 345, 490
Dṛḍhā, goddess of the earth, 487
Dul-va, one of the sections of the Kahgyur, 60, 298—Dul-va is the Sanskrit *vinayavastu*, 88
Dundubhīśvara, name of one of the four buddhas, 485
Dur khrod pa (meaning of the Tibetan expression), 307

E

Effort (meaning of the word), according to the Yātnikas, 416
Eight parts (path of). See Path.
Eighteen distinct conditions of a buddha, 437
Eighty-four thousand, edicts of the law, 84, 354, 357
Eighty signs, secondary, of beauty, 335
Ekāpanikaḥ (meaning of the word), 304—We must change it to *etāsanikaḥ*, 305
Ekottarāgama, collection of religious treatises, 62
Elements (six), 458, 589
Emancipation (final). See Nirvāṇa.
Epi, Chinese transcription of Upasena. See this word.

F

Fan (language), in Chinese, the language of India, 65
Faxian, Chinese traveler, 148ff.
Fayi, Chinese name of Dharmavivardhana, 587
Female energies of the Buddhas and Śiva, 482ff., 498
Five advantages assured to one who has heard much, 319
Five attributes, 470. See Skandhas.
Fives causes of misery, 393
Five Objects, that one does not grow tired looking at, 314
Five parts of the body, 471
Form, opposed to illusion, 441
Four intrepidities, 437
Four manners in which birth occurs, 455
Four supports of memory, 126
Four tathāgatas of the four points of the horizon, 485
Four truths (sublime), 291, 583

G

Gaṇḍaka, name taken by Prince Kāla, 198. See Kāla.
Gaṇḍavyūha, narrative work, 100—The *Gaṇḍavyūha* is one of the nine dharmas, 111, 158, 494
Gandhamādana, name of a mountain, 200, 376, 378
Gandhāra, name of a province, 405
Gāthā, discourse in verse, 101
Gati. See the Six Paths.
Gautama, one of the names of Śākyamuni, 121
Gautamaka, name of one of the nāga kings, 274
Gayākāśyapa, name of an arhat, 184
Geya, religious works written in a modulated language, 98, 141
Girika, name of a man, 350
Gītapustakasaṃgraha, Summary of the Book of Songs, 98
Gnas brtan, Tibetan translation of *sthavira*. See Sthavira.
Gośīrṣa (meaning of the word), 569
Gopā, name of a woman, 281, 489
Gopālī, the name of a woman, 360
Gṛdhrakūṭa, name of a mountain, 485
Guanshiyin, Chinese name of Avalokiteśvara, 14
Guṇakaraṇḍavyūha (two treatises called), 234ff.—The epoch of their composition, 242
Guṇamati, name of an ācārya, 515
Guptika, name of a sthavira, 468
Gzhi ji bzhin pa (meaning of the Tibetan expression), 307

H

Haimavatāḥ, philosophical school, 418
Hells, Buddhist (sixteen), 219, 351ff.
Hemacandra, Sanskrit vocabulary later than Buddhism, 481
Heruka, name of a divinity, 491
Hospitality, recommended to monks, 327
Human actions (where they accumulate), 277, 325—Black and white, 278, 407—That bring about metamorphosis, 319—No one can avoid their influence, 389
Human body (what it is), 359

I

Iddhipāda (four). See Ṛddhipāda.
Illusion (what is), 441
Indra, his relations with Śākyamuni, 163, 205
Insignia (five) of royal power, 191
Investiture (conditions to receive), 280, 431
Īśvara (meaning of the word), 520, 565
Ityukta, collection of accounts and explanations, 105

J

Jainas (sect of), 295—They are unclothed, 309
Jalagarbha, name of a man, 488. See Ānanda.
Jalāmbara, name of a man, 488
Jalāmbugarbha, name of a woman, 489
Jalavāhama, name of a man, 488
Jambudvīpa, one of the divisions of the world, 118, 314, 315
Jarāmaraṇa (meaning of the word), 454
Jātaka, collection of legends, 106, 506
Jātakamāla, Garland of Births, 106
Jāti (meaning of the word), 454
Jātiṃdhara, name of a doctor, 488
Jayaśrī, name of a Buddhist scholar, 234
Jetārāma, name of a place, 236
Jetavana, name of a monastery in the Kośala country, 72, 72n, 73n, 74, 130
Jetavanīyāḥ, philosophical school, 418
Jewels (seven), 333
Jiashe wei, Chinese transcription of Kāśyapīyāḥ, 418
Jina (meaning of the word), 209, 582
Jinas, 221, 363
Jinaśrī, name of a king, 235
Jñānaprasthāna, philosophical treatise, 419
Jyotiṣka (legend of), 217
Jyotiṣprabha, name of a Buddha, 139

K

Kah-gyur, collection of Tibetan Buddhist works, 59—Presumed epoch of the translation of the Kah-gyur, 526
Kākaṇi (meaning of the word), 372
Kākavarṇin, name of a prince, 345
Kakuda Kātyāyana, name of a man, 188
Kāla, name of a prince, 197
Kālacakra, name of a tantra, 493
Kālakarṇin, nickname of Pūrṇa, 263
Kālika, name of a king of the nāgas, 368
Kalpa, age or duration of a world, 118, 450
Kāmadhātu, name of a superior region, 552
Kāmāvacara, gods who live in the first of the three regions, 122, 550, 552
Kanakamuni, name of an ancient sage, 313
Kanakavarṇa, name of a king, 131
Kanakavatī, name of a city, 131
Kāñcanamālā, name of a woman, 382, 386
Kaniṣka, name of a king, 516, 527
Kapila (system of the ascetic), 227
Kapilavastu, name of a city, 164, 366
Karaṇḍakanivāpa, name of a place, 426
Karaṇḍavyūha, religious treatise, 13. See *Guṇakaraṇḍavyūha.*
Kārikās, memorial axioms, 509
Kārmikas (sectarians), 413
Kārṣāpaṇa (meaning of the word), 545
Karuṇapuṇḍarīka, name of a sūtra, 116
Kāśmīra, name of a city, 375—Name of a country, 495, 517
Kāśyapa, disciple of Śākyamuni and compiler of the Abhidharma, 92, 277, 313, 371, 406, 526—Chief of a philosophical school, 418—A brahman, 418
Kāśyapīyāḥ, philosophical school, 418
Kaṭhināvadāna, treatise of religious discipline, 88
Kātyāyana, chief of a philosophical school, 418, 424
Kātyāyanīputra, philosophical writer, 419, 513
Kaurṇkullakāḥ, philosophical school, 418
Kāvya, one of the divisions of Buddhist works, 97
Khagarbha, name of a bodhisattva, 507
Khalupaśvāddhaktiṃkaḥ (meaning of the word), 305
Khumbhāṇḍa (meaning of the word), 548
Kings (list of), 345
Kola (Kalinga?), 207
Kolita, one of the names of Maudgalyāyana, 371. See Maudgalyāyana
Kośa, dictionaries, 97—One of the divisions of Buddhist works, ibid.
Kośala and Kosala, name of a kingdom, 175, 197, 226
Koṣṭhaka, name of a place, 404
Krakuchanda, name of an ancient buddha, 238, 313, 390
Kṛkin, name of a king, 506, 514
Kṛmisena, name of a man, 404

Kṛṣna (cult of), later that Śākyamuni, 167—King of the nāgas, 274
Kṣāntivādin, name of an ancient ṛṣi, 236
Kṣatriyas (caste of), its relations with Buddhism, 172
Kṣemaṃkara, name of a buddha, 187
Kṣemendra, name of a Buddhist writer, 506
Kṣitigarbha, name of a bodhisattva, 507
Kṣudraka, treatise of religious discipline, 514
Kukkuṭārāma, name of a hermitage, 235, 351, 357, 401ff.
Kunāla, name of a prince, 178, 379ff.—His other name, 587
Kuṇḍopadhāna, name of a place, 267
Kuśigrāmaka, name of a city, 127
Kuśinagarī, name of a city, 196, 370
Kūṭāgāra, the name of a hall, 118

L

Lalitavistara, life of Śākyamuni, 56, 59—Is a gāthā, 102—One of the nine dharmas, 111—A developed sūtra, 158—Quotation from the *Lalitavistara*, 450
Laṅkāvatāra, philosophical treatise, 59—Chinese translation of the *Laṅkāvatāra*, 61—Is one of the nine dharmas, 111, 145—Details on the *Laṅkāvatāra*, 411, 472, 494
Lichavi (tribe of), 486
Liṅga, found in the tantras, 492
Liṅgaśarīra (meaning of the expression), 459
Lokapāla. See Caturmahārājakāyika.
Lokapradīpa, name of a buddha, 139
Lokeśa, name of a bodhisattva, 507
Lokeśvararāja, name of a buddha, 138
Lokottaravādinaḥ, philosophical school, 418, 423
Lotsavas, Tibetan interpreters and translators, 68
Lotus of the Good Law. See *Saddharmapuṇḍarika*
Lūhasudatta, name of a man, 202, 396
Lumbinī, name of a garden, 364

M

Ma mo. See Yum.
Madhyadeśa, name of a country, 148
Madhyamika, philosophical system, 418ff., 467, 469, 509—*Madhyamakavṛtti* (treatise of Madhyamika doctrine), 512
Magadha, name of a country, 174
Mahābhikṣu, one of the names of Śākyamuni, 74, 279
Mahābrahmāṇa, gods of the heavens where Brahmā rules, 557
Mahābuddha, 235
Mahākāla, name of a tantra, 492—Name of a divinity, 495, 502
Mahākālī, name of a goddess, 502
Mahākaruṇapuṇḍarīka, name of a sūtra, 116
Mahākāśyapa, name of an arhat, 184. See Kāśyapa.
Mahākauṣṭhila, name of an arhat, 419, 513
Mahākāvya. See *Buddhacarita*.
Mahāmaṇḍala, name of a prince, 345
Mahāmati, name of a bodhisattva, 473
Mahāmāyā, name of a woman, 365
Mahāparinibbāna Sutta, Pāli canonical work, 118
Mahāprajāpatī, name of a woman, 281, 366
Mahārājā, gods of the Buddhist hierarchy, 551
Mahāratha, name of a king, 490
Mahāsaṃghikāḥ, philosophical school, 418, 423
Mahāsattva (meaning of the word), 434, 442ff.
Mahāśramaṇa, one of the names of Śākyamuni, 74
Mahāsthāna or Mahāsthānaprāpta, name of a bodhisattva, 139
Mahāvaipulyasūtra, name of various canonical works, 100, 107, 110, 117
Mahāvaṃsa, Sinhalese life of the Buddha, 524, 537 passim.
Mahāvana, name of a forest, 375
Mahāvastu, collection of legends, 66, 423, 491
Mahāvihāravāsinaḥ, philosophical school, 418
Mahāyāna (sect of) 156, 534—Epoch of its development, 156
Mahāyāna sūtra, canonical work, 66, 117, 411, 494
Maheśvara, name of a yakṣa, 263
Mahīśāsakāḥ, philosophical school, 418
Maitrāyaṇī, name of a woman, 443
Maitreya, name of a bodhisattva, 101, 139, 490—The future buddha, 145, 235
Maitrīnātha (Ārya), name of a sage, 495
Mallas, name of a people, 128
Maming, name of a Chinese Buddhist monk, 230
Manas (meaning of the word), 461

Mandākinī, name of a pond, 322
Maṇḍala (meaning of the word), 479, 507
Māndhātṛ,name of a king, 118, 129
Mañjughoṣa. See Mañjuśrī.
Mañjuśrī, name of a bodhisattva, 148, 291, 490
Mañjuśrīmūlatantra, religious and prophetic treatise, 493
Mantra, in six letters, 494
Mantra, magical formulas, 155, 494
Mānuṣi buddhas, 151
Māra (the Sinner), 120, 164, 377—Battle with Śākyamuni, 190
Marīcika, name of a universe, 275
Markaṭahrada, name of a pond, 118
Marriage, according to Buddhist law, 179
Marvelous horse, 237
Maskarin, name of a man, 188
Mātanga, name of a caste, 222
Māṭhara, name of a man, 426
Mathurā, name of a city, 175, 360
Mātṛkā, synonym of Abhidharmapiṭaka, 95
Maudgalyāyana, disciple of Śākyamuni, 148, 203, 274, 308, 371, 419, 513
Maurya, name of a man, 357
Mauryas (family of), 357 passim.
mDo sde, one of the parts of the Kah-gyur, 59—Corresponds to the sūtras, 87
Meṇḍhaka (legend of), 209, 212
Meru (divisions of the mountain), 548
Metamorphosis (causes of), 321
Metaphysics. See Abhidharmapiṭaka.
Milindapaṇṇa, Pāli philosophical work, 574
Mishase, Chinese transcription of Mahīśāsaka, 418
Moha (meaning of the word), 496
Mohe sengzhi (monks named in Chinese), 423
Moheyan, Chinese transcription of Mahāyāna, 148
Mṛgāra, name of a king, 267
Mūlagrantha, book of the text, 85, 91, 98. See Buddhavacana.
Mūlasarvāstivādāḥ, philosophical school, 418
Muṇḍa, name of a prince, 345
Musalaka, name of a mountain, 227

N

Nāgābhibhu, name of a buddha, 139
Nāgārjuna, the founder of a philosophical school, 419, 421, 518—His system, 467, 478—Predicted in a tantra, 493—Most celebrated among the writers who dealt with mantras, 507, 508—His doctrine, 509
Nāgas, their role in Buddhist mythology, 312–326
Nāgasena, Pāli name of Nāgārjuna, 518
Nairañjanā, name of a river, 120
Naiṣadikaḥ (meaning of the word), 307
Nālanda, name of a place, 426, 582
Nāmarūpa (meaning of the word), 462
Nāmatikaḥ (meaning of the word), 304
Namuci, name of a king, 369
Nanda, name of a prince, 345
Nandā, name of a woman, 368
Nandabalā, name of a woman, 368
Nandikeśvara, name of a divinity, 495
Nandimukhasughoṣāvadāna, Nepalese work, 230
Naṭabhaṭikā, name of a place, 361
Naturalist (school). See Svābhāvikas.
Nature (what the Svābhāvikas understand by this word), 414
Nesajjikaṅga (meaning of the Pāli word), 307
Nidāna, category of philosophical works, 104
Nidāna (theory of), 449, 589
Nidānas (twelve), 592. See Twelve causes of existence.
Nine parts of the law, 98ff.
Nirgrantha, name of a religious, 188—Meaning of the word, 516
Nirgranthaśāstra, Sanskrit work opposed to Buddhism, 516
Nirmāṇarati (meaning of the word), 554
Nirupadhiśeṣa (meaning of the word), 536
Nirvāṇa, the final deliverance, 68—Interpretation of this word by Tibetans and Hindus, 69—Definition of this word, 473ff., 535ff.
Nirvṛtti (meaning of the word), 414, 476
Nisazhi, Chinese treatise called, 300
Nissaggiyā dhammā, Pāli religious treatise, 301

O

Observances (Book of the Twelve), 302–309
Oṃ maṇi padme hūm (meaning of this formula), 238
Organs (six), of the senses, 590

P

Pācittiyā dhammā, Pāli religious treatise, 301
Padmapāṇi, name of a bodhisattva, 151

Padmavatī, name of a queen, 381
Paiśācika (dialect), 418
Pāli (dialect), used by Sinhalese Buddhists, 142
Pāṃśukūlikaḥ (meaning of the expression), 303
Pañca dhyāni buddhas, 151. See Dhyāni buddhas.
Pañcakrama and Pañcakramaṭippanī, work on mantras and its commentary, 507, 538
Pañcaraṣa or rakṣa, division of the Nepalese treatises, 431
Pañcaskandhaka, Nepalese work, 516
Pāñcika, chief of the Yakṣas, 206ff., 582
Pāṇini, Buddhist writer, 493
Pannattivadas (sectarians). See Prajnāptivādinaḥ.
Panthaka, name of a man, 169
Parahitarakṣita Paṇḍita, Buddhist writer, 508
Pārājika or Phārājika, Pāli religious treatise, 300
Paranirmitavaśavartin (meaning of the word), 556
Parinirvṛta (meaning of the word), 536
Parīttābha (gods of the first level of the second sphere), 559
Parīttāśubha (gods of the first level of the third sphere), 560
Pāṭaliputra, name of a city, 177, 345 passim—Legend about Pāṭaliputra, 405ff.
Path, sublime, composed of eight parts, 126
Pāṭidesanīyā dhammā, Pāli religious treatise, 301
Pātimokkha Sutta. See Prātimokṣa Sūtra.
Philosophical schools of Nepal (four), 413, 421—Philosophical schools of Nepal (four others), 418, 588
Phyag dar khrod kyi gos (meaning of the Tibetan expression), 304
Phyag dar khrod pa (meaning of the Tibetan expression), 303
Phying ba can (meaning of the Tibetan expression), 304
Piṇḍapātikaḥ and Piṇḍapātikaṅga (meaning of the Pāli words), 304
Piṇḍapātrāvadāna, a religious treatise, 88
Piṇḍola, name of a man, 376
Pingalavatsājīva, name of a mendicant, 346ff.
Piṭakas (or three collections), 85
Piyadassi, one of the names of Aśoka, 587
Pocuo fuluo, Chinese transcription of *vātsīputrīya*, 418, 518
Potaraka and Potala, name of a city, 495
Pradānaruci, name of a man, 399
Pradhāna (meaning of the word), 520
Prajñā (meaning of the word), 235, 415
Prajñāpāramitā, a great Buddhist compilation, 57—Its two redactions, 84, 433—Its importance, 98—One of the nine dharmas, 111—Difficulty of explaining its philosophical terms, 412—Foreign to the theist school, 417—Its relations with the sūtras, 426—Meaning of the word, 432—Its four sections, 433—What it teaches, 447, 469
Prajñaptiśāstra, philosophical treatise, 419
Prajñāptivādinaḥ, philosophical school, 418
Prakaraṇapāda, philosophical treatise, 419
Prakṛti, name of a woman, 222, 224
Prasenajit, name of a king, 174, 191, 223, 345
Prātihārya Sūtra, collection of legends, 298
Prātimokṣa Sūtra, philosophical treatise, 299, 301
Pratītyasamutpāda (meaning of the word), 449ff., 577
Pratyekabuddha (what it is), 133, 296, 411—How one reaches the state of pratyekabuddha, 435
Pravṛtti (meaning of the word), 414, 475
Principles (four) of supernatural power, 118, 579
Production of the successive causes of existence. See Pratītyasamutpāda.
Pṛthagjana (meaning of the word), 291
Pudgala (meaning of the word), 462, 467, 538
Pūjā (meaning of the word) among the Buddhists, 330
Pūjākhaṇḍa, religious treatise, 110
Puṇḍravardhana, name of a country, 378, 397, 586
Puṇyaprasava, gods of the second level of the fourth sphere, 561
Purāṇa, weight of silver, 545
Purāṇa Kāśyapa, name of an ascetic, 162, 197, 207
Purāṇas, ancient books, 97
Pūrṇa, name of a monk, 164, 513—His legend, 247–278—Author of the *Dhātukāya*, 419
Pūrṇāvadāna, philosophical treatise, 88
Puruṣa (meaning of the word), 520
Pūrvaśailāḥ, philosophical school, 418

Puṣpabherotsa, name of a man, 405
Puṣpamitra, name of a prince, 403
Puṣyadharman, name of a prince, 403

R

Rādhagupta, name of a man, 347, 378, 396, 400
Rāhula and Rāhulabhadra, son of Śākya and chief of a philosophical school, 418, 588
Rājagṛha, name of a city, 138, 145, 331, 426
Rājikā (meaning of the word), 585
Rakṣabhagavatī, metaphysical treatise, 431
Rāktākṣa, name of a mendicant, 195
Rāma. See Bhadanta Rāma.
Rāmagrāma, name of a place, 356
Rambhaka, name of a man, 202
Ranjā, ancient script, 492
Ratnacūḍāparipṛcchā, canonical work, 510
Ratnaka, name of a man, 200
Ratnākara, name of a Buddha, 139
Ratnaketu, one of the tathāgatas, 485
Ratnakūṭa Sūtra, philosophical treatise, 511
Ratnapāṇi, name of a bodhisattva, 152
Ratnarakṣita, Buddhist writer, 242
Ratnasaṃbhava, name of a future buddha, 152
Ratnaśikhin. See Śikhin
Rāvaṇa, name of a king, 472
Ṛddhila, name of a man, 202
Ṛddhipāda (the four portions on which supernatural power rests), 118
Receptacles (six), 420
Religious discipline of the Buddhists, 297. See Vinaya
Revataka, name of a chariot, 375
Rgyun du zhugs pa, Tibetan translation of *srotāpatti*. See this word.
Roruka, name of a country, 174, 331
Rosary (mendicant having a rosary), 437
Ṛṣis converted by Śākyamuni, 201, 271, 317
Ruciraketu, name of a bodhisattva, 485
Rudrāyaṇa, name of a king, 174, 331
Rukkhamūlikaṅga (meaning of the Pāli word), 306
Rurumuṇḍa, name of a mountain, 361

S

Ṣaḍāyatana (meaning of the word), 461, 592
Saddharmalaṅkāvatāra. See Laṅkāvatāra.
Saddharmapuṇḍarīka, philosophical treatise, 59—Chinese translation of the *Saddharmapuṇḍarīka*, 61—What the *Saddharmapuṇḍarīka* is, 65—Its importance, 78 —Its special title, 100—One of the nine dharmas, 111—A developed sūtra, 159, 411, 494
Sahālin or Sapālin, name of a prince, 345
Sahalokadhātu (meaning of the word), 541
Sahāṃpati (meaning of the word), 543, 588
Sākala. See Śākala.
Śākala, name of a place, 404, 573
Sakṛdāgāmin (state of), 292ff.
Śaktis. See Female energies.
Śākyamuni, last of the seven human buddhas, 91—Opinion of the Nepalese on the buddhas previous to Śākyamuni, 92—Opinion of the Tibetans and the Sinhalese on his books, 92—His mission, 165—His teaching, 180, 477—His education, 181—His preaching, 183, 213—His miracles, 188–209—Calls the ignorant and the poor to him, 214, 216—Rejects the distinction among the castes, 222, 226—Śākyamuni's predictions, 238—His assemblies, 285ff.—His representation, 331, 336—His relics, 337—His funeral, 339—Legends related to his stūpas, 342, 356—His various trainings, 366—His method of dialectic, 426ff.—His borrowings from the Sāṃkhya system and from Brahmanical opinions, 477—Epoch of the three redactions of the books of Śākya, 526, 529ff. See Buddha.
Śākyaprabha, Buddhist writer, 242
Samādhirāja, narrative work, 100—One of the nine dharmas, 111, 411, 494
Samantabhadra, name of a bodhisattva, 152, 154, 507
Saṃgha (meaning of the word), 235, 285
Saṃgha (Ārya), chief of the Yogācāra school, 493, 521
Saṃghādisesa, a philosophical treatise, 300
Saṃgharakṣitāvadāna (legend called), 88
Saṃgītiparyāya, philosophical treatise, 419
Saṃjaya, chief of the armies of yakṣas, 487
Saṃjayin, name of a man, 188
Saṃjñā (meaning of the word), 470
Śaṃkarācārya, Vedānta philosopher, 421
Sāṃkāśya, name of a city, 194, 377
Saṃkhya (relation of the system) to that of Śākyamuni, 477—Atomist school, 517

Saṃmatāḥ, assembly of the disciples of Upāli, 418
Saṃpadī, name of a prince, 401ff.
Saṃskāra (meaning of the word), 464
Samuccayā, name of a goddess, 488, 499
Samudra, name of a man, 352
Samutpāda. See Pratītyasamutpāda.
Saṃvarodaya, name of a tantra, 491
Śaṇka, name of a king, 170
Sapadānacārikaṅga (meaning of the Pāli word), 307
Saptakumārikāvadāna, name of a legend, 506
Śāradvatīputra. See Śāriputra.
Śaraṇagamana. See Trīśara.
Śārdūlakarṇa (legend of), 155, 222, 494
Śāri, name of a woman, 426
Śāriputra, one of the first disciples of Śākyamuni, 95, 196, 310, 371, 419, 513
Śarīra (meaning of the word), 337
Sarvajña, name of a Buddhist writer, 495
Sarvanivaraṇaviṣkambhin, name of a bodhisattva, 235, 507
Sarvasattvapriyadarśana, name of a man, 486
Sarvāstivādāḥ, philosophical school, 418
Śatarudrīya, work opposed to Buddhism, 516
Śatasāhasrikā, collection of metaphysical treatises, 431
Sattādhikaraṇasamathā, Pāli religious treatise, 301
Sautrāntika (school of), 123, 418ff., 420
Sects born from Buddhism, 528
Sekkhiyā dhammā, Pāli religious treatise, 301
Sengjia fa shisha, Chinese religious treatise, 300
Śerīṣaka, name of a palace, 375
Shambala, name of a city, 493
Shelifo, Chinese transcription of Śāriputra. See this word.
Sher phyin or Sher chin, one of the sections of the Kah-gyur, 59
Shier toutuo jing, Chinese treatise on discipline, 302
Shing drung pa (meaning of the Tibetan expression), 306
Siddhārtha, name of the young Śākyamuni, 170
Śikhin, name of an ancient Buddha, 235, 313, 487
Sikkhāpada. See Śikṣāpada.
Śikṣāpada (meaning of the word), 302, 585
Siṃhala, name of a man, 236
Six paths of birth or existence, 455
Six seats of sensible qualities, 451
Skandhas (five), or attributes of birth, 454ff., 471, 538
Smāśānikaḥ (meaning of the word), 306
Sosānikaṅga (meaning of the Pāli word), 307
Sotāpatti, Pāli for *śrotāpatti*. See this word.
Sparśa (meaning of the word), 461
Sphuṭārtha, commentary of the *Abhidharmakośa*, 512
Sragdharā. See Āryatārā
Sragdharāstotra, poem by that name and its commentary, 507
Śramaṇa, ascetic who tames his senses, 121, 279, 297
Śrāmaṇera, small monk, 279
Śrāvaka, listener, 122, 411ff.—Mahāśrāvaka, 297
Śrāvastī, name of a city, 72, 130, 193, 247, 310
Śreṇya, another name of Bimbisāra. See this word.
Śrīlābha. See Bhadanta.
Śrīvajradatta, Buddhist writer, 495
Śronāparāntaka (country of), 261
Śrotāpatti (state of), 292
Stavakarṇin, name of a man, 249
Sthavira (meaning of the word), 289, 297, 513
Sthavirāḥ sthavirāṇām (meaning of the word), 289
Stotras or praises, 495
Stūpas (towers named), 148, 271, 338ff., 372—Manner of honoring them, 399
Subaranaprabhā, one of the nine dharmas, 111
Subhadra, name of a man, 121, 196
Śubhakṛtsna, gods of the third level of the third sphere, 561
Subhūti, name of a sthavira, 434ff.
Sudarśana, gods of the seventh level of the four sphere, 564
Śuddhodana, name of a king—Father of Śākyamuni, 164, 170, 173, 366
Sudṛśa, gods of the sixth level of the fourth sphere, 563
Sugata, one of the names of the Buddha, 120, 580 passim.
Sujāta, name of a man, 267
Sūkarikāvadāna, religious treatise, 88
Sukhavatī, name of a universe, 139, 235
Śukhavatī, name of a universe, 541

Sukhāvatīvyūha, one of the Mahāyāna sūtras, 138
Sumāgadhā, the name of a woman, 308, 378
Sumāgadhāvadāna, name of a legend, 516
Sumukha, gods of the eighth level of the fourth sphere according to the Nepalese, 564
Sundara, name of a man, 405
Śūnya, Śūnyatā (meaning of the words), 414, 431
Supriya, name of a man, 121
Sureśvara, name of a king, 488
Sūrpāraka, name of a city, 247–274
Sūryaśataka, one hundred stanzas in praise of the sun, 495
Susaṃbhava, name of a king, 487
Susīma, name of a prince, 345ff.
Sūtra, one of the divisions of the Buddhist scriptures of Nepal, 59—Sūtrapiṭaka, 85—Explanation of the word *sūtra*, 85—Sūtras attributed to Śākyamuni, 86—Their character, 86, 98—Their importance, 115—Two classes of sūtras, 141, 155, 157, 232, 242—Style of the sūtra, 144
Sūtranta. See Sūtra.
Suvarṇabhujendra, name of a king, 486
Suvarṇaprabhāsa, philosophical treatise, 60, 61—A tantra, 484—There are two, 484
Suvarṇaratnākarachatraketu, name of a future buddha, 488
Svabhāva (meaning of the word), 414, 587
Svābhāvika (system of), 152, 413ff., 449
Svāgata, name of a man, 216
Svaśa (country of), 348
Svayaṃbhū, name of Ādhibuddha, 235
Svayaṃbhūpurāṇa, religious treatise, 529

T

Takṣaśilā, name of a city, 348, 357, 383ff.
Tāmradvīpa (island of), 237
Tāmraparṇa. See Tāmradvīpa.
Tāmraparṇīya (sectarians), 517
Tāmraśāṭīyāḥ, philosophical school, 418
Tanmojuduo, Chinese transcription of Dharmagupta, 418
Tantras, ascetic rituals, 97, 109—Not counted among the sacred books, 111—Contain magical formulas, 479—Borrowings from Śivaist beliefs, 482—Epoch of their introduction in Nepal, 500—Their doctrine, 508ff.—Divided in Tibet in four categories, 593
Tathāgata, one of the names of the Buddha, 119, 145, 580. See Buddha.
Tathāgataguhyaka, one of the nine dharmas, 494
Teles Dhūtaṅga, treatise of Pāli discipline, 303
Ten abstentions. See ten rules of the novice.
Ten strengths (sage with), 369ff.
Terasa Dhūtaṅga. See Teles Dhūtangga
Thirty-two characteristics of beauty, or characteristic signs of a great man, 335
Three kinds of sensations, 429
Three precious objects. See Triratna
Three subjects of opinions, 427
Three supports, 334, 584
Thūpavaṃsa, Pāli treatise on the Stūpas, 339, 543
Tīrthikopāsaka (meaning of the word), 283
Tīrthyas and Tīrthakas (battle of), against Śākyamuni, 188–213
Tiṣya, name of a man, 426
Tiṣyarakṣitā, name of a woman, 178, 373ff.
Topes (buildings named), 338. See Stūpas.
Traicīvarikaḥ (meaning of the expression), 304
Trapukarṇin, name of a man, 249
Trapuṣa, name of a man, 369
Trayastriṃśa (gods), 552
Trembling of the earth (eight causes of), 123—Six different kinds, 269
Trikaṇḍaśeṣa, Sanskrit vocabulary later than Buddhism, 481
Tripiṭaka, assemblage of the three categories of Buddhist collections, 85, 513
Triratna, three precious objects, 235
Triśangku, name of a king, 223—His legend later than the time when Śākyamuni lived, 230
Triśaraṇa (meaning of the word), 584
Tṛṣṇā (meaning of the word), 459
Tsog pu pa (meaning of the Tibetan expression), 307
Tulakuci, name of a prince, 345
Turuṣka (kings), 542
Tuṣita, gods of the fourth heaven, 145, 547, 554
Twelve causes of the existence, according to the Mongols, 588ff.

U

Udāna, philosophical treatises, 102—Meaning of the word *udāna*, 103
Udāyi. See Ujāyin.
Udayibhadra. See Ujāyin.
Udraka, name of a ṛṣi, 367
Ujāyin, name of a prince, 345
Upādāna (meaning of the word), 456
Upadeśa, treatises about esoteric doctrines, 109—Meaning of the word *upadeśa*, 579
Upadhi (meaning of the word), 538
Upagaṇa, name of a man, 370
Upagupta, name of a monk, 164, 175, 235, 238, 360, 398, 406
Upāli, disciple of Śākyamuni and compiler of the Vinaya, 92, 527—Chief of a philosophical school, 418, 517
Upāsaka, Upāsikā (meaning of the words), 282
Upasena, the name of a monk, 582
Upendra, one of the names of Viṣṇu, 163
Urumuṇḍa, the name of a mountain, 361
Uruvilvā, the name of a place, 120
Utkaṭā, the name of a city, 224
Utpalā, Utpalavarṇā, names of a nun, 201, 281, 377
Uttara, name of a man, 199, 326
Uttarakuru, name of a continent, 200, 492

V

Vaibhāṣika, philosophical system, 418ff.
Vaipulya (treatises named), 106—Are later than the sūtras, 158, 159, 411
Vairocana, name of a buddha, 152, 507
Vaiśālī, name of a place, 118, 127
Vaiśeṣika (school of), 517
Vaiśravaṇa, name of a divinity, 164
Vajrācārya, Nepalese priest, 328
Vajracchedikā, philosophical treatise, 60—Translated from Tibetan, 117—A summary of the *Prajñāpāramitā*, 433, 539
Vajrahṛdaya, name of a dhāraṇī, 495
Vajrakukṣi, name of a cave, 236
Vajramaṇḍā, name of a dhāraṇī, 495
Vajrapāṇi, name of a bodhisattva, 152, 507—Son of Akṣobhya, 492
Vajrasattva, name of the sixth dhyāni buddha, 481
Vajraśuci, polemical treatise, 230, 507
Vakkalin, name of a ṛṣi, 272, 372
Vakkula, name of a sthavira, 372
Vāsavadattā, name of a woman, 175
Vasiṣṭa, name of a ṛṣi, 495
Vasubandhu, the author of the *Abhidharmakośa*, 512, 519
Vasudharā, name of a goddess, 495
Vasumitra, philosophical writer, 419, 515, 516
Vasus (eight), their place in the Buddhist pantheon, 553
Vātsīputrīyāḥ, philosophical school, 418, 517
Vedanā (meaning of the word), 460
Vedas, rejected by the Buddhists, 499
Vehicle. See Mahāyāna.—Great vehicle, 442
Vibhājyavādinaḥ, philosophical school, 418
Vibhāṣā, philosophical school, 516
Videha, name of a country, 395
Vidyāṣaḍakṣarī (magical formula called), 238
Vigatāśoka, son of Bindusāra, 346
Vihāra (monasteries named), 287, 585—Religious life in the vihāras, 309
Vijñāna (meaning of the word), 463—Sixth organ, 591
Vijñānakāya, philosophical treatise, 419
Vinayakṣudrakavastu, collection of treatises about religious discipline, 514
Vinayapiṭaka, treatise of discipline, 85—Vinayasūtra or Patra, a Nepalese work, 48, 85, 509
Vipaśyin, name of an ancient buddha, 235, 313
Virajaprabha, name of a buddha, 139
Viṣkambhin, name of a bodhisattva, 237
Viṣṇu, his role in the Buddhist mythology, 163
Viṣṇumitra and Visṣumitra (?), the name of a monk, 516
Viśvabhū, name of an ancient buddha, 236
Viśvapāṇi, name of a bodhisattva, 152
Vītāśoka, name of a prince, 391ff.
Vṛhaspati, name of a prince, 403
Vṛhatphala, gods of the third level of the fourth sphere, 562
Vṛji, name of a building, 118
Vṛkṣamūlikaḥ (meaning of the word), 306
Vṛṣasena, name of a prince, 403
Vyākaraṇa, grammars, 97—Narrative works, 100—Explanation of the word, 100
Vyākaraṇa Kauṇḍinya, name of a Brahman, 486
Vyāsa (work attributed to), 516

W

Wenshu shili, Chinese transcription of Mañjuśrī, 148

Y

Yakṣas, their place in the Buddhist pantheon, 548
Yāma, their place in the Buddhist pantheon, 553
Yamāntaka, name of a divinity, 502
Yaśas, name of a sthavira 357, 376ff.
Yaśodharā, name of a woman, 281
Yaśomitra, name of a Buddhist writer, 512, 514—Quotations from his commentary on the *Abhidharmakośa*, 519ff.
Yāthāpaṃtari (meaning of the word), 307
Yathāsanthatikaṅga (meaning of the Pāli word), 307
Yātnikas (sect of), 413, 416ff.
Yoga tantra, magical formulas, 507
Yogācāra, philosophical system, 418ff., 469
Yonaka, inhabitant of the country of Yona, 583
Youposai, Chinese transcription of *upāsaka*. See this word.
Yum, Tibetan translation of *mātṛkā*, 95

Z

Zas byis mi len pa (meaning of the Tibetan expression), 306

CPSIA information can be obtained
at www.ICGtesting.com
Printed in the USA
LVOW11s1414300418
575393LV00001B/100/P

9 780226 269689